E-Commerce

A Guide to the Law of Electronic Business

E-Commerce

A Guide to the Law of Electronic Business

Third edition

Edited by:

ROBERT WEGENEK

GED O'NEILL

JONATHAN MOORE

Hammond Suddards Edge

Members of the LexisNexis Group worldwide

United Kingdom	LexisNexis Butterworths Tolley, a Division of Reed Elsevier (UK) Ltd, Halsbury House, 35 Chancery Lane, LONDON, WC2A 1EL, and 4 Hill Street, EDINBURGH EH2 3JZ
Argentina	LexisNexis Argentina, BUENOS AIRES
Australia	LexisNexis Butterworths, CHATSWOOD, New South Wales
Austria	LexisNexis Verlag ARD Orac GmbH & Co KG, VIENNA
Canada	LexisNexis Butterworths, MARKHAM, Ontario
Chile	LexisNexis Chile Ltda, SANTIAGO DE CHILE
Czech Republic	Nakladatelství Orac sro, PRAGUE
France	Editions du Juris-Classeur SA, PARIS
Hong Kong	LexisNexis Butterworths, HONG KONG
Hungary	HVG-Orac, BUDAPEST
India	LexisNexis Butterworths, NEW DELHI
Ireland	Butterworths (Ireland) Ltd, DUBLIN
Italy	Giuffrè Editore, MILAN
Malaysia	Malayan Law Journal Sdn Bhd, KUALA LUMPUR
New Zealand	LexisNexis Butterworths, WELLINGTON
Poland	Wydawnictwo Prawnicze LexisNexis, WARSAW
Singapore	LexisNexis Butterworths, SINGAPORE
South Africa	Butterworths SA, DURBAN
Switzerland	Stämpfli Verlag AG, BERNE
USA	LexisNexis, DAYTON, Ohio

© Reed Elsevier (UK) Ltd 2002

A CIP Catalogue record for this book is available from the British Library.

First edition published 1999

Second edition published 2000

ISBN 0 406 94879 8

Typeset by Doyle & Co, Colchester

Printed and bound in Great Britain by William Clowes Limited, Beccles and London

Visit Butterworths LexisNexis *direct* at www.butterworths.com

Editor's foreword

A project such as this is a credit to the whole of Hammond Suddards Edge. To invest the time of around 40 lawyers is a huge commitment. This indicates that e-commerce was never viewed by this firm as an opportunistic fad. We never had a separate department to deal with the Internet and this book is a reflection of the fact that all departments of the firm are expert in e-commerce.

From a personal perspective, I recall well the first sets of instructions, back in 1994, that I had from clients relating to the Internet and the sense of genuine excitement that I was at the forefront of something new and important. At the time it was satisfying to be involved in a project as high profile as the Guinness 'dancing man' screensaver. Eight years on, I find it remarkable that the law and technology have progressed to such an extent that we have produced a tome as substantial as this one.

Thanks are due to a number of people other than the contributors. I would thank Liz Machin for her work in proofing, David Llewellyn and Sue Pembridge for her secretarial assistance. I would like to thank Paul Lyons for his support and analysis for the last three years in helping me to understand the dynamics behind this sector. I would also thank those who helped on previous editions of this book, such as Emma Beattie, Aine Davies and Noreen Grant. Most of all in this respect, Daniel Tunkel continues to deserve huge credit for his lasting contribution to this rolling project.

Robert Wegenek
Hammond Suddards Edge
July 2002

Preface

The first edition of this book was published in November 1999 and was the first legal commentary on the rapidly developing world of e-commerce, aimed primarily at the UK market. The fact that, two-and-a-half years later, we are publishing the third edition illustrates how much has changed, both in terms of law and practice.

Our firm was instructed on its first matter relating to commercial exploitation of the Internet in the autumn of 1994. At the time, only three Internet companies had IPO'd in the USA and even the earliest of stalwarts, such as Amazon, Excite and Yahoo, were 18 months from coming to market. For some years after our initial involvement, law firms had to combat the popular misconception that the Internet was not regulated and that materials posted on it were not subject to any kind of restriction or limitation. It was this kind of naivety that subsequently manifested itself in the notion that Internet businesses were not subject to the same economic rules and influences as the 'old economy'.

Since early 2000, we have witnessed a substantial downturn in corporate and investment activity relating to e-commerce. Yet the size of the e-commerce market has grown at an impressive rate when judged against any normal standards of economic comparison. There is a greater need than ever for this book to help practitioners and businessmen alike. Forty lawyers from my firm have made contributions, demonstrating from a legal perspective that the same legal principles that apply to off-line businesses apply to on-line businesses.

This book is intended to be of interest to lawyers, businessmen and investors. This new edition updates the last one extensively and includes two entirely new chapters. The first of these deals with brands separately from other intellectual property rights and the second reflects the growing importance of the betting and gaming industry to interactive commerce.

Since the second edition of this book, Hammond Suddards Edge has itself made huge progress as a firm. The Internet is itself a manifestation of an increasingly global focus for business and in the last 18 months we have announced mergers with firms from, or opened offices in, six European cities and in Hong Kong.

While demonstrating glimpses of what will be possible, as this book is published, broadband technology is still in its infancy in the United Kingdom. As this technology and other technologies develop and have increasing influence over our daily lives and business practices, everyone at our firm hopes that this book will prove a valuable companion and will help to provide some insight into a fascinating and constantly developing subject.

Richard Burns
Senior Partner
Hammond Suddards Edge
July 2002

List of contributors

EDITORS

Robert Wegenek
Ged O'Neill
Jonathan Moore

GLOSSARY		David Cannel and Paul Lyons
1	**E-WORLD**	Robert Wegenek and Paul Lyons
2	**E-CONTRACT**	Mike Butler and Robert Wegenek **Competition law:** Robert Vidal
3	**E-LIABILITY**	**Contract and negligence, obscenity:** Paul Jinks and Mike Henley **Defamation:** Robert Wegenek and Tim Pritchard **Data protection:** Caroline Egan and Charlotte Colman **Secure communications:** David Savage **Secure delivery:** Mike Butler and Greg Pryor
4	**E-RIGHTS**	**Patents, trade marks and trade secrets:** Jonathan Moore **Copyright, database rights and design rights:** Hubert Best
5	**E-BRAND**	Linda Gibbons and Robert Wegenek
6	**E-MARKETING**	Robert Wegenek and Jo Searle
7	**E-DISPUTE**	Miryana Nesic **Evidence:** David Savage
8	**E-TAXATION**	Michael Ridsdale and Beverley Tanner
9	**E-FINANCE**	Nick Williams, Dearbhla Quigley and Nick Butcher
10	**E-BANKING**	Gwyneth Macaulay and Matthew Ingram
11	**E-INSURANCE**	Steven Reynolds and Lynne Atherton
12	**E-CORPORATE**	Nadim Meer and Ged O'Neill
13	**E-PROPERTY**	Chris Brigstocke, Lesley Haworth and Robert Holland
14	**E-GAMBLING**	Steven Burton, Robert Wegenek and Ieuan Jolly

Contents

Contents

9   E-FINANCE

10   E-BANKING

Table of statutes

Table of statutory instruments

Table of European legislation

Table of cases

C

E

F

M

MP3 'MPEG-1 Audio Layer-3'. This is a format for compressing a sound sequence into a very small file while preserving the original level of sound quality when it is played. MP3 allows CD-quality music to be **downloaded** onto a user's computer from the **Internet**. However, that computer will need to be equipped with an MP3 player in order to listen to the files[17].

MPEG 'Moving Pictures Experts Group'. Originally this referred to the research group responsible for developing technology for the compression of files containing video and audio format materials (eg feature films). It has come from this to refer to material in a format which the MPEG has designed (so a film buff collecting material over the **Internet** might tell you that he has a lot of MPEGs stored on his hard drive).

Newsgroup A public forum for exchanging information and views on a particular subject over the Internet. There are by now tens of thousands of different topics covered by public newsgroups. There is some capacity for forming further newsgroups in the public domain, though of course it is equally common to find private services (run as e-mail distribution services or via **websites**). To view and post messages to a newsgroup requires appropriate posting software (which most **ISPs** provide as a part of their basic service) and a capacity to communicate using **NNTP**.

NewsML A version of **HTML** very recently developed and released by Reuters, which is expected to become a standard for the delivery of news and information services on-line.

NGI 'Next-Generation Internet Project', a US Government-funded institution set up to develop systems for the next generation of the Internet.

NNTP 'Network news transfer protocol'. NNTP is a series of rules which govern the manner in which news messages posted to **newsgroups** are transferred around the **Internet**. NNTP is supported by **Usenet**.

Node Any connection, routing or end point on a computer **network**. A node (or, more accurately, the computer hardware and software operating at that node) has the capacity to recognise and process or forward transmissions to other nodes.

Nominet A non-profit organisation set up by the British Internet industry, which administers the allocation of **domain names** with suffixes such as .co.uk, .org.uk, etc.

NSP 'Network service provider'. An NSP provides **Internet** access to **ISPs**.

NTS 'Number transmission service' or 'number transmission system'. This is in effect the set of rules which determine how much of a telephone user's bill should be allocated to the telecom network provider (eg British Telecom), the service operator (eg Cable & Wireless) and, if relevant, the **ISP**.

Packet A unit of data routed between a source and a destination on the **Internet**. Every file sent over the **Internet** is broken down into packets which are then individually numbered and 'routed' to their destination by a **router** mechanism, where they are then reassembled.

Pagejacking The process of stealing the contents of a **website** by copying some of its pages, putting them on a **website** that appears to be legitimate, and then inviting people to it by deceptive means (eg by having the contents indexed by a major **search engine**). Users linking to the illegitimate site may find themselves redirected to a pornographic or other unwanted site. As an additional annoyance, users subjected to pagejacking may also encounter **mousetrapping**.

PDA 'Personal digital assistant'. Handheld device that synchronises with PCs. Seen by many as the best method for accessing the Internet on the move, hence **convergence** with mobile phones.

PKI 'Public key infrastructure'. This includes the **certificate authorities** (who issue **digital certificates**) and their management and directory systems (which enable the use of public key **encryption**).

Plug-in A software program that adds to, and is used as part of, a user's **browser**. Plug-ins are recognised automatically by **browsers** and their function integrated into the main **HTML** file that is being prepared.

POP 'Point of presence'. A POP is the location of an access point to the **Internet**. All **ISPs** necessarily have POPs on the **Internet**. The private user who dials up to gain access to the **Internet** is in effect accessing one of his **ISP**'s POPs (most **ISPs** maintain several, and the larger **ISPs** have POPs in many different countries).

Portal	A **website** that offers an entry point to other sites, or services, on the **web**. Portals such as *Yahoo!* and *Excite* give links to news, sports, weather and entertainment pages. Many portals let you personalise the main page so that each time you access the portal it gives you the information you want to see. Portals often offer free e-mail accounts[18].
Proxy server	Within an organisation with many individual users, a proxy server acts as an intermediary between such users and the **Internet**, to enable the organisation to ensure security and administrative control. Proxy servers can also have **caches**, so that if a user requests a **web** page that has previously been **downloaded** within the organisation, the proxy server can find it in its **cache**, thus avoiding the need to forward the user's request to the **Internet**.
Public key encryption	This refers to an extremely secure system of **encryption** that uses two keys, one public and one private, to encode messages. Public and private keys are created and issued to applicants by a **certificate/certification authority**. The details of a user's public key are contained within his **digital certificate**. If a user wishes to send a message to a certain recipient he can use the recipient's public key (which can be discovered from a control administrator) to encrypt the message. The recipient can then use his corresponding private key (that is never shared with anyone or sent across the **Internet**) to decrypt it. This can also work in reverse, with the sender using his own private key to encrypt a message and the recipient then using the sender's public key to decrypt it. This enables the recipient to verify the sender's identity. Public key encryption is also known as asymmetric encryption.
Pull technology	A medium by which the customer can request that material is sent to him. The **World Wide Web** has conventionally worked on the basis of pull technology, since nothing is sent to a PC user until and unless he has requested it (by loading a **website**, searching for it, etc).
Push technology	A medium which sends data to a customer without his having specifically requested it. Radio and TV broadcasting are examples: the programmes are broadcast regardless of whether anybody tunes in. Push technology is coming into its own on the web as well, however (for example with the use of webcasting services and services that send customised news to a user's computer).
PVR	'Personal video recorder'. Uses a PC hard disk to record programmes digitally. The more sophisticated devices allow live broadcasts to be paused or automatically record programmes of a specific interest area.
Router	A device positioned at various points on a computer network, which recognises **packets** and routes them on course for their intended destinations. Routers are found at **gateways** and at points at which component networks of the **Internet** intersect.
RSA	The de facto worldwide standard **public key encryption** algorithm, developed by RSA Data Security Inc. The algorithm has been incorporated into a number of major protocols including **S/MIME** (where it is used for initial authentication) and **SSL**.
SAT	'SIM alliance toolbox'. SAT technology enables the **downloading** of **Java** mini-**applets** to a **GSM** phone's SIM card, allowing **WAP**-compliant **web** pages to be viewed, without graphics, on non-**WAP**-compliant **GSM** phones. SAT technology uses **SMS** text messaging as its communications pathway.
Search engine	A software device on the **Internet** that allows the user to search potentially the entire **World Wide Web** for pages or information on defined subjects. Search engines themselves trawl the **web** constantly looking for new **web** pages to include for the purposes of future user searches[19].
Second-level domain	In the address www.abcde.com, the 'abcde' represents the second-level domain; it is that aspect of the **URL** as a whole which is personal to the owner or controller of that **URL**.
Server	At its most basic, a server is a computer (and the programs within it) that provides services to other computers (and the programs within them). In the context of the **web**, a **web** server is a programme that supplies **HTML** pages to the **browsers** that request them on behalf of their users.
SET	'Secure electronic transmission'. SET is a system for ensuring the security of financial transactions over the **Internet** through the use of **digital certificates**, which effectively act as electronic credit cards.

S/MIME	'Secure multipurpose Internet mail extensions'. S/MIME is an addition to MIME protocol that supports the exchange of encrypted e-mail via the **Internet**. It uses **RSA encryption** for the initial authentication and, once a secure connection is established, an exchange of symmetric **encryption** algorithm keys takes place.
SMS	'Short message service'. SMS is a service for sending short messages to mobile phones that use **GSM**. SMS messages are limited to 160 characters at a time and the user is usually charged per message by the network operator. SMS can be sent person to person (as a sort of miniature mobile e-mail) or from content provider to consumer.
SMTP	'Simple mail transfer protocol'. SMTP is the set of rules governing the sending and receiving of e-mail over the **Internet**.
Spam	Unsolicited junk e-mail. Senders of spam generally obtain user addresses from lists of subscribers to discussion groups or from companies that specialise in creating e-mail distribution lists.
SSL	'Secure sockets layer', which is an **Internet** security standard widely supported by leading **web browsers** and **web servers**. SSL is said to be 'application independent', meaning that it works with all **Internet** tools. SSL functions at network layer level rather than application layer level. Applications using SSL use **RSA encryption**, **digital certificates** and **digital signatures** to establish the identity of the parties to a transaction. If used with 128-bit keys (as within the US) it is considered nigh-on impossible for encrypted transactions to be decoded. However, the 40-bit version used in most popular **browsers** is not secure and is not recommended for commercial transactions.
Stickiness	This term (now somewhat archaic) has come to be used in relation to **websites** that are successful in keeping the interest of users in paying return visits. Good content is the obvious way of obtaining stickiness. Other methods include allowing the personalisation of the site by individual visitors, building on-line communities and discussion groups and providing interactive features such as games.
Streaming	Streaming technology allows multimedia files to begin playing seconds after they are received, removing the need to wait minutes for an audio or video file, MPEG for instance, to download.
TCP/IP	'Transmission control protocol/Internet protocol'. TCP/IP is the basic language of the **Internet**. It is an agreed communication standard, hence the use of the term 'protocol', and all computers or devices connected to the **Internet** must support it.
Top-level domain	That component of a **URL** which describes the organisational character of the **URL**. It is a suffix, such as '.com', '.org', '.ac', etc.
Trojan Horse	A seemingly harmless computer programme which carries within itself a means to allow its creator access to the system using it.
UMTS	'Universal mobile telecommunications system'. UMTS is the standard for mobile telephone users around the world planned to be in use by 2002. It is based upon the **GSM** communication standard and will enable users of mobile computers and phones to be constantly and consistently attached to the **Internet** as they travel.
Upload (to)	To send data or software from your computer to another computer. Opposite of **download (from)**.
URL	'Uniform resource locator'. This is the official terminology for an **IP address** on the **web**. Every single **web** page has a unique URL. The full URL of a **web** page may have a lot of extensions, which indicate the detail which the author of that page needs to attribute to it in order to give it a unique and purposeful reference. Thus one might see http://www.websitename.com/homepage as a generic example of the sort of URL that applies to the home page on a **website**.
Usenet	A worldwide bulletin board system that consists of a network of thousands of newsgroups. Usenet follows **NNTP** to post, distribute and retrieve notes between **servers**. Most **browsers** support Usenet.
Virus	A program designed to replicate and spread undetected through computer systems. Many are annoying rather than harmful and are commonly transferred via e-mail attachments. Most harmful are viruses which attack and corrupt software and data stored on a computer's hard drive or within a network. Some are designed to spread through detecting e-mail distribution lists stored on a network and sending harmful messages to each address found there.

Vortal	A **portal** established by a so-called 'vertical industry' (ie a particular industry or sector of the market, where those at the top of the vertical structure have an interest in relating to those in levels lower down and ultimately to consumers at the bottom of the structure). A vortal might be used to allow people to relate to components of the industry or sector in question, to disseminate news, etc.
VPN	'Virtual private network'. A VPN is a private data network that makes use of the public telecommunication infrastructure. Various security procedures, including **encryption**, are used to maintain privacy.
VRML	'Virtual reality modelling language'. VRML is an extension of **HTML** which gives virtual reality effects. For example, using VRML, a user can view a room and use controls to move the room so it appears as if the user is actually walking through it in real space.
W3C	'World Wide Web Consortium'. W3C is the recognised body for approving and standardising revisions of **HTML**.
WAN	'Wide area network'. A WAN is a network of interconnected computers, or computer networks, in different areas. For example, several **LANs** can be joined together to form a WAN. Service speed across a WAN is likely to be slower than across a **LAN**, for obvious reasons.
WAP	'Wireless applications protocol'. WAP is a set of rules that governs how hand-held digital wireless devices (eg mobile phones) can send and receive data. WAP technology takes **Internet** content and turns it into a format capable of being displayed on the screen of a mobile phone by using a special stripped-down version of **HTML** called WML. One advantage WAP phones have over the **Internet** is that phone network operators can locate each phone to within about 40 square metres, thus enabling information, for example about travel and entertainment, to be personalised according to the user's location.
The web	The **World Wide Web**. The **web** is probably the most popular aspect of the **Internet** (or **WWW**) and is the main driving force for e-commerce on the **Internet** today. **Websites** enable businesses and private individuals to advertise themselves to customers, enquirers and friends. The **web** supports hypertext links, thus enabling you to navigate from one **website** to another.
Webcast	A sound or video broadcast over the **web**. It can be live or after the event. To view a webcast a user needs to **download** an appropriate video viewing application[20]. Webcasting is an example of a **push technology**.
Web hosting	Refers to the hosting of **websites**. **Web** hosts maintain **server** connections, thus ensuring reliability, offer disk storage and high-speed connection to a site. **Web** hosting is a growth area so most **web** hosts now offer various support services to their clients as well.
Website	A collection of connected **web** pages, all having the same **IP address**.
Webvertising	Jargon for advertising on a **website**.
Wireless technology	Technology that uses electromagnetic or acoustic waves to carry signals through atmospheric space rather than along a wire. Examples of the use of wireless technology include GSM and cellular phones.
Worm	A type of self-propagating virus, designed to spawn in network environments.
XBRL	'Extensible business reporting language'. This is a version of **XML** which has been developed for the purpose of facilitating the on-line publication of corporate annual reports and accounts and similar corporate financial data in a fashion that corresponds with current accounting standards and practices for the presentation and appearance of financial data of this nature.
XML	'Extensible mark-up language'. This is a more sophisticated version of **HTML**, in that in addition to being able to tell a **browser** how to display data **downloaded** from a **website**, it can tell the **browser** what type of data this is (for example, it can recognise prices, names, measurements, etc). Data of this type is termed 'metadata'.
Zip file	A file containing data which has been compressed. This makes files less memory-hungry and quicker to send across the **Internet**. Zip files have the .zip suffix. Special software is needed to 'zip' and 'unzip' files[21].

1 Taking its name from Thomas Boole, the 19th century mathematician.
2 For example, to look for references to any London other than the one in England, you might search for 'London NOT England'.
3 The current version of which is 7.0.
4 The current version of which is 6.0.
5 The analogy in the jargon is with a shrink-wrap software licence agreement that one finds attached to software purchased over the counter, where it is a term of the agreement that the purchaser is bound by it as soon as he removes the wrapping.
6 See further in Chapter 5, E-brand.
7 Such as www.flowers.com, which it is understood that Interflora in the US were required to pay a large amount of money to purchase from the entity which had originally registered the name
8 See further in Chapter 9, E-finance.
9 See further in Chapter 2, E-contract.
10 For example, DNS reads 195.67.49.54 as www.yahoo.co.uk.
11 Some e-merchants are using systems of this nature: for example, Amazon.com allows you to build a profile of yourself which is used on future visits to its website to offer new titles that match (in its opinion) your characteristics. For a discussion of how intelligent agent software is likely to revolutionise financial services on-line, see Chapter 9, paragraph 9.71.
12 Of the major ISPs, AOL is the one most commonly associated with this type of communication, though generally AOL users can only communicate with other AOL users using it.
13 ISO is not an acronym, but is simply derived from the Greek *isos*, meaning 'the same'.
14 For example, FreeServe and Netscape-On-Line.
15 For example, Netscape 3 or earlier.
16 Generally, only later editions of the more common browsers support JavaScript.
17 For example, the more advanced versions of RealPlayer.
18 Portals are also springing up in a more commercial context, eg www.easyodds.com, which offers access to the best odds from a range of bookmakers.
19 Popular search engines include *Alta Vista*, *Hotbot* and *Lycos*. Some search engines are appearing now for the purposes of specific areas of interest.
20 For example, NetShow or RealVideo.
21 For example, winzip.

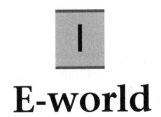

E-world

I. INTRODUCTION

1.01 The dot.com revolution began at some indefinable point during the mid-1990s. Its epitaph has since been written many times, but the start of the collapse in investor sentiment can be traced back to the spring of 2000 and the first of the dot.com insolvencies. The short period in between gave way to a frenzy of excitement which, looking back, seems (and was) unreal. The market has matured since those days and this, the third edition of *E-Commerce: A Guide to the Law of Electronic Business*, unlike its predecessors, is concerned with a body of law that has developed quickly and also reached a certain level of maturity.

The enduring image of the dot.com boom is the newly launched business headed up by a young and middle class 'dot.com millionaire', aimed at a consumer market, focusing on retail or sports content.

In reality, the world of electronic business and the subject matter of this book is very much wider. In this book you will see references to m-commerce, t-commerce and SMS[1]. Indeed, the editors and the publishers of this book engaged in some debate as to whether the title of the book should be changed to reflect the fact that e-commerce is more than simply Internet and whether it should reflect the subject matter of 'interactive commerce' in its widest sense.

1   Mobile phone commerce, television commerce and short messaging services (ie text messages) respectively.

2. 'DOT.COM TO DOT.BOMB'

1.02 During the mid-1990s, the Internet's use as a tool for commercial purposes was still limited. It was seen as being the domain of a company's IT director and perhaps the occasional, adventurous, marketing director. Within two to three years, the Internet had assumed board room importance as, for any company, declaring an Internet strategy was a way of achieving massive growth in share valuations. The subsequent collapse in market sentiment has meant a time for reappraisal. There is a continuing sobriety and scepticism about all matters relating to e-commerce which detracts from the continuing and growing importance of the Internet and e-commerce in all of our lives.

In his magnificent dissection of the rise and fall of the dot.com boom, John Cassidy[1] uses priceline.com's[2] initial public offering (IPO) as a prime example of the ridiculous overvaluation achieved by dot.com stocks. In retrospect, there is clearly no debate that these stocks were overvalued. In retrospect, there is no debate that the dot.com era was a short-lived speculative bubble. However, as Cassidy points out, speculative bubbles are only apparent with hindsight. For a period of two or three years at the end of the 1990s, there was extravagant talk of a 'new economy' and one could list scores of instances of companies' stock prices leaping following the announcement of their new Internet strategy.

Priceline.com IPO'd on 30 March 1999 on NASDAQ. The business consisted of a website enabling holiday companies and airlines to sell excess availability for airline tickets, where consumers could name their own price. During 1998 the company had lost more than $114m. Priceline.com owned few assets other than computer hardware, software, its brand name, domain name registration and its customer lists and databases. (The lack of tangible assets is something that has subsequently become all too obvious when acting on any dot.com insolvency.) Within several weeks of IPO, this new and unprofitable company was worth nearly $25 billion. This was more than the valuation at the time of the entire US airline industry.

Oddly, in the circumstances, priceline.com's prospectus had not sought to paper over the financial cracks. In fact, quite the opposite. The prospectus stressed 'we are not profitable and expect to continue to incur losses' and caveats throughout the prospectus warned that the business model was unproven and that the brand would not necessarily achieve the recognition necessary to succeed.

1   John Cassidy, *Dot.con – the greatest story ever sold* (2002) Allen Lane, the Penguin Press.
2   www.priceline.com.

3.   REASONS BEHIND THE COLLAPSE OF THE DOT.COM BOOM

1.03   As would be expected with a book such as this, there is little incentive to conduct a detailed post-mortem as regards the collapse in market sentiment; the purpose of this chapter is to look at areas of growth and continued optimism. Nevertheless, in addition to obvious factors such as ignorance and greed, it is worth identifying several factors which contributed to the ultimate collapse of the dot.com boom.

(a)   The 'herd' mentality of investors

1.04   John Cassidy[1] cites the following approach as being the basis behind the successful picking of shares:

> 'John Maynard Keynes compared stock picking to a newspaper beauty contest in which readers are asked to pick the six prettiest girls from 100 photographs, the winner being the person whose choices correspond most closely to the selections of the entrants as a whole.'

The point made by Keynes is that success is not determined by an objective and informed calculation of which company is to be the best investment, but by correctly anticipating public opinion. If this public opinion drives up share prices, then following the herd itself brings success as those prices continue to rise. Hence the priceline.com example (see section 2 above). One cannot seriously believe that investors in priceline.com believed at the time that their shares were intrinsically worth the value that they paid for them at the peak of the market.

In retrospect, financial commentators talk glibly of a notional '99% club', which has a distressingly long membership list and which represents those companies (on both sides of the Atlantic) whose share prices are now less than 1% of their peak value.

1   See footnote 1 to paragraph 1.02 above.

(b)   The battle for 'clicks'

1.05   It became a perceived wisdom that what was most important of all in order to succeed, not only for Internet companies but also for new media platform owners such as digital television and mobile phone companies, was the battle to win subscribers at all costs. Valuation models of Internet companies began to focus on the number of subscribers which they had and this, in turn, would fuel the battle for critical mass The perceived wisdom was that Internet companies had to battle for 'clicks'[1] and that once a large customer base was developed profit would inevitably follow. Adopting a similar strategy, mobile phone companies began to offer pre-payment services with subsidised handsets. This strategy has now been abandoned by all the of major players and the emphasis now for the mobile telephone networks and for media companies adopting a subscription model (such as BSkyB) is to concentrate less on customer numbers and more on increases in ARPU[2].

A knock-on effect as regards the battle for consumer numbers was that it became a truism that 'content is king'. To attract subscribers and to maintain their interest, it was felt necessary to provide top quality information and entertainment. This, in turn, inflated the value of premium content (such as the value of sports rights).

In May 2000 the UK Government awarded 'third generation' (or 3G) mobile phone licences to five operators: BT (now MM02), Vodafone, Orange, One2One (T-Mobile) and Hutchison (now '3'). These licences would allow these companies to operate third generation mobile telephony services for a period of 20 years. The total figure raised for the five licences following an auction was in the region of £22 billion. To put it into perspective, at the time, this figure represented twice the volume of sales generated by e-commerce in the whole of Canada during the whole of 1999.

Again, in retrospect, we can see that this auction was held at the peak of the market. This chapter goes on, briefly, to examine the state of play as regards these companies' 3G operations and aspirations. However, the operators themselves will face an interesting strategic battle to persuade consumers to upgrade their existing mobile phones to the superior platform while avoiding a repetition of the mistake that subscriber volumes are paramount. In doing so, they are expected to concentrate on the value generated by each customer, as opposed simply to volumes of customers.

1   That is, the number of visitors and/or subscribers to the website in question.
2   'Average revenue per user'.

(c)   The discrediting of the Internet advertising revenue model

1.06   Much of the dot.com boom and the focus on aggregation of subscribers and users was based around a misconception as to the amount of revenue which could be generated from advertising. Chapter 6, E-marketing examines the growing sophistication of the on-line advertising market and how interactive advertising has matured in a comparatively short period of time. The focus of that chapter is on the use of the Internet and interactivity as a marketing tool rather than as a generator of revenues. Banners and pop-ups are an unwelcome distraction to Internet users and the click through rate is not high. It became clear that the advertising revenue generated by most websites was comparatively insignificant, partly due to the sheer volume of sites available. It quickly became apparent that banner ads were not going to sustain whole businesses which themselves were making huge expenditure in traditional media in order to attract the subscribers at which the banner advertising was aimed[1]!

1   John Cassidy explains that the average costs of an Internet advertisement was, contrary to popular belief, expensive when judged by click through rates compared with advertising in conventional media (*Dot.con – the greatest story ever sold*).

(d) The cost of building a brand

1.07   The dot.com boom was remarkable for the large number of new consumer-facing businesses which were launched on the back of a new, untried and unproven brand name. Each of them was engaged in the battle for 'clicks' (see paragraph 1.05 above) and the only way this could be achieved was by throwing money into building brand awareness.

Established businesses are no strangers to diversification and when developing a new operating channel or diversifying their range of products they have ongoing revenues which enable them to invest in the new enterprise. In particular, established businesses are 'media owners', in the sense that they have existing customers and are able to communicate with those existing and potential customers through their traditional operations.

In retrospect, established businesses had a huge advantage over the new dot.coms. Boo.com, the fashion retailer which has become synonymous with the excesses of dot.com millionaires, raised £100m of venture capital during 1998. By May 2000 this had all been spent. There is only so much that can be spent on expensive cars and lavish parties and the vast majority was used in a failed attempt to build the boo.com brand in order to attract subscribers and to move the business into profit before funds ran out. On a smaller level, stepstone.co.uk (the recruitment site) closed in November 2001 having spent £20m on advertising and marketing since the beginning of 2000. During the same period, its revenues had only been £8m[1].

Neither stepstone.co.uk nor boo.com had retail premises, but they had much investor cash. In contrast, Tesco, in setting up its on-line operation did not have £100m of venture capital to spend. We know now which of these players has been successful in building an Internet business[2]. Along similar lines, Ladbrokes.com has moved into profit, as has the Internet bank Egg. In both cases, their on-line activities had been supported by their existing off-line activities.

Lastminute.com is perhaps the UK dot.com which is the most enduring symbol of the era. It too has now achieved profitability with a sales and marketing strategy which has deliberately moved away from the initial focus on vastly expensive mass media advertising. In terms of ongoing marketing it has redirected its efforts towards its own database and towards targeting its spend in a more focused way. Its activities have been greatly assisted by the media coverage and public relations activities before, during and after its IPO in March 2000, which achieved levels of publicity which would have cost tens of millions of pounds had this been done in an advertising context. Lastminute.com is not the owner of retail outlets, but it has deliberately changed its initial advertising strategy in order to survive and to succeed.

1   Figures reported in the *Evening Standard Internet for Business Supplement*, June 2002.
2   Tesco.com leads the on-line grocery sector in terms of visitors to its website and claims to be profitable (reported in *Revolution* 6, June 2002).

4.   THE WIDER REPERCUSSIONS

1.08   Digital TV is regarded as a crucial platform as regards interactive commerce, and the UK Government has very publicly set itself a target of migrating the vast majority of UK television viewers onto this platform[1].

Digital TV has recently faced something of a collapse in sentiment. Both ITV Digital in the UK[2] and QUIERO TV in Spain went into liquidation in April 2002. Studies and surveys continue to show the UK public being sceptical as to the future of digital television and in one recent study 29% of consumers stated that they would never subscribe to a digital television platform[3].

The effect of the collapse of the dot.com boom on the website design industry has been nothing short of disastrous, with redundancies continuing unabated from the middle of 2000 onwards. Many highly regarded creative agencies with prestigious client bases have failed to survive[4]. The website design agencies which have managed to withstand the collapse of the dot.com boom would appear to be, by and large, those which are part of much larger marketing services groups.

The difficulties faced by the interactive sector in the widest sense, be it Internet businesses, interactive television or telecoms, have manifested themselves in a lack of investment funds. In particular, the development of broadband technology and its take-up by users in the United Kingdom has been disappointing and the UK has fallen behind its competitors. This, in itself, is not merely a symptom of the collapse of the dot.com boom (other jurisdictions faced similar economic conditions), as the UK broadband industry has faced a number of other practical and regulatory issues which are beyond the scope of this book. Various studies show the extent to which the UK is lagging behind, not only in take-up of broadband, but also the levels of use by those who actually have broadband access[5]. Section 6 below examines the state of play as regards broadband technology in the UK in more detail.

1   This is to enable it to auction off the existing analogue spectrum for commercial purposes.
2   In the final few months of its operation, ITV Digital had abandoned its original brand identity (On Digital), in order to improve brand awareness. Paragraph 1.07 includes a discussion on the cost of building a new brand.
3   Mediaedge: CIA's report on digital television in *New Media Age*, 20 June 2002. Contrast the projections made by strategyanalytics.com (see paragraph 1.13 below).
4   For example, Deep End Group's international reputation for outstanding and prestigious creative work was not enough to prevent them from going into liquidation in August 2001.
5   Netvalue.com study (reported in *New Media Age*, 14 February 2002) suggests that in the UK only 3.1% of all Internet connections are made by broadband users, in comparison with 8.9% in France and 13.1% in Germany.

5. AREAS FOR OPTIMISM

1.09 In the same way that e-mail proved itself to be the 'killer application' in respect of the Internet, SMS (text messaging) has proven itself to be the equivalent in respect of mobile phone technology. In January 2002 a record 1.4 billion text messages were sent in the UK[1]. The number of text messages sent is somewhere in the region of one per person per day for everybody living in the UK. The UK Government's e-Envoy recently announced a plan for children to have their exam results notified to them in the form of text messages[2]. The concept of using a mobile device for an ever wider range of functions is catching on. Vodafone is reported to have signed more than 50 companies to its mobile micro billing system, allowing content providers to bill for web or WAP content[3]. It appears that the major operators are looking to adopt a consistent standard across their networks and Vodafone recently announced that it would be teaming up with T-Mobile in this respect[4].

E-mail has become more popular than post in the UK and the number of e-mails sent and received between UK households now exceeds the number of letters. Helped also by the predominant use of the English language on the Internet, Britons are also the highest e-mail users in Europe[5]. On-line retail sales continue to grow and there are many supporting statistics:

- By December 2002, on-line retail is expected to account for 4% of all UK retail sales[6]. Indeed, e-commerce sales are currently growing 2.5 times faster in the UK than in the US. The figures show that in the fourth quarter of 2001, UK e-commerce sales represented 2.37%[7] of all retail activity, compared with 1.07%[8] in the US.

- The global Internet population grew by 18% during the period April 2001–April 2002, meaning that 420 million individuals worldwide have Internet access[9].

- Eurotunnel sells 40% of all its tickets through its website, offering a £2.00 on-line discount[10].

- Argos doubled its e-commerce sales to a total of £164m in the year ending 31 March 2002[11] and is also reported to be planning an own-brand digital satellite shopping channel[12].

- Internet use is spreading across social groupings. *The Sun* attracts 24 million page hits monthly on its website located at thesun.co.uk from social groups A, B and C[13].

1 Figures from MDA – Mobile Data Org (www.mda-mobiledata.org).
2 Reported in *The Independent*, 16 May 2002.
3 Reported in *Revolution*, 14 February 2002.
4 Reported in *The Independent*, 15 March 2002.
5 Figures from netvalue.com reported 550 million e-mails were sent in the UK in January 2002, compared to just 258 million domestic letters handled by Royal Mail.
6 Figures from the Interactive Media in Retail Group (www.imrg.org).
7 Figures from the Interactive Media in Retail Group.
8 Figures from US Department Of Commerce.
9 Neilson/Net Ratings Global Internet Index June 2002.
10 Reported in *Revolution*, 1 May 2002.
11 Reported in *Revolution*, 5 January 2002.
12 Speculation reported in *Marketing Week*, 13 June 2002.
13 Reported in *New Media Age*, 13 June 2002.

1.10 During the height of the dot.com boom, the UK Government publicly declared its stated policy to be for the UK to become the best place in the world to engage in e-commerce. By the end of 2000, Tony Blair famously ordered all central government services to be available on-line by 2005. The Government appears to be making progress in respect of its own activities[1]. Objectively, one independent report[2] suggests that the UK is making steady progress in terms of the facilitation of on-line government and that the UK occupies fourth position in the world in this respect (up from sixth the previous year). Certainly, the Government has made very public spending commitments in this regard[3]. In certain respects, the Government is certainly seizing the initiative. In particular, Chapter 14, E-gambling examines one area where the Government is deliberately seeking to make the UK a haven for a particular business sector. The on-line betting and gaming sector is a particularly lucrative one and a number of profitable businesses have emerged in this arena. For example, Ladbrokes.com and Ladbrokescasino.com have more than 260,000 customers in 160 countries and they are available in 11 languages. Financial results for the period ending 31 December 2001 revealed an operating profit of around £2m[4].

The 2002 FIFA World Cup was billed as the 'Internet World Cup'. Partly due to the timing of the games (early morning through to lunchtime), European audiences found themselves increasingly reliant on following developments on-line. During the period 31 May–29 June 2002, Fifaworldcup.com claimed more than 1.7 billion page views in aggregate. At times, traffic to the site exceeded 125 million page views in a single day[5].

Perhaps the most remarkable statistic brings us back to that enduring survivor of the dot.com boom. At the time of writing, the stock markets around the world have suffered something approaching a collapse. It is surprising that the best performing shares traded on the London Stock Exchange during 2002 are lastminute.com[6]. Lastminute.com's share price has seen a 217% rise during the course of 2002 to 96 pence[7].

1 Progress is outlined on a monthly basis at www.e-envoy.gov.uk.
2 Accenture report on e-government leadership.
3 £1 billion per annum is to be spent in each of the three years commencing from April 2001 in order to further this aim.
4 Reported in *Revolution*, 21 March 2002.
5 Reported in *Revolution*, 10 July 2002.
6 Reported in *The Independent*, 29 July 2002.
7 However, this is well down on the issue price at the time of the IPO, which was £3.80.

6. DEVELOPING TECHNOLOGIES

1.11 The second edition of this book looked at the pace with which new technologies were developing and attempted to predict how these would impact on the interactive world. As a consequence of depressed economic conditions progress has slowed immensely, as the funding for such investment and rollout is simply much less available than before. This section attempts, briefly, to set out an overview as to the current state of play in respect of a number of technologies.

(a) Fixed broadband

1.12 There are three main ways in which fixed (ie not mobile) broadband services are being delivered to customers (whether consumers or businesses) in the UK: via telephone lines, cable and satellite. Broadband technology allows for the transmission of significantly higher levels of data, allowing for an improved service for the recipient. Broadband can accommodate much more data than traditional Internet connections using a dial-up modem, because it makes use of multiple channels to transmit data simultaneously. It is often compared to the volume of traffic on a motorway as opposed to a single track road. Broadband is approximately ten times faster than the connection using a standard 56k dial-up modem. Broadband technology will have a huge impact, particularly in respect of distribution of the type of content which is owned by media companies, for example allowing for video clips to be downloaded with much greater speed.

Each of the delivery technologies for fixed broadband have their pros and cons and, generally, there is little availability for customers to be able to choose between the technologies at present. At present, no single technology can cover the United Kingdom, let alone Europe, and the Government will need to be technology neutral in terms of how it encourages take-up of breakdown, to ensure that roll out of broadband technologies is as rapid as possible. Currently, the maximum reach of cable broadband will be around 70% of UK homes and 90% by satellite. Approximately 60% of UK telephone exchanges (numerically as opposed to by population average) are now broadband-enabled.

Unfortunately, whatever the technology, the UK is lagging behind in respect of broadband take-up. At the start of 2002, the UK was in 26th place on the global league table of broadband penetration, with 0.24 digital subscriber lines (DSL) for every 100 people. In contrast, South Korea led the way with 11 DSL lines for every 100 inhabitants[1].

BT, however, is optimistic that its broadband operations are generating momentum. BT recently claimed that it was receiving 12,000 orders a week for broadband connections and that it already has 280,000 users connected[2]. By summer 2003 BT expects to have 1 million broadband customers. Within four years, BT claims that 25% of UK households will be using broadband.

It is to be seen which sectors will benefit most from broadband technology. Certainly, content and media owners will be able to benefit from another platform for distribution of content. It is generally agreed that the entertainment and media sectors will be a key beneficiary. A major beneficiary may turn out to be the owners of sports rights in that the technology will facilitate the live broadcast of events around the world. Interestingly, the threat to the entertainment sector (in particular music) of piracy and unauthorised use of copyright material is less of an issue for the sports sector on the basis that the revenue models for sports rights focus on the live event – and media values decrease the further the live event is removed in time. Section 11 of Chapter 3, E-liability outlines some of the practical commercial issues facing copyright owners.

Interestingly, the broadband sector's own lobbying group, the Broadband Content Coalition, which is made up of telecoms companies, content suppliers and IT firms, is urging the Government to push for a change of its broadband strategy and to focus attention on building awareness of the attractiveness of broadband content, such as games, music and films, rather than simply promoting the availability of fast access[3].

1   Research from PointTopic reported in *Revolution*, 29 May 2002.
2   Reported in the *Financial Times*, 18 July 2002.
3   Reported in *New Media Age*, 23 May 2002.

(b)   Digital TV

1.13   In section 4 above, some of the current difficulties faced by digital television were outlined. It is expected that digital television will be a key driver of interactivity going forward, and analysts in the sector believe that the collapse of companies such as ITV Digital and QUIERO TV in Spain will only make a small impact on the overall take-up of digital television. One study suggests that nearly three quarters of all European homes will have digital television by 2008[1].

One difficulty faced by digital television in the UK has been that until now availability has only been on a subscription basis. The recent announcement by the BBC that it will team up with BSkyB to try to create a digital terrestrial television service to replace ITV Digital[2] may facilitate take-up of digital TV. It is likely that a number of free digital channels will be available through receivers costing viewers less than £100.

It has also been recently reported that all of London's boroughs are teaming up to offer a range of public services via interactive television to be rolled out over the next two years[3].

1   Research from Strategy Analytics, June 2002 (www.strategyanalytics.com).
2   (2002) Times, 12 June.
3   Reported in *New Media Age*, 14 February 2002.

(c)   Wireless broadband

1.14   Paragraph 1.05 above highlighted the likely difficulties facing those companies which were awarded 3G mobile phone licences by the UK Government in May 2000. One of the difficulties faced by 3G operators is that the intermediate technology of GPRS (commonly known as 2.5G) is likely to offer a similar range of functions to 3G, albeit to a lower technical standard. The 3G operators are faced with a crucial strategic decision of whether or not they should push GPRS technology and whether doing so will make users less likely to take up 3G.

Mobile phone operators are looking to diversify their content offerings in order to encourage the take-up of such services. MMS[1] is a recently launched service which operators are heavily promoting. It is an extension of SMS, allowing the user to send pictures and sounds together with text, a service enhanced by the recent introduction of colour screens. The mobile phones used for MMS technology make use of cameras (either built-in or as an add-on). A new mobile phone is required to take advantage of the service.

In terms of content diversification, intriguingly, Hutchison 3G appointed a 'head of adult services' in 2001, to explore a range of content opportunities including gambling and soft core pornography. Recently, Virgin Mobile was reported to be in discussions with Playboy to offer its customers access to soft core pornography via mobile handsets[2].

Another area being explored by mobile operators is that of the potential for exploiting digital radio content on hand held devices. MM02 are reported to have linked with Virgin Radio and other partners to explore the potential for delivering digital radio through mobile phones[3].

With the gradual switch to GPRS and 3G, most mobile phone operators are reported to expect that their revenues are likely to be coming increasingly from the supply of content rather than traditional telephony[4].

At the time of writing, 3G mobile telephony in the UK is still very much in the experimental stages. The only operating service is a service being trialled by MMO2 on the Isle of Man. The aim of the trial is not only to test the technology but also to ascertain customer requirements in respect of the services offered. This trial represents the world's only 3G service other than in Japan[5].

A recent study predicts that 27% of all mobile phone users in Western Europe will own a 3G handset by the end of 2007[6]. The figures represent a sobering in attitudes from previous studies due to a growing awareness from consumer trials that users are not as enthusiastic about the potentials of this technology as previously predicted. The other reason for a lowering of expectations are continuing technological setbacks[7].

It will be intriguing to see how 3G operators rise to the challenge. It is generally accepted that customers will not simply trade one superior technology once it has superseded its predecessor without justification by way of superior services at an acceptable price[8]. Lessons learned from the hype which met the launch of WAP technology are apparent.

3G operators may well look to the valuable lessons to learn from iMODE, which was launched in Japan in February 1999 by NTT DoCoMo. This is a mobile Internet access system which has been an enormous success in Japan in terms of distribution of content. This technology allows subscribers to access the Internet through their mobile phones (80% of NTT DoCoMo's 40 million subscribers do so, compared to only 3% of mobile phone users in Europe). The technology allows e-mail access and web browsing and, very basically, consists of an additional layer of technology over NTT DoCoMo's ordinary mobile phone system.

The relative failure of WAP and slow take-up of data services in Europe has encouraged NTT DoCoMo to export iMODE and it is expected that, by the end of 2002, this service should be available in Germany, France, Belgium and The Netherlands as well as in Taiwan and the United States. This may represent a further challenge to the 3G operators.

1   Multimedia Messaging Service.
2   Reported in the *Financial Times*, 11 March 2002.
3   Reported in the *Sunday Times*, 7 July 2002.
4   Data is expected to account for a quarter of ARPU by 2006. Current levels are approximately 10%.
5   Vodafone's service is expected not to launch until 2003 and Hutchison 3G's projected launch is December 2002 (*The Independent*, 16 August 2002).
6   Research from the Worlds Market Research Centre at www.wmrc.com.
7   The Isle of Man trial was widely reported to be experiencing difficulties as regards the 'handover' of the handset from transmitter to transmitter.
8   Hence the lobbying of the Broadband Content Coalition outlined in paragraph 1.12.

7. CONCLUSIONS

1.15   During the height of the dot.com boom, Tesco's Internet strategy was widely ridiculed. Whereas many of its competitors and most aspiring on-line businesses were developing their own warehouses and concentrating on logistical issues, Tesco was accepting orders on-line while satisfying deliveries by having assistants in its local stores taking items from supermarket shelves.

With the benefit of hindsight, the strategy has worked: Tesco.com was spun off as a separate business in April 2000 and now operates not only in the UK but in the US, South Korea and the Republic of Ireland. It made sales of approximately £250m in the year to September 2001. In certain Tesco stores, 10% of sales are made via the web and Tesco is now considering revisiting how it satisfies orders[1]. In fact, there are many examples of traditional businesses succeeding in their Internet operations where they have pursued a gradual policy of re-education of their existing customer base or have focused on their core businesses. For example, Abbey National has reportedly seen an increase in user traffic on its website by 12% since it abandoned attempts to create an on-line financial portal and simplified its site by ridding itself of much third party content. Most importantly, product applications were up by 20%[2]. In retrospect, it is clear that businesses which did not go all out to develop an on-line strategy during the late 1990s have not missed the boat at all. No doubt buoyed by Tesco.com's success, the supermarket group Waitrose has recently launched its own Internet venture located at ocado.com.

Existing businesses no longer see their e-business as being a way to increase their share price or as a separate business which could be hived off for vast rewards. Rather, they view them increasingly as another arm of their existing operations and as a convenient way for transacting business at a reduced cost. The trend is to treat e-commerce as something different and special, as opposed to another aspect of a company's core activities. A recent CBI study suggests that in 2002 only 16% of member firms conducted a separate e-business. The comparative figure for 2001 had been 38%[3].

A post-mortem of brands such as boo.com, excite.com, stepstone.co.uk and letsbuyit.com suggests that they saw the potential of the Internet and, seeing that potential, took a gamble which did not pay off. One inevitable consequence, though, has been that the dot.coms helped prepare consumers to do business on-line and to lose their fear of the unknown. However, it is the tried and trusted brands that look as if they will benefit.

Broadband technology will clearly have an important impact on all of our lives. At this stage it is difficult to envisage how quickly this will happen and who the commercial winners will be.

What is evident, however, from the brief overview in this chapter, and from the chapters which follow, is that our lives have already changed and that the impact of the Internet and interactive media cannot be ignored or disregarded merely due to current economic difficulties.

1 *Revolution*, 19 June 2002.
2 www.abbeynational.co.uk (reported in *New Media Age*, 28 February 2002).
3 Reported in the *Evening Standard Internet for Business Supplement*, June 2002.

E-contract

I. INTRODUCTION

2.01 The ability to enter into valid and binding contracts on-line is crucial if the digital revolution is to continue and for businesses and consumers alike to benefit from e-commerce. This chapter looks at how existing concepts of contract law may apply to cyberspace in a variety of contractual situations and also how the function of a signature in traditional contractual relations can be replicated in an on-line environment. Later chapters will look at contracts entered into in specific situations, where the subject matter of the contract or the nature of and relationship between the parties calls for special further consideration.

This chapter looks in particular at the new Electronic Commerce (EC Directive) Regulations 2002[1] that transpose into English law the majority of the provisions of the E-Commerce Directive[2]. The consultation period for the Regulations closed on 2 May 2002 and the E-Commerce Regulations came into force on 21 August 2002, with the exception of regulation 16 (which comes into force on 23 October 2002). Unfortunately, neither the E-Commerce Directive nor the E-Commerce Regulations clarify beyond doubt the strict legal position as to when an on-line contract is concluded. Accordingly, lawyers will be required to look both at the common law and legislation when analysing on-line contracting at a technical level. However, at a practical level, the new legislation reinforces the common law position that, for the vast majority of goods and services, there is nothing in English law which prevents an on-line seller from concluding contracts on-line.

In England and Wales the law of contract is a creature of the common law[3], which has developed over centuries largely through the decisions of the judiciary in relation to disputes brought before them[4]. While in the nineteenth and twentieth centuries some changes to the law of contract had been introduced under Acts of Parliament[5], the law of contract still has its roots firmly embedded in the 'judge-made' common law. This has a distinct advantage, namely that of flexibility: courts are much freer than Parliament to address changes in business practice and technology. For example, the courts were always in the best position to take into consideration the effect on the development of contract law of new delivery methods. When at the start of the nineteenth century it became much more common to assume that a contract might be 'concluded' by postal delivery, rather than face-to-face, the courts formulated rules governing when offers were validly accepted[6]. The more recent innovations of the telegraph and telex called for further legal innovation in this respect[7] and, equally, it is likely that it will be the courts which will consider whether on-line contracting calls for a new approach to be adopted as to when acceptance takes place and a binding contract is formed[8].

1 SI 2002/2013.
2 Directive (EC) 31/2000 on certain legal aspects of Information Society Services, in particular electronic commerce in the Internal Market.
3 Scotland is a civil law jurisdiction and its laws of contract are somewhat different from those in the rest of the UK.
4 The current conception of the law of contract started to emerge from the middle of the fourteenth century (eg *The Humber Ferry Case* (1349)), when the common law courts began to recognise an action for what we think of as damages payable by a party who had undertaken (assumpsit) to do something and had failed to do so or (through further evolution of the principle) had done so in an inadequate fashion. This in turn was a reaction to the courts insisting that the early medieval writ of covenant, the common law's first attempt to regulate commercial agreements between parties, was not available to litigants who were unable to produce evidence in writing under seal of the terms they had agreed. For a fuller discussion of the evolution of the common law of contract, see Chapter 1 of *Cheshire, Fifoot & Furmston's Law of Contract* (13th edition, 1999).
5 For example, the Sale of Goods Act 1893, subsequently re-enacted in 1979 (as amended) (regulating aspects of the sale of goods, including the introduction of implied warranties), the Consumer Credit Act 1974 (CCA 1974) (providing a regime for regulation of two party and three party consumer credit transactions), the Unfair Contract Terms Act 1977 (UCTA 1977) (the first measure in the UK to provide for the avoidance of certain unfair terms sought to be introduced into consumer contracts) and, most recently, the Contracts (Rights of Third Parties) Act 1999 (which for the first time afforded a mechanism for third parties to sue on contracts in certain cases).
6 *Adams v Lindsell* (1818) 1 B & Ald 681, discussed in paragraph 2.33.
7 For example, *Tenax Steamship Co Ltd v Reinante Transoceania Navegacion SA, The Brimnes* [1975] QB 929.
8 The E-Commerce Directive will also impact here – see paragraph 2.18 below.

2.02 In addition to the issues of actually contracting in an on-line environment, parties may contract in a traditional way in order to put themselves in the position to contract on-line by entering into agreements with Internet service providers (ISPs), designers and maintainers of websites and providers of advertising services in an on-line environment. We will consider these issues in outline in paragraph 2.20 below.

This chapter closes with a section on competition regulation. Whereas parties are generally free to contract to carry on business together, or to supply each other with goods or services, in a completely free and unrestricted fashion, regulations have evolved over recent years which control practices and commercial relationships which are considered to be against the interests of fair competition in the market. Paragraph 2.22 looks at how the UK and the EU are regulating such activities in general terms, and how these general principles are being applied to e-commerce.

2. WHAT IS A CONTRACT?

2.03 A contract has been defined in a variety of ways; but essentially it is an agreement or bargain between two or more parties which a court will enforce. A full analysis of the law of contract is beyond the scope of this chapter. However, we need to address certain basic concepts in order to understand how these subsist in relation to on-line trading activities.

The basic requirements to create a contract are as follows:

■ offer;

■ acceptance;

■ consideration; and

■ intention to create legal relations.

In all probability, the formal requirements of consideration and intention to create legal relations will be present in a typical on-line bargain. What is more problematic, and where care needs to be taken, is when and where (or if) offer and acceptance take place and who makes the offer and who accepts.

(a) Invitations to treat, offers and acceptances

2.04   As a general rule, a contract is concluded when an offer is accepted. Although this appears to be a simple rule, there have been many legal problems in the past over how to characterise and identify 'invitations to treat', offers, counter-offers and acceptances. This problem is relevant to e-commerce and may indeed be exacerbated because of the use made of automation by businesses who use websites and other e-commerce methods as part of their operation.

For example, if the price of a product is incorrectly advertised on a web page then it is likely that a large number of orders may be placed by customers before the mistake is rectified. This was illustrated by an incident in September 1999 involving Argos, the UK retailer, where £299 21-inch televisions were accidentally advertised for £2.99 on its website. Almost £1m of orders were taken before the mistake was noticed, with one opportunistic buyer placing an order for 1,700 sets alone. Argos subsequently declined to fulfil the orders. Whether Argos was entitled to do so depended partly on whether the price on its website was an 'invitation to treat' so that the customers' orders only constituted an offer to buy, or whether the web page was an offer which the customers could have accepted by placing their orders to conclude the contract. Examples of other such occurrences are not uncommon and this highlights the danger of using automated responses to confirm acceptance of an order.

The website is a virtual shop window and just as the display of goods in a supermarket is regarded as an invitation to treat and their presentation at the checkout counter is regarded as an offer which is accepted by the cashier[1], a web page, which serves an analogous purpose, should probably also be regarded only as an invitation to treat. The on-line seller can take further steps to reinforce this conclusion. For example, it can state that it requires confirmation of payment before dispatch of goods (for instance credit card authorisation) or that it reserves his right to decline to supply goods to certain jurisdictions or to underaged customers. Most on-line sellers will take prudent steps to make their websites stand out as invitations to treat, for fear of otherwise binding themselves to an obligation to supply to all-comers where they may have insufficient stock to meet the demand. For example, the on-line seller should make a clear statement that it will not be bound until the on-line seller accepts the customer's offer.

However, where the on-line seller intends to be bound immediately by its response to its customer then it will be considered to have actually made an offer. The on-line seller's intention will always be judged objectively. For example, what construction should be placed on an expression such as: 'Special Offer! £50 off for the first 50 customers'? This problem can, of course, arise in relation to the sort of offer which stands out from the language used, even if perhaps the offeror might not have intended it to be read thus[2]. As well as possibly being a unilateral offer, such a statement may well be regarded as a continuing offer[3]. It may not, therefore, always be appropriate to consider a website as an invitation to treat. For example, if there is a link to a database which indicates the number of products available, it may be correct to view this as an offer. Making a unilateral or continuing offer on the Internet could create many issues as to when acceptance takes place.

1   See *Pharmaceutical Society of Great Britain v Boots Cash Chemists (Southern) Ltd* [1952] 2 QB 795; *Fisher v Bell* [1961] 1 QB 394. Likewise, generally, price lists, circulars and advertisements, which are analogous to the website, are often regarded as invitations to treat. See *Grainger & Son v Gough* [1896] AC 325, HL; *Partridge v Crittenden* [1968] 2 All ER 421. But contrast these decisions with *Carlill v Carbolic Smokeball Co* [1893] 1 QB 256, CA.
2   *Carlill v Carbolic Smokeball Co* [1893] 1 QB 256, CA. It is worth noting that under article 14(2) of the United Nations Convention On Contracts For The International Sale Of Goods (Vienna, 1980) (the Vienna Convention), a proposal other than one addressed to one or more specific persons is to be considered merely as an invitation to make offers, unless the contrary is clearly indicated by the person making the proposal; details are available at www.unictral.org.
3   *R v Warwickshire County Council, ex p Johnson* [1993] AC 583, HL.

2.05   The customer will make an offer in response to the on-line seller's invitation to treat. An offer is any statement, by words or conduct, which unequivocally indicates that the person making the offer ('the offeror') is willing to be bound by the terms if the other person ('the offeree') accepts. An offer may be withdrawn at any time prior to its acceptance, unless the promise to keep it open is supported by consideration[1]. An acceptance is any indication, by words or conduct, that the person accepting agrees to be bound by the terms of the offer.

Even if the initial web page is considered to be an invitation to treat rather than an offer, careful planning is required with respect to the response generated to the customer's offer. A contract could be formed inadvertently if the on-line seller's system issues an automatic confirmation or acknowledgement of an order, as this could be deemed to be an acceptance. However, if the response that is generated is nothing more than an acknowledgement that an order has been registered by the system, or is expressly subject to wording such as 'goods supplied subject to availability and the terms and conditions set out on the site', then this will probably not amount to a contractual acceptance and may allow for some flexibility in the event of manifest error or supply shortages. As an 'acceptance' must be an unequivocal assent to all the terms, the addition or modification of any term makes the on-line seller's reply a 'counter-offer' and, strictly speaking, no contract is formed until that counter-offer is accepted[2].

1   In contrast, the Vienna Convention, art 16(2) states that where an offer is stated to be open for a fixed time, it is irrevocable until that period expires regardless of consideration. This is a common feature of most civil law systems.
2   See *Hyde v Wrench* (1840) 3 Beav 334; but compare the approach of Lord Denning MR to that of Lawton LJ in *Butler Machine Tool Co Ltd v Ex-Cell-O Corpn (England) Ltd* [1979] 1 All ER 965, CA, where Lord Denning was prepared to try to reconcile the differences between the parties and find a contract.

(b) Counter-offers and the 'battle of the forms'

2.06   Where the e-commerce system is not entirely web-based but the on-line seller is willing to accept orders by e-mail as well, then additional care should be taken to avoid a 'battle of the forms'. This can arise where each party appends its own terms and conditions to its e-mails, so that the customer sends a purchase order by e-mail with its standard terms of purchase and the on-line seller replies 'accepting' the order but appending its own terms and conditions of sale. This is more likely in business-to-business transactions where parties are used to negotiating and have their own standard terms.

One possible solution to this problem may be for the parties to choose to apply the 1964 Uniform Law on the Formation of Contracts for the International Sales of Goods[1], which provides that, where the added or modified terms in the reply do not materially alter the terms of the offer, the reply will constitute an acceptance unless the offeror promptly objects to the discrepancy. If the offeror does not object then the terms of the contract shall be the terms of the offer with the modifications contained in the acceptance[2]. This will not solve the problem where the added or modified terms are materially different and, given the declining number of countries which are now part of the 1964 Hague Convention and the lack of experience of the UK courts in applying the Uniform Law, most UK businesses do not choose this option.

1   See Schedule 2 to the Uniform Laws on International Sales Act 1967. The Vienna Convention applies to the formation of contracts of sale of goods which, if they were concluded, would be governed by the Uniform Law on the International Sale of Goods (see the 1964 Hague Convention) (the Uniform Law). The UK will apply the Uniform Law only to contracts in which the parties have chosen the Uniform Law as the law of the contract.
2   Article 7 of the Vienna Convention.

2.07   Another possible solution is to apply the 1980 Vienna Convention on Contracts for the International Sale of Goods. Article 19(2) of the Vienna Convention provides that:

> 'a reply to an offer which purports to be an acceptance but contains additional or different terms which do not materially alter the terms of the offer constitutes an acceptance, unless the Offeror, without undue delay, objects orally to the discrepancy or dispatches a notice to that effect. If he does not so object, the terms of the contract are the terms of the offer with the modifications contained in the acceptance.

Additional or different terms relating, among other things, to the price, payment, quality and quantity of the goods, place and time of delivery, extent of one party's liability to the other or the settlement of disputes are considered to alter the terms of the offer materially.'

The Vienna Convention has not, however, yet been ratified by the UK[1] and will only govern the formation of international non-consumer contracts for the sale of goods if expressly incorporated, if it is incorporated by choice of law of a ratifying state or if both parties are from states which have ratified it[2].

1   As of 19 July 2002, 63 states, including the US, Australia, most EU Member States and China, have adopted the Vienna Convention.
2   The Vienna Convention applies to contracts of sale of goods between parties whose places of business are in different states: (a) when the states are Contracting States, or (b) when the rules of private international law lead to the application of the law of a Contracting State. The Vienna Convention does not apply to sales of goods bought for personal, family or household use, unless the seller, at any time before or at the conclusion of the contract, neither knew nor ought to have known that the goods were bought for any such use. In short, the Vienna Convention is only ever likely to govern business-to-business e-commerce relationships.

(c) Steps to avoid problems

2.08   Where an incorrect offer has been made and accepted, the on-line seller can only rely on the doctrine of mistake to avoid the contract. At common law, this will depend on a court finding that the customer knew[1] that the offer must have been made on the basis of a mistake. Given the number of 'free' or deeply discounted deals available on the Internet, this may nowadays be a difficult argument for the on-line seller to sustain.

To avoid such problems, the on-line seller should state clearly the procedure to be followed for a binding contract to come into existence so that the customers have actual knowledge that it does not intend to be bound until that procedure is completed. The E-Commerce Regulations now specifically require an on-line seller to provide to customers certain information, including in particular the different technical steps to follow to conclude the contract – see paragraph 2.18 below.

1   It is not clear whether the mistake must actually be known to the customer or whether it is enough that the mistake ought to have been apparent to any reasonable man: see *Centrovincial Estates plc v Merchant Investors Assurance Co Ltd* [1983] Com LR 158, CA, which suggested the latter test could apply at common law, compared to the requirement of actual knowledge for rectification in equity in *Agip SpA v Navigazione Alta Italia SpA* [1984] 1 Lloyd's Rep 353, CA; *Olympia Sauna Shipping Co SA v Shinwa Kaiun Kaisha Ltd* [1985] 2 Lloyd's Rep 364.

3.   CAN A CONTRACT BE FORMED ELECTRONICALLY?

2.09   The short answer is yes (except where there are specific regulations affecting the formation of a contract which require writing, etc). Under English law, in most cases there are no particular formal requirements nor is there a need for a contract to be in writing or to be in tangible form. The courts will often construe a contract to exist between two parties on account of an undocumented course of dealing between them[1]. This is all, of course, very helpful in the context of e-commerce where such requirements can be difficult to create, even by analogy.

However, care should still be taken in the meantime as there remains within English law a number of types or classes of contract which are subject to specific legislation and which may, therefore, require formalities which cannot be accommodated on-line[2]. Furthermore, other countries have their own requirements regarding contracts, which may have the effect of requiring a verbal contract to be reduced to writing (for example, that in order to give effect to some aspect of the contract in another country, it is required to be notarised).

1 Courts are generally keen to help rather than hinder businessmen and look to give effect to commercial expectations as far as possible, even if the agreement appears incomplete or imprecise: *Hillas & Co Ltd v Arcos Ltd* (1932) 147 LT 503, HL; *Foley v Classique Coaches Ltd* [1934] 2 KB 1, CA.

2 For example, consumer credit bargains under the CCA 1974 must be entered into through the use of elaborate printed forms and signed with a pen in the usual fashion, which, therefore, precludes such agreements – for the time being – from being entered into on-line. However, the DTI has indicated in its Consultation Document on Modernising the Consumer Credit Act 1974 ('Tackling loan sharks – and more') that until 21 June 2002 it was to be consulting on various substantive issues, including removing the requirement for all credit agreements to be concluded in writing. In its Progress Report, it stated that focus group discussions on this issue would begin in the second half of 2002 and that a consultation paper will be issued.

(a) Need for a deed

2.10 The legal form used to effect an English law agreement is not usually of concern to the courts in considering the status or enforceability of that agreement. However, certain contracts are subject to rules as to their legal form. Certain contracts must be executed as deeds[1] (for example, a lease of real property for more than three years[2]).

The historic requirement that deeds be sealed was abolished by the Law of Property (Miscellaneous Provisions) Act 1989, but the Act made it clear that for a contract to qualify as a deed it has to be clear from the terms of the contract that the parties intend it to be executed as such[3]. In addition, there is a requirement for the presence and signature of a witness to each person executing the deed (who also signs his name).

It is at least arguable that the requirements of section 1(2) and (3) of the Law of Property (Miscellaneous Provisions) Act 1989 in relation to 'sign' could be extended by analogy to include a digital equivalent of a signature[4]. However, even if an electronic deed might in fact be valid and enforceable where electronically 'signed' by the parties and their witnesses, the law has yet to be clarified on this point, and it would be more advisable for the time being for any contract required to be executed in deed format to be printed out on paper and signed by the parties and witnesses in the time-honoured fashion.

1 This is a throwback to the medieval 'covenant', which by the early fourteenth century had evolved into a written agreement under seal. Nowadays, the principal function of a deed of agreement (rather than a 'parole' agreement, ie one that is not expressed to be a deed) is that the execution of the deed connotes the parties' consideration and intention to be bound. Thus, the deed is often used to give effect to arrangements where there is nil or negligible valuable consideration.

2 The Law of Property Act 1925, ss 52 and 54(2). A recent e-conveyancing paper has proposed that e-conveyancing be made possible under section 8 of the Electronic Communications Act 2000 (ECA 2000). For further examples, see the Law Commission's Report on the Execution of Deeds and Documents by or on behalf of Bodies Corporate (Law Com Report No 253).

3 The attestation provision usually commences with the words 'Executed as a Deed by ...'.

4 Subject, of course, to the law being capable of recognising the concept of a digital signature simpliciter. See further, paragraph 2.26 below.

(b) Need for contract to be in writing

2.11 While very few legal documents require execution as deeds, rather more must still be in writing. It has been estimated that there may be as many as 40,000 references to 'writing' and 'signature' alone in existing legislation[1].

Some examples of contracts that must be 'in writing' include:

■ assignment of a copyright (see section 90(3) of the Copyright, Designs and Patent Act 1988);

- regulated consumer credit agreements (see section 61 of the CCA 1974)[2];

- contracts for marine insurance (see section 22 of the Marine Insurance Act 1906);

- contracts for the sale or disposition of interests in land (see section 2(1) of the Law of Property (Miscellaneous Provisions) Act 1989);

- contracts of guarantee (see section 4 of the Statute of Frauds 1677); and

- certain contracts for the provision of investment services under the Financial Services Act 1986 regime (governed pursuant to the terms of the relevant regulatory bodies operating under that Act).

In respect of all these contracts, the issue as to what constitutes 'writing' is now governed by Schedule 1 to the Interpretation Act 1978, which contains a definition for writing as follows:

> 'Writing includes typing, printing, lithography, photography and other modes of representing or reproducing words in a visible form, and expressions referring to writing are construed accordingly.'

Although this is a fairly broad definition, its origins predate the computer age, and certainly predate the age of e-commerce and on-line dealing. In fact, there is a good case to be made for saying that if the terms of an on-line agreement appear on your computer screen (and, indeed, it can be saved by you to a hard disk or printed out), this amounts to 'writing' within the broad scope of the above definition. However, it is unclear whether this requirement would be satisfied if all one were to do would be to click on an 'I accept' button when asked to do so, bypassing in the process the actual terms of the agreement, because you did not choose to follow a hyperlink to the relevant page. In this respect, see further the discussion at paragraph 2.26 which examines the common law requirements for incorporating written terms into a contract.

In view of the rapid pace of e-commerce development, there are a number of initiatives (both on an international front and within the UK) aiming to address concerns over this question.

1   See, for example, Copeland, 'Digital Signatures: Throw Away your Pens?' [2000] ENTLR 112.
2   See footnote 2 to paragraph 2.09.

4.   THE E-COMMERCE DIRECTIVE AND E-COMMERCE (EC DIRECTIVE) REGULATIONS

2.12   The Electronic Commerce (EC Directive) Regulations 2002[1] transpose into English law the majority of the provisions of the E-Commerce Directive.

In broad terms, the E-Commerce Regulations apply to on-line trade and advertising (eg over the Internet, by e-mail or by mobile phone) irrespective of whether the goods or services in question are themselves delivered electronically. The Regulations do not apply to the goods or services themselves. They address the following key principles:

- 'country of origin principle';

- information requirements when contracting on-line;

- treatment of on-line contracts; and

- liability of intermediary service providers.

1   SI 2002/2013. The Regulations came into force on 21 August 2002, with the exception of regulation 16 (which comes into force on 23 October 2002).

(a) Where do the E-Commerce Regulations apply?

2.13 The E-Commerce Regulations apply to 'information society services' within the 'co-ordinated field'.

Information society services are defined as having the meaning set out in article 2(a) of the E-Commerce Directive, and as summarised in recital 17 to the E-Commerce Directive as covering any service normally provided for remuneration at a distance, by means of electronic equipment for the processing (including digital compression) and storage of data, and at the individual request of a recipient of a service.

The Guidance on the E-Commerce Regulations published by the DTI (Guidance)[1] notes that this definition spans a wide range of economic activities that take place on-line, including selling goods and services on-line as well as video on demand and services consisting of the transmission of information via a communication network, providing access to a communication network, hosting information provided by a recipient of the service or providing commercial communications by e-mail.

The Guidance also notes that the requirement for an information society service to be 'normally provided for remuneration' does not restrict its scope to services requiring monetary payment. It would also extend to services that are not directly remunerated by those who receive them – for example, those offering advertisements on-line.

The co-ordinated field is defined by the E-Commerce Regulations as:

> 'requirements applicable to information society service providers or information society services, regardless of whether they are of a general nature or specifically designed for them, and covers requirements with which the service provider has to comply in respect of:
>
> - the taking up of the activity of an information society service, such as requirements concerning qualifications, authorisation or notification; and
>
> - the pursuit of the activity of an information society server, such as requirements concerning the behaviour of the service provider, requirements regarding the quality or content of the service including those applicable to advertising and contracts, or requirements concerning the liability of the service provider,
>
> but does not cover requirements such as those applicable to goods as such, to the delivery of goods or to services not provided by electronic means.'

---

1 'A Guide for Business to the Electronic Commerce (EC Directive) Regulations 2002' Guidance July 2002, available from the DTI website, at www.dti.gov.uk.

(b) Country of origin principle

2.14 Under regulation 4(1) and (2), information society services provided to a person in another state in the European Economic Area (EEA) by a service provider from an establishment in the UK must comply with any applicable UK law that falls within the co-ordinated field and for which the enforcement authorities are responsible for ensuring compliance.

The Guidance notes that the effect of this regulation is a shift in responsibility for enforcement. That is, UK enforcement authorities will now regulate information society services provided from the UK, wherever in the EEA they are delivered. This will not affect UK consumers of information society services provided by UK-established service providers. However, it does mean that UK-established service providers will need to comply with UK law when they are providing information society services to consumers *elsewhere* in the EEA.

Regulation 4(3) provides that any applicable UK law that falls within the co-ordinated field may not be applied to an information society service provided by a service provider established *elsewhere* in the EEA, *if* this would restrict the freedom to provide that service into the UK. Accordingly, inbound information society services are subject to a restrictions test: UK law *may* apply to the service provided it does not restrict the freedom to provide the service in the UK.

Regulation 4(4) provides that regulation 4(1), (2) and (3) do not apply to the following fields:

- copyright, neighbouring rights, rights referred to in the Semiconductor Topographies Directive (EEC) 54/87 and the Databases Directive (EC) 9/96 and industrial property rights;

- the freedom of the parties to a contract to choose the applicable law;

- contractual obligations concerning consumer contracts;

- formal validity of contracts creating or transferring rights in real estate where such contracts are subject to mandatory formal requirements of the law of the Member State where the real estate is situated; and

- the permissibility of unsolicited commercial communications by e-mail.

It must be stressed that regulation 4 does *not* provide for what might be termed a 'pure' country of origin regulation (that is, regulation only in the service provider's home country and not in the consumer's). In particular, the wide exception for 'contractual obligations concerning consumer contracts' will mean that a UK-based website selling to consumers will need to make sure that its terms and conditions comply with the laws of the country in which the consumer is based. The Guidance has additionally gone further than the terms of the E-Commerce Directive by stating that the exception for consumer contracts includes requirements to do certain things *before* entering into a contract. This Guidance has been criticised by industry as going further than the E-Commerce Directive requires, especially as the E-Commerce Directive does not itself result in a country of origin principle as a result of the exceptions noted above.

(c) Information requirements

2.15   One of the key elements of the E-Commerce Directive is to enhance the transparency of information for those buying on-line, with the intent that this will increase confidence in on-line commercial media. Regulation 6(1) of the E-Commerce Regulations states that a person providing an information society service must make available to the recipient of the service, in a form and manner that is easily, directly and permanently accessible, the following information:

- the name of the service provider;

- the geographic address at which the service provider is established;

- the details of the service provider, including his e-mail address;

- if the service provider is registered in a trade or similar register available to the public, the register in which the service provider is entered, along with his registration number;

- where the provision of the service is subject to an authorisation scheme, the particulars of the relevant supervisory authority.

There are additional information obligations in respect of 'regulated professions' (for example, professional bodies). If the service provider is subject to value added tax, he must also provide his VAT number.

The Regulations do not prescribe how the requirement to make information 'easily, directly and permanently accessible' should be met. The Guidance notes that, where technical restraints mean that information may not be readily accessible (for example, on mobile phone text messages), on-line suppliers may still have met the criteria if the information is accessible by other means (for example, inclusion on a website).

(d) 'Commercial communications'

2.16 As well as the general information requirements noted above in paragraph 2.15, the E-Commerce Regulations go further by imposing additional requirements on service providers who send 'commercial communications'. This definition spans a wide range of on-line forms of communication, including websites and e-mails. To fall within the definition, the communication must be 'designed' to promote the goods or services of the service provider; it is not yet clear whether certain types of communication (such as mobile text 'welcome messages') will be considered to be 'designed' to promote the service provider.

A service provider must ensure that a 'commercial communication':

- is clearly identifiable as a commercial communication;

- clearly identifies the person on whose behalf the commercial communication is made;

- clearly identifies as such any promotional offer (including any discount, premium or gift) and ensures that any conditions which must be met to qualify for it are easily accessible, and presented clearly and unambiguously; and

- clearly identifies as such any promotional competition or game and ensures that any conditions for participation are easily accessible, and presented clearly and unambiguously.

The E-Commerce Regulations do not prescribe how the requirement for information about commercial communications to be 'clearly identifiable' should be met.

(e) Electronic contracting

2.17 Article 9(1) of the E-Commerce Directive states:

'Member states shall ensure that their legal system allows contracts to be concluded by electronic means. Member states shall in particular ensure that the legal requirements applicable to the contractual process neither create obstacles for the use of electronic contracts nor result in such contracts being deprived of legal effectiveness and validity on account of their having been made by electronic means.'

This requirement is subject to certain exceptions. Member States are not required to ensure that the following types of contracts can be concluded by electronic means:

- contracts that create or transfer rights in real estate, except for rental rights;

- contracts requiring by law the involvement of courts, public authorities or professions exercising public authority;

- contracts of suretyship granted and on collateral securities furnished by persons acting for purposes outside their trade, business or profession; and

- contracts governed by family law or by the law of succession.

The E-Commerce Regulations do *not* transpose article 9(1) of the E-Commerce Directive into UK law. The Guidance notes[1] that:

> 'The Government believes that the great majority of relevant statutory references (eg to requirements for writing or signature) are already capable of being fulfilled by electronic communications where the context in which they appear does not indicate to the contrary.'

Where obstacles do exist to on-line contracting, the Guidance states that the Government will address these on a case-by-case basis – for example, by making orders under section 8 of the ECA 2000[2].

1   The Guidance Note, para 5.12.
2   See below, paragraph 2.20.

(f)   Contract requirements

2.18   The E-Commerce Regulations (in transposing the E-Commerce Directive into English law) contain yet further obligations on service providers in relation to the information that they must provide to customers on-line. The requirements (which are not limited to dealings with consumers) will need to be read in conjunction with the requirements of the Distance Selling Directive (see paragraph 2.43 below).

Regulation 9(1) provides that, unless parties who are not consumers have agreed otherwise, a service provider must, prior to an order being placed by the recipient of a service, provide to that recipient in a clear, comprehensible and unambiguous manner the following information:

- the different technical steps to follow to conclude the contract;

- whether or not the concluded contract will be filed by the service provider and whether it will be accessible;

- the technical means for identifying and correcting input errors prior to the placing of the order; and

- the languages offered for the conclusion of the contract.

Importantly, Regulation 9(3) provides that where terms and conditions applicable to the contract are provided to the recipient, they must be made available to him in a way that allows him to 'store and reproduce them'.

Regulation 11(1) provides that, unless parties who are not consumers have agreed otherwise, where the recipient of the services places his order through technological means, a service provider must:

- acknowledge receipt of the order to the recipient of the service without undue delay and by electronic means; and

- make available to the recipient of the service appropriate, effective and accessible technical means allowing him to identify and correct input errors prior to the placing of the order.

Regulation 11(1) is a key element of the E-Commerce Regulations. On-line suppliers engaged in business-to-business transactions are likely to wish to contract out of the above regulation, especially given the consequences of failing to comply with this regulation (see paragraph 2.19 further below).

The Regulations further provide (regulation 11(2)) that the order and acknowledgement of receipt will be deemed to be received when the parties to whom they are addressed are able to access them. The Regulations do not specify what is meant by 'access', nor is there any assistance provided in the Guidance concerning this point. It is also unclear how this regulation will impact on the common law rules concerning when a contract is formed (see paragraph 2.23 below). In this respect, regulation 12 states that an 'order' *may* be but need not be the contractual offer for the purposes of regulation 11.

In effect, the regime set out in regulation 11 will interact with (but not replace) the common law regarding offer and acceptance. If the on-line seller's acknowledgement does constitute contractual acceptance (as determined by the common law), the time of contract formation will be as specified in regulation 11(2). Accordingly, on-line sellers will wish to clarify the position as to what constitutes offer and acceptance in their terms and conditions wherever possible.

(g) Cancellation right

2.19 A key provision introduced by the E-Commerce Regulations (as included in the E-Commerce Directive) is a right of cancellation now given to recipients of on-line services. Regulation 15 provides that where a person has entered into, or proposes to enter into, a contract to which the E-Commerce Regulations apply and:

■ the terms and conditions of the on-line seller have not been made available to him in compliance with regulation 9(3); or

■ the service provider has not acknowledged receipt of the order or made available means of allowing the customer to identify and correct input errors in compliance with regulation 11(1),

then the contract shall not be enforceable against the customer and the customer may give notice of cancellation of the agreement to the service provider at any time.

This is a significant modification to the common law concerning contractual formation. In particular, there is no time limit (other than general time limits available under the Limitation Act 1980) under which the customer can exercise his option to cancel the contract. Accordingly, on-line sellers will need to ensure in particular compliance with regulations 9(3) and 11(1) of the E-Commerce Regulations.

5. THE ELECTRONIC COMMUNICATIONS ACT 2000

2.20 The ECA 2000 received Royal Assent on 25 May 2000. It does not directly address contractual issues. However, section 8 of the Act gives power to the 'appropriate Minister', by order made by Statutory Instrument, to 'remove restrictions in other legislation which prevent the use of electronic communication in place of paper, and to enable the use of electronic communications to be regulated where it is already allowed'. Although the Act and the E-Commerce Directive (and E-Commerce Regulations) address the same issues, there is no real overlap between them.

Section 8(1) gives the appropriate Minister the power to authorise or facilitate the use of electronic communications or electronic storage (instead of other methods of communication or storage) for any purpose mentioned in section 8(2) (ie the doing of anything which is required to be done in writing, by any specified means of delivery, signed or sealed, under oath or by statutory declaration, for which records must be kept, information published or payment made).

This power is limited by section 8(3), which places a duty on the Minister not to make such an order unless he is satisfied that it will be possible to produce a record of anything that is done by virtue of the authorisation. It is also limited by section 8(6), so that a person cannot be required to abandon paper unless he has previously chosen to do so. When someone has previously chosen the electronic option, restrictions or conditions may also be imposed on the variation or withdrawal of such a choice. The intention is that the Minister's power should be used selectively, to offer the alternative of electronic contracting to those who want it.

The Act contemplates that secondary legislation may provide, in relation to cases in which the use of electronic communications or electronic storage is so authorised, for the determination of any of the following matters, or as to the manner in which they may be proved in legal proceedings, namely:

- whether a thing has been done using an electronic communication or electronic storage;

- the time at which, or date on which, a thing done using any such communication or storage was done;

- the person by whom such a thing was done; and

- the contents, authenticity or integrity of any electronic data.

2.21 The first use of the section 8 power was made when Parliament approved, at the end of 2000, an Order which amends the Companies Act 1985 in a number of respects, so as to enable electronic communications of different types to take place between companies and their investors in prescribed circumstances[1]. Subsequently, the following orders have been made:

- the Unsolicited Goods and Services Act 1971 (Electronic Communications) Order 2001 (SI 2001/2778);

- the Local Government and Housing Act 1989 (Electronic Communications) (Wales) Order 2001 (SI 2001/605);

- the Prescription Only Medicines (Human Use) (Electronic Communications) Order 2001 (SI 2001/2889);

- the National Health Service (General Medical Services) (Electronic Communications) Order 2001 (SI 2001/2890);

- the National Health Service (Charges for Drugs and Appliances) (Electronic Communications) Order 2001 (SI 2001/2887); and

- the National Health Service (Pharmaceutical Services) and (Misuse of Drugs) (Electronic Communications) Order 2001 (SI 2001/2888).

The Value Added Tax (Electronic Communications) (Incentives) Regulations 2001 (SI 2001/759) are in force, although not released under the ECA 2000 but by the Commissioners of Customs & Excise (in exercise of the powers conferred on them by Schedule 38 to the Finance Act 2000).

1   The Companies Act 1985 (Electronic Communications) Order 2000 (SI 2000/3373), in force 22 December 2000. The scope of the Order is considered in more detail in Chapter 11, E-insurance.

6.   THE UNCITRAL MODEL LAW ON ELECTRONIC COMMERCE

2.22 The United Nations Commission on International Trade Law (UNCITRAL)'s proposed Model Law on Electronic Commerce[1] deals with a number of matters in relation to e-commerce, including requirements for signatures and writing. Article 11 provides that:

'In the context of contract formation unless otherwise agreed by the parties an offer and the acceptance of an offer may be expressed by means of data messages. Where a data message is used in the formation of a contract, that contract shall not be relied upon for validity and enforceability on the sole ground that a data message was used for that purpose.'

It should be noted that the model law not only applies to data messages sent by electronic mail but also by electronic data interchange (EDI), telegram, telex or telecopy (fax). The model law is not binding but the UN recommends that members give careful consideration to the Model Law when they enact or revise their own laws.

1 The Model Law with Guide to Enactment 1996 is available at www.unictral.org.

7. WHEN AND WHERE IS THE CONTRACT FORMED?

2.23 In most transactions the precise timing and/or place where the contract is formed is not an issue and most legal problems revolve around cases where one party wishes to withdraw the offer after the other party tried to accept it or vice versa.

The place of formation may, however, make a significant difference in e-commerce transactions which cross national boundaries as it may subject the on-line seller (or, indeed, its customer) to a different tax and legal regime which the respective parties may not desire or even have envisaged.

The common law has evolved two different approaches to the process of offer and acceptance, which have been alluded to above. Under the so-called 'receipt' (or 'delivery') rule, the offer will be deemed to have been accepted when the purchaser receives the seller's acceptance[1], whereas under the rather older 'postal' (or 'mailbox') rule, this occurs merely at the point when the seller sends his acceptance[2]. There is uncertainty in England as to which of these rules applies in e-commerce situations. There are arguments in favour of applying each rule, based generally on which party has control over the selection of method of transmission and who should bear the risk of the messages being delayed, garbled or lost. The postal rule had been developed to deal with the vagaries of the early postal system and the receipt rule was developed later to deal with the advent of the telephone, telex and facsimile, which provided continuous communications over the same long distances. In as much as the Internet is a continuous communications medium in many circumstances, it is undeniably true that e-mail still gets regularly 'lost' or delayed in cyberspace, or bounces back from the intended recipient due to computer error of some sort[3]. Time will no doubt tell whether in fact e-mail contracts and web contracts should be treated differently. E-mail is still not as reliable as post and it is often hard to assess whether an e-mail was received. Websites are based more on a real-time link and communication is more or less instantaneous. The time a contract is concluded will depend on the site more than law. Thus, in both cases it is clearly advantageous to include clear statements in the terms and conditions on how offer and acceptance are to be communicated and how and when they will be received, in accordance with the requirements under regulations 9 and 11 of the E-Commerce Regulations.

As noted above, in paragraph 2.18, the common law rules will now need to be read in conjunction with regulation 11(2) of the E-Commerce Regulations, which provides that the order and acknowledgement will be deemed to be received when the parties to whom they are addressed will be able to 'access' them. This rule will only apply where the acknowledgement amounts to contractual acceptance – as determined by the common law. There is therefore a lack of harmonisation at two levels: first, the laws of each country will still determine the requirements for contractual formation; second, the national courts of each country will be left to determine what is meant by 'access' to an order and acknowledgement.

1 *Entores Ltd v Miles Far East Ltd* [1955] 2 QB 327, CA; *Brinkibon Ltd v Stahag Stahl und Stahlwarenhandel GmbH* [1983] 2 AC 34, HL. In other words, it is necessary for the acceptance to have come to the notice of the offeror (or at least to have come constructively to his notice, so that he cannot claim to have failed to receive the acceptance merely because he did not look for it in the obvious place).

2 *Adams v Lindsell* (1818) 1 B & Ald 681. This case, decided at the time when postal delivery services were becoming much more commonly used in commercial practice, holds in effect that if the parties contemplate that the acceptance will come by post, then the offeror and the offeree are bound by the latter giving up his letter of acceptance to the postal service for delivery (whether or not the letter arrives). The logic driving this case is simply that at the point in question each party has done everything he personally needs to do in order to commit to agreement. Equally, it was true in those early days of postal delivery that the service was not nearly as reliable as today. In effect, the case decides upon whom the risk falls that the postal service fails to deliver a letter in the normal way.

3 In the US, the default rule for acceptance is the 'mailbox' rule, unless the offeror specifies that acceptances will only be effective on receipt. In contrast, for contracts governed by the Uniform Law on the Formation of Contracts for the International Sale of Goods, the receipt rule will apply. The Vienna Convention also applies the receipt rule. Under article 24, 'an offer, declaration of acceptance or any other indication of intention "reaches" the addressee when it is made orally to him or delivered by any other means to him personally, to his place of business or mailing address or, if he does not have a place of business or mailing address, to his habitual residence'.

2.24 Even if the laws as to where and when contractual acceptance took place were harmonised in the EU (such that it was clear whose laws applied in every case), in the business-to-consumer market place, on-line sellers may still not be able to rely on compliance only with the laws of the country in which they are established. Many countries in the EU will impose their own consumer protection laws to protect their citizens even if there is an express choice of the law of a different country[1]. While there is substantial harmonisation of consumer protection legislation, there will be discrepancies in national laws resulting from differing implementation of the various Directives.

This position is not rectified under the E-Commerce Directive. As noted above[2], there is a specific exception to the 'country of origin principle' for consumer contracts in both the E-Commerce Directive and Regulations. Accordingly, on-line sellers offering goods and services to consumers throughout the EU will need to achieve compliance with the laws of each of the countries in which they offer those goods and services.

The requirement that the service provider is obliged 'without undue delay' to send the acknowledgement of receipt of the purchaser's order indicates that automated processes must be put in place. This will mean that the on-line seller's systems ought to be set up to be able automatically to decide such matters as whether there is sufficient stock to fulfil the order, or whether the order for that particular purchase should be rejected because local law prohibits dealing with the purchaser on account of his residence or age, and to process quickly any payment authorisations. There is also a risk that where the 'order' contains additional or different terms, sending back an acknowledgement may constitute acceptance of what is actually a counter-offer[3].

Finally, in deciding how it would wish to implement its order acceptance system, the on-line seller should also consider the tax implications of forming a contract in or outside its home country. These considerations are dealt with in Chapter 8, E-taxation.

1 In the UK, the Unfair Contracts Terms Act 1977 and the Unfair Terms in Consumer Contracts Regulations 1999 (SI 1999/2083) apply, for example, notwithstanding any contract term which applies or purports to apply the law of a non-EEA Member State, if the contract has a close connection with the territory of an EEA Member State. (The Regulations came into force on 1 October 1999, replacing the Unfair Terms in Consumer Contracts Regulations 1994 (SI 1994/3159) which originally came into force on 1 July 1995.)

2 See paragraph 2.14.

3 See *Butler Machine Tool Co Ltd v Ex-Cell-O Co Corpn (England) Ltd* [1979] 1 All ER 965, CA.

8.   THE PRACTICALITIES OF CONTRACTING ON-LINE

2.25 There are essentially three different ways of contracting on-line. The first is akin to a negotiation of one or more infrequent transactions by exchange of letters and documents, whereby parties can exchange e-mails and perhaps attachments setting out more detailed terms of their contract and the exchange of those e-mails will represent the offer and acceptance between the parties.

The second is similar to mail order, whereby one party maintains the website at which he advertises his goods and services and a prospective purchaser finds out details of those goods and services on the website and then completes an electronic form, similar to an order form, through which he orders goods and services from the seller. In this situation, the general law of contract holds that the website display is not an offer, but merely an invitation to treat[1]. The order form sent in by the customer constitutes an offer to purchase and the website citation owner is at liberty to accept that offer or not, but in general must communicate such acceptance to the prospective customer.

The third is where parties trade under the framework of an EDI agreement, usually using dedicated bespoke software and private value added networks linking businesses. The exchange of messages between the parties, which are effectively mini-orders and acceptances, will be governed comprehensively by the terms of the EDI agreement.

All three methods can be and are used in business-to-business e-commerce but it is the second of those two types which is the most common model for business-to-consumer e-commerce where a seller is looking to sell goods and services on an ad hoc basis to a wide variety of customers. Given the likely small value of the transactions and their high volume, the only practical way to conduct business is on a standardised basis.

In considering how to structure its e-commerce site, the on-line seller should take into account the following legal considerations:

- the distinction between invitations to treat, offers and acceptances;

- the use of digital signatures; and

- the use of 'click-wrap' contracts.

1 Generally, price lists, circulars and advertisements, which are analogous to the website, are often regarded as invitations to treat: *Grainger & Son v Gough* [1896] AC 325, HL; *Partridge v Crittenden* [1968] 2 All ER 421, but contrast these decisions with *Carlill v Carbolic Smokeball Co* [1893] 1 QB 256, CA.

(a) Digital signatures

2.26 As we have seen above, in the majority of cases a contract can be concluded by the simple exchange of messages. No further formalities are required. Indeed, in non-consumer transactions, the on-line seller may accept an offer by performance alone, ie shipping the goods or rendering services ordered, without first confirming the order with an acceptance message[1].

Terms of contract mean, obviously, that parties have obligations and they will want reliable information on the other parties. However, the essentially anonymous nature of the Internet creates a risk of subsequent repudiation of the contract by the purchaser (for example, the use of the 'someone else was using my credit card number' argument by the supposed purchaser). The on-line seller needs some protection against this risk. This is where digital signature of an on-line order or agreement is of potentially very significant value. Additionally, in business-to-business transactions, where the value of any given transaction is likely to be rather higher than will be the case for most business-to-customer bargains, the corporate purchaser or seller can ensure that its employees and agents do not exceed their authority through the obligatory use of digital signatures which encode the limit of the relevant persons' contracting authority.

1 *Smit International Singapore Pte Ltd v Kurnia Dewi Shipping SA, The Kurnia Dewi* [1997] 1 Lloyd's Rep 552.

(i) General considerations on signatures and contracts

2.27 Conventionally, what a signature does is to authenticate the document on which it appears. When a signature is affixed to a document or a contract of sale it symbolises the intention of the signatory to be legally bound by the terms thereof. The signatory to a contract may not later deny either the existence of that contract or its terms[1].

1 Subject, always, to considerations of mistake on the face of the contract, misrepresentation, etc, and, of course, the possibility that the signature was forged or obtained under duress. Having said this, other than in the case of misrepresentation, these are all classically quite difficult matters to prove in the law of contract.

(ii) The rise of digital signatures

2.28 Other than where a deed is required to form the contract (see the discussion at paragraph 2.10 above) or in certain specific instances (eg consumer credit agreements[1]), the law does not require that the parties to a written contract should sign it, even in circumstances where the terms of the contract are required to be in writing.

The need to create a verifiable alternative to the handwritten signature on the face of a contract document has been most pressing in relation to on-line transactions. By definition, such transactions are not amenable to the traditional concept of paper-based written signature, but verification of a party's identity and willingness to be bound remains.

The technology for achieving verification has normally been referred to as facilitating a 'digital signature', or 'electronic signature'. The latter expression is preferred in the European Commission's Directive on a Community framework for electronic signatures, known as the Electronic Signatures Directive[2].

Commercially, the development of digital signature technology has been driven by the banking industry, for fairly obvious reasons. Currently, most banking transactions only become legally valid after the relevant parties have signed appropriate paper documentation. Given the desirability to effect transactions from a remote computer or terminal, how should technology and law work together to effect a digital signature in an on-line environment?

Despite the adoption of the Electronic Signatures Directive and the ECA 2000 the answer to that question is currently being considered by the user commercial organisations, representative bodies and legislators/regulators at national and supra-national level.

1 See footnote 2 to paragraph 2.09.
2 Directive (EC) 93/99. See paragraph 2.35 for further details.

(iii) Functions of digital signatures

2.29 A digital signature can serve the following purposes:

■ it can fix the identity of the party entering into the contract. This is potentially important where pre-contractual dialogue may have been conducted electronically, screen to screen, and where one party, while knowing the machine from which a message is being transmitted, may not know whether the machine is being operated by someone with whom the recipient individual wishes to contract (for example, a home-based personal computer may be being used by a child rather than the adult owner of that machine).

■ it can act as confirmation of the identified individual's acceptance of the terms on offer.

In addition to these two functions (which are analogous to the central functions of the handwritten signature on a paper document), a digital signature also has the advantage of being able definitively to imprint 'time' into the signature 'stamp'. The 'time' stamp can be combined with the 'identity' stamp in a way that is not normally possible in a 'physical' signature, where a date may be added after a signature on a contractual document, and the signature itself cannot evidence the time at which agreement was reached in respect of contract terms.

(iv) Key requirements of a digital signature

2.30 Before examining the current position, it is useful to identify the key features in ideal circumstances for a digital signature:

- **uniqueness,** such that it can only be created by the user;

- **impossibility of forgery,** so that unauthorised users should encounter intractable numerical, time and resource difficulties in trying to effect forgery;

- **ease of authentication,** allowing the receiver of information to be able to identify the transmitter/author of such information authoritatively, even after the passage of significant time;

- **impossibility of denial,** such that authors of digital signatures should not be able to deny true authorship on the basis of forgery, even after the passage of significant time;

- **economy of generation,** in that it clearly matters that the technology should be inexpensive to introduce and to use, in order to encourage the level of take-up needed to ensure that the concept is commercially successful; and

- **ease of generation,** so that the technology is easy for people (often unskilled private individuals) to use for broadly similar reasons – in much the same way as the average person can easily sign his own name to a document today.

(v) Technical basis for digital signatures

2.31 Digital signatures are based on the application to electronic data of an algorithm contained within the data stream which authenticates the identity of the sender by encoding the document until the intended recipient unlocks the data stream.

The ability to create digital signatures relies on the technology of cryptography (discussed in Chapter 3, E-liability). In particular, the technology of public/private key cryptography (of which the most widespread is RSA[1]) allows individuals to 'sign' electronic documents. A message which has been encrypted with the individual's or organisation's 'private key' can be decrypted with the 'public key' from that key pair.

If the public key is applied to a message or document which has been encrypted with any key other than the 'private key' of that particular individual or organisation, it will produce gibberish. It is this phenomenon and technology which has come to be known as a 'digital signature'. Hence an individual or organisation which wishes to 'sign' an electronic document can add a statement of acceptance to it and then encrypt it by applying their private key. The encrypted version is, therefore, effectively capable of being treated as a signed contract, because it could only have been encrypted by using the 'signer's' private key.

Unlike a handwritten signature, which remains the same for all or any documents which the signatory executes, a digital signature may vary according to both the text of the document being authenticated and the person signing it. While a written signature is appended to a particular document, this is not possible with an electronic document sent on-line (because of the possibility of alteration of the message during transmission), and hence the 'signature' is 'applied' to the whole message, rather than being an appendage to it.

1   After Ron Rivest, Adi Shamir and Leonard Adleman, who invented the technique in 1976.

2.32   The verification of identity process underlying a digital signature can be seen as precisely the inverse of the process between Mr B and Ms A when they were wishing to communicate secretly by encrypting a message from Ms A to Mr B. Instead of Ms A encrypting with a public key which Mr B then decrypts with a private key, the process is now:

■   Mr B generates a public and private key;

■   Mr B gives Ms A (and the public) the public key;

■   Mr B 'signs' an electronic document by encrypting it with his private key and sends the signed document to Ms A; and

■   Ms A uses Mr B's public key to decrypt the signed document, thus establishing that it was authentically signed by Mr B.

(vi) *Verification of identity*

2.33   Since the whole purpose of digital signatures is to confirm the mutual intention of contracting parties (rather than simply encryption per se) the methods used for signature generation must allow for the resolution of any dispute as to the authenticity of a 'signed' communication. Two possible authentication methods are:

■   authentication by the recipient directly (direct signature authentication); and

■   authentication by third parties acting as referees/arbiters (indirect signature authentication).

It will be immediately obvious why it is preferable to have digital signatures amenable to authentication by a third party. Such a third party could keep the public data generated by senders and used by receivers to validate signatures.

Such an arrangement potentially overcomes the significant problem otherwise associated with digital signatures whereby a sending party could deliberately reveal its private key in circumstances where it wished (for whatever commercial reasons) to repudiate authorship of its own genuine digital signatures generated before publication of its private key.

To avoid this, on-line sellers can incorporate as part of their digital signature scheme a 'trusted third party' who acts as an arbiter to settle disputes between senders and receivers. All such schemes assume that the arbiter acts with integrity and honesty in respect of both parties (in effect performing a similar role in the third millennium to that performed by notaries in the latter centuries of the second).

Given that, by definition, e-commerce involves distance selling with merchants trading together with little or no prior knowledge of each other, the requirement for public keys to be accessible is regarded as central to the success of e-commerce generally.

A mechanism is clearly required to make public keys widely available by centralising the keys alongside the information on the companies and individuals wishing to trade electronically. This will rapidly become as indispensable a directory of data as the old-style telephone book and more recent electronic variations on it, from which the telephone, fax, e-mail and address details of businesses and customers are made available[1].

There is also the obvious but integral requirement that the public keys are trusted as belonging to the companies or individuals to whom ostensibly they relate.

These two functions of centralising information on public keys and vouching for the integrity and reliability of them have been combined and offered to the e-commerce public by a number of companies[2] which have come to be known as 'Certification Authorities'. In addition to private sector initiatives between companies, there have also been moves to create legally binding systems for digital signatures on forms submitted electronically to the British Government[3].

1   Though it must as a matter of policy be right to require that such public key directories cannot operate on the same 'ex-directory' basis as currently applies in relation to telephone number listings.
2   The best known of which are probably Verisign (www.verisign.com) and Cyberscript.
3   For example, NatWest and Barclays Banks' agreement with the UK Government.

(vii) Digital signatures and English case law

2.34   There are currently no decided cases that indicate whether an English court would treat a document as 'signed' electronically in circumstances where the sender had previously provided the recipient with the means of deciphering the encrypted data in that document for the purposes of authenticating the identity of its sender.

Nevertheless, on the basis of existing precedent relating to the use of handwritten signatures, there is a basis for arguing for a flexible judicial approach to new forms of technology such as that represented by digital signatures.

In the case of *Goodman v J Eban Ltd*[1] the general principle was expressed:

> 'The essential requirement of signing is the affixing, either by writing with a pen or pencil or by otherwise impressing on the document, one's name or 'signature' so as to personally authenticate the document.'

Whereas this dictum predates the age of e-commerce and digital signature, it is not wholly unrealistic for us to expect that today a court would construe this as authority for the proposition that what matters is that a document is *authenticated*, rather than signed in any conventional sense. As we have seen, the technology of public/private key encryption is a means of authenticating a document. However, it does this by reducing the whole document to an apparently meaningless and indecipherable stream of data whilst simultaneously providing the intended reader with the means to decipher it[2]. In this sense, using a digital signature is not on 'all fours' with the concept of 'impressing on the document' which might appear to envisage the addition of a distinctive mark, rather than a distinctive process, to the document being authenticated.

On the other hand, the essential elements identified within the passage quoted above would appear to be the personal identification of a particular document. As the ECA 2000 now provides a statutory basis for recognition of digital signatures, the courts might well be receptive to the argument that a digital signature verified the identity and authenticity of a particular document, subject to the usual considerations applying to the admissibility and weight to be afforded to computer evidence[3].

1   [1954] 1 All ER 763, CA.
2   Incidentally, while the indecipherability of a handwritten signature might not affect the validity of a written contract, a process that renders the whole document indecipherable and, pursuant to which, it remains this way for some reason most certainly would do so. See *Falck v Williams* [1900] AC 176, in which the litigants contracted with each other in code, but reached a point in relation to a specific transaction where neither party could establish as against the other what a specific term of their agreement required the parties to do. The Privy Council held that the plaintiff's action, therefore, failed as the contract was void for uncertainty; but moreover, had the defendant in fact sued or counterclaimed, then his suit would equally have been held unenforceable.
3   See also *Re a Debtor (No 2021 of 1995), ex p IRC v Debtor* [1996] 2 All ER 345, where a faxed copy of a signature was held to satisfy the statutory requirements of the Insolvency Act 1986 and rule 8.2(3) of the Insolvency Rules 1986 (SI 1986/1925). Laddie J held that a proxy form is signed for the purposes of rule 8.2(3) if it bears upon it some distinctive or personal

marking which had been placed there by, or with the authority of, the creditor and said '[if] it is legitimate to send by post a proxy form signed with a rubber stamp, why should it not be at least as authentic to send the form by fax?'.

(viii) The Electronic Signatures Directive[1]

2.35 The Electronic Signatures Directive clearly recognises that electronic communication and commerce necessitate 'electronic signatures' and related services allowing data authentication, and that electronic signatures will be used in a large variety of circumstances and applications, resulting in a wide range of new services and products related to or using electronic signatures, such as registration services, time-stamping services, directory services, computing services or consultancy services.

The Directive makes a distinction between 'advanced electronic signatures', which are guaranteed to be legally effective and admissible in legal proceedings, and 'electronic signatures', which qualify for certain purposes but can be denied recognition on additional grounds.

Article 5(1) provides that Member States shall ensure that 'advanced electronic signatures' which are based on a qualified certificate and which are created by a secure signature-creation device:

'(a) satisfy the legal requirements of a signature in relation to data in electronic form in the same manner as a handwritten signature satisfies those requirements in relation to paper-based data; and

(b) are admissible as evidence in legal proceedings.'

An 'advanced electronic signature' is defined as an electronic signature which:

'(a) is uniquely linked to the signatory;

(b) is capable of identifying the signatory;

(c) is created using means that the signatory can maintain under his sole control; and

(d) is linked to the data to which it relates in such a manner that any subsequent change of the data is detectable.'

A 'qualified certificate' is defined as a certificate which meets the requirements laid down in Annex I to the Directive[2] and is provided by a certification service provider who fulfils the requirements laid down in Annex II.

A 'secure signature-creation device' is defined as a signature-creation device which meets the requirements laid down in Annex III to the Directive[3].

Article 5(2) in contrast provides that Member States shall ensure that an electronic signature is not denied legal effectiveness and admissibility as evidence in legal proceedings solely on the grounds that it is:

■ in electronic form;

■ not based upon a qualified certificate;

■ not based upon a qualified certificate issued by an accredited certification service-provider; or

■ not created by a secure signature-creation device.

1 See footnote 2 to paragraph 2.28.
2 Annex I provides that qualified certificates must contain:
   • an indication that the certificate is issued as a qualified certificate;
   • the identification of the certification service provider and the state in which it is established;
   • the name of the signatory or a pseudonym, which shall be identified as such;
   • provision for a specific attribute of the signatory to be included if relevant, depending on the purpose for which the certificate is intended;

- signature verification data which correspond to signature creation data under the control of the signatory;
- an indication of the beginning and end of the period of validity of the certificate;
- the identity code of the certificate;
- the advanced electronic signature of the certification service provider issuing it;
- limitations on the scope of use of the certificate, if applicable; and
- limits on the value of transactions for which the certificate can be used, if applicable.

3 Annex III states that secure signature-creation devices:
- must, by appropriate technical and procedural means, ensure at the least that:
  - the signature creation data used for signature generation can practically occur only once and that their secrecy is reasonably assured;
  - the signature creation data used for signature generation cannot, with reasonable assurance, be derived and the signature is protected against forgery using currently available technology;
  - the signature creation data used for signature generation can be reliably protected by the legitimate signatory against the use of others; and
  - must not alter the data to be signed or prevent such data from being presented to the signatory prior to the signature process.

(ix) The Electronic Communications Act 2000

2.36 Member States were due to implement the Electronic Signatures Directive before 19 July 2001. Although the ECA 2000 implemented some of the key requirements of the Directive, parts of the Directive remain to be implemented.

In particular, Part 1 of the Act (which provides for a statutory voluntary approvals regime) was not enacted. Moreover, section 16(4) of the Act specifically provides that if Part 1 of the Act is not brought into force within five years, it will be deemed repealed at the end of that period.

In March 2001 the DTI issued a consultation paper on proposals to implement the remaining parts of the Directive[1]. The DTI has now advised that it is unlikely that these remaining parts of the Directive will ever be implemented as Government favours an industry-led scheme rather than a statutory one. This is wholly in accordance with the Directive (see recitals 11 and 13).

The Government favours the scheme established by the Alliance for Electronic Business known as 'tScheme'[2]. tScheme exists as a non-statutory voluntary approvals regime for trust service providers. The DTI's consultation document makes the point that tScheme appears to fulfil the broad objectives for voluntary accreditation schemes that might be introduced in line with the Directive. tScheme states the following as one of its objectives:

> 'tScheme will seek to work closely with HMG [Her Majesty's Government] to make [the] UK the "best and safest" place in the world for e-commerce and will provide an effective voluntary approvals regime for cryptographic services, making it unnecessary for the Secretary of State to invoke his powers under Part I of the Electronic Communications Act 2000 to establish a statutory authority.'

As the Trade and Industry Committee's Report on the Electronic Communications Bill recognised[3], the common law treats a signature in terms of its purpose (did the signatory intend to indicate his assent to what was in the document?) rather than its form (does the signature meet certain requirements?). This means that the law is already flexible enough in most cases to be capable of accommodating electronic signatures.

Although the consultation document suggested the creation of a rebuttable presumption for the validity of any type of electronic signature, the Government has decided not to follow this suggestion. Instead, section 7 of the Act makes it clear that all types of electronic signature, whether facilitated by 'approved' providers or not and irrespective of the jurisdiction where they were issued, will be legally admissible in court. This area is addressed in more detail in section 9 of Chapter 7, E-dispute.

1   Department of Trade and Industry Consultation on EC Directive 1999/93/EC of the European Parliament and Council on a Community Framework for Electronic Signatures, March 2001.

2 See www.tscheme.org. tScheme was incorporated in May 2000.
3 See 'Building Confidence in Electronic Commerce' (March 1999), available at www.dti.gov.uk/cii/ecommerce/ ukcommercestrategy/archiveconsultationdocs/summary.shtml.

(x) The Electronic Signatures Regulations 2002[1]

2.37 The Electronic Signatures Regulations came into force on 8 March 2002. They implement those provisions of the Electronic Signatures Directive relating to the supervision of certification service providers, their liability in certain circumstances and data protection requirements concerning them. In essence, these Regulations implement article 5 of the Electronic Signatures Directive[2]. In particular, the Regulations provide that a certification service provider who issues a 'qualified certificate' will, in certain prescribed circumstances, be held liable for loss suffered by a person relying on that certificate *unless* the certification service provider proves that he was not negligent. This reverses the burden of proof from the normal negligence standard, which requires the person suffering loss to prove negligence.

1 SI 2002/318.
2 See paragraph 2.35 above.

(xi) The UNCITRAL Model Law on Electronic Signatures

2.38 The United Nations Commission on International Trade Law's Model Law on Electronic Signatures was adopted on 5 July 2001[1]. The Model Law is not binding but is available to assist countries in establishing a legislative framework in relation to electronic signatures. The Model Law deals with a number of matters in relation to electronic signatures, including compliance with a requirement for a signature, conduct of the signatory, the certification service provider and the relying party, and recognition of foreign certificates and electronic signatures.

'Electronic signature' is defined and under article 6 must be as reliable as is appropriate for the message concerned in order to be legally valid as a signature. The signature must be linked to the signatory and no other person and the data must have been under the control of the signatory at the time of signing. Alterations to the signature made post-signing must be detectable.

It will thus be left to the court to decide in a particular case whether an electronic signature has been correctly used and what weight it should be given (eg in relation to the authentication or integrity of a message) against other evidence.

Under section 8 of the ECA 2000, Ministers will have the power to pass secondary legislation to remove any remaining legal obstacles in other legislation which prevent the use of electronic signatures (see paragraph 2.20).

1 The Model Law is available at www.uncitral.org/english/texts/electcom/ml-elecsig-e.pdf.

(b) Click-wrap and other contracts of adhesion

2.39 The terms of a contract may include:

- **express terms,** ie those specifically agreed by the parties and which are usually, but not necessarily, in writing;

- **implied terms,** ie terms which are implied by conduct, trade customs or law (under the last of these, see, for example, the various implied warranties as to title, satisfactory quality, fitness for purpose and conformity to description in the Sale of Goods Act 1979);

■ **mandatory terms**, ie terms mandated by law and which the parties cannot contract out of (these may be express terms, but are more likely to be implied terms in most cases).

The effect of some of these implied and mandatory terms is dealt with in Chapter 3, E-liability.

As a general rule, express terms override any implication of further terms in a contract that conflict with them. (However, this is subject to exceptions and qualifications in itself. For example, where the UCTA 1977 applies.) The on-line seller will wish as far as possible to ensure that its standard terms and conditions apply to all transactions into which it enters, in order to minimise its exposure to liability to the customer or third parties.

The problem that the on-line seller faces, in common with those providing goods and services in the conventional world, is how to draw the customer's attention to its standard terms *before* the contract is concluded and to incorporate them into any agreement without driving that customer away.

It is not generally sufficient for the on-line seller to make the terms available somewhere on its website, as the customer will only be bound by those terms if he actually knew that the transaction was subject to them or if the on-line seller 'did what was reasonably sufficient to give him notice of it'[1].

1 This conclusion may be construed from numerous cases on the law of exclusion and limitation clauses, eg *Thornton v Shoe Lane Parking Ltd* [1971] 2 QB 163, CA. What is 'reasonably sufficient' in terms of the architecture of a website has yet to be considered by the courts, however.

2.40 The safest approach is, therefore, to require the customer to read through the applicable terms and conditions and signify his acceptance of those terms before proceeding. This typically involves using the 'scroll down and click' dialogue boxes which are becoming increasingly common[1]. Requiring the customer to affix his digital signature to signify acceptance will obviously afford the on-line seller even greater protection. It would be extremely tedious and off-putting to have to do this for every transaction. As the design of the website should be a balance of being attractive and affording adequate protection to the on-line seller through use of disclaimers and conditions, etc, it may be preferable to have a registration process. Once the user agrees to the terms and obtains an ID and password he is free to use the site again and again without re-reading the terms until the terms are altered, which is when the original process should be repeated.

Terms which limit or exclude liability should in particular be clearly highlighted and brought to the attention of the customer[2].

Under regulation 9(3) of the E-Commerce Regulations, where terms and conditions are provided to a customer, they must also be made available in a way that allows the customer to store and reproduce them.

Undoubtedly this is unattractive and cumbersome, and interferes with the smooth flow of web design. Given that in a typical transaction the customer is currently required to enter what may amount to several screens of information (to provide the on-line seller with his name, billing and shipping addresses, credit card details, etc), adding an appropriate dialogue box at the end of the ordering process, together with an appropriate data protection notice and opt-out, may not after all present such an unattractive option. As the customer has spent time inputting all his personal information already, this would be psychologically the best time to ask him to acknowledge the legal terms of the transaction. It is understood that leading on-line sellers are looking to standardise the ordering process and thus reduce the need to re-input the same data for each transaction. This may have a bearing on how the on-line seller's terms of business are presented to customers on-line.

The on-line seller may, of course, wish to adopt a lower level of certainty to increase the attractiveness and ease of use of its website by using, for example, hyperlinks to its 'legal' page. For less onerous terms, this may be sufficient notice[3], but data protection issues, exclusion/limitation of liability clauses and other unusual terms should still be incorporated on the order page or otherwise brought clearly to the customer's attention before the contract is formed.

It is important that the on-line seller maintains full records of all transactions, including the relevant terms and conditions applicable at the time of conclusion of each on-line contract. Terms and conditions, statements and disclaimers are frequently updated, and it is advisable to keep a copy of old or updated versions. With the adoption of the ECA 2000, digital storage of data is now acceptable. However, it is advisable to be aware of conditions relating to admissibility of electronic evidence in the event of disputes at a later date.

1 For these purposes, it is likely to be 'reasonably sufficient' to afford the customer the opportunity to read the terms relevant to the transaction and it is, therefore, at the customer's risk if he chooses to skip through them without doing so. What is clear is that the on-line seller should not impede the customer's ability to read the terms. The document must be of a type reasonably expected to contain conditions, and what is reasonably sufficient is a question of law on the evidence.

2 The flexibility of HTML and web architecture makes it entirely realistic to give effect to the delightful dictum of Lord Denning in *Thornton v Shoe Lane Parking Ltd* [1971] 2 QB 163, CA, that '[i]n order to give it sufficient notice, it would need to be printed in red ink with a red hand pointing to it – or something equally startling'.

3 In *Parker v South Eastern Rly Co* (1877) 2 CPD 416, CA, a notice on the front of a railway ticket to 'see back' for the terms and conditions was held to be sufficient notice. This sort of analogy may well apply in terms of website architecture, provided that the on-line seller has not been disingenuous in the manner in which the terms of business are shunted out of primary view.

(c) Future developments

2.41 As with the recognition of electronic contracts generally, there are various initiatives on an international[1] level in relation to the recognition of digital signatures.

Article 7 of the UNCITRAL Model Law on Electronic Commerce, set out below, establishes the general conditions under which data messages would be regarded as authenticated with sufficient credibility and enforceable in the face of signature requirements which currently present barriers to electronic commerce.

'7(1) Where the law requires a signature of a person, that requirement is met in relation to a data message if:

(a) a method is used to identify that person and to indicate that person's approval of the information contained in the data message; and

(b) that method is as reliable as was appropriate for the purpose for which the data message was generated or communicated, in the light of all the circumstances, including any relevant agreement.'

Paragraph 58 of the Guide to Enactment to the Model Law provides some explanation of how these provisions could be interpreted:

'In determining whether the method used under para (1) is appropriate, legal, technical and commercial factors that may be taken into account include the following:

(1) the sophistication of the equipment used by each of the parties;

(2) the nature of their trade activity;

(3) the frequency at which commercial transactions take place between the parties;

(4) the kind and size of the transaction;

(5) the function of signature requirements in a given statutory and regulatory environment;

(6)   the capability of communication systems;

(7)   compliance with authentication procedures set forth by intermediaries;

(8)   the range of authentication procedures made available by any intermediary;

(9)   compliance with trade customs and practice;

(10) the existence of insurance coverage mechanisms against unauthorised messages;

(11) the importance and the value of the information contained in the data message;

(12) the availability of alternative methods of identification and the cost of implementation;

(13) the degree of acceptance or non-acceptance of the method of identification in the relevant industry or field both at the time the method was agreed upon and the time when the data message was communicated; and

(14) any other relevant factor.'

The mere signing of a data message by means of a functional equivalent of a handwritten signature is not intended, in and of itself, to confer legal validity on the data message. Whether a data message that fulfilled the requirement of a signature has legal validity would have to be determined under the law applicable outside the Model Law[2]. As mentioned, the Model Law is not binding on members but provides guidance when enacting domestic legislation.

The UK is developing an industry-led scheme and details of this are still emerging.

1   For example, there are various model codes and laws being adopted as well as moves at national levels. China, for example, seems to be developing its own policy which includes market entry restrictions (see PLC Vol X1 no 5 and www.chinaonline.com/refer/legal).
2   Other international moves include those in Canada. In June 1999 the Uniform Conference of Canada adopted a model law (the Uniform Electronic Commerce Act 1999). It is not binding but most provinces have introduced draft legislation to reflect it. Saskatchewan has recently adopted its Electronic Information and Documents Act 2000 based on this Uniform Act, which allows for recognition of digital signatures and e-contracts. Quebec has objected to implementation of the model law but has other options in place. Japan is also taking similar steps (see, for example, www.miti.go.jp).

9.   THE RIGHT TO WITHDRAW FROM A CONTRACT

2.42   The position in English law has traditionally been that, once parties had contracted, they were bound to complete the bargain. However, in certain circumstances, even when a contract has been concluded, a party may extract itself from the contract without penalty, for example by mutual agreement, or where further performance is discharged by breach or frustration. However, there is no basic rule of English common law that has the effect of allowing one party to unilaterally cancel his participation in an agreement.

To address this issue in areas where high-pressure selling techniques were coming more and more into use, various statutes have created rights of cancellation or 'cooling-off' in certain specific cases (for example, the CCA 1974 in relation to certain types of consumer credit agreement, the Consumer Protection (Cancellation of Contracts concluded away from Business Premises) Regulations 1987[1], the Mail Order Transactions (Information) Order[2] and rules made pursuant to section 51 of the Financial Services Act 1986 in relation to the sale in particular circumstances of life assurance and certain other types of personal investment).

1   SI 1987/2117.
2   SI 1976/1812.

(a) The Distance Selling Directive and UK implementation

2.43 The European Commission's Directive on the protection of consumers in respect of distance contracts, known as the Distance Selling Directive[1] imposes certain requirements on consumer contracts concluded where the parties are not in each other's presence. The Consumer Protection (Distance Selling) Regulations 2000[2] implement the Distance Selling Directive and came into force on 31 October 2000.

The Regulations apply to all 'distance selling contracts', which are essentially consumer contracts concluded without face-to-face contact between the supplier and consumer. 'Distance contract' is defined as:

> 'any contract concerning goods or services concluded between a supplier and a consumer under an organised distance sales or service-provision scheme run by the supplier who, for the purpose of the contract, makes exclusive use of one or more means of distance communication up to and including the moment at which the contract is concluded.'[3]

A 'consumer' is defined as 'any natural person who, in contracts to which these Regulations apply, is acting for purposes outside his business'.

The Regulations cover e-commerce, as well as sales made by mail order, telephone or fax.

Excluded from the scope of the Regulations, by virtue of regulation 5(1) are, for example, contracts:

- or the sale of land;

- concluded by means of an automated vending machine or automated commercial premises;

- concluded at an auction[4]; or

- relating to financial services, which are covered by a separate proposed Directive[5].

1 Directive (EC) 7/97 of 20 May 1997 (replacing former Directive (EEC) 577/85). See also Commission Recommendation (EEC) 295/92 of 7 April 1992 on codes of practice for the protection of consumers in respect of contracts negotiated at a distance (distance selling): OJ L156 10.06.92, pp 21–22 (the Distance Selling Directive).
2 SI 2000/2334. This is by no means the first intervention of regulation into the operation of consumer contracts, and various other instances will be referred to in other parts of this book.
3 Regulation 2(1).
4 Therefore excluding contracts negotiated through Internet auction houses such as Aucland, eBay, QXL and Sothebys.
5 See COM 0385/99 final – COD 0245/99: OJ C177E 27.6.2000.

2.44 The key aspects of the Consumer Protection (Distance Selling) Regulations 2000 are the imposition of requirements to provide certain information to the consumer at specified times and the establishment of a 'cooling-off' period or right of cancellation for the consumer.

Note that regulations 7 to 19(1) (ie the bulk of the requirements, including the information and cooling-off provisions) do not apply to:

- contracts for the supply of foodstuffs, beverages or other goods intended for everyday consumption supplied to the consumer's residence or to his workplace by regular roundsmen[1] (eg Internet grocery shopping), because of the perishable nature of the goods concerned;

- contracts for the provision of accommodation, transport, catering or leisure services, where the supplier undertakes, when the contract is concluded, to provide these services on a specific date or within a specific period[2] (eg hotel and travel bookings); and

- other contracts to which only part of the Regulations apply (and which are also listed in regulation 6(1) and (3), eg 'timeshare agreements' and 'package' holidays).

The growing number of on-line auction houses and grocery stores will no doubt experience relief at falling within the exemptions in this way. The white goods and automotive industries have been less fortunate, however, in spite of extensive lobbying. A position has been reached where the purchaser of a car through an website may be able to cancel the transaction and return the car having already clocked a significant number of miles, thus wiping hundreds or thousands of pounds off its new value. The fact that the consumer has taken good care of the vehicle during the cancellation period is immaterial (see regulation 17). It remains to be seen how the automotive industry will adjust to this unwelcome complexity.

1 Regulation 6(2)(a).
2 Regulation 6(2)(b).

(b) The Consumer Protection (Distance Selling) Regulations 2000

(i) Information to be provided prior to conclusion of the contract – regulation 7

2.45 Under regulation 7(1)(a), a supplier must in good time, prior to the conclusion of the contract (ie before the contract is made, not before performance) and in a manner which is clear, comprehensible and appropriate to the means of distance communication, provide to the consumer the following information:

■ identity of the supplier and, if the contract requires payment in advance, the supplier's address;

■ description of the main characteristics of the goods or services;

■ price of the goods or services (including all taxes);

■ delivery costs;

■ payment, delivery or performance arrangements;

■ existence of a right of cancellation (subject to regulation 13);

■ cost of using the distance communication (if calculated other than at basic rate);

■ period that the offer/price remains valid; and

■ minimum duration of contract (in the case of contracts for goods or services which are to be to be performed permanently or recurrently).

Under regulation 7(b) and (c) the supplier must also inform the customer if he proposes, in the event of the requested goods or services being unavailable, to provide substitute goods or services of equivalent quality and price, and inform the customer that the supplier will meet the cost of returning any substitute goods in the event of cancellation by the consumer.

(ii) Additional information requirement (in writing) – regulation 8

2.46 Under regulation 8(2), the supplier must provide to the consumer in writing or in some other durable medium (see further below) the information set out below. The information must be provided either prior to the conclusion of the contract, or in good time thereafter, and in any event at the time of delivery at the latest:

■ the information in regulation 7(I)(a)(i)–(vi) above;

■ information about the conditions and procedures for exercising the right to cancel under regulation 10 (see below), including:

- – notification of any contract term that requires the consumer to return goods to the supplier in the event of a cancellation;

- – notification of whether the supplier or the consumer is responsible for the cost of returning goods, or of the supplier recovering them, if the consumer cancels the contract under regulation 10;

■ the geographical address for the supplier where the consumer may address any complaints;

■ information about any after-sales service and guarantees;

■ conditions for exercising contractual right to cancel the contract where the contract is of an unspecified duration or of a duration exceeding one year.

Under regulation 8(3), which applies in relation to contracts for the supply of services, the supplier must inform the consumer that he will not be able to cancel the contract under regulation 10 once performance of the services has begun.

Posting this information on the website or giving it verbally is not sufficient to comply with regulation 8.

Commentary on the Regulations suggests that the DTI considers that confirmation by electronic mail would meet the requirements where the order has been placed by means of e-mail. This has not been specified in the Regulations as the DTI believes 'the Directive is not specific on the point, and only a court can determine the meaning of the wording'. Although this non-specific approach does have the benefit of being vague enough to keep up with fast moving technological developments in communication, clearly some clarification will be required. For the time being, however, on-line sellers are advised to provide any information in writing or at least in a printable form. It remains to be seen how pragmatic a view suppliers take of the extent of the detail required to be provided. 'Famous name' suppliers may rely on the recognition of their names and brands to supply less information. Arguably, such an approach would defeat the object of the Regulations in providing for a regime that is transparent and fully protective of consumers.

(iii) Right to cancel (the cooling-off period) – regulation 10

2.47   The customer may cancel the contract without explanation or penalty if he gives notice of cancellation within the cancellation periods set out in regulations 11 and 12 (summarised below).

The effect of such a cancellation is that the contract is treated as if it had not been made.

Regulation 13 contains a list of exceptions to the right to cancel (see below). If any of these apply the consumer is deprived of the right to cancel.

A notice of cancellation must be a notice in writing or other durable medium accessible to the supplier which indicates the intention of the consumer to cancel the contract. It can be hand-delivered, posted, faxed or e-mailed to the last known contact point for the supplier.

The consumer, then, is given a wide right to cancel. Upon cancellation, the supplier has to repay the money and there are detailed provisions on return of goods (see below).

(iv) Cancellation period for contracts for supply of goods – regulation 11

2.48   The period during which the consumer may cancel the contract begins with the day on which the contract is concluded and ends seven working days from the day after the consumer receives the goods.

This period is extended by up to three months if the supplier fails to meet the written information requirements of regulation 8.

'Working days' are all days other than weekends and public holidays.

(v) Cancellation period for contracts for supply of services – regulation 12

2.49 The period during which the consumer may cancel the contract begins with the day on which the contract is concluded and ends seven working days from the day after the contract is concluded.

This cancellation period is again extended by up to three months if the supplier has not met the regulation 8 information requirements.

(vi) Exceptions to the right to cancel – regulation 13

2.50 Unless the supplier agrees otherwise, the consumer will not have the right to cancel a contract in respect of the following contracts:

- for supply of services if the supplier has complied with regulation 8(3) and performance of the contract has begun with the consumer's consent prior to the end of the cancellation period specified under regulation 12;

- for the supply of goods or services if the price is dependent on fluctuations in financial market;

- for the supply of goods made to the consumer's specifications or clearly personalised or which, by reason of their nature, cannot be returned or are liable to deteriorate/expire rapidly;

- for the supply of audio-visual recordings or computer software if they are unsealed by the customer;

- for the supply of newspapers, periodicals and magazines; or

- for the supply of gaming, betting and lottery services.

(vii) Recovery of sums paid by consumer – regulation 14

2.51 Where a contract has been cancelled under regulation 10, the supplier must reimburse any sum paid by or on behalf of the consumer free of any charge, less any permitted charge for the costs of recovering any goods (see below).

The supplier may make a charge not exceeding the direct costs of recovering the goods, if the supplier's terms stated that the consumer had to return the goods, and the consumer has either failed to do so or has returned them at the supplier's expense. However, the supplier may not levy a recovery charge if:

- the consumer cancels where he has a right to reject the goods under a contract term (including a statutory implied term);

- the contractual term requiring the consumer to return the goods on cancellation was 'unfair'; or

- the returned goods were substitutes for the goods ordered.

Reimbursement must be made as soon as possible and in any event within 30 days of the date of cancellation.

(viii) Restoration of goods – regulation 17

2.52 If the consumer cancels the contract under regulation 10 after he has received the goods, the consumer is deemed to have been under a duty throughout the period prior to cancellation to retain possession of goods and to take reasonable care of them.

On cancellation, the consumer is also under a duty to restore the goods to the supplier (in accordance with the rest of regulation 17) and, in the meantime, to retain possession of the goods and take reasonable care of them (subject to the time limits on that duty set out below).

The Regulations do not require the consumer actually to return the goods, just to make them available for collection at his own premises following a written request from the supplier given either prior to or at the time of collection.

If the consumer delivers the goods to the supplier (at his premises or elsewhere) or sends the goods at his own expense to the supplier, he is discharged from any duty to retain possession of the goods or restore them to the supplier. Where he sends the goods back to the supplier, he is under a duty to take reasonable care to see that they are received by the supplier and not damaged in transit.

Under regulation 17(7), if within 21 days of cancellation the supplier asks to collect the goods, but the consumer unreasonably refuses or fails to comply with that request, the consumer's duty to take reasonable care of the goods will continue until he delivers the goods to the supplier (at his own premises or elsewhere) or he sends them to the supplier at his own expense.

Under regulation 17(8), if the terms of the contract require the consumer to return the goods to the supplier upon cancellation, and the consumer is not otherwise entitled to reject the goods under the terms of the contract or under any statutory implied terms, regulation 17(7) applies as if the 21-day period is extended to six months.

(ix) Performance – regulation 19

2.53 Under regulation 19(1), the supplier must perform the contract within 30 days from the day after which the consumer sent his order to the supplier, or within such other period for performance as the parties agree (the 'period for performance').

Subject to the right to provide substitutes (set out below), if the supplier is unable to perform the contract within the period for performance because the goods or services ordered are not available, the contract falls away, as if it had never existed, other than any rights that the consumer may have in respect of the non-performance. The supplier must inform the consumer and must reimburse any sum paid by or on behalf of the consumer within 30 days of the end of the period for performance.

Where the supplier is unable to supply the goods or services ordered by the consumer, the supplier may perform the contract by providing substitute goods or services of equivalent quality and price, if:

■ this possibility was provided for in the contract; and

■ the supplier gave the consumer the information required by regulation 7(1)(b) and (c).

(x) Protection of the consumer against payment card fraud – regulation 21

2.54 The consumer can cancel a payment if fraudulent use has been made of his payment card in connection with the contract. If this happens, the consumer shall be entitled to be re-credited, or to have all sums returned by the card issuer. If there are proceedings it is for the card issuer to prove the use was authorised.

In this regulation, 'payment card' includes credit cards, charge cards, debit cards and store cards.

This regulation amends the provisions of the CCA 1974. At present, under the CCA 1974, a credit cardholder has a potential liability for the first £50 of loss suffered by the card issuer where the card has been used fraudulently. In theory, the cardholder may have liability greater than £50 if he has been grossly negligent.

Under the Regulations, a credit cardholder is completely protected, and that protection has been officially extended to cards which are not strictly speaking credit cards (eg debit cards).

(c) Enforcement

2.55 The DTI regards failure to inform consumers of the right of withdrawal in writing as a serious matter and proposals regarding the implementing legislation suggested such failure would be a criminal offence (which is similar to the sanction already used in the Consumer Protection Regulations 1987 and 1998[1]). However, the adopted Regulations are silent on the sanction for non-compliance, unless dealt with via an enforcement authority. These bodies are given powers to take proceedings by way of an injunction against offenders to prevent further breaches. The DTI considers that the extended cancellation period, and the availability of injunctions in the event of non-compliance (together with associated negative publicity) should be sufficient to ensure compliance. However, the DTI is considering whether consumers should be given a right of compensation for losses suffered from non-compliance. The Regulations will be amended at a later stage if this approach is adopted. The need for criminal sanctions will also be under review. The Regulations also create a remedy for breach of statutory duty.

Member States remain free to stipulate the language(s) which may or must be used in on-line contracts. This may prove problematic if assessing what an on-line seller must do to comply with the Distance Selling Directive. In addition, for consumer contracts there is a requirement that contracts are in plain intelligible language[2], which may amount to a requirement to translate information or terms into all languages of the Member States. Perhaps a more viable option is to consider translating terms and conditions and any required information into the main languages of any target states.

One issue which is not resolved through the Directive or the Regulations is the practicality of enforcing remedies against on-line sellers in different Member States. Broadly, the consumer will wish to sue in the courts of his home state, but the relatively low cost or value of the contract involved means that enforcement of the judgment will not be worthwhile unless the on-line seller has assets in that state also. Cross-border enforcement of judgments is something that is not usually worthwhile in low value cases. The matter of enforcement of judgments is more fully considered in Chapter 7, E-dispute.

The scope of the Regulations is very broad, although they do not apply to business-to-business transactions or to one-off transactions[3]. It may be that the Regulations merely provide statutory backing for the good business practices which many on-line businesses already observe[4]. Clearly, the obligation to provide information and the 'cooling-off' provisions will be extremely onerous on suppliers and may even act as a deterrent to offering on-line business to consumer transacting facilities[5], since it wipes out many of the advantages of providing low margin services on-line and interferes with the implementation of the obligation to perform the contract within 30 days. The delay in implementation of the Directive into UK law (the Directive should have been implemented by 4 June 2000) was partly as a result of the extended consideration of the impact there will be on business-to-consumer transactions. The cooling-off period seems anomalous in e-commerce: although useful where consumers are relying on descriptions, the rationale for such provision is clearly to allow consumers to reconsider after being subjected to pressure selling. Such pressure selling as might be experienced through telesales, for example, is absent in e-commerce transactions, and it seems excessive to include such provision in these transactions. This certainly seems at odds with the UK's desire to become the pre-eminent venue for e-commerce and to reduce the burden on on-line sellers. Quite how the UK will police such a requirement remains to be seen.

1   SI 1987/2117 and SI 1998/3050.
2   Article 5 of Directive (EEC) 12/93 on Unfair Terms in Consumer Contracts.
3   Regulation 9.
4   DTI Press Release P/2000/599.
5   The Outline Regulatory Impact Assessment of implementing legislation (www.dti.gov.uk) suggests compliance costs for businesses will be huge: one company has estimated compliance costs would be £250,000 to £500,000, while one bank estimated costs would be a one-off £1.05m.

10. SPECIFIC ON-LINE CONTRACTUAL TERMS

2.56   So far this chapter has dealt with contracting on-line in an abstract context. Most prudent on-line sellers will have a set of standard terms and conditions or a standard licence agreement which they already use off-line and which could be adapted to meet the requirements of trading on-line. We have already discussed some of the specific e-commerce issues which the on-line seller will have to address in its terms and conditions, relating to:

■   the status of its website, ie whether it is an invitation to treat only or a contractual offer;

■   the procedure by which a contract will be formed (offer, acceptance, acknowledgement, incorporation of terms, where and when effective); and

■   the other requirements of the E-Commerce and Distance Selling Directives.

The on-line seller should also consider:

■   **price and other essential terms** Regulation 6(2) of the E-Commerce Regulations requires that when an on-line seller refers to prices, 'these shall be indicated clearly and unambiguously and, in particular, shall indicate whether they are inclusive of tax and delivery costs'.

■   **payment terms** For consumer transactions, payment will usually be in advance by credit card, especially where international sales are made, given the difficulty in enforcing a small debt overseas[1]. Regulation 7(1)(a)(v) of the Distance Selling Regulations requires arrangements for payment to be stated in advance.

■   **choice of law** For obvious reasons, the on-line seller will usually want to choose the law of its home country. However, the on-line seller should bear in mind that this may be varied by other countries' consumer legislation[2].

■   **implied terms** The on-line seller must consider the extent to which any on-line contract into which it enters contains implied terms. For example, as goods will usually be purchased on the basis of a description contained on the website, and the buyer will not generally have seen the goods at the time of contract, there will be an implied term that such goods will comply with such description[3]. In business-to-consumer contracts, liability for breach of this implied term cannot be excluded or restricted. In other cases, liability may be excluded or limited by reference to a contract term only in so far as such clause satisfies the requirements of reasonableness[4]. Traditionally, courts have taken a wide view of the meaning of 'description' – so that it covers, for example, weight, measurements, volume, packaging. There are also issues such as implied rights which may accrue under the Contracts (Rights of Third Parties) Act 1999. These are excludable; however, such exclusion must be handled carefully.

- **other requirements of the distance selling legislation** In addition to the information to be provided prior to contracting and the right to cancel, the Distance Selling Regulations impose obligations in respect of returning sums paid and security, cancellation of related credit agreements and time of performance, which must be observed. There are also provisions relating to recovery of goods from consumers supplied under a contract which is subsequently cancelled. Details of any after sales services and guarantees as well as information relating to terminating indefinite or long-term (ie longer than one year) contracts must be provided[5].

- **dispute resolution procedures and jurisdiction** This is considered further in Chapter 7, E-dispute.

- **exclusion and limitations of liability** As in any off-line transaction, the on-line seller must deal with limiting its liability very carefully and should take care to ensure it complies with any applicable legislation. See further in Chapter 3, E-liability.

1 It is noteworthy that article 8 of the Distance Selling Directive requires Member States to ensure that appropriate measures exist to allow a consumer to request cancellation of a payment where fraudulent use has been made of his payment card in connection with distance contracts falling within the scope of the Directive and, in the event of fraudulent use, to be recredited with the sums paid or have them returned.
2 See footnote 1 to paragraph 2.24 above in relation to the Unfair Terms in Consumer Contracts Regulations 1999.
3 See the Sales of Goods Act 1979, s 13 and the Supply of Goods and Services Act 1982, s 3.
4 The UCTA 1977, s 6.
5 The DTI has prepared a short guide for business (www.dti.gov.uk/CACP/ca/bisguide.htm) and is intending to prepare a guide to frequently asked questions by consumers and an information leaflet for consumers.

2.57 Briefly, where English law is chosen to govern the contract, the Unfair Contracts Terms Act 1977 will apply with the following effects:

- the on-line seller will not be able to exclude or limit its liability for personal injury or death caused by negligence. This is a standard provision that will affect all types of contract;

- the on-line seller can only exclude or restrict its liability for other loss or damage caused by negligence in so far as the term is reasonable;

- for business-to-business transactions, where written standard terms of business apply, any exclusion or limitation of liability must be reasonable[1];

- for business-to-consumer transactions, any exclusion or limitation of liability must be reasonable and the consumer cannot be made to indemnify anyone unless it is reasonable. Where consumer goods are supplied, a clause should be included that any 'guarantee' given does not affect the consumer's statutory rights[2]. The Unfair Terms in Consumer Contracts Regulations 1999 will also apply and the on-line seller should check the list of terms which may be regarded as unfair in Schedule 2 to the Regulations to make sure that they are not included[3].

Although the UCTA 1977 will not apply to international contracts for the sale of goods, the on-line seller should still draft its standard terms fairly, as most countries will impose similar restrictions, especially where consumer contracts are concerned.

Although we have largely looked at the position of the on-line seller as a seller, it may also wish to purchase over the Internet. Most of the considerations above will still apply in reverse and the on-line seller should treat the on-line purchase just as it would a regular purchase by:

- making appropriate enquiries before dealing with a supplier, taking up references, etc, to determine whether it is generally reputed to be able to deliver on time, etc;

- if possible, negotiating in advance the terms of supply, especially in relation to payment and warranties. This may have to be done in part off-line and, if so, the on-line seller should take care to ensure that these amended terms are incorporated when it eventually places the order on-line;

- ensuring that regular proper approval procedures are followed on-line; and

- keeping proper records.

In Europe, at least, it is probably fair to say that the legal regimes for business-to-business and business-to-consumer on-line contracting have diverged sufficiently to affect the design of websites used for e-commerce and also raise the question as to whether e-commerce should be undertaken at all[4].

1 Guidelines for the application of the reasonableness test are set out in Schedule 2 to the Unfair Contracts Terms Act 1977 and look to bargaining power, availability of other suppliers, insurance and whether legal advice was sought, for example when assessing reasonableness.
2 Article 4 of the Consumer Transactions (Restrictions on Statements) Order 1976 (SI 1976/1813).
3 One may also refer to the Office of Fair Trading website, where details of terms which have been regarded as unfair may be obtained (www.oft.gov.uk).
4 However, UK businesses seem undeterred by this trend. The DTI has reported (Press Release P/2000/614) that small businesses have exceeded Government targets for getting on-line. 1.7 million small and medium sized enterprises are now on-line, which represents a 1.1 million increase since 1999. 'On-line' for these purposes means using external e-mail frequently, using a website or using electronic data interchange. Trading on-line means using both on-line payment and on-line ordering with customers and suppliers. Businesses accounting for 27% of UK employees are now trading over the Internet. UK Online For Business (formerly the Information Society Initiative) is providing £25m funding to increase this figure. There are advice centres and business advisors available to assist with this process of getting businesses on-line.

II. SUPPORTING AGREEMENTS

2.58 Other agreements which an on-line seller may need to enter into include the following.

(a) Website development agreement

2.59 The main aims of a website development agreement are to ensure that the on-line seller gets the website it wants, on time, within budget and with all the rights necessary for it to use, modify and adapt the website later. It is probable that the development work will involve the appointment of an external supplier, be it freelance programmers or a website or design development agency. Simple websites may not need as much 'protection' because they can be easily redeveloped, but a larger project should be treated as if it were a mixture of a large bespoke software development agreement and an appointment to carry out creative work.

Crucially, it is important to remember that an assignment of copyright is not effective unless it is in writing and signed by or on behalf of the assignor (section 90(3) of the Copyright, Designs and Patents Act 1988). This can easily be overlooked and, having commissioned and paid for the project, the website 'owner' is left reliant on implied licences to carry on operating the site. In practice this is likely to tie the on-line seller to the website developer on an ongoing basis. The agreement between them should deal with the following points (among others):

1. The developer's obligations to create the website, preferably according to a full written specification and project plan. As technology develops further, WAP and GPRS compatibility will need to be considered.

2. The on-line seller's obligation to co-operate with the developer and to provide instructions and basic materials, eg logos, graphics and text.

3. The on-line seller's obligation to pay the charges, preferably linked to milestones in the project. From the on-line seller's point of view, a specific proportion of the fee should be held back until the project has been completed to its satisfaction.

4. 'Change control' procedures for agreeing variations to the initial specification.

5. Acceptance testing and initial error correction work during the 'guarantee period'.

6. Transfer of ownership to the on-line seller of copyright in all bespoke elements of the 'touch and feel' of the website or, at the minimum, an exclusive licence on a royalty-free basis.

7. A royalty-free, non-exclusive licence in respect of the copyright in all of the developer's basic scripts, graphics and other web elements used in the website. For bespoke development work in respect of programming, this is also the more usual approach. The developer will usually insist that this licence will only be for the purposes of maintaining, operating or updating the website.

8   An obligation on the developer to place source codes in escrow or, ideally, to disclose them to the on-line seller on an ongoing basis.

9. A further assurance clause that the developer will execute all necessary documents to vest in the on-line seller all intellectual property rights related to the project.

10. Whether the overall look and feel of the website is to be an 'exclusive' design, which, if so, has the effect of preventing the developer from creating a substantially similar site for a third party.

11. Acknowledgement that no licence is granted to the developer to reuse any of the materials provided by the on-line seller.

12. Warranties and indemnity that bespoke works to be transferred are original and the developer has a right to grant licences in respect of the remaining intellectual property rights. The developer can rightfully expect to have a similar warranty and indemnity from the on-line seller in respect of content which it has provided for inclusion on the website.

13. Whether the developer should be allowed to place a credit on the site and use it as a reference site. The developer should waive all other moral rights.

14. Termination and the effects of termination. This is especially important if the developer is also to host or update the site, as in such circumstances the on-line seller will want to build in the right to move the website to a different ISP and a matching obligation on the developer to co-operate and provide assistance, especially in relation to scripts and other coding.

15. Commercially, the on-line seller may wish to impose a restriction on the developer providing similar services to a direct competitor of the on-line seller during the term of the project.

16. Ideally, the issue of copyright in content of the site and legal clearances should be addressed. In the recent case of *Antiquesportfolio.com plc v Rodney Fitch & Co Ltd*[1] it was held that in the absence of agreement to the contrary, there was an implied term in a website development contract that a website developer would use 'reasonable skill and care not to use and supply material that infringed third party copyright'. It may be that the parties would agree that the developer may simply identify what issues arise and leave it for the on-line seller to obtain the necessary legal clearances. As regards other content, the on-line seller will usually have to accept that the developer cannot be responsible for compliance of the website with worldwide legal requirements.

17. Data protection clauses if personal data is processed by the website.

18. Dispute resolution and choice of law.

Other issues are likely to arise depending upon the circumstances. It is frequently the case that two different contractors will be involved in the development work relating to the look and feel and visual content of the site ('front end') and the programming work relating to its functionality ('back end'). In such circumstances, the on-line seller will need to establish who will take overall responsibility for the integration and testing of the two aspects of the work carried out. If this is to be the responsibility of one of the contractors, then the on-line seller will wish to make clear that the primary contractor has dealt with copyright issues with its subcontractor to the on-line seller's satisfaction.

1   (2000) Times, 21 July, LTL 10/7/2000, (2000) IPD November 23092.

(b) ISP agreement

2.60   Unless the on-line seller has its own server and direct Internet connection, it will need to contract with an Internet service provider (ISP) to obtain Internet access and hosting of its website. Although there are many 'free' offers available now, these are largely directed at the general public and usually relate to volumes of web space that are too small to be adequate for e-commerce use.

The main concern for the on-line seller will be to ensure that the ISP will be able to support the volume of traffic which its site is likely to generate, that it is stable and scalable and that there is sufficient security to ensure that its site is not hacked into. The website is an advertisement for the on-line seller, so a constantly 'unavailable' or sluggish site may have a serious effect on the on-line seller's goodwill. The on-line seller should also try to ensure that it can move its site easily to another ISP if necessary.

The main concern for the ISP will be to ensure that it will not become liable for any unlawful activity on the website and that it has the right to suspend or terminate its services in the event that, for example, defamatory or obscene material or material in breach of another's copyright is found on the website.

In this respect, ISPs have greater protection as a consequence of the E-Commerce Directive. The Directive (and E-Commerce Regulations) specifically exempt service providers from liability in damages in the following circumstances:

- where the service provider plays a passive role as a conduit of information for content providers (ie it is a 'mere conduit') – regulation 17;

- where the service provider 'caches' information (ie stores information to enable a more efficient onward transmission of that information) – regulation 18;

- where the service provider hosts information (for example, the provision of server space for a website or newsgroup) and does not have actual knowledge that the information breaches any law or is not aware of any circumstances from which it would have been apparent to the service provider that the activity or information was unlawful – regulation 19.

The agreement should deal with the following points (among others):

1.   The amount of storage space, bandwidth and provision for scaling up.

2.   The availability of the system (which the ISP and the on-line seller will generally want to be on an all-day every-day basis), redundancy and downtime for maintenance.

3.   Whether it can run scripts, Java applets and other executables.

4.   E-mail forwarding if required.

5.   Access numbers for connection and help desk support.

6. Security and passwords and procedure for uploading materials.

7. Reports and statistics to analyse hits and performance.

8. A confidentiality clause and a data protection clause if the ISP will be the data processor.

9. Restrictions on illegal or harmful content – the procedure to be adopted to deal with allegations that the site contains copyrighted, defamatory or pornographic materials and when the right to suspend or terminate service arises.

10. Indemnities.

11. If the domain name is provided by the ISP, whether the on-line seller can transfer the domain name to another ISP on termination.

12. Assistance in transfer of materials on termination.

13. Clarification that suitable backup/disaster recovery facilities are in place in the event of unavailability of the server.

(c) 'Webvertising' or 'linking' agreement

2.61 The on-line seller will want to advertise its website both in the traditional media and on other websites. It may also wish to allow others to advertise on its website. This advertising can be in the form of banner adverts, hyperlinks and browser windows which start up automatically.

The main issues for the advertiser will be to ensure that the adverts are displayed appropriately (eg to a targeted segment, not next to 'unsuitable' content) and that this link to its site works. The advertiser will usually also require a certain degree of exclusivity as regards its business sector. The website owner will want to make sure that it is paid correctly (for example, if it is on a 'click through' basis, how that will be verified) and that it does not suffer any additional liability for displaying the advert (for example, because of trade mark or copyright infringement).

Both parties should do some due diligence – the advertiser will not want to be seen to 'endorse' some unsuitable site where it has a particularly famous brand and a good website will want to make sure similarly that the advertising is appropriate. It will not want, for example, banner advertising for a pornographic site suddenly appearing on its website and this may happen where the images are being fed from a separate server over which it has no control.

Points which should be dealt with in the agreement include:

1. Technical issues relating to the display of graphics, their execution and provenance, and ensuring links to the advertiser's site function properly.

2. Limited licences for the use of graphics and/or text and trade marks used in the advertisements.

3. Responsibilities of the parties regarding appropriateness of adverts and content of the website.

4. Payment structure and triggers (eg base fee, per display, click through, visitor, ultimate sale), how payment obligations are to be verified and other reporting obligations.

5. Indemnities or limitations of liability, in particular in respect of the infringement of third party rights by the advertising.

6. How the agreement can be terminated and the effects of termination, eg materials to be destroyed, web pages to be changed within the stated period and payment of outstanding amounts to become immediately due and payable.

7.   Data protection and privacy obligations of each of the parties, eg regarding the use of cookies and data collected on visitors and customers.

8.   The format and timetable for the supply of advertising content.

In practice, the owners of popular websites will contract with advertisers on the basis of standard rate cards which include non-negotiable standard terms and conditions. The advertiser may well not contract with the website owner direct, but by using a media buying agency. Industry standard practice dictates that the media buyer will contract as principal with the website owner and that the contractual terms between them will correspond with and be incorporated in the contract between the advertiser and its media buyer.

(d) Content provision agreement

2.62 Most e-commerce websites will offer information of some sort. These can range from sites whose sole purpose is to sell electronic content (movies, software and information) to those sites where information is provided free of charge but ancillary to the sale of other goods (eg sales and technical information).

The content provider will either own or have the right to sub-license the copyrights and/or database rights in the information. Even where the information is to be provided free of charge, the content provider should still carefully define the terms of the licence it grants to users of the information to protect its existing rights and limit its liabilities. The user of the website should similarly check what it is allowed to do with the information to ensure that it is not subject to future lawsuits: although the user will have an implied licence of some sort, the licence will be limited and may be terminable at will. The terms and conditions on the website may impose express restrictions or limitations on use.

A useful example which can be applicable to most e-commerce sites is the multi-level structure used by many newspaper sites. This consists of:

1.   pages with no access restrictions, usually the home page, what's new page and the marketing and corporate background pages;

2.   pages available only to registered users, which are usually today's or the week's news or perhaps just the summaries of the news and which are password protected; and

3.   one or more different levels of 'premium' pages, accessed through a secure server, which could be back issues, special reports, third party materials, usually on a pay-per-download basis.

2.63 Even for the on-line seller who only wishes to provide technical information to customers who have already bought its goods, this structure can be useful as it encourages its customers to register, allows the on-line seller to know who has accessed the information and when and, as the user will have agreed to the on-line seller's terms and conditions as part of the registration process, to enforce those express terms and increase its chances of limiting its liabilities, rather than relying on terms on a different part of its website. The on-line seller could also use 'premium' pages to support customers who had contracted for maintenance, rather than charging on a per use basis.

The content provider should consider the following issues:

■   **Scope of the licence,** eg to download and store on a single local drive and to use the materials for internal business purposes or personal non-commercial use only, to print one copy of the materials, to play the music/movie in private, not to further redistribute the materials.

■   **Term of the licence,** eg single use, during a limited period only, until the licence is terminated.

- **Integrity of the materials**, eg materials to be kept as a whole, no extracts without acknowledgement, no substantial extracts without written permission, no removal or modification of copyright management information, no incorporation into another database.

- **Whether it wishes to allow the information to be subsequently 'shared'**, eg to be copied to others within the same organisation, stored on a network drive or otherwise cache. The content provider may wish expressly to prohibit this where it obtains revenue for each page 'hit' (for instance, on a pay-per-display basis or where advertising revenue is earned per page hit) as this will reduce the number of visitors to its site. It may also wish to track individual accesses.

- **Payment terms.**

- **Right to suspend service and termination.**

- **Limitations and exclusion of liability**, eg information supplied 'as is' with no guarantee as to accuracy, timeliness, completeness, fitness for purpose or satisfactory quality.

- **Data protection** Whether registration details and usage of site will be used for any other purposes.

- **Confidentiality** Some suppliers, such as Intel, use secure sites to distribute confidential materials to their customers. Provided this is done properly, there is no reason why even an essentially 'open' medium like the Internet could not be used for this purpose. The content provider should ensure that:

  - a confidentiality agreement is in place before the materials are disclosed to the user – this can be done either off-line or on-line. It may also be useful to remind the user each time it accesses or downloads the materials that the terms of the confidentiality agreement apply to that material;

  - the materials are clearly marked 'confidential' with a statement that any use is governed by the terms of the confidentiality agreement;

  - access to the materials is restricted by technical means, eg passwords, encryption, etc;

  - records are kept of the contents and timing of each download and of the identity of the persons downloading the materials, eg IP address, electronic signature, etc;

  - the materials cannot easily be modified, eg by distributing them in secured PDF files.

12. COMPETITION LAW

2.64 Companies developing on-line e-sales platforms will have to consider potential competition law issues. This should come as no surprise, but it does involve posing the familiar competition law questions within a new context, a context with which regulators are just coming to grips.

(a) The context

2.65 Broadly, e-competition issues seem to divide down two lines:

- first, there are the structural issues, such as those relating to access to the Internet and the web user contracts between content providers, intermediary ISPs and network providers; and

- second, there are issues relating to the mechanics of on-line trading, such as restrictions companies may wish to place on distributors in terms of e-sales and the very popular trend of companies in the same industry joining together to set up joint procurement or sales platforms (so-called 'B2B market places').

After an overview of the relevant legal provisions, we will look at some of the more important competition issues. For example, what kind of restrictions, if any, can a supplier impose on distributors? May a supplier choose to reserve all on-line sales to itself, through its own website? How should companies set up and operate joint buying or selling platforms?

(b) Sources of law

2.66 For most companies operating in the UK, the relevant competition provisions can be found in the Competition Act 1998 (CA 1998). The CA 1998 incorporates into domestic UK law the prohibitions found in articles 81 and 82 of the EC Treaty, referred to in the CA 1998 respectively as the Chapter I and Chapter II prohibitions. The CA 1998 requires UK authorities to ensure there is noinconsistency with the principles of European competition rules and UK authorities must have regard to any relevant decision or statement of the European Commission. This means that EU competition law will be of increasing relevance to regulating competition domestically within the UK.

- Chapter I of the CA 1998 prohibits all agreements between undertakings that have as their object or effect the prevention, restriction or distortion of competition, which may affect trade within the UK or a part thereof. This covers, in particular, concerted practices involving price-fixing and market sharing.

- Chapter II prohibits any abuse by one or more undertakings of a dominant position on the relevant market. Dominance will always depend on the definition of the relevant geographic and product market. Taking the market for book sales as an example, it will be germane to ask whether the market for on-line books is UK restricted, European or even global, and whether on-line book sales are to be considered as part of the same market as books sold in high street bookstores. Where a company has a market share of 40% or more, this will typically be considered to amount to a dominant position. Abuse of a dominant position may consist of imposing unfair purchase or selling prices, limiting or refusing supply or attaching additional conditions to contracts that companies would otherwise not be able to apply.

The CA 1998 took effect from March 2000. It applies to agreements and practices the effects of which are felt mainly in the UK. However, where there is an appreciable effect on trade between Member States of the EU, articles 81 and 82 of the EC Treaty will themselves be the applicable provisions and, for example, companies risking falling foul of the article 81 prohibition will have to look for negative clearance or ensure the agreement falls within one of the 'block exemptions' issued by the European Commission. As with the Office of Fair Trading in the UK, the European Commission has broad enforcement powers in terms of both article 81 and 82 prohibitions, with the power to impose fines of up to 10% of company turnover.

(c) Relevant issues

2.67 With the main provisions in mind, we can turn to the e-competition issues themselves. First, we should look at some of the structural issues. These relate mainly to Internet access and the marketing and sale of software and technology. Although these are perhaps not issues of immediate relevance to companies setting up e-trading platforms (rather, these are primarily issues for ISPs and network companies), it is important to have an understanding of the issues involved. Indeed, if potential customers are frustrated by anti-competitive practices in gaining access to the Internet, they may not be able to visit your website, let alone buy your product. The remaining sections look at the interesting issues of the mechanics of on-line trading in terms of e-commerce and the creation of B2B market places.

(i) Access to the Internet

2.68   Access to the Internet is of course typically obtained through an ISP. A variety of organisations offer ISP services, ranging in size from large organisations (eg telecoms companies) with their own networks, to smaller providers who are, in effect, local resellers of capacity on a large ISP's network. Competition authorities both in the EU and the US have been concerned with the so-called 'bundling' of access and software services. Although WAP Internet access for mobile phones and multimedia cable networks is now on the market, the vast majority of e-trading is still conducted via the telecommunications networks with customers dialling up to their ISPs through their 'local loops' (ie via their local telephone exchanges). The networks and the local loops are traditionally owned by the incumbent telecoms operators, placing them in a dominant position for the provision of Internet access services[1]. Indeed, many telecoms operators have set up ISPs as subsidiaries, prompting fears that the parent company may be able to distort competition by affording favourable treatment to, or even subsidising the operations of, its ISP subsidiary. Competition rules require the incumbent operator to provide all ISPs with access to the local loops to enable them to provide Internet services to their customers, even where this is in direct competition with the telecoms operator. This opening of access is referred to as the 'unbundling' of the local loop and is required so as to stimulate the provision of telecommunications services, including broadband multimedia and high-speed Internet connections. The European Commission, despite proclaiming a 'light touch' approach to regulating innovative markets, is concerned that new markets are not foreclosed by dominant players. National competition authorities, and in particular the UK's OFTEL (Office of Telecommunications), are under strong pressure to ensure the fast development of Internet services.

1   This is certainly the case in the UK, where the vast majority of the network for these purposes is controlled by British Telecom.

(ii) Distribution of browser software

2.69   Broadly similar competition issues apply in relation to the distribution of software. One of the best examples of competition policy in practice concerns Microsoft and its marketing and sale of its browser software, *Internet Explorer*. In May 1999, the European Commission approved Microsoft's agreements with some European ISPs for the licensing and distribution of its *Internet Explorer* browser and related products. The Commission was concerned that restrictions in those agreements might have the effect of preventing the marketing of Internet browser software by Microsoft's competitors (eg Netscape)[1]. The Commission eventually cleared the agreements by way of a 'comfort letter' after Microsoft agreed, first, to delete a provision under which it would have been allowed to terminate its agreement with an ISP if the latter did not attain minimum distribution sales of *Internet Explorer* and, second, to allow such ISPs to promote and advertise competing browser software. However, with the launch of Windows 2000 in February 2000, the Commission has taken a tougher line with the new series of licensing agreements, which were allegedly allocated according to a so-called 'friend-enemy' scheme depending on whether the ISP offers its customers other browser software in addition to *Internet Explorer*.

1   One particular concern with respect to the manner in which browser software is distributed is its capacity, when installed onto a computer, to interfere with the working of other software already resident there. It is within the realms

of acceptability for a computer user who installed browser X to then install browser Y (as a result, say, of signing up with a second ISP and receiving its software bundle) and be offered the opportunity to specify which of X or Y is his preferred (or default) option. But it is not in principle acceptable for the effect of installing Y to be that the computer automatically selects Y or makes X difficult or impossible to use properly.

(iii) Refusal to supply software information

2.70 Microsoft is also in trouble with regard to its refusal to supply software information, which can constitute abuse of a dominant position. Microsoft has a market share of about 95% in the market for personal computer operating systems, and thus enjoys a practically undisputed market dominance. Most PCs today are embedded into networks, which are controlled by servers. Interoperability (ie the ability of the PC to talk to the server) is the basis for network computing. Interoperability can only function if the operating systems running on the PC and server can talk to each other. To enable competitors of Microsoft to develop server operating systems which can talk to the dominant Windows software for PCs, interface information must be known. Without that information computers running on Windows operating systems would de facto be obliged to use Windows server software to ensure full interoperability. This phenomenon is known as *'the client (PC) dragging the server'*. In December 1998, Sun Microsystems submitted a complaint to the European Commission alleging that Microsoft's dominance in the PC operating system market created an obligation on Microsoft to disclose its interfaces to allow full interoperability with non-Microsoft server software. The launch of Windows 2000 prompted the Commission to officially warn Microsoft that it believed Microsoft was abusing its dominant position in the market for PC operating systems software by leveraging this power into the market for server software[1]. Additional proceedings were initiated against Microsoft in August 2001 for tying its Media Player product with its dominant Windows operating system[2]. The investigation continues.

1 Commission Press Release IP/00/906, 3 August 2000.
2 Commission Press Release IP/01/1232, 30 August 2001.

(iv) Competition issues in the mechanics of on-line trading

2.71 Turning away from structural e-competition issues, we can now look at certain issues relating to the mechanics of on-line trading, such as the restrictions companies may wish to place on distributors in terms of e-sales and the creation of B2B market places. We are concerned here primarily with agreements between undertakings and are, therefore, in the realms of article 81 of the EC Treaty and the Chapter I prohibition under the CA 1998. In EU competition law terms, such agreements are generally distinguished as being either 'vertical' or 'horizontal'.

- 'Vertical' denotes agreements or concerted practices between companies at *different* stages in the production chain, the best example being distribution agreements between supplier and retailer.

- 'Horizontal', on the other hand, denotes agreements or concerted practices between companies operating at the *same* level in the market, ie who are effectively competitors.

The European Commission's rules and accompanying guidelines on vertical agreements do not deal specifically with e-commerce. As a general rule, however, a supplier cannot restrict his distributors from using the Internet to advertise and sell his products. Two important exceptions apply:

- first, a restriction may be imposed on the use of the Internet where the promotion of e-sales would lead to 'active' selling into another distributor's territory or customer group. So, for example, a Belgian distributor acting for a UK-based company can be prohibited from 'actively' selling into France if the UK company already has its own French distributor (or distributes in France himself). However, the supplier cannot prevent the Belgian distributor from what is termed 'passive' selling in equivalent circumstances, ie where a French customer solicits the goods via the Belgian distributor's website; and

■ second, so long as they can be objectively justified, a supplier may always place conditions on the sale of his product through a distributor's website, in the same way as he may impose quality standards for a shop or for advertising and promotion in general.

(v) The creation of B2B market places

2.72 In contrast to vertical agreements, B2B market places are usually horizontal in nature. In other words, they characteristically involve forms of co-operation between competitors operating at the same level on the market. Hence, for example, a number of multinational companies such as Scottish Power, Northern Electric and United Utilities recently teamed up with technology providers to form an Internet-based 'procurement exchange'. The pace of development of these kind of on-line exchanges has taken the regulatory authorities by surprise. The European Commission has created a team of officials to address the issue and deal with the mounting number of notifications. The main concern is that such exchanges may operate as little more than disguised cartels in which competitors can co-ordinate their market behaviour, dividing markets and sharing information on price and other sensitive market issues.

There are three main regulatory processes of which e-businesses should be aware when establishing joint venture arrangements.

■ Where there is a potential effect on trade between Member States and the joint venture is intended to operate as a separate and autonomous legal entity from its parents, notification of the joint venture agreement is required under the EU Merger Control Regulation where the turnover Merger Control Regulation thresholds are met[1].

■ Where the joint venture is not intended to operate as a separate and autonomous legal entity (for example, where the joint venture is simply a contractual arrangement rather than a specially formed corporate entity), the agreement may nevertheless have to be notified to the European Commission under article 81 of the EC Treaty if there is a potential effect on trade between Member States[2].

■ Where there is no potential effect on trade between Member States, but the effects are likely to be purely domestic to the UK, UK competition law applies and similar notification procedures and competition rules are applied by the UK competition authorities pursuant to the CA 1998[3].

To benefit from negative clearance or exemption from the article 81 (or Chapter I) prohibition, the companies entering into the joint venture arrangement need to be able to demonstrate that the joint venture will be pro-competitive and that any restrictions on competition are necessary to make the arrangement work. Moreover, the companies must show that the efficiencies resulting from the new market place will be passed on to consumers. In the European Commission decision on the creation of Volbroker.com[4] (a joint venture e-market place established by six major banks to provide first brokerage services for automated trading in foreign currency exchange options), the Commission also required that the market place be open to other competitors and requested guarantees that sensitive market information would not be passed between members. It is likely that these kinds of conditions will be applied more forcefully if there is a risk that the e-market place will result in a significant degree of market concentration.

1 Council Regulation (EEC) 4064/89: OJ L395 30.12.89, as amended by Council Regulation (EC) 1310/97: OJ L180 9.7.97.
2 Council Regulation (EEC) 17/62: OJ L13 21.2.62, as amended. See http://europa.eu.int/comm/competition/index_eu.html.
3 For further information see www.oft.gov.uk.
4 See Press Release in 'Agence Europe (Bulletin Quotidien Europe)', 3 August 2000, p 6.

3

E-liability

I. INTRODUCTION

3.01 A website is accessible by anyone in the world who has access to the Internet and this opens up new avenues for doing business which were not available before the advent of the Internet and e-commerce. But these opportunities carry with them a range of risks.

This chapter examines a range of legal 'liabilities' which affect those who market goods or services on-line. We will summarise the common law and statutory regimes which govern the various duties arising from the legal relationship between those who operate businesses on the Internet and those who visit websites.

2. SCOPE OF THIS CHAPTER

3.02 In this chapter, we will examine the following implications of engaging in e-commerce:

■ common law liability related to contract: for example, what is the on-line seller's liability for failing to deliver goods or services as contracted? We examine how this is affected by matters such as terms implied in a contract or claims by the purchaser for loss above the purchase price of the goods or services in question;

■ common law liability for negligence, including negligent misstatements made on-line;

■ the statutory regime regulating liability for defective products;

■ the statutory regime regulating the gathering, retention, processing and protection of data;

■ the common law and statutory regime regulating defamation; and

■ the criminal offences related to obscenity and obscene or harmful publications.

Accordingly, it will be important to look at issues such as:

■ the types of liability[1] and risks a seller faces;

■ how liability can arise and for how long the seller can be held liable; and

■ how to minimise or deal with liability when it arises.

---

1 It will be apparent from what follows that there can be overlap between the various categories itemised above. For example, a negligent misstatement at common law might also be a misrepresentation that undermines a contract. Defamatory material might also be obscene (or vice versa).

3. LIABILITY ISSUES COVERED IN OTHER CHAPTERS

3.03 This chapter is not an exhaustive list of the criminal or civil liability issues that the on-line seller or Internet user faces. For example:

- Chapter 4, E-rights and Chapter 5, E-brand deal with a range of intellectual property rights and liabilities. Chapter 6, E-marketing examines certain issues related to copyright and advertising law;

- criminal offences in relation to the making of false and misleading statements inducing investment transactions and the issue of unauthorised investment advertisements are matters considered in Chapter 9, E-finance, and criminal offences relating to the provision of on-line betting or gaming services are looked at in Chapter 14, E-gambling; and

- Chapter 13, E-property contains a section which looks at certain rights that attach to ownership of land as these might, for example, affect those laying Internet cables or those complaining of electromagnetic interference from adjoining premises.

4. THE IMPORTANCE OF THE CONTRACT

3.04 The principle legal tool between two or more parties doing business together for managing risk is the contract into which they enter[1]. What follows is not a discussion of the law of contract in general – if it were, there would be a significant number of areas that could be reviewed here. We restrict this chapter to a review of four aspects of contract law, the development of which in relation to e-commerce gives rise to significant issues for contracting parties:

- **Implied terms** A contract need not be in writing and the parties' course of conduct, the history of their relationship and the nature of the contract and its performance may allow for contractual terms not explicitly agreed between the parties to be implied.

- **Remoteness of damage** The contract may limit liability for matters arising separately from the contract itself (for example, indirect or consequential losses a party may sustain as a result of a breach but which are not directly attributable to the breach in question).

- **Choice of law** The parties can use a contract to choose the law by which they wish to contract – which is an essential issue where the parties are subject to different legal systems. If the parties do not do so, or if they have no written agreement at all, there are rules and procedures which will determine the choice of law for them – often to the disadvantage of one party.

- **Excluding or limiting liability** Contracts, particularly those in standard form, often contain clauses which expressly exclude or limit the liability of a contracting party. Sometimes, exclusions or limitations of this nature are introduced into contracts by implication or surrounding circumstances. Traditionally, the courts have taken a harsh view of exclusions and limitations that have been relied upon in apparently unfair or oppressive circumstances, and latterly statute and European law have intervened to further qualify the basis for exclusion of liability.

---

1 Formation of the e-contract is dealt with in Chapter 2, E-contract. It should be remembered that a contract will exist between any persons carrying on business with each other and that most contracts (particularly in the ordinary course of business) do not need to be in writing. The writing or recording of the parties' contract stems from the need for certainty in the future as to the terms agreed, particularly in complex circumstances.

(a) Implied terms[1]

3.05 The general rule in English law is that if a contract has been reduced to writing, the court must give effect to the agreement between the parties as set out in the express terms contained in

arising under the contract, to the detriment of the consumer'[4]. The court has a wide discretion therefore to consider the fairness of clauses, applying very loose assessment criteria. The challenge for on-line sellers in B2C markets is to position their contracts through their standard terms in order to minimise their exposure to liability, and the best way to do so will be to establish and adhere to the best practice exercised in the relevant market.

The Unfair Terms in Consumer Contracts Regulations 1999 also emphasise the importance of using plain, intelligible language in standard form contracts and small print. If it is not used, then the court actually has the power to review such matters as to whether the price paid by the consumer was fair.

Subject to local laws relating to 'unfair contract terms', liability can generally be limited in the contract to one or more of the following:

- a specified maximum amount;

- direct losses only; or

- repairing the defect or replacing the defective product under guarantee.

These are all highly relevant considerations for on-line business, and should be automatic issues for consideration in production of terms for trading on-line.

1 The UCTA 1977, s 11 and Sch 2.
2 See paragraph 3.07.
3 See paragraph 3.07.
4 The Unfair Terms in Consumer Contracts Regulations 1999, reg 5(1).

5. LIABILITY FOR DEFECTIVE PRODUCTS

3.22 Defective products are a good example of an area where an on-line seller could face potential liability in contract, in tort or under a statutory regime[1]. We shall consider these areas in turn (and, as will be seen, this in some respects focuses the discussion on contractual content at paragraph 3.17).

1 See for example *Lexmead (Basingstoke) Ltd v Lewis* [1982] AC 225, HL.

(a) Contractual liability

3.23 Where there is a direct contractual relationship, the on-line seller may be liable to his customers for supplying defective products because this may be a breach of:

- an express term of the contract, for example to deliver goods of a specified description and/or quality;

- an implied term of the contract; and

- a collateral warranty, for example where pre-contractual assurances are given to induce the other party to enter into the contract.

These obligations are absolute: the seller will be liable even if he took all possible care.

Damages in contract are intended generally to put the claimant in the position he would have been in had the contract been performed and there is scope for contractual damages to provide for 'loss of expectation'.

Actions brought in contract generally have a six-year limitation period. This is extended to 12 years where the agreement is by way of a deed. The question of when the limitation period runs from is of potential interest and, although a discussion of this issue is necessarily outside of the scope of this book[1], it should be noted that in certain circumstances the limitation period will not run from the date of purchase but instead from some date in the future.

1   See section 2 of the Limitation Act 1980, but see also sections 14A and 14B (added by the Latent Damage Act 1986).

(b) Tortious liability

3.24   The vast majority of common law tort claims concern the tort of negligence. While it is possible for a claim in respect of a defective product to be founded in deceit (basically, fraud), it is relatively unlikely to be relevant, and in relation to defective products we shall consider the impact of negligence alone.

(i)   General principles in negligence

3.25   Before discussing defective product liability, a few general words should be said about the law of negligence. The standard ingredients of the tort of negligence include the following (though there may be other issues of a more specialised nature to take into account in relevant circumstances)[1]:

■   there must be a duty of care owed by the defendant to the claimant[2]. How this duty is characterised may vary from situation to situation. For example, a considerable degree of skill and care is expected from persons who profess to have a particular skill[3];

■   clearly, this duty must have been breached, for otherwise there is no cause of action;

■   the nature of the loss must be foreseeable. What this means has been the subject of complex litigation over the years. Does it mean that the physical nature of the loss must be foreseeable[4], or the extent[5]? Special rules apply in cases where the claimant is unduly susceptible to damage (the so-called 'eggshell skull rule')[6]. Equally, persons who put themselves into extraordinary positions cannot expect to claim for foreseeable loss which arises from such an extraordinary situation[7];

■   the claimant must also show that the defendant caused the loss. To the extent that the claimant would have suffered that loss anyway, he cannot recover from the defendant[8];

■   the damage must not be too remote. This point is analogous with the discussion at paragraph 3.10 above with respect to remoteness in contractual claims, though (as indicated there) the courts generally take a slightly different view of remoteness in negligence cases[9];

■   finally, there must not be a public policy reason for the case failing. This is a conceptually very wide head, and is beyond the scope of this book[10].

1   Once again, this is an enormous area of the law, and each of the points identified below merits significant further discussion. See generally, for example, *Winfield and Jollowicz on Tort* (15th edn, 1998), Chapter 5.

2   Unquestionably, the most famous statement of which (the famous 'neighbour' principle) is set out in the landmark case of *Donoghue v Stevenson* [1932] AC 562 at 580, HL (per Lord Atkin).

3   Thus, a doctor is expected to show a very high degree of skill in the exercise of his calling (and is similarly allowed a latitude for the exercise of professional judgment): *Whitehouse v Jordan* [1981] 1 WLR 246, HL; however, a learner driver is expected to demonstrate less competence behind the wheel than a trained driver who has passed a driving test: *Nettleship v Weston* [1971] 2 QB 691, CA.

4   *The Wagon Mound* [1961] AC 388, HL.

5   See for example *Vacwell Engineering Co Ltd v BDH Chemicals Ltd* [1971] 1 QB 88, where a small chemical explosion at the claimant's premises was foreseeable as a consequence of the defendant's negligence, and the defendant was therefore held liable for the full extent of what was actually a catastrophically large explosion.

6   The classic case being *Smith v Leech Brain & Co Ltd* [1962] 2 QB 405.

7   *Cutler v United Dairies (London) Ltd* [1933] 2 KB 297, CA (the claimant was injured by a horse belonging to the defendant when he went to what he thought was the rescue of the horse's rider, and was in effect held to have needlessly involved himself in a situation not of his concern).

8 *Barnett v Chelsea and Kensington Hospital Management Committee* [1969] 1 QB 428 (although the defendant hospital breached its duty of care by not admitting the claimant when he complained of symptoms of vomiting, his subsequent death was held to have been caused by poisoning, which the hospital would, on the balance of probability, have been able to do nothing about: hence no causation and no damages for his estate).

9 See *H Parsons (Livestock) Ltd v Uttley Ingham & Co Ltd* [1978] QB 791, CA.

10 An interesting example is *McKay v Essex Area Health Authority* [1982] QB 1166, where the court refused to entertain a claim from a child born with Downs' Syndrome that had his mother been warned in time of the defect she could have had an abortion and, as it were, saved him the trouble of being born.

(ii) Negligence applied to defective products

3.26 An on-line seller can be liable for negligent acts and omissions, for example where there are manufacturing defects in the products he supplies and these cause personal injury or physical damage to property. The premise is that the on-line seller has a duty of care to supply non-defective products and breaches that duty by supplying defective ones – clearly his customer is foreseeable as a claimant. Moreover, where the on-line seller is a wholesaler, the ultimate consumer may still fall within the scope of foreseeability[1]. This liability has been characterised as one for 'dangerous' goods rather than simply 'defective' goods. This means that, if a hidden defect is discovered before any damage can be caused by it, there will be no liability as there is no longer any danger[2].

Generally in tort, the courts have been reluctant to entertain claims for economic loss in cases where damages for the basic direct or 'physical' loss is just compensation. The general principle in the most recent cases in this area is that where a claimant wishes to sue for lost profit, economic loss or the like, he has to rely on a contract with the defendant[3].

There does not need to be a direct contractual relationship, so a manufacturer can be sued by an end-user who bought the product from a supplier several steps down the supply chain. The courts in the UK have been willing to extend the duty of care owed by manufacturers, repairers, fitters, erectors and assemblers to anyone who could foreseeably suffer damage by a defect in the product, for example members of the purchaser's family, passers-by or donees, who would have no claim in contract either directly or indirectly.

Damages in tort are intended to put the claimant in the position he would have been in had the tort not been committed. These will exclude pure economic loss (unless there is a special relationship of proximity imposing a duty on one party to safeguard the other from economic loss) and loss of the defective product itself. Failing to warn of a known defect will not produce the necessary close proximity[4].

1 This, in effect, was the basis of the claim in *Donoghue v Stevenson* [1932] AC 562, HL, where there was no contractual relationship between the claimant who drank the contaminated beer produced by the defendant drinks company.

2 *D & F Estates Ltd v Church Comrs for England* [1989] AC 177, HL.

3 The House of Lords flirted with the idea of a head of economic loss in negligence in *Junior Books Ltd v Veitchi Co Ltd* [1983] 1 AC 520, HL. But this is now regarded as an oddity: the law has been reaffirmed in the more recent cases of *Muirhead v Industrial Tank Specialities Ltd* [1986] QB 507, CA (the claimant could not recover the value of lost business from his fish sales from the manufacturers of defective pumps on his tanks, with whom he had no contract) and *Murphy v Brentwood District Council* [1991] 1 AC 398, HL (defective premises claims are matters of contract only, not negligence).

4 *Hamble Fisheries Ltd v L Gardner & Sons Ltd* [1999] 2 Lloyd's Rep 1, CA.

3.27 Applying these principles more specifically to the e-commerce arena, we may perhaps draw the following conclusions:

■ what the consumer buys on-line may cause the on-line seller to be liable, or indeed the supplier at the top of the chain from whom the on-line seller acquired the material for onward sale. The on-line seller has the advantage of having a contract with the consumer, and (subject to the restrictions on exclusion clauses discussed at paragraph 3.17 above) he has the ability to limit his liability accordingly.

- once again we encounter the problem over whether a supply by an on-line seller amounts to a sale of a product or a provision of a service where, for example, the substance is a data feed that the consumer can reconstitute into software or music or some other digital medium. From the common law perspective, this may not actually matter much and, if the music or software supplied is defective, there will be issues of liability for the on-line seller and his supplier to consider. Whether this holds in relation to claims falling within the realm of statute and regulation is not as clear, and we shall turn to this area next.

- the notion that if the nature of the damage is foreseeable the negligent party is liable in tort for the full extent of the damage[1] has profound consequences in relation to the use of the Internet for disseminating software. It seems that if the defendant provided software to a corporate user for use on a small part of the user's network, but the nature of the defect disabled the entire network, then the claimant has ground for recovering damages related to the effect on the network as a whole. The same may apply where unauthorised software is released and passed around a system via interchanges of e-mail between the system's users (because surely the passing of e-mails between friends and work colleagues is a foreseeable matter these days).

1 *Vacwell Engineering Co Ltd v BDH Chemicals Ltd* [1971] 1 QB 88.

(c) Statutory liability

3.28 Since 1987, every producer in the EU has been obliged to make good any damage to health, safety and property caused by a defective product on a no-fault basis under the Defective Products Liability Directive[1], which was implemented in the UK by the Consumer Protection Act 1987 (CPA 1987). The more recent adoption of Directive (EC) 34/99[2] means that producers of non-processed agricultural products are also liable without fault for damage to individuals' health caused by defective products.

The following types of persons can be liable under the Directive/the CPA 1987:

- manufacturers of a finished product;

- producers of any raw materials;

- manufacturers of a component part of a finished product;

- 'own branders', ie supermarkets, chain store retailers, mail order merchants;

- first importers into the EU; and

- each supplier in the supply chain, unless he informs the injured person within a reasonable time of the identity of the producer or of his supplier.

The CPA 1987 covers death or personal injury and damage to other property over £275 caused by the commercial supply of a defective product. Under the CPA 1987, there is no liability for loss or damage to the defective product itself or the whole or any part of any product which has been supplied with the defective product comprised in it. The defective product must be of a type ordinarily intended for private use and intended by the person suffering loss and damage primarily for his own private use. There will be a 'defect' if 'the safety of the product is not such as persons generally are entitled to expect'. The safety of the product is judged by reference to standards prevailing when it was put into circulation (a defect will not be inferred simply because the safety of the product is later improved).

1 Directive (EEC) 374/87.
2 Directive (EC) 34/99 on the approximation of the laws, regulations and administrative provisions of the Member States concerning liability for defective products The text of SI 2000/2771, which implements Directive (EC) 34/99, is available at www.legislation.hmso.gov.uk/si/si2000/20002771.htm.

3.29 Liability under the CPA 1987 cannot be excluded by any contractual term or notice. However, warnings over the manner of use can affect what will be treated as a defect. Apportionment of liability will be made if the injured party was contributorily negligent[1], for example by failing to follow genuine and clearly drafted instructions.

For jurisdiction purposes, liability under the CPA 1987 is treated as liability in tort. The same limitation rules for personal injuries generally apply but no action can be brought in any case more than ten years after the date the product was put into circulation.

Further significant amendments to the Defective Products Liability Directive were proposed by the European Parliament and its Environmental Committee during 1998. These proposals included reversal of the burden of proof and deletion of the 'developments risks' defence. As yet, these proposals have not been adopted.

The European Commission issued a Green Paper on 28 July 1999[2] and will examine how the Defective Products Liability Directive is being implemented. It will look in particular into detailed arrangements implemented regarding the burden of proof imposed on the victims, the existence of financial limits (compensation is provided for damage in excess of €500), the justification for the ten-year deadline, the effects of any change on the lack of any obligation on producers to obtain insurance, the dissemination of information on cases arising from defective products, the supplier's liability and the type of goods and damage covered.

The Opinion of the Economic and Social Committee of the Council of Ministers (ECOSOC) has been delivered[3] in relation to this Green Paper and proposals for further Directives may follow. The ECOSOC raises concerns about the short length of time over which the original Directive's effectiveness has been monitored. We will not discuss the Opinion in depth at this stage; however, it is clear that the ECOSOC has reservations about altering the system too soon and stresses the need for further evaluation, education, development and prevention.

The CPA 1987 also makes it a criminal offence to supply, offer to supply or expose or possess for supply in the UK consumer goods which fail to comply with 'the general safety requirement'. The offence is punishable by six months' imprisonment and/or a fine on summary conviction[4].

1 In other words, if there is more than one person in the supply chain and each has in some fashion contributed to the defect. By way of hypothetical example, the product may have been poorly made to start with (implicating the maker), damaged in transit (implicating the carrier) and stored incorrectly (implicating the warehouseman) – and all of these factors may be deemed to have contributed to the defective nature of the product once supplied to the consumer.
2 COM 0396/99 final, July 1999; and see http://europa.eu.int/comm/dg15/en/update/consumer/greenen.pdf.
3 OJ C117 26.4.2000, p 1; and see www.europa.eu.
4 See also Council Directive (EEC) 59/92 of 29 June 1992 on general product safety (OJ L228 11.8.92, pp 24–32). DGXXIV (which is responsible for consumer policy) is to issue a report of the implementation and effects of the Directive.

6. LIABILITY FOR INFORMATION

3.30 Most e-commerce websites will contain information which is relied upon by visitors to the site. This information can range from on-line product catalogues which lead a purchaser to order a product and press releases to tax and investment advice and medical self-help remedies. Many websites are not vetted from a legal standpoint and, if unchecked, a marketing department's 'enthusiasm' may increase the risk of an on-line seller being sued.

Negligence in relation to the provision of information has become a major area in English litigation, the principles of which are largely derived from the seminal House of Lords judgment in *Hedley Byrne & Co Ltd v Heller & Partners Ltd*[1]. As a consequence of this case, and several which have flowed from it, the law in relation to negligence in the making of statements, reports, etc, has become highly developed, and there should be no difficulty in applying basic principles to the making of statements in negligent fashion where these are on-line.

However, we are concerned in relation to statements on-line with other areas of the law, including:

- contract (where the material in question relates to the formation or performance of a contract);

- defamation (where the information published by one person on-line defames another or others); and

- the criminal jurisdiction in relation to obscenity and obscene publications.

The remainder of this section will examine the impact of the law of contract and of negligence on information on-line. The current law and practice in the UK in relation to defamatory material is considered in section 7, while the criminal liability of on-line service providers for obscene and harmful content is considered in section 8.

1 [1964] AC 465, HL. What is interesting about this case from a jurisprudential viewpoint is that the claim that the defendant had made a negligent misstatement was itself unanimously rejected on the facts; yet their Lordships unanimously pronounced that as a matter of law such a concept was admissible.

(a) Contractual liability

3.31 We need not dwell at length on this point, since the general principles that relate to the breach of a contract to supply products or services will apply if the product provided is information. If A contracts on-line with B for the provision of material in the form of a feed of data and this data is corrupt, or does not arrive in time for a purpose specified in the contract, or is simply not delivered at all, then B is in principle liable under the contract. This may, of course, be qualified by clauses which limit liability in relation to certain facts or situations, and A's measure of damage will be governed by the *Hadley v Baxendale* principles explained at paragraph 3.11 where A seeks to recover for consequential losses.

(b) Liability for negligence

3.32 In passing, we should mention that a party would be liable in the tort of deceit[1] (rather than negligence) if he *knows* that his statement is false, or is reckless or consciously indifferent as to whether his statement is true or not[2]. Where a statement is made truthfully but the maker subsequently becomes aware of its falsehood and does nothing about it, the same principles apply[3]. In such circumstances in order to bring a case, the claimant must of course prove that he has suffered loss[4].

The principles that were stated or which have since evolved from the *Hedley Byrne* case, in relation to negligent misstatement, provide that liability will only arise if there is a 'special relationship' between the parties (for example, if the maker of the statement was in the business of supplying information and advice or had claimed to possess the necessary skill to do so and it can be said that the maker is deemed to have 'assumed responsibility' to a person who acts upon the advice). It is important, though, to appreciate that such a relationship can exist in law as between the statement-maker and a third party of whose identity he is unaware. It need not be the person to whom the statement was made – or for whom it was expressly made or published who has a right to sue for negligence[5]. The consequences for this concept in relation to the flow of information around the Internet is significant. Nobody with an open-access website can be certain all of the time who is seeing what is published there. The same could apply to a newsgroup, bulletin board or chat room, where the moderator might be implicated along with contributors or participants for the appearance of material whose foundation is negligent[6].

Although primarily concerned with the issue of defamation, the recent case of *Totalise plc v Motley Fool Ltd*[7] has gone some way in clearing the muddied waters surrounding the duties of providers of services such as newsgroups and bulletin boards. In this case an anonymous user carried out a concerted campaign of defamation against the claimants on a discussion website run by the defendant. It was obvious to any user of the site that the information posted was defamatory of Totalise and its officers and accordingly Totalise sought to force the defendants to disclose the identity of the author. The court held that the only factor which prohibited the claimant from requiring the defendants to identify the author was the inability of the defendants to identify the author. It is also interesting to note that the court held that the Data Protection Act 1998 (DPA 1998) did not prohibit this type of disclosure. The court made clear that when assessing whether a refusal by an ISP to identify an alleged defamer was 'reasonable' it would have reference to the strength of the claimant's case, the gravity of the defaming material and whether there was any other means of obtaining redress without the assistance of the ISP in question.

Disclaimers of liability and 'of responsibility' for liability caused by negligence in the course of a business will be subject to the requirement of reasonableness under sections 2(2) and 13 of the UCTA 1977, discussed at paragraph 3.21 above.

1 Discussed more fully in. for example, *Winfield and Jollowicz on Tort* (15th edn, 1998), pp 354–365.
2 *Pasley v Freeman* (1789) 3 Term Rep 51; *Derry v Peek* (1889) 14 App Cas 337, HL.
3 *Bradford Third Equitable Benefit Building Society v Borders* [1941] 2 All ER 205, HL.
4 *Briess v Woolley* [1954] AC 333, HL.
5 See example *Yianni v Edwin Evans & Sons* [1982] QB 438 (where the negligent report prepared by the surveyor of a private house ostensibly for the sole purpose of the mortgagee lending to the purchaser was held to entitle the purchaser to recover damages as well).
6 However, the passivity of an ISP in relation to unreviewed material passing through its systems ought not to lead to its implication in the purveying of negligent representations. See also the cases of *Godfrey v Demon Internet Ltd* [1999] 4 All ER 342 (discussed at paragraph 3.41); *Sir Elton John v Countess Joulebine* (2001) unreported and the application by Thus plc in relation to the injunction against the press in disseminating and publishing information concerning the two Jamie Bulger killers.
7 [2001] EMLR 750.

(c) Misrepresentation

3.33 Where statements are made in pre-contractual negotiations and the injured party enters into the contract and suffers loss as a result, he has various remedies under the Misrepresentation Act 1967:

■ where the misrepresentation is innocent (that is, the representor is not at fault in any way), then the representee has the remedy of rescission of contract. Rescission means, simply, an unravelling of the contractual arrangements (in so far as this is possible). Where, for example, A has paid cash to B for the purchase of goods, rescission means that A returns the goods to B and B repays A the cash.

■ if the misrepresentation was fraudulent in character then, in addition to the remedy of rescission, A in the above example would be entitled to claim damages (where he can prove he has lost or suffered as a result of the contract).

These remedies apply in parallel with common law principles of contractual and tortious remedies. So, for example, if a misrepresentation inducing a contract also happened to be a negligent misstatement (and the other qualifications in *Hedley Byrne* and subsequent cases are satisfied), then the representee can sue for damages in negligence, as well as for rescission of the contract itself.

(d) Strict liability

3.34 In spite of the abandonment of the original 1991 proposals for a draft Council Directive on the liability of suppliers of services[1], which would have imposed strict liability similar to that imposed under the CPA 1987[2], it seems the European Commission is still examining the issue of how to reinforce the safety of services and is following up on its 1994 Communication[3] on a new approach to services. The Opinion of the ECOSOC on the Green Paper 'Liability for Defective Products' (discussed at paragraph 3.29) expressly mentions that the European Commission is planning a new measure to address the specific nature of the issues involved so that the deficiency in relation to liability for defective services would be remedied. Therefore, we can expect further EU initiatives to be proposed to address both service safety and the liability of service providers.

The Commission has put forward a proposal entitled 'Proposal for a Directive of the European Parliament and of the Council on General Product Safety' (GPSD)[4], which it is hoped will deal with the issue of strict liability, not only in relation to product safety, but also in relation to the safety of services as distinct from products.

The GPSD states that the Commission will seek to prepare specific proposals relating to the area of services and an investigation is underway aimed at identifying priority areas. Pending the outcome of these investigations, it is proposed that the scope of the GPSD be limited only to products related to services. This would cover:

- products supplied to consumers in the course of a service; and

- products used to provide a service.

As yet there is no indication as to when the proposals of the Commission will be adopted. In the meantime in the field of e-commerce, it is not clear if defective program files would fall within the CPA 1987 as they might in fact be considered goods. For example, if a Java applet is transferred onto a customer's computer and causes personal injury or physical damage to property because it produces unsafe medical or repair information, there could still be no fault liability.

1 OJ C12 8/91.
2 See paragraphs 3.28 and 3.29.
3 Communication from the Commission on new directions on the liability of suppliers of services COM 260/94 final, 23 June 1994.
4 See http://europa.eu.int/eur-lex/en/com/pdf/2000/en_500PC0139.pdf.

7. DEFAMATORY CONTENT AND COMMUNICATIONS[1]

3.35 Having considered the impact of the tort of negligence, we move now to consider two further torts, those of libel and slander, which collectively fall under the heading of defamation[2].

The Internet provides a medium in which anyone can easily publish a message which will reach a large number of people virtually instantly, without having to go through an intermediary like a newspaper or book publisher who would be in a position to vet it[3]. Individuals tend to treat the Internet as a more informal medium than other forms of communication. There is a risk to employers, who may be liable for the actions of their employees[4]. There is also an increased risk for anyone who operates a website (particularly one which invites visitors to engage in a message forum or chat room) or moderates a newsgroup.

1 For a fuller discussion, see for example *Winfield and Jollowicz on Tort* (15th edn, 1998), Chapter 12.
2 It is, perhaps, appropriate for completeness to mention that 'defamatory libel' is also a criminal offence: see the Libel Act 1843, s 5. There are a number of differences between the tort and the crime in terms of scope: (i) defamation as a criminal offence is limited to libel (slander is insufficient: *R v Burford* (1669) 1 Vent 16); (ii) though truth is a defence to the tort of libel, in criminal libel the defence must also prove that publication was for the benefit of the public; and (iii) publication in the crime is sufficient if to the person defamed, whereas in tort the publication has to be wider

(*R v Perry* (1883) 15 Cox CC 169). There are certain other less important distinctions. For further reading, see *Smith and Hogan: Criminal Law* (10th edn, 2002).

3 That said, there are clearly issues for organisations involved with aspects of the flow of data and the administration of the Internet who may also need to consider their position. We will consider the position of the ISP, for example, below.

4 This is part of the doctrine of vicarious liability in tort, where if the tort was committed by the employee in the course of the employment, the employer will be held liable on his account. For further information see, for example, *Winfield and Jollowicz on Tort* (15th edn, 1998), Chapter 20.

(a) Elements

(i) *Defamatory statement*

3.36 Just like any other form of speech or communication, a statement published on-line may be actionable as a libel if it is defamatory in that it 'would tend to lower the plaintiff in the estimation of right-thinking members of society generally or cause him to be shunned or avoided or tend to expose him to hatred, contempt, or ridicule'[1].

A defamatory statement need not allege some scandalous conduct[2]. Nor need the victim be an individual: corporations can be defamed as well. Two cases, settled before the trial of the issues, provide illustrations of the sort of problems which arise in this area. In the *Western Provident v Norwich Union*[3] case, Norwich Union made a High Court apology and paid £450,000 to settle Western Provident's action. A statement agreed by both sides said:

> 'In the middle of 1995, rumours circulated that Western Provident was insolvent, in financial difficulty and under investigation by the Department of Trade and Industry. These rumours were disseminated by some of Norwich Union's staff via its internal e-mail systems with the result that they could be used to the detriment of Western Provident in order to obtain new business.'

Similarly, in *Duffield and Exoteric Gas Solutions Ltd v British Gas plc*[4], British Gas plc paid out £101,100 for an internal e-mail sent by an area director to the staff of its Transco subsidiary that 'as a result of a high level complaint', they were 'to have no further dealings with this company or its principal until further notice'.

1 *Partmiter v Coupland* (1840) 6 M & W 105; *Youssoupoff v Metro-Goldwyn-Mayer Pictures Ltd* (1934) 50 TLR 581, CA; *Sim v Stretch* [1936] 2 All ER 1237, HL.

2 *Tolley v J S Fry & Sons Ltd* [1931] AC 333, HL is a famous example, which involved a successful claim for libel by an amateur golfer that inclusion of his image in advertising by the defendant compromised his amateur status.

3 Unreported.

4 LTL 24/9/99.

(ii) *Publication*

3.37 The defamatory statement must be 'published' by communicating it to at least one person other than the person defamed. A posting on a Usenet site would definitely count as publication, as would statements on a web page. Furthermore, each time the posting or statement is accessed a separate actionable publication occurs[1]. This issue is particularly relevant to the maintenance of archive materials on web pages. However, an appropriate notice attached to the statement warning against treating it as the truth may be sufficient to prevent liability for defamation[2]. An e-mail containing a statement which is defamatory only to the addressee cannot normally be sued upon by the addressee unless it can be proved that a third party did in fact read the e-mail and the defendant intended or should have foreseen that the e-mail would or could be read by someone other than the intended recipient. Where there is no actual proof that a third party has read the defamatory statement, the court can be asked to infer from the surrounding circumstances that some third party has read it[3].

Publication may occur where the addressee's (or even the sender's) employer 'intercepts' and reads the e-mail in line with its stated policy of screening all incoming and outgoing e-mails. Methods to overcome the problem could be to attach the message within another e-mail which, if opened, would alert the reader to the nature of its attachment, or by deliberately encrypting the message with the public key of the addressee[4].

The fact that the addressees may be 'internal', eg other members of the same organisation, does not matter[5]. In both the *Norwich Union* and *British Gas* cases, the defamatory statement was circulated by internal e-mails. It is not clear if the defence of qualified privilege would have succeeded if the cases had proceeded to trial.

In litigation an e-mail containing defamatory content is a document that the other side may require to be disclosed to it in any proceedings[6]. In addition, a court may order that the identity of an individual responsible for sending an anonymous defamatory e-mail[7] or making a defamatory posting on a website[8] is to be revealed by an ISP, notwithstanding the confidentiality provisions in an ISP's terms and conditions.

The court, in deciding whether to make the order, will have regard to the rights and freedoms and the legitimate interests of the data subject[9], and will assess whether the order unjustifiably invades the right of an individual to respect for his private life[10]. The costs incurred in taking action to obtain the identity of the author of the defamatory statement will in general be recoverable from the wrongdoer.

An ISP should ensure that its terms and conditions provide for the disclosure of the identity of a user in the event of court proceedings requiring such. However, it is legitimate, and advisable bearing in mind human rights legislation, for an ISP who agrees to keep information confidential and private to refuse to voluntarily hand over such information until an order is made by the court.

1 *Loutchansky v Times Newspapers Ltd (No 2)* [2001] EWCA Civ 1805, [2002] QB 783.
2 *Loutchansky v Times Newspapers Ltd (No 2)* [2001] EWCA Civ 1805, [2002] QB 783.
3 The fact that the web is a public place may give rise to an inference that the public have seen defamatory material published there.
4 In *Grappelli v Derek Black (Holdings) Ltd* [1981] 1 WLR 822, CA, the defamatory material was not in the defendant's native language, though with the aid of a dictionary he was able to decipher the material and it thereby became actionable.
5 *Riddick v Thames Board Mills Ltd* [1977] QB 881, CA, but see the dissenting judgment of Lord Denning.
6 CPR Part 31.
7 *Takenaka (UK) Ltd v Frankl* [2001] EWCA Civ 348, [2001] EBLR 40.
8 *Totalise plc v Motley Fool Ltd* [2001] EMLR 750.
9 Pursuant to section 35 and Schedule 2, paragraph 6 to the DPA 1998.
10 Pursuant to article 8 of the European Convention on Human Rights.

(iii) Malice and qualified privilege

3.38 Where malice can be shown, that is there is a dominant motive in the maker or publisher of the statement which is dishonest, actions can also be brought for malicious falsehood, slander of title and slander of goods. There would not be malice, however, if the maker of the statement spoke or wrote honestly believing the words to be true, even if this was done wrongly or carelessly or for the purpose of advancing the sale of the maker's own products.

Where the statement is made in good faith, without any improper motive and there is a duty or interest on the part of the person making the statement to disclose information to the person(s) receiving the statement, the defence of qualified privilege could exist[1].

The defence of qualified privilege in relation to matters of public concern has been the subject of two recent appeal court decisions[2]. In *Loutchansky v Times Newspapers Ltd (No 2)* the defendant published two articles, both of which were posted on the Internet at a later stage, alleging the claimant was the head of a Russian criminal organisation. The Court of Appeal assessed the corresponding parts of the duty-interest test as being the interest of the public in a democracy in free expression and the promotion of a free and vigorous press to keep the public informed. The duty was that of the journalist to behave responsibly. This approach reflected the jurisprudence relating to article 10 of the European Convention on Human Rights (freedom of expression), to which the court must have regard[3]. Both the interest and the duty need to be present in order to justify publication; however, in relation to cases involving the press there is no onus to establish an honest belief in what is published.

The defendant failed to establish qualified privilege in relation to the articles it had published on the Internet since its failure to attach a notice of qualification following the assertion of their defamatory nature could in no way be described as responsible journalism. The duty on the journalist to act responsibly effectively pre-empts any question of malice.

In assessing the duty to publish statements in multi-jurisdictional cases, the international dimension of the matter is taken into account. Where statements are published in a number of countries including England the focus is on whether there is a duty to publish the information to the world at large, rather than just in England. Consequently, if there is a duty and interest for publication in a number of countries, then it would be artificial to say that there was no duty and interest in England[4].

1 See *Pullman v Walter Hill & Co* [1891] 1 QB 524, CA.
2 *Reynolds v Times Newspapers Ltd* [2001] 2 AC 127, HL; *Loutchansky v Times Newspapers Ltd (No 2)* [2001] EWCA Civ 1805, [2002] QB 783.
3 Section 12(4) of the Human Rights Act 1998 (HRA 1998).
4 *Lukowiak v Unidad Editorial SA* (2001) Times, 23 July.

(iv) Author, editor or publisher

3.39 In the UK, liability for defamation at common law extends to editors and publishers as well as the original author of the defamatory matter. Accordingly, as far as the Internet is concerned, the possible scenarios in which a company could be liable in defamation include:

- 'official' statements made by the company itself, for example on its own website or in its own press releases, because it is the 'author';

- statements made by the company's employees acting within the scope of their apparent or actual authority for which the company would be liable under the normal principles of vicarious liability, because the employees are regarded in law as one and the same with the 'author';

- statements made by the company's employees (for example in personal e-mails which they send) because it is acting as a 'publisher' by providing those employees with the hardware and the link to the Internet; or

- statements made by third parties which occur on the website of the company or in any newsgroup or bulletin board the company hosts as either an editor or publisher[1].

1 This applies in relation to the publisher of a website or the moderator of a newsgroup or chat room, whether that person is a corporate or a natural person.

3.40 The Defamation Act 1996 (DeA 1996), s 1(3) provides a series of presumptions that a person shall *not* be considered the author, editor or publisher of a statement if they are *only* involved, among other things:

> '(c) in processing, making copies of, distributing or selling any electronic medium in or
>   on which the statement is recorded, or in operating or providing any equipment,

system or service by means of which the statement is retrieved, copied, distributed or made available in electronic form; ...

(e)   as the operator or provider of access to a communications system by means of which the statement is transmitted, or made available, by a person over whom he has no effective control.'[1]

This distinction is important because section 1(1) of the DeA 1996 provides a statutory defence for a person who is *not* the author, editor or publisher of a defamatory statement.

The defence (discussed below) could be lost if, for example:

■   the statements are 'reviewed' (even if they are simply cut and pasted manually) for inclusion into a web page; or

■   the statements are moderated before or soon after they are posted on a forum.

It is unclear whether simply selecting the newsgroups to provide with material could impose liability as an 'editor' (it is arguable that the decision to exclude certain newsgroups without having seen the content of the others is not the same as having editorial responsibility for those carried).

In most cases, the editor or publisher will find itself to be the target for proceedings in respect of defamatory material posted by a third party because:

■   the identity of the author may have been disguised or stripped out of the message by an 'anonymous re-mailer' (via the Internet), making it easier to identify and, potentially, sue the 'distributor' of the message; and

■   it will often have 'deeper pockets' than the real author.

However, it is not only large ISPs and bulletin board service providers who should be wary of defamatory material posted to them or held on their websites. Simply forwarding a defamatory e-mail onto others would make an individual liable as a re-publisher of the statement and possibly also his employer if the employer could be held to be vicariously liable.

1   Even if a web host does not fall within one of the presumptions, it may still be able to argue that it is not an 'author, editor or publisher' by analogy to one of the other presumptions and definitions, eg in relation to films, sound recordings and broadcastings.

(v) Reasonable care

3.41   The DeA 1996, s 1(1) defence is limited because a party can only rely on it if:

■   he took reasonable care in relation to the publication; and

■   he shows that it did not know, and had no reason to believe, that what it did caused or contributed to the publication of the defamatory statement.

The limits of this defence were shown in the UK in 1999, when the High Court held in *Godfrey v Demon Internet Ltd*[1], in relation to an application to strike out parts of the defence[2], that Demon could not rely on that defence in relation to defamatory material published on the 'soc.culture.thai' newsgroup because it failed to remove the offending material (despite repeated requests) once it had been notified by Mr Godfrey. (It is unclear whether attaching a qualification to the defamatory statement warning not to treat it as the truth would be a defence.) This must be regarded as a strong precedent, particularly in light of the fact that Demon more recently agreed to settle the action prior to a full trial.

One-off e-mails sent by an employee, in cases where the principle of vicarious liability does not apply, are not likely to be a problem, provided that the employer has taken reasonable care, for example:

■ by informing its employees of the terms of use of its e-mail system, that defamatory messages should not be sent and that e-mail is for business use only; and

■ by taking steps to destroy all copies of any defamatory messages once it learns of their existence to prevent them from being forwarded again.

The problem is more difficult where the message is posted on a Usenet newsgroup which may or may not be fully under the control of the host being sued (most newsgroups are automatically replicated regularly and, even if deleted, a message could reappear or be included in a forwarded message or reply).

Thus, even if the host is not considered to be an 'author, editor or publisher' in relation to a forum or Usenet newsgroup, it may still be liable for not taking reasonable care by allowing a forum to continue or simply re-publishing an entire Usenet newsgroup which had a reputation for being defamatory or which is known to carry postings of defamatory materials.

The *Demon* ruling appears to be in line with recent cases in European jurisdictions which seem to suggest that a person may be held legally accountable for 'illegal' material posted on his website if he has 'knowledge' of the nature of the material. These are discussed elsewhere, in Chapters 6 (E-marketing) and 7 (E-dispute).

1 [1999] 4 All ER 342.
2 The case was scheduled to proceed to trial on other grounds, but Morland J had already strongly hinted that damages were likely to be 'very small' and, on a second application to amend the defence, allowed the addition of particulars of the claimant's own conduct in mitigation of damages.

(vi) Jurisdiction

3.42 The issue of jurisdiction is clearly not relevant where the statement is published in the UK by a UK resident which is defamatory of another UK resident. However, in the case of web pages/newsgroups, whose readership may be worldwide, can a statement made by a foreigner be sued on in the UK?

The question of jurisdiction is discussed in more detail in Chapter 7, E-dispute. Briefly, the starting point is that a claim may be served out of the jurisdiction with the permission of the court if 'the claim is made in tort where the damage was sustained within the jurisdiction, or the damage sustained resulted from an act committed within the jurisdiction'[1].

It is clear from several cases that even if the statement is originally posted outside the UK, a person with a substantial connection in the UK will be entitled to bring proceedings in the UK against foreigners who were aware that their publication would be sent to/received by persons in the UK, even though the circulation of the statement alleged to be defamatory was extremely limited in the UK and there was much larger publication elsewhere[2].

The UK courts will refuse jurisdiction where the claimant's personal connection with the UK is more tenuous[3].

Where there is more than one defendant, for example the author and the publisher, the UK courts will have jurisdiction over all defendants under article 6(1) of the Brussels Convention as long as one defendant is in the UK.

1 CPR Part 6, r 20(8).
2 In *Godfrey v Demon Internet Ltd* [1999] 4 All ER 342, the claimant was a lecturer resident in the UK. See also *Berezovsky v Forbes Inc* [1999] EMLR 278, CA; *Schapira v Ahronson* [1998] IL Pr 587, CA.
3 Using the test in *Spiliada Maritime Corpn v Cansulex Ltd* [1987] AC 460, HL. See also *Parvinder Chadha & Oiscom Technologies Inc v Dow Jones & Co Inc* [1999] EMLR 724, CA.

(vii) Limitation period

3.43 Any action in defamation must be brought generally within one year from the date when the cause of action accrued[1]. The court has discretion to allow a case to proceed outside this time limit if it would be equitable to do so having regard to the relative prejudice to the claimant and the defendant. The fact that a defamatory statement is published each time it is accessed as described above is at odds with some of the reasons for the introduction of the one-year time limit. However, it was the court's view in *Loutchansky v Times Newspapers Ltd (No 2)* that it was justified bearing in mind the likely scale of the subsequent publication and the resulting damage[2].

1 The Limitation Act 1980, s 4A as substituted by the DeA 1996, s 5.
2 [2001] EWCA Civ 1805, [2002] QB 783.

(b) Reducing the risk of liability

3.44 It is instructive to consider the scope of the E-Commerce Directive[1] and the new Electronic Commerce (EC Directive) Regulations 2002[2], produced by the DTI in relation to the liability of 'intermediaries'. Now the E-Commerce Directive has been given effect, 'intermediaries' and 'hosts' should be provided with a measure of immunity from suit similar to that granted to ISPs in the US under the Communications Decency Act of 1995 (47 USC, s 230).

Regulation 19 (hosting), which is based closely on the wording of article 14 of the E-Commerce Directive, provides that:

> 'Where an information society service is provided which consists of the storage of information provided by a recipient of a service, the service provider (if he otherwise would) shall not be liable for damages or for any other pecuniary remedy or for any criminal sanction as a result of that storage where—
> (a) the service provider—
>   (i)   does not have actual knowledge of unlawful activity or information and, where a claim for damages is made, is not aware of facts or circumstances from which it would have been apparent to the service provider that the activity or information was unlawful; or
>   (ii) upon obtaining such knowledge or awareness, acts expeditiously to remove or to disable access to the information, and
> (b) the recipient of the service was not acting under the authority or the control of the service provider.'

The E-Commerce Regulations also deal with 'mere conduits' (regulation 17) and 'caching' (regulation 18). Regulation 20 provides that:

> '(1)   Nothing in regulations 17, 18 and 19 shall—
>   (a) prevent a person agreeing different contractual terms; or
>   (b) affect the rights of any party to apply to a court for relief to prevent or stop infringement of any rights.
> (2)   Any power of an administrative authority to prevent or stop infringement of any rights shall continue to apply notwithstanding regulations 17, 18 and 19.'

1 Directive (EC) 31/2000 on certain legal aspects of Information Society Services, in particular electronic commerce in the Internal Market. The E-Commerce Directive has already been reviewed in the context of on-line contracting in Chapter 2, E-contract.
2 SI 2002/2013. The Regulations came into force on 21 August 2002, with the exception of regulation 16 (which comes into force on 23 October 2002).

3.45 The E-Commerce (EC Directive) Regulations provide important protection for on-line service providers against liability for the defamatory content they convey or store for users where:

■ they do not initiate or select the receivers of any transmission (or where this is done automatically at the request of the user);

■ they do not modify the information they transmit or store; or

■ where they act expeditiously to remove or prevent access to information on receiving actual knowledge of any defamatory content[1].

In light of this, it is advisable for any on-line service provider to consider the following precautionary steps:

■ to include a disclaimer on its website along the lines that it takes no responsibility for any statements made by third parties and does not necessarily share their views;

■ if it does vet incoming e-mails before they are published, not to post any messages which are clearly defamatory;

■ once it receives any notice that messages are defamatory, to remove them promptly from the website; and

■ if necessary, to consult any aggrieved parties and offer to settle the matter (perhaps by publishing a rebuttal in an agreed form).

Hosts should consider:

■ vetting dubious newsgroups and forums regularly – although the host may not be able to rely on the presumptions, a prudent host is more likely to show that it took reasonable care and it is likely to face claims less often;

■ ensuring that each of its members provides a full name and address even if these are not available to other members before entering each forum (that is, not allowing anonymous guest members) to make it more likely that members will be careful about what they post;

■ having a 'hotline' or emergency e-mail address for members to report defamatory statements so that they can be removed quickly if necessary and correction made (a copy of the allegedly defamatory material should be attached for quick consideration);

■ obtaining an indemnity from each of its members as part of the terms and conditions of membership (even if it may not be worth much) and the right to remove posted material at the host's sole discretion;

■ withdrawing an allocated password which appears to be subject to misuse;

■ taking out insurance (the host may be able to reduce its insurance premiums if it takes some editorial responsibility); and

■ where necessary, quickly making an 'offer of amends' under section 2 of the DeA 1996 by e-mail (suitable correction, sufficient apology, compensation plus costs).

1 Guidance on the regulations is available at http://www.dti.gov.uk/cii/ecommerce/europeanpolicy/ecommerce_directive.shtml.

(c) The Human Rights Act 1998 and the European Convention on Human Rights

3.46 The HRA 1998 came into force on 2 October 2000, and since that date the UK courts in deciding defamation cases have had to give effect to its provisions and those in the European Convention on Human Rights. The Convention protects, among other things, the individual's right to privacy[1] and the right to freedom of expression[2]. Aside from the effect this has on judicial decisions, you need to be aware of the rights when formulating and pursuing an anti-defamation policy.

As discussed above, it is legitimate for an ISP asked to disclose the details of an anonymous individual who posts a defamatory statement on a website to withhold this information until an Order of the Court is made, and any terms of conditions should provide for this. The court decides whether the disclosure represents a justified invasion of the individual's right to privacy; however were the ISP to voluntarily hand over the information, prior to the Order, it could find itself contravening the individual's right to privacy.

Companies wishing to limit their liability for defamation are likely to pursue a policy of monitoring the e-mail and Internet communications of its employees. However, any policy will have to respect the employees' right to privacy and ensure that any monitoring is necessary, for legitimate reasons, proportionate and in accordance with the provisions of the Regulation of Investigatory Powers Act 2000 (RIPA 2000), the Telecommunications (Lawful Business Practice) (Interception of Communications) Regulations 2000[3] and the DPA 1998.

The court is required to have particular regard to the importance of the Convention right to freedom of expression[4]. The defence of qualified privilege in particular focuses on this right and on the limits that can legitimately be placed on a person's right to say what they wish, and is particularly relevant to the operation of news web pages. The right is also relevant to the ISP's obligation to remove potentially defamatory material posted on a web page as it needs to be aware of what material it may legitimately remove and when the removal of material may involve an unjustifiable and disproportionate restriction on the right to freedom of expression. The importance given to the right was shown in *O'Shea v MGN Ltd and Free4Internet.net Ltd*[5] relating to the strict liability offence of unintentional defamation where a 'look a like' photograph of the claimant was used to advertise an adult site. It was held that a finding of defamation would be an unjustifiable interference with the right of freedom of expression disproportionate to the protection of the claimant's reputation.

1 Article 8 of the European Convention on Human Rights.
2 Article 10 of the European Convention on Human Rights.
3 SI 2000/2699.
4 Section 12(4) of the Human Rights Act 1998.
5 [2001] EMLR 943.

(d) What if you are defamed?

3.47 Companies often find themselves the subject of defamatory statements by disgruntled ex-employees, customers and activists who set up '.sucks' websites or post statements on newsgroups trashing their organisation, goods and services. It may be worth carrying out occasional searches of your company name and brand names with a view to seeing exactly what is being said about you on the Internet. More substantial organisations may be prepared to appoint a specialist to provide such a monitoring service on a regular basis.

The options open to anyone who has been libelled are to:

■ sue the author of the statement for damages and take out an injunction to stop further publication;

■ sue his employer, if vicarious or publisher liability can be established; and/or

■ try to get the ISP hosting the website or the moderator of the newsgroup to suspend and/or remove the offending material and possibly sue it for damages as well.

(i) Offending websites

3.48 The first step the libelled person should consider taking is to draw the contents of the offending site to the attention of the ISP(s) hosting the website (there may be one or more 'mirror' sites set up for maximum impact). This may 'encourage' the ISPs voluntarily to stop hosting the site, especially where the statements are clearly false and offensive and the ISP has clear rules regarding the use of websites by its customers. Some ISPs and portals even have on-line 'Content Violation Reporting Forms' for lodging complaints.

If that fails, then it may be necessary to bring a claim against the maker of the defamatory statement and/or the ISP from whose system the statement is being published. Where the statements are obviously false, then neither of them is likely to have an arguable defence and it may be possible to obtain a summary judgment. However, there is always the risk of further adverse publicity being generated by simply bringing the action, especially if there is a risk that any aspect of the statement made proves to be true or subject to privilege. The makers of the statement may be individuals with a 'mission', with time on their hands, and may force the on-line seller to conduct lengthy and expensive proceedings against litigants in person against whom they are unlikely to recover their costs even if they technically win the legal proceedings. The celebrated 'McLibel'[1] case is an example of this risk. Costs in libel hearings are substantial, as a rule, since the advocacy is the province of skilled lawyers who command high retainer fees[2].

Even if a defamed party is successful in getting an ISP to suspend the site, it is possible that the potential defendant will attempt to relocate their website to a friendlier web server, who may be in another jurisdiction. Any advantage gained may therefore be temporary.

1 *McDonald's Corpn v Steel and Morris* 19 June 1997, 31 March 1999.
2 It should also be borne in mind that defamation trials take place before judge and jury (defamation is one of the last few civil jurisdictions where juries are involved) – something which itself tends to spin out the proceedings.

(ii) Other types of action

3.49 In some cases, the authors may have used the trade marks or logos (either in the actual visible body of the web page or in the metatags that draw the page to the attention of search engines) and other materials which may be protected by copyright. The legal issues involved in such circumstances are discussed in Chapters 5 (E-brand) and 6 (E-marketing).

(iii) Inducing breach of contract

3.50 If you are successful in getting an ISP to suspend a website where the ISP is not contractually entitled to do so there is also a risk that a potential defendant may try to bring an action against you for inducing breach of the contract between it and its ISP[1]. If the ISP is alert it will also ask for an indemnity from you against meeting the cost of any action by the potential defendant. Many good ISPs have a clause in their customer agreements requiring the customer, for example, 'not to use or permit the usage of the service in an unlawful manner or in contradiction of published legislation and regulations governing the Internet' as well as allowing them to suspend the site at will.

1 This is based on the tort of interference with contract. See *Lumley v Gye* (1853) 2 E & B 216 and more generally, for example, *Winfield and Jollowicz on Tort* (15th edn, 1998), pp 623–634.

8. OBSCENITY[1] AND HARMFUL CONTENT

3.51 'Obscene' is a very strong word. It carries the connotation of something which is filthy, vile and disgusting, offensive to the senses, etc, particularly in a sexual context. Since the turn of the eighteenth century the common law has recognised 'obscene libel' as a misdemeanour[2]. The principal sources of current UK law regulating criminal conduct amounting to obscene behaviour derive from the Obscene Publications Acts 1959 and 1964, as amended. However, a common law offence of outraging public decency still exists[3].

Although obscenity is generally unlikely to be relevant to most entities concerned with the Internet, this section will have relevance in certain situations:

- entities who provide access to 'adult' content on-line clearly expose themselves to the risk of prosecution under obscenity laws;

- increasingly, issues arise with respect to the distribution of pornographic or other extreme information as between private individuals, on account of the servers and systems through which such traffic passes. As an employer granting a measure of private access to the Internet for your employees, you may be concerned that your company could be held responsible if your employees download, store and/or e-mail such 'sensitive' materials using your company's systems. Or as an ISP, the issue may arise as to the measure of control over such traffic through your server that you can have or (which is a different matter) can be expected to have.

It is easy these days to find pornographic material on the Internet (it is understood that 'sex' is the second most commonly searched keyword among the various Internet search engines) and most research shows that sex is big business on the Internet. Moreover, shadier corners of the Internet have become homes for communication between people with interests in a variety of extreme political, religious and other views, all reflective of the fact that on the Internet it is possible, to a certain extent, to hide from the reach of law enforcement in individual countries.

In this section, we are principally concerned with the UK legal regime for controlling the publication of obscene materials. By way of comparison, we will also look at the US position in this area, as well as at European initiatives with respect to the regulation of harmful content on the Internet.

1 For a fuller discussion, see *Smith and Hogan: Criminal Law* (10th edn, 2002).
2 *R v Curl* (1727) 2 Stra 788.
3 The cases primarily concern acts of perversion in public, or in the presence of others. Private diaries of an obscene nature are insufficient: *R v Rowley* [1991] 4 All ER 649, CA (and hence so, too, are private computer records). However, since liability appears to be strict (see *R v Gibson* [1991] 1 All ER 439, CA), this looks like the sort of offence where prosecutions for abuse of the Internet might be entertained, assuming that there was no clear path towards proving that the defendant intended to corrupt or deprave. In *Gibson* itself, the defendant mounted a display of earrings made out of freeze-dried human foetuses. But had he directed persons to view pictures of this exhibition on a website, arguably he would have been just as culpable.

(a) What does 'obscene' mean?

3.52 The definition of this actually quite complex word is set out in section 1(1) of the Obscene Publications Act 1959 (OPA 1959) as follows:

> 'For the purposes of this Act, an article shall be deemed to be obscene if its effect or (where the article comprises two or more distinct items) the effect of any one or more of its items is, if taken as a whole, such as to tend to deprave and corrupt persons who are likely, having regard to all relevant circumstances, to read, see or hear the matter contained or embodied in it.'

The suggestion is that this actually removes or mitigates the need for the article in question to have an inherently filthy or lewd context, if it will merely deprave or corrupt *as such*. Two important points are of relevance here:

- depravity and corruption may be relative terms. However, courts have upheld convictions in cases where the defence tried to argue that the only recipients were persons already depraved and corrupted[1].

- sexual depravity is not the only sort which is inherent within the meaning of these words. See, for example, *John Calder (Publications) Ltd v Powell*[2], with respect to the capacity of a publication advocating drug-taking to corrupt and deprave.

1 *DPP v Whyte* [1972] 3 All ER 12, HL, and see in particular at 19, per Lord Wilberforce.
2 [1965] 1 QB 509, DC.

(b) Obscene publications

3.53 The Criminal Justice and Public Order Act 1994 extends the scope of the OPA 1959 to cover the electronic transmission of data which, on conversion into viewable form, is obscene.

The test of obscenity as set out above will be satisfied even if a file sent across the Internet is encrypted and is not viewable by the general public, on the basis that it is decrypted by a person on whom it has, or is intended to have, the requisite effect[1].

In 1999 a new Obscenity Bill was introduced before Parliament which would have amended the OPA 1959 by specifically identifying as obscene something which was referable to one or more of 39 specific sexual activities specified in the Bill's Schedule. The list apparently included much of the 'hard-core' pornography currently available on the Internet (including within various Usenet newsgroups). The Bill did not, however, progress and lapsed at the end of the 1998/99 Parliamentary session. To date, the Government has given no indication that it intends to resurrect this Bill at a later date.

A person publishes an article for the purposes of the OPA 1959 if, in the case of an article containing matter to be looked at or a record, he shows, plays or projects it or, where the matter is data stored electronically, transmits that data. While the ISP will generally not have to consider its position in relation to material of this nature which passes through its systems unbeknown to it, a service provider which knows that it is hosting a website that intends to promote this sort of material should be concerned that it may be implicated either as a secondary party or (depending on the level of its involvement) a co-principal in the commission of the offence[2].

1 Where material of this nature is sent to a person, identified to the sender, on whom it is known or understood that it will not have an corrupting or depraving effect, there is a strong argument for a defence under the 1959 legislation. This defence was successful in *R v Clayton and Halsey* [1963] 1 QB 163, CCA, in relation to a supply of materials to an undercover policeman who was held as a matter of fact in the case to be of an incorruptible nature. However, the mere attempt to supply such material to a person whom you believe to be capable of being corrupted by it (even if for some reason not known to you he is somehow immune from this) is now an offence under the Criminal Attempts Act 1981.
2 This concept is expanded on at paragraph 3.56 with reference to the 'Notify and take down' procedure.

(c) Child pornography

3.54 Within the realm of obscene and harmful publications, paedophile pornography undoubtedly attracts the most concern[1]. Thus, we find that it is an offence under:

- section 1 of the Protection of Children Act 1978 to take, distribute, show, have in possession with a view to their being distributed or shown to others, or advertise that you intend to do so, any indecent photographs or image, whether made by computer graphics or otherwise, which appears to be a photograph of a child;

- the Children and Young Persons (Harmful Publications) Act 1955 to print, publish, sell or let on hire a book, magazine or other work which is of a kind likely to fall into the hands of children or young persons and consists wholly or mainly of stories told in pictures portraying the commission of crimes, acts of violence or cruelty or incidents of a repulsive or horrible nature which as a whole would tend to corrupt a child or young person into whose hands it might fall[2]; and

- section 160 of the Criminal Justice Act 1988[3] to possess any indecent photograph or pseudo-photograph (a photograph doctored to look as if of a child) of a child, unless you have a legitimate reason for having the photograph or pseudo-photograph in your possession or you have not yourself seen the photograph or pseudo-photograph and did not know, nor had any cause to suspect, it to be indecent, or that the photograph or pseudo-photograph was sent to you without any prior request on your part and that you did not keep it for an unreasonable time.

1 The Internet Watch Foundation (www.iwf.org.uk) plays a particularly prominent role in policing illegal material on the Internet, with a particular focus on child pornography. The focus is to put pressure on ISPs and hosts to take down dubious content and the IWF operates a hotline to facilitate the process. This is done with commendable speed. There have also been a number of highly publicised police raids on paedophile networks which have been exchanging material over the Internet. Recent focus by legislators appears to be to tackle the issue of adults posing as children in Internet chat rooms.

2 The offence would in principle be applicable even if access was restricted only to adults as, even if they were not deliberately stored by the adult onto his hard disk, the pictures would be cached automatically by the browser and could therefore be made available easily to a child with basic computer literacy skills where such a child has access to the machine in question.

3 Punishable by a fine or six months in prison or both.

(d) Corporate liability

3.55 The liability for transmission of obscene material extends to the organisation whose facilities are used to access the Internet if it facilitates, by storing, the transmission of an obscene file. The OPA 1959 applies to the 'producer' of a website in the same way as it does to other forms of publication. A company which provides access to the Internet to its employees could accordingly be liable as publisher.

(i) Notify and take down

3.56 There is a defence in section 2(5) of the OPA 1959 which provides that a person shall not be convicted of an offence if he proves that he had not examined the article in respect of which he is charged *and* had no reasonable cause to suspect that it was such that its publication would make him liable.

While most companies may not have problems with the second limb of section 2(5) in relation to acts of their employees when they are clearly acting in a capacity outside their scope of employment, most ISPs now have an obvious difficulty with this defence given that the police have supplied ISPs with a list of newsgroups known to contain dubious files (on the assumption that such newsgroups remain available through those ISPs).

Faced with the risk of prosecution, the UK's ISPs decided to opt for a self-policing scheme and the Internet Watch Foundation (IWF), representing most of the ISPs, was launched in September 1996 following discussions between the Home Office, the police and the ISPs.

The IWF has established a unified national hotline so that users can report the presence of pornography on the Internet. When they do, the IWF will establish whether the particular Internet newsgroups in question carry illegal material. If so, it will forward the information to the relevant service provider who will trace the originator and ask for its removal. This allows the ISPs to co-ordinate deletions of indecent material and help the police track down offenders. In all cases, details are passed to the police, or to the National Criminal Intelligence Service if the originator is abroad[1].

The 'success' of the IWF's 'notify and take down' scheme has removed a measure of the pressure to police the Internet from ISPs for the time being, and may in the future form the basis for EU-wide legislation[2]. Companies should follow the same basic principle – once notified of possible pornography, they should investigate promptly and remove the material from their systems[3].

1 The IWF handled 2,407 reported cases of illegal content in 1998, compared with 898 in 1997, and although more recent figures are not yet available, it seems likely the IWF will handle an ever increasing work load as more people go on-line.

2 On 25 January 1999 the European Parliament and the European Council adopted Decision 276/99, which comprises an action plan for promoting safer use of the Internet (available at www.europa.eu.int).

3 The point is analogous with *Godfrey v Demon Internet Ltd* [1999] 4 All ER 342, referred to at paragraph 3.41.

(ii) Finding a host

3.57 If your business wishes to offer access to adult content, you will need to find a host who is willing to carry your traffic and not shut you down too quickly. This may be a problem in the UK given that the Internet Service Providers' Association has a Code of Practice for its members which states that:

'**1.1**   Members shall use their reasonable endeavours to ensure the following:

1.1.1   Services and promotional material do not contain anything which is in the breach of the law, nor omit anything which the law requires.

1.1.2   Members, their services and promotional material do not encourage anything which is in any way unlawful.

1.2   Members shall use their reasonable endeavours to ensure the following:

1.2.1   Services and promotional material do not contain material inciting violence, sadism, cruelty or racial hatred.

1.2.2   Services and promotional material are not used to promote or facilitate prostitution.'

The other main body representing UK ISPs is the London Internet Exchange Ltd (LINX)[1], which provides guidance to its 180 members in the form of the July 1998 'LINX Best Current Practice Handling of Illegal Material'.

LINX's main Memorandum of Understanding also contains the general restriction that:

'Members must not carry out any illegal activities through the LINX.'

Most ISPs will have a clause in their contract enabling them to suspend a site in the event of any illegality.

1 www.linx.net.

(e) Overseas communications

3.58 The position in the UK with respect to traffic coming from, or aimed at, other countries is obviously more complicated. The key issue will be where any offence may be deemed to have been committed.

(i) ISPs and conduit providers

3.59 Conduit providers such as telecoms companies and other intermediaries are probably not liable for the mere mechanical transmission of any illegal materials. In Europe, at least, ISPs appear to have won the battle for the same exemption. The E-Commerce Directive provides that an ISP which acts as a mere conduit or provides caching or hosting services shall not be liable for information transmitted (articles 12–14). The E-Commerce Directive also provides that the ISP is not under a duty to monitor content if it is acting in those capacities (article 15). Content providers such as authors and publishers of illegal material will probably be liable provided the court has jurisdiction and the materials are illegal under the laws of the relevant state.

(ii) Individuals

3.60 The case of *R v Waddon*[1] concerned the publication by the defendant of material on a website in California. For the purposes of the OPA 1959 it was held that this occurred in the UK, even though the server was located in a country where such material would be legal. The trial judge appears to have directed as a matter of law that the transmission of the materials in question amounted to a publication (interpreting the words in section 1(3)(b) of the OPA 1959 inserted by the Criminal Justice and Public Order Act 1994). It is not clear what view the judge took of any argument to the effect that lawful publication in California implied that the material did not have a corrupting influence there. Although this is an interesting potential development for the future, the case should probably be treated as having little clear legal authority at this stage.

An altogether more interesting case is *Gold Star Publications Ltd v DPP*[2], where the House of Lords was asked to consider the position of 150,000 hard-core pornographic magazines seized in the UK from a warehouse where, it was accepted, they were intended for export sale only (that is publication for gain outside the UK). By a four-to-one majority, their Lordships upheld the decision of the magistrates' court to order seizure of the magazines. But it is instructive to compare the logic of Lord Wilberforce (for the majority) with Lord Simon of Glaisdale (dissenting). Basically, two arguments were rehearsed:

- **The jurisdictional and economic argument** Lord Wilberforce emphasised that Parliament can have intended the wording of the OPA 1959, and in particular what was meant in section 3(3) by 'publication for gain', to provide for circumstances where publication takes place overseas. It was not paternalistic for the UK to appear in this fashion to be making laws with application to the conduct of individuals overseas, since Parliament was required to have regard to the economic impact of the hard-core pornography trade on the UK, and this necessitated taking a view as to the contribution of exports to that trade. Lord Simon's dissent was based on the argument that express words are required for the legislation of the UK to be deemed to have jurisdictional effect in relation to other countries.

- **The moral argument** The defence raised the argument that Parliament is not competent to legislate, nor indeed interested in legislating, for the protection of the moral standards of inhabitants of other countries. What may or may not corrupt a UK person may not have the same effect in another country. Lord Wilberforce dismissed this suggestion, on the basis that the power to seize the materials in question vested in the magistrates, and they were entitled to infer from the seized materials that they were intended for persons who would understand what they were. Lord Simon's dissent revolved around the implausibility of English magistrates having any sort of objective capacity to determine what is likely to corrupt or deprave persons outside the same moral environment as the UK.

The *Gold Star* case leaves unanswered questions. The main problem is that the House of Lords majority seemed happy to allow the seizure in the case to stand on the basis that the magistrates must have had a sufficient idea of the situation before them to reach a defensible conclusion. How this would apply in relation to a situation where pornographic or other obscene material is being transmitted overseas (so that no seizure powers are in issue) remains to be seen; but there is a strong rationale for favouring Lord Simon's dissenting views – unless, of course, this issue is addressed through legislative reform.

1 Crown Court at Southwark, July 1999 as reported in [1999] ITCLR 422, [1999] Masons CLR 396. Of some interest, however, is that the trial judge ruled that it was sufficient for police to certify that their computer was working and that similar certification for the network of computers outside the UK that carried the material was not necessary, when adducing evidence under section 69 of the Police and Criminal Evidence Act 1984. No formal report of this case exists, however.

2 [1981] 2 All ER 257.

(iii) Liability outside the UK

3.61 An interdepartmental group comprising representatives from the Crown Prosecution Service and other interested government departments and the police commissioned a research study comparing controls on obscene material in England and Wales, Scotland, the Republic of Ireland, Germany, The Netherlands, Australia, New Zealand, Canada and the USA. This was published in July 1996, and makes for a useful introduction to this subject[1].

Broadly speaking, different standards apply throughout Europe ranging from the more liberal definitions of obscenity in The Netherlands to the anti-porn, anti-neo-Nazi propaganda crusade in Germany.

In late 1995, CompuServe tangled with Bavarian government prosecutors who threatened criminal action if CompuServe did not shut down newsgroups that used the word 'sex'. Authorities charged that the content violated German pornography laws. CompuServe placated Bavarian prosecutors by giving German-language speakers localised filtering software.

This solution seems to have been adopted in the German Federal laws aimed at regulating the 'Conditions for Information and Communications Services' (the Multimedia Law) (the final version of which was published on 29 June 1997), and which provides an exemption from liability if 'technical measures have been taken so that the offer or dissemination in Germany can be limited to adult users' and 'if dissemination to or access by children or minors is excluded by technical or other means', amending the earlier Law on the Dissemination of Writings and Other Media Harmful to Minors.

However, in 1997 a Munich court convicted the executive of Compuserve Deutschland, Felix Somm, of distributing pornography because customers could use Compuserve to download child pornography from Internet sites in the United States[2].

The local court in Munich dismissed Compuserve's claims that it was helpless to block German customers access to so many deemed offensive sites and sentenced Somm to two years of probation and fined him 100,000 marks (around £40,000). These initial proceedings, in which Somm was found guilty, were characterised by numerous errors of law and were criticised worldwide as being unfair.

On 17 November 1999, the Landgericht München (Regional Court of Munich) finally acquitted Felix Somm of the accusation, overturning a verdict that had horrified the Internet industry in Germany and had worried the industry the world over. The Landgericht München clarified that Somm was not responsible for the illegal content upon which the charge was based. Furthermore, it created some legal certainty for the information and communications service industry by confirming exemption from punishment for providing access to the Internet.

1 HORS 157 *Testing* Obscenity: *An International Comparison of Laws and Controls Relating to Obscene Material*. Available from the Home Office.

2 See Roger Boyes, 'Computer Firm to Fight Bavarian Charges of Internet Pornography' (1997) Times, 18 April and the commentary at www.digital-law.net/somm/commentary.html.

3.62 Similar cases have come before the French courts in respect of the on-line sale of Nazi memorabilia, most notably against the ISP Yahoo!. In a protracted case[1], the French courts ordered Yahoo! to take all necessary steps to block the access of French citizens to sites hosted on the

American website Yahoo.com which offered for sale Nazi memorabilia (an offence under French law). In addition, Yahoo! were ordered to put in place a warning system whereby French Internet users who access Yahoo.com through the French-based Yahoo.fr are warned that accessing certain material on the American website may contravene French law.

This case has yet to be resolved, as Yahoo! have lodged appeals questioning the jurisdiction of a French court to rule on content located on an American site. However, the case serves as a pertinent reminder that compliance with local obscenity laws will not guarantee freedom from the interference of a foreign court.

Such a concept of filtering software is also included in the French proposal for an OECD Agreement on international co-operation with regard to the Internet, which calls for a voluntary code of conduct based on guiding principles including 'the principle of respect for human dignity and public order, in particular by making filtering software available to users, by designing classification systems or defining a corpus of key words'.

There have been calls for international harmonisation and the setting of minimum standards for defamation, obscenity and blasphemy laws for interstate and international Internet traffic. Until such harmonisation is achieved, as discussed in paragraph 3.61, even if materials are not obscene in the jurisdiction they originated, they may be in the jurisdiction in which they are downloaded and viewed, exposing the provider to liability.

In the US, successful prosecutions have been brought in one State against individuals supplying material in another State: see *US v Thomas* (material downloaded from California to Tennessee was not obscene in California but an offence in Tennessee, as a different community test applied[2]).

The moral of the story is that specific legal advice must be sought in respect of each relevant jurisdiction into which your business might be involved in transmission of suspect material, given the fast-changing pace of the law.

1 *UEJF and LICRA v Yahoo! Inc and Yahoo France* 22 May 2000, available at www.juriscom.net/txt/jurisfr/cti/yauctions20000522.htm.
2 1996 FED App 0032P (6th Cir), 74 F 3d 701, cert den 117 S Ct 74 (1996), available at www.jmls.edu/cyber/cases/thomas.html. In the US, in order to be obscene, and therefore outside the protection of the First Amendment, an image must:
   • appeal to a prurient (that is, unhealthy or shameful) interest in sexual activity;
   • depict real or simulated sexual conduct in a manner that, according to an average community member, offends contemporary community standards; and
   • according to a reasonable person, lack serious literary, artistic, political or scientific value.
   However obscene or not, visual depictions of children engaged in sexual conduct are not constitutionally protected. Because the government interest identified by the Supreme Court as justifying removing child pornography from the protection of the First Amendment is more urgent than the government interest which justifies denying protection to obscenity, and because the child pornography standard is far less vague than the obscenity standard, law enforcers and prosecutors are not bound by any unique procedural burdens here.

(f) European initiatives against harmful content

3.63 The European Commission has firmly stated that it intends to take a back seat in the regulation of the registration and management of domain names, and leave the private sector to formulate its own rules as far as is possible. As long as the registration process for domain names remains broad and open, the Commission is unlikely to intervene.

Instead, the Commission is concentrating on regulating the content of the Internet in order to curtail the amount of harmful and illegal content. The Commission's initiatives in this area follow a request by the Council of Ministers responsible for telecommunications, cultural and audio-visual policy in November 1996[1]. The Council's call followed a Commission working party report on the illegal and harmful content on the Internet. This report was subsequently updated in

October 1997[2] and recommended a series of actions which led to the publication of a proposed European Parliament and Council Decision for an action plan on promoting safer use of the Internet. The proposal was amended on 11 September 1998[3] and adopted on 25 January 1999[4].

At the same time as the Commission's report on illegal and harmful content on the Internet, it also published a Green Paper on the protection of minors and human dignity in audio-visual and information services[5]. The Green Paper covered all audio-visual information services, including the Internet, and examined the current rules concerning the protection of minors and human dignity. The Commission concluded that the centralised services, and primarily the Internet, merit its main attention and urgency. Faced with the limits of purely national solutions, there is a need to devise and apply worldwide solutions in which the EU must play a fundamental role.

1   See Resolution adopted at the Telecommunications Council of 28 November 1996.
2   COM 518/98 final.
3   OJ C324/98, p 6.
4   Decision (EC) 276/99 adopting a multinational Community action plan on promoting safer use of the Internet by combating illegal and harmful content on global networks: OJ L33 06.2/99, pp 1–11.
5   COM 483/96 final and COM 570/97.

3.64   The Commission's action plan[1] sets out various initiatives to deal with undesirable Internet content. It covers a period of four years which commenced on 1 January 1999 and has a financial framework for implementation of €25m. The plan points out that the vast majority of information on the Internet poses no problem. However, it must be appreciated that the Internet can be used for illegal activities and the distribution of illegal information. The action plan aims to:

■   empower the user to protect himself and his family from undesirable and harmful materials;

■   strengthen reporting mechanisms for illegal material to be dealt with by existing legislation;

■   ensure that the specific multicultural and multilingual needs of Europe are addressed adequately;

■   build trust in the new environment so that the consumer can benefit from the new services, and industry can use the opportunities of electronic media; and

■   promote safer use of the Internet and encourage, at European level, an environment favourable to the development of the Internet industry.

These objectives will be carried out within the framework of the following actions:

■   the promotion of industry and user self-regulation and the implementation of schemes to monitor and combat illegal and harmful content on the Internet which may jeopardise national security, the protection of minors, protection of human dignity, financial security, data protection and protection of privacy, reputation, public health and intellectual property;

■   encouraging industry to provide filtering tools and rating mechanisms, which will allow parents or teachers to select content appropriate to children in their care while, at the same time, allowing adults to decide what legal content they wish to access;

■   promoting activities fostering international co-operation in the areas listed above to ensure compatibility between the approach taken in Europe and elsewhere; and

■   supporting initiatives, including websites for information and assistance, by organisations that are active in the protection of human and citizens' rights and in counteracting violence and the abuse of women and children.

1   COM 518/98 final.

3.65   When the proposal set out above was debated in the European Parliament, it was sought to include provisions relating to the legal liability for illegal information contained on the Internet. However, the Commission did not accept these amendments as it felt they were not appropriate in an action plan which focused on non-regulatory measures. However, the Commission did amend the adopted proposal so that it will now have to undertake an assessment of the current legal instruments available to challenge illegal use of and content on the Internet. The assessment will examine the extent to which changes are needed to police law in EU Member States in order to ensure preventative action in relation to Internet content and use.

All the Commission's actions are overseen by a committee consisting of representatives from each of the Member States and Commission officials. On adoption of the Decision[1], the Commission was obliged to issue tenders to organisations to run projects fulfilling the aims and objectives of the action plan. The Commission General Report of 2000[2] stated that as a result of this process, ten projects had been selected for EU funding totalling €6m and in December 2000 a new call for further proposals was issued[3].

For the on-line seller, these initiatives mean that there is, and they can continue to expect, a greater degree of self-regulation in the industry. In addition to the Internet Watch Foundation (see footnote 1 to paragraph 3.54 above), which was set up in the UK to provide a hotline for the public to complain about illegal content and a 'notify and take down' procedure (see paragraph 3.56), there is already a similar Copywatch scheme which has been set up to cover copyright materials. On-line sellers can also expect privacy programmes similar to TrustE[4] to be set up in the EU and other consumer kite mark programmes like the Consumer Association's 'Which? Web Trader' scheme. The DTI and the Alliance for Electronic Business have set up an industry-led body called TrustUK. The aim of this body is to ensure that e-commerce hallmarks meet a consistent standard so that:

> 'The presence of a TrustUK hallmark on a website will offer users the re-assurance that they are dealing with an authentic, trustworthy trader who will respect the consumer's privacy, follows good information security practices, will not display any illegal or immoral content and will have a clear policy concerning its contracts and dispute resolution.'[5]

On-line sellers may also have to rate their content to ensure that it is not filtered out automatically because browsers are set up to allow only rated content through.

1 Council Decision (EC) 276/99: OJ L33 6.2.199; Commission General Report 1999, point 423 (see http://europa.eu.int/ abc/doc/off/rg/en/1999/index.htm).
2 Commission General Report 2000, Chapter III, Section 9, para 323 (see http://europa.eu.int/abc/doc/off/rg/en/2000/ index.htm).
3 OJ C345 2.12.2000.
4 See section 9 of Chapter 6, E-marketing.
5 See Recommendation 10.2 of the Report published by the Cabinet Office's Performance and Innovation Unit in September 1999 (at http://www.cabinet-office.gov.uk/innovation/1999/ecomm.shtml).

9. DATA PROTECTION AND PRIVACY

3.66 This section examines issues of liability of a different sort, namely those which arise primarily under the framework of UK and European data protection legislation. For the on-line seller, compliance with data protection legislation is increasingly important. Breach of the UK legislation (the DPA 1998) may ultimately lead to criminal sanctions, liability in damages and a ban on processing data about living individuals, the cumulative effect of which would stop most businesses in their tracks – e-businesses in particular. Moreover, individuals are increasingly aware of their rights in relation to data protection and are prepared to exercise them. As the Data Protection Commissioner (the official charged with policing the DPA 1998) has the specific obligation of informing the public of their rights, and has already begun running a series of television advertisements doing so, public awareness can only be expected to increase. In light of this, a more immediate risk for all businesses, but particularly e-businesses, is the potential for adverse publicity. If individuals lose confidence in the security and proper processing of their data, it can have a significant adverse effect on any e-business[1]. Chapter 6, E-marketing looks at more specific data protection issues relating to the use of data for advertising and marketing purposes.

The DPA 1998 relates only to information about individuals. The HRA 1998, which came fully into force on 1 October 2000 and enacts into English law the principles in the European Convention on Human Rights, is also likely to be a significant force for the development of data protection law. The DPA 1998 was drafted bearing in mind the provisions of the HRA 1998, and in particular the interplay between article 8 (the right to privacy) and article 10 (the right to freedom of expression). The English courts have already held that a company can have private activities which need protection from unwarranted intrusion, ie a right to privacy[2]. We may see further developments in this area.

1 Witness, for example, the serious adverse publicity during the summer of 2000 for companies such as PowerGen and Barclays, when it was found that personal data of their customers was somehow becoming widely available to visitors to their websites.
2 *R v Broadcasting Standards Commission, ex p BBC* [2000] 3 All ER 899, CA.

(a) Background

3.67 The concept of privacy and data protection dates back centuries[1]. The unlawful processing of personal data, the processing of inaccurate personal data and the abuse or unauthorised disclosure of such data are all considered to be violations of *fundamental* human rights and are legislated against in a number of countries. The risk of abuse rises with the increasing sophistication of technology – new technology increases the amount of information generated on each individual and allows the easy and often invisible collection, analysis and dissemination of the information by governments, commercial organisations and private citizens (including, in the last two categories, criminals).

The 'information superhighway' collects, processes and transfers enormous amounts of personal data each day and one of the key issues to users is the need for their privacy to be protected. Simply tracking a user as he surfs the web may reveal to the tracker his interests, tastes, religion, sexual inclinations and purchasing intentions, all of which can be easily abused. The DPA 1998 regulates not only the overt collection of data over the Internet, but also such invisible tracking, whether by means of the use of 'cookies' or otherwise.

If you wish to trade responsibly and respect your customers' rights, ask yourself how you would like private information on you and your family to be used.

1 For an amusing nineteenth-century example of privacy protection in action, see *Prince Albert v Strange* (1849) 2 De G & Sm 652, which concerned the restraint of an artist who wanted to publish drawings he had made of the Prince Consort.

(b) EU and UK legislation

3.68 In the EU, the regulation of data protection exists at several different levels: the European Convention on Human Rights, Directive (EC) 46/95 on the protection of individuals with regard to the processing of personal data and on the free movement of such data (the EU DP Directive), and national implementing legislation like the DPA 1998.

The EU DP Directive was required to be implemented by Member States by 24 October 1998. The majority were, however, very slow to implement it. As at 28 August 2002, France, Ireland and Luxembourg had yet to implement the EU DP Directive (though they were taking preliminary steps towards implementation)[1]. The DPA 1998 came into force on 1 March 2000, replacing the Data Protection Act 1984 (DPA 1984).

The DPA 1998 significantly increases the obligations on a data controller (ie anyone who alone, or with others, determines the purposes for which and the manner in which any personal data are processed), and gives considerably greater rights to individuals and powers to the Data Protection Commissioner. Importantly, unlike the DPA 1984, it now applies to *manual* as well as computerised records, provided that they form part of a 'relevant filing system'.

The DPA 1998 applies to you if:

■ you are 'established' in the UK, ie are ordinarily resident, a UK-incorporated body, partnership or unincorporated association, or have an office, branch or agency which carries on any activity or a regular practice in the UK;

■ you are not established in the EEA but use equipment in the UK for processing data (unless the information is merely in transit, for example if the information is routed over the Internet via a UK node); and

■ practically, data is exported to you from the UK.

Elsewhere in the EEA, local data protection legislation will apply similarly, subject to the variations permitted by the EU DP Directive.

This means that a website hosted in the US and controlled by a US entity will not be caught by the DPA 1998 even if it processes information obtained from a UK customer. It will, however, continue to be subject to other applicable Acts and regulations, eg in relation to advertising, which may impose similar obligations[2].

1   The status of the implementation of the EU DP Directive can be found at http://europa.eu.int/comm/internal_market/ dataprot/law/impl.htm.
2   Further commentary on advertising and website consent can be found in Chapter 6, E-marketing.

(c) The basic requirements

3.69   The types of information about which the DPA 1998 is concerned are *personal data*, ie data which relate to a living individual who can be identified directly or indirectly from those data alone or from those data and other information which is in, or is likely to come into, the possession of the data controller. These living individuals could include your employees, suppliers, customers and personal contacts.

The DPA 1998 requires a *data controller* to:

■ except in very limited circumstances, notify the Data Protection Commissioner of his identity, and provide a description of, and the purposes for which, personal data are to be processed by or on behalf of the data controller;

■ process the personal data fairly and comply with the eight Data Protection Principles (see paragraph 3.70 below); and

■ provide access to the data which he holds on a person (the *data subject*) so that the data subject can check and correct his records and prevent certain types of processing.

Even if a data controller is not required to notify the Data Protection Commissioner, he is still obliged to comply with the remainder of the DPA 1998.

(d) The Data Protection Principles

3.70   The eight Principles enshrined in the DPA 1998 and derived from the EU DP Directive which must be followed are:

- personal data shall be processed fairly and lawfully and, in particular, shall not be processed unless:

  - at least one of the conditions in the DPA 1998, Sch 2 is met, and

  - in the case of sensitive personal data[1], at least one of the conditions in the DPA 1998, Sch 3 is also met;

- personal data shall be obtained only for one or more specified and lawful purposes and shall not be further processed in any manner incompatible with that purpose or those purposes;

- personal data shall be adequate, relevant and not excessive in relation to the purpose or purposes for which they are processed;

- personal data shall be accurate and, where necessary, kept up to date;

- personal data processed for any purpose or purposes shall not be kept for longer than is necessary for that purpose or those purposes;

- personal data shall be processed in accordance with the rights of data subjects under the DPA 1998;

- appropriate technical and organisational measures shall be taken against unauthorised or unlawful processing of personal data and against accidental loss or destruction of, or damage to, personal data; and

- personal data shall not be transferred to a country or territory outside the EEA unless that country or territory ensures an adequate level of protection for the rights and freedoms of data subjects in relation to the processing of personal data.

1 Sensitive personal data is defined in section 2 of the DPA 1998 as being data relating to the racial or ethnic origin of the data subject, his political opinions, his religious beliefs or other beliefs of a similar nature, whether he is a member of a trade union, his physical or mental health or condition, his sexual life, the commission or alleged commission by him of any offence or any proceedings for an offence.

(e) Penalties

3.71 Failure to comply with the DPA 1998 may result in criminal penalties for companies and their individual managers. It is a criminal offence, to which there is no defence, for you to process personal data without having an appropriate registration or notification, unless you fall within the limited category of persons exempt from the registration or notification requirement.

The Data Protection Commissioner has the power to:

- issue enforcement notices in the event of any contravention of the Data Protection Principles – an enforcement notice can require a data controller to refrain from processing any personal data (which would stop most businesses in their tracks), or to rectify, supplement or destroy inaccurate or outdated data; or

- serve an information notice requiring a data controller to provide information which may be reasonably required to determine whether he is complying with the Data Protection Principles.

A person who fails to comply with an enforcement or information notice is guilty of an offence[1] unless he can prove he exercised all due diligence. It is also an offence knowingly or recklessly to supply materially false information in purported compliance with an information notice.

Additionally, it is a criminal offence for anyone, without the consent of the data controller, to obtain or disclose personal data or to procure the disclosure to another person of the information contained in personal data[2]. Data processors (discussed in more detail below) will need to take particular care not to exceed the authority given to them in relation to processing personal data.

1 The DPA 1998, s 47(1), (2), (3).
2 The DPA 1998, s 55.

(f) Practical steps[1]

3.72 Data protection compliance requires that you:

- understand your responsibilities;

- know what information you are processing;

- except in limited circumstances referred to below, notify the Data Protection Commissioner and keep your notification up to date; and

- put in place systems to enable you to achieve compliance.

Data protection legislation is not intended to stop the processing of all personal data. It requires that any processing is done *fairly*, at each stage from its collection, storage, manipulation, analysis and disclosure, until its destruction. Full compliance may require you not only to change the design and content of your website, but also your business processes. Most e-businesses will not be entitled to take advantage of the transitional provisions under the DPA 1998 and must, therefore, comply in full from the outset. It is important that e-businesses put in place appropriate systems to operate as soon as they first start trading so as to ensure that compliance with the DPA 1998 becomes an automatic part of doing business.

1   Hammond Suddards Edge has developed a DPA 1998 compliance product, *Dataedge* (for more details, please refer to www.hammondsuddardsedge.com/dataedge), which is available for purchase. It includes a brief overview of the DPA 1998, detailed checklists taking you through matters such as notification, compliance with the Data Protection Principles, security, third party processors and transfers outside the EEA, a data protection compliance policy, instructions for insertion in employee handbooks, specimen consent clauses, a data processor security questionnaire and data processor agreement, and an agreement incorporating necessary safeguards for when personal data are transferred outside the EEA, all with guidance notes. It is updated annually.

(i) *What are your responsibilities?*

3.73 As an e-business, you should:

- read the Data Protection Commissioner's guidance notes – there is a general note and specific notes on areas including the Internet, direct marketing, franchises, financial services, credit referencing, debt tracing and collection and a draft code of conduct for employers, which set out a summary of what is expected from you[1];

- audit your usage of personal data;

- establish a manual and/or code of practice setting out clearly your internal rules for processing data;

- ensure that your managers and employees are aware of your organisation's responsibilities under the data protection regime and the penalties for non-compliance. You might, for example, run regular training sessions;

- designate a member of your management (or a responsible person within the organisation directly answerable to management) who will be responsible for learning about the DPA 1998 regime and supervising your organisation's compliance with it;

- audit the security status of your data processors, and put in place written agreements with them; and

- make appropriate amendments to your contractual documentation to address data protection compliance.

1 For the guidance notes, see http://www.dataprotection.gov.uk/dpr/dpdoc.nsf.

(ii) How do you determine what data you already process?

3.74 Unless yours is a new business, you should in fact already be registered under the DPA 1984 (except where all you have kept are paper records, to which the DPA 1984 did not apply). If so, your registration under the DPA 1984 will continue in force until it would normally expire (three years from the date of registration), when you will need to renew it under the DPA 1998 regime.

Even if you have registered, you are under a continuing duty to keep your registration up to date. Unless you fall within one of the exemptions[1], you are required either to be registered or to notify. Failure to do so amounts to the criminal offence of processing without registration[2], to which there is no defence.

It is also an offence to fail to notify changes to the basis for your registration within 21 days of their occurring[3], although it is a defence to show that you have exercised all due diligence to comply with that duty[4].

To determine properly what your notification should cover or whether your existing registration is correct, you will need to collect information on what, how, from whom and by whom data in your organisation is or may be:

- **collected** This includes electronic and manual data, so you will need to obtain copies of the forms or scripts used on your web pages for data collection;

- **kept** You will need to be aware of the format and location of data, who maintains it and what security measures have been put in place;

- **disclosed to** This includes disclosure to other group companies and to credit reference agencies; and

- **destroyed** You will need to be aware of your organisation's document and data retention and destruction policies.

This information might be collected in some cases through an interview process and in other circumstances through the use of a data protection audit questionnaire.

The types of information you will need to consider include:

- electronic records, eg from your website or e-mails;

- manual records, eg customer files, card indexes and paper lists of customer contacts; and

- e-mails, voicemails and CCTV recordings.

It does not matter if the data is 'confidential'. Under the DPA 1998, expressions of opinion and your intentions regarding the data subject are included within the definition of personal data. It is important to bear this in mind as such personal data must be disclosed to the data subject on request.

1 See the Data Protection (Notifications and Notification Fees) Regulations 2000 (SI 2000/188).
2 The DPA 1998, s 17(1).
3 The DPA 1998, s 21(1).
4 The DPA 1998, s 21(3).

(iii) Do the transitional provisions apply to you?

3.75 The DPA 1998 contains complex transitional provisions, a full analysis of which is beyond the scope of this chapter. Basically, in order to be able to rely on the transitional exemptions, personal data must have been the subject of processing that was 'already under way' immediately before 24 October 1998[1]. It is not clear precisely what this phrase means. The Data Protection

Commissioner's Office has indicated, in relation to employees, that if data that is processed about an employee who commenced employment after 24 October 1998 is the same as information processed about employees employed before that date, that counts as existing processing. A change to the scope, nature or purposes of the processing, however, is likely to mean that the transitional exemptions are not available.

As we have already said, most e-businesses commenced trading after October 1998, so the transitional exemptions will not be available to them, and they must comply in full with the DPA 1998 from the outset. If you operated a conventional business prior to October 1998 and have added an e-commerce arm subsequently, you will have to decide whether it is feasible to run a 'twin-track' system of compliance, where the new business is DPA 1998-compliant from day one, while the old business benefits from the transitional regime.

If transitional exemptions are available, then in the case of computerised data, a data controller was exempted from complying with some, but not all, of the requirements of the DPA 1998 until 23 October 2001. Such a controller still had to comply with the fair processing requirements under the DPA 1984.

In the case of manual data, if the transitional exemptions apply, the controller is exempt from a few of the requirements of the DPA 1998 until 24 October 2007.

The transitional provisions under the DPA 1998 are highly complicated, and it is recommended that they should not be relied upon without taking professional advice. In any event, you should keep a record of the steps you have taken in arriving at any conclusion so that you can rely on the transitional exemptions.

1   That is, not the date on which the DPA 1998 itself came into force in March 2000.

(iv) Now, it is time to notify

3.76   Once you have collected and assessed the audit information, unless you fall within the category below, you must take steps to notify the Data Protection Commissioner or, if necessary, update your existing registration.

The Data Protection Commissioner has sought to streamline and simplify the process of notification. The Commissioner has produced a Notification Handbook, which seeks to take an applicant through the procedure[1]. Notification can be undertaken on-line[2].

Unlike registration under the DPA 1984, which was for three years for a fee of £75, there is now an annual fee of £35 and, provided you continue to pay the annual fee, your notification continues indefinitely.

When making a notification, you will need to have at least the following information available:

- the business's name and address (note that in the case of a group of businesses, each company or entity in the group may need a separate registration if it processes data);

- if you wish to nominate a representative, the name and address of the representative;

- a description of the personal data being/to be processed and of the category(ies) of data subject to which they relate;

- a description of the purpose(s) for which the data are being/are to be processed;

- a description of any recipient(s) to whom you intend or may wish to disclose the data;

- the name or a description of any countries or territories outside the EEA to which you transfer or intend or may wish to transfer the data;

- if you hold exempt data (ie manual data held in a relevant filing system) or accessible data (ie health records, educational records, local authority housing records or local authority social services records) and decide not to notify in respect of such data, your notification will need to include a statement that the notification does not extend to such data; and

- a general description of the security measures taken to protect the personal data (this will not appear on the public register).

Under the DPA 1984 you would be registered under one or more 'purposes'. The old list of standard purposes has been reduced by more than half, with the description of data subjects, data, recipients and third country transfers being linked to purpose only. The option to describe a purpose other than by using a description from the standard list has been retained, but applicants are advised to use it only where it is clearly not possible to use a standard description of purpose.

1   Contact the Data Protection Commissioner's Office on 01625 545745 to obtain a copy.
2   The Data Protection Commissioner's website is at www.dpr.gov.uk and the Notification Handbook is also available on-line.

3.77   The *Guidance Note on the Internet* published under the DPA 1984 by the Data Protection Registrar (as the Commissioner then was), noted that:

'Generally, use of the Internet is not in itself a purpose. The Internet is a means to facilitate some other business purpose, such as marketing. The data user needs to consider whether the use of the Internet significantly changes the purpose. In many cases, the answer will be that it does not; for example, marketing of an organisation's products or services is the same purpose whether it is done by direct mail, by telephone selling or via the Internet.'

Because of the nature of the Internet, however, the Registrar recommended that the following disclosures be made where appropriate:

'Personal data held for this purpose is accessible over the Internet. Disclosure may, therefore, be made to any person having access to the Internet, worldwide.'

'Personal data held for this purpose may be transmitted over the Internet. Transfers of personal data may, therefore, take place, potentially, to any country in the world.'

The Data Protection Commissioner is now taking a stronger line. It may be necessary also to make clear that many countries worldwide do not have regimes for the protection of personal data as strong as those within the EEA.

You may also be required by your industry code of conduct or by membership of certain organisations to register certain purposes. Members of the Internet Service Providers' Association (ISPA) are, for example, required by the ISPA Code of Practice to state that data may be used for regulatory purposes, which should read along the following lines:

'Personal data held for this purpose may be made available to the Internet Service Providers' Association (ISPA) where necessary to enable ISPA to carry out its regulatory function.'

(g) Checklist for fair and lawful processing

3.78   The overriding principle of the DPA 1998 is that processing must be 'fair and lawful' (the first Data Protection Principle). This means that any processing of personal data must be justified. Part II of Schedule 1 to the DPA 1998 sets out in greater detail the implications of the Data Protection Principles. Schedule 2 sets out the conditions (at least one of which must be met if processing is to be fair) and Schedule 3 sets out further conditions (at least one of which must also be met if the processing of sensitive personal data is to be considered to be fair). You need to consider whether you have legitimate grounds for your processing operations:

■ Is data obtained from a person authorised or required by legislation to supply data?

■ If not, has the specific and informed consent of the data subject been obtained?

  – Non-response is not enough.

  – Consent must be explicit if sensitive data are involved.

  – Consent must be properly obtained (ie not coerced or obtained on the basis of misleading information).

  – Consent must not have been withdrawn.

  – Consent should cover current processing, ie if processing after the end of the original transaction.

■ If not, is processing necessary:

  – for performance of a contract with the data subject?

  – as a preliminary step to entering into a contract in response to a request made by the data subject?

  – because you are under a legal (non-contractual) obligation to do so?

  – in order to protect the vital interests of the data subject (ie matters of life and death)?

  – to carry out a public function?

■ Do you have a legitimate business interest for processing the data which is not prejudicial to the interests of the data subject?

■ If data are obtained from the data subject, have you as soon as you start processing the data, as far as practicable, provided or made readily available to the data subject fair processing information, ie:

  – your identity (and that of any other data controllers);

  – your representatives (if any);

  – the purpose or purposes for which the data are intended to be processed; and

  – any necessary further information so that the data subject understands the purposes for which their personal data is going to be processed, the likely consequences of such processing and whether particular disclosures can reasonably be envisaged.

■ If data is obtained from a third party, you should:

  – take reasonable steps to ensure the accuracy of the data; and

  – provide data subjects with the fair processing information either before the data is first processed, or within a reasonable time if you intend to disclose the data to a third party (or even if you plan to do nothing else with the data except hold it indefinitely), unless:

    • it would involve a disproportionate effort, eg if the time, expense and difficulty outweighs the benefit to the data controller and the data subject is not prejudiced;

    • it is necessary for you to record the information to be contained in the data or to disclose the data to comply with any relevant legal (non-contractual) obligation;

■ If use of the personal data is not reasonably foreseeable, have you supplied the data subject with further information to ensure processing is fair?

- If the data subject indicates that the data obtained from a third party is inaccurate, your records must reflect that.

(h) Obligations on the registered business

3.79 Having registered under the DPA 1998, what now are your obligations with respect to the collection and processing of data?

(i) Obtain the data fairly

3.80 Data which is collected can only be used for the purpose for which it is collected initially. If the information was collected to enable a contract to be performed (eg obtaining the shipping address of a data subject who is your customer), then even though the information was provided with the consent of the customer, it cannot be later used for any non-obvious purpose without the informed consent of the data subject. It would not be obvious to the data subject, for example, that his personal data would then be posted on the Internet (eg in a list of satisfied customers).

The best practice is to make it clear to the customer:

- what the data collected will be used for, including in particular any non-obvious purposes (eg for credit scoring, profiling, direct marketing by other companies): see *Innovations (Mail Order) Ltd v Data Protection Registrar*[1];

- for whom the information is being collected, where this may not be clear;

- to whom the data may be disclosed (eg group companies, credit reference agencies, regulatory bodies, web page advertisers);

- that the data subject has an opt-out (eg 'I do not wish to receive any further marketing information from you or any other company').

Excessive or irrelevant data should not be collected – if communications are intended to be conducted by e-mail then consider whether postal addresses and fax numbers need to be asked for. Visitors to your website should not be automatically asked for personal details. The European Commission has issued a recommendation entitled *Anonymity on the Internet*[2], which concludes that:

'The sending of e-mail, the passive browsing of World Wide Websites, and the purchase of most goods and services over the Internet should all be possible anonymously. Some controls over individuals contributing content to on-line public fora (newsgroups, etc) are needed, but a requirement for individuals to identify themselves is in many cases disproportionate and impractical. Other solutions are to be preferred.'

1 Data Protection Tribunal, September 1993.
2 Commission Recommendation (EC) 3/97, XV D/5022/97 final. See http://www.open.gov.uk/dpr/502297an.htm.

(ii) Use of cookies

3.81 Most sophisticated sites will use cookies, ie files that track a customer's preferences and even the pages they visit so as to leverage the opportunity to market further products and services to the customer based on their interests. As this process clearly amounts to the collection of personal data, your website will need to contain a fair processing notice, stating that such information is being collected and for what purposes this is being undertaken. You will also need to consider the basis on which you can justify the collection of such data. For ordinary data, if the data subject will not be prejudiced by the use of the data, it may be sufficient to rely on the 'legitimate business interests' provision. If sensitive personal data is involved, however, the explicit consent of the data subject is needed. Collection of personal data via cookies will also be a form of direct marketing and the customer may at any time (even if he has consented previously) request in writing that you cease such processing. You must respond in writing within 21 days of receiving such notice and your system must be able accordingly to allow either:

■ cookies to be switched off for a specific customer, but still allow the system to work; or

■ preferably flag that the customer has exercised his rights and that no further marketing should be attempted.

Problems may arise if the customer requests that only certain information be stopped, so one way could be to implement a preference screen which would enable the customer to signify the types of information he would like to be presented with automatically, allowing him easily to opt in/out at will.

(iii) Special conditions for sensitive personal data

3.82 Sensitive personal data (ie data that relates to the data subject's racial or ethnic origin, political opinions, religious beliefs or other beliefs of a similar nature, trade union membership, physical or mental health or condition, sexual life or criminal record) must be treated with additional care and can generally only be processed if the data subject has given his *explicit* consent.

If you are handling such data in relation to data subjects in different EU Member States, you will need to check the laws in each relevant Member State as they may prohibit altogether some forms of processing of these data. There are a number of exceptions, however, which allow for the processing of these data in certain cases (though only as far as *necessary*) subject to particular safeguards. These cases include the processing of data mandated by employment law, the cases in which it is impossible for the data subject to consent (eg blood-testing of the victim of a road accident), processing of data manifestly made public or processing of data about members by trade unions, political parties or churches, for certain legal and medical purposes and to further racial or ethnic equality.

(iv) 'Bare processing'

3.83 The DPA 1998 restricts the disclosure of personal data. As information will only be personal data if a living individual can be identified from it, this will not prevent a subset of the data stripped of all personal identifiers from being disclosed, eg a database of sales by region to middle-aged men. If, however, codes are included which could lead to the identity of the individual being worked out, eg a look-up table which can be accessed, then this will constitute a disclosure of personal data.

Where data is transferred outside the EU, it is arguable that the restrictions will apply even if in such a case the look-up table is not supplied to the data importer so long as some personal identifiers are left in the data. 'Personal data' is defined under the DPA 1998 as 'data which relate to a living individual who can be identified from those data and other information which is in the possession of, or is likely to come into the possession of, the data controller'. It is 'the duty of a data controller to comply with the data protection principles in relation to all personal data with respect to which he is the data controller'[1]. The DPA 1998 defines a data controller as 'a person who (either alone or jointly or in common with other persons) determines the purposes for which and the manner in which any personal data are, or are to be, processed'. As a 'data exporter' must be considered to be a data controller of the data, the DPA 1998 obliges it to prevent the 'unsafe' export of personal data in the first place. Practically, however, it is recommended that, wherever possible, names and addresses be removed in any case from the data prior to export if they are not strictly required to enable the data importer to process the data, and to reduce the chance of such data being misused.

1   The DPA 1998, s 4(4).

(v) Automated decisions

3.84 In relation to credit checking or any other decision which 'significantly affects' the data subject (for example, in relation to the initial decision whether to take on a new customer or whether to accept new dealing instructions based on creditworthiness or to reduce a person's credit limit or trading limit), automatic decision-making is permitted. If, however, the automatic processing results in a decision which significantly affects the individual (eg financially, emotionally, etc) then either:

- a human should be involved in making the final decision; or

- the customer should be notified as soon as is reasonably practical that the decision was taken on that basis. The customer can require the decision to be reconsidered within 21 days by written notice.

The requirement to notify the data subject of the decision as soon as reasonably practicable need not be given before the decision is implemented. However, best business practice would be to notify the data subject of a decision and withhold implementation until the data subject has an opportunity to object.

This means that the system cannot be fully automated and will need some human supervision, not least as a channel for customer communications. If the system is intended to be operational 24 hours a day, or if the anticipated volume is such that it will be impracticable for a human to review every decision which would significantly affect each potential customer, then practically the only choice would be to use an automated response making it clear that the decision was based on an automated procedure, and providing the facility for a human override if there are complaints.

If a written complaint is received, you must respond in writing within 21 days specifying the steps you are intending to take to comply with the notice. Strictly, verbal complaints can be ignored but, from a customer relations standpoint, they should be treated similarly.

It is possible for an individual to prohibit, by written notice, a data controller from taking any automated decision about them at any time.

(vi) Use of credit referencing agencies

3.85 The fact that personal data may be disclosed to and retained by credit reference agencies should be made clear to a data subject at the time the personal data is obtained, whether in an application form or otherwise. The information you give should be tailored according to whether you intend only to file initial information with the agency for credit searching, or whether you will also file default information or full account information. A DPA 1998 notification will require the applicant to state the sort of entities with whom the applicant proposes to share data which it has received. You would therefore need to add to your notification a specific reference to disclosures to these agencies and/or other lenders.

(vii) Security

3.86 The seventh Data Protection Principle requires that 'appropriate technical and organisational measures shall be taken against unauthorised or unlawful processing of personal data and against accidental loss or destruction of, or damage to, personal data'.

The objective of security of information systems is the protection of the interests of those relying on information systems from harm resulting from failures of availability, confidentiality and integrity.

You will, therefore, need to ensure that adequate procedures are in place to ensure the security of personal data. These will include specific procedures for manual and automated data.

The seventh Data Protection Principle also requires that if you, as a data controller, use a third party data processor to process personal data for you, you must vet their security procedures before appointment.

If you are satisfied with the processor's security measures, you should implement a written agreement to ensure all security conditions and control requirements you require are complied with. The obligation to vet processors is an ongoing one and it is therefore important to periodically monitor the security procedures of all processors.

The typical on-line seller is likely to appoint a number of data processors. These include external organisations (including other companies within the same group) who act as website developers or hosts or who maintain software. General business activities that may involve external data processors include outsourcing, payroll processing and using external delivery agents.

(viii) Establishment of subject access procedures

3.87 You must put in place systems which will allow you to respond to written requests from a data subject (for a small fee) within 40 days, stating whether personal data on him is being held by you and, if so, their contents, the purposes for which they are being processed and the recipients to whom the data may be disclosed; where the data is inaccurate, you need to allow him to make corrections or add a statement of the true facts to supplement the records.

Where the request cannot be entertained without disclosing information relating to another individual (for example, if it is not possible to omit references to the other individual's name or particulars, or if it would be obvious from the information who the source was), you do not have to comply, provided you have reasonable grounds for refusing (eg on confidentiality grounds or express refusal of consent by the other individual). Accordingly, you may wish to consider designing your database structures to indicate the source of the data and whether it is confidential and/or should not be disclosed, and put in place guidelines for responding to data subject access requests.

E-businesses involved in financial services will be interested to know that a security guideline entitled *Keeping Customer Information Safe* is available from the Data Protection Commissioner.

(i) Export of personal data

3.88 The eighth Data Protection Principle states that personal data shall not be transferred to a country outside the EEA (ie the 15 EU Member States plus Norway, Iceland and Liechtenstein) unless that country ensures an adequate level of protection in relation to the processing of personal data.

Switzerland and Hungary have recently been declared by the European Commission to provide an adequate level of protection for data. However, no other countries outside the EEA have been given this 'white' status.

The European Commission continues to assess countries, and is currently determining whether Canada's new privacy laws provide adequate protection. Other countries with protection laws which may be declared adequate by the Commission in the future include Hong Kong, New Zealand, Japan and Australia. It is particularly noteworthy, however, that to date the US has not been added to the 'white' list (however, see below regarding the US Safe Harbour scheme).

(i) When can personal data be transferred outside the EEA?

3.89 Personal data can only be transferred to a country which does not provide adequate protection if it falls within one of the categories in Schedule 4 to the DPA 1998. In brief, these are:

- the data subject has given his (informed) consent to the transfer;

- the transfer is necessary:
    - for the performance of a contract between the data subject and the data controller; or
    - for the taking of steps at the request of the data subject with a view to his entering into a contract with the data controller (eg transferring personal data on a potential licensee to obtain the consent of the licensor);

- the transfer is necessary:
    - for the conclusion of a contract between the data controller and a person other than the data subject which:
        - is entered into at the request of the data subject; or
        - is in the interests of the data subject; or
    - for the performance of such a contract;

- the transfer is necessary for reasons of substantial public interest, eg:
    - for the purpose of, or in connection with, any legal proceedings (including prospective legal proceedings);
    - for the purpose of obtaining legal advice; or
    - is otherwise necessary for the purposes of establishing, exercising or defending legal rights

- the transfer is necessary in order to protect the vital interests of the data subject;

- the transfer is part of the personal data on a public register and any conditions subject to which the register is open to inspection are complied with by any person to whom the data are or may be disclosed after the transfer;

- the transfer is made on terms which are of a kind approved by the Data Protection Commissioner as ensuring adequate safeguards for the rights and freedoms of data subjects[1]; and

- the transfer has been authorised by the Data Protection Commissioner as being made in such a manner as to ensure adequate safeguards for the rights and freedoms of data subjects (ie on a case-by-case basis until general guidelines are issued).

1 None have been approved yet but the Commissioner is consulting various interested parties and various proposed model clauses have been issued, eg by the International Chamber of Commerce.

(ii) The US Safe Harbour scheme

3.90 The European Commission has adopted a decision approving a US Safe Harbour scheme. US organisations receiving personal data can voluntarily adhere to a binding set of data protection principles recognised by the Commission. This commitment to safe harbours will provide a presumption of an adequate level of protection for transfers of personal data.

The US Department of Commerce implemented the scheme on 2 November 2000.

EU data exporters wishing to check the status of their US recipient can refer to a publicly available list maintained by the US Department of Commerce. Complaints about data handling are referred to an independent dispute resolution mechanism, while it is also possible in certain cases to bring cases in the US courts. The bodies empowered to investigate complaints and obtain relief are the Federal Trade Commission (FTC) and the US Department of Transportation. It is important to note that banks, and savings and loans and credit unions, are not subject to the powers of either of these regulatory bodies and will not appear on a list of companies with safe harbour status.

Data transfers to US organisations outside the safe harbour are still possible but will need an exemption to apply or alternative safeguards to be put in place.

Without the benefit of the Safe Harbour scheme or an alternative means of compliance, this will mean, for example, that a UK subsidiary cannot report back regularly to its US parent with a list of new customers' details, key accounts, major defaulters, etc.

(iii) 'Model' contracts

3.91 The Safe Harbour scheme only applies to transfer of data to the US. In relation to transfers to other countries (other than on the EU 'white' list), contracts will need to be put in place between the sending and receiving parties to establish a similar level of protection (ie effectively making the receiving party subject to all the provisions of the DPA 1998). The exceptions in Schedule 4 set out at paragraph 3.89 are likely to be narrowly construed (ie to allow for the export of data that is strictly necessary and no more)[1].

The Data Protection Commissioner is particularly keen to see the development of model contract clauses to guarantee the protection of personal data, and a number of bodies in the UK which represent businesses are currently looking at the issue of model contracts with a view to preparing clauses for approval by the Data Protection Commissioner. The main doubts over the acceptability of any contractual solution relate to the historic inability of third parties to take the benefit of rights under an English law contract due to doctrine of the privity of contract. However, this has, in part at least, been addressed by the introduction of the Contracts (Rights of Third Parties) Act 1999[2].

The International Chamber of Commerce Model Contract, for example, contains:

- provisions requiring the data importer to submit to verification or audit procedures of its processing facilities and information handling (which could be at the insistence of the data protection authority in the country where the data exporter is established);

- provisions requiring submission by the data importer to the jurisdiction of a country's courts for certain reliefs;

- provisions requiring the data importer to permit the data subject the same rights it would have had against the data exporter in respect of the data prior to its export;

- an indemnity for violations of contractual provisions;

- rights of termination clauses if the data importer is in breach of contract; and/or

■ return of, or deletion of, the personal data on termination of the relationship for any reason.

1 It should also be pointed out that, in many cases, a business is likely to wish to transfer categories of data, or to transfer data for purposes, which are wider in scope than those which fall under the US Safe Harbour scheme.

2 In force since May 2000, but not with retrospective effect or with effect in relation to any contract where the rights of non-contracting parties are expressly excluded.

3.92 The Data Protection Commissioner will pay particular attention to transfers which have been identified as of particular risk to privacy, including:

■ transfers which carry the risk of financial loss (eg credit card payments over the Internet);

■ transfers made for the purposes of making a decision which significantly affects the individual (such as the granting of credit);

■ transfers which may result in specific actions which constitute a significant intrusion into an individual's private life (such as unsolicited telephone calls);

■ repetitive transfers involving massive volumes of data (such as transactional data processed over telecommunications networks, the Internet, etc); or

■ transfers involving the collection of data in a particularly covert or clandestine manner (eg Internet cookies).

It is likely that any trans-border e-commerce solution will involve one or more of these types of transfers and there will need to be strong and appropriate procedures and safeguards set up in the receiving offices.

The transitional provisions under the DPA 1998 provide that, until 23 October 2001, the eighth Data Protection Principle will not apply in relation to personal data which was being processed before 24 October 1998. As indicated above, the precise extent of the 'existing processing' provision is unclear. In any event, many e-businesses will not be able to rely on the transitional exemption, as they will have been set up after October 1998.

The Data Protection Commissioner's preliminary view on the Eighth Data Protection Principle and Trans-border Dataflows provides some helpful legal analysis and a suggested 'good practice' approach which should be taken into consideration.

(j) Privacy policies

3.93 In concluding this section on data processing, it is appropriate to make some suggestions with respect to privacy policies for website operators. Best practice is for you to have a clearly defined privacy policy on your website covering:

■ what personal information you are gathering;

■ how the information will be used;

■ who the information will be shared with, if anyone;

■ whether the information will be exported outside the EU;

■ what choices are available to your visitors regarding how collected information is used;

■ what safeguards you have put in place to protect information from loss, misuse, or alteration; and

■ how your visitors can update or correct inaccuracies in their information.

You should also consider joining one of the 'On-line Privacy Oversight Programs' like TRUSTe[1] or CPA WEBTRUST[2].

It is arguable that this is the only way a website can properly obtain the 'informed consent' of its data subjects required by the EU DP Directive.

In contrast, the US Federal Trade Commission's June 1998 report entitled *Report to Congress on Privacy On-line* concluded that 'industry's efforts to encourage voluntary adoption of the most basic fair information practices have fallen short of what is needed to protect consumers' as only 14% of commercial US websites disclosed their information collection practices.

1 www.truste.org. See Chapter 6, E-marketing, section 9 for further details.
2 www.cpawebtrust.org.

10. SECURE COMMUNICATION

3.94 We turn now to the consideration of a crucial issue in relation to Internet communication: security. This section will examine issues involving security in relation to methods of communication. Section 11 below looks at content security.

E-commerce requires a certain degree of trust. Given a choice, customers will choose to transact with on-line sellers they trust to give them their money's worth. Chapter 1, E-world has outlined the success of established brands in achieving this trust. Where trade is not face-to-face, that trust must be established remotely, and the trustworthiness of the means of communication becomes critically important. The customer needs to know that his message has been sent to and received by (and only by) the correct addressee, without being garbled, and is being acted upon. For e-businesses it will also be important that the contents of the message are kept secret to prevent trade rivals from intercepting and exploiting the information communicated remotely.

For e-commerce to succeed and develop, the identity and trustworthiness of the parties needs to be securely established (by authentication) and the content of messages and data communicated needs to be kept confidential and securely transmitted (via encryption).

Authentication and encryption are particularly necessary in a global computer network, such as the Internet, because:

■ on-line identities can be easily faked;

■ there is no good reason to believe that the actual channels over which data travels in such a network are physically secure;

■ the scale of connectivity which constitutes the Internet means that potentially unlimited numbers of people from around the world could try to attack the integrity of the data you wish to communicate; and

■ unlike telecommunication networks, the Internet is not 'owned' by anyone and there is therefore no direct line of accountability for information being communicated, which may well be handled by numerous different service providers in geographically diverse locations.

The perceived lack of security is often quoted as the main reason why consumers have been reluctant to trust e-commerce transactions. Apart from the many good business reasons for putting in place authentication and encryption systems, legally the on-line seller is exposed to the following risks if he does not do so:

■ having the sale disputed if he cannot prove that the customer made the order ('I did not send that e-mail or click on "buy"') or what he agreed to ('that was not what I wrote/ ordered');

■ not getting paid; or

■ being sued for breach of contract or negligence if the information was misused due to inadequate security provisions (for example, if credit card details were obtained from the supplier's supposedly secure system).

The issue of authentication is intrinsically linked to the development, both legally and technically, of 'digital signatures', and is discussed in Chapter 2, E-contract, para 2.26, in relation to contracting on-line.

(a) Encryption

3.95 The Internet is an 'open' network and as even 'closed' intranets or dedicated electronic data interchange (EDI) networks are not 100% secure from hacking, some form of cryptography may be required to make more secure information in respect of which illegal and/or undesirable access may be possible. Cryptography is the science of developing, analysing and deciphering techniques applied to data to produce secure communication. In the past such techniques would have included the application of codes and ciphers to data.

However, the primary tool of modern cryptography is encryption. Encryption is the application to data of particular mathematical computations that are intended to have the effect of rendering that data meaningless for all parties other than the intended recipient.

The various mathematical qualities of modern encryption technologies can be used in respect of a communication to:

■ protect the information content;

■ establish the authenticity of the sending party;

■ prevent undetected modification of the message;

■ prevent repudiation; and

■ prevent unauthorised use.

For the purposes of e-commerce, encryption will most commonly be used:

■ during secure communications sessions – this is usually effected by the use of secure sockets layer (SSL) technology (see below);

■ to encrypt specific communications – one of the more common packages used is Pretty Good Privacy (PGP) (also considered below); and

■ to sign communications digitally (this is dealt with in Chapter 2, E-contract in para 2.26, in respect of execution electronically of binding agreements).

3.96 Most web-based on-line purchases and monetary transactions are now secured by SSL. SSL was developed by Netscape Communications and RSA Data Security and is used to form a secure information 'tunnel' between a web browser and a web server. This is indicated by the unbroken 'key' appearing at the bottom of most browsers during a secure session and a URL beginning with 'https' instead of the normal 'http'. There are many Internet server/client products that support SSL connections. To set up shop on the Internet, all an on-line seller needs is access to one of these servers and to acquire a digital certificate to enable SSL. Customers should already have the technology as SSL is built into recent versions of both the Microsoft and Netscape Internet browsers.

Other solutions include S-HTTP (or Secure Hypertext Transfer Protocol), proposed by Enterprise Integration Technologies. This application has the benefit of two additional features:

- client certificates allowing the server to authenticate the identity of the customer; and

- a choice of cryptographic options to be used.

S-HTTP would be used where it is important to verify the identity of the customer, for example in an e-finance transaction before money was allowed to be transferred or confidential information released.

SET™ (or Secure Electronic Transactions) standards developed by Visa and MasterCard go a few steps further. While SSL websites basically collect the information from the customer (using SSL to protect the information during transit) and then independently verify the payment information via separate credit card authorisation networks, SET links together the banks and credit card issuers as well as the on-line seller and customer.

Some hardware vendors, notably Intel and Hewlett Packard, incorporate digital identities into their hardware to facilitate encryption and authentication. This avoids some of the need for individuals to obtain digital certificates, but does in turn raise obvious privacy implications as users can be tracked across the Internet.

(i) Encryption of specific communications

3.97 While it may well be the case that most e-mail communication is mundane and not commercially sensitive, the increased use of e-mail for sending documents that are commercially sensitive by way of 'file attachments' (such as word processing files, spreadsheet files, photographs or other graphical images) means that companies should look seriously at routinely implementing encryption software in respect of their e-mail communication.

In addition, many businesses may be unaware how difficult it is to actually delete an e-mail. Pressing the 'delete' button at one's own computer is no guarantee that an offending or potentially prejudicial e-mail has actually been deleted from the system as a whole. In most instances it can easily be recovered, as the message continues to exist in a number of forms, especially where the system carries out regular back-up routines. The message may also have been stored by the recipient's Internet service provider on a back-up system, stored on anything from tape to CD-ROM or other electromagnetic media.

Depending on the archival system of the ISP, e-mail communications from as far back as ten years could in principle be retrieved. Given these technical constraints arising from the basic structure of the Internet, it is far easier to apply encryption to e-mail communication as generated, rather than attempt to delete an unencrypted e-mail after it has been sent.

The best advice for businesses must be that if confidential information has to be sent by e-mail, it should be encrypted. 56-bit encryption is the lowest level of encryption that should routinely be used for such sensitive information.

PGP (Pretty Good Privacy) is the most commonly used package and has been in the market for a few years. Alternatives include PEM (Privacy-Enhanced Mail) and S/MIME (secure MIME messaging). PGP allows encryption without author signature, allowing you to create anonymous, encrypted messages. PEM does not support this, but as the PEM message signature is outside the encryption envelope, it allows anyone to verify the sender of the message without reading the message.

If public key encryption is used, you will need first to obtain the public key of the recipient (see the 'How encryption works' example below). Ideally this should be obtained directly from the recipient so you can verify its source. If it is obtained indirectly, eg from a public key directory (or even the end of an e-mail), you will need to carry out the same due diligence as you would for a normal distance transaction to link the key to a real person or organisation.

There are currently two solutions to the certification issue:

■ relying on a 'web of trust', where the recipient's public key is 'signed' by other people (eg his bank or solicitor) whom you trust and who can vouch for them; or

■ relying on official key issuing authorities, that is what is referred to as a Trusted Third Party (TTP) or Certification Authority (CA). Many governments are looking to enact legislation dealing with the authorisation of TTPs.

3.98 Breach of confidence is an area of English law in which litigation is complicated by the difficulty of producing sufficient evidence to support a claim[1]. Legally, therefore, it is prudent for businesses to routinely ensure that any e-mail containing confidential information (whether encrypted or not) should include an initial paragraph identifying it as such and stating that it is intended for the named recipient only. In addition, many businesses operating without the benefits of encryption now issue e-mail warnings stating they cannot guarantee the security or confidentiality of such communication.

For example, the current Hammond Suddards Edge standard e-mail notice reads:

'This message is confidential and may be legally privileged or otherwise protected from disclosure. If you are not the intended recipient, please telephone or e-mail the sender and delete this message and any attachment from your system; you must not copy or disclose the contents of this message or any attachment to any other person.

Copyright in documents created by or on behalf of this firm remains vested in the firm, and we assert our moral rights, unless the terms of our relevant client's engagement provide otherwise.'

1 Consider, for example, the problem over what is meant by whether ostensibly confidential information has entered the public domain. With regard to drawing a demarcation line between the public and the private domain in relation to information, it is interesting to note here the position in *Schering Chemicals Ltd v Falkman Ltd* [1981] 2 All ER 321, where the second defendant was held to have breached a confidential relationship with the plaintiff by producing a TV programme about the plaintiff's affairs based wholly on research into the plaintiff's affairs derived from external sources already in the public domain (including press coverage in the *Sunday Times*).

How encryption works

There is an ancient Chinese saying that 'the best way to keep a secret between two people is if one of them is dead'. While this is undeniably true, the next best thing is probably modern 'strong' encryption technology.

The basic explanation

Modern encryption relies on the particular mathematical properties of prime numbers (numbers that only have factors of themselves and one). If you multiply two large (say 56 digit) prime numbers, you create a third number which, whilst not prime itself, only has the factors of the two original prime numbers, except for itself and one. The mathematical difficulty in obtaining the two original prime factors in circumstances where you only know the product of these numbers is the fundamental mathematical basis for all modern encryption methods.

Virtually all cryptosystems now rely upon the difficulty of reversing encryption computations based around such prime number mathematics, when all that is available is the meaningless encrypted data. A simple way of expressing the phenomenon is to think of the process of encryption as a 'one way function': easy to achieve forwards, but enormously hard to carry out backwards. A purely analogous example would be smashing a pane of glass with a brick: while it is easy to smash the window into tens of thousands of pieces, the restoration of the window from those shards of glass, while not theoretically impossible, is so difficult as to render its reconstruction wholly impracticable.

Encryption achieves the same result on data by making use of an algorithm selected from a group of invertible transformations known as a cryptosystem. The variable component which selects the particular transformation from within the group is known as 'the enciphering key', normally abbreviated to simply 'the key'. The reversal of the resulting 'ciphertext' into its original 'plaintext' (even when knowing the key in the encryption algorithm) is known as 'cryptoanalysis'. Successful cryptoanalysis renders the encrypting system 'compromised'. Effectively, cryptoanalysis is a system identification problem and therefore the aim of cryptography is to construct systems that are hard to identify. The best of such systems will have applied a cipher that so obscures the qualities of the plaintext natural language that it cannot be distinguished from purely random 'bit strings' of meaningless data by a cryptoanalyst.

The 'key'-based explanation

Encryption, like any code, requires 'a key' in order to decipher the message. Obviously, the 'key' required to decipher an encrypted message cannot be sent with the message itself! The requirement to send a key separately to the message recipient represented an additional security risk and resulted in cryptography being largely limited to parties amongst whom there already existed a relationship of trust.

It was not until 1976 that a new development in encryption mathematics introduced the 'public key' concept. This concept of a 'private key/public key' system of encryption represented a quantum leap forward in cryptography, in that the new public key system allowed communicating parties to exchange encrypted data without the requirement of having to share a secret key in advance. This had the obvious security benefit of there being no risk that a secret key, obtained improperly, might be used by an unintended third party to compromise the security of the encrypted communication. In contrast, the public key, which could be disclosed to the public, was used to encrypt the data being communicated, and a corresponding 'private key' (known only to the recipient party) was used to decrypt the communication.

- Mr B generates public and private key.
- Gives Ms A (and public) the public key.
- Ms A uses Mr B's public key to encrypt message.
- Sends encrypted message to Mr B.
- Mr B uses private key to decrypt message.

The public and private keys are generated from the original two prime numbers. The process is represented above. Ms A uses a public key to encrypt a message to Mr B. Once Ms A's message is encrypted, no one other than Mr B can decrypt it, including Ms A herself (albeit she already knows the message). Whilst there is a mathematical relationship between the public and private keys, that relationship is the 'wrong side' of the 'one way function' (described above in relation to prime number factorisation) from the point of view of a hostile interceptor. There is therefore, effectively a completely secure communication between Ms A and Mr B without the need for communication of a pre-existing 'secret' key. This breakthrough is known by a range of descriptions:

- RSA (after Ron Rivest, Adi Shamir and Leonard Adleman who invented the technique in 1976);
- asymmetric key encryption; and
- public key encryption.

The most public recognition of the technology is via the PC-based communication security software product known as PGP (Pretty Good Privacy), which was written by Philip Zimmerman in 1992, and widely distributed across the world following its placement on the Internet.

The future of encryption?

In August 2000 researchers from Toshiba working with Cambridge University in the UK announced a breakthrough in sending secure communications which raises the prospect of 100% secure e-mail and e-commerce[1].

The technique they reported is called 'quantum communication', and uses particles of light (photons) to transmit data along optical fibres, which are detected by a sensor at the recipient's end.

Unlike traditional 'prime number'-based encryption techniques, which can eventually be deciphered given enough time and computing power, the 'quantum cryptographic system' relies on the laws of quantum mechanics which make it impossible for a third party to intercept the sequence of photons being transmitted without corrupting the sequence and thus reading some of them incorrectly. This disruption also alerts the intended recipient to the compromise of security represented by the third party.

The system also avoids the difficulties of securely communicating a key for a strong encryption cipher, which currently requires the use of a weaker encryption cipher.

The scientists have predicted that the system will be capable of commercial application within three to five years. One of the current difficulties rendering the system uneconomic is the requirement to operate the photon detector at a temperature equivalent to that of liquid nitrogen.

1   For a full account, see http://www.newsfactor.com/news/articles2000/000823-sml.shtml.

(b) Cryptography service providers and the Electronic Communications Act 2000

3.99   On 25 May 2000 the Electronic Communications Act 2000 (ECA 2000)[1] came into force. The Act provides for:

- the arrangements for registering approved cryptography service providers; and

- the legal recognition of electronic signatures and the way in which they are created, communicated or verified[2].

The provisions relating to recognition of electronic signatures are discussed in Chapter 2, E-contract, para 2.26. The capacity for orders to be made under section 8 of the ECA 2000, allowing for electronic means of contracting and communication to be introduced as opt-in substitutes for existing paper-based methods, is also discussed elsewhere in this book, notably in Chapter 12, E-corporate in relation to corporate communications with shareholders.

Under the ECA 2000, the Secretary of State has an obligation to establish and maintain a register of approved providers of cryptography support services[3]. Section 6 of the ECA 2000 defines a 'cryptography support service' as:

> 'any service which is provided to the senders or recipients of electronic communications, or to those storing electronic data, and is designed to facilitate the use of cryptographic techniques.'

The approval of support services does not extend to the supply of, or any right to use, computer software or hardware, unless the supply is integral to the provision of the service[4].

Examples of cryptography services eligible for approval would include companies providing services such as certifying the public key of an individual, managing encryption keys, time-stamping electronic signatures, key storage, and the creation of directories of certificates.

No specific criteria for approval are provided for in the ECA 2000, but details required to be provided include the technology being offered, the identity of the applicant himself and his background, and the way he intends to provide the technology to the public.

The key point to note in relation to this legislation however, is the voluntary nature of the scheme. The decision to reject a mandatory register represented a considerable reversal of initial government policy in this area, following extensive industry lobbying. Therefore any provider of cryptographic support services will be able to trade notwithstanding the fact that he has not applied to be listed on the register, or even if his application has been rejected by the Secretary of State.

On the other hand, the register will be open to the public for inspection, and it is hoped it will provide a useful 'benchmarking' and quality control function for service providers in this area.

1 The ECA 2000 implements the EC Electronic Signatures Directive (EC) 93/99, designed 'to facilitate the use of electronic signatures and to contribute to their legal recognition' (article 1).
2 Two essential features of the legal recognition of electronic signatures concern 'authenticity' (confirmation to the recipient that the communication came from who it was supposed to come from) and 'integrity' (that the communication has not been tampered with).
3 Section 1 of the ECA 2000.
4 Section 6(2) of the ECA 2000.

(c) Policing electronic commerce: the Regulation of Investigatory Powers Act 2000

3.100 The Regulation of Investigatory Powers Act became law in July 2000[1]. The stated purpose of the Act was to ensure that the UK's law enforcement authorities and security agencies had sufficient powers to intercept communication taking place via the Internet, to discharge their responsibilities effectively. The RIPA 2000 also aimed to provide the necessary protection to individuals' rights and the interests of businesses consequent upon such actions by state bodies.

The RIPA 2000 contains provisions relating to four distinct functions:

■ the interception of communications;

■ the undertaking of intrusive surveillance;

■ regulation relating to human intelligence sources; and

■ the compulsory disclosure of encrypted information.

Subject to the provisions of the RIPA 2000, service providers are now under a legal obligation to give access to targeted transmissions and to disclose any protected (for example, encrypted) electronic communication or data storage services in an intelligible form. ISPs have therefore had to develop quick and easy access facilities to ensure compliance with valid requests made by the law enforcement authorities and security agencies.

In view of recent decisions at the European Court of Human Rights (ECHR), the RIPA 2000 represents welcome clarification of the powers given to agencies authorised to carry out interception and surveillance activities.

In relation to the line taken in ECHR decisions in this area, the conduct under warrants granted by the Home Secretary to the police, security services or Customs & Excise must be 'proportionate to what is sought to be achieved by that conduct'. Under the RIPA 2000, the issue of a warrant must be based on a validly held belief that the granting of the warrant is:

■ in the interest of national security;

■ needed for the detection of serious crime; or

■ needed to ensure the economic interest of the UK.

1 Many provisions of the RIPA 2000 were due to come into force on 2 October 2000 (to precede the coming into force of the HRA 1998), but the rules proposed by the Department of Trade and Industry have been condemned by the Alliance for Electronic Business (AEB), which includes the Confederation of British Industry. Therefore, the rules have currently been delayed. A central issue concerns legally distinguishing between private and business e-mails because, if no difference can be made, then companies will be intercepting private e-mails, which most companies will not want to do (according to the Chamber of Commerce): *Financial Times*, 25 August 2000, p 1.

3.101 The global nature of the Internet has led to provisions being included within the RIPA 2000 to provide for interception warrants to be granted in respect of foreign law jurisdictions in addition to the UK.

Confidentiality and encryption

Global governmental attitudes to strong encryption, interception and export issues

The United Kingdom

In 1996 the UK Government proposed compulsory licensing of Trusted Third Parties as providers of data encryption services (containing the so-called 'key escrow' provision, which required each organisation to give a copy of any private encryption keys to an 'escrow agency').

Mandatory key escrow has now been expressly prohibited under the ECA 2000 (see paragraph 3.99 above) following heavy criticism (for example, the idea of centralised locations holding keys to so much secure communication was deemed too much of a security risk).

The RIPA 2000 obliges providers (under warrant) to disclose private encryption keys (or their location). This provision was originally included in the draft Electronic Communications Bill, but was transferred to the RIPA Bill because of concern that the original provisions might contravene the European Convention on Human Rights.

The relevant provisions are to be found in Part III of the RIPA 2000. The power can be given:

- if an intelligence service, the police or Customs & Excise have lawfully obtained encrypted data (article 49(1));
- if decryption is necessary in the interest of national security, crime prevention or detection, or the UK's economic well-being, or if it is necessary for the effective exercise or proper performance of a statutory power or duty, and if requiring decryption is proportionate and the only reasonably practicable means (article 49(2) and (3));
- if the person addressed is believed to be in possession of the decryption key (article 49(2)(a)); and
- in principle, by requiring the person to decrypt himself (article 50(1)), or, in special circumstances, by requiring the person to provide the decryption key (article 50(3)(c) and article 51) – but not a key that is only used as an electronic signature key (article 49(9));

Control of exports/imports

Export of encryption technology is regulated by the EU Dual-Use Regulation[1] and the Wassenaar Arrangement (pre-December 1998) (see below). There is freedom to export encryption technology over the Internet provided there is no export to embargoed countries, and provided it does not represent breach of the Official Secrets Act. The DTI recommend that a licence should be granted and legal advice obtained.

The United States

The US has been a world leader in its efforts to regulate encryption technology, but it has been forced to relax export laws in response to the adverse effect on e-commerce for US firms which did not have the same market advantages as their foreign counterparts.

In September 1999, the US Government proposed the Cyberspace Electronic Security Bill, which provides for law enforcement and intelligence agencies to order third parties to disclose encryption keys and other information. The Bill contains provisions for key recovery and escrow, measures strongly supported by the Federal Bureau of Investigation. The Bill also proposes new funding for the FBI's Technical Support Centre which develops techniques to obtain encryption keys. The legislation has not yet been implemented.

Control of exports/imports

Export is regulated by the Wassenaar Arrangement, which does not implement the (pre-December 1998) General Software Note and generally maintains stricter controls. There is no control given to import. The US Department of Commerce's Bureau of Export Administration issued amendments to the Export Administration Regulations (EAR) on 12 January 2000[2] (further relaxed on 17 July 2000[3]), allowing US firms to export encryption products to any end-user without a licence in the EU countries, Australia, the Czech Republic, Hungary, Japan, New Zealand, Norway, Poland and Switzerland. The 'seven terrorist countries' (Cuba, Iran, Iraq, Libya, North Korea, Sudan and Syria) were not included. There was no government/non-government end-user distinction.

US exporters may ship products immediately following the filing of a request for commodity classification by the National Security Agency, based on the Commodity Control List[4]. Prior to these amendments, a licence was required under the Arms Export Control Act and the International Traffic in Arms Regulations (ITAR). The ITAR contained an exemption for public domain information and information taught in educational institutions. The amendments to the EAR have helped to clarify the case law in this area[5].

Russia

Legislation in Russia is at an embryonic stage, but should gain pace following the creation of the Russian Association for Electronic Commerce (November 1998) and the US–Russian Institute for the Development of E-Commerce.

Control of exports/imports

Importation of encryption products requires a licence from the Ministry of Trade[6]. The Russian Government is under pressure to relax control over the Internet and to allow e-commerce to flourish in the country. Microsoft was ordered in February 2000 by one of the former departments of the KGB FAPSI (Federal Bureau for Government Information) to release a version of Windows 2000 in Russian, but without any strong encryption being included[7].

Export is controlled through the Wassenaar Arrangement and tight domestic law in the form of a decree which prohibits unauthorised encryption[8]. There is prohibition against the development, production, implementation and use of encryption products without a licence. Based on its own guidelines, the FAPSI is authorised to issue licences to State organisations and enterprises to use encryption for authentication, secrecy, storage and transmission.

China (including Hong Kong)

China endorses severe restrictions on the manufacture of national encryption products. On 15 October 1999 the Chinese Government published State Council Order No 273 entitled 'Commercial Use Password Management Regulations'. Under this provision, officially designated manufacturers are required to seek approval from the State Encryption Management Commission (SEMC) in respect of both the type and model (including key length) of all encryption products. Only SEMC approved encryption products may be used by individuals, the sole exemption from this provision being in respect of foreign diplomats and consulates. Encryption products may not be distributed abroad by organisations or individuals.

In Hong Kong there are no domestic controls on the use of encryption. The September 2000 Report of the Inter-departmental Working Group on Computer Related Crime recommended that it be made a crime to refuse to provide an encryption key, where necessary and justified, when requested by the police.

Control of exports/imports

Under State Council Order No 273, import and export of encryption products requires a licence from the SEMC. However, the Order only relates to hardware and software where encryption and decoding are core functions. Therefore, systems containing encryption as an ancillary function do not appear to be so restricted. The regulation does not contain any provision for key escrow as applied to foreign encryption products. Foreign companies and individuals had to apply for permission to use encryption products by 31 January 2000, although this does not apply to visitors carrying laptops with normal software containing some encryption capability.

In Hong Kong, encryption products using a key length larger than 56 digits require a licence to import or export under the Import and Export (Strategic Commodities) Regulations, following amendment to the regulations in October 1999. This has caused great concern and fear that China's restrictive Internet legislation may harm business opportunities in the region. There is an exception for access-control equipment and authentication encryption products not used for encryption text or files. 'Import by electronic means' is not, however, included in the definition of 'import' in the regulations.

Japan

Japan has no domestic restrictions on the private use of encryption products. The Government has been very slow to regulate encryption technology and has not yet decided upon what type of legislation to implement[9]. The Ministry of Posts and Telecommunications oversees Government policy in respect of encryption technology via private and commercial use of the national telecom networks.

Japan makes a reference to cryptography in its proposed Wiretap Law: if encryption renders partial eavesdropping or wiretapping difficult, law enforcement is allowed to record all communications.

On the other hand, the Ministry of International Trade and Industry published a draft in May 1997 stating that encryption and authentication technologies should be promoted and developed for ensuring security.

Control of exports/imports

Export is regulated through the Wassenaar Arrangement, including the General Software Note. Tighter export controls have been implemented since October 1996. Decisions are made on an individual basis and businesses are obliged to seek approval for an encryption product export order larger than 50,000 yen.

The Wassenaar Arrangement

The Wassenaar Arrangement on Export Controls for Conventional Arms and Dual-Use Goods and Technologies is an international arrangement covering conventional weapons and dual-use goods and technologies (those that may be used for civilian and military purposes). An encryption product is an example of a dual-use good. The Agreement to establish the Wassenaar Arrangement was reached on 19 December 1995, and the inaugural Plenary Meeting of the Wassenaar Arrangement was held in April 1996 in Vienna, Austria. There are now 33 participating states to the Arrangement[10].

The purpose of the Arrangement is to assist national and international stability and security through introducing uniformity and issuing guidelines in the transfer of conventional arms and dual-use goods and technologies. The arrangement is implemented through national legislation.

The General Software Note was abolished by the December 1998 amendments made to the Arrangement. The note exempted mass-market and public domain encryption products from control. The main provisions of the arrangement are:

■ free export for all *symmetric* encryption products up to 56 bits, all *asymmetric* encryption products up to 512 bits, and all *subgroup-based* encryption products (including elliptic curve) up to 112 bits;

■ free export for mass-market symmetric encryption software up to 64 bits;

■ relaxation upon export of products using encryption to protect intellectual property (eg DVD technology); and

■ the requirement of a licence for the export of all other encryption products.

The export of all encryption products in the public domain is permissible. 'Electronic export' still needs to be defined.

---

1   SI 1996/2721.

2   See the US Department of Commerce Press Release at http://204.193.246.62/public.nsf/docs/
      60D6B47456BB389F852568640078B6C0.

(b) What is patentable?

4.06 For an invention to be patentable it has to fulfil certain criteria. The accepted criteria of almost all industrial countries basically are that the invention:

- is new;

- involves an 'inventive step', that is, something that is not obvious;

- is capable of industrial application; and

- is not an expressly excluded subject matter[1].

There is some variation of approach as to what can be the subject matter of patent protection. The approach in Europe and the UK is that computer programs and methods of doing business cannot be accorded patent protection unless there is a technical effect, and, until recently, 'technical effect' has been construed rather narrowly. On the other hand, in the US and Japan patent protection is granted to computer programs and business methods more liberally. In fact, the US is probably the most liberal jurisdiction in this regard, where the basis of assessing patentability for such subject matter is 'commercial utility' rather than 'technical effect'. For example, Amazon.com has been granted a patent for its 'one-click' ordering method. Similarly, priceline.com has been granted a patent for its Internet action system. IBM, whose IBM text handling patents were invalidated in the European Patent Office (EPO), was granted patents by the US Patents and Trademarks Office. So, it may be beneficial for an on-line seller to consider obtaining a patent in the US.

Novelty is assessed on the basis that the invention is not known or does not form any part of the state of the art. This means that, at the date of registration of the patent (priority date), the subject matter is not found in any product, process, information or otherwise used or described anywhere in writing or orally.

A concept or process is inventive if it is not obvious to a person with ordinary skill in the art concerned. An invention involving computer technology would therefore have to be non-obvious to a computer engineer or programmer who is totally familiar with the 'prior art' in the computer technology field. Furthermore, whether or not an invention is obvious is determined as at the date when the first application for patent registration is filed (the priority date).

The concept of industrial application is concerned with whether or not a particular subject matter can be capable of patent protection. A computer program is not regarded as being industrially applicable. However, as explained in paragraph 4.10 below, both under the European Patent Convention (EPC) and by the UK Patent Office, a computer program which achieves a 'technical effect' may be allowed patent protection.

Computer programs are also expressly excluded as subject matter which can be accorded patent protection. Also in the list of excluded subject matter in the PA 1977 are works protected by copyright (literary, artistic, dramatic and musical works), schemes, rules or methods for performing mental acts, playing a game or doing business, discoveries, scientific theories, mathematical methods and presentation of information.

1 The PA 1977, s 1(1).

(i) Software and business methods

4.07 To an on-line seller, the two subject matters that are likely to be of most relevance in terms of their patentability are computer programs and methods of doing business.

Neither computer programs nor methods of doing business are in themselves regarded as patentable in Europe and the UK. But if there is a 'technical effect' involved with a program or a business method, both the European Patent Office and the UK Patent Office will in principle grant patents.

'Computer program' is a relatively broad term, encompassing basic algorithms for conversion of binary code into pure binary to detailed instructions for solutions to specific problems. Computers use mathematical instruction when selecting information and performing mathematical manipulations to produce the desired results. The view has historically been that a computer program is nothing more than a set of instructions to perform tasks resulting in production or manipulation of information and therefore not really an invention. However, it has always been the position that converting instructions into a technical process merits protection. In May 1999, the UK Patent Office published a practice note[1] confirming that it is prepared to accept applications for computer programs, either themselves or on a carrier (such as disk or CD-ROM) which, when run on a computer, results in producing a technical effect. However, it is to be noted that this represents a change in form rather than substance. The effect of this note is to confirm that the Patent Office will have regard to the nature of an application, and will not determine what is patentable purely in terms of the substance of the application.

Some examples of programs that were not considered to have a technical effect, and therefore were not capable of being granted patent protection, are:

- a program for analysing data in relation to shares and similar securities. The program caused data to carry on legal transactions[2]; and

- software to calculate square roots in the binary functioning of a computer by eliminating division and restricting multiplication to specified binary functions[3].

Examples of computer programs that have been considered to have technical effect, and therefore have been granted protection, are:

- x-ray apparatus controlled by a computer program so as to secure optimal exposure without overloading the x-ray tube[4]; and

- a program that processes digital images in accordance with a given mathematical procedure[5].

1 *Practice Note* dated 19 May 1999.
2 *Merrill Lynch's Application* [1989] RPC 561, CA.
3 *Gales's Application* [1991] RPC 305, CA.
4 Application T26/86, a Technical Board of Appeal Decision of the European Patent Office.
5 *Vicom Systems Inc's Application* [1987] 2 EPOR 74.

(ii) The IBM cases[1]

4.08 In 1999, IBM made two patent applications to the EPO under the EPC.

Application T0935 was for a method and system in a data processing system windowing environment for displaying obscured information. The program code stored on a computer-readable medium enabled display of information in a window to be altered if that window was obscured in part by another window. This was done by arranging the information in the first window so that it was still visible in parts of the window which were not obscured.

Application T1173 was for a method to achieve resource recovery in a computer system running a software application such that the application could run even though a particular procedure had not executed.

Both of the applications were rejected by the EPO's Examination Board. IBM appealed and the Technical Board upheld the appeal. It held that a computer program by itself was not excluded from patentability when running or loaded into a computer; it produced or was capable of producing a further technical effect which went beyond the normal physical interactions between the software and the hardware on which it was run. Furthermore, there was no bar on whether or not what was claimed was a computer program by itself or as a record on a carrier such as a CD-ROM or disk in which the program is recorded.

As a result of the IBM decisions, the position is now as follows:

- For software to be patentable, it must be capable of industrial application which has a technical effect.

- In order to have a technical effect the software must do something. However, merely running software is not sufficient. There must be a result or effect. Provided the software produces a technical result, it is in principle patentable. It is then necessary to examine whether the other conditions of patentability are satisfied. As discussed in paragraph 4.06 above, these are whether the software, which is akin to a process control when used in conjunction with the process to produce the result, is new and has an inventive step.

- A technical result expressed on a carrier such as a disk, CD-ROM or other media will not be excluded.

What could be 'technical effect' can be illustrated as follows. A patent has been granted to a squash ball with a particular shade of blue because it makes it more visible. That particular shade of blue solves the technical problem[2]. The shade of blue has a secondary function, that of giving the squash ball colour, which cannot in itself render the squash ball patentable. If the only basis of the choice of colour was a pleasing shade, the patent application would doubtless have been refused on the grounds of lack of an inventive step (even assuming that the blueness of the ball amounted to a novelty).

Similarly, an engineering drawing, for example for a piece of machinery, is not patentable as a drawing (although the drawing itself is or may be the subject of copyright). The principles behind the piece of machinery, if new and if they have an inventive step and provide a useful result, are patentable. However, not every mechanical device is patentable – nowadays something as mundane as a cup would not be patentable unless it had the necessary novelty and inventive step. Merely being a device with a handle to hold fluid is insufficient to support patentability, notwithstanding that such a mechanical device can be drawn and the drawing itself may attract copyright protection and, in three dimensions, design right protection.

1 *IBM's European Patent Applications*; TO935/97 and T1173/97 [1999] EPOR 301.
2 *ITS Rubber Ltd's Application* [1979] RPC 318.

(iii) Business method

4.09 Similarly, methods of doing business which have a technical effect are now also considered to be patentable. It is possible that where a technical result is achieved (for example, the creation of order in something where there was disorder before) and it can be expressed in general terms and produce a technical result which is useful, then – with the benefit of clever and somewhat disguised claims – a method of doing business can be patented[1].

The following are examples of some applications for patents in relation to e-commerce in different countries around the world:

- A system relating to the facility of making purchases over the Internet by credit card. The buyer registers its credit card number with the vendor. The vendor terminal is able to transmit a part of the registered number to the buyer's terminal, sufficient to enable identification but insufficient for it to be misused by an unauthorised interceptor[2].

- A customer rewards system for purchases made over the Internet[3].

- A system for the purchase of airline tickets in which facilities are provided for users to purchase an 'option to buy' for a certain ticket at a certain price[4].

- A computer system having facility for purchasers to specify the price at which they are willing to buy goods or services[5].

■   BT claims ownership in the hyperlinks that separate pages of information into an interconnected whole. It claims to have filed an application in the US in 1976 which was granted in 1989. If successful, BT would have monopoly over this technology until 2006.

1   *Sohei* ER 209, 907B and *Reuters* EP 407, 0267.
2   Application EP 829,056.
3   *Amazon Inc's Applications* US 5,774,870.
4   *Priceline.com Inc's US Application* US 5,797,127.
5   *Priceline.com Inc's US Application* US 5,794,207.

(c) How do you apply for a patent?

4.10   In the UK, the procedure of application for patents is governed by the PA 1977.

A choice of routes is available for securing a patent. A UK patent can be obtained either through the UK Patent Office or through the EPO in Munich, Germany. It is also possible to enter the systems by filing an international application under the Patent Convention Treaty (PCT). The route to be adopted would depend upon the extent of the territories in which patent protection is required and commercial validity.

If the patent is required only for the UK, then the patent application could be made through the UK Patent Office.

If the patent is required for various countries in Europe, then an application to the EPO may be the most appropriate route. A European patent, which also covers the UK, will be treated as a patent under the UK PA 1977 as if granted by the UK Patent Office. For all practical purposes, a European application ranks as a UK application. The advantage of making a single European application is that, for a single application fee, protection can be obtained in several countries within Europe. The disadvantage is that it has an all-or-nothing outcome. In relation to PCT applications, one application is made for the signatory countries to the Treaty, which in practice are most countries of the world, including the US and Japan.

Generally, whichever route is ultimately adopted, a UK on-line seller will start by making an application by filing the requisite form in the appropriate patent office. The form will need to be accompanied by a patent specification. This is a very important document as it contains the description and the scope of the invention. The invention must be described in such a manner that it can be sufficiently performed by an appropriately skilled person, and clearly sets out the scope of the monopoly sought. A patent specification is an important document and it is best that it be drafted by a patent agent.

Once an application is made, it takes between about a year to 18 months for initial processing. An applicant is also given a grace period, generally a year, to amplify or amend the application without losing priority. It is also within this period that a further application may be lodged in other jurisdictions in reliance upon the priority of the first application. For example, if an application is first made in the UK Patent Office, the date of this application will become the 'priority date' of the patent and, if a further EPO application or PCT application is to be made, it would have to be within 12 months from this date.

The 'priority date' is also the date on which a patent is tested against 'state of the art' to determine whether or not it is new or inventive and this is the date from which the 20-year term of a patent is computed.

The patent application is examined in the relevant patent offices for form and patentability by requesting a search for prior art. After 18 months from the earliest priority date the patent application is published. Assuming the patent application passes through the examination stage, it will be granted. So, a European Patent Application can become a granted patent in up to 23 European countries[1], each one of which enforces it in its own national court.

1   Austria, Belgium, Bulgaria, Cyprus, the Czech Republic, Denmark, Estonia, Finland, France, Germany, Greece, Ireland, Italy, Liechtenstein, Luxembourg, Monaco, The Netherlands, Portugal, Slovakia Spain, Sweden, Switzerland and the UK.

(d) Protection and exploitation

4.11 Having obtained a patent, an on-line seller would want to protect it against any unauthorised use or infringement and would want to exploit it as well.

(i) Infringement

4.12 The fundamental right granted to an owner of a patent is to prevent someone else from infringing it. Acts which amount to infringement of a patent include making, importing or keeping, whether for disposal or otherwise, any product which comes within the scope of any claim of the patent. It is also an infringement to use a patented process within the jurisdiction and to import a product made out of the jurisdiction directly by an infringing process.

Finally, it is also an infringement to import or sell a product which is an essential means for putting an invention into effect, when the infringer knows or it is obvious to a man skilled in the art that the product is intended to be used and is an essential element of the invention as claimed. There is an exception for staple commercial products and dual use products where one use may infringe but where other uses are non-infringing and there is an absence of clear instructions not to use the product in an infringing way.

Patents are territorial in nature. A UK patent is infringed only by acts done in the UK, its territorial waters and the designated continental shelf. If the infringing acts are done in Germany then the patent holder would have to sue in Germany, provided that the patent protection covers Germany as well. A UK patent cannot be enforced in Germany.

There are certain acts that are not considered as infringing acts. These include acts done privately and for non-commercial reasons and acts done for experimental purposes.

The scope of the monopoly granted by a patent will depend on its interpretation. Where the patent product or process has been imitated in its entirety, that would fall within the core of the monopoly. But where it has been imitated partially in an attempt to design around it, then scope of monopoly will become an important issue. A patent is given what is called a purposive construction. This means that a description of the patent is construed more widely than the narrow literal meaning of the words of the claim. This is in order to give effect to the purpose of the patentee determined from the limitations in the claims and the specification (text) of the patent.

The test as to whether a variant comes within the scope of the patent can be characterised as follows:

- Does the variant have a material effect upon the way the invention works? If yes, the variant is outside the claim. If no –

- Would this (that is, that the variant had no material effect) have been obvious at the date of publication of the patent to a reader skilled in the art? If no, the variant is outside the claim. If yes –

- Would the reader skilled in the art nevertheless have understood from the language of the claim that the patentee intended that strict compliance with the primary meaning was an essential requirement of the invention? If yes, the variant is outside the scope of the claim.

(ii) Who is an infringer?

4.13 A person who commissions or directs an infringement may also be an infringer. Mere supply of a product outside the jurisdiction is not an infringement, even where the supplier knows that the product will be imported into the jurisdiction and is an infringement. However, where additional steps are taken by the foreign supplier to secure the UK market for the importer, he may be an infringer. It is not easy to decide where the dividing line lies so as to make a person out of the jurisdiction liable as a tortfeasor.

(iii) Common carriers

4.14 A person is not an infringer merely by transporting someone else's infringing product. The same is applicable to a warehouseman who has no knowledge of the contents of a particular product. So the capacity in which an infringing product is held may be important.

It is likely, but not certain, that a similar view will be taken of an electronic carrier over a public network (for example, an ISP). The question may be whether the carrier uses an infringing programme in the course of his business, in which case there is infringement, or merely acts as a conduit, like a parcel carrier, in which case there is probably no infringement.

It is very unlikely that a carrier such as a network will be liable for a third party offer to supply an infringing product in which the network carrier is not actively participating.

However, where the carrier does work on the signal by reproducing, compressing or modifying it, he may be liable as an infringer of an appropriately worded software or other patent, where the result is transmitted by the carrier into the UK.

(e) Validity

4.15 Even after a patent is granted, it can be revoked on various grounds. A patent often comes under attack in circumstances where the owner of the patent has started proceedings against someone who is believed to be infringing the patent, and the latter in his defence attacks the basis for the original grant.

There are three grounds of invalidity of a patent:

- that the subject matter is not novel;

- that it is not inventive; and

- insufficiency. (This means that the patent specification does not describe the invention clearly enough or completely enough for it to be performed by the person skilled in the art.)

(f) Who can obtain a patent?

4.16 There are three categories of person who can be granted a patent:

- the inventor or the co-inventor;

- the employer of the inventor where the invention is made during the course of employment; and

■ the legal owner of the subject matter – this might, for example, mean an assignee of the original invention. In relation to this third category, where an on-line seller commissions a third party to develop any technology or software, it may well be worth his while to agree that patentable rights in the technology should pass to him by way of an express assignment.

(g) Employee inventions

4.17 The employer is the owner of all rights in an invention made by an employee in the course of his normal or specifically assigned duties provided that an invention might be the reasonable outcome of such duties. Employees in this category would include designers, research and development personnel, computer system designers.

The employer is also entitled to employee inventions where the employee has special obligations to further the interests of the employer's organisation because of the nature of his duties and the particular responsibilities arising from them. Employees occupying senior management positions who owe a general duty and fidelity to the company would be included here, such as the chief technician employed to give technical advice.

It is common practice for employers to include provisions in employment contracts requiring employees to give over rights in all inventions made in relation to the duties performed during the employment. This is always subject to the invention relating to the employer's business, otherwise such a provision may be an unreasonable restraint of trade.

An employee could be entitled to 'compensation', that is, some sort of bonus for any invention made by him even though it is owned by the employer. This situation might arise where the resulting patent is of outstanding benefit to the employer and it is fair that compensation should be awarded. The guarantee of compensation is assessed so as to allow the employee a fair share on an arm's length basis.

(h) Checking what rights exist

4.18 It would be worthwhile for an on-line seller who is involved in the development of an invention or who wishes to adopt a piece of technology to try and find out whether or not it is patented. Under UK law, all patents are by definition registered and the same is true of patents elsewhere. The Register contains many details, including the name, address and title of the patent and details of any licences granted by the patentee for exploitation of the patent. It also tells the enquirer whether the renewal fees to keep the patent in force have been maintained.

This information is useful as it enables a check to be carried out on what patents are in force covering a specific subject matter. The Register would also contain a list of patents applied for. In Europe, there is early publication of patent applications, so searching can be done for any application more than 18 months after its earliest application date. In the US, there is a problem with so-called 'submarine' patents as patent applications are not published and so the first a third party may know about the patent is when it is granted. This problem was once extremely serious, when a US patent was granted just as the same patents elsewhere were expiring. Now, because US patent life is 20 years from the earliest application or 17 years from grant (whichever is the shorter), this is less of a concern.

There are many ways of searching for patents and, as might be expected, searches are now computerised[1]. Most searching vehicles will list all foreign equivalent patents from a single source.

1 See, for example, www.delphion.com.

(i) Dealing with the patents

4.19 Apart from preventing infringement, an owner of a patent may wish to exploit it. A patent is a personal property that may be assigned, mortgaged, licensed or sub-licensed. It is possible either to assign partial rights in the patent or to assign partial rights for a particular field of use or assign rights for a particular territory.

There are two types of licences – exclusive or non-exclusive. An exclusive licence is one under which the licensor agrees not only that he will not grant another licence in relation to the subject matter to any one else in the licensee's territory, but also agrees not to manufacture or use the subject matter of the licence in the territory himself. Also, the exclusive licensee is authorised to take action for infringement. A non-exclusive licence contemplates the grant of similar such licences either in different territories or fields of use, or to several parties (for example, manufacturing rights). The terms and conditions of a licence will depend upon the commercial arrangement between the parties. However, it is important to ensure that there are no terms in the licence that may fall foul of applicable competition laws.

Also, it should be noted that any 'tying' provisions in the licence which require the licensee to obtain additional products or services from the licensor or any of his nominees which the licensee does not want would not be enforceable and would be void.

Generally the owner has the discretion as to whether or not to grant a licence in relation to a patent. However, in certain circumstances the owner can be compelled to grant a licence. Such patent licences are called 'compulsory licences'. The various grounds for granting such licences are:

- if the patent is not being 'commercially worked' in the UK or not being worked to its fullest extent;

- if it is a product patent and the demand for it is not being met on reasonable terms or is being met through imports; or

- if the patent is being prevented from being 'commercially worked' because of imports.

(j) Licences

4.20 Ensuring the information on the Register is kept up to date is particularly important for an assignee or a licensee. There are a number of reasons for this, not least because the Register is conclusive as to its contents, so a second assignee without notice of an earlier assignment takes ahead of the first assignee. Also, an unregistered licensee's rights are ignored and there is a restriction on claiming damages where a licence is not registered within six months of its creation. So, there are real incentives to register patent licences, at least in the UK.

4. TRADE MARKS

(a) Introduction

4.21 Trade marks, and particularly domain names, are extremely valuable e-rights. Chapter 5, E-brand deals with the rapidly growing body of law relating to domain names in more detail. Trade marks, which include signs such as brands, business names, logos, get up as well as domain names, serve as symbols that enable consumers to distinguish the goods or services of one competitor from those of another, and between competing products and services. Trade marks can be built up as extremely valuable assets of any business. Brands and domain names play a significant role in the provision and selling of goods and services and the value of established brands can be most valuable to an e-business. A trade mark may fulfil any of the following functions:

- indication of origin. A trade mark signifies that the goods or services bearing a certain trade mark come from a particular source.

- product differentiation. Trade marks distinguish the goods or services of one trader from those of another.

- quality assurance. Goods or services sold under a particular trade mark are of a certain quality or standard.

- advertising and marketing.

Rights in trade marks can be acquired in two ways – either by registering them in accordance with the provisions of the TMA 1994 or by using them in course of trade in relation to goods or services (in which case they remain as unregistered trade marks). There are several benefits in registering a mark. Registration is a proof of entitlement; monopoly in a mark can be acquired by the party registering it without his having actually used it first; and a third party can be prevented from using it without the registering party having to prove that he has suffered damage or loss.

If the on-line seller intends to use a trade mark on the Internet or expects to provide goods or services or advertise them in various counties, then ideally the trade mark should be registered in as many countries as possible. This implies obtaining separate registrations in various countries, at a potentially huge overall cost. It is, however, possible to make a single application for a Community Trade Mark (CTM) for the 15 EU Member States. Also, registering a trade mark in the home country of the business concerned, as well as in certain relevant jurisdictions where the mark is most used, may in itself provide adequate protection.

(b) Which marks can be registered?

4.22 Any sign which is capable of being represented graphically and of distinguishing goods or services of one trader from those of another may in principle be registered[1]. Such a sign may be words, designs, mixed designs with words, or even a smell, a tune or the distinctive shape of packaging or slogans or logos. On the Internet it is commonly a logo or a word that is used. Generally, ordinary English words are used in domain names. A sign which does not have a capacity to distinguish will not qualify as a registrable trade mark (for example, common words like 'shoe' for shoes or 'soap' for soaps). Long use of a particular sign may render registrable an inherently unregistrable mark, as the mark acquires distinction as a result of that use (for example, geographical words).

1   The TMA 1994, s 1.

(c) Registration

4.23 Where the on-line seller requires protection only for the UK market, his objective would be to obtain UK registration. If the objective is Europe-wide protection then the route would be through the Office of Harmonisation of Internal Market (OHIM) in Alicante, Spain, for a Community Trade Mark.

In the UK there are two routes to registration of a trade mark. A mark can be applied for registration through the UK Patent Office for protection only in the UK or it can be registered as a CTM under European Community law[1] to obtain protection in all Member States.

Apart from the UK or CTM route, an international application could be made through the route of the Paris or Madrid Conventions mentioned in paragraph 4.27.

1 Council Regulation (EC) 40/94.

(i) Registrability

4.24 There are two categories of grounds upon which a trade mark may be refused registration. These apply to UK and CTM applications and are as follows.

So-called 'absolute grounds' of refusal are that the trade mark:

- is devoid of any distinctive character[1];

- consists exclusively of signs or indications which designate the kind, quality, quantity, intended purposes, value, geographical origin, the time of production of goods or rendering services or other characteristics of goods or services; or

- consists exclusively of signs or indications which have become customary in the current language or in the bona fide and established practices of the trade.

So-called 'relative grounds' are the existence of earlier rights in relation to the trade mark sought to be registered or in relation to the goods or services which are sought to be registered.

1 In *eFax.com Inc v Ogelsby* [2000] Masons CLR 28, it was held that 'e-fax' was descriptive in nature, and therefore devoid of distinctive character. But the court commented that the use of 'e'-terminology of this sort was clearly increasing, so that the concept of 'common stock language' could become more difficult to apply in the future, meaning that such marks might in time be capable of registration as distinctive trade marks.

(ii) The UK route

4.25 Applications are made to the Registrar of Trade Marks. Registration can be sought only in relation to those classes of goods or services for which the mark is used or intended to be used.

There are 42 recognised international classes of goods and services – 34 being for goods and eight for services. Each class requires a separate registration, although multi-class registrations are permitted. It is quite possible for the same trade mark to be registered by two separate parties for quite different goods or services, for example 'Prince' for sports goods and for computer services.

A trade mark is examined in the Trade Marks Registry for distinctiveness, where a search is made for prior similar marks and also to verify that the class of goods claimed is correctly stated having regard to what else is on the Register. Prior unregistered rights can also defeat an application to register a trade mark, but it may be difficult for the Registry to determine their existence.

The grant process in the UK takes several months and, in the case of refusal by the Registry, there are appeal procedures. When the application has been accepted by the Registry, it is advertised for opposition. Any person may oppose the grant of a trade mark by lodging a notice of opposition within three months of the advertisement. If there is no opposition to grant, the trade mark will be granted. The registration is then of retrospective effect and is deemed to date from the time of the lodging of the application for registration.

The grounds for opposition at this stage are broadly the same as the grounds on which the Registry can refuse to grant a trade mark in the first place. These include lack of capability of distinguishing the goods or services of the proprietor from those of others, prior vested rights, and that the mark was registered in bad faith.

Opposing the grant of a trade mark registration can take several years. The obvious difficulty is that neither side can be certain of its position and a non-infringing position may become infringing, or the applicant may not have the rights he thought he had. Either way, an opposition can create great commercial uncertainty.

Upon grant, a trade mark is registered for a period of ten years and may then be renewed for a further ten years by payment of renewal fees. However, it can be revoked on various grounds, including that it has not been used for a continuous period of five years or has become non-distinctive or deceptive.

(iii) The Community Trade Mark route

4.26 The Community Trade Mark was set up by the EC Trade Marks Directive[1] and is a system for granting trade marks on an EU-wide basis. It is possible to register a single CTM which applies throughout the EU. The mark has to be available for each of the EU Member States. A single CTM, having all of the features required by the Trade Marks Directive as enshrined into UK domestic law by the TMA 1994, results on grant. However, it is an all-or-nothing grant. If the mark is not available in any Member State for reasons of existence of an earlier identical or similar mark or otherwise, the application will fail in its entirety (that is, in relation to *all* Member States). This does not rule out the possibility of applying for separate national rights by continuing the process through a series of separate national applications, but of course this is likely to be a great deal more expensive to prosecute.

If a CTM is declared invalid after grant either by the OHIM or as a result of a counterclaim on infringement in any national court, the CTM may be disqualified either in its entirety or in respect of only some of the goods and services sought to be covered. It is possible to convert the CTM to a national trade mark. The tests for registrability for CTM applications are the same as for UK applications. After the application is filed, the OHIM examines it and carries out various searches. The CTM search comprises of searching earlier applications or registrations for residential or similar marks in relation to identical or similar goods or services. It also searches the International Register maintained by the World Intellectual Property Organisation (WIPO). Searches are also made at the national trade mark offices of the countries that have elected to operate national searches.

The OHIM only examines the application to ensure that there are no absolute grounds of refusal and does not examine it for relative grounds. These are left to be raised by way of opposition.

After substantive examination, the CTM application is published in the CTM Bulletin. Anyone wishing to oppose the application is entitled to launch opposition proceedings within three months after the publication in the Bulletin.

A CTM mark is registered for ten years and can be renewed at ten-year intervals upon payment of requisite fees, although it is open to revocation.

1   Directive (EEC) 104/89.

(d) International trade mark application systems

4.27 There are two relevant international trade mark convention systems.

(i)   The Paris Convention

4.28 The relevance of this Convention is that it sets up a priority system for trade mark applications, pursuant to which signatories recognise that a trade mark application made in one signatory state can form the basis of priority for a trade mark in another signatory state provided that the latter is applied for within six months of the date of the earliest application of the former. The effect of establishing a priority date is that any event occurring after the priority date does not count for the purpose of invalidating the trade mark.

(ii) The Madrid Convention

4.29 The Madrid System is made up of the Madrid Agreement and the Madrid Protocol. These set up a system, until recently much used by continental European trade mark practitioners, which enables an application to be made in one Member State to carry over to other Member States (and so to have multi-state applications). The UK was not a signatory, because it operated a system by which pre-grant oppositions were permitted. This was not reconcilable with the non-opposition first-to-file systems of continental Europe. The Madrid Convention has now been largely superseded by the Community Trade Mark system.

(e) Should trade marks be applied for first-to-file or first-to-use?

4.30 There is a tension between the two European traditions of trade mark applications. The UK and common law countries grant trade marks on the basis that the person entitled to grant is the first to use the mark, even if the application for registration takes place many years after the first use. The theory is that, as at the date of application, only the mark of the earlier user can have been capable of distinguishing its goods from those of others. In practice, if there are two users of precisely or nearly the same mark and the same goods, neither is likely to be distinctive as at the date of application, so registration may fail. In the UK there is provision for an honest concurrent user, so that the same mark can be registered by two different people for the same goods, but the practice is unsatisfactory as the later applicant needs the consent of the earlier trade mark owner – a consent which is not likely to be given.

Under the alternative system of continental Europe, the first person to apply for registration is entitled to register the mark. This system is not absolute, as registration may be refused or found invalid if there are prior vested rights. However, the fact of registration establishes rights which may prove difficult to dislodge.

(f) Infringement

4.31 As in the case of patents, an owner of a registered trade mark acquires the exclusive right to use it in the territory where it is registered in relation to goods or services for which it is registered, and is entitled to prevent someone else from infringing his rights. The territorial nature of trade mark rights and the global nature of the Internet create unique problems of infringement on the Internet, where the same trade mark may be used by different parties in different jurisdictions. For example, the mark 'Express' in relation to widgets owned by an on-line seller in the UK may be used on a website which is available in the US, where 'Express', also in relation to widgets, is used by someone else. This could raise cause of complaint of trade mark infringement in the US. The approach of the courts in such situations has been to consider the degree to which the website targets a particular jurisdiction before adjudicating whether the use is an infringement.

An on-line seller can take some steps to prevent such conflicts:

- if he is aware that his trade mark is registered by somebody else in another jurisdiction, he should ensure that the website clarifies that it is not targeted at individuals in the conflicting jurisdiction;

- he should not accept orders or enquiries from prospective customers in that jurisdiction;

- he should acknowledge the rights of the other party in the conflicting jurisdiction.

In the UK, acts that are considered acts of infringement are the application of the mark or sign to unauthorised goods, their packaging, advertising materials, business papers, circulars (and similar materials which relate to the goods). In the case of e-commerce, this includes advertisements and offers for the goods on the Internet and electronic order forms. The unauthorised use of a domain name is a matter discussed in Chapter 5, E-brand. It is also an infringement to import materials with an infringing sign on them. The test of infringement is the comparison between the mark as registered and the sign as used by the defendant. The packaging around the use is irrelevant. The comparison is mark for mark, regardless of extraneous factors, not mark against the packaging as a whole. That is the purview of the common law tort of passing off (see paragraph 4.44).

4.32 There are three sets of circumstances which constitute trade mark infringement:

- using an identical mark registered in relation to goods or services identical to which it is registered;

- using an identical mark in relation to similar goods or services for which it has been registered, a similar mark in relation to identical goods or services for which it has been registered, or a similar mark for similar goods or services to those for which it has been registered. In each case there is a requirement that the use of the offending sign causes or is likely to cause confusion with the claimant's mark. Mere association with the registered mark is not sufficient;

- using an identical or a similar mark in relation to goods or services which are dissimilar to the goods or services for which the mark has been registered, provided that the reputation of the registered mark is such that it would take unfair advantage of or is detrimental to the character or reputation of the registered mark except in accordance with honest business practices[1].

'Similar goods' in this context means goods likely to be thought of as being in the same category as each other. The infringer need not be applying a trade mark of his own, provided that what he has used is a sign of some sort in relation to goods or services which engenders the confusion with the infringed mark. This point is illustrated by the following case study.

Case Study – Same or similar name trade mark infringement claim

The trade mark Beefy is registered in Class 29 for meat pies containing beef and for these purposes we should assume that the mark has been in use sufficiently long for it to have obtained a secondary meaning: namely, to consumers it means meat pies containing beef from the manufacturer who is the owner of the mark.

Scenario 1: The defendant sells meat pies containing beef under the mark 'Beefy' This is clear infringement as an identical mark is used in relation to identical goods.

Scenario 2: The defendant sells 'Beefy' meat pies containing lamb but no beef In this case the issue is whether meat pies containing lamb are similar goods to meat pies containing beef. The question is one of fact, in which burden of proof is on the claimant. The issue is how products are sold. In this example the overwhelming likelihood is that, since lamb pies and beef pies are likely to be sold from the same freezer and next to each other in a supermarket, they are likely to be similar products. The test which has to be satisfied is whether lamb pies and beef pies are goods of the same description. As this test is liable to be satisfied, it is likely that there will be infringement provided that the claimant can also show a likelihood of confusion by consumers, which includes a likelihood of association with the mark.

By contrast, crockery sold under the name 'Beefy' is unlikely to satisfy the above test. Even if there is a likelihood of association of the defendant's mark with the mark which has been registered, that will only be sufficient where there is also a likelihood of confusion. So, if the consumer is not confused, there will be no infringement under this head.

Scenario 3: The defendant sells beef pies under the trade mark 'Beefeater' In this case, also under section 10(2) of the TMA 1994, the goods are the same, but the mark is only similar to the registered mark. The claimant must prove that the defendant's use of its mark gives rise to the likelihood of confusion, including likelihood of association with the registered mark. It is a question of fact which the claimant must prove as to whether the defendant's use is going to give rise to a likelihood of confusion. This is usually proved by a combination of survey and oral evidence. The comparison is mark for mark.

Scenario 4: The defendant sells 'Beefo' brand cat and dog food In this scenario where the use is of a similar mark and similar goods, at least as the claimant would allege, the question of infringement is governed by section 10(3) of the TMA 1994. The question under section 10(3) is whether the claimant's mark is sufficiently well known and the use made of it by the defendant takes unfair advantage of the reputation of the mark. This is equivalent to a famous mark right. It will be a question of fact and argument in each case as to whether the claimant's mark is sufficiently famous that a significant number of people think that the defendant's product, although not put on similar goods to the goods for which the mark is registered, originates from or is licensed by the claimant. Such an enquiry is never likely to be easy, involving, as it would, both the establishment of the extent of the claimant's reputation in his own mark and the use by the defendant being such as to give rise to the generally held belief amongst the public (and therefore the judge) that the use is unfair.

1   The TMA 1994, s 10.

(g) Defences

4.33   Certain uses of a registered trade mark will not amount to infringement and will be valid defences in any action for infringement.

The use of the following marks is permitted even if there is a conflict with a registered mark, provided they are used in accordance with most commercial practice:

- a person's own name or address;

- indications of kind, quality, quantity, intended purpose, value, geographical origin, time of production or rendering, or other characteristics of goods and services;

- the mark itself, where it is intended to indicate the purpose of the product or service; or

- use for an honest descriptive purpose[1].

We will examine some of these in more detail.

1   The TMA 1994, s 11.

(i)   Descriptive quality

4.34   Section 11(2) of the TMA 1994 states that it is not an infringement of a registered trade mark to use the trade mark to describe the kind, quality, contents or origin of goods. So, referring back to the case study (paragraph 4.32), a description of a meat product as 'beefy' may well be considered to relate to a normal English use of the word describing the quality of the contents. The conflict becomes particularly acute where the alleged infringement is of the 'identical mark on identical goods' variety because, as we have seen, there is typically no need for the claimant to demonstrate likelihood of confusion or association. The issue is also important because a claimant must prove infringement under section 10, but the defendant has the onus of establishing the defence under section 11.

The use of the sign to describe the claimant's goods must be in accordance with honest business practices. It would therefore follow that, in the case study example above, if the product was not 'beefy' (whatever this is held by the court to mean, but let us assume that the word conveys the impression of the associated product being fibrous and looking like beef), a trade mark infringement could be upheld on the grounds that the defendant was not honestly describing the quality or other attributes of the contents. This conclusion raises problems since, in effect, it indicates an interaction between the TMA 1994 and the Trades Descriptions Act 1968, which is an area of the law that still has to be fully explored.

(ii) Legitimate use

4.35   Use of a third party mark is legitimate where such use is necessary to describe the third party's goods, the person using the mark does not take unfair advantage of the mark and the use is in accordance with honest business practices.

This category of use arises in two different contexts. These are:

- **Where spare parts or associated parts are being described** However, there is a distinction between describing, for example, non-genuine razor blades as blades for Gillette razors (which is permitted) and describing them as Gillette razor blades (which remains impermissible as a false statement of origin). Further, in the list of products for which the part in question is suitable, undue prominence should not be given to the product of one manufacturer over and above the products of all the manufacturers, otherwise the description will not be in accordance with honest business practices. An on-line seller who offers genuine products under brand names on its websites would be entitled to do so. If a repairer of 'Zanussi' or 'Bosch' appliances advertises simply that, he does not infringe Zanussi's or Bosch's trademarks; but if he adopts either of these brand names as his trading name then there is no defence of legitimate use. Similarly, if he represents or advertises that he is an authorised dealer or repairer of 'Bosch' or 'Zanussi' when he is not, this is not legitimate use.

- **Comparative advertising** Section 10(6) of the TMA 1994 permits use of a registered trade mark to identify goods as those of the owner of the trade mark. The burden of proving infringement and all its elements lies on the person alleging infringement. It is a question of fact as to whether a comparison is fair. The court will consider the advertisement as a whole. If the comparison is fair, weighted for what really matters to the audience, then there will be no infringement even though the claimant's product or service is mentioned by name. If it is not fair or is significantly misleading, then the use of the mark will not be in accordance with honest practices in business, and the court is likely to hold that an infringement has occurred.

There have been many comparative advertising cases which set out what is thought to be fair. It is an issue of balance as to what the consumer would want to know. A misleading advertisement which takes unfair advantage of the distinctive character or repute of the registered mark will be an infringement. For products which are price-sensitive, such as credit cards and mobile telephone charges, a comparison of charges or interest rates is likely to be, and has been held to be, fair – provided the comparisons are fair and accurate. The test of honesty is objective. The test of honest business practice is set high enough that there is a real hurdle to climb to establish honesty, but not so high as to preclude most comparative advertising. A more detailed discussion of this area can be found in Chapter 5, E-brand.

(h) Harmonisation and exhaustion of rights

4.36 One of the more important issues for an on-line seller is to determine the degree to which he can service orders from outside his home country or, conversely, restrict others from selling into his exclusive territory. Where the on-line seller is an official distributor, he will obviously need to check the express terms of his distribution agreement to see whether he can sell goods outside his contractual territory. This would also apply to a manufacturer who may have granted exclusive rather than sole distribution rights to third parties in particular territories. Although these contractual issues are often important, most disputes are in relation to the rights to resell goods which are bought legitimately from a manufacturer/distributor/reseller but are then exported (that is, by a parallel importer). In such cases, there is likely not to be any contractual nexus between the trade mark owner and the importer, and the extent to which the parallel importer can resell the imported legitimate goods will be determined by the existence of intellectual property rights in the territory, usually trade marks and/or patent rights.

Many large and small corporations may trade in more than one country of the world. Very few trade under different trade marks in different countries, although different trade marks may be used within different trading blocs. It is virtually impossible to ensure uniformity of pricing within one country, let alone across a trading bloc, or across the world. The effect is that cheaper goods manufactured or sold in a low cost country will move to markets in a high cost country. This is called parallel importing or grey goods.

Because intellectual property rights are national in character, it is important to consider the principle known as 'exhaustion of rights': to what extent does use by the trade mark owner in one country of his mark on goods exhaust the rights of the owner elsewhere in relation to those goods? What it means is that the owner of rights in respect of a product put on the market in, say, France with its trade mark cannot use its trade mark rights to stop that product being imported into England.

The question which is always raised is, 'What can be done to stop or limit parallel imports?'. This poses a number of further questions:

■ are all intellectual property rights treated the same?

■ are goods from all sources treated the same?

■ what is the position on repackaged goods marked with a trade mark?

The short answer to the first question is that not all intellectual property rights are treated in the same way. Neither are all geographic areas treated in the same way. In Europe, the important distinction is between goods first put on the market in the EU or the European Economic Area (EEA) with the consent or licence of the owner of the intellectual property right, and those which were not. The principle of exhaustion of rights applies throughout the EEA in respect of goods first put on the market anywhere in the EEA by the owner of the right or with his consent. It may also apply to goods put on the market by the owner of the rights or with his consent elsewhere and subsequently imported into the EEA. A trade mark is regarded as a badge or certificate of origin, so that it certifies where the goods came from.

4.37 The doctrine of exhaustion of rights has long applied within the EEA, so goods put onto the market in one Member State (State A) by the rights owner or with his consent (that is, by a licence) can circulate freely into another Member State (State B):

■ where there are parallel rights in States A and B; and

■ where the right subsists in State A, whether or not such a right is available in State B.

These rules have applied irrespective of the nature of the right involved (trade mark, patent, copyright). The exception has been in respect of rental rights for videotape and the like, where it has been held that putting a pre-recorded videotape on the market in one Member State where rental rights do not exist does not exhaust rental rights in Member States where such rights do exist.

There are three types (or, perhaps, degrees) of exhaustion:

- no exhaustion at all, so that the putting of a product on the market by the rights owner does not act as a bar to him using the parallel rights to stop importation of that product;

- local exhaustion of rights within a limited geographic area, so goods are free-traded within that area, but parallel imports from outside the area can be prevented by the rights owner (the EEA is a typical example of such a limited free trade area); and

- international exhaustion, where once the goods have been put on the market anywhere by the rights owner or with his consent, they may be freely traded elsewhere no matter their origin.

The rules that protect free trade within the EU and EEA mean that parallel rights may not be used to impede the free movement of goods within the EU and EEA. The position regarding the relationship between the EU/EEA and the rest of the world is more complex: where there is a pan-European harmonised right, local exhaustion applies, and where the rights owner's goods are put on the market outside the EU/EEA by the rights owner or with its consent, it can probably use its right to stop the parallel import from outside the EU/EEA. Trade marks are an example of just such a harmonised right and some elements of copyright are harmonised.

By contrast, where there is no pan-European harmonisation, as is the case with patents, each Member State is entitled to decide whether to apply local or international exhaustion. As some EU Member States, including the UK, apply international exhaustion to such rights, the standard tends to be international exhaustion, due to the free movement of goods provisions.

(i) Parallel imports from outside the EU

4.38 The UK courts and many other EU courts have traditionally taken a liberal view of importation of goods from outside the EU, applying the doctrine of exhaustion of rights worldwide and not just within the EU. So, in the UK, in many trade mark cases it has been held that provided the goods were put on the market by the trade mark owner or with his consent, they could be imported into the UK.

One might have thought that the sensible view is that if the same mark can be applied by any member of a group of companies forming a multinational whole, the man in the street who sees a trade mark on the goods of a multinational will not be concerned with the fine detail of the group structure. But some courts have unfortunately pulled in a different direction. Until recently, Germany held the same liberal interpretation of exhaustion of rights as the UK. More recently, however, its jurisprudence has undergone a volte-face. In several cases there, and in The Netherlands, the courts have held that, in respect of trade marks, the principle of exhaustion is limited to trade within the EEA and does not apply to trade from outside the EEA into the EEA.

These injunctions preventing parallel importing have been justified on the basis of article 7(1) of the EU Trade Marks Directive[1] and the national statutes which have been adapted to conform to it.

Article 7(1) reads:

> 'The trade mark shall not entitle the proprietor to prohibit its use in relation to goods which have been put on the market in the [EEA] under that trade mark by the proprietor or with his consent.'

Since the exception is limited to goods put on the market in the EEA, the argument is that it does not apply to goods put on the market outside the EEA and hence goods from outside the EEA do not take the benefit of the doctrine. This view has been upheld by the European Court of Justice and so it is an infringement of a trade mark registered in the EU to market genuine products bought outside the EU. This conclusion has been subjected to so much criticism, however, that a change in European law to reverse its effect cannot be discounted.

1   Directive (EEC) 104/89.

(i)   Harmonisation, exhaustion and e-commerce

4.39   The doctrine of exhaustion of rights has important implications for the Internet and e-commerce. It may be argued that merely being able to access a web page displaying a trade mark may be an infringement of the trade mark owner's rights. It will certainly be argued that an offer to supply goods of the trade mark owner marked with its trade mark across boundaries where harmonisation does not apply (for example, from the US into the EEA) is a trade mark infringement and so can be stopped. The law is not clear in this regard, but this seems to be the current view. It follows that goods offered for supply across harmonisation boundaries (for example, US into the UK) should be offered free on board, ex works or ex retailer, so that the import is a private import and the issue of infringement of rights by importation becomes solely the customer's problem (since he is unlikely to be sued) rather than that of the retailer (who is vulnerable to a lawsuit).

The position with respect to services is also that where a service has to be provided across a harmonisation boundary, then the trade mark or copyright owner may well be able to sue for infringement, as his local rights are not exhausted. This could be a particular problem where trade marks for services are licensed. The problem can be manifested both ways: where a licensor provides services into the territory of his exclusive licensee (which is a breach of contract) and where the licensee provides the services into an unlicensed territory (which is an infringement, as well as probably being a breach of contract).

(j)   Repackaging

4.40   The position of a trade mark owner is complicated by the prohibition, except for good cause, against using different trade marks in different Member States to divide the Single European Market. The same principle applies to the prohibition on using regulatory devices to divide markets. Laid on top of the general rules relating to parallel imports under the doctrine of exhaustion of rights, and of particular importance to trade mark owners, is the extent to which parallel importers have the right to repack trade marked goods (for example, by repackaging into smaller packets) and to sell them under or by reference to the original trade mark by re-affixing the same.

The governing rule is that a trade mark acts as a certificate of origin. This means that a customer can be certain that the goods have not been subsequently interfered with in a way that may impair their quality, including the quality of the packaging. This fundamental right conferred in the trade mark owner overrides the principle of free movement of goods enshrined in article 36 of the Treaty of Rome, pursuant to which the doctrine of exhaustion of rights was developed within Europe.

(i)   Rules relating to repackaging

4.41   Rules relating to the application and use of the original trade mark owner's trade mark on the repackaging of goods have now been established. Use of the original trade mark owner's mark will be permitted where:

- reliance on the trade mark right by the owner, having regard to the market system he has adopted, will contribute to the artificial partitioning of the markets between Member States;

- it is shown that repackaging cannot adversely affect the original condition of the goods;

- the owner of the mark receives prior notice before the repackaged product is put on sale; and

- it is stated on the packaging by whom the product has been repacked.

The burden of proof is on the parallel importer to show it has satisfied these requirements.

The European Court of Justice has recently examined these issues and put forward the following propositions:

- there is no requirement to prove the parallel importer has deliberately set out to divide the market – it is sufficient that there is a division by reason, for example, of markets preferring different sized or formatted packs;

- the repackaging must be necessary or appropriate to enable the parallel import to take place at all;

- provided the operations of the parallel importer are such that they involve no risk to the product (for example, by removing only the outer packaging or blister packs without exposing the contents to any risk of contamination);

- provided no important information relating to the product is omitted from the repacked product or is misleading on the new packaging;

- the new packaging clearly states who repackaged the product in a way that an ordinary careful person examining the packaging is not misled;

- the presentation of the product is not so poor as to damage the reputation of the trade mark owner, that is the packaging must not be defective, of poor quality, or untidy;

- where there is an extra article with the repackaged product, the importer must not give the impression that the trade mark owner has anything to do with that additional product; and

- the importer gives notice to the trade mark owner before the repackaged product is put on sale and, on demand, supplies him with a sample of the repackaged product.

Each of the above questions of fact are for the national court to determine. The ultimate issue is whether the consumer is being deceived as to the origin of the goods or their actual or potential condition on sale.

The principles in relation to a mark as a sign of origin and quality were also used by the European Court of Justice to defeat the argument of a trade mark owner that the exception to article 7(1) of the Trade Marks Directive (that is, that the principle of exhaustion of rights applies within the EEA) does not apply where legitimate reasons arise for not applying it, especially where the condition of the goods has been changed or impaired after they have been put on the market. It was held that this exception provides relative rights and it is a question of fact for the national court whether this condition has been met, having regard to the above principles.

(k) Trade marks as property

4.42 Trade marks can be bought and sold, assigned or charged as property. The Trade Marks Register contains many details helpful to the enquirer, including the name and address of the trade mark, the mark itself and details of any licences granted. It also tells the enquirer whether the renewal fees to keep the trade mark in force have been maintained.

This information is useful as it enables a check to be carried out on what trade marks are in force and where, covering specific classes. As trade marks are classified according to their subject matter, this also enables a search for subsisting registered marks to be carried out.

There are many ways of searching for registered trade marks and, as might be expected, searches are now computerised. Some searching vehicles will list some foreign equivalent trade marks. Searching for device marks is more difficult.

The comments in relation to the Patents Register made at paragraph 4.18 are equally applicable to the Trade Marks Register.

(l) Invalidity, revocation and non-use

4.43 A trade mark may be found invalid or may be revoked. The difference is important: revocation is backdated only to the date on which the application to revoke was made, so it may still be possible to have infringed a revoked trade mark. Invalidity means that the trade mark never should have been registered, so dates back to the time of application.

The grounds for invalidity are the same as those for refusal to grant a trade mark and for opposing the grant. The primary ground for revocation is that the trade mark has not been used and there is no reasonable excuse for the non-use. There must have been five years' continuous non-use, starting with the date on which the formalities for grant were completed, which is the earliest date from which non-use runs, but resumed use within three months of the date of the application for revocation does not count as use. This is because otherwise the trade mark owner could resume use after a warning letter and save his trade mark. Any use to oppose the revocation application must be a genuine commercial use. What that amounts to is a question of fact in each case. Non-use where there is a genuine commercial reason will be excused.

5.   PASSING OFF

(a) The localisation of common law and statutory trade mark protection

4.44 English law has always recognised local goodwill and provided protection by means of actions for passing off. It has also recognised unregistered trade marks. Both depend on the existence of local rights.

The law of passing off is well established and is designed to prevent one trader trading off the goodwill of another (the more precise features of passing off are set out below). Precedent shows that the broader the trader's goodwill, the wider the relief to which he will be entitled. The trade mark Kodak for bicycles, although unregistered, has been the subject of a successful passing off action[1].

English courts, however, have been unwilling to recognise foreign goodwill in respect of unregistered marks. In *Athletes Foot Marketing Associates Inc v Cobra Sports Ltd*[2] the Athlete's Foot mark for sports shoe stores was well known in the US. The mark was known in the UK, but the claimant did not trade in the UK and, as a result, it had no protectable goodwill. That case is typical of very many in which the English courts have failed to recognise foreign goodwill. The law was recently reviewed in *Jian Tools for Sales Ltd v Roderick Manhattan Group Ltd*[3].

1 *Eastman Photographic Materials Co Ltd v John Griffiths Cycle Corpn Ltd* (1898) 15 RPC 105.
2 [1980] RPC 343.
3 [1995] FSR 924.

(b) Passing off defined

4.45 Passing off in English law is tantamount to a tort of unfair competition and protects unregistered trade marks. Technically, passing off actions protect the goodwill in the mark as a matter of property. The fundamental definition is that no man may pass off his goods or services as those of another. That definition was expanded in two leading cases, popularly referred to as the *Jif Lemon* case[1], and in the older *Advocaat* case[2].

In *Jif Lemon*, passing off was defined in terms of three elements which a claimant has to prove for his claim to succeed. These are:

- that there is a goodwill or reputation attached to the goods or services of the claimant in the mind of the purchasing public by association with their appearance or presentation;

- that there has been a misrepresentation to the public likely to lead the public to believe the goods or services offered by the defendant were the goods or services of the claimant; and

- that the claimant is suffering or is likely to suffer damage by reason of the erroneous belief engendered by the defendant's misrepresentation. Whether or not the public is aware of the claimant's identity as the manufacturer or supplier of the goods in question is irrelevant, as long as the goods are identified with a particular source.

1 *Reckitt & Colman Products Ltd v Borden Inc (Jif Lemon)* [1990] 1 All ER 873, [1990] RPC 341, HL.
2 *Erven Warnink Besloten Vennootschap v J Townend & Sons (Hull) Ltd (Advocaat)* [1979] AC 731, HL.

(c) The definition of goodwill

4.46 Goodwill was classically defined almost 100 years ago as follows[1]:

'What is goodwill? It is a thing very easy to describe, very difficult to define. It is the benefit and advantage of the good name, reputation and connection of a business. It is the attractive force which brings in custom ... The goodwill of a business must emanate from a particular centre or source. However widely extended or diffused its influence may be, goodwill is worth nothing unless it has power of attraction sufficient to bring customers home to the source from which it emanates ...

If there is one attribute common to all cases of goodwill it is the attribute of locality. For goodwill has no independent existence. It cannot subsist by itself. It must be attached to a business. Destroy the business, and the goodwill perishes with it, although elements would remain which may perhaps be gathered up and revived again.'

It follows that if there are no customers there is no goodwill, and if there is no goodwill, it cannot be harmed, so an element essential to a passing off action is missing.

1 *IRC v Muller & Co's Margarine Ltd* [1901] AC 217, HL.

(d) The territorial nature of passing off

4.47 This is a very important issue for e-commerce, as brands which are unregistered in a local jurisdiction are suddenly accessible to the public in a different country, so the question is whether a person who has no local business can still protect his rights.

In the *Advocaat* case, Lord Fraser stated[1] that for the cause of action to subsist, 'the claimant must be a member of the class of those who sell the goods and who is the owner of goodwill *in England*[2] which is of substantial value' (*emphasis added*).

The fundamental question of territoriality was posed most clearly in the *Athlete's Foot* case[3], where Walton J posed the question, 'What connection with this country is required before a claimant can successfully maintain an action for passing off?' The judge generalised the answer in the following terms:

> 'it would appear to me that, as a matter of principle, no trader can complain of passing off as against him in any territory – and it will usually be defined by national boundaries, although it is well conceivable in the modern world that it will not – in which he has no customers, nobody who is in a trade relation with him. This will normally shortly be expressed by saying that he does not carry on any trade in that particular country (obviously, for present purposes, England and Wales) but the inwardness of it will be that he has no customers in that country: no people who buy his goods or make use of his services (as the case may be) there'[4].

1　[1979] AC 731, HL.
2　England is referred to in this dictum, as this was an English case. The same principles apply elsewhere in the UK.
3　[1980] RPC 343.
4　In support of that proposition Walton J relied on a significant body of prior case law, namely *IRC v Muller & Co's Margarine Ltd* [1901] AC 217, HL; *Anciens Etablissements Panhard et Levassor SA v Panhard Levassor Motor Co Ltd* [1901] 2 Ch 513; *Ewing v Buttercup Margarine Co Ltd* [1917] 2 Ch 1, CA; *Poiret v Jules Poiret Ltd* (1920) 37 RPC 1773; *R & J Pullman Ltd v Pullman* (1919) 36 RPC 240; *R J Reuter Co Ltd v Muhlens* (1953) 70 RPC 235; *T Oertli AG v E J Bowman (London) Ltd* [1957] RPC 388, CA; affd [1959] RPC 1, HL; *Sheraton Corpn of America v Sheraton Motels Ltd* [1964] RPC 202; *Alain Bernardin et Cie v Pavilion Properties Ltd* ('Crazy Horse') [1967] RPC 581; *Amway Corpn v Eurway International Ltd* [1974] RPC 82; *Globelegance BV v Sarkissian* [1974] RPC 603; *Star Industrial Co Ltd v Yap Kwee Kor* [1976] FSR 256, PC; *Baskin-Robbins Ice Cream Co v Gutman* [1976] FSR 545; *Maxims Ltd v Dye* [1977] 1 WLR 1155 and *C & A Modes v C & A (Waterford) Ltd* [1978] FSR 126.

(e)　Passing off without a local business

4.48　Passing off actions protect goodwill and, as the cases examined above indicate, to have goodwill protectable in England a person normally has to have customers in England as well. However, there has been some relaxation of that strict position. This arises where the goodwill is so strong that, despite having no business in the UK, the owner of the goodwill has customers in the UK.

This was raised in *Baskin-Robbins Ice Cream Co v Gutman*[1]:

> 'It may well be very difficult if not normally impossible for a claimant to establish such a reputation of goodwill to support a passing off action without showing he has used his mark for get up in this country.

> Some businesses are, however, to a greater or lesser extent truly international in character and the reputation and goodwill attaching to them cannot in fact help being international also. Some national boundaries such as for example those which are members of the EEC are in this respect becoming ill defined and uncertain as modern travel and Community Rules make the world grow smaller. I believe myself that the true legal position is best expressed by the general proposition ... that the existence and the extent of the claimant's reputation and goodwill in every case is one of fact however it may be proved and whatever it is based on.'

This approach was followed in *C & A Modes v C & A (Waterford) Ltd*[2]. In that case, the claimant did not operate from business premises in the Republic of Ireland (the location in suit) but did have a very substantial number of customers in the Republic. The court held that the claimant had sufficient customers to claim a vested right to retain and expand that custom, no matter where the claimant's business was based. The claimant was held to be entitled to be protected against that custom being taken away or dissipated by someone whose deceptive conduct is calculated to create confusion of identity in the minds of existing or potential customers.

1　[1976] FSR 545.
2　[1978] FSR 126.

(f) Summary of passing off

4.49 In *Athlete's Foot* Walton J stated the position in law on the territorial nature of passing off to be 'relatively clear'. He said:

'That is to say, it does not matter that the claimants are not at present actually carrying on business in this country, providing they have customers here. Equally, it is of no moment, if they have no customers here, that they have a reputation in the general sense of the word in this country. It is also of no moment that the reputation may have been brought about by advertising: this can be of no moment unless it brings in customers, when, of course, there is once again no need to rely upon it.'

That proposition of law has not been seriously challenged in the 20 years since it was expounded. In the law of passing off, goodwill is local, and without local goodwill in the form of a UK presence or at least British customers, there is no goodwill capable of protection. This formulation was considered by Knox J in *Jian Tools for Sales Inc v Roderick Manhattan Group Ltd*[1], where he held that:

- in order to succeed in a passing off action, a foreign claimant who does not have a place of business in the UK must at least show that he has customers in the UK;

- the nature of the goods or services provided by the claimant was to be taken into account when deciding whether the customer base in the UK was sufficient to support goodwill locally situate within the jurisdiction; and

- in assessing the customer base, sales generated by foreign sources (such as advertising in foreign publications) were to be disregarded.

1 [1995] FSR 924.

(g) Extra protection for famous marks

4.50 This is of importance for domain name protection and for protecting famous foreign marks. If the owner of the foreign goodwill has registered a trade mark but not used it and the trade mark is famous in the UK, he may have additional protection. The UK has finally honoured its treaty obligation under the Paris Convention, art 6[bis] through section 56 of the TMA 1994. This provision is of direct applicability to famous marks[1]. Section 56 reads as follows:

'(1) References in this Act to a trade mark which is entitled to protection under the Paris Convention as a well-known trade mark are to a mark which is well known in the United Kingdom as being the mark of a person who—
    (a) is a national of a Convention country, or
    (b) is domiciled in, or has a real and effective industrial or commercial establishment in, a Convention country,
    whether or not that person carries on business, or has any goodwill, in the United Kingdom. References to the proprietor of such a mark shall be construed accordingly.
(2) The proprietor of a trade mark which is entitled to protection under the Paris Convention as a well-known trade mark is entitled to restrain by injunction the use in the United Kingdom of a trade mark which, or the essential part of which, is identical or similar to his mark, in relation to identical or similar goods or services, where the use is likely to cause confusion.
    This right is subject to s 48 (effect of acquiescence by proprietor of earlier trade mark).
(3) Nothing in subs (2) affects the continuation of any bona fide use of a trade mark begun before the commencement of this section.'

The law therefore now provides that:

- the mark must be well known in the UK (if it is well known elsewhere, that does not count);

- there is no need for any local business or goodwill to support a well-known mark in the UK;

- protection is (apparently) extended to include unregistered trade marks[2];

- to be actionable, the defendant's use must be likely to cause confusion.

There has been one failed case[3] in England and one successful case in South Africa[4] in relation to this conception. In the South African *McDonald's* case, the claimant, the well-known fast food franchiser, had registered 52 trade marks in South Africa, but had not traded in or used any of the trade marks. The McDonald's trade marks were held on the evidence to be well known in the Republic of South Africa[5]. McDonald's therefore retained their trade mark registrations even though they had no business in South Africa. Once established, this proved fatal for the defendants, Joburgers, and their applications for registration were refused. McDonald's accordingly obtained a permanent injunction to restrain infringement of their marks. It was therefore apparent that, in a broad sense, McDonald's had goodwill because there were many people in South Africa who would have purchased from the real McDonald's without the need for advertising.

1   Trade Marks Directive, art 4(2)(d).
2   By section 2(2) of the TMA 1994, the right to prevent infringement or recover damages is limited to trade marks registered under the Act. A trade mark is widely defined in section 1(1) as any sign capable of being represented graphically and of distinguishing goods or services of one undertaking from those of another. Section 56 uses the term 'mark'. This is probably loose drafting, but appears to open up more scope in passing off.
3   *Philips Electronics BV v Remington Consumer Products* [1998] RPC 283. This case related to a registered trade mark to Philips' well-known three-headed electric shaver. Remington introduced a rival product with three heads. The case failed because no confusion was proved and, anyway, section 56 does not cover three-dimensional products.
4   *McDonald's Corpn v Joburgers Drive-Inn Restaurant (Pty) Ltd* 1997 (1) SA 1.
5   It is significant for this purpose that the South African Trade Marks Act, s 35(1) is the same as the TMA 1994, s 56(1).

(i)   *Famous marks and passing off compared*

4.51   Section 56 of the TMA 1994 puts the claimant who has a reputation in a famous mark but no business presence in the UK in the same position as if he had an operation there. It does not extend to protect a claimant from non-deceptive use of its mark, but neither does passing off. So, it puts the owner of a famous registered trade mark in a slightly better position than the owner of a famous unregistered mark. The former does not need to prove the existence of local customers, whereas the latter does to have any hope of protection in the absence of a local business.

6.   COPYRIGHT

4.52   More than any other form of intellectual property, copyright works will constitute much of the valuable subject matter of e-commerce. An on-line seller is bound to use various copyright works on a website, such as graphics, texts, animations, video clips, HTML coding, photographs, etc. Such features are all capable of being protected by copyright. Digital technology facilitates transmission and use of a wide range of information and products in digital form over interactive networks. Transmission of text, data, commentaries, music, images and other material is commonplace and it is only a matter of time, with the increasing availability of broadbrand technology, until films, television programmes and sporting fixtures (such as football matches) will be commonly available on the Internet as well.

Unlike patents and trade marks, copyright protection does not confer a monopoly. It grants to the owner the right to prevent any third party from copying or doing any of the other 'restricted acts' (detailed below) to the work (see 'Scope of copyright' at paragraph 4.61) without permission of the right owner.

Another significant difference between copyright on the one hand and patent and registered trade marks on the other is that copyright applies automatically upon creation to all types of original expression provided various conditions are met (also detailed in paragraph 4.54 below).

Copyright protection does not prevent the copying of mere ideas; it prevents the copying of the permanent forms (such as printed page, film, computer programme) in which ideas are expressed.

In order for a work to be protected by copyright it must be (a) original and (b) recorded in permanent form, for example writing or otherwise (such as film, audio or video tape or computer disk). 'Original' does not mean that the work must be an expression of original or inventive thought but that the expression must be original and created by the author and not copied (thus, for example, an arrangement or edition of an eighteenth century piece of music which is produced today can be the copyright work of the arranger or editor, even though the original music will not be protected by copyright).

Copyright as applied to a specific end product is apt to describe a bundle of different rights. Thus, for example, a website may well embody text, graphics, sounds, video clips, HTML codes, software, etc. Each of these components may be the copyright work of one or more persons, and the right protecting each of those works may have a different duration or other characteristics different from the others.

(a) Copyright legislation

4.53 The law relating to copyright in the UK is based on statute. In 1988 the law was consolidated into the CDPA 1988, which came into force on 31 July 1989. A significant number of features of the CDPA 1988 carry across from earlier legislation and it covers a very broad area including:

- traditional copyright;

- design right;

- moral rights; and

- the copyright tribunal.

The provisions of the CDPA 1988 have been amended as a result of EC Directives in the copyright field. These Directives, and the legislation implementing them in the UK, are:

- Directive (EEC) 250/91 on the legal protection of computer programs, implemented by the Copyright (Computer Programs) Regulations 1992[1], which came into force on 1 January 1993. This requires computer programs to be treated as literary works for copyright purposes.

- Directive (EEC) 100/92 on rental, lending and neighbouring rights in the copyright field, and Directive (EEC) 83/93 on copyright and related rights in relation to cable retransmission and satellite broadcasting, both implemented by the Copyright and Related Rights Regulations 1996[2], which came into force on 1 December 1996.

- Directive (EEC) 98/93 on the Copyright Duration and related rights, implemented by the Duration of Copyright and Rights in Performances Regulations 1995[3], which came into force on 1 January 1996. This harmonises upwards the terms of authors' rights to the highest terms in a Member State, namely the author's own life plus 70 years.

- Directive (EC) 9/96 on the Legal Protection of Databases, implemented by the Copyright and Rights in Databases Regulations 1997[4], which came into force on 1 January 1998. This introduces protection of databases as a sui generis right and is further discussed in section 7 below.

■ Directive (EEC) 94/98 on the legal protection of conditional access services, which was implemented by sections 297A and 298 of the CDPA 1988.

■ Directive (EC) 29/2001 on the harmonisation of certain aspects of copyright and related rights in the Information Society (the Infosoc Directive), which was adopted by the European Parliament and Council on 22 May 2001 and must be implemented in UK law by 22 December 2002.

■ Directive (EC) 84/2001 on the resale right for the benefit of the author of an original work of art, which was adopted by the European Parliament and Council on 27 September 2001.

Other Directives and proposals – such as the E-Commerce Directive[5] – aimed at limiting the liability of service providers, and which will have a particular impact on e-commerce, are referred to in the relevant parts of this book.

The Infosoc Directive presents a special problem at the time of writing. The Directive entered into force throughout the EU on 22 May 2001, however it has not yet been implemented into UK national law, and the UK has until 22 December 2002 to implement it. The consultation period ends on 31 October 2002, leaving a very tight turnaround time until implementation. In principle Directives take effect through national legislation, although it is possible that even where a Member State has not yet implemented a Directive, some of its provisions could have direct effect. If a Directive confers direct rights upon individuals, then individuals could rely on the Directive before a judge in a national court without having to wait for national legislation to implement it[6]. Individuals may be able to rely on this provision before the implementation date, 22 December 2002. Further, if sufficiently serious losses have been incurred because a national authority failed to implement a Directive, individuals could be able to sue the authority for damages[7]. This would apply after 22 December 2002.

Therefore as the Directive is in force in the EU, what follows should incorporate its provisions. Some Infosoc Directive provisions allow considerable scope for variety in national laws – for example, the provisions relating to exceptions to copyright. Moreover, it does not go without saying that all national laws implement Directives in accordance with the Commission's intention. For example, the Commission will refer the UK to the European Court of Justice (ECJ) for incomplete implementation of Directive (EEC) 100/92 (Rental and Lending Right Directive) because the UK considers it impossible at this stage to foresee with precision the amendments which will be made to the CDPA 1988. At the time of writing, the DTI has published a Consultation Paper on the Infosoc Directive (7 August 2002)[8] and proposed draft amendments to the CDPA 1988[9]. The draft amendments may be altered following the consultation, therefore it has been decided that, except where stated, the following text will refer to the 1998 Act as it stands at the time of writing, and paragraph 4.87 deals with the Infosoc Directive separately. The E-Commerce Directive is treated in the same way at paragraph 4.91. Please refer to those sections frequently if you are using this chapter for reference.

1 SI 1992/3233.
2 SI 1996/2967.
3 SI 1995/3297. Article 4 of this Directive is implemented by SI 1996/2967.
4 SI 1997/3032.
5 Directive (EC) 31/2000.
6 Case C-104/89: *Nimz v Freie and Hansestadt Hamburg* [1991] ECR I1-1 297, [1992] 3 CMLR 699, ECJ.
7 'The Member States are obliged to make good loss and damage caused to individuals by breaches of Community law for which they can be held responsible' in cases of sufficiently serious breach – joint Cases C-6/90 and C-9/90: *Francovich and Boniface v Italy* [1991] ECR I-5357, [1993] 2 CMLR 66, applied in the UK courts by (inter alia) *R v Secretary of State for Transport, ex p Factortame Ltd (No 5)* [2000] 1 AC 524, HL; *(No 7)* [2001] 1 WLR 942 (The Spanish Fishermen); *Scullion* [1999] 3 CMLR 798 (sex discrimination and pensionable age). In Case C-128/92 *Banks* [1994] ECR I-1209, the Advocate General argued that individuals are also liable for breaches of directly effective provisions of Community law which place a duty on them. Could a national collecting society under an obligation imposed by Community law to collect royalties arising from certain uses of rights assigned to it also be liable for failing to do so, if the national law has not implemented the requirement?
8 www.patent.gov.uk/about/consultations/ecopyright/index.htm.
9 www.patent.gov.uk/about/consultations/ecopyright/index.htm.

(b) Copyright subsistence

4.54 Copyright arises automatically upon the creation of a work in a tangible permanent form. There are no forms to fill in or fees to pay and in the UK it is a non-registrable right[1].

The following are the general categories of copyright[2]:

- **Literary works,** encompassing any work, other than dramatic or musical work, which is written, spoken or sung. It includes a table or compilation and computer programs. Examples of literary works would include (apart from obvious materials such as newspapers, magazines and books) works such as software, software documentation, flow charts, tables and electronic directories, graphics, HTML coding and JavaScript. A text of a document reproduced on the Internet would constitute a literary work as would texts of e-mails and texts appearing on websites and the layout of a web page. It would also include directories, translations, abridgements, adaptations, etc, provided that sufficient 'skill, labour and judgment' has been expended in their creation.

- **Computer programs,** including websites as a whole and/or the individual elements of the sub-paragraphs, would constitute literary works.

- **Titles of web pages and hypertext links,** which could be considered copyright works if sufficiently substantial. In the *Shetland Times* case[3] the court accepted that a headline of 'eight or more words put together for the purposes of imparting information' could be protected by copyright. On the other hand, in the case of *Exxon Corpn v Exxon Insurance Consultants International Ltd*[4] the claimant was refused copyright protection in relation to the name 'Exxon' alone.

- **Dramatic works,** including works of dance or mime and scenarios or scripts of films. Some of these may exist separately as literary works. However, titles would be excluded on the basis that they are too insignificant (unlike, for example, Italian copyright law which specifically protects titles of work)[5].

- **Musical works,** including works consisting of music, exclusive of any words or action intended to be sung, spoken or performed with it. Certain secondary activities such as arrangement of scores and orchestrating would qualify as protectable copyright works provided sufficient skill, labour and judgment is involved in their creation. They may exist in various physical forms, such as sheet music, CDs, audio and digital tapes or any other electric medium.

- **Artistic works,** irrespective of artistic quality this includes all manner of graphic art, photography, sculpture and collages, works of architecture and works of artistic craftsmanship, bitmaps, diagrams, engravings, architectural and technical drawings. Graphics, photographs and artwork used within a website would constitute artistic work.

- **Film,** including recordings in any medium from which a moving image made by any means may be produced. It includes an accompanying soundtrack (but has not always done so). Moving images include video clips on websites.

- **Broadcasting,** meaning broadcasting by wireless telegraphy (as defined in the Wireless Telegraphy Act 1949), whether by way of sound broadcast or of television. Contents of a radio and television broadcast which are digitally reproduced over the Internet would amount to broadcasting.

- **Sound recording:** recording of sounds, from which sounds may be reproduced, or a recording of the whole or any part of a literary, dramatic or musical work, from which sounds reproducing the work or part may be produced. Sound tracks are included and the sounds do not have to be musical or have any meaning to the listener. Digital sound effects would constitute sound recordings. However, the sound recording has to be original, and should not be a copy of a previous sound recording or film.

- **Cable program**, including any item comprised in a cable programme service. Cable programme service means a service which consists of visual images, sounds or other information through a telecommunication system other than by wireless telegraphy for reception at two or more places or for presentation to members of the public. Home banking services and stock market communications to private subscribers would not constitute cable programmes but home shopping services would. In the *Shetland Times* case the Scottish court accepted that a website was capable of constituting a cable programme service.

1 Compare the position in the US where the owner of a work of US origin cannot sue anyone for infringing his copyright until he has registered his work with the Copyright Office. Where the work is registered within three months from the date of first publication, or at least prior to the date of infringement, the owner can collect statutory damages from the infringer of up to $100,000, plus attorney fees and court costs. Otherwise, he will only be able to recover actual damages, which may be only nominal.
2 Rights are afforded to the creators of these categories of subject matter under the CDPA 1988, s 1(1).
3 *Shetland Times Ltd v Jonathan Wills & Zetnews Ltd* [1997] FSR 604, discussed more fully in Chapter 5, E-brand.
4 [1981] 3 All ER 241, CA.
5 Copyright could not exist in words merely because they could be described as 'original', 'literary' and 'work'; the work must offer information, instruction or pleasure in the form of literary enjoyment: *Exxon Corpn v Exxon Insurance Consultants International Ltd* [1982] Ch 119, [1982] RPC 81, CA.

4.55 Databases and compilations need special mention. A database is defined as a collection of independent works, data or other materials which (a) are arranged in a systematic or methodical way, and (b) are individually accessible by electronic or other means. A systematically arranged collection of independent data which is original in creation would qualify as a copyright work. If a database is not original in terms of its selection or arrangement of data, it could constitute a database right under the Copyright and Rights in Databases Regulations 1997 but would not attract copyright protection. It has been suggested that the threshold of originality for UK copyright protection of a database may be higher than the threshold which applies to other copyright works, because article 3.1 of the Database Directive refers to 'the author's own intellectual creation', a concept which does not apply to UK copyright in general.

In order to be protected by copyright, a work must be original; but the threshold for originality in the UK is very low. Its author must not have merely copied it slavishly from another work. Sufficient 'skill, judgment and capital' must have been expended in creating it. It is not necessary that the work be a result of some inventive thought – an input of a substantial amount of purely routine mental labour will suffice[1]. Examples of this might include compilations and originally created fonts. However, databases are considered original only if, by reason of the selection or arrangement of the contents, the database constitutes the author's own intellectual creation.

In addition to the requirement of originality for literary, dramatic, musical or artistic works (but not for other kinds of work) copyright will be protected within the UK only if:

- the author is a qualifying individual;

- the country in which the work was first published is a qualifying country; or

- in the case of broadcast or cable programmes, the country in which the broadcast was made or the cable programme was sent is a qualifying country (the CDPA 1988, ss 153–156).

'Qualifying individual' means a British national, a UK resident or a UK body corporate. It also includes the subjects of some British colonies. 'Qualifying countries' include the UK, EEA and countries with which the UK has a treaty obligation. As the UK is a party to the Berne Convention for the Protection of Literary and Artistic Works, the Rome Convention (the International Convention for the Protection of Performers, Producers of Phonograms and Broadcasting Organisations) and the Universal Copyright Convention, there will be very few works which do not qualify. The UK is also a member of the World Trade Organisation and adheres to the agreement on Trade-Related Aspects of Intellectual Property Rights (TRIPS).

1   This is best illustrated by the street and trade directory cases. For example, in *Waterlow Directories Ltd v Reed Information Services Ltd* [1992] FSR 409, a list of all practising solicitors was held to be protected by copyright. The position in the US is different and in the leading case of *Feist Publications Inc v Rural Telephone Service Co Inc* 499 US 330 (1991), the Supreme Court held that 'the white pages do nothing more than list Rural's subscribers in alphabetical order. This arrangement may, technically speaking, owe its origin to Rural; no one disputes that Rural undertook the task of alphabetising the names itself. But there is nothing remotely creative about arranging names alphabetically in a white pages directory. It is an age-old practice, firmly rooted in tradition and so commonplace that it has come to be expected as a matter of course. It is not only unoriginal, it is practically inevitable.'

(c) Copyright life

4.56

Summary of copyright durations

Literary, dramatic, musical or artistic work (including a photograph)	70 years from end of the calendar year when the author dies[1]. If author is unknown, 70 years from end of the calendar year when made or when first made available to the public (CDPA 1988, s 12)
Computer generated work	50 years from end of the calendar year when made (CDPA 1988, s 12(7))
Sound recording	50 years from end of the calendar year when made or released (CDPA 1988, s 13A)
Film	70 years after the death of the last to survive of the principal director, the authors of the screenplay and dialogue, and the composer of any music specially created for the film (CDPA 1988, s 13B)
Broadcast and cable programme	50 years from end of the calendar year when broadcast or included in cable programme service (CDPA 1988, s 14)
Published edition	25 years from the end of the calendar year from which the edition was first published (CDPA 1988, s 15)

These terms of protection apply to works originating in the UK or another EEA Member State. In other cases, the term of protection granted in the UK is that given by the country of origin of the work, which may be shorter.

One particular problem in relation to copyright is its very longevity. This has recently been increased for literary, dramatic, musical and artistic works from life of the last surviving author plus 50 years to life plus 70 years. This means that not only does an enquiry have to be made as to who owns the relevant copyright, but such ownership may have passed on to heirs and assignees, making title searches particularly complicated. There are many works made in the early years of the twentieth century which remain in copyright or in which copyright has revived.

1   Jointly authored copyrights last 70 years from the end of the calendar year of the death of the last known author.

(d) Ownership of copyright

4.57 The first owner of copyright is the author (CDPA 1988, s 11(1)). The author is the person who creates the work (CDPA 1988, s 9(1)). In relation to the following types of works, the creator is taken to be:

■   literary works – the writer;

- sound recordings – the producer;

- photographs – the photographer;

- films – the producer and principal director;

- broadcast – the person transmitting the programme (if he has any responsibility for its contents) and any person providing the programme, who makes with the person transmitting it the arrangements for the transmission;

- cable programme – the person providing the cable programme service in which the programme is included;

- typographical arrangement of a published edition – the publisher; and

- computer generated works – the person by whom the arrangements necessary for the creation of the work are undertaken.

4.58 It is also possible to have works of joint authorship where a work is produced by the collaboration of two or more authors whose respective contributions are not distinct from that of the other author or authors[1]. This is of particular relevance to websites as they comprise various composite works created by different people who could claim authorship. In order to do so, the contribution of each author has to amount to sufficient skill and labour. Helping fix errors or carrying on testing or suggesting ideas would not constitute sufficient skill and labour to justify joint authorship[2].

Where a literary, dramatic, musical or artistic work is created by an employee in the course of his employment, the employer is the first owner of any copyright in the work, subject to any agreement to the contrary[3].

It is important to note that there is no work for hire doctrine in English law. This is a particular problem with software development, where assignments have to be taken from independent or freelance contractors, even if under local law the commissioner owns the copyright in the work. This means that if an independent contractor is used to generate a copyright work, he (orhis employer) will be the first owner of the copyright. If the party commissioning the work wishes to become owner, then he must take an assignment. Otherwise at best he either has equitable title or is an equitable exclusive licensee. (Only in relation to design rights is the commissioner the first owner of the right.)

Tip

An on-line seller should own or have an exclusive licence to use as much of his website as possible. An assignment (giving ownership) or an exclusive licence of copyright must be in writing, signed by the party granting the right. To ensure first ownership, he needs to take care that all material (such as text, images, sounds, etc) are either created by him or his employees. If a service provider or a website designer is engaged to create such material, they will own copyrights in such works. The on-line seller should obtain an assignment or exclusive licence in the copyright work. These should include the right to exploit the work electronically and extract appropriate warranty and indemnity protection[4].

It is important to acquire the rights from the outset as the commissioner of the works cannot sue a third party for infringement unless he owns or has exclusive licence to use the copyright work. In any event, the commissioner, subject to all the circumstances, would have an equitable title and may be in a position, depending on the contractual relationship between the parties, to call for an assignment; this could arise only years later where the contractors can no longer be traced or have been wound up.

Any works made by authors, whose identity cannot be ascertained by reasonable inquiry, are protected by copyright. It is essential for the on-line seller to review any material to be used in a website carefully to ensure he has all necessary rights before incorporating them in his website or products.

1 The CDPA 1988, s 10.
2 *Fylde Microsystems Ltd v Key Radio Systems Ltd* [1998] FSR 449; *Ray v Classic FM plc* [1998] FSR 622.
3 The CDPA 1988, s 11(2).
4 For further commentary on the applicable content for a website design contract, see Chapter 2, E-contract, paragraph 2.59.

(e) Dealing in copyrights

4.59 Copyright is a property right which can be dealt with. Copyright may be transmitted by assignment, by disposition or operation of law. It is personal or movable property and may be charged or licensed[1]. An assignment can be partial. Even future copyright works can be assigned or licensed[2]. A copyright may be licensed exclusively, but an exclusive licence must be in writing signed by or on behalf of the copyright owner[3]. A non-exclusive copyright licence need not be in writing.

1 The CDPA 1988, s 90(1).
2 The CDPA 1988, s 91.
3 The CDPA 1988, s 92(1).

(f) Copyright notices

4.60 Although a few countries require that a work be marked with the international © mark followed by the name of the copyright owner and year of publication, this is not essential in most countries, including the UK. There is, however, no disadvantage in inserting a copyright notice. It helps to make known that the work is a copyright work. However, marking it in this way may assist in infringement proceedings by putting third parties on notice that the work is protected by copyright.

(g) Scope of copyright

4.61 The CDPA 1988 confers upon the owner of a copyright exclusive rights to do, or authorise others to do, certain acts in relation to the work. These are to[1]:

■   copy the work;

■   issue copies of the work to the public;

■   perform, show or play the work in public;

■   broadcast the work or include it in a cable programme service; or

■   make an adaptation of the work or do any of the above in relation to an adaptation.

It is important to bear in mind, however, that these are not positive rights. They are rights to stop others from infringing the rights of the owner.

1 The CDPA 1988, s 16(1).

(h) Copyright infringement

4.62 Copyright in a work is infringed by a person who, without a licence from the copyright owner, does or authorises another to do, any of the acts restricted by the copyright, as set out above[1]:

- in relation to the whole work or a substantial of part of it; and

- either directly or indirectly[2].

The CDPA 1988 divides infringement into two categories, termed primary infringement and secondary infringement. Broadly, acts of primary infringement can be distinguished from acts of secondary infringement because a person who engages in an act of primary infringement will be strictly liable to the copyright holder (without the requirement to prove fault on the part of the infringer).

1 The CDPA 1988, s 16(2).
2 The CDPA 1988, s 16(3).

(i) Primary infringement

4.63 Broadly, in the context of e-commerce, primary infringement of copyright is likely to impact upon the copyright holder's reproduction right, and his right to control the distribution, public performance, broadcasting or cable transmission of the copyright work (see also the right of communication to the public below, in paragraph 4.65).

Reproduction

4.64 In relation to literary, dramatic, musical or artistic works, the work is copied if it is reproduced in any material form, which includes storing the work by electronic means[1]. Copying includes the making of copies of a purely temporary nature or copies which are incidental to the use of the work[2]. However, note the exception for temporary acts of reproduction conferred by the Infosoc Directive, in paragraph 4.53.

Copying in relation to films, broadcast or cable programmes includes such actions as making a photograph of the whole or any substantial part of any image forming part of the film, broadcast or cable programme (video-grabbing).

'Reproduction' means reproduction 'in any material form', which includes storing the work in any medium by electronic means[3]. Delivery of content over the Internet (whether a word-processed document sent as an e-mail attachment, the content of a website, or a piece of software or application downloaded from another server) by definition involves both reproduction of the original content and its distribution to others. But the original work is never transferred: what is transferred is a copy in a digital form. Therefore, in principle, every transmission of any material over the Internet amounts to a potential copyright infringement. Electronic storage is also a form of copying. Similarly, making a copy in the computer's RAM for the purposes of viewing it on the computer screen or saving it on a floppy disk are acts of reproduction. Many of these reproductions fall within the exception conferred by the Infosoc Directive mentioned above. Further examples of acts of reproduction which do not fall within that exception include:

- downloading a web page or software into your computer's memory;

- automatic web page caching – a standard feature of practically all browser software;

- printing of a web page;

- reproducing material downloaded from a website[4];

- simple web linking, where a website operator provides a reference hyperlink[5] in one of his web pages to another website allowing the user to activate the link and gain direct access to the targeted linked website;

- so-called 'deep-linking', which goes further than simple linking because the link includes not only a destination URL but also, by implication, copyright material from the destination website (as the latter's home page is bypassed and the user is taken directly to a specific page);

- web posting, that is the routine process of placing somebody else's material on your website and thereby making it available on the Internet;

- webcasting, that is broadcasting via the Internet musical recordings, radio and television programmes. 'Subscription transmissions', which are generally subject to a statutory licence, are treated in the same way as traditional radio broadcasts, in that their 'primary purpose is to provide audio or other entertainment programming'[6]. On-demand transmissions, where the listener specifically chooses the material to be broadcast, are becoming increasingly popular for the distribution of music and film; and

- simple screen displays[7].

Other techniques which are used to import the content of one website into another, such as those involving framing, the use of metatags, spamdexing and word-stuffing, are dealt with in Chapter 5, E-brand[8].

1 The CDPA 1988, s 16(1).
2 The CDPA 1988, s 16(2).
3 The CDPA 1988, s 16(3).
4 See *Nottinghamshire County Council v Gwatkin* (unreported), where three journalists who published an edited version of an enquiry report taken from the Internet were held to have infringed the copyright in the report.
5 It would have, in principle, to be an actual hyperlink, however. Merely inserting the name of the other website or even its full URL as plain text would probably not be sufficient.
6 Webcast transmissions in the US made by Federal Communications Commission (FCC) licensed terrestrial broadcast stations are exempted there from the exclusive performance rights of copyright owners.
7 In *Galaxy Electronics Pty Ltd v Sega Enterprises Ltd* [1997] FCA 403, an Australian court held that computer game images are 'films' and are therefore capable of copyright protection.
8 From which it will be apparent that some of these give rise to questions of trade mark abuse as well as infringement of copyright.

Issuing copies to the public, or distribution

4.65 This involves putting into circulation, or distributing, in the UK or elsewhere within the EEA, copies of the work (including copies of a temporary or transient nature) not previously put into circulation. This in turn implies that a copy has material form.

The right to put into circulation 'exhausts' when it is legitimately exercised on distribution of the copy of the work (for example, book, DVD) within the UK or any other EEA Member State. This means that the right holder has no control over further distribution of the copy (for example, he cannot control second-hand sales). However, other rights do not exhaust. Therefore, the purchaser of the second-hand book may not copy (or rent, perform in public, adapt, etc) the copy he has bought without the right holder's consent[1].

'On-line distribution', such as making a copy available over the Internet, is controlled by the new right of making available under the Infosoc Directive, which does not exhaust (see paragraph 4.87). Consequently when a copy is 'distributed' over the Internet, an Internet user who legitimately browses the document may not (without licence) distribute it further, say by e-mail.

1 The CDPA 1988, s 18(2) and (3) was amended to introduce EEA-wide exhaustion (replacing international exhaustion) by the Copyright and Related Rights Regulations 1996 (SI 1996/2967), ie by secondary legislation. It has been suggested that this amendment was effected ultra vires the powers relating to secondary legislation conferred on the Secretary of State by section 2(2) of the European Communities Act 1972. Be that as it may, Directive (EEC) 100/92 (Rental Rights Directive) obliges the UK's domestic law to provide EEA exhaustion, and this is confirmed in the Infosoc Directive. The Patent Office have said that the CDPA 1988 will be amended by Statutory Instrument, that is further secondary legislation pursuant to the European Communities Act. Perhaps the same objection will be raised again in the same quarters.

Broadcasting

4.66 The definition of 'broadcasting' for these purposes cannot apply to Internet transmission, to the extent that this is not conducted by means of wireless telegraphy as required by the CDPA 1988 but through a network of cables[1].

1 As a premise, this remains the case while computers require to be connected to the Internet via telephone cables. How true this remains as technology develops will depend on the degree to which wireless systems for Internet traffic come into use. Developments such as WAP, i-mode and bluetooth, for example, all indicate a move towards wireless systems, or hybrid systems which involve a combination of radio transmissions and telephone lines. Other important developments in this area will come in the field of set-top box technology, once again involving an interaction between signals transmitted along telephone cables and signals received via the TV aerial or satellite dish.

Cable programmes

4.67 It is an infringement to use or include without permission a copyright work in a cable programme service. The definition of 'cable programme service' is wide enough to include a website whose operator makes available an on-demand service of the sort operated through a cable network (distribution of films, music, etc). Similarly, where an Internet service provider provides access to material through its home page, it would be deemed to be providing a cable programme service. However, where an ISP is merely a 'host' to digital files placed on its server, then it is unlikely that the ISP would be held to be providing cable programme services[1].

1 Though the persons who maintain those files on the server might be so implicated.

No implied consent to copy material found on the Internet

4.68 It is so easy to download material from a website that many PC users have developed (incorrectly) the notion that anything that is on the Internet is lawfully in the public domain and can be taken and reproduced without the permission of the owner. The idea is current that because web pages can be cached or because certain browsers have a built-in 'file save as' function, the material copied or saved in this way can be used without restriction – that is fundamentally incorrect. All material you may find on the Internet is potentially copyright work and its use beyond the allowed parameters without permission is an infringement. MIDI files (containing sound or musical data), text in general, HTML coding itself and JavaScript files found in many typical websites are all copyright works. Similarly, graphic images provided as 'free' or as 'linkware' should not be considered as being provided for you to download and keep in copy form for ever, since they are usually only licensed for the PC user to use or copy in accordance with the owner's terms and conditions. The owner may impose a condition on the use of a graphic or photograph such as 'do not alter' (so that any alteration is a breach of contract) or that the graphic is 'only for personal home use' (so that any published or commercial use is prohibited). Similarly, scanning photographs taken from a magazine and pasting them on your own website[1] amounts to infringement of the copyright of the photographer or magazine. All of these are examples of different sorts of plagiarism in the context of the Internet. Plagiarism is not allowed: it is important that copyright clearance to use material found on the Internet is sought from the owner, and there is no concept of implied consent to use that material merely because you found it on somebody else's website.

1 Or arranging for them to be stored on a server to which you establish hyperlinks on your website.

Whom can the copyright owner sue?

4.69 In this context, the copyright owner can in principle proceed for infringement against:

- the person responsible for producing and operating the infringing website (that is, both the person who holds himself out as the website owner and, if different, the person who drafted it);

- the ISP hosting the website;

- any person responsible for a computer or server on which the relevant web pages are cached in the course of their being downloaded and viewed; and/or

- simply, any person browsing the website, because there is no implied licence to browse if the reproduction of the material is unauthorised[1].

Recognising a right of action against the hosting ISP is a paramount concern of content owners such as film and music companies because the ISP is a more visible legal target, and one against whom a court order or an award of damages is much more capable of routine enforcement.

The need for a right to take action against persons who cache a web page is, however, more contentious, because caches are needed for the efficient functioning of the Internet.

Liability for caching and hosting are both considered in the E-Commerce Directive and the Infosoc Directive, in slightly different terms (see paragraph 4.85). Liability for caching and hosting under US law (1998's Digital Millennium Copyright Act) is subject to compliance with the statutory take-down procedure.

Copying could also take place where text from one site, for example news headlines, is used as a hyperlink to content on the other site. In the *Shetland Times* case[2], the court found that the claimants had a prima facie case of copyright infringement under the CDPA 1988, ss 7 and 20 and accordingly issued an interim interdict stopping the defendants from copying the claimant's headlines and using them as a 'deep' hyperlink directly to the news item, bypassing the *Shetland Times*' homepage and advertising. Unfortunately, this case was settled before full trial, so as yet we do not have a decision from a court in the UK to provide definitive judicial guidance on the practice of hyperlinking in this fashion[3]. However, there is at least guidance from the interlocutory judgment of the *Shetland Times* case to be able to form the view that best advice is always to ask permission before deep-linking so as to bypass a home page on another website[4].

1 Having said that, the latter two categories are likely to be questions of degree. If the copyright infringed is in a single graphic on a complex website, then the creator, operator and ISP host may all be liable because of their relationship with the website as a whole; but the caching system operator and the viewer will probably not be liable unless they see and take advantage of that very graphic.
2 Paragraph 4.54, and see also Chapter 5, E-brand.
3 The *Ticketmaster* litigation in the US, considered in Chapter 5, E-brand, paragraph 5.73 and dealing with a related matter, was also settled before a final trial of the issue.
4 See, however, *Futuredontics Inc v Applied Anagramatics* No 97-56711, 1998 (US Ct of Apps (9th Cir), 1998), Case No CV 97-6991, 1998 *ABC (Manx)* (CD Cal, 30 January 1998), where the Court of Appeals for the 9th Circuit held that the plaintiff had failed to show that it was or would be injured by the defendant's conduct and so was not entitled to injunctive relief.

Other forms of reproduction

4.70 Other forms of reproduction protected by copyright include:

- in relation to artistic works, making a copy in three dimensions of a two-dimensional work and making a copy in two dimensions of a three-dimensional work[1]. This means that the on-line seller cannot take a picture of a sculpture, for example, and include it on his website without the permission of the sculptor; and

- in relation to films, television broadcasts or cable programmes, taking a photograph of the whole or any substantial part of any image forming part of the film, broadcast or cable programme[2]. This means that the on-line seller cannot also take a still image captured from a movie and use it on his website without permission (so-called 'video-grabbing').

1 The CDPA 1988, s 17(3). But see section 51 in relation to design documents or models, discussed below.
2 The CDPA 1988, s 17(4).

Adaptations

4.71 An adaptation is made when it is recorded in writing or otherwise[1] and includes:

■ in relation to literary or dramatic works (other than a computer program), a translation of the work, a version of the dramatic work in which it is converted into a non-dramatic work, or vice versa, and a version of the work in which the story or action is conveyed wholly or mainly by means of pictures in a form suitable for reproduction in a book, newspaper, magazine or periodical;

■ in relation to computer programs, an arrangement or altered version of the program or a translation of the program into another language, computer language or code; and

■ in relation to a musical work, an arrangement or transcription of the work.

It is important to note that although making an unlawful adaptation is an infringement of the copyright in the original work, the adaptation will also acquire a separate copyright. The on-line seller commissioning a translation of his website into a different language should obtain a written assignment of the copyright(s) in the translation(s) concerned.

1 The CDPA 1988, s 21(1).

Authorisation

4.72 Not only is the actual making of an unauthorised copy of copyright material prohibited, it is also prohibited to authorise another to do so. Where a person authorised others to copy Microsoft software without consent, he was found to have infringed the copyright work[1]. On the other hand, Amstrad's supply of dual cassette players from which music cassettes could be made did not amount to authorisation of tape duplication because Amstrad had no control over the way the equipment was used after sale[2].

In recent US litigation[3] a number of major record companies (Universal, Warners, EMI, Sony and BMG) successfully obtained an injunction prohibiting Napster from 'engaging in or facilitating in copying, downloading, uploading, transmitting or distributing copyright and sound recordings protected by Federal or State law without express permission of the rights owner'. The preliminary injunction was subsequently modified, requiring the record companies to inform Napster of infringing material before Napster had a duty to disable access to it. Throughout the litigation Napster 'pretty much acknowledged' that end-users infringe at least two of the copyright owners' exclusive rights: of reproduction and distribution. Napster itself does not make, receive or store any copies of the music files, even transiently. Therefore Napster does not directly infringe copyright. Instead, Napster was found liable for contributory and vicarious infringement of copyright. Liability for contributory infringement is found if one 'with knowledge of the infringing activities induces, causes or materially contributes to the infringing conduct of another' (that is, Napster's facilitation of identifying/downloading files). Vicarious liability for copyright infringement can be found if one 'has the right and ability to supervise the infringing activity and also has a direct financial interest in such activities' (that is, Napster could allow or filter out music files, but had not).

Under UK law, given the structure of Napster's service, it is not possible to target it with an action for primary infringement of copyright. The CDPA 1988 does not provide for the US Copyright

Code's offences of contributory and vicarious copyright infringement. However section 16(2) of the CDPA 1988 provides that copyright is infringed in the UK if a person authorises any of the primary acts. Liability for authorisation is difficult to establish. Whitford J in *CBS Inc v Ames Records and Tapes Ltd*[4] was cited with approval in *Amstrad v BPI*[5] and *CBS Songs Ltd v Amstrad Consumer Electronics plc*[6], stating that authorisation 'can only come from someone having or purporting to have authority, and an act is not authorised by someone who merely enables or possibly assists or even encourages another to do an act but does not purport to do any authority'. Lord Templeman in *Amstrad* (which concerned the manufacture and sale of twin deck tape recorders) said, 'by selling the recorder Amstrad may facilitate copying in breach of copyright but do not authorise it ...'.

With this background, proving in a UK court that Napster has authorised copyright infringement within section 16(2) of the CDPA 1988 would certainly be problematic unless the courts took this as an opportunity to develop this area of law.

Subject to the law being developed by the court, Napster's activities do not fall entirely within section 23 of the CDPA 1988 (secondary infringement), although these provisions could be of some limited assistance provided that the requisite degree of knowledge on the part of the infringer could be proved.

Given the international scope of the Internet, UK providers of file-swapping protocols clearly need to be wary of being sued in the US, and the judgements thus obtained in the US being enforced against them in the UK[7]. Other relevant US cases are *Universal City Studios Inc v Reimerdes*[8] (the Motion Picture Association of America claimed that use of DeCSS Software on the Internet infringed the provisions of the Digital Millennium Copyright Act); *RealNetworks Inc v Streambox Inc*[9] (recording streaming media files); and the DeCSS cases[10].

1 *Microsoft Corpn v Computer Future Distribution Ltd* [1998] ETMR 597.
2 *Amstrad Consumer Electronics plc v British Phonographic Industry Ltd* [1986] FSR 159, CA.
3 *RIAA v Napster* 2000 US Dist LEXIS 6243 (ND Cal, 2000).
4 [1982] Ch 91 at 106.
5 *Amstrad Consumer Electronics plc v British Photographic Industry Ltd* [1986] FSR 159, CA.
6 [1988] AC 1013, HL.
7 Note however, *McDonough v Fallon McEllighott Inc* 1996 US Dist LEXIS 15139 (SD Cal, 1996) in which a Minnesota corporation was not subject to Californian jurisdiction where the infringing act (use of a copyright photograph) did not occur in and was not directed towards California. That the website was accessible in California was not sufficient to support personal jurisdiction: 'the fact that [the defendant] has a website used by Californians cannot establish jurisdiction by itself'. Likewise, in *Subafilms Ltd v MGM-Pathe Communications Co* 24 F 3d 1088 (9th Cir, 1994), cert den, 513 US 1001 (1994), mere authorisation within the United States of infringing acts which occurred entirely outside of United Stated did not give rise to a claim for copyright infringement under the US Copyright Act. This case concerned reproduction of film, not an Internet communication, however.
8 82 F Supp 2d 211 (SDNY, 2000).
9 2000 US Dist LEXIS 1889 (WD Wash, 2000).
10 Multiple courts, filed December 1999 to January 2000.

(ii) Secondary infringement

4.73 Actions which amount to secondary infringement[1] include:

- importing into the UK, otherwise than for private or domestic use, an article which constitutes a breach of copyright (this does not apply to articles made by or with the right holder's consent in another EU Member State);

- possessing or dealing with an infringing copy in the course of a business (this includes selling and hiring);

- providing the means for making infringing copies;

- transmitting the work by means of a television or other communication system (for example via the telephone network), knowing or having reason to believe that infringing copies of the work will be made by means of the reception of the transmission in the UK or elsewhere;

- permitting the use of premises for an infringing performance;

- providing apparatus for a public performance or playing or showing the work in public; or

- supplying a copy of a sound recording or film knowing or having reason to believe that infringing copies of the work will be made directly or indirectly.

There is a presumption in favour of copyright subsisting in the work at the time the infringing article was made[2].

For a person to be liable for acts of secondary infringement, the primary criterion is that that person should have knowledge or reason to believe that the work is an infringing copy. This is in contrast to primary infringement where liability is strict and lack of knowledge (that the material was subject to copyright) is not a defence. Further, in the case of secondary infringement, a claimant is not entitled to recover damages against a secondary infringer unless the claimant can prove that the infringer actually did have knowledge, although the claimant may still apply for an injunction to restrain the secondary infringer from future acts of infringement.

Since the infringer will have express notice of subsisting copyright from a notice to that effect on the material concerned, it is for this reason advisable to append such a notice (even if as a matter of law this is not necessary in the UK).

1   The CDPA 1988, ss 22–26.
2   The CDPA 1988, s 27 (4).

(iii) Indirect infringement

4.74   Finally, we should consider a further concept, which may be described as 'indirect infringement'. There are two circumstances in which this concept is relevant:

- first, the person dealing in infringing goods may not himself have copied or authorised the copy that infringes the claimant's rights, but his dealership in such goods nevertheless amounts to an infringement (for example, by possessing them in the course of business). It is not an infringement of copyright to deal in infringing goods unless the person dealing in such goods knows or has reason to believe that there has been a copyright infringement with reference to them. It must be emphasised that lack of knowledge or lack of reason to believe is not a defence as such, but rather his dealing in such goods is simply not an infringement at all. It is therefore prudent for the right holder to take whatever steps he can to put such infringers on notice of subsistence of copyright[1].

- second, there is an indirect infringement where a copy of copyright material is taken indirectly, not from the original itself but from an intermediate document or source. Infringement of copyright occurs even if copying is not taking place directly[2]. Thus, even if the work is copied down from one's own memory at a later date, the result will be an infringement. In *Sega Enterprises v Maphin*[3], the defendant was held liable for allowing users to upload and download Sega games from his bulletin board.

1   See *Linpac Mouldings Ltd v Eagleton Direct Exports Ltd* [1994] FSR 545, CA.
2   The CDPA 1988, s 16(3)(b).
3   (unreported).

(i)   Defences to infringement

4.75   Certain acts cannot constitute infringement and those relevant to the Internet are considered below.

(i) Licence

4.76 Copyright in a work is not infringed if the copying is done with the consent of the copyright owner. Where there is an express licence, the matter is straightforward. An exclusive licence must be in writing. However, a non-exclusive licence may be granted orally, and there are situations where it is possible to claim the existence of an implied licence. This might apply, for example, where a work has been commissioned but the commissioner has not obtained any express assignment or licence. In such a case, the commissioner would be entitled, having regard to all the surrounding circumstances, to use the work (although not exclusively) for the purposes for which it was created. In *Saphena Computing Ltd v Allied Collection Agencies Ltd*[1], a purchaser of software, who had also acquired the source code, was deemed to have a licence to copy and adapt it for the purposes of his business. Further, where the material has been put on the Internet, there is an implied licence to the user to browse and view. The extent to which this implied licence may extend to making 'transient' copies for viewing or downloading under English law is clarified by the 'caching' regulation in the E-Commerce Regulations (regulation 18). However, it is unlikely that an implied licence exists to hypertext link to another website. In the US it has been widely argued that hypertext linking to the claimant's website is within the parameters of an implied licence[2], and an aggrieved right holder has redress under the take-down provisions of the Digital Millennium Copyright Act.

In relation to licences granted before Internet use was prevalent – in these instances the publication of newspaper articles on the Internet – the French and US courts have held that a further licence is required from the right holder[3].

1 [1995] FSR 616, CA.
2 Again, however, this sort of practice might also amount to a trade mark infringement, eg if the link makes use of a term which the claimant can show was registered to him as a trade mark.
3 *If SNJ v Le Figaro* (Tribunal de Grand Instance de Paris, 4/3/98); *USJF v SA SDV Plurimedia R.Com* MO 9700919 Jonction: R.COM.97-918 (Tribunal de Grand Instance de Strasbourg, 2/3/98; *Tasini v New York Times* 192 3d 356 (2d Cir NY, 1999).

(ii) Insubstantial part

4.77 It would not be an infringement to copy or reproduce an insubstantial part of any work. The test of substantiality is one of quality and not quantity. Substantiality is not defined and the courts assess it on the basis of individual cases. For example, a 'sample' of a musical work and sound recording incorporated into a new dance music track can be a substantial part of the original by virtue of its quality even though it lasts for only a few seconds.

(iii) Public policy

4.78 Section 171(3) of the CDPA 1988 states that 'nothing in this part affects any rule of law which prevents or restricts the enforcement of copyright on grounds of public policy or otherwise'. The scope of this section was explored in *Hyde Park Residence Ltd v Yelland*[1] (newspaper publication of stills from security videos showing Diana, Princess of Wales and Mr Dodi Fayed visiting a villa in Paris). The CDPA 1988 does not give the court a general power to enable an infringer to use another's copyright without consent, in the public interest. However section 171(3) preserves the court's inherent jurisdiction to refuse to enforce an action for infringement of copyright where enforcement would offend against the policy of the law, for example where the work in question is immoral, scandalous or injurious to public life or the administration of justice. In this instance the Court of Appeal did not refuse to enforce copyright on this group. (The Court of Appeal distinguished the basis of this jurisdiction from the basis of public interest in a breach of confidence action.)

As a hypothetical example, in the e-commerce sphere, suppose X were to post on to a website information concerning computer viruses which Y was known or understood to be causing to circulate around the Internet. Some of that information might breach Y's copyright in his virus programs, or in web literature which describes them, but given the desire to restrict the manner in which this sort of material circulates, because of its destructive potential, it seems plausible that X's publication of Y's copyright material might attract the public policy defence[2], so the court might refuse to enforce Y's copyright.

1   [2001] Ch 143, CA.
2   Clearly, the posting of this sort of material to a website raises other legal issues, such as the potential for a claim of defamation, as to which see Chapter 3, E-liability.

(iv) Fair dealing

4.79   The fair dealing concept is an important element in several exceptions to copyright, including the first four exceptions considered below, which conceptually predate the computer age. Three further instances are of more recent origin and have a specific frame of reference for users of computer systems, suppliers of software and programs and therefore for the Internet and the web in general:

- Fair dealing for the purposes of research or private study[1]. This is the primary exception which will be relied on by most individual domestic web users. This exception does not extend to films, sound recordings, broadcasts or cable programmes, however, and an on-line seller cannot use these on its website without permission.

- Fair dealing for the purposes of criticism, review or reporting current events, provided it is accompanied by a sufficient acknowledgement of the author and the title of the work[2]. The exception for news reporting does not cover photographs. No acknowledgement is required if the reporting is by means of a film, sound recording, broadcast or cable programme.

- Incidental inclusion of copyright material, for example musical works and words spoken or sung with music, and pieces of a sound recording. If broadcast or cable programmes include such music deliberately, the copyright material will not be regarded as incidentally included[3]. A news broadcast which catches a snatch of a piece of music played at an event covered in the news will typically fall within the scope of this exception. But this is unlikely to benefit the on-line seller, as the inclusion of even very short video and sound clips on a website is unlikely to be incidental.

- Copying (other than by reprographic means) in the course of instruction or preparation for instruction by the person giving or receiving instruction[4]. Essentially the copying must be done by hand (one thinks of a teacher writing something down on the classroom blackboard, for example) and the work cannot be photocopied or copied and stored using electronic means, so it is of limited application to the Internet.

- The making of back-up copies of a computer programme by a lawful user[5].

- Decompiling a computer program to obtain information necessary to create an independent interoperable program where the information is not readily available[6]. One solution which the on-line seller may adopt is to state clearly in its licence terms that interoperability information will be made available on reasonable request.

- Copying and adapting a computer program where the copying is necessary (for example, for error correction) and not expressly prohibited[7]. This right can be excluded by the supplier of the program in its licence terms; when supplying such software, a supplier should carefully consider whether it is appropriate to do so.

There are further exceptions for education establishments[8], librarians and archivists[9] and for public administration purposes[10].

The principle of fair dealing under the CDPA 1988 is strictly confined to the scope of each exception to which it applies, for example reporting current affairs, criticism or review. When considering in which jurisdiction to bring an action for infringement, or whether a use of copyright material may be legitimate, it is often useful to consider the more flexible fair use provisions of the US Copyright Code[11]. Four criteria are considered to determine whether a use for purposes such as criticism, comment or teaching is fair: the purpose and character of the use, the nature of the copyright work, the amount and substantiality of the proportion used, and the effect of the use on the market of the copyright work. For example, in *Kelly v Arriba Soft Corpn*[12], the transformative way in which the original work was used made its use fair. (The Infosoc Directive lists an exception to copyright for the purpose of caricature, parody or pastiche[13].)

1 The CDPA 1988, s 29.
2 The CDPA 1988, s 30.
3 The CDPA 1988, s 31.
4 The CDPA 1988, s 32.
5 The CDPA 1988, s 50A. In fact, in shrink-wrap and click-wrap licence agreements, there may well be an express licence for the making of a single such back-up copy.
6 The CDPA 1988, s 50B.
7 The CDPA 1988, s 50C.
8 The CDPA 1988, ss 33–36A.
9 The CDPA 1988, ss 37–44.
10 The CDPA 1988, ss 45–50.
11 Title 17 US Code s 107.
12 77 F Supp 2d 1116 (CD Cal, 1999).
13 The Infosoc Directive, art 5, 3(k).

(j) Copyright licences

4.80 Subject to the fair dealing exceptions listed in paragraph 4.79, a licence is required to do any of the acts restricted by the copyright in a work. As the terms of a licence can be express or implied, it is preferable for the on-line seller to set out fully the rights which it intends to grant to its licensees so it can retain control. Aspects of the protection of copyright in content and the capacity to control its licensing to others have been considered in Chapter 2, E-contract, paragraph 2.62.

It will also be important for the on-line seller in taking a licence from a copyright owner to check equally that it has all the rights it may need. Different rights can be licensed to different persons. In relation to a published work, it may be the case that one party has the exclusive right to develop electronic publication but another has the exclusive right to publish in any format in a particular country. Taking a licence from one and not also from the other may lead to an inadvertent conflict between the rights of the different licensees and/or the licensor. Where multimedia works are concerned, the on-line seller may need a licence from a number of different parties.

Many copyright owners will be represented by a 'collecting society'. In the UK these include:

Authors' Licensing and Collecting Society Limited (ALCS)	Secondary rights in literary, dramatic, musical and artistic works
British Equity Collecting Society Limited (BECS)	Performers
Compact Collections Limited	Film and television producers
Copyright Licensing Agency Limited (CLA)	Reprographic rights of authors and publishers
Design and Artists' Copyright Society Limited (DACS)	Rights in artistic works
Directors' and Producers' Rights Society (1992) Limited (DPRS)	Film and television directors and producers
Educational Recording Agency Limited (ERA)	Recording by educational establishments of broadcasts and cable programmes
Mechanical Copyright Protection Society (MCPS)	Sound-bearing copies of musical works
Newspaper Licensing Agency Limited (NLA)	Reprographic rights of newspaper publishers in the typographical arrangement of news articles[1]
Performing Artists' Media Rights Association Limited (PAMRA)	Performers' recorded performances
Performing Rights Society Limited (PRS)	Non-dramatic performing rights in musical works, film synchronisation rights
Phonographic Performance Limited (PPL)	Public performance and broadcasting rights in sound recordings for record producers
Video Performance Limited (VPL)	Music video producers

1 See *Newspaper Licensing Agency Ltd v Marks & Spencer plc* [2001] UKHL 38, [2001] 3 All ER 977.

4.81 Thus, for example, if an on-line seller wants to use recorded music, in most cases licences will be required from:

- the MCPS for the right to make a copy of the composition on its server; and

- the PRS for the public performance in a cable programme service of the composition.

The PRS and the MCPS have formed a Music Alliance to deal with licensing on the Internet, and the New Technologies Division of the MCPS can issue a separate licence in respect of each organisation's rights for Internet use. The PRS is currently operating trial licences for the broadcast or provision of a cable programme service embodying copyright music in an on-line environment[1]. There are five types of usage for which blanket licences are available for on-line music use from the PRS, namely clips, short audio-only productions, continuous productions, extracts of broadcast programming and music on broadcast-related websites, and audio-visual music productions.

In March 1999, ASCAP (US), BumaStemra (Netherlands) and the MCPS-PRS Alliance (UK) agreed to create a shared service centre to handle music rights processing in the digital age[2]. The European

Commission has addressed the issue of collective management of copyright and related rights in several studies and it is likely that the Commission will continue to favour collective societies in order to ensure that users do not face unreasonable difficulties in identifying the person(s) who can grant or refuse them a licence.

1 See www.prs.co.uk/DocsRepository/894.
2 See www.mcps-prs-alliance.co.uk/DoscRepository/1352.

(k) Moral rights

4.82 In addition to the rights of ownership, the author of a literary or artistic copyright work has certain so-called 'moral rights' which are protected under the law. Moral rights cannot be assigned or licensed, but remain with the author and his heirs. The copyright in a book is likely to be exploited by its publisher, whilst the author has the moral rights described below. It may be to the advantage of the licensee or assignee to obtain a written waiver of the moral rights of an author or director[1], in order to be assured of complete freedom in exploiting the work.

Moral rights include the right to be identified as author when the work is published or director in a film, a right to object to derogatory treatment in the work and false attribution of the work. There is also the right to privacy of certain photographs and films (which are limited to those commissioned for private and domestic purposes[2]). All of the above rights continue to subsist as long as the copyright subsists in the work, apart from the right to avoid false attribution of the work, which continues to subsist until 20 years after the death of the holder of that right.

1 Which is allowed under the CDPA 1988, s 87, although moral rights cannot be waived in some other countries.
2 The CDPA 1988, s 85.

(i) Identification as author/director

4.83 The right to be identified as author arises whenever the work is published commercially or included in a film. To be enforced, the right must be asserted in writing. Published copies frequently contain a notice identifying the author or director as such and stating that the right is asserted. There are provisions stating how the rights may be asserted[1]. Generally, assertion is by notice signed by the author or director.

The right to be identified as author or director does not apply to computer programs, the design of a typeface, any computer generated work, or to anything done by or with the authority of the copyright owner where the copyright owner is the employer of the author or director.

1 The CDPA 1988, s 78.

(ii) Objection to derogatory treatment

4.84 The right to object to derogatory treatment[1] means that the author's consent may be required to make an alteration to or editing of the work, other than a translation or transcription. The treatment of the work is derogatory if it amounts to distortion or mutilation or is otherwise prejudicial to the honour or reputation of the author or director. It does not, however, apply to computer programs or computer generated works or for the purpose of reporting current events, publication in newspapers, magazines or periodicals, encyclopaedias, dictionaries, yearbooks or other reference works. It does not apply where the employer owns the copyright unless the author or director has been identified at the time of the relevant alteration. The right is infringed by a person who possesses what he knows to be infringing copies in the course of a business.

1 The CDPA 1988, s 80.

(iii) Prevention of false attribution

4.85 Finally, there is the right to prevent false attribution of a work[1]. A third person may not be falsely identified as the author of literary, dramatic, musical or artistic work or as the director of a film.

1 The CDPA 1988, s 84.

(I) European legislation in the field of copyright law

4.86 Recognising the need for continued harmonisation and for law reform in the light of technological developments and globalisation, the European Commission has proposed legislative changes. In the intellectual property area the three most important initiatives to be considered are:

■   the Infosoc Directive[1];

■   the E-Commerce Directive[2]; and

■   the Conditional Access Directive[3].

1 Directive (EC) 29/2001.
2 Directive (EC) 31/2000.
3 Directive (EC) 84/98.

(i) The Infosoc Directive

4.87 Directive (EC) 29/2001 on copyright and related rights in the Information Society was adopted on 9 April 2001. It was published in the *Official Journal*. It entered into force on 17 June 2001. Member States must implement it by 22 December 2002.

The Infosoc Directive is intended to extend copyright protection to, and harmonise copyright protection in, the digital environment throughout the EU, and provide protection for anti-copying devices and electronic rights management systems. It also implemented the provisions of the 1996 WIPO Copyright and Performers and Phonograms Treaties.

The Patent Office has indicated that amendments will be necessary to CDPA 1988 and, at the time of writing, the DTI has published a Consultation Paper on the Infosoc Directive (7 August 2002)[1] and proposed draft amendments to the CDPA 1988[2]. The draft amendments may be altered following the consultation, which expires on 31 October 2002.

■   **Reproduction right** In relation to copyright, this is likely to remain unchanged. Section 17(2) of the CDPA 1988 includes storing all work in any medium by electronic means. Section 17(6) includes transitory and incidental copies. However, text may be added to clarify that temporary acts of reproduction also cover copies of recordings of performances.

■   **Right of communication to the public** The Infosoc Directive gives authors the exclusive right to authorise or prohibit any communication of their works to the public, by wire or wireless means. Radio and television broadcasts, cable programme services and communications via the Internet are currently dealt with in section 20 of the CDPA 1988 but are likely to be amended in order to include unambiguously all on-line Internet services and wireless Internet services. (Similar rights are given to performers, and section 183 will need to be brought into line.)

■   **Distribution right** This applies to physical copies only, and the rules of EEA exhaustion apply to such physical copies. 'On-line distribution' is in fact controlled by the right of communication to the public, therefore it does not exhaust.

1 www.patent.gov.uk/about/consultations/ecopyright/index.htm.
2 www.patent.gov.uk/about/consultations/ecopyright/index.htm.

(m) Exceptions to copyright

4.88   There is an exhaustive list of exceptions.

The exception for temporary acts of reproduction is mandatory. This exception applies only to the reproduction right. To qualify, acts of reproduction of work must:

- be transient or incidental;

- be an integral and essential part of a technological process;

- have the sole purpose of enabling:

  - transmission in a network between third parties by an intermediary; or

  - a lawful use of the work;

- have no independent economic significance;

- not conflict with normal exploitation of the work; and

- not unreasonably prejudice the legitimate interests of the right holder[1].

There is a list of five further exceptions to the reproduction right, and 14 to both the reproduction right and the right of communication to the public. Member States are not obliged to provide these exceptions. In addition, Member States may retain exceptions 'of minor importance' which are not listed in the Infosoc Directive, but only in relation to analogue use, and provided they do not affect free circulation of goods and services within the Community[2].

Few of these listed exceptions correspond exactly with the exceptions to copyright provided by the CDPA 1988. The UK will be obliged to adjust the scope of exceptions to copyright provided by the CDPA 1988.

1   The last three points embody the 'three step test', which is contained in the TRIPS Agreement (WTO 1994, article 13) and the WIPO Copyright Treaty (article 10) and introduced by article 5.5 of the Infosoc Directive in relation to all exceptions. However, it is not currently proposed to introduce this text explicitly into the CDPA 1988. The exception for temporary acts of reproduction provided by article 5 of the Infosoc Directive described here is not the same as the exception provided by article 13 of the E-Commerce Directive – 'automatic and intermediate temporary storage do not attract liability if the specified conditions are met'.

2   The Commission appears to be intent on bringing the specific subject matter of copyright into the ambit of Community competition law, or at least in defining liberally the 'exceptional circumstances' where the free market purpose set out in article 82 of the EC Treaty should prevail over intellectual property rights. However, at the time of writing the ECJ has suspended execution of the European Commission's Decision of 3 July 2001 requiring IMS Health to make copyright sales information available to its competitors on competition grounds, pending the final hearing.

4.89   'Technological measures' are anything designed to prevent the commission of unauthorised restricted acts, such as copying or the database unfair extraction right. These include encryption, access control and copy control technology, and are 'effective' if a right holder uses them to control access. Member States are obliged to provide adequate legal protection for any effective technological measures, against manufacture, importation, distribution, sale, rental, advertisement for sale or rental, or possession for commercial purposes of:

- devices, products, components or the provision of services which are promoted, advertised or marketed for the purpose of circumvention;

- have limited commercially significant purpose or use other than circumvention; or

- are primarily produced to enable or facilitate circumvention.

Whilst the Infosoc Directive defines to find technological measures as preventing unauthorised acts – in other words the definition of technological means, and thus the extent of the protection afforded to them excludes permitted acts, such as exceptions to copyright – in reality the vast majority of currently available technological measures prevent access altogether. In these instances, not only access for copyright restricted acts, but also access by those legitimately wishing to exercise permitted exceptions, is controlled by the party who controls the technological measures which protect the work.

The Infosoc Directive obliges Member States to ensure that right holders are able to benefit from certain exceptions to copyright, in the absence of voluntary agreements by which the right holders grant such access. The Directive does not state how this is to be achieved.

Exceptions to copyright which must be ensured by Member States under this provision include the exceptions for temporary acts of reproduction, libraries and archives, ephemeral recordings (but not domestic time shifting), hospital broadcasts, teaching and research, disability and public security, but exclude the exception for reporting current events by the media.

(i) *Rights management information*

4.90 This is information which identifies the work, author, terms of use, etc. It includes digital code containing that information. For example, electronic rights management information can be used to enable right holders to trace the use of or obtain payment for their works on the Internet. Member States are obliged to provide adequate legal protection against:

■   unauthorised removal or alteration of electronic rights management;

■   exploitation of works from which electronic rights management information has been removed; and

■   a person doing those acts, if he knows or has reasonable grounds for knowing that he is inducing, enabling, facilitating or concealing an infringement of copyright.

The following technological protection is already provided for Information Society services by UK law:

■   the Conditional Access (Unauthorised Decoders) Regulations 2000[1] amend sections 297A and 298 of the CDPA 1988 and section 42A of the Telecommunications Act 1984 (TA 1984). The Regulations provide for protection and criminal sanctions against illicit devices which enable or facilitate the circumvention of technological measures designed to protect television and radio subscription services and conditional access services.

■   section 297A of the CDPA 1988 makes it an offence to make, import, sell or let for hire or offer or expose for sale or hire any unauthorised decoder. (Unauthorised access is not an offence under this section[2].)

1 SI 2000/1175.
2 Other relevant legislation currently in force:
   • the Computer Mis-Use Act 1990 (s 1 – unauthorised access to computer material; s 2 – unauthorised access with intent to commit or facilitate commission of further offences);
   • section 296 of the CDPA 1988 (devised as a design to circumvent copy protection);
   • section 297A of the CDPA 1988 (unauthorised decoders);
   • section 298 of the CDPA 1988 (rights and remedies in respect of apparatus, etc, for unauthorised reception of transmissions);
   • section 42 of the TA 1984 (fraudulent use of telecommunication system);
   • section 42A of the TA 1984 (control of anything used for obtaining a service covered by section 42(1));
   • section 55 of the Data Protection Act 1998 (unlawful obtaining, etc, of personal data);
   • section 42 of the TA 1984 (dishonestly obtaining a service);
   • section 297 of the CDPA 1988 (fraudulently receiving broadcasts or cable programme services); and
   • section 5(b)(1) of the Wireless Telegraphy Act 1949 (offence to use any wireless telegraphy apparatus to obtain information as to the content of any message whilst the person is not authorised to receive – this could include WAP and other wireless Internet services).

(ii) The E-Commerce Directive

4.91 The E-Commerce Directive, which has been adopted by the European Council of Ministers and was implemented in the UK in August 2002, is considered in various different respects in a number of chapters in this book[1]. In relation to the law of copyright, one particular aspect of the Directive and its impact should be mentioned, which is in relation to limiting the liability of ISPs when they act as unknowing intermediaries in relation to unlawful acts of others. The activities for which the Directive indicates that the ISP should not be liable are conduit, caching and hosting of material which is produced by third parties. We will look at each in turn.

1 See in particular Chapter 2, E-contract (with respect to contractual relations on-line) and Chapter 6, E-marketing.

Conduit

4.92 Conduit implies the passive transmission of, or passive allowing of access to, information provided by third parties. The ISP's liability for content transmission would be excluded where the service consists of transmission of information provided by a user of the service or the provision of access to a communication network. But this would be limited to circumstances where the ISP does not monitor the transmission, does not determine to whom the transmission is sent and does not edit or modify the information being transmitted.

The exclusion applies also to automatic, intermediate and transient storage of information in the network for the purpose of carrying out these acts.

Caching

4.93 An ISP will be exempted from liability for caching if done within the sole purpose of making the onward transmission of information to recipients of the service more efficient, and provided it is automatic, intermediate and temporary.

There are further conditions that the ISP must satisfy to benefit from this protection:

- it must not modify the information;

- it has to comply with any conditions for access to the information;

- it must comply with industry standards relating to the updating of the information;

- it must not interfere with the industry recognised technology to obtain data for the use of the information; and

- it has to act quickly on receiving knowledge that the information at source has been removed or disabled.

Hosting

4.94 Hosting refers to the provision by an ISP of space on its server to users for content (websites, bulletin boards, etc). An ISP will not be liable for information stored at the request of persons contracted to it for the provision of hosting services, provided that it does not have knowledge of any illegality and acts quickly to remove or disable access upon obtaining knowledge of any illegality[1].

Note the analogous but not identical provisions of the Infosoc Directive, which also cover these activities and which are described in paragraph 4.87. Neither Directive corresponds exactly with the take-down provisions of the US Digital Millennium Copyright Act. It may not be realistic to hope that implementation of these differing provisions in the laws of each EU Member State will result in a fully harmonised legal environment for ISPs within the single European Market[2].

1 In this context, we are concerned with material which breaches copyright. In Chapter 3, E-liability, we have also considered the parallel position with respect to material of an obscene or offensive nature.
2 Member States' courts are already establishing case law on take-down. For example, *Netherlands Church of Scientology v Dataweb* Cause No 96/1048, Dist Ct of The Hague, 9 June 1999: an ISP could be liable for copyright infringement by hosting infringing material if notice had been given, unless it acted quickly to remove the material.

(iii) The Conditional Access Directive

4.95   Chapter 3, E-liability contains commentary on the Conditional Access Directive and how it will affect the management of copyright, so it is not proposed to elaborate further in this chapter.

(n) Interrelationship with other intellectual property rights

4.96   In addition to, or instead of copyright, digital and physical products can be protected by one or more other potentially overlapping intellectual property rights[1]. Briefly:

Databases	Rights in a set of information can be protected by copyright and/or database rights. These are discussed in section 7 below.
Designs	Copyright and design rights can subsist in a design document. Design rights can protect the shape or configuration of an article, while copyrights can protect the surface decoration on the article.
Trade marks	A device trade mark will start with a drawing and the drawing itself will attract copyright. This is the defence against exact or substantial copiers during the first years of the trade mark. Copyright also protects the design in a trade dress. If that trade dress generates sufficient goodwill to be recognisable, it can be protected as an unregistered trade mark.
Patents	Copyright does not protect ideas as such. Copyright may protect a work that expresses an idea but not the idea behind it. An inventive idea may be protectable by a patent.

1 For protection by non-intellectual property rights, see paragraph 4.88 and the footnotes to that paragraph.

7.   DATABASE LAW

(a) Copyright and database rights

4.97   The Copyright and Rights in Databases Regulations 1997, which came into force on 1 January 1998, created database rights in the UK for the first time. These were derived from the EC Database Directive[1]. Sui generis database rights operate under a separate framework from conventional copyright[2].

Database rights subsist under the Regulations if:

■   there is a 'database', which is defined as a collection of independent words, data or other materials, which is arranged in a systematic or methodical way and where relevant entries are 'individually accessible' by electronic or other means. Certain collections of data do not fall within this definition, such as linked records, unsorted data, and data which cannot be individually accessed[3];

- a 'substantial investment' has been made in obtaining, verifying or presenting the contents of a 'database'.

A further requirement is that one of the 'makers' of the database must be an EEA national, habitually resident in the EEA, a body incorporated or formed under the laws of an EEA Member State with its principal place of business a registered office within it, or have ongoing links with the EEA at the time that the database is created.

The database rights subsist for a period of 15 years after the end of the calendar year in which the database is completed or first made available to the public and give a limited right to prevent a third party from

- unfairly extracting; and

- reusing for commercial purposes all or substantially all of the database contents. A fair dealing exception to the use of another's database allows for third party access or use of data where this relates to insubstantial parts of the contents or to extraction for teaching and research purposes. Subsequent substantial changes to the database will qualify it for new 15-year terms of protection.

1 Directive (EC) 9/96.
2 In relation to Internet use of data and the sui generis database rights, in *British Horseracing Board Ltd v William Hill Organisation Ltd* [2001] 2 CMLR 215, at first instance, regardless of copyright, the database owner who could show substantial investment in compilation of the database was entitled to restrain indefinitely unauthorised re-use of a substantial part or any unauthorised repeated re-use of an insubstantial part of the database. The Court of Appeal overturned this injunction (31 July 2001, unreported), CA, and referred the case to the ECJ on the interpretation of the Database Directive.
3 They may, however, be subject to copyright protection as a table or compilation.

(b) Modified copyright protection

4.98 A 'database' will also be protected by copyright if 'by reason of the selection or arrangement of the contents of the database the database constitutes the author's own intellectual creation'. This copyright subsists for 70 years from the end of the year in which the author dies.

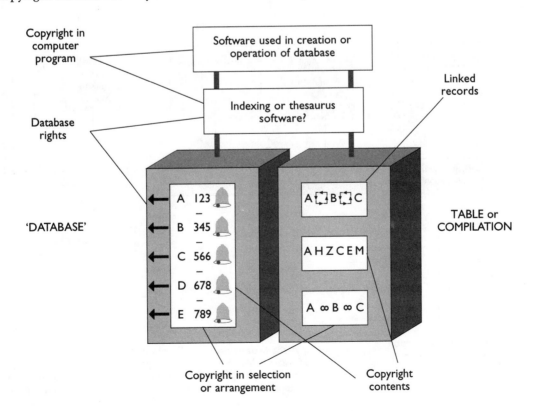

It is important to make a clear distinction between the software used to create and access the information, the way the information is presented, the indexes used and the information itself. These are all distinct, and may be protected by different rights.

(c) How to protect your rights

4.99 Practical tips for a database owner include:

■ ensuring that the name of the maker and date of first publication clearly appear on the database;

■ keeping good records evidencing the quantity and quality of the financial, human or technical resources invested in the making of the database; a database notice similar to a copyright notice would be useful. Wording along the lines 'Database rights of ABC dated [ ]' would be appropriate;

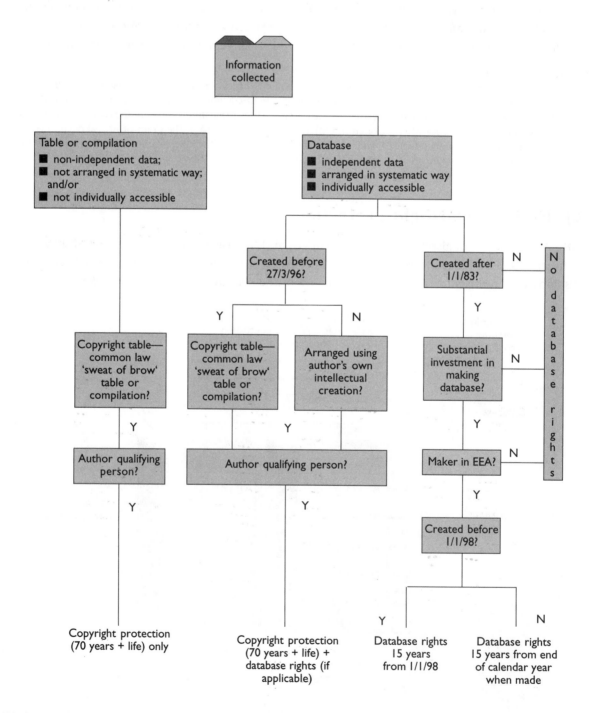

- continuing to get *copyright* assignments from contractors – although the 'maker' and so therefore the owner of the database will usually be the commissioner, any copyrights will still be owned by the contractor; and

- checking licences for terms which may now be void.

It follows that, for all practical purposes in the UK, rights in a database can be treated as literary copyright if the selection or arrangement of the contents constitutes the author's own intellectual creation. Otherwise, if it is a mere listing made through a substantial investment by the maker, the rights would be the sui generis database rights.

8. REGISTERED DESIGNS AND DESIGN RIGHTS

4.100 Design rights, which are akin to copyright, protect features of shape, configuration, patterns or ornaments applied to articles. The design is not distinct from the article in which it is embodied. Design rights subsist as registered designs or as unregistered designs. Both are separate and distinct rights.

(a) Registered designs

4.101 Directive (EC) 71/98 of the European Parliament and of the Council dated 13 October 1998 on the legal protection of designs has been implemented in the UK by the Registered Designs Regulations 2001, which came into force on 9 December 2001.

Registered designs are granted a life span of 25 years for the appearance of all or part of a product resulting from its features (for example lines, contours, shapes, ornamentation) in two or three dimensions, and including texture and materials. There is no requirement for aesthetic appeal. A 'product' is any industrial or handicraft item. The whole or any part of a product can be registered, even if the part will not be sold separately (for example, an external part of a car, such as a wing mirror). Multiple designs cannot be registered, only single applications. Designs are no longer registrable in relation to a particular product (this is called 'dematerialisation'). Only features which remain visible in normal use are protected.

A design has individual character if overall impression on an informed user is materially different from the impression made by another design. A product can be on the market for up to one year prior to application for registration, and this 'period of grace' is not considered as disclosure (this replaces the previous provision for four months' certified exhibition). This one-year 'period of grace' only applies within the EEA. Registration cannot protect designs which:

- are solely dictated by the design's technical function; or

- must be reproduced exactly to permit the product (or the product which it is beside or to which it is connected) to perform its function (the 'must fit' exception) – but parts of a modular product can be registered (the 'Lego exception').

The creator of the design is the first owner. However, the employer of the designer is the first owner where it is created in the course of employment. Commissioned work is owned by the commissioner, which is different from the analogous situation relating to copyright works (where the 'creator' and not the 'commissioner' is the first owner).

The rights granted to the owner include exclusive rights to manufacture and commercial dealings with the design.

4.102 Any unlicensed commercial activity carried out within the UK's jurisdiction will constitute an infringement. However, there is a list of deemed non-infringing uses:

- private and non-commercial use;

- experimental use;

- teaching and citations (if properly acknowledged and not commercially unfair nor commercially prejudicial); and

- body parts (the 'must match' exceptions) for re-instatement or repair.

Exhaustion of rights is international.

Registration protects the design in respect of any use (so registration of a Beetle car also protects a model Beetle car and a Beetle key-ring).

The changes in registered design law will mean that there is greater overlap with other intellectual property rights: trade marks (for example, shapes – such as a dishwasher tablet registered as a design and a trade mark); copyright (literary and artistic materials are no longer excluded – old rule 26 – so posters, collectibles, etc, can now be registered as designs).

(b) Design rights

4.103 As well as the harmonisation of national laws covering protection of registered designs, the project for harmonising the laws on the protection of designs in the EU includes a new Community Design System containing an unregistered design protection. This will be administered by the Office of Harmonisation for the Internal Market (OHIM) in Alicante.

The current law in relation to unregistered design rights combines features of copyright and registered design right law. These rights are available only to European designers. The right protects any aspect of the shape or configuration of an article. It does not apply to surface decorations and there is no requirement of 'appeal to the eye'. Unregistered designs protect three-dimensional designs to complete items and their individual components. To qualify as a protectable design it has to be original, which means that it should not be commonplace at the time it was created or commonly used in the trade.

The following also do not qualify:

- methods or principles of construction;

- features of shape or configuration which enable the article to be connected to, or placed around or against another article, so that either article may perform its function, ie 'must fit'; and

- features which are dependent upon the appearance of another article of which the article is intended by the designer to form an integral part, ie 'must match'.

However, discrete components can be taken alone and unless their design is dictated by some general standard or other design (eg the shape of an electrical connector or plug into a standard socket), the component is entitled to design right protection. Even components which are partially required to fit some standard shape may have design right protection for the remainder of their shape.

(c) Primary and secondary infringement

4.104 The act of infringement is that of copying or substantially reproducing the design. As with copyright, there are different tests for primary and secondary infringement. Primary infringement consists of the making of an article or a design document. A primary infringer is liable without notice of the design right, but there is a defence available of innocent infringement, where the copier did not know and had no reason to believe that the design right subsisted.

An importer or a distributor of an article is only an infringer if he knew or had reason to believe that the design right existed, so it is necessary to put the putative infringer on notice of the design right, and to give him the opportunity to cease the infringing activity after investigating the claim. Two weeks is a fair time to investigate any allegation of infringement. Without such 'knowledge or reason to believe' there is no infringement.

(d) Threats

4.105 Where an unjustified threat is made other than in respect of the reproducing or importing of an article made in accordance with a design, any person aggrieved by the threat is entitled to seek an injunction to prevent a recurrence and damages. This is considered in more detail in paragraph 4.118.

(e) Spare parts

4.106 The question often arises as to the right to make spare parts. There is no current EU harmonisation on this issue, although there are proposals. Everyone is entitled to buy spare parts from any source to keep their goods in working order; however, design rights may subsist in components and this causes some doubt over whether manufacturers of spare parts are entitled to supply them.

The position on spare parts is uncertain. European law is in disarray on this point and there is no inherent exhaustion of rights to enable spare parts to be made for public sale. So while English law does provide for local exhaustion with respect to spare parts, this has been untested in design right law.

(f) Confidential information[1]

4.107 Information which is substantial and secret, in the sense that it is not available to the public, is protectable as confidential information. This is of great relevance and value to an on-line seller who is able to protect know-how, technical know-how, commercial information and trade secrets which would not otherwise qualify for protection as patent or copyright. Information may be confidential even if each part of it could be put together by the public so that, although the 'building blocks' are available, they have not previously been put together publicly. Whether information is treated as confidential is a matter of law which depends on how the owner has treated it. If the owner has taken proper steps to protect information as confidential information, the law will respect that information. Information may also be of the kind which is inherently confidential.

The law recognises two kinds of confidential information:

■ An employee should not disclose the information which is confidential commercially during the course of his employment. Confidential commercial information includes price lists, delivery routes and commercial plans in a general sense (such as areas of proposed expansion or contract of a business). After the contract of employment has come to an end the information is no longer confidential in the absence of any express term stating otherwise.

■ Technical information is information such as secret recipes, formulae, processes and confidential methodologies and know-how used in a business. In these cases the source code is generally kept secret and therefore the information in the source code is usually regarded as confidential information. This kind of confidential information is regarded by the courts as secret and protectable, even without a specific contractual obligation, where it appears from the circumstances that the information is of the kind that the courts will protect.

1 See also aspects of Chapter 3, E-liability with respect to data protection rights and the overlap with confidential information.

4.108 If confidential information is published on the Internet, it then becomes available to the public and can no longer be considered confidential[1]. It does not have the benefit of protection because it is in the public domain, having been published on the Internet, and there can be no control over those who have had access to it. It is immaterial that no-one may have actually accessed it because it is the availability that destroys the confidentiality.

A person unlawfully putting confidential information on the Internet is unlawfully publishing it. That person is liable in damages to the owner of the confidential information. Although an injunction is also a remedy for breach of confidence, if the confidence has been comprehensively breached, as it would be by putting it on the Internet, it may be too late for an injunction.

Even where a corporation has put the confidential information on the Internet, actions may lie against individuals (such as the corporation's directors or senior executives) for breach of duty.

The position of a carrier such as an ISP is that no cause of action subsists until the ISP has noticed the breach of confidence. At that point the ISP should remove the confidential information from the server, for if it does not do so it risks being jointly liable for breach of confidence with the publisher of the information. However, it is arguable that the confidentiality has been so thoroughly destroyed that the information is no longer confidential, in which case the ISP may be fortunate enough to escape liability[2].

1 For a view as to how the English courts treat claims of confidentiality applying to information which in some sense has appeared in the public domain, see *Schering Chemicals Ltd v Falkman Ltd* [1981] 2 All ER 321, CA. This is a pre-Internet era case, which related to the subsequent use of 'confidential' material concerning the claimant which had appeared in the *Sunday Times*. It remains to be seen what actual view the courts would now take if a case on similar facts involved the use of 'confidential' information derived from Internet websites.
2 However, see again the *Schering Chemicals* case, which may be considered to provide a measure of guidance on this point.

9.   PROCEDURE FOR INFRINGEMENT

4.109 This section outlines the remedies available to a right holder against another person for conduct prejudicing the rights of the rightholder.

(a) The causes of action

4.110 Broadly, the causes of action are as follows:

- An action for infringement is the main procedure by which an on-line seller may enforce his registered intellectual property rights. An action for infringement is commenced by initiating proceedings in an appropriate court.

- Infringement of an unregistered trade mark, trade name, trading style, etc, where the claim is in the tort of passing off.

- The equitable remedies associated with breach of confidentiality.

- In relation to an intellectual property right where the claimant maintains that a wrongful registration favours the defendant, the claimant will want to bring revocation or invalidity proceedings.

(b) What sort of proceedings to bring

4.111 It would always be the desire of a claimant to find the quickest and most cost-effective procedure. There are several routes to consider. The question is often asked as to what is the most appropriate procedure where a claim is urgent. Much depends on the strength of the claimant's case as well as the nature of the course of action. There are five alternatives, each of which has its place:

- **Full trial** Anybody seeking redress through the mechanism of a process before the courts should bear in mind that trials are now taking about a year from the claim being served on the defendant to reach judgment, sometimes less. The courts have been diligent in speeding up matters, but court litigation in England involves high costs, especially in comparison with other European countries.

- **Speedy trial** This is available in cases of great urgency, for example where the issue of a claim is equivalent to an interim injunction, as no one will buy the product because of the high risk of a final injunction. Speedy trials are currently taking about four to five months from the issue of proceedings to judgment.

- **Summary judgment** The rule is that summary judgment can be granted where there is likely to be no successful defence, either on the facts or on the facts and law jointly, or the defendant is unlikely to succeed in its defence. The defence need not be totally unarguable. Summary judgment is not available where libel forms part of the claim, even if summary judgment is not being sought for that part.

- **Interim injunction** This is an injunction pending trial. It is customarily granted or refused on the balance of convenience, provided the claimant has an arguable case but, in practice, especially in trade mark and passing off cases, the court always sets a higher standard than that of an arguable case because the grant or refusal of an interlocutory injunction is likely to be the end of the matter.

- **A split trial** It is possible to have a split trial on the merits, so that an issue which will be conclusive can be heard ahead of other issues.

Given this choice, and the effectiveness of English remedies, England is becoming a more inviting jurisdiction in which to litigate intellectual property disputes. It should, however, be noted that mini trials are firmly discouraged. We will now look at some of these issues in more detail.

(c) Interim injunctions

4.112 The criteria for granting or refusing an interim injunction have recently been revisited. As a result, the inflexible bar on examining the merits has been removed. The current guidelines are:

- The grant of an interim injunction is a matter of discretion and depends on all the facts of the case.

- There are no fixed rules as to when an interim injunction should or should not be granted. The relief must be kept flexible. Because of the procedure adopted on the hearing of applications for interim relief, the court will rarely attempt to resolve complex questions of disputed fact or law.

■ Major factors the court should bear in mind are:

    – the extent to which damages are likely to be an adequate remedy to either party and the ability of the other party to pay;

    – the balance of convenience between the parties;

    – the maintenance of the status quo; and

    – the clear view the court may reach as to the strength of the parties' cases.

In summary, we have returned to a merit-based regime for the granting of interlocutory injunctions and the remedy may be just as effective as the *kort gedding* remedy of the Dutch court, provided the English courts are willing to grant pan-European injunctions like their Dutch brethren under harmonised rights such as trade marks.

The advantages of an interim application include the fact that the parties have a preliminary view from a judge and the setting out of the merits is likely to result in earlier, and therefore cheaper, dispute resolution.

(d) Substantive and procedural remedies

4.113 English law provides useful substantive and procedural remedies in relation to infringement. The remedies sought and generally granted consist of an injunction to escape further infringement, damages for past infringement or, at the claimant's option, an account of profit in lieu of damages and, with respect to copyright, additional damages for flagrancy, or an account of profit.

(i) *Damages and account of profits*

4.114 The English court has the power to award damages arising out of infringement. Damages are a statutory right. The fundamental rule is that damages are designed to compensate the claimant for the losses he has suffered and not to punish the defendant[1]. This is a point of some significance when compared in particular with the US, where the attitude to punitive damages awards in appropriate cases has always been much more tolerant.

Damages are awarded in intellectual property cases on the basis of the level of sales the claimant would have made but for the infringing activities of the defendant. The measure of damage is the claimant's loss of profit. Where he would not have made the sale, the measure of damages is a reasonable royalty. Any other relevant head of damage which is not too remote should be included, such as the need to advertise heavily to recover the market position. Where there are dependent sales which have also been lost (for example, spare parts and consumables), loss of these may be included in the claim.

It can often be difficult to ascertain the quantum of reasonable royalty. Sometimes this is institutionalised, such as in the case of the taking of a song or music score without consent, where a song or music score has been freely licensed in the past. In those circumstances, the royalty will be the going rate, but on other occasions the court may have to make an informed guess based on the evidence.

However, because copyright infringement is so easy, for example by replicating CDs, liability for compensatory damages may be an inadequate deterrent to defendants, given the profit available to the defendant after paying compensatory damages may be inadequate. Thus the court has power[2] to award additional damages having regard to the flagrancy of the infringement and the state of knowledge of the defendant at the relevant time. To date, awards of additional damages for flagrancy have not been large but there is no reason in principle why they should not be substantial in nature. Because of the availability of additional damages for flagrancy, it is doubtful whether exemplary or punitive damages at common law can be awarded in copyright infringement cases.

Instead of damages, a party which is successful as a claimant may also apply to the court for an account of profits. This means an account of the profit which the defendant has made by virtue of the infringement. An account of the claimant's profit is a head of damages and is treated as such under English law. Accounts of profits are rare, because it is thought to be relatively easy for a defendant to deflate profit to zero and, in any event, it is only for that proportionate part of the profit which relates to the infringement that an account of profits can be claimed. However, where copying is low cost and profits high, an account of profit is a remedy perhaps worth utilising.

1   *General Tire and Rubber Co v Firestone Tyre and Rubber Co Ltd* [1975] 2 All ER 173, HL.
2   Pursuant to the CDPA 1988, s 97(2).

(ii) Injunction

4.115   An injunction is available for infringement of any intellectual property rights. The usual order is that an injunction is granted after trial, although an interim injunction may also be granted, pending trial. Interim injunctions have been discussed at paragraph 4.112 above. Substantive and final injunctions are definitive outcomes of litigation. A stay of an injunction, even pending appeal, may be requested by a defendant.

An injunction is a remedy available as of right after trial[1]. The usual rule is that an injunction will be granted after trial. If there is some reason to stay pending appeal, a stay may be granted, but if the claimant wishes to have his injunction pending trial he has to provide a cross undertaking in damages[2].

Injunctions are also available to prevent infringement of moral rights, for example allowing an author to prevent derogatory treatment of the work being published.

The injunction will cover all infringing acts, and breach of the terms of an injunction constitutes a contempt of court, rendering the breaching party potentially liable to fines or imprisonment.

1   The CDPA 1988, s 96(2).
2   That is, that if the injunction should as a result of the trial be discharged, then the claimant will compensate the defendant for the damage he has sustained through the imposition of the injunction in the first place.

(iii) Cease and desist, confiscation and destruction

4.116   It is usual that after trial the court will order delivery to the claimant of any infringing copies. Infringing copyright[1] relates to infringing copies of work in the possession, custody or control of a defendant in the course of a business or where the defendant has in his possession, custody or control an article specifically designed or adapted for making copies of a particular copyright work knowing or having reason to believe that this has been or is to be used to make infringing copies.

Such an application is usually made on judgment, but may be made pursuant to an application for interim relief[2].

The infringing product may be delivered, or alternatively destroyed upon oath. Where it is delivered, it is for the person then in possession of it to do what they will. In copyright cases the court may order infringing copies to be forfeited to the copyright owner or destroyed as the court thinks fit[3].

However, no right of delivery is available later than six years after the date in which the infringing copy or article was made in the absence of fraud or legal disability of the copyright owner.

1 See the CDPA 1988, s 99(1).
2 Such as that on a civil service order under the Civil Procedure Act 1997, s 10.
3 The CDPA 1988, s 114.

(e) Criminal sanctions and seizure powers

4.117 Infringement of copyright or a trade mark in English law is a criminal offence with a maximum sentence on summary conviction of up to six months or a fine, or on conviction on indictment for a term of imprisonment not exceeding two years.

Each act which is a similar offence is also a criminal offence. Securing criminal convictions is more difficult than in the civil courts because allegations have to be proven beyond all reasonable doubt. In relation to each offence it is necessary to prove that the accused knew or had reason to believe that the article was an infringing copy of the copyright work. There are therefore relatively few convictions in England for criminal offences. In practice, prosecutions brought from time to time are likely to be dealt with in a summary jurisdiction, and sentences are likely to involve fines at most.

There are also criminal sanctions for those who interfere with copy protection equipment[1] by making, importation of, selling, letting or hiring any unauthorised decoder, or dishonestly receiving a programme, including a broadcasting for cable programme service provided from a place in the UK, with intent to avoid payment of any charge applicable to reception of the programme[2].

It is also an offence to make, import, sell, offer or expose for sale or advertise for sale or hire any device designed or adapted to avoid copy protection, or to publish information to enable or assist persons to avoid copy protection[3].

The CDPA 1988 also grants customs officers power to seize and impound material which is in breach of copyright.

1 The CDPA 1988, s 297(8).
2 The CDPA 1988, s 297 generally.
3 The CDPA 1988, s 296(2).

(f) Threats

4.118 Where a person is alleged to be an infringer of a patent, trade mark, registered design (in respect of old law, secondary infringing acts) or design right, any notice to him must be circumspect. This is because any person aggrieved by an unjustified threat can sue for an injunction and damages. The risk that the claimant might himself be sued for damages for the making of an unjustified threat can be avoided by his issuing proceedings first and then issuing a threat to serve the proceedings if appropriate undertakings are not given.

The basis of the right of action to sue if threatened is that customers and, in the case of design rights, the importer should not be threatened with legal action without justification. The claimant in such a situation is usually the manufacturer or importer of the goods and the person threatened is usually the customer or a third party.

There is a defence that the person threatened is an infringer, but patentees should not be defendants in their own patent action. There is an important exception to this rule, namely that it is not actionable to threaten a manufacturer or importer in respect of patent infringement for the manufacture or import of the infringing goods, even though it is actionable to threaten the manufacturer for selling or supplying the goods in question. Express threats must therefore be limited to importing or making the infringing goods or carrying out an infringing process.

In trade mark cases the threat is not actionable where the threat is in respect of the application of the trade mark to the goods, or the importation of goods or their packaging to which the trade mark has been applied, and the supply of services under the mark.

For design right and registered design right the permitted acts for which threats can be made are the making of or importing of an article.

The action for an unwarranted threat may be brought against the person who wrote the threatening letter as well as the right owner. Legal advisers may find themselves added as defendants to threats actions[1].

Mere notification of a patent, registered trade mark, design right or registered design is not an actionable threat. Any allegation not within the permitted categories is actionable, even if confirmed only with a permitted threat.

1 In the recent case of *L'Oreal (UK) Ltd v Johnson & Johnson* [2000] FSR 686, the defendants were found liable for unjustified threats contained in a solicitor's letter before action.

10. SOME SPECIFIC INTELLECTUAL PROPERTY ISSUES FOR E-COMMERCE

(a) How and where do infringement rights arise?

4.119 This is a major issue in intellectual property law and the same principles apply as apply for domain names. The position appears to be that a person offering goods or services over the Internet will offer them out of a location. So, for a UK-based company using a UK-based Internet provider which will probably have a URL that ends with .co.uk, the location from which those goods and services are offered will be the UK. The Internet itself is a directory which can be accessed so that someone in another country might access the website. Obtaining information on a website, having looked it up on a directory (whether by browsing or otherwise) is a positive act by a third party. Goods or services may be ordered via the Internet, and the order form should be worded so delivery of that order takes effect where the goods or services are provided and not where the website (or its hosting server) is itself located.

Any infringement of intellectual property rights arising out of the offer to supply or the supply of goods or services therefore ought to be an infringement in the place of the website and not an infringement in the place of delivery if different. However, if the services are supplied locally or the goods are supplied CIF (Carriage Insurance and Freight) or by some other means so that property (title) in the goods does not pass until the goods have been delivered (or at least have entered the third country), then there may be infringement of rights by reason of importation in that third country.

Taking the above example, a person who offers goods or services over the Internet should do so on the basis of supply out of the country of offer. In that way infringement risks are minimised as it is the customer who is the importer into the third country and not the service provider. If the service provider is the importer then the offer to supply goods outside the territory of the advertiser will be an infringement if such acts are acts of infringement in the third country.

This analysis provides a rationale for the supplier to seek to ensure that the act of importation into a foreign country is that of the customer, not his own. Of course, there may be conflicting commercial reasons for the supplier to wish to be considered to be the person causing that importation, such as retention of title or taxation treatment. The analysis above is complicated further by factors outside the supplier's control. What, for example, is the position where, under the law of the country of the customer's residence, the supplier is deemed to import the material concerned into that country, regardless of what the supplier attempts to provide in the terms of his agreement? These issues are considered further in Chapter 7, E-dispute.

(b) Downloading copyright material and databases

4.120 The rule is that if it is an infringement of copyright to copy all or a substantial part of a copyright work without the licence of the copyright owner, then it is an infringement irrespective of the media in or through which the copying occurs. So, unlawfully putting music or computer software on the Internet is a copyright infringement. A claim for infringement is best prosecuted where the person who has the website is based. It may also be appropriate to take proceedings against the ISP hosting the website given the nature of the materials on the server which have to be copied each time the website is accessed. As we have seen above, that itself may be a separate infringement.

It will also be an infringement to copy by a person accessing the website. The obvious difficulty with the nature of this infringement, however, is that of policing.

(c) Is injunctive relief a useful remedy in cyberspace?

4.121 This is a question which is also far from resolved. Much depends on whether technical means exist to make an injunction effective. The general principle is that the court will not grant an injunction where it cannot be policed or where the person who is the subject of the injunction does not know with certainty whether or not he is infringing. The reason for this is that the penalty for breach is a fine or imprisonment. So means have to be found to police an injunction effectively.

This is an issue which has arisen with respect to pornography, and CompuServe in Germany has been subject to criminal prosecution[1]. The sanction, which is technically feasible, is to block any offending website source and not allow it into the system. So it may well be a requirement that, while infringing material is being offered from a particular website, that website may be blocked by ISPs by order of the court until such time as the offer of infringing material has ceased.

1 See Chapter 3, E-liability.

(d) Fighting a software patent action

4.122 The World Wide Web, by definition, is worldwide. There may therefore be occasions when a software program is the subject of patent protection in one country (often in the US) but not elsewhere, or a method of doing business may be patentable in one country (the US) but not in another. It becomes necessary to consider where the act of infringement is committed and who is committing that infringement.

For example, the owner of an Australian website uses a particular software program to produce a technical result. A third party, in the UK as part of a business, visits that website. That third party will carry out the steps which will result in the patent to the software program which belongs to a UK patentee being infringed. As the third party accesses the program as part of business, no issue arises as to whether it is done for private non-commercial purposes. But if this was the case, recall is not an infringement[1].

Where the program is accessed for commercial purposes (subject to a viable defence of innocent infringement), infringement proceedings may lie in the UK against the user of the program, but would they also lie in the UK against the Australian website owner? This is not a matter which is free from doubt but, applying first principles, it would appear to be no different from the supply of a process where the process can be used freely. All the cases on joint tortfeasorship suggest that where a person buys a product abroad and then imports it into the UK, even if the exporter knows that it is an infringing product in the UK, the exporter is not liable if title passes outside the jurisdiction of the UK courts unless something special was done between the importer and exporter to make the exporter liable as a joint tortfeasor.

A different theory could be applicable, which is that software patents are process patents and the end product on the screen is what could be termed a 'product'. On this basis, the importation would be that of an infringing product because it is an infringement to make a product abroad directly by an infringing process. However, the person who made the product would be the user and catching the user is difficult.

While it may be very difficult to catch infringers of software patents, it may also be difficult to prove that patents are invalid. The difficulty which arises is one of the prior art, since patenting software is a relatively new subject. The traditional place to look for prior art is a combination of prior art patents and journal articles, and generally neither format exists in great quantity in this relatively new area of patent law development.

1 Under section 60(5)(a) of the PA 1977.

5

E-brand

1. INTRODUCTION

5.01 This E-brand chapter is new to the third edition of this book. It explains how a new pseudo intellectual property right (IPR) can be created by registering a domain name identifying what a domain name is, who is entitled to one and how they are protected. It also explains how a person may use this domain name in conjunction with his own brand and those of third parties for his own e-activities, for instance by comparative advertisements, hyperlinks or metatags.

In previous editions of this book these issues were dealt with in the E-communicate and E-rights chapters. However, as issues surrounding domain names in particular have become so complicated and widespread, they now warrant a chapter to themselves. This chapter should, however, be read together with Chapter 4, E-rights, which deals with IPR (and in particular trade marks) and Chapter 6, E-marketing, which deals exclusively with advertising and sales promotion issues. Together, these three chapters highlight the issues to consider when creating and exploiting a brand in new media.

2. DOMAIN NAMES

5.02 To establish a presence on the Internet, the first step for a business is to choose a domain name. A domain name is a user friendly alias for an Internet address. The real address (the Internet protocol address) is a string of numbers that are difficult to use and remember, for example 207.46.130.150 is the Internet protocol address for www.microsoft.com. Each domain name is composed of a series of labels separated by dots, with the rightmost label referring to the domain name's top-level domain. Top-level domain names are either generic top-level domain names (gTLDs) or country-code top-level domain names (ccTLDs). Each of these top-level domains can be divided into second or third level domain names.

With the growth of the Internet, registration and/or use of domain names has, to a certain extent, conflicted with trade marks. One of the reasons for such conflict can be attributed to the lack of connection between the system for registering trade marks and the system for registering domain names. The former is a system granting territorial rights enforceable only within the designated territory. The latter is a system of granting rights that can be enforced globally.

The management of the domain name system is undertaken by the Internet Corporation for Assigned Names and Numbers (ICANN). ICANN is the non-profit corporation formed in September 1998 to assume responsibility for co-ordinating the assignment of protocol parameters, the management of the domain name system, the allocation of Internet protocol address space and the management of the root server system previously performed under US Government contract by the Internet Assigned Numbers Authority (IANA) and other entities[1].

1   For more detailed information on ICANN and/or IANA, visit their websites at www.icann.org and www.iana.org. A Michael Froomkin's article entitled 'Wrong Turn in Cyberspace: Using ICANN to route around the APA and the Constitution' (2000) 50 *Duke Law Journal* 17 may be found at www.personal.law.miami.edu/~froomkin/articles/ icann-main.htm. This offers a detailed analysis of the history of ICANN. In addition, ICANN Watch's website at www.icannwatch.org provides an excellent read entitled 'ICANN for Beginners'.

3.   GENERIC TOP-LEVEL DOMAINS (gTLDs)

5.03   In November 2000, the Board of Directors of ICANN approved the introduction of seven new gTLDs to the Internet. As discussed in the previous edition, it was of paramount importance to ICANN that the introduction of the new gTLDs be in a measured and responsible manner, with due regard to the need to minimise the infringements of IPR that is prevalent with the original gTLDs. Hence, a rejection of the first-come first-served approach to the allocation of domain names and a pre-launch priority registration period for IPR owners[1]. Recognition of the unknown effect that new gTLDs would have on the stability and reliability of the domain name system was also to occupy much of the debate on the introduction of the new gTLDs by ICANN[2].

So, in addition to the .com, .net, .org, .edu, .int, .gov and .mil gTLDs that were introduced in the 1980s, there are now .aero, .biz, .coop, .info, .museum, .name and .pro gTLDs. These must not be confused with the non-ICANN approved alternative gTLDs such as .kids and .sport that have been introduced by New.net and which are discussed at paragraph 5.13.

Of the original gTLDs, four are closed, which means that restrictions apply on who may register these and unless you fall within the restrictions, you will not need to consider these gTLDs when deciding which gTLD to register. These are:

■   .edu (restricted to specified educational institutions in the US);

■   .gov (restricted to US Government);

■   .int (restricted to organisations established by international treaties between governments); and

■   .mil (restricted to US military).

The other three original gTLDs are not restricted and are open to the Internet public for registration. These are:

■   .com (for international commercial organisations);

■   .net (for network organisations); and

■   .org (for miscellaneous organisations).

1   The problem with the first-come first-served approach is that a given domain name will be allocated to the first person who submits an application for that name. As highlighted by paragraph 5.46, those who are too 'slow off the mark' will often find that the domain name they are applying to register has already been registered by a third party. This is demonstrated by the domain name baa.com. Prior to its transfer, Internet users looking for the website for BAA plc (one of the world's leading airport companies) may have expected to find BAA plc at www.baa.com. However, an Internet user would have found that this was actually a sheep site, not an airport management site. BAA plc was to be found at www.baa.co.uk. Now BAA plc may be found at both these websites.
2   For information on the ICANN Board of Directors' adoption of a new top-level domains policy, see the ICANN website at www.icann.org/yokohama/new-tld-topic.htm, which provides a background and overview to the meeting on 16 July 2000 in Yokohama adopting this policy. Up-to-date information on the gTLDs may be found at www.icann.org/tlds and Internic's website at www.internic.net/faqs/new-tlds.html. Section 7 below and Chapter 4, E-rights consider the infringement of IPR by domain names.

5.04 For each gTLD there is a corresponding database of names. The database of names in the above three gTLDs is managed by the ICANN approved registry, VeriSign Inc (formerly Network Solutions Inc, which is now a subsidiary of VeriSign Inc). Each of the new gTLDs has its own individual ICANN approved registry, which should correspond to the organisation that submitted the proposals to ICANN for the new gTLD.

In accordance with ICANN's objectives, each new registry is required to devise a system of introducing the new gTLD in a considered manner, which is incorporated into the Registry Agreement that they enter into with ICANN. The Registry Agreement will either be sponsored or unsponsored.

A Sponsored Registry Agreement is needed where an organisation acts as a sponsor for the gTLD, that is where the sponsor represents the sponsored gTLD community that is most affected by the gTLD. For example, MuseDoma is the sponsor for .museum and the Society for International Telecommunications for Aeronautics (SITA) for .aero. Under this type of Registry Agreement, ICANN will delegate specific policy formulation to the sponsor, which would ordinarily have been under the remit of ICANN. By creating a charter for the sponsor, ICANN can ensure that the sponsor will act to ensure that the gTLD operates for the benefit of its sponsored gTLD community. The relevant new gTLDs are:

- .aero (for the air transport industry);

- .coop (for co-operatives); and

- .museum (for museums).

In contrast, under an Unsponsored Registry Agreement, the sponsor will operate under policies that represent the Internet community as a whole through ICANN. The relevant new gTLDs are:

- .biz (for businesses);

- .info (for all uses);

- .name (for individuals); and

- .pro (for professionals such as accountants, lawyers and physicians).

Save for .pro (whose Registry Agreement was signed by ICANN on 8 May 2002 and is expected to be launched late 2002/early 2003), all registries are operational, with .biz, .info and .name registries accepting live registrations. To assist in determining which gTLD to register, an overview of the new gTLDs can be found at paragraphs 5.05 and 5.08. Since sponsored gTLDs are representative of particular sections of the Internet community, a brief overview of each sponsored gTLD, together with advice on where more detailed information may be obtained, is provided.

(a) Unsponsored gTLDs

(i) .info

5.05 The .info registry was the first of the new gTLDs to be launched by Afilias Limited (Afilias), the ICANN registry for .info, on 1 October 2001. Over 500,000 domain names have already been registered and with Afilias' mission to expand the Internet as a global resource that fosters communication, commerce and community for the people of the world, they expect this number to increase significantly as on-line applications are accepted.

Afilias maintain that .info represents an opportunity for businesses, individuals and organisations to reach a worldwide audience with information about their products, services and ideas. Used either as a means of supplementing an existing website or for creating a new website, Afilias consider

.info to be a truly global gTLD, in contrast to .com[1]. While it is true that the pre-launch interest in and demand for .info domain names was high, it is premature to say whether this was a result of demand for a domain name address that could be used by a business to provide tailored information to their e-customers, or whether it was a pre-emptive strike against third parties willing to take advantage of a reputable name[2]. Information on Afilias and .info can be found at Afilias' website at www.afilias.info.

1 Afilias do not qualify this statement; perhaps it is a reflection of the misplaced perception that .com is a US domain name.
2 The difficulties encountered on the launch of .info are discussed below under 'Proof of concept' at paragraph 5.12.

(ii) .biz

5.06 After a number of delays, the .biz registry was launched by NeuLevel Inc (NeuLevel), the ICANN registry for .biz, in November 2001. In contrast to .info, which has no restrictions on use, .biz gTLDs are subject to key restrictions, which are detailed at NeuLevel's website at www.neulevel.biz. The key restriction is that domain names must be used or intended to be used primarily for bona fide business or commercial purposes. That is to say:

■ to exchange goods, services, or property of any kind;

■ in the ordinary course of trade or business; or

■ to facilitate the above.

NeuLevel make it clear that using or intending to use .biz exclusively for personal, non-commercial purposes or (to the welcome of IPR owners) the expression of non-commercial ideas, does not constitute bona fide business or commercial purposes. For example, registering www.microsoftsucks.biz to criticise the products or services of Microsoft, with no other intended business or commercial purpose would not be acceptable[1].

As with .info, the pre-launch demand for .biz was high. Critics argue that .biz is too young sounding, appealing to young businesses in contrast to the more traditional businesses. Time will tell whether .biz will prove as popular as .com for traditional businesses, who submitted pre-launch applications[2].

1 See also paragraph 5.27 on domain name dispute policies for the attitude of ICANN toward such domains and a discussion of, amongst others, the NatWest Bank dispute concerning the domain name natwestsucks.com.
2 The difficulties encountered on the launch of .biz are discussed below under 'Proof of concept' at paragraph 5.12.

(iii) .name

5.07 Global Name Registry Limited (GNR), the ICANN registry for .name, launched the .name registry in January 2002. The .name registry is aimed exclusively at individuals and provides both a domain name and e-mail forwarding service. GNR's website at www.gnr.com explains how it intends to use .name as a global platform for digital identity services whereby individuals can store, retrieve or distribute personal information on the Internet.

.name is a positive development for gTLDs, providing an alternative to .com that is more meaningful for individuals. The .name gTLD may appear in a number of ways. For example, firstname.lastname.name (robbie.williams.name), lastname.firstname.name (williams.robbie.name), or initial.lastname.name (r.williams.name). By inserting @ between the two names, an e-mail forwarding address is created (for example, robbie@williams.name). Since fictional characters, such as Harry Potter, are registerable by their IPR owners, .name will be of particular relevance to media and publishing houses and their clients[1].

1 See also paragraph 5.34 on domain name dispute policies, which discusses the recent spate of Harry Potter domain name disputes.

(b) Sponsored gTLDs

(i) .pro

5.08 RegistryPro Limited (RegistryPro), the registry for .pro, believe that the .pro gTLD will help Internet users all over the world locate professionals on-line by creating a virtual directory to enable consumers to perform searches for professionals by area of speciality and geographic location. Since domain name applicants must verify that they are qualified professionals in good standing, RegistryPro maintain that consumers will be assured they are dealing only with credentialed entities. If you are a certified professional (that is, accountant, doctor, lawyer), then .pro is a gTLD that you should consider registering, particularly as RegistryPro intend to establish a global awareness of .pro through extensive marketing campaigns aimed at .pro's target audience. For further information on .pro, visit RegistryPro's website at www.registrypro.com.

(ii) .coop

5.09 The National Cooperative Business Association (NCBA) are the sponsor for .coop, which is restricted to businesses and organisations that operate according to co-operative principles. If you are a co-operative, then the NCBA's website at www.ncba.org provides detailed information on .coop.

(iii) .aero

5.10 .aero has been created for the air transport industry. Air transport industry operators should visit SITA's website at www.nic.aero. This provides detailed information on .aero and SITA's plans (SITA is the sponsor for .aero) for implementation of the new gTLD. As SITA intend that .aero will establish global standards to enable Internet technologies to be fully exploited, the development of .aero will be of interest to the wider Internet community if they succeed in improving the efficiency and security of e-transactions within the air transport industry.

(iv) .museum

5.11 MuseDoma are the sponsor for .museum, which is restricted to museums, as defined by the International Council of Museums. Should you fall within this definition of museum, it is recommend that you visit Musedoma's website at www.musedoma.museum, where detailed information on .museum and advice on domain name applications may be found.

(c) Proof of concept

5.12 The introduction of the new gTLDs is described by ICANN as a proof of concept of the technical and business feasibility of the introduction of new gTLDs into the domain name system. While it was clear that there was an overwhelming demand for the introduction of new gTLDs (since the most popular domain names had nearly all been registered), it was less clear how the domain name system would cope with the millions of new domain names that would be introduced.

Enhancing the domain name system while maintaining the stability of the Internet is an objective that each new gTLD registry must facilitate. When .biz, .info and .name were launched, each registry disregarded a free for all registration launch date and gave priority to IPR owners. Although each registry adopted a different policy, effectively, these all centred around a pre-launch period within which IPR owners could either register a claim to a trade/service mark, register an application for a domain name for that trade/service mark or block the trade/service mark from registration[1].

By monitoring the new gTLDs, ICANN will be able to determine whether further gTLDs should be introduced at some point in the future. It is clearly premature to speculate on ICANN's determination. However, what is apparent is that, despite their best endeavours, Afilias and NeuLevel were the subject of much criticism.

NeuLevel were involved in legal actions in the US, which centred on the system under which NeuLevel randomly selected the winner of contested pre-launch domain names[2]. Complaints were also levied that restricted domain names (that is, those that were placed on a reserved list by ICANN and NeuLevel) were allocated to domain name applicants during the pre-launch domain name period. NeuLevel blamed the registrars[3], including the registrar Register.com, who they say should have filtered out such applications.

Afilias were also the subject of a number of complaints, particularly with regards to pre-launch bogus IPR applications, forcing Afilias to introduce a procedure under which they could submit challenges to the World Intellectual Property Organisation (WIPO) in respect of unqualified domain name registrations. Following concerns raised by ICANN for ccTLDs, Afilias registered English language ccTLDs and their equivalents in official languages, including the EU, that had not been registered pre-launch. One report went so far as to suggest that between 15 to 20% of pre-launch domain name applications were fraudulent (particularly for desirable domain names and generic domain names such as bank.info, sports.info and newyork.info)[4]. Post launch, Afilias' system was overwhelmed by the demand for real-time registrations and Whois enquiries[5], which forced them to close their registry while they tried to rectify its problems.

These problems are hardly surprising when you consider, as highlighted in a recent article, that it took over five years for the number of domain names in .com to reach over 500,000, yet Afilias managed to achieve this in their first 90 days[6].

Regardless of ICANN's final determination, there are those that consider that more gTLDs are needed, and fast.

1 Domain names were (as explained at paragraph 5.03) historically registered on a first-come first-served basis. The result of this was that domain names were registered by people which included trade marks (including company names, brands and famous individuals names) and disputes arose as the owners of the trade marks tried to get the domain names back. Paragraph 5.27 discusses domain name disputes in more detail. Information on the various launch processes may be obtained from each of the registry's websites.
2 IPR owners were provided with a period within which to submit intellectual property claims and pre-launch domain name applications. Where there was more than one applicant for the same domain name, NeuLevel needed to be able to award the domain name to an applicant. A random selection procedure was created. It was alleged that this system was an illegal lottery. See, for example, Bob Sullivan's article entitled 'Controversy dogs .biz domain launch' at www.msnbc.com/news/, CNN.com's article entitled 'L.A. judge bars lottery for ".biz" Web domain' at www.cnn.com and MSNBC's article 'Dot-biz domain launch stalls in court' at www.msnbc.com.news/642106.asp?cp1=1, which discuss the Amazon.com declaratory judgment and the Smiley litigation. It is submitted that the pre-launch procedure adopted by Afilias (based on a sole domain name application) was less complex, costly and cumbersome than that of NeuLevel.
3 Section 6 below explains the role of a registrar in the domain name system.
4 See the article entitled 'One fourth of .info addresses may be frauds – study' by David McGuire in *Newsbytes*, 29 August 2001, which refers to Professor Robert Connor's study at www.newsbytes.com.
5 Section 5 below explains what a Whois enquiry is.
6 McAuliffe, 'Dot-info making a name for itself' *ZD Net News*, 25 October 2001.

(d) New.net

5.13 New.net is a domain name registry that have introduced their own alternative gTLDs for sale. These have not been approved by ICANN and, consequently, are the cause of much concern to ICANN. By approaching Internet service providers (ISPs) directly, New.net have been able to persuade ISPs to modify their servers to recognise New.net's alternative gTLDs[1].

There are over 30 alternative gTLDs offered by New.net (with further domain names planned). These include .chat, .club, .family, .free, .gmbh, .game, .hola, .inc, .kids, .ltd, .law, .med, .mp3, .shop, .sport, .soc, .travel, . tech, .video, and .xxx; and, more recently, .arts, .auction, .agent, .church, .golf, .love, .llp, .llc, .school and .scifi. They also offer a number of alternative gTLDs in French, Spanish and Portuguese, such as .amor, .boutique and .esporte to correspond with New.net's English language gTLDs.

New.net maintain that their alternative gTLDs have been created to meet the market demand for Internet addresses with logical, easy to remember extensions that make Internet navigation simpler. They do not consider that alternative gTLDs will threaten the domain name system, which they consider under serves Internet users[2].

ICANN's discussion draft entitled 'A Unique, Authoritative Root for the DNS' (DNS refers to the domain name system)[3] presents an argued case as to why the alternative route and the domain names offered by companies such as New.net has the potential for seriously disrupting the reliable functioning of the domain name system. The discussion draft explains that as a globally distributed database of information, including domain name information, a primary objective for the domain name system is to provide the same answers to the same queries from any source on the Internet. This requires predictable routing of Internet communications through a unique root, the DNS root. It identifies a number of key reasons why the alternative routes that are emerging have a potential for seriously disrupting the reliable functioning of the domain name system. This includes the possibility that a search for a website on two different computers that have been configured to reference different roots may result in different websites being reached.

ICANN remains committed to a single authoritative root for the domain name system and the belief that new gTLDs cannot be made on an ad hoc basis by entities or individuals which are not accountable to the Internet community. Hence the introduction of the proof of concept for the new gTLDs described at paragraph 5.12 above. ICANN acknowledges that the community-based policy development is not without its faults (namely being too slow) but consider that this pales into insignificance on the realisation that it serves to benefit the global community, as opposed to the self-interests of the minority.

In turn, New.net are highly critical of ICANN and remains confident that its alternative domain names will be recognised universally. Arguably the alternative domain names offer greater relevance and meaning than the official gTLDs. However, in light of ICANN's reservations, it is questionable whether the creation of domain names in this manner will make the Internet an easier place for Internet users to find what they are looking for. It goes without saying that a huge potential for future conflict between ICANN and companies such as New.net will arise, particularly if ICANN were to adopt, say, .kids as an official gTLD[4].

1 Internet users may need to activate their Internet browsers to recognise these alternative gTLDs. For a detailed explanation on the modification of servers, see New.net's website at www.new.net.
2 New.net's paper 'A Proposal to Introduce Market-Based Principles into Domain Name Governance' is published on ICANN's website at www.icann.org/correspondence and offers a useful insight into New.net's standpoint.
3 9 July 2000. Available at www.icann.org/icp/icp-3.htm.
4 ICANN rejected .kids in November 2000. Regard should be had to the current measures in the US for an official .kids gTLD. See ICANN Watch's website at www.icannwatch.org for a review of the US Dot Kids Domain Name Act.

(e) Internationalisation of domain names

5.14 In Melbourne in 2001, ICANN's Public Forum discussed the introduction of internationalised domain names, referred to as IDNs or multilingual domain names. The domain name system has largely operated with the use of Roman characters, which means that the billions of people who cannot read these are not catered for. In November 2000, VeriSign began a domain name test bed with non-Roman characters and in February 2001, the registrar JPNIC began one with Japanese characters. These are just a couple of the initiatives that are assessing the need for the Internet to accommodate Arabic, Chinese, Hebrew characters, etc. Hence, there may be domain names that are fully Arabic (including the .com) or partly Arabic (excluding the .com). In recognition of the technical measures that will need to be overcome, ICANN has created a working group to assess the feasibility of IDNs. A more detailed discussion of IDNs may be found at ICANN's website at www.icann.org[1].

1 WIPO and the International Telecommunication Union (ITU) held a Multilingual Domain Name Joint ITU/WIPO symposium in Geneva in December 2001. Visit www.itu.int for the latest position.

(f) Which gTLD should I register?

5.15 In theory, there is an infinite choice of domain names. To enable customers (and potential customers) to locate them on the Internet easily, most businesses try to choose one or more domain names which include either their corporate name, their main brand or a name which describes the goods and services being offered. The logic for this is simple: although a search engine might find the business's website by using a conceptual searching method, the majority of Internet users are more likely to try to guess your domain name before resorting to a search engine. A UK company like the Virgin Group, with its diverse services and brands, could decide, for example, to register one or more of:

■ virgin.com, virgin.biz, virgin.info (as its main domain name);

■ virgin.net (to provide Internet services); and

■ virgincola.com, virginmegastores.info, virginatlantic.aero (for its sub-brands).

Registration of gTLDs is a purely personal choice. Although .com was created with international commercial organisations in mind, prior to the introduction of the seven new gTLDs, it accounted for 80% of registrations in .com, .net and .org. There is no doubt that this is due to the perception that .com is the top domain name. Individuals searching for a company on the Internet, such as Marks & Spencer will more often than not key in www.marksandspencer.com before trying www.marksandspencer.co.uk (.co.uk being the ccTLD for the UK).

It will be interesting to see how the introduction of the new gTLDs affects this perception. Even if .com were to become displaced from the top spot, the practice of preventative registrations will continue until the likes of cybersquatters are stamped out. This is evident from the introduction of .biz and .info, which has seen businesses registering their business name and/or variations and/or abbreviations of their business name, such as www.marksandspencer.info and www.mands.info. Doubtless these are in addition to registrations for domain names in all the original gTLDs and in the most relevant ccTLDs. So even if a business has no intention of using .com or .org, preventing a third party from using that domain name either to draw a searcher's attention away from the business, or in some instances to be derogatory about the business, is a factor that needs to be considered. (The practice of cybersquatting is discussed in more detail in section 7 below).

Business registrants fall into two broad categories. The first category, which comprises nearly all the big brand companies, take an aggressive approach to domain name registrations and will register nearly all variations of their domain name in nearly every gTLD and ccTLD. The second category, which comprises a small number of big brand companies, simply register the gTLD that they will use in everyday business. The big brand companies that fall into the second category often find that they are forced to take action against third party registrants who have registered variations of the big brand company's name, product or services. That is not to say that this does not happen to the first category: no matter how many domain names a business chooses to register, the fact remains that someone will inevitably hit upon a variation that the business discounted or overlooked. It remains to be seen which is the best approach.

Generally speaking, applying for a .com and/or .info domain name is a sensible first move. If a business choses to register an alternative gTLD, it is important to remember ICANN's warning that these domain names create a risk that the name resolver is unable to determine at which Internet protocol address a given name should point. Simply because something looks like a gTLD does not, as ICANN stresses, mean it is one. A business should not mistakenly think that registration of one of these domain names will entitle it to preferential rights to these domain names as if they were part of ICANN's authoritative domain name system.

4.   COUNTRY-CODE TOP-LEVEL DOMAINS (ccTLDs)

5.16   There are more than 240 ccTLDs, which are also referred to as two-letter codes because the two letters represent the names of countries, territories or other geographic locations. For example, .uk means that it is a UK-based Internet domain name, .fr for France, .ps for Palestinian territories, etc. A full list of available ccTLDs may be found at IANA's website[1]. Some ccTLDs have qualifying criteria and may, for example, be restricted to persons domiciled in that particular country. Information on qualifying criteria can be found by visiting the national registry responsible for the ccTLD that you are considering[2].

As the demand for domain names continues to explode, a number of countries have been willing to drop their restrictions. This is particularly so for countries with catchy ccTLDs, such as .tv (which is the ccTLD for Tuvalu in the Pacific Islands)[3]. It is interesting to note that .us (the ccTLD for the US) has not taken off in the way that .uk has in the UK. No doubt this is due to the popularity of .com in the US but also, as reported in a recent article, there has been no consistent rules applied to .us. It is mooted that the patriotic emotion following the events of 11 September 2001 may see an increase in its popularity when the US appoints the new operator for .us[4].

1   See www.iana.org. IANA maintain the database of ccTLDs and are responsible for the delegation and re-delegation of ccTLDs.
2   In addition, WIPO maintain a ccTLD database that contains links to all of the ccTLD at ecommerce.wipo.int/databases/cctld/index.html.
3   For further reading, see Ellen Rony and Peter Rony, *The Domain Name Handbook: High Stakes and Strategies in Cyberspace* (1998) R&D Books. The .tv Corporation is the registry for .tv (see www.tv).
4   McGuire, 'Commerce Dept On track for October .us decision', 18 October 2001 at www.newsbytes.com.

(a) .uk

5.17   The ccTLD .uk is divided into a number of sub-categories (second-level domains or SLDs), which are available for registration in addition to .uk and which are managed by Nominet UK (Nominet), which is the national registry for the UK. These include:

■   .co.uk (for commercial enterprises);

■   .ltd.uk (for registered companies);

■   .net.uk (for ISPs);

■   .org.uk (for non-commercial organisations that do not fall within the other categories);

■   .plc.uk (for registered companies); and

■   .sch.uk (for schools).

For more detailed information on SLDs and the applicable restrictions on registration, see Nominet's website at www.nominet.org.uk. With regards to .ltd.uk and .plc.uk, particular attention should be made to Nominet's guidance on registration, which requires that the domain name is the same as that which is registered with Companies House. Nominet's website also provides details and links to SLDs that are not managed by Nominet[1], which include:

- .ac.uk (for academic establishments);

- .gov.uk (for Government bodies);

- .mod.uk (for Ministry of Defence);

- .nhs.uk (for NHS organisations); and

- .police.uk (for UK police forces).

Businesses should also be aware that in addition to .uk, ccTLDs exist for the British Channel Islands (.gg or .je) and the Isle of Man (.im).

1 Nominet assumes responsibility for the delegation of new SLDs. Proposals for the introduction of .me.uk and .scot.uk have recently been made and are due for consideration by the Policy Advisory Board of Nominet.

(b) .eu

5.18 In the second edition of this book, we discussed the European Commission's proposal for a new .eu ccTLD[1]. In July 2001, the European Parliament approved the proposal and a report on the .eu top-level domain name is expected, with the launch of the .eu registry, in 2002[2]. At the time of writing, the European Parliament had approved the .eu domain name, and the Commission anticipates that registration of .eu domain names can begin in early 2003. The Commission see the introduction of a specific European identity as a means of strengthening the image and infrastructure of the Internet in Europe. It hopes that it will serve to monitor businesses' compliance with European legislation, such as the data protection and competition legislation. As with the introduction of other gTLDs, the speculative and abusive registration of domain names is a concern for the Commission and measures to counter such activities are being proposed. For continued information on its development, the Official Journal of the European Communities and IANA's website should be reviewed.

1 For background information on the .eu top-level domain and proposed consultation with ICANN, see the European Commission's 'Working Paper on the Creation of a Top-Level Domain Name for the European Union' (COM 153/2000 final) and Communication entitled 'Internet Domain Name System – Creating the .eu top-level domain' (COM 421/2000 final).
2 4 July 2001. Position of the European Parliament on the Implementation of the Internet Top Level Domain .eu. (0328/2000 (COD) – PE1).

(c) Which ccTLD should I register?

5.19 As with gTLDs, a large percentage of ccTLDs are registered purely as a preventative measure by businesses, often redirecting the consumer direct to the business's main website. That is not to say that a number of businesses do not choose to have an overseas website that is targeted to that individual country. ccTLDs are important when the country that you are operating in has strict laws on, say, alcohol. By registering a ccTLD in that country and removing alcohol from your website you can tailor your website to that particular country[1].

Since some countries require an operating company in that country, it is important to check the ccTLD's qualifying criteria. If you are planning on carrying on your business in the UK, or marketing it in the UK, it is advisable to register .uk or a .uk SLD. To use the Virgin Group as an example again, it could decide, for instance, to register one or more of:

- virgin.co.uk (as its main domain name);

- virgin.co.net (to provide Internet services); and

- virgin.tv or virgin.fr (to establish local overseas sites).

1 See Chapter 6, E-marketing for advertising compliance and website tailoring.

5. HOW DO I FIND OUT IF THE DOMAIN NAME I WANT IS AVAILABLE?

5.20 If you want to see whether a domain name that you are considering using is already registered to another entity, then you should carry out an on-line 'Whois' search. This will reveal the identity of the registered holder of a domain name, known as the registrant. Depending on the type of domain name involved and the website that you use, the search can reveal not only the name of the registrant but also their address, administrative and billing contacts, the date the record was created and updated and the domain name servers[1].

Network Solutions provide a helpful Whois database that allows you to search .com, .net and .org gTLDs by either the domain name, domain name owner, contact name owner, handle and Internet protocol address[2]. For .uk ccTLDs, Nominet's Whois is a good starting point, although it only carries limited information due to data protection reasons. If further information is required you could contact Nominet directly (contact details can be found on their website at www.nic.uk) and, depending on the circumstances, they may be able to give further assistance.

Better Whois[3] is a system that is capable of carrying out multiple Whois queries across various registrars. The advantage given by such multiple search systems is that a more in-depth search is made and you are more likely to get an accurate domain report. Better Whois claims to look up the domain name in the shared domain registry, locate which registrar has reserved the domain name and visit and query that registrar's database for the correct information. Geektools[4], The Big Whois[5] and Netnames[6] are all useful search engines that can do multiple gTLDs and ccTLDs in a single search. You can also use the Saegis.com service for a fee[7].

If the domain name that you are considering is in one of the new gTLDs that has yet to be launched (for example, .pro), we recommend that you monitor ICANN's website for announcements on the launch of the relevant registry[8]. You will then be in a position to submit a domain name application at the appropriate time.

It is recommended that you do not limit your search to only one gTLD. You should search the relevant gTLDs and also the ccTLDS for .co.uk (whether you will search .fr, etc, will depend on the international presence (proposed or otherwise) of your company). If you find, for example, that the .co.uk is available but not the .com, you should consider carefully whether the operation of a website at .com will be counter productive to your business. Visiting the existing website should assist you. If you find that there is a likelihood of confusion between the existing website and your proposed website, for example because you provide the same or similar services, then you should not register the domain name. Registering the domain name runs the risk of a common law action for the tort of passing off and may be contrary to the ISP's terms and conditions[9]. Nor should you choose a domain name by reason of its association to a well-known third company, individual or product, for example, Marks & Spencer, Playboy magazine or Madonna[10].

If you are a new company, are developing a new product or are perhaps re-branding, then it is also advisable to check with Companies House to see whether a limited company has already been incorporated under that name. This search may be carried out on-line at the Companies House website at www.companies-house.gov.uk.

If the domain name that you are considering is available, then you will need to submit a domain name application form to an approved registrar. Section 6 below provides further information on domain name registrations. However, if the domain name is not available, you will need to consider section 7 below, which explains how disputes over domain names may be resolved.

1 There is no centralised Whois system, hence the format of each Whois database search is different. There has recently been considerable debate about the quantity of detail provided by a Whois search, which varies from one registry to another. This may largely be attributed to data protection reasons, together with the misuse of these databases by third parties as a source of sales and marketing leads. The restriction on this information has an obvious impact on IPR owners who, when their IPR is infringed, will need to know the details of the registrant in order to take the appropriate action to protect their rights.
2 See www.netsol.com/cgi-bin/whois/whois.
3 See www.better-whois.com.
4 See www.geektools.com/cgi-bin/whois.cgi.
5 See www.thebigwhois.com.
6 See www.netnames.co.uk.
7 See www.compu-mark.com.
8 ICANN's website is found at www.icann.org.
9 See Chapter 4, E-rights for an understanding of the tort of passing off. WIPO recommended the use of WIPO's trademark Database portal published at ecommerce.wipo.int/databases/trademark/. This enables individuals wishing to register a domain name to perform a trade mark search on the existing on-line trade mark databases maintained by IP offices throughout the world.
10 See Chapter 4, E-rights and section 7 below on domain name disputes that arise out of such registrations.

6. HOW DO I REGISTER A DOMAIN NAME?

5.21 It is now relatively quick and easy to register a domain name. Registration will be for a specified period, with a minimum of one year and a maximum of ten years available, subject to renewal. Registering a domain name does not mean that you actually own the domain name. Rather, your name is entered into the corresponding database registry as the registrant for a certain period of time.

(a) gTLDs

5.22 Registration of a gTLD is through one of ICANN's accredited registrars, a list of which can be found at the registrar directory at InterNIC's website[1]. VeriSign are the sole registry through which an ICANN accredited registrar can submit a domain name application on your behalf for .com, .net and .org. For new gTLDs, accredited registrars can submit a domain name application to the gTLD's corresponding registry. For example, .info, .biz and .name will be submitted to Afilias, NeuLevel and GNR respectively.

Following the establishment of ICANN and the introduction of competition in domain name registration via the Shared Registration System, ICANN reports that competition at the accredited registrar level is robust, leading to significantly lower prices and a larger array of service offering from which to choose[2]. There are now over 80 different operational accredited registrars (more than 170 have been accredited) that receive equivalent access to the central registry for .com, .net and .org. All offer competitive domain name registration services to customers in these domains.

1 See www.internic.net/regist.html or at ICANN's website at www.icann.org/registers/accredited-list.html. UK registrars include Easyspace Limited, NetBenefit plc and Virtual Internet, which can be found at www.easyspace.com, www.netbenefit.com and www.virtualinternet.com respectively.
2 Prior to the establishment of ICANN and the introduction of competition in domain name registration via the Shared Registration System, Network Solutions Inc (now VeriSign Inc) had been the sole accredited registrar. It remains the sole registry and has an authorative database that maps names with gTLDs to Internet protocol addresses for .com, .net and .org. Further information on VeriSign and VeriSign's global registry services may be obtained from their website at www.verisign.com. As regards competitive pricing, note the controversy surrounding AltaVista and their thwarted launch of an unmetered Internet access service in June 2000 in the UK. See, for example Anne Young, 'AltaVista fails to deliver on free Internet promise' *Total Telecom* at www.totaltele.com/vprint.asp?txtID=30148.

(b) ccTLDs

5.23 Each ccTLD has its own national registry that will process domain name applications and maintain the database of domain names. For the UK, this is Nominet[1]. Although not specifically accredited by ICANN, the ccTLD registries are appointed by the ccTLD's corresponding country, territory or geographic locality.

A domain name application may be submitted directly to Nominet or indirectly through an ISP (who effectively acts as your agent). With hundreds of ISPs to choose from, Nominet's website provides useful guidance on choosing an ISP. Although we do not propose to repeat that guidance here, it is advisable to shop around before choosing your ISP, as the services that are offered by ISPs will vary. A list of Nominet members that provide registration services can be obtained from Nominet's website.

Nominet and IANA provide useful links to overseas registries, should you wish to register a ccTLD other than .uk.

1   See section 4 above and paragraph 5.38 for further information on Nominet.

7.   WHO IS ENTITLED TO A DOMAIN NAME?

5.24 Unfortunately, unlike the real world where people and companies can generally co-exist with the same or similar names, each domain name must necessarily be unique and there may be multiple parties who might wish to use the same domain name and are willing to fight over it. SCRABBLE (the board game) serves as a useful illustration of the difficulties that are encountered by a first-come first-served domain name registration system.

In the US and Canada the IPR in and to SCRABBLE is owned by Hasbro Inc and Hasbro Canada Corporation respectively, while in the UK and elsewhere in the world, this is owned by J.W. Spear & Sons Limited (a subsidiary of Mattel Inc). As would be expected, the domain name www.scrabble.com is the preferred choice of each of these companies. A sensible approach to resolving this issue was adopted by the courts as a result of a dispute over the domain name[1]. If you type in www.scrabble.com, you will find the official SCRABBLE worldwide website, which will redirect you either to Hasbro's SCRABBLE website or to Mattel's SCRABBLE website (depending which icon you choose to click on). Since the stylisation of SCRABBLE by Hasbro and Mattel differ, the joint website serves to avoid any potential customer confusion[2].

The law as to who is entitled to a domain name varies from country to country. Although this is not yet fully decided amongst the various courts of the world, it is likely that it will be dealt with in the courts of the location where the registrar is located, unless all the parties to a domain name dispute are within the same jurisdiction[3]. This may be impracticable, particularly if there are countries without a well-developed legal system which are trafficking in domain names that are well-known trade marks.

Generally, domain name disputes can be handled in four ways:

- by agreement (for example, purchasing the rights);

- using the registrar's domain name dispute policy (for example, the ICANN policy);

- employing a form of alternative dispute resolution (for example, mediation)[4]; and

- court proceedings.

1   *Mattel Inc v Hasbro Inc* (CD Cal, 1997). The US court found that the parties were jointly entitled to the domain name and are now joint registrants of www.scrabble.com (Hasbro Inc being the original registrant).
2   The individual SCRABBLE websites for Hasbro and Mattel are to be found at www.hasbroscrabble.com and www.mattelscrabble.com respectively.

3 In this regard see the US Anticybersquatting Consumer Protection Act 1999 discussed later in this chapter.
4 As Chapter 7, E-dispute deals with the process of alternative dispute resolution in general terms (whether before the courts or by alternative methods) we do not discuss alternative dispute resolution in this chapter.

(a) Agreement

5.25 Given the high cost of litigation, if you have difficulty over a domain name because it is already registered and perhaps already in use, it is always preferable to try to open channels of communication, to see if the registrant is willing to transfer the domain name to you. There may be commercial advantages in negotiating a settlement with the current registrant, even if your legal position (which is more fully discussed below) to challenge the registration is strong.

A Whois search (see section 5 for details on these searches) will have identified the individual or company (known as the registrant) who has registered the domain name(s) in question. Before approaching the registrant, it is essential to seek to establish whether the registrant has a legitimate competing right to the domain name. The results of such domain name searches need to be carefully evaluated as the registrant may have used a pseudonym and/or given false contact details. Depending on the registrar involved there may be provision for cancelling/deleting a domain name if the contact details provided are incorrect. Visiting the corresponding website should help you assess this. For example, John Smith & Son butchers of Southport may have found that John Smith & Son booksellers (since 1751) were operating a website at johnsmith.co.uk to advertise their bookselling services. As such, John Smith & Son butchers of Southport may opt for a different domain name, perhaps johnsmithbutchers.co.uk.

If the registrant does not appear to have any connection to the domain name, check if the registrant has registered other domain names. This is not conclusive but it may suggest that the registrant is a cybersquatter and evidence of such trafficking in domain names will be good evidence if court proceedings or dispute resolution procedures are commenced. Predictably, domain name registrations by cybersquatters (who we first alluded to at paragraph 5.15, where we discussed the practice of preventative registrations by businesses[1]) account for a large percentage of domain name disputes.

The results of your findings are likely therefore to determine if the registrant is to be approached. If you are going to challenge the registrant's rights to the domain name on the basis of a trade/service mark, care must be taken to avoid threatening another party with proceedings for infringement of a trade mark[2]. Chapter 4, E-rights, which discusses the limited situations in which allegations of trade mark infringement may be made, should be reviewed.

1 The registration of company/brand names (and/or variations/abbreviations/misspellings) as domain names to prevent these domain names falling into the hands of third parties who are prepared to use the domain names for monetary gain and/or to abuse/discredit the company/brand. (The same is true for 'celebrity' figures, such as actors, politicians and sportsmen.)
2 In this regard see *Prince plc v Prince Sports Group Inc* [1998] FSR 21.

5.26 It is strongly advisable to seek legal advice, particularly when dealing with a cybersquatter. A strongly worded letter requesting not only the transfer of the domain name in question, but also undertakings that no further infringement of your trade/service mark will be made, should be sent by your lawyers. There are usually four different responses to such a letter:

■ the registrant has no legitimate rights to the domain name and, realising the severity of the situation, agrees to transfer the domain name and provide the undertakings requested. This is the most preferred response but unfortunately it is not the most frequently received;

■ the registrant agrees to provide the undertakings requested and to transfer the domain name, but requests a financial reimbursement. Obviously it will depend on the circumstances whether a payment is justified. For instance, the registrant may have a competing right to the domain name yet is willing to transfer it to you for a fee, in which case payment would be justified. If the registrant has no legitimate right to the domain name, such as a cybersquatter, we do not, in principle, advise making any payment. From a commercial point of view it is not advisable to let it be known that you are in the habit of paying when being held to ransom to such demands. If this becomes known it may encourage, or indeed lead to, further incidents of cybersquatting with similar demands. However, you must always take a commercial view of such situations. If the amount being requested would, for example, cover the initial registration fee and any transfer costs, then it may be prudent to pay such an amount in order to resolve the situation without further legal action (not to mention the consequential costs arising from such action)[1];

■   the registrant defends his right to the domain name in question and is unwilling to come to a settlement; or

■   no response is received.

If attempts to negotiate a settlement have failed then further action needs to be contemplated. Consideration should first be given to the commencement of proceedings under the dispute resolution procedure available for the particular domain name.

1   See paragraphs 5.28 and 5.38 for a discussion of cybersquatting cases.

(b) Registrar's domain name dispute policy

5.27   Disputes relating to domain name registrations present unusual features for which ordinary judicial systems may not be able to provide comprehensive solutions. Moreover, ordinary litigation can be slow and expensive. There are alternative systems available for resolving disputes relating to domain names. Which one to use will depend on the circumstances of the case, the time available to resolve the dispute, the registry involved, the financial and commercial considerations and the evidence that can be adduced.

It was because of these inherent difficulties that WIPO recommended to ICANN that ICANN introduce a uniform dispute resolution procedure that was capable of resolving domain name conflicts, specifically those registered in bad faith (that is, by cybersquatters) [1]. This provides an expedited administrative procedure to allow the dispute to be resolved without the cost and delays of court litigation and was adopted by ICANN on 26 August 1999.

A second WIPO report has recently been published[2]. This is aimed at preventing conflicts in relation to a range of identifiers other than trade marks, such as personal names, geographical identifiers, names and acronyms of international government organisations, trade names and international non-proprietary names. Recognising that the international legal framework for the protection of these identifiers is not as developed as that for trade marks, WIPO's second report makes a number of findings and recommendations that remained unanswered following WIPO's first report[3]. It will be interesting to see how ICANN responds to the second report's recommendations on how the issue of bad faith and misleading domain name registrations that make use of these identifiers can be addressed.

On purchasing a domain name, a registrant is required to enter into a registration agreement with the domain name registrar. This details the terms and conditions that will be invoked by the registrar in the event of a dispute between the registrant and a third party over the registration and/or use of a domain name. These are discussed below.

1   Report on the First WIPO Internet Domain Name Process, published April 1999. This may be found at www.wipo.org.
2   Report on the Second WIPO Internet Domain Name Process, published September 2001. This too may be found at www.wipo.org.
3   These issues were in fact considered beyond the scope of the first WIPO report.

(i) gTLDs

ICANN's Uniform Domain Name Dispute Resolution Policy

5.28 Pursuant to WIPO's first report, ICANN adopted its Uniform Domain Name Dispute Resolution Policy (UDRP) on 26 August 1999, approving the implementation documents on 24 October 1999. Prior to its adoption, complaints were resolved in accordance with Network Solution Inc's dispute policy. The development of ICANN's UDRP has since made this policy redundant[1].

ICANN's UDRP establishes the legal framework for resolution of disputes between a registrant and a third party relating to the abuse of a domain name which is either a .biz, .com, .info, .name, .net or .org gTLD. It should be noted that an increasing number of national registries for ccTLDs have also submitted to the jurisdiction of this dispute policy, including .tv (Tuvalu), .fj (Fiji) and .mx (Mexico).

All ICANN accredited registrars that are authorised to register the above gTLDs (and ccTLDs that have adopted the UDRP on a voluntary basis) have agreed to abide by and implement the UDRP for those domain names. Any person or entity wishing to register a domain name using any of these gTLDs or ccTLDs is required to consent to the terms and conditions of ICANN's UDRP and submit to mandatory administrative proceedings if any dispute arises.

Proceedings under ICANN's UDRP are conducted in accordance with the rules of procedure and are subject to any supplemental rules of the selected administrative dispute resolution service provider accredited by ICANN (provider[2]) that will administer the proceedings. (ICANN does not become involved in the administration or conduct of proceedings (in contrast with Nominet, discussed below).) There are four such providers: WIPO[3], the National Arbitration Forum[4], eResolution[5] and CPR Institute for Dispute Resolution[6]. Commencing administrative proceedings does not prevent the complainant bringing court proceedings, either before or after the administrative proceedings have been concluded[7].

1 See footnote 2 to paragraph 5.22 for a discussion of Network Solution Inc's role in the development of the domain name system as both registry and registrar. ICANNs UDRP is intended to overcome the shortcomings in Network Solution Inc's dispute policy.

2 Information on providers can be found at www.icann.org/udrp/approved-providers.htm. See also the provider's websites, which provide further information (including a list of the independent and impartial panelists and their qualifications).

3 WIPO was approved as the first provider of ICANN dispute resolution services on 29 November 1999, and the service opened for business on 1 December 1999. The first application was lodged the very next day, and at the time of publication, over 3000 gTLD cases and over 60 ccTLD cases have been subject to these proceedings. Of the completed cases, over 70% of gTLDs have been transferred or cancelled (20% of complaints were denied). WIPO maintain a table of case results at their website. A geographical distribution of parties table is also available. In 2001, of the 1,414 complaints, over 600 were of US domicile (making the US the country of most use), the second highest country was the UK (over 120 complainants). See www.arbiter.wipo.int/domains.

4 See www.arbforum.com/domains.

5 See www.eresolution.ca/services/dnd/arb.htm.

6 See www.cpradr.org/icann-menu.htm.

7 Paragraph 18 of ICANN's UDRP describes the effect of court proceedings on these administrative proceedings. If initiated either prior to or during administrative proceedings, the panel has the discretion to suspend, terminate or proceed through to a decision.

Procedure

5.29 To initiate ICANN'S UDRP procedure, a complainant must complete and file a complaint (in hard copy and in electronic form) with a provider, together with the initial fee. The complaint must specify the remedies sought (that is, cancellation or transfer of the domain name) and should attach evidence in support[1]. The fees payable differ between the providers and are also dependent upon whether the complainant elects to have the dispute decided by a single-member or a three-member panel[2]. Prompt payment is advisable: if the complainant fails to pay the requisite fee to the provider within ten days of the provider's receipt of the complaint, the complaint will be deemed withdrawn and the proceedings will be terminated.

1   See paragraph 3 of ICANN's UDRP for further information. A copy of ICANN's complaint form may be found at WIPO's website at www.wipo.org.
2   For example, WIPO charge a fee of $1,500 for one to five domain names included in a complaint and eResolution charge a fee of $1,250 for one to two domain names or $1,500 for three to six domain names. The complainant is required to make this election at the time of submitting the complaint. If he elects to have three panelists, the complainant will be required to pay an additional fee. In the case of WIPO this is $3,000 (for one to five domain names included in a complaint) and for eResolution $2,900 for one to two domain names or $3,250 for three to six domain names. The complainant will need to provide the names and contact details of three candidates to serve as one of the panelists from ICANN's list of providers. Upon appointment of the panel, the provider will refund the appropriate portion, if any, of the initial fee to the complainant.

Grounds of complaint

5.30   The complaint must, in accordance with paragraph 4(a) of ICANN's UDRP, demonstrate the following three elements:

■   that the complainant has rights in a trade/service mark that is identical or confusingly similar to the domain name in question[1];

■   that the registrant has no rights or legitimate interests in the domain name in question[2]; and

■   that the domain name in question has been registered and is being used in bad faith.

Registration and use in bad faith is defined at paragraph 4(b) to include the following circumstances:

■   the domain name was registered or acquired primarily for the purpose of selling, renting or otherwise transferring it, either to the complainant or a competitor of the complainant, for consideration in excess of the registrant's out-of-pocket expenses[3];

■   the domain name was registered in order to prevent the owner of the trade/service mark from obtaining a corresponding domain name (provided that the registrant has engaged in a pattern of such conduct)[4];

■   the domain name was registered primarily for the purpose of disrupting the business of a competitor[5]; or

■   the registrant, by using the domain name, intentionally attempted to attract for commercial gain, Internet users to its website or other on-line location by creating a likelihood of confusion with the complainant's mark as to the source, sponsorship, affiliation or endorsement of the registrant's website or location or of a product or service on the website or location[6].

These circumstances are not definitive but serve as helpful guidance as to the kind of evidence in support of a complaint that a complainant will need. If you have difficulty with a domain name and wish to commence proceedings under ICANN's UDRP, you need to be confident that your complaint can satisfy the three elements of paragraph 4[7].

Within three days of receipt of the complaint and the requisite fee, the provider will review the complaint for compliance with ICANN's UDRP before sending the complaint to the registrant. The registrant then has 20 days from the date of commencement of proceedings[8] within which to submit a response (again, in hard copy and in electronic form) to the provider and the complainant[9]. This must respond to the complaints raised and assert (within the prescribed word limit) why the registrant should retain registration and use of the domain name.

1   The addition of geographical designations, generic or descriptive terms or words designating the goods or services with which the mark is used does not alter the fact that a domain name is confusingly similar to a trade/service mark: see *United States Olympic Committee v MIC* Case no D2000-0189. Misspellings fall within this element (see *Encyclopedia*

Britannica Inc v John Zuccarini Case no D2000-0330 and *Nicole Kidman v John Zuccarini* Case no D2000-1415 (discussed at paragraph 5.36)), as do phonetically identical domain names (see *Hewlett-Packard Co v Cupcake City*, File No FA000200093562). *Wal-Mart Stores Inc v Richard MacLeod d/b/a, For Sale* Case no D2000-0662 concluded that a domain name (in this case, wal-martsucks.com) is identical or confusingly similar to a trade mark when the domain name includes the trade mark, or a confusingly similar approximation, regardless of other terms in the domain name. A discussion of sucks domain names may be found in paragraph 5.35.

2 For example, the registrant is a cybersquatter (see the cases at paragraph 5.35) or is a competitor or person with a grievance: see *Reg Vardy plc v David Wilkinson* Case no D2001-0593 (paragraph 5.35). Legitimate interest includes use of one's own name: see the reverse domain name hijacking cases (paragraph 5.37). See also *Victorias Secret v Victorias Cyber Secret NAF* Claim no FA 010100009653L, which concerned domain names such as victoriasexysecret.com and victoriasexsecret.com.

3 That is, cybersquatters. See *National Westminster Bank plc v Purge I.T. and Purge I.T Ltd* Case no D2000-0636 (discussed at paragraph 5.35), where one of the registrant's reasons for the registration was to make a modest return for their initiative. See also *G A Modefine and Ward S.A. v A.R. Mani* Case no D2001-0537 for an example of a case where the consideration requested was found to be relatively modest.

4 See *Bruce Springsteen v Jeff Burgar and Bruce Springsteen Club* Case no D3000-1532, which found that brucespringsteen.net (registered by the complainant) was a corresponding website to brucespringsteen.com (registered by the respondent). A pattern of conduct has been shown to exist where four and 100 domain names have been registered: see *Potomac Mills v Gambit* Case no D200-0062 and *Time Warner v Harper Stephens* Case no D2000-1257, respectively (both discussed at paragraph 5.34).

5 There has been disagreement as to the interpretation of competitor. *Mission KwaSizabantu v Benjamin Rost* Case no D2000-0279 held that the natural meaning of the word was one who acts in opposition of another and the context does not imply or demand any restricted meaning such as commercial or business competitor. *Britannia Building Society v Britannia Fraud Prevention* Case no D2001-0505 (discussed at paragraph 5.35) followed *Tribeca Film Center Inc v Lorenzo Brusasco-Mackenzie* Case no D2000-1772, finding that a 'competitor' is a person or entity in competition with the complainant for the provision of goods or services, not merely a person or entity with an interest opposed to the complainant. In *Reg Vardy plc v David Wilkinson* Case no D2001-0593, while recognising that the registrant was not a competitor of the complainant (the registrant being a dissatisfied customer of the complainant), the panel still found that the domain name was registered in bad faith.

6 See *Nicole Kidman v John Zuccarini, Cupcake Party* Case no D2000-1415, discussed at paragraph 5.36. See also various Harrods cases, such as *Harrods v Dorgan* Case no D2001-1165 and *Harrods v Harrod's closet* Case no D2001-1027.

7 Where a complaint is brought in bad faith, a declaration of reverse domain name hijacking may be found (see paragraph 5.37).

8 The proceedings commence on the date the provider completes all responsibilities in connection with forwarding the complaint to the registrant.

9 The registrant is compelled to participate in the proceedings by virtue of the registrant's domain name registration agreement. At this stage, the registrant has the option to elect a three-member panel, if the complainant has so declined. If elected by the registrant he will be required to pay half the fee of the three-member panel (the claimant must pay the other half) at the time the response is submitted. These fees are outlined at footnote 1 to paragraph 5.29 above.

Registrant's rights to and legitimate interests in a domain name

5.31 Paragraph 4(c) of ICANN's UDRP identifies the circumstances that the registrant may rely upon to demonstrate that the registrant has rights and/or legitimate interests in the domain name. These include any of the following:

■ before notice of the dispute, the registrant's use of, or demonstrable preparations to use, the domain name or a name corresponding to the domain name was in connection with a bona fide offering of goods or services[1];

■ the registrant has been commonly known by the domain name (even if no trade/service mark rights have been acquired[2]; or

■ the registrant is making a legitimate non-commercial or fair use of the domain name, without intent for commercial gain to misleadingly divert consumers or to tarnish the trademark or service mark at issue[3].

1 See *CMG Worldwide Inc v Naughtya Page*, NAF Caim No FA 00090000956641, brought by the authorised representative for The Diana Princess of Wales Memorial Fund in relation to the registration of princessdi.com and princessdiana.com. See also *Bruce Springsteen v Jeff Burgar and Bruce Springsteen Club* Case no D2000-1532.

2 Again, see comments in paragraph 5.34 on the *Bruce Springsteen* case.

3 *Universal City Studios Inc v G.A.B Enterprises* Case no D2000-0416 found that this means the kind of confusion that arises in the context of trade mark infringement, where a competitor diverts consumers (and potential sales) to its website. *Wal-Mart Stores Inc v Richard MacLeod, For Sale* Case no D2000-0662 affirms that 'legitimate interest' and 'bad faith' insulates true protest sites from vulnerability under ICANN's UDRP. Criticism websites are discussed at paragraph 5.35.

The panel

5.32 The panel will be appointed by the provider. Where there is a single-member panel, the provider will appoint the single panellist from its list of panelists within five calendar days of receipt of the response or the lapse of the time period for the submission of one. A three-member panel is also appointed within five calendar days, although the procedure for appointment differs since the complainant and registrant will have nominated a panellist[1]. Once appointed, the provider notifies the complainant and the registrant of the panelists and the expected date of the decision[2].

The panel will consider the complaint on the evidence presented in the complaint and the response (forwarded to the panel by the provider)[3]. (In the event that the registrant fails to submit a response, the dispute will be decided by the panel solely on the basis of the complaint.) There is therefore no in-person hearing, the proceedings being conducted entirely on the papers.

Each decision of the panel will detail the reasons on which it is based (including, in the case of a three-member panel, any dissenting opinion[4]) and will be forwarded to the provider within 14 days of appointment. The panel may only transfer or cancel a domain name pursuant to a complaint and are not entitled to award money judgments or legal costs. Once the provider has forwarded the decision to all the parties concerned, including the registrar and ICANN, the registrar will inform all the parties of the due date of implementation.

The panel's decision is binding, although the parties can challenge it by commencing court proceedings. The decision will be implemented within ten business days after its notification to the relevant domain name registry, unless court proceedings have been commenced in the meantime[5].

All decisions are published by the provider and are also available at ICANN's website, where they are categorised for ease of reference[6].

1 See ICANN's UDRP in this regard. See also the article by Matt Loney entitled 'Cybersquatting cases branded as biased', 21August 2001 at news.zdnet.co.uk/story10,t269-s2093539,00.html. This discusses Professor Geist's Report, 'Fair.com? An examination of systematic unfairness in the ICANN UDRP' (August 2001, University of Ottawa, available at http://aix1.uottowa.ca/~geist/geistudrp.pdf), on the differences in decisions by one and three-member panels.
2 It is intended that the proceedings be completed within 45 and 50 days of receipt of the complaint.
3 The panel does, however, have the discretion to request further documents or statements from the complainant and the registrant.
4 A majority decision only is needed for a three-member panel.
5 If the registry has been notified of court proceedings, it will take no action until the court's decision is announced, or until there is a resolution between the parties or the court proceedings are withdrawn or dismissed.
6 See www.icann.org/udrp/proceedings-list-name.htm to review any of the ICANN decisions. See also WIPO's website at arbiter.wipo.int/domains/cases/index.html.

Cases under ICANN's UDRP

5.33 In the last year alone, there have been over a thousand decided ICANN cases. A discernible picture on issues, such as what may constitute 'identicality', 'similarity', 'competitor' or 'tarnishment' is now emerging. Many of these cases have been identified during the course of this chapter as the elements that are required to be proved by the complainant or relied upon by the registrant have been discussed. Nevertheless it is helpful to expand upon some cases that we consider to be of consequence.

Bad faith

5.34 When vast sums of money can be made from film and book merchandising, the registration of a domain name that incorporates the name of the film or book in question, or perhaps one of its characters, is not something that the publisher or distributor wishes to be made by a third party. The hugely successful children's books (and now films) Harry Potter is an obvious example.

In October 2000, WIPO awarded 107 domain names containing the Harry Potter trade mark to Time Warner[1], which holds the film's production and merchandising rights. The panel found that HarperStephens had acted in bad faith by registering the majority of these domain names within two days of Time Warner's announcement that it had secured the film rights. Significantly, the panel stated that the registration of over 100 such domain names is sufficient to constitute a pattern of conduct[2].

Unsurprisingly, a number of sports and entertainment stars such as Madonna, Julia Roberts and Nicole Kidman have filed complaints with WIPO regarding the use of their names in domain names. While the decisions may indicate a preference towards the complainant (understandable given that ICANN's UDRP was initiated to thwart cybersquatters) there are a number of decisions which undermine the rationale of these decisions. It is debatable whether these are an attempt at 'back-peddling' (in the sense that famous name cases have too readily determined common law rights in famous names) or are simply narrower in their analysis and interpretation of ICANN's UDRP.

Bruce Springsteen's complaint[3] against the registrant of brucespringsteen.com was unsuccessful since the registrant had demonstrated that he had some rights or legitimate interest in the domain name on the grounds of the use of the name 'Bruce Springsteen Club'[4]. The panel considered that the decisions in the *Julia Roberts* and *Jeanette Winterson* cases (discussed below) were flawed[5]. The panel maintained that since a search under the name Bruce Springsteen would give rise to many thousands of hits, even a relatively unsophisticated Internet user would be aware that not all of these hits would be directly associated (in an official and authorised capacity) with Bruce Springsteen himself. They dismissed the likelihood that any Internet user would go straight to the website at www.brucespringsteen.com in the hope of reaching the official Bruce Springsteen website[6]. Were they to do so, they would soon realise that was not the case and move on[7].

While Internet users may not expect all websites bearing the names of celebrities, famous historical figures or politicians to be authorised or in some way connected with that person (recognising the existence of websites placed independently by advisers or critics), the expectation of an official website at www.brucespringsteen.com should not have been so readily dismissed by the panel[8].

Russell Boyd, the registrant in the *Julia Roberts* case was not successful in establishing any rights or legitimate interest in the domain name as the panel found that Julia Roberts had common law trade mark rights to her name and that Russell Boyd had registered the domain name in bad faith[9]. Similarly, Madonna (who had common law and registered rights in the 'Madonna' trade mark) won back her name[10], as did British writer Jeanette Winterson, who was successful because, despite the fact that her name is unregistered, it constituted a trade mark[11]. Sting, however, failed in his complaint because the name 'Sting' was not a registered trade mark, while at the same time being a word in normal English usage[12].

1 *Time Warner Entertainment Company, LP v HarperStephens* Case no D2000-1254. See the article by Alastair Alexander entitled 'The Potterwar Campaign' at web.ukonline.co.uk/bringers/temp/c-potter.html. This discusses the complaints made by Time Warner to teenage registrants. A British teenager, Claire Field, received a letter stating that her website www.harrypotterguide.co.uk was likely to cause confusion or dilution of IPR. Singapore teenager Catherine Chang surrendered all rights to the domain name www.thepn.com.

2 See also *Potomac Mills Limited Partnership v Gambit Capital Management* Case no D2000-0062, which held four domain names to be sufficient. The panel in *Time Warner* comment on the belief that the Owl Post System employed by wizards and students of wizardry in the Wizarding World is often referred to as 'The Way of the Wizarding World', alternatively 'www'.

3 *Bruce Springsteen v Jeff Burgar and Bruce Springsteen Club* Case no D2000-1532. Bruce Springsteen relied upon common law rights in his name.

4 Bruce Springsteen considered this to be evidence of bad faith as the name was, in his opinion, purely fictitious (the domain name was just one of more than 1,500 domain names allegedly registered by the registrant). Whilst the panel commented that there may be some element of bad faith, this was not sufficient to satisfy the necessary burden under ICANN's UDRP.

5 *Jeanette Winterson* for indicating that the burden is on the registrant to demonstrate that the domain name has been used in good faith, when it is for the claimant to demonstrate bad faith. *Julia Roberts* for placing reliance upon a lack of 'permission' to the registrant to use the name, when it is irrelevant.

6 The official Bruce Springsteen website is at www.brucespringsteen.net.

7 The domain name www.brucespringsteen.com resolves to the website www.celebrity100.com.

8 See the opinion of the dissenting panellist in this regard, who concluded that the average Internet user would not sift through thousands of hits searching for information on Bruce Springsteen; rather, they would go directly to www.brucespringsteen.com. See also his opinion on the personal name 'Bruce Springsteen' acquiring a secondary meaning.

9 That is, the name 'Julia Roberts' has acquired a distinctive secondary meaning giving rise to common law trade mark rights: *Julia Fiona Roberts v Russell Boyd* Case no D2000-0210. The defendant had registered over 50 domain names comprising the names of famous people, including alpacino.com. He then attempted to auction the website, which at that time did not contain any material relevant to the actress, on Ebay. He challenged the assumption that Julia Roberts had any rights in her name but admitted that he chose the name because of her celebrity status.

10 *Madonna Ciccone p/k/a/Madonna v Dan Parisi and 'madonna.com'* Case no D2000-0847.

11 *Jeanette Winterson v Mark Hogarth* Case no D2000-0235. Jeanette Winterson was able to demonstrate sufficient goodwill and reputation in her name to sustain a claim for passing off. Moreover, Mark Hogarth had also registered the names of a number of other authors and offered to sell them in return for royalty payments from the authors concerned, or indeed to auction them. He was held to have acted in bad faith, even though he claimed he intended also to set up websites employing these registrations.

12 *Gordon Sumner, p/k/a Sting v Michael Urvan* Case no D2000-0596.

Criticism websites

5.35 It is accepted that those with genuine grievances or a wish to express criticisms of others (whether commercial or financial institutions, governments, charitable, sporting or cultural institutions, or whatever) must be at liberty (within the confines set by the laws of the relevant jurisdictions) to express their views. If they use a website or e-mail address for this purpose, they are entitled to select a domain name which leads others easily to them[1].

Rights or legitimate interests in and to a domain name may therefore be demonstrated by the registrant making a legitimate non-commercial or fair use of the domain name (without intent for commercial gain to misleadingly divert consumers or to tarnish the trade/service mark at issue)[2]. However, it is evident from the reported cases that there is a lack of consensus in approach by the panels, resulting in inconsistent decisions[3]. Contrast the complaints brought by NatWest Bank[4], the Britannia Building Society[5] and Reg Vardy[6].

NatWest Bank complained that the registrant had registered the domain name natwestsucks.com to obtain financial gain from NatWest Bank by seeking to transfer the domain name to them for a substantial sum. The registrant argued that their motivation in registering the domain name was to protect the complainant against a disgruntled person acquiring the domain name[7]. As there was no justification for this role of 'officious interferer' and it was evident to the panel that the prime purpose in acquiring the domain name was to transfer it at more than cost to the complainant, the panel ordered that the domain name be transferred to NatWest Bank.

The complaint brought by Britannia Building Society concerned the domain name britanniabuildingsociety.org. There was an active website at this address, which was highly critical of the Britannia Building Society. The panel concluded that the registrant was making a legitimate non-commercial use of the domain name because he maintained the website as a site critical of the policies of the management of Britannia Building Society[8]. The panel reiterated that genuine criticism websites are protected by ICANN's UDRP and, as such, do not constitute tarnishment[9]. It found that a low level of confusion was a price worth paying to preserve the free exchange of ideas on the Internet.

A dissatisfied customer of the car dealership Reg Vardy was not, however, allowed to exchange his opinions on Reg Vardy at his 'Customer Driven Complaints Site'[10]. The panel concluded that the registrant had registered the domain names with the primary purpose of disrupting the business of the complainant, motivated solely by the desire to create bad publicity. This is in marked contrast to the views expressed by the panel in *Britannia Building Society*, which concluded that 'a genuine criticism site, undertaken by its proprietors with no intent other than to protest, ridicule and mock its targets, does not fall astray of the dictates of the [ICANN] Policy, regardless of the outrageousness of the allegations or the vigorousness with which they are made'[11].

Where a criticism site is used as a pretext for cybersquatting, the ICANN Policy will not protect the registrant[12].

Arguably all of the above domain names satisfied ICANN UDRP's first two criteria (identical/ confusingly similar to a third party trade mark without any legitimate rights to the name). It is the interpretation of the third criteria (registered and being used in bad faith) that has resulted in different conclusions under the UDRP. At first sight, it seems illogical that a website that is critical of the owner of the rights in the domain name is not an abusive registration, yet (in the case of *Natwest*) a domain name per se is[13]. This, however, is too simplistic an approach to take. The Internet was created to allow the free exchange of information. As a newspaper or a television programme may criticise a third party (libel/slander notwithstanding), so too can a website (see Chapter 3, E-liability). However, how you choose to index (that is, register) your website may, in some circumstances, define whether your registration is abusive[14].

Domain names and/or websites that are critical of well-known companies and individuals, such as natwestsucks.com, clearly pose a dilemma for ICANN.

1 *National Westminster Bank plc v Purge I.T. and Purge I.T. Ltd* Case no D2000-0636. The registrant in *Bruce Springsteen* argued that the mere use of the name of a celebrity on the front page of a magazine does not mean that the magazine is claiming any kind of specific rights in relation to the name, but merely that it features an article about the individual in question. The Internet, he argued, is of a similar nature.

2 Paragraph 4(b)(iv) of ICANN's UDRP.

3 *Britannia Building Society v Britannia Fraud Prevention* Case no D2001-0505 recognised that no consensus has emerged. Further, that where a consensus has developed, it is incumbent on the panel to follow this, so as to promote consistent application of ICANN's UDRP.

4 *National Westminster Bank plc v Purge I.T. and Purge I.T. Ltd* Case no D2000-0636.

5 *Britannia Building Society v Britannia Fraud Prevention* Case no D2001-0505.

6 *Reg Vardy plc v David Wilkinson* Case no D2001-0593.

7 This domain name was just one of 18 such domain names that had been registered by the registrant, including directlinesucks.com and dixonsucks.com. It was irrelevant that that there was no active website at www.natwestsucks.com. The registrant's motivation was found to fall within the definition at paragraph 4(b)(i) of ICANN's UDRP. That is, the registrant's argument that mere registration without more cannot amount to use failed.

8 The WIPO panel rejected the assertion that the website tarnished the complainant. Specific reference was made to *Nicole Kidman v John Zuccarini d/b/a Cupcake Party* Case no D2000-1415 and *Etam plc v Alberta Hot Rods* Case no D2000-1654, which established that tarnishment refers to such unseemly conduct as linking unrelated pornographic, violent or drug-related images or information to an otherwise wholesome mark (see paragraph 5.36).

9 See *Wal-Mart Stores Inc v Richard MacLeod d/b/a For Sale* Case no D2000-0662.

10 The 'Customer Driven Complaints Site' explained that the website had been created by 'an unhappy Reg Vardy Customer' and referred to phrases such as 'shit-service at reg-vardy.com' and a 'slag your manager off' section. (The trade mark Reg Vardy was also included in the metatags, a discussion of which can be found at section 9 below.) No response was submitted by the respondent in this case, so the case was determined solely on the evidence put forward by the complainant.

11 *Britannia Building Society v Britannia Fraud Prevention* Case no D2001-0505.

12 *Rolex Watch U.S.A. Inc v Spider Webs Ltd* Case no D2001-0398 and *Wal-Mart Stores Inc v Richard MacLeod d/b/a, For Sale* Case no D2000-0662.

13 See *Wal-Mart Stores Inc v Walsucks and Walmarket Puerto Rico* Case no D2000-0477, which found that although potential customers of the complainant are not likely to conclude that the complainant is the sponsor of walmartcanadasucks.com, it is likely that users would visit the sight out of curiosity, thereby achieving the registrant's objective of diverting potential customers of the complainant. The intention here was not to criticise but to exact money.

14 ICANN's approach should be contrasted with the approach taken by the courts and Nominet, which are discussed at paragraphs 5.38 and 5.46.

Tarnishment

5.36 We touched upon tarnishment earlier in the context of genuine criticism websites. Tarnishment refers to unseemly conduct, such as the linking of a name with pornography.

Nicole Kidman v John Zuccarini d/b/a Cupcake Party[1] concerned nicholekidman.com and nicolekidmannude.com. Although no goods or services were offered at the websites, the Internet user arriving at these websites would have to click on a series of windows containing advertisements before exiting (known as 'mousetrapping'). The advertisements at nicolekidmannude.com were for sexually explicit websites. Since Nicole Kidman has appeared nude on stage and in film, the panel was satisfied that some Internet users would be confused into believing that the website was affiliated with Nicole Kidman[2]. The sexual implications of the domain name and the sexually explicit advertisements to which it was connected threatened to tarnish Nicole Kidman's image[3].

1 Case no D2000-1415.
2 Zuccarini had registered thousands of domain names (the majority being misspellings of famous names). It was submitted that Zuccarini's business was to charge fees to advertisers for each advertisement that mousetrapped users needed to click through. That is in itself bad faith. No response was filed.
3 *Rita Rudner* Case no D2000-0581 followed.

Reverse domain name hijacking

5.37 The panel may, upon consideration of the complainant's and registrant's submissions, conclude that the complaint was brought in 'bad faith'. In this context, 'bad faith' includes an attempt by the complainant to deprive the registrant of a domain name (known as reverse domain name hijacking) or an attempt at harassing the registrant. When such a conclusion is reached, the panel will make a declaration that the complaint was brought in bad faith, thereby constituting an abuse of ICANN's UDRP[1]. One such finding was made in *G.A. Modefine S.A. v A.R. Mani*[2], the *Armani* case.

The *Armani* case concerned the domain name www.armani.com, registered by the graphic artist Mr Anand Ramanath Mani, who traded under the name A.R. Mani. Although there was no website at the domain name address, e-mail addresses (such as info@armani) were used by the registrant. The complainant (the registered proprietor of the ARMANI, GIORGIO ARMANI and EMPORIO ARMANI trade marks) complained that the domain name failed to correspond to the registrant's name, surname, name and surname or an acronym of his initials[3]. The panel considered that this was not a case that concerned an 'opportunistic' registrant, adopting a name to give a 'spurious air of legitimacy to an otherwise questionable registration'. Rather, it was felt to be a case that was brought before the panel because the complainant had come up against a respondent with a legitimate use of a variant of its own name, who it had been pursuing without success. As such, the complaint was brought in bad faith and constituted an abuse of ICANN's UDRP[4].

The *Armani* case was relied upon in *Societe des Produits Nestle S.A. v Pro Fiducia Treuhand AG*[5], the *Nestle* case. In much the same way that the complainant in *Armani* had failed to appraise the courts of the full circumstances surrounding the registration of the domain name, so too had Nestle. Regardless of the fact that the domain name (www.maggi.com) was originally registered by Mr Romeo Maggi using his company name (Pro Fiducia Treuhand, a Swiss financial and management consulting firm) as opposed to his personal name, the registrant had a legitimate interest in the domain name[6]. The panel shared the registrant's view that the complainant knew of the registrant's rights to use his name as a domain name, yet insisted on a 'campaign of intimidation' to dispossess the registrant of his domain name. This lack of legal merit, coupled with a lack of candour with regards to material facts, constituted an abuse of ICANN's UDRP[7].

For a case in which the registrant unsuccessfully raised this equitable remedy, see *Britannia Building Society* discussed earlier at paragraph 5.35. The panel found that the registrant had failed to show that the equities weighed in his favour, not having respected and followed ICANN's UDRP or acted equitably himself.

A predilection for IPR rights cannot therefore be taken for granted.

1 Paragraph 3 (xiv) of ICANN's UDRP: A complainant is required to state in the complaint that the complaint has not been brought for any improper purpose, such as to harass the registrant.
2 Case no D2001-0537.
3 *Valazquez Jimenez v Velazquez-Perez* Case no D2001-0342 recognised that a person has a legitimate interest in a domain name that corresponds to that person.

4 The panel also commented on the correspondence between the parties, where the complainant's offer to purchase the domain name for Canadian $1,250 was met with a counter offer of US $1,935. Whilst the sum was more than the registration costs of the domain name, it did not constitute bad faith. It was a relatively modest sum (compared with the sums sought by cybersquatters at that time (1997)) and was entirely reasonable in view of the costs that would be incurred in changing business stationery.

5 Case no D2001-0916.

6 Nestle was aware of Romeo Maggi's application to record himself as the registrant and his intention to use the website for the Maggi family's personal use. Nestle nonetheless complained that the domain name infringed the MAGGI trade mark used by its subsidiary for various food products.

7 See also *Aspen Grove Inc v Aspen Grove* Case no D2001-0798, in which the software company Aspen Grove was unsuccessful in 'reclaiming' the domain name www.aspengrove.com from the registrant who had chosen the domain name on account of the fact that it reminded him of the Aspens around his home. A legitimate right and interest in the domain name was found as it had been used as an address for personal communication, including e-mail and the sharing of family photos, for more than four years. Note that since the domain name registration pre-dated Aspen Grove's trade mark application and company incorporation, no rights were found to have been shown in the trade mark. The filing of a complaint without a 'colourable' claim was an abuse of ICANN's proceedings.

(ii) ccTLDs

5.38 As explained at paragraph 5.28, ICANN's UDRP has been adopted by a number of national registries. To determine whether the domain name with which you are concerned is subject to ICANN's UDRP, you will need to visit the website of the national registry in question[1]. Nominet (the national registry for .uk ccTLDs) has not adopted ICANN's UDRP and it is necessary therefore to discuss its policy.

1 Alternatively, see IANA's website at www.iana.org/cctld/cctld.htm or WIPO's website at www.wipo.org. WIPO have published voluntary guidelines for the development of practices and policies to curb abusive and bad faith registrations (The WIPO ccTLD Best Practices for the Prevention and resolution of Intellectual Property Disputes), visit: ecommerce.wipo.int/domains/cctlds/bestpractices/index.html. See also WIPO's ccTLD databases at ecommerce.wipo.int/databases/ccltd.

Nominet's dispute resolution service

5.39 Nominet has operated a dispute resolution service (DRS) since April 1997, details of which may be found at Nominet's website (www.nic.uk). The current DRS was adopted in September 2001 and modifies the original DRS, which was the subject of much criticism. One of the failings of the original DRS was that Nominet did not have the power to transfer a disputed domain name without a court order or the consent of the registrant. The new DRS provides Nominet with the power to transfer, cancel or suspend a domain name registration[1].

Commencement of the DRS will not prevent the dispute being brought before the courts, should this be required. Nominet will need to be notified, and proceedings will be suspended pending the outcome of the court proceedings.

1 As with ICANN's UDRP, no damages or legal costs can be awarded. Information on Nominet's original DRS can be found on Nominet's website, at www.nic.uk.

Procedure

5.40 The complainant is required to submit a complaint (in hard copy and electronic form) to Nominet[1]. This must include details of the grounds on which the complaint is made, including the rights the complainant asserts in the name or mark, why the domain name is, in the complainant's mind, an 'abusive registration' (defined below) and must specify the required outcome (that is, transfer, suspension, cancellation).

1 A copy of Nominet's complaint form may be found at Nominet's website. The complaint must not exceed 2,000 words.

Abusive registration

5.41 Abusive registration is defined at paragraph 1 of the DRS policy[1] as including a domain name that has been registered, used or otherwise acquired in a manner that takes unfair advantage of or is unfairly detrimental to the complainant's rights. Guidance as to the factors that may be evidence of such a registration can be found at paragraph 3 of the DRS policy. This list is a non-exhaustive list of factors and includes circumstances that indicate that the domain name was registered (or otherwise acquired):

■ primarily for the purposes of selling, renting or otherwise transferring it to the complainant or to its competitors at a premium (that is, in excess of the registrant's out of pocket registration expenses);

■ as a blocking registration against a name/mark in which the complainant has rights; or

■ primarily to unfairly disrupt the complainant's business.

Or is being used:

■ in a way which has confused people or businesses into believing that the domain name is registered to, operated by or otherwise connected with the complainant.

Or is:

■ (in combination with other circumstances) part of a pattern of making abusive registrations by the registrant; or

■ (independently verified as such) made with false contact details.

Failure by the registrant to use the domain name for the purposes of e-mail or a website will not in itself be evidence of an abusive registration.

Within three days of Nominet's receipt of the complaint, Nominet will verify that the complaint complies with the DRS and forward it to the registrant (by post, fax or e-mail), thereby commencing proceedings under the DRS.

The registrant has 15 days within which to submit a response to Nominet (again, in hard copy and electronic form)[2]. The grounds upon which the registrant seeks to rebut the complaint, such as 'fair use', must be detailed.

1 This can be found at www.nic.uk/ref/drs-policy.html.
2 A copy of Nominet's response form may be found at Nominet's website. The response must not exceed 2,000 words.

Non-abusive registration

5.42 Paragraph 4 the DRS policy provides a non-exhaustive list of factors that the registrant may raise to demonstrate (by way of evidence) that the domain name is not an abusive registration. For example, prior to the complaint the registrant has:

■ used or made demonstrable preparations to use the domain name or one similar in connection with a genuine offering of goods or services; or been commonly known by the name or legitimately connected with a mark which is identical or similar to the domain name, or made a legitimate non-commercial or fair use of the domain name.

Further:

■ the domain name is generic or descriptive and the registrant is making 'fair use' of it. Fair use may include websites operated solely in tribute to or in criticism of a person or business provided that if the domain name is identical to the name in which the complainant asserts rights without any addition and the registrant is using or intends to use the domain name for the purposes of a tribute or criticism website without the complainants' authorisation. The burden of proof will shift to the registrant to show that the domain name is not an abusive registration.

Within three days of Nominet's receipt of the response, Nominet will forward it to the complainant. If the complainant so chooses, the complainant has five days within which to submit a reply to Nominet. After five days of the claimant's receipt of the response (or three days of Nominet's receipt of a reply), a ten-day confidential informal mediation period will commence.

Informal mediation

5.43 This is initiated and conducted by Nominet without charge to either the complainant or the registrant in an attempt by Nominet to find an acceptable resolution to the dispute. Nominet values this open channel for negotiation, which is conducted on a without prejudice basis and, apart from possible financial and time savings, it can produce solutions which the courts cannot order. For example, the parties can agree to share the domain name by having two frames side by side which link to each of their websites, and agree how incoming e-mails should be directed.

If a mediated resolution is not possible, Nominet will notify the complainant and the registrant that Nominet will, upon payment of a fee of £750 (plus VAT)[1] by the complainant, refer the dispute to an independent expert[2].

1   If six or more domain names are involved, Nominet will, in consultation with the complainant, set a different fee.
2   If the complainant fails to make this payment within ten days of receipt of notification that the dispute is to be referred to an expert, Nominet will deem the complaint to have been withdrawn.

Determination by expert

5.44 Within five days of receipt of the fee, Nominet will appoint an independent and impartial expert[1]. Save for the informal mediation documents (which are without prejudice), Nominet will forward all documents to the expert[2].

Determination by expert will also occur where the registrant has failed to submit a response to Nominet within the time period described above. In this case, informal mediation will be bypassed[3]. The decision will be communicated to Nominet within ten days of the expert's appointment (and within three days of this, by Nominet to the complainant and registrant).

The complainant must show to the expert (on the balance of probabilities) that: (1) he has rights in respect of a name/mark that is identical or similar to the domain name; and (2) the domain name is, in the hands of the registrant, an abusive registration (defined above). As with ICANN's UDRP, there are no in-person hearings (although the expert does have a discretion to order such a hearing).

Any decision in favour of the complainant (that is, transfer, suspension or cancellation of the domain name) will be put into effect by Nominet after ten days of the expert's decision (unless there is an appeal or legal proceedings are commenced, in which case no action will be taken until those are concluded or resolved). Alternatively, the expert may find that the complaint was brought in bad faith, for example in an attempt at reverse domain name hijacking (concept also used by ICANN)[4]. Regardless of the outcome of the DRS, Nominet cannot order damages or payment of legal fees.

The complainant and registrant have the right to appeal a decision. This must be made to Nominet by submitting written grounds (maximum 2,000 words) together with the fee of £3,000 (plus VAT) within five days of Nominet's communication of the decision. Three experts (appointed by Nominet) will decide the appeal at the earliest opportunity. It will be considered on the basis that a matter be re-examined on the facts and that procedure has been incorrectly followed. Interestingly, appeal decisions (which will also be published) will not become precedents, although they can be persuasive.

Nominet advises that the DRS should last no longer than two or three months provided that its strict timetable is adhered to. However, as this is a new DRS, it is unclear whether this timetable is practicable.

1   Nominet maintains a list of experts (including qualification details) on their website at www.nic.uk.
2   The expert has the authority to request further documents or statements from the complainant or registrant.
3   Again, the complainant is required to pay a fee of £750 (plus VAT).
4   If within a two-year period, the experts have, on three separate occasions, found that a complainant has brought a complaint in bad faith, Nominet will not accept any further complaints for a two-year period.

Cases under Nominet's DRS

5.45   Nominet reports that less than 0.05% of .uk domain name registrations are disputed. It will be interesting to see whether this figure increases in light of the improvements that Nominet has made to the DRS.

Since decisions under the old DRS were confidential, only a few of Nominet's decisions have been reported in the press and are open to discussion. Decisions under the new DRS are published on Nominet's website at www.nominet.org.uk/drs/decisions.html. At the date of publication 80 decisions have been published on the website. The vast majority of these find in favour of the complainant and suggest that the new DRS will produce results that compare favourably with those given under ICCANN's UDRP (in that they will also strongly support the rights of brand owners[1]).

As only a few decisions have so far been published, if proceedings are to be commenced, it is advisable to consider how that issue has been addressed under ICANN's UDRP. Even though the dispute policies are distinct from each other (you cannot use ICANN's UDRP for a .uk domain name and vice versa), there are parallels between the policies, which enable guidance to be obtained on the type of evidence required in a dispute[2].

Of the reported decisions under the old DRS that are available, *Financial Services Authority v Findlay Steele Associates*[3] warrants discussion. The complaint concerned the domain name www.fsa.co.uk, which was representative of the acronym 'FSA' used by both parties to the complaint. The small family business, Findlay Steele Associates, was first to register the domain name and since registration had used it for e-mail purposes[4]. A chronology of the events, as seen through the eyes of Findlay Steele Associates, is available at their website (including a copy of Nominet's decision and the written recommendations of the independent expert appointed by Nominet). The written recommendations conclude that the registrant had attempted to minimise or obviate the risk of material levels of confusion. Notwithstanding that the ground relating to actual or likely confusion was well-made out before Nominet, there is reason to recommend to Nominet that it now revoke its decision (to suspend the domain name) based on this ground.

1   See, however, *Fiat S.p.A and WDOT Internet Limited* DRS 0066.
2   For example, both require identicality or similarity with a trade/service mark, both recognise the 'blocking' and reverse domain name hijacking concepts, both recognise registrations for the purpose of selling, renting and so on. In fact, the new DRS is noticeably modelled on ICANN's UDRP. Nevertheless, decisions under ICANN's UDRP are not regarded by Nominet as persuasive and so should not be relied upon for any complaint.
3   See www.news.zdnet.co.uk/story/0,t269-s2097308,00.html.
4   The Financial Services Authority was known by a different name at the time of registration. Their website is at www.fsa.gov.uk.

(c) Court proceedings

5.46   There will invariably be instances where the dispute over the alleged unauthorised registration of a domain name would be better decided by a court. Examples of where a court forum would be more appropriate to decide a case are as follows:

- when there are legitimate competing trade mark interests, perhaps where trade marks are held by different owners in different classes for different goods and services, or for different countries;

- when trade mark rights exist but there is no actual evidence of bad faith/abusive registration as these are not requirements for trade mark infringement or passing off cases before the courts;

- where the facts of the case are strongly contested and are not clear from the documents available;

- if an injunction is required perhaps to prevent further use of a trade mark within metatags or website content; and

- if recovery of costs and damages is required.

In these circumstances, it is advisable to contact the relevant domain name registry to request that a 'lock' is placed on the domain name. This will ensure that the registrant cannot transfer or use the domain name until the lock has been removed. Whether the registry will choose to place a lock on the domain name will be dependent upon the circumstances of the case. The issuance of court proceedings will generally be sufficient[1].

Basically, to win in court, the claimant must prove that its registered trade mark has been infringed and/or the registrant's acts amount to passing off and/or unfair competition. This means that trade mark law has to be applied to situations where there has been no application of the mark to goods or services. For example, where the domain name has just been registered and there is not even a functioning website yet, or where the website is just a very basic site, giving the address and perhaps a map direction or an e-mail address to the registrant.

1 Where parallel proceedings have been commenced under the registrar's domain name dispute policy, the registrar should be notified.

(i) *Position in the UK*

Cybersquatters

5.47 Unlike the US, which is discussed at paragraph 5.51 below, the UK does not have any specific legislation concerning cybersquatters, such as the US AntiCybersquatting Consumer Protection Act 1999. There are, however, a number of significant cases dealing with the issue and which take a firm stance against their activities. Such cases are brought on the basis of trade mark infringement and/or the common law tort of passing off.

The most significant UK decision to date is that in *British Telecommunications plc v One in a Million Ltd*[1], commonly referred to as *One in a Million*. This is the leading cybersquatting case in the UK and its determinations on passing off and trade mark infringement merit detailed discussion.

One in a Million were dealers in domain names. As part of their business they secured registrations of prestigious names (whether they be company names or brand names) as domain names without the consent of the organisation owning the goodwill in those names. They intended to make a profit by either selling them to the owners of the goodwill, using the blocking effect of the registration to obtain a reasonable price, or selling them to collectors or other persons who could have a legitimate reason for using them. Amongst the domain names registered were bt.org, marksandspencer.com, sainsbury.com and virgin.org. Consequently, BT, Marks & Spencer, Sainsbury, Virgin and others relying on their trade mark rights brought an action for trade mark infringement and passing off.

With regards passing off, the court found that the mere creation of an 'instrument of deception' without either using it for deception or putting it into the hands of someone else to do so, is not passing off. (There is no such tort as going equipped for passing off.) Thus, mere registration of a deceptive domain name is not passing off. But where a domain name is registered with the intention, or is calculated, to infringe in the future, then mere registration will amount to passing off.

The court found that, since it is accepted that the name Marks & Spencer denotes Marks & Spencer and nobody else, anybody hearing the name realises that what is being referred to is the business of Marks & Spencer. It followed that the registration of a domain name including the name Marks & Spencer makes a false representation that (the registrant, One in a Million) is associated or connected with Marks & Spencer.

Since a person who carries out a Whois search will be told that the registrant is One in a Million, a substantial number will conclude that there must be a connection or association with Marks & Spencer. This false representation the court found constituted passing off[2]. Furthermore, the registration of the domain name including the words Marks & Spencer is an erosion of the exclusive goodwill in the name, which damages or is likely to cause damage to Marks & Spencer[3].

The court rejected the defendants' argument that the domain names were being used in the course of trade (that is, trading in business names) and was thus fair use. Although not actively using the domain names, by registering them they were blocking the registration of such names by the respective claimants. It was quite clear that the defendants' intention was to offer to sell the domain names back to the respective claimants. The defendants were 'equipping themselves' for misrepresentation, and so were involved in passing off.

As for trade mark infringement, assuming section 10(3) of the Trade Marks Act 1994 (TMA 1994) required the use to be trade mark use and confusing use, threats to infringe had been established. The defendants sought to sell the domain names, which were confusingly similar to registered trade marks. The domain names indicated origin (that is, the purpose for which they were registered) and they would be used in relation to services provided by the defendants who traded in domain names. The domain names were therefore registered to take advantage of the distinctive character and reputation of the marks, which was in the court's opinion unfair and detrimental.

The threat of passing off and trade mark infringement and the likelihood of confusion arising from the infringement of the mark were, in the court's opinion made out beyond argument in this case[4].

1 *British Telecommunications plc v One in a Million Ltd* [1998] FSR 265; on appeal [1999] FSR 1, CA. For the leading authorities pre-*One in a Million*, see *Harrods Ltd v UK Network Services Ltd* (1997) EIPR D-106 (the first UK cybersquatting case), *Pitman Training Ltd v Nominet UK* [1997] FSR 797 and *Prince plc v Prince Sports Group Inc* [1998] FSR 21.

2 The placing on the domain name register of a distinctive name (such as marksandspencer.com) makes a representation to persons who consult the register that the registrant is connected or associated with the name registered and thus the owner of goodwill in the name.

3 The registrant registered domain names without any distinguishing words because of the goodwill attaching to the names; it was the value of that goodwill which caused the registrant to register the domain names.

4 The High Court decided in favour of the claimants and this decision was upheld by the Court of Appeal.

5.48 The position in the UK after *One in a Million* is that where the registration of a domain name is intended or calculated to infringe the rights of another, even in the future, the registration amounts to passing off. Domain names comprising names such as Marks & Spencer are instruments of fraud; any realistic use of them would result in passing off. Mandatory injunctions have accordingly been ordered against such cybersquatters.

The attitude of the courts in *One in a Million* has been followed in other decisions, such as *Britannia Building Society v Prangley*[1]. Britannia Building Society, who own various trade marks, domain names and addresses for providing services over the Internet, objected to the registration of the domain name britanniabuildingsociety.com by the defendant. The defendant claimed that the domain name had been registered since it was appropriate to a business that he was intending to carry out in Iran, providing the services of British builders to Iranians. The court regarded the defendant's evidence as 'wholly incredible' and had no doubt that the defendant registered the domain name on account of the fact that it represented the name of the claimant. It was in the court's opinion, perfectly plain from the evidence before them, that the domain name in issue was to be regarded as an instrument of fraud in the same sense that Aldous LJ in the Court of Appeal described the domain names in *One in a Million*. Any use of the domain name in the UK would lead to a serious risk, if not certainty, of confusion in the mind of anybody who saw the domain name as to whether or not the user was connected with the claimant.

Where the domain name may not be regarded as a sole reference to the trade/service mark owned by the claimant, such as FCUK; or where the claimant is unable to demonstrate significant goodwill in the trade/service mark, such as the letters FCUK, the action for trade mark infringement may fail, as it did in *French Connection Ltd v Sutton*[2]. So, despite the use by French Connection of FCUK since 1997 in its advertising campaigns and the offer for sale of the domain name (fcuk.com) by the defendant, the domain name was not an instrument of fraud or deception within the meaning of *One in a Million*[3].

Following *One in a Million* as seen, if the intention in registering a domain name (in this case, www.radiotaxis.com) and in creating an automatic direct link to another website (in this case, www.dialacab.co.uk) was to pass itself off as or associated with a third party, it was concluded in *Radio Taxicabs*[4] that this fact would probably be the decisive factor in determining whether the domain name should be delivered up to the claimant. The parties were two of the four radio circuits for licensed black cabs in London. The claimant owned the domain name radiotaxis.co.uk, from which it operated its website. The court rejected the contention that there was an intention to divert business from the claimant to the defendant, finding that the domain name had been registered for the purpose of promoting the defendant's supply of radio taxis. Without a finding of an intention to deceive, the claimant's claim for a transfer of the domain name failed[5].

Where there is a threat to sell a domain name to pornographers if the trade/service mark owner does not purchase the domain name from the registrant, then the transfer of the domain name (and damages) may be awarded by the courts[6].

1 LTL 12 June 2000.
2 [2000] ETMR 341. The court held that the letters were not a name of anybody or anything and were in use on the Internet before French Connection Limited started using them.
3 The court remarked that given the tasteless implications of the mark, there might even be public policy grounds for the registration to be revoked. While the tasteless implications of the mark have been considered by some as a factor in French Connection Limited losing this action, it should be noted that the Court of Appeal in *One in a Million* conceded that the names Cellnet, Sainsbury, Ladbroke, Virgin and BT could, unlike Marks & Spencer, relate to entities (or individuals in the case of Sainsbury) other than the registered trade mark holders. However, since the defendants had registered a host of domain names of famous trade marks, the intention to deceive was evident in *One in a Million*.
4 *Radio Taxicabs Ltd (t/a Radio Taxis) v Owner Drivers Radio Taxi Services Ltd (t/a Dial-a-Cab)* (12 October 2001, unreported), Ch D.
5 Note that the court regarded Radio Taxis as a generic term and followed *Office Cleaning Services Ltd v Westminster Office Cleaning Association* (1946) 63 RPC 39, HL in this regard. (No secondary meaning had been acquired.) Note also that the defendant did not register radiotaxis.co.uk, which was available for registration at the time radiotaxis.com was registered. The Internet was also disregarded as a means of gaining business for the services provided by the parties.
6 *Cosmopolitan v England* (26 March 2000, unreported).

Competing legitimate interests

5.49 The earlier example of johnsmith.co.uk exemplifies the inherent 'weakness' of the domain name system[1]. Whereas John Smith & Son butchers of Southport and John Smith & Son booksellers have been able to co-exist in the 'real' world, on the Internet this is not always possible. It is of course feasible for each company to provide Internet services quite independently from each other at johnsmith.co.uk and johnsmith.com (which is often the case)[2]. However where for instance the products/services are identical/similar to each other and/or where the reputation of one company outshines another, disputes will inevitably arise.

In *Pitman Training Ltd and PTC Oxford Ltd v Nominet UK Ltd and Pearson Professional Ltd (t/a Pitman Publishing)*[3], the trade mark PITMAN was legitimately used by Pitman Training Ltd, its franchisee PTC Oxford Ltd and Pearson Professional Ltd. Pitman Training failed to establish that the registration of the domain name pitman.co.uk by Pearson Professional (registered in relation to its publishing division, Pitman Publishing) constituted passing off. Pitman Publishing had been using the mark PITMAN for a very long time and there was no evidence that the prior use of the domain name by Pitman Training for a few months had caused the public to associate the domain name with Pitman alone[4]. Nor was there evidence of confusion on the part of the public.

In *Prince plc v Prince Sports Group Inc*[5], the US company Prince Sports Group Inc (owner of UK and US trade mark registrations for PRINCE) threatened legal action against Prince plc, a UK computer services company and registrant of prince.com. In response, Prince plc commenced court proceedings in the UK seeking a declaration that it had not infringed any rights of Prince Sports and that its letter of demand was an unjustified threat. The UK court held in favour of Prince plc, which resulted in Prince Sports commencing proceedings in the US, only for Prince Sports to later withdraw them.

More recently, the World Wrestling Federation found itself fighting with the World Wide Fund For Nature over an agreement in 1994 which had limited the World Wrestling Federation's use of the initials WWF (used by the World Wide Fund For Nature since 1961)[6]. Upholding the World Wide Fund For Nature's rights over its name and trade mark, the court found that the agreement did not permit the worldwide use of the World Wresting Federation's website at www.wwf.com.

1 This being the limited scope for the domain name system to allow multiple use of the same brand or trading name by businesses operating in different sectors.
2 Unless, that is, one company has registered both of these domain names (not to mention domain names in each of the remaining gTLDs).
3 [1997] FSR 797.
4 Nominet had mistakenly allocated the domain name to Pitman Training.
5 [1998] FSR 21.
6 *WWF – World Wide Fund for Nature (formerly World Wildlife Fund) and World Wildlife Fund Inc v World Wrestling Federation Entertainment Inc* reported at www.newlawonline.com/cgi-bin/nlo.dll/dFn9bbmmKmo/60184601j.htm. Judgment dated October 2001.

Jurisdiction – Internet 'use' in the UK

5.50 Merely operating a website that is accessible in the UK will not of itself be sufficient to constitute passing off and/or trade mark infringement in the UK. Though there is no specific legislation in this regard, this is the view currently held by the courts, as exemplified by *1-800 Flowers Inc v Phonenames Ltd*[1] (*1-800 Flowers*) and *Euromarket Designs Inc v Peters*[2].

1-800 Flowers concerned an opposition to an application for the service mark 800-FLOWERS. Reliance was placed on Internet use of 1-800 FLOWERS. It was submitted that any use of a trade mark on any website (wherever the owner of the website was located) was potentially a trade mark infringement anywhere in the world, because website use is an omnipresent cyberspace. Placing a trade mark on a website was 'putting a tentacle' into the computer user's premises.

Jacob J questioned this by way of the following example:

> 'A fishmonger in Bootle who put his wares and prices on his own website, for instance for local delivery, can hardly be said to be trying to sell fish to the whole world or even the whole country. And if any web surfer in some other country happens upon that website he will simply say "this is not for me" and move on.'

He went on to state that:

> 'For trade mark laws to intrude where a website owner is not intending to address the world but only a local clientele and where anyone seeing the site would so understand

him would be absurd. So I think that the mere fact that websites can be accessed anywhere in the world does not mean, for trade mark purposes, that the law should regard them as being used everywhere in the world. It all depends on the circumstances, particularly the intention of the website owner and what the reader will understand if he accesses the site.'

The claimant in *Peters* was the US company Crate & Barrel, proprietor of the CRATE & BARREL trade mark. The second defendant was an Irish company run by the first defendant, which had one store in Dublin also called Crate & Barrel. The case concerned two alleged acts of infringement in the UK: (1) an advertisement in the magazine Homes & Gardens; and (2) the defendant's website at www.crateandbarrel.ie ('.ie' being the country code for Ireland). It should be appreciated that neither party traded in the UK and that the first defendant stated that she always intended to sell only to the Irish market.

Jacob J found that the point about the locality of the trade was clear:

'Now a person who visited that website would see "ie" … the reference to four floors is plainly a reference to a shop so what would the visitor understand? Fairly obviously that this is advertising a shop and its wares. If he knew that "ie" meant Ireland, he would know the shop was in Ireland. There is no reason why anyone in this country would regard the site as directed at him. So far as one can tell, no one has.

Whether one gets there by a search or by direct use of the address, is it rational to say that the defendants are using the words "Crate & Barrel" in the UK in the course of trade in goods? If it is, it must follow that the defendants are using the words in every other country of the world. Miss Vitoria says that the Internet is assessable to the whole world. So, it follows that any user will regard any website as being "for him" absent a reason to doubt the same. She accepted that my Bootle fishmonger example in 800-Flowers is that sort of case but no more. I think it is not as simple as that. In 800-Flowers I rejected the suggestion that the website owner should be regarded as putting a tentacle onto the user's screen. Mr Miller here used another analogy. He said using the Internet was more like the user focusing a super telescope into the site concerned; he asked me to imagine such a telescope set up on the Welsh hills overlooking the Irish Sea. I think Mr Miller's analogy is apt in this case. Via the web you can look into the defendant's shop in Dublin. Indeed the very language of the Internet conveys the idea of the user going to the site – "visit" is the word. Other cases would be different – a well-known example, for instance, is Amazon.com. Based in the US it has actively gone out to seek worldwide trade, not just by use of name on the Internet but by advertising its business here, and offering and operating a real service of supply of books to this country. These defendants have done none of that.'

1 *800-FLOWERS Trade Mark* [2000] FSR 697.
2 [2001] FSR 288.

(ii) Position in the US

5.51   The fact that more than half the domain name complaints made to WIPO are made by US citizens and concern domain names registered by US citizens highlights the severity of the problem in the US[1]. It is not surprising therefore that the US has taken an aggressive stance towards cybersquatting with the enactment in 1999 of the AntiCybersquatting Consumer Protection Act[2]. The effectiveness of this AntiCybersquatting Act will no doubt be monitored by many countries, particularly the UK, where the courts have effectively followed the US courts' approach to applying trade mark laws to domain name disputes.

Since the position in the UK on domain name disputes is fairly established, an in-depth analysis of the US cases pre-dating the AntiCybersquatting Act is unnecessary[3]. It is, however, worthwhile to run through one or two essential principles.

Panavision International LP v Toeppen[4] established that the registration and subsequent offer for sale of a domain name that incorporates the trade mark (in this case Panavision's trade marks) to the owner of the trade mark dilutes the trade marks[5]. Furthermore, the trading of recognised trade marks is sufficient for the purposes of trade mark dilution (regardless of whether the domain name is sold or licensed)[6].

1 See the earlier analysis of complaints to WIPO.
2 15 USC 1125(d). This amended the Lanham Act of 1946 (the US Trade Mark Act).
3 See for example, *eToys.com v etoy.com* (LA Sup Ct, 1999); *Toys 'R' Us Inc v Feinberg* 26 F Supp 2d 639 (SDNY, 1998); reversed on appeal 1999 US App LEXIS 29833 (US Ct of Apps (2d Cir), 1999); *People for the Ethical Treatment of Animals v Doughney* 2000 US Dist LEXIS 9474 (ED Va, 2000); and *New York State Society of Certified Public Accountants v Eric Louis Associates Inc* 79 F Supp 2d 331 (SDNY, 1999).
4 141 F 3d 1316 (9th Cir) 1998, LA Sup Ct, 1999; *Toys 'R' Us Inc v Feinberg* 26 F Supp 2d 639 (SDNY, 1998); reversed on appeal 1999 US App LEXIS 29833 (US Ct of Apps (2d Cir), 1999).
5 The argument that the defendant's actions were non-commercial (a requirement for trade mark dilution) were rejected by the court, who considered that this was a commercial transaction. See also *Playboy Enterprises Inc v Calvin Designer Label* C-97-3204 (ND, 1997), where Playboy successfully objected to the registration of the domain names playboyxxx.com and playmatelive.com on the basis of its registered trade mark rights in PLAYBOY and PLAYMATE.
6 *Avery Dennison Corpn v Sumpton* 999 F Supp 1337 (CD Cal, 1998). Approximately 12,000 domain names comprising common surnames were registered by the defendant, which were then licensed as e-mail addresses. The court concluded that trade mark law applied equally to these domain names, the effect of course being that an individual could be prevented from registering their own name as a domain name if there is a corresponding trade mark. (Note that decisions under ICANN's UDRP recognise the legitimate use of one's own name.)

The AntiCybersquatting Consumer Protection Act 1999

5.52 The AntiCybersquatting Act serves to 'protect consumers and promote electronic commerce by amending certain trade mark infringement, dilution and counterfeiting laws'. Key to this is the creation of a new cause of action for trade mark owners and the protection of personal names. It is specifically concerned with 'bad faith' registrations and use.

Under the AntiCybersquatting Act liability is imposed on a person who has:

■ a bad faith intent to profit from a trade/service mark[1]; and

■ registered, trafficked in, or used a domain that in the case of a trade/service mark is distinctive at the time of registration of the domain name or is identical or confusingly similar to such mark; or, in the case of a famous trade/service mark at the time of registration of the domain name is identical or confusingly similar to or dilutive of such marks; or is a trade/service that has specific protection under US legislation.

In determining whether there is bad faith intent, a court may consider but is not limited to factors such as:

■ the trade mark or other intellectual property rights of the person, if any, in the domain name;

■ the extent to which the domain name consists of the legal name of the person or a name that is otherwise commonly used to identify that person;

■ the person's prior use, if any, of the domain name in connection with the bona fide offering of any goods or services;

■ the person's legitimate non-commercial or fair use of the mark in a site accessible under the domain name[2];

■ the person's intent to divert consumers from the mark owner's on-line location to a site accessible under the domain name that could harm the goodwill represented by the mark, either for commercial gain or with the intent to tarnish or disparage the mark, by creating a likelihood of confusion as to the source, sponsorship, affiliation, or endorsement of the site;

- the person's offer to transfer, sell, or otherwise assign the domain name to the mark owner or any third party for substantial consideration without having used, or having an intent to use, the domain name in the bona fide offering of any goods or services;

- the person's intentional provision of material and misleading false contact information when applying for the registration of the domain name; and

- the person's registration or acquisition of multiple domain names which are identical or confusingly similar to trademarks or service marks of others that are distinctive at the time of registration of such domain names, or dilutive of famous trademarks or service marks of others that are famous at the time of registration of such domain names, without regard to the goods or services of such persons.

1 See *Northand Insurance Companies v Blaylock* 2000 US Dist LEXIS 14333 (D Min, 2000), where no bad faith intent to profit from the domain name was found.
2 In *Northand Insurance Companies v Blaylock* 2000 US Dist LEXIS 14333 (D Min, 2000), the defendant's use of the domain name for criticism of the plaintiff did not constitute infringement, the right of free speech outweighing any initial interest confusion.

5.53 Thus, in a US case involving the registration or use of a domain name[1] that is not itself the trade mark of the registrant or is sufficiently similar to another trade mark so as to be likely to cause confusion, mistake, deception or dilution of the distinctive quality of a famous trade mark, the plaintiff may, at any time before final judgment, instead of actual damages and profits, elect for:

- statutory damages of $1,000 to $100,000 per domain name (as the court considers just)[2]; or

- in instances of wilful registration and use, statutory damages of $3,000 to $300,000 (as the court considers just) per domain name; and

- costs and reasonable lawyer's fees.

Unique to the AntiCybersquatting Act is the concept of 'in rem'[3] jurisdiction. Its uniqueness lies in the ability of a complainant to commence proceedings against the domain name itself, as opposed to the registrant. This is particularly beneficial for situations were the registrant cannot be served with proceedings, for instance the registrant is outside of the US or cannot be traced, having provided false details.

Hence, where a plaintiff cannot secure personal jurisdiction over the registrant, the plaintiff may bring an in rem action against the domain name in the jurisdictional court in which the domain name registrar is located, provided the domain name violates any registered trade/service mark of the plaintiff and the court finds that the plaintiff has not been able to obtain in personam jurisdiction[4].

Although damages are not available in in rem proceedings, the court can order the transfer or cancellation of a domain name, which is in reality the primary objective of the plaintiff.

The current US legislation gives rise to a civil claim both in respect of registered and unregistered trademark rights. The difference comes in the manner of enforcing those rights. Registered trade marks may be enforced both in a personal action against a registrant and in an in rem against the domain name; whereas unregistered trade marks may only be enforced in a personal action against the registrant.

The effectiveness of the AntiCybersquatting Act is also demonstrated by the successful case brought by Harrods Limited[5]. This case concerned the registration in Virginia, USA by an English company trading in Argentina called Harrods (Buenos Aires) Limited (HBA). There were not sufficient contracts between HBA and the USA to establish personal jurisdiction so the action was brought by Harrods Limited against the domain names themselves, invoking the in rem jurisdiction of the AntiCybersquatting Act. After a full trial of the action, the district court judge found that the domain names were registered with a bad faith intent to profit and thus ordered their transfer to the plaintiff. Whilst the case was peculiar on its facts given the historical relationship between the parties, one of the factors that clearly swayed the case in the plaintiff's favour was the fact that

HBA had registered nearly 300 domain names incorporating the word Harrods. In August 2002 the US Court of Appeals for the 4th Circuit affirmed the decision of the district court in relation to 54 domain names and reversed the decision in relation to six.

To conclude, a domain name is effectively a form of branding, fiercely protected by its owners, in the same way as traditional brand names. Aldous LJ stated in the court of Appeal in *One in a Million*:

> 'Any person who deliberately registers a domain name on account of its similarity to the name, brand name or trade mark of an unconnected commercial organisation must expect to find itself on the receiving end of an injunction to restrain the threat of passing off.'

Accordingly, if you are considering using a third party's domain name and/or website material to promote your own e-activities, whether by way of comparative advertising, banner advertisements, hyperlinks, metatags and so on, you need to be aware of the legal issues involved.

1   In *Bihari v Gross* 2000 US Dist LEXIS 141800 (SDNY, 2000) it was held that the AntiCybersqutting Act applies to marks included in domain names but not metatags.
2   *Electronics Boutique Holding Corpn v Zuccarini* 2000 US Dist LEXIS 15719 (ED Pa, 2000) saw one of the largest (if not the largest) statutory awards to date when the defendant (who earns up to $1m per year through the registration of misspelled domain names) was ordered to pay $530,000 in damages and lawyers' fees.
3   That is to say, an act available against the world at large, in comparison to an in personam jurisdiction, which is an act directed against a specific person.
4   In *Lucent Technologies v lucentsucks.com* 98 F Supp 2d 528 (ED Va, 2000) the court held that because the plaintiff had located the owner of the website and could have exercised in personam jursidiction, in rem jurisdiction was not permitted.
5   *Harrods Ltd v Sixty Internet Domain Names* 157 F Supp 2d 658 (ED Va, 2001).

8.   COMPARATIVE ADVERTISING

5.54   Consumers regularly scan the newspapers and pound the streets to compare prices and products offered on the high street. The Internet makes comparison shopping much easier due to the ease of clicking from one competing website to another via comparison search engines such as Kelkoo. In the future, shopping 'webbots' could largely automate this task and so it will be important for a business to try to distinguish its goods and services from its competitors.

An advertisement is comparative if in any way, either explicitly or by implication, it identifies a competitor or goods or services offered by a competitor[1]. For example, take such statements as:

> 'Probably the best lager in the world.'

> 'These thingys are 10p cheaper than them Wotsits.'[2]

Comparative advertising is more prevalent today than ever before. It is becoming increasingly difficult to turn on a television, pick up a newspaper or read a magazine without finding at least one prominent example of it. Comparison, explicit or implied, specific or vague, is a crucial component of modern marketing. Certain sectors lend themselves particularly well to commercial battles based on comparisons of prices or tariffs and it is no surprise that the leading English cases in recent years here come from the credit card, mobile phone and 'no-frills' airline sectors. Comparative advertising can be a legitimate, useful and effective marketing tool to convey a major competitive advantage. Where this is done fairly then this practice should not be discouraged. However, where it is done unfairly then the company being unfavourably compared should have recourse.

1   Regulation 2(2A) of the Control of Misleading Advertisements Regulations 1988 (S1 1988/915) as amended by the Control of Misleading Advertisements (Amendment) Regulations 2000 (SI 2000/914), which implement the Comparative Advertising Directive (EC) 55/97. (Direct comparative advertising is when the advertising clearly describes a particular product by making specific comparison to competing products, whereas indirect comparative advertising is more subtle, making a general or indirect comparison to competing products.)
2   This slogan was apparently part of the big brand battle between Golden Wonder and Walkers (unreported).

(a) The position in the European Union

5.55 In the UK we have been familiar traditionally with advertisements which explicitly or implicitly compare the goods or services of one competitor with another. The judiciary, government and Advertising Standards Agency (the ASA) have favoured such advertisements on the basis that they stimulate competition and inform the consumer in a way that is easy to understand. Other Member States have not been so favourably disposed, and have heavily restricted comparative advertising or outlawed it altogether (for example, Germany). The alternative view is that comparative advertising is characterised by the selective use of facts presented with an ulterior motive. Brand owners are more likely to be of the opinion that comparative advertising by a competitor is an attempt to 'ride on the back' of their well-known and successful product and use the reputation of their products as a platform from which to generate sales of that competitor's product.

The Council of the European Communities recognised that the differing views of Member States towards comparative advertising hindered the execution of advertising campaigns beyond national frontiers and constituted an obstacle to the free movement of goods and services. The Comparative Advertising Directive[1], which amends the 1984 Misleading Advertising Directive[2] by including provisions relating to comparative advertising, was introduced as a means of harmonising such laws in the EU as well as helping to stimulate competition[3].

It is perhaps not surprising (given Germany's previous position on comparative advertising) that the German courts have already had cause to refer to the European Court of Justice (ECJ) for guidance on what constitutes a comparative advertisement[4]. The advertisement in question appeared in Katun's catalogues and consisted of Toshiba Europe's product numbers appearing alongside the equivalent Katun product number. By printing the specification numbers of its competitor's products, the advertisement not only constituted a comparative advertisement but also a positive statement that the two products have equivalent technical features[5].

Before discussing the position in the UK, a brief comment on the case of *Pfizer Inc and Pfizer BV v Lestre Nederlandse Reformadriegbureau ENRA BV*[6] is warranted as one of the first cases decided on the basis of the Comparative Advertising Directive. The comparison in question appeared in an enclosure contained in the defendant's VIGRO/VIGORA product[7]. This claimed that the product was for the same medical complaint as that of the claimant's VIAGRA product[8]. As the defendant had failed to substantiate adequately (for example, by way of scientific proof) that its product VIGRO was just as effective for erection problems as VIAGRA, the advertisement was found not to have complied with the requirements of the Comparative Advertising Directive. The judge found that the claimants had made it sufficiently plausible that VIAGRA was a safe medicine, so the suggestion that VIAGRA still has unknown secondary effects wrongly discredited the defendant's product. It is clear therefore that where there is a claim made about a product or competitor's product, the onus will be on the defendant to provide adequate substantiation (that is, a reversal of the usual burden of proof).

1 Directive (EC) 55/97.
2 Directive (EEC) 450/84.
3 All Member States were required to bring into force laws necessary to comply with the Comparative Advertising Directive no later than 23 April 2000.
4 Reference from Landgericht Düsseldorf, Germany: Case C1-1 112/99: *Toshiba Europe GmbH and Katun Germany GmbH* [2002] All ER (EC) 325.
5 That is, a comparison of material, relevant, verifiable and representative features of the products.
6 Ruling of the District court of Utrecht, Belgium: [2001] ETMR 15.
7 The enclosure stated the following (inter alia): 'Finally justice for men and women. Therefore, preferably no more messing around with those "modern" chemical products, which have secondary effects which are still hardly clear at all, and, nota bene: only for men! The positive effect of the chemical preparations which have been on the market since recent times is established, but they must surely have secondary effects which are not at all clear at this time.'
8 VIAGRA was not explicitly stated in the enclosure, hence the comparison was an implicit comparison.

(b) The position in the UK

5.56 The Control of Misleading Advertisements (Amendment) Regulations 2000 came into force in the UK on 23 April 2000, amending the Control of Misleading Advertisements Regulations 1988 and implementing the Comparative Advertising Directive in the UK.

Pursuant to the implementation of the Comparative Advertising Directive, an addendum to the tenth edition of the ASA Codes has been issued to incorporate the new Regulations. Until the revised clauses are produced, clause 19.2 (clause 19 deals with comparisons in advertisements) must be read in conjunction with the addendum[1].

To be lawful, a comparative advertisement should not only be clear and fair (clause 19.2) but must also comply with Regulation 4A(1), which permits comparative advertising provided that the following conditions are met:

- the comparison is not misleading;

- the comparison compares goods or services meeting the same needs or intended for the same purpose;

- the comparison objectively compares one or more material, relevant, verifiable and representative features of those goods and services, which may include price[2];

- the comparison does not create confusion in the market place between the advertiser and a competitor or between the advertiser's trade marks, trade names, other distinguishing marks, goods or services and those of a competitor[3];

- the comparison does not discredit or denigrate the trade marks, trade names, other distinguishing marks, goods, services, activities, or circumstances of a competitor;

- for products with designation of origin, the comparison relates in each case to products with the same designation;

- the comparison does not take unfair advantage of the reputation of a trade mark, trade name or other distinguishing marks of a competitor or of the designation or origin of competing products; and

- the comparison does not present goods or services as imitations or replicas of goods or services bearing a protected trade mark or trade name[4].

In the case of a comparative advertisement referring to a special offer, Regulation 4A(2) permits such an advertisement provided that the advertisement indicates in a clear and unequivocal way:

- the date on which the offer ends;

- that the offer is subject to the availability of the goods or services (where appropriate); and

- the date on which the offer begins (where the special offer has not yet begun) or other specific conditions shall apply[5].

1 Clauses 4.1, 8.1, 19.2, 20.1, 20.2, 21.1, 22.1, 30.1 and 37.1c of the ASA Codes should also be read in conjunction with the addendum. As at August 2002 no such revised clauses have been issued.
2 See, for example, *Toshiba Europe GmbH and Katun Germany GmbH* for a European perspective.
3 See for example, *Pfizer v Lestre Nederlandse Reformadriegbureau* for a European perspective.
4 Regulation 4A(1) repeats article 3(a) of the 1984 Misleading Advertising Directive (as amended). See also clause 22.1 (no advertisement should so closely resemble any other that it misleads or confuses the public), clause 20.1 (advertisers should not unfairly attack or discredit other businesses or their products) and clause 21.1 (advertisers should not make unfair use of the goodwill attached to the trade mark, name, brand, or the advertising campaign of any other organisation) of the ASA Codes.
5 Regulation 4A(2) implements article 3a(2) of the Misleading Advertising Directive (as amended).

5.57 The Control of Misleading Advertisements (Amendment) Regulations 2000 present a significant change in UK advertising laws that must not be overlooked by businesses. The requirement that advertisements compare objectively 'verifiable' features of the goods or services in question may well signal the end of trade puffery and humorous comparisons. So, we could actually see statements such as 'probably the best lager in the world' falling foul of the new Regulations! Since advertisements must compare objectively 'representative features', it will not be permissible for a business whose goods are clearly inferior to another's to choose as a 'comparator' the one feature which is not inferior as the basis of a comparative advertisement. One area in which comparisons are often subjective by their very nature is the performance of different ISA funds (which formed the subject matter of the case *Jupiter Unit Trust Managers v Johnson Managers plc*, discussed below at paragraph 5.59 in connection with the TMA 1994).

Regulation 4A(2) may well become the 'housewives' favourite'. A business which deliberately adjusts prices/conditions for a short period to take advantage of the new pricing/conditions to issue an advertisement claiming superiority over competing goods or services will fall foul of the new Regulations.

Notably, the new Regulations do not provide for brand owners to sue their competitors for advertisements considered to contravene the new Regulations. (Although a complaint to the Director General of Fair Trading may, if appropriate, result in an injunction preventing further publication of the offending comparative advertisement.) For a summary of the Codes and ramifications of non-compliance see Chapter 6, E-marketing.

Clearly, from a European viewpoint, the Comparative Advertising Directive is a liberalising measure, allowing the publication of comparative advertisements in Member States where they were previously prohibited (as is recognised by the ASA). The ASA acknowledges that, for UK advertisers, whether targeting the UK or European markets, the new Regulations will have an immediate impact on the actions to be taken to ensure their comparative advertisements are not illegal, although the Director General of Fair Trading has to date not taken any action in the courts to prevent any such advertisements.

Unsurprisingly, the main legal issue with comparative advertising is trade mark infringement. By its very nature, an advertisement of one company comparing itself to another must incorporate the other company's name and/or trade mark. For example, a comparison between Burger King and McDonalds inevitably involves the use of the names and trade marks 'Burger King' and 'McDonalds' along with, possibly, subsidiary brands such as 'Whopper' and 'Big Mac'.

(c) Comparative advertising under the Trade Marks Act 1994

5.58 Following consultation with the Patent Office, the DTI determined that, notwithstanding the requirements of section 10(6)[1] of the TMA 1994 (which deal with comparative advertising), which were arguably less restrictive, implementation of the Comparative Advertising Directive did not give rise to an amendment to section 10(6). According to the DTI, where the use of a registered trade mark is by a person other than the owner or licensee, such use will continue to be subject to the TMA 1994 unless such use is in a comparative advertisement, when it will also be subject to the more restrictive provisions of the Comparative Advertising Directive (as implemented by the Control of Misleading Advertisements (Amendment) Regulations 2000). It is necessary, therefore, to consider the position of comparative advertising under the TMA 1994 and its respective case law as well as under the new Regulations. Section 10(6) of the TMA 1994 provides that:

> 'Nothing in the preceding provisions of this section [infringement provisions] shall be construed as preventing the use of a registered trade mark by any person for the purpose of identifying goods or services as those of the proprietor or a licensee.

> But any such use otherwise than in accordance with honest practices in industrial or commercial matters shall be treated as infringing the registered trade mark if the use without due cause takes unfair advantage of, or is detrimental to, the distinctive character or repute of the trade mark.'

Although less restrictive, this section is hardly a model of clarity – in the words of Laddie J[2], 'it is a mess'. This is highlighted by the fact that the phrases 'honest practices', 'without due cause' and 'takes unfair advantage' are not defined in the TMA 1994 and are new to English law. As a result the interpretation of these expressions is something of a grey area. (Similarly, it is expected that the phrase 'meeting the same needs or intended for the same purpose' may be something of a grey area and give rise to differences in construction between Member States.)

Nevertheless, the current leading cases concerning section 10(6) (*British Airways plc v Ryanair Ltd*[3], *Emaco Ltd and Aktiebolaget Electrolux v Dyson Appliances Ltd*[4], *Barclays Bank plc v RBS Advanta, Vodafone Group plc v Orange Personal Communications Services Ltd*[5] and *British Telecommunications plc v AT&T Communications (UK) Ltd*[6]) all seem to follow a common thread, which establishes the following principles:

- The onus is on the trade mark proprietor to show that the third party's use which is complained of is not in accordance with honest practices in industrial or commercial matters or takes unfair advantage of or is detrimental to, the distinctive character or reputation of the trade mark[7]. (This position may be reversed by the new Regulations, which in effect places the onus on the third party to show that the comparison is legal.)

- '[U]se in accordance with honest practices' – the test here is an objective one: if the use is considered honest by members of a reasonable audience, then it will not infringe. Honesty has to be gauged against what is reasonably to be expected by the relevant public of advertisements for the goods or services in issue. If, however, a substantial portion of the members of a reasonable audience are likely to say, on being given the full facts, that an advertisement is not honest, or is significantly misleading, then the protection from trade mark infringement is lost. (While this may not be echoed by the new Regulations, it is certainly within their spirit[8].)

- Mere 'trade puffery' does not amount to trade mark infringement as Jacob J highlighted in the *McDonalds v Burger King*[9] case. There is, though, a fine line between, on the one hand, merely puffing one's own goods or services at the expense of a competitor and, on the other hand, disparaging the competitor's goods or services. This line always turns on the circumstances of the case. It is generally accepted in consumer circles that a certain amount of self-glorification over one's competitor is an important and necessary strategy to gain that all-important competitive edge in today's market place. In essence, the public expects hyperbole and the courts are not there to be puritanical. (Nonetheless, the new Regulations may throw a question mark over the use of trade puffery and it will be interesting to see how the UK and European courts interpret this point[10].)

- The degree of hyperbole acceptable would depend on the nature of the product. For example, it is more tolerated in the food marketing sector than in the pharmaceuticals sector. It is also necessary to consider the target audience to gauge the likely response. (The interpretation of 'verifiable' will again be key.)

- The advertisement must in all cases be considered as a whole and not be broken down into minute detail. Minute textual examination of an advertisement is not something on which the reasonable reader would embark and therefore neither should the courts.

- The omission of certain facts may in certain circumstances be dishonest if, for instance, it would be significantly misleading.

- The more precise the claim, the more likely it is to be construed as a serious claim by the public and therefore would almost certainly be seen as misleading or dishonest if not entirely true.

1 Use by one company of another company's trade mark in any way was historically trade mark infringement. By the 1990s this official disapproval of comparative advertising had relaxed. In the new atmosphere of 'consumerism', advertisers and the media found it circumspect to agree in principle that 'fair' comparisons ought to be allowed. The TMA 1994 further loosened the reins around comparative advertising and codified UK law relating to registered trade marks. In essence, 'the primary objective of section 10(6) was to legalise comparative advertising' (*Barclays Bank plc v RBS Advanta* [1996] RPC 307, per Laddie J).

2 In *Barclays Bank plc v RBS Advanta* [1996] RPC 307.
3 [2001] FSR 541.
4 [1999] ETMR 903.
5 [1997] FSR 34.
6 (18 December 1996, unreported).
7 See also the *Pfizer* case discussed above for the position in Europe under the Comparative Advertising Directive.
8 See for example, *British Airways plc v Ryanair Ltd* [2001] FSR 541.
9 [1987] FSR 112, CA.
10 See, however, *Jupiter Unit Trust Managers Ltd v Johnson Fry Asset Managers plc* (19 April 2000) LTL 12.5.00, which does not involve trade marks.

5.59 Some commentators have suggested that as comparative advertising will potentially increase in the more permissive era of the TMA 1994 (and the Control of Misleading Advertisements (Amendment) Regulations 2000), claims alleging malicious falsehood or trade libel may increasingly come into play in an attempt to protect brand reputation. An example of such a case is *British Airways plc v Ryanair Ltd*[1], which concerned malicious falsehood and trade mark infringement[2].

The Irish airline company Ryanair had published two advertisements entitled 'Expensive BA .... DS' and 'Expensive BA' respectively, which included fare comparison tables. It was held that British Airways' argument that Ryanair had exaggerated how expensive British Airways' fares were was unsuccessful (British Airways being only three, as opposed to five, times more expensive than Ryanair)! Although the advertisements pre-dated the implementation of the requirements of the Comparative Advertising Directive in the UK[3], the judge applied these requirements and held that the average consumer would not think the advertisement had fallen foul of the requirements (notwithstanding that the advertisements were offensive).

Although the following case did not involve any trade mark use (it involved libel and malicious falsehood), it is clearly of relevance in this context. In *Jupiter Unit Trust Managers Ltd v Johnson Fry Asset Managers plc*[4], the judge stated that if a statement was made regarding the way a company conducted its business as to lead 'people of ordinary sense' to the opinion that 'the company conducts its business badly and inefficiently', this will be libellous[5]. In this instance, the judge found that this was not the case. Surprisingly, the judge said that in comparative advertising a degree of puffing the advertiser's own product was inevitable (with a consequent disparagement of the compared product). The advertisement in question seemed to go beyond earlier comparative advertisements found in the market, which provided merely an objective comparison, leaving it up to the viewer to infer a conclusion and to decide for themselves which was the 'winning horse'. As regards the malicious falsehood element, the judge was unable to make a finding of malicious falsehood. He did not find that the financial service provider in puffing his own product had overstepped the permissible limit of denigration or disparagement of his rival's product so that a reasonable man would take the claim seriously[6].

Therefore the more objective and transparent the comparison, the easier it will be for the judge to make a finding of malicious falsehood, if that line has been deemed to have been crossed.

1 [2001] FSR 541. Even before the court ruling, the ASA upheld a complaint from a member of the public against the advertisement.
2 Malicious falsehood is more fully discussed in Chapter 4, E-rights. In this case, it should be noted that the judge stated that in the absence of proof of malice, careful thought must be given to including such a claim in these cases.
3 The advertisements in question were published in 1999. The Control of Misleading Advertisements (Amendment) Regulations 2000 came into effect on 23 April 2000. The judge indicated that compliance with most of these requirements would be necessary to comply with section 10(6) of the TMA 1994.
4 (19 April 2000) LTL 12.5.00.
5 The test in the libel claim was whether the meaning of the words used were defamatory. To determine this the judge again used an objective test – what is the ordinary meaning of the words conveyed to the ordinary viewer? (From the guidance of the Master of the Rolls in *Skuse v Granada Television Ltd* [1996] EMLR 278, CA). The Master of the Rolls also stated that 'a statement should be taken to be defamatory if it would tend to lower the plaintiff in the estimation of right-thinking members of society generally ...'.
6 The claimant's case was that the advertisement made a number of false claims about its company. The bases of these claims was a table of weighted performance figures for small unit trust groups for the year to 31 December 1998 showing the claimant's company ranked third behind the defendant. These performance claims were inevitably subjective and depended on the benchmark used, timings and reinvestment of gross dividends.

(d) Other relevant codes

5.60 The International Chamber of Commerce (ICC) promotes high standards of ethics in marketing and advertising on the Internet via self-regulatory codes, which are intended to complement the existing framework of national and international law. Advertisements containing comparisons should be so designed that the comparison is not likely to mislead and should comply with the principles of fair competition, and national laws and regulations concerning comparative advertising. Points of comparison should be based on facts which can be substantiated and should not be unfairly selected. For more detailed information on the ICC, visit their website at www.iccwbo.org.

(e) Practical points and examples

5.61 The following points should be kept in mind when embarking on this sort of advertising:

- run a trade mark search on the competitor's mark to see if it has been registered and, if registered, determine what for;

- if using a competitor's trade mark, ensure that it falls into the guidelines described in this section in order to be able to benefit from the statutory defence to infringement and avoid being caught by the proviso to section 10(6) of the TMA 1994 and the Control of Misleading Advertisements (Amendment) Regulations 2000;

- beware of the common law tort of passing off. Even if your competitor's mark is not registered a campaign can still fall foul of this tort, which protects a brand owner from a competitor passing off a mark or get-up as his own. For example, in *McDonalds Hamburgers Ltd v Burger King (UK) Ltd*[1], the defendant's statement 'It's Not just Big, Mac' in an advertisement for a Whopper hamburger was held by the court to contain a risk of confusion as to the origin of the Whopper, so this advertisement was held to constitute passing off;

- take care that your comparative advertisement does not infringe a competitor's copyright (for example, the logo, packaging or its price list). There is no statutory defence in the Copyright Designs and Patents Act 1988 equivalent to section 10(6) of the TMA 1994;

- does the advertisement comply with the relevant industry and regulatory codes? Remember that these are only a guideline and not a categorical indication that an advertisement is honest for the purposes of section 10(6) of the TMA 1994; and

- do not stray into the realms of trade libel or malicious falsehood. Make sure statements can be substantiated and are not merely designed to rubbish your competitors. The test here is an objective one – would the reasonable man take the claim being made as one being made seriously?[2]

So, compare if you wish, but compare with caution!

1 *McDonald's Hamburgers Ltd v Burger King (UK) Ltd* [1986] FSR 45, 4 Tr 226 L; revsd [1987] FSR 112, CA.
2 *Jupiter Unit Trust Managers Ltd v Johnson Fry Asset Managers plc* (19 April 2000) LTL 12.5.00.

9.   METATAGS

5.62 Metatags are hidden Hypertext Markup Language (HTML) code which are intended to describe the contents of a website. 'Description' metatags are intended to describe the website, whereas 'keyword' metatags contain keywords relating to the contents of the website (although there are no actual constraints on the words that can be used). As hidden code, metatags will only be visible to an Internet user if he specifically views the source of the document[1].

Given the enormity of the World Wide Web, unless a user knows the domain name of the website he is looking for, the user will either hazard a guess at the domain name or utilise an Internet search engine such as Alta Vista or Yahoo! As a number of Internet search engines use the information within metatags as part of their indexing formulae, one recommended way of increasing the chances of a web page appearing on the list of hits returned by a PC user's search is by using keyword metatags[2].

This practice is largely legitimate but problems may arise when these metatags include the trade marks of another party. Trade mark owners often object to this practice because, just like similar domain names, they divert customers away from their own websites. For instance, Cartier, the designer and manufacturer of jewellery, watches and other accessories, has keyword metatags such as 'cartier watches, swiss watches, diamonds and engagement rings'. Such keywords are logical given the nature of the business and its clientele. Were Cartier to use, say, Rolex as a keyword then, depending on the circumstances surrounding such use, Cartier may find that Rolex take objection to the metatag, if the metatag lures Rolex customers to Cartier's website. The sections below consider whether this type of metatag would entitle Rolex to a cause of action in respect of this hypothetical use.

1　In Microsoft Internet Explorer, for example, this is done by selecting Source from the View menu.
2　Search engines generally operate on the basis of either indexing every word on your website (Alta Vista) or by surfers categorising sites into subjects (Yahoo!) and it is estimated only 40% of sites are registered by the search engines.

(a)　The position in the US

5.63　The US courts have already determined many cases in favour of the trade mark owner, most notably *Brookfield Communications Inc v West Coast Entertainment Corpn*[1], which concerned use of Brookfield's registered trade mark 'MovieBuff' by West Coast. The court considered that the question here was whether West Coast could use 'MovieBuff' or 'moviebuff.com' in the metatags of its website at 'westcoastvideo.com' or at any other domain other than 'moviebuff.com' (which the court had already determined West Coast could not use). The court found that although there was no source confusion (in the sense that consumers knew they were patronising West Coast rather than Brookfield), there was initial interest confusion[2]. By using 'moviebuff.com' or 'MovieBuff' to divert people looking for 'MovieBuff' to its website, West Coast improperly benefited from the goodwill that Brookfield developed in its mark. In effect, 'using another's trade mark in one's metatags is much like posting a sign with another's trade mark in front of one's store'. The court made the following analogy:

> 'Suppose West Coast's competitor ... puts up a billboard on a highway reading – West Coast Video: 2 miles ahead of Exit 7 – where West Coast is really located at Exit 8 but Blockbuster is located at Exit 7. Customers looking for West Coast's store will pull off at Exit 7 and drive around looking for it. Unable to locate West Coast, but seeing the Blockbuster store right by the highway entrance, they may simply rent there. Even consumers who prefer West Coast may find it not worth the trouble to continue searching for West Coast since there is a Blockbuster right there. Customers are not confused in the narrow sense: they are fully aware that they are purchasing from Blockbuster and have no reason to believe that Blockbuster is related to, or in anyway sponsored by, West Coast. Nevertheless, the fact that there is only initial interest confusion does not alter the fact that Blockbuster would be misappropriating West Coast's acquired goodwill.'

Whilst the court agreed that West Coast could legitimately use an appropriate descriptive term in its metatags, 'MovieBuff' was not such a term. Although 'MovieBuff' differs from 'Movie Buff' by only a single space, the difference is pivotal. 'Movie Buff' is a descriptive term used to describe a movie devotee, whereas 'MovieBuff' is not a word to be found in the English language. When the term 'MovieBuff' is employed, it refers to Brookfield's products and services, not a movie devotee. Thus, as West Coast used Brookfield's trade mark to attract people to its website and not as a reference to Brookfield's products, such use was not considered fair.

It is important to understand that the court emphasised that it was not restricting West Coast's right to use the mark in a manner which would constitute fair use under US trade mark legislation and referred to the case of *Playboy Enterprises Inc v Terri Welles*[3]. Welles, a former Playmate of the Year, was using 'Playboy' and 'Playmate' not as trade marks but as descriptive terms fairly and accurately describing her website, which advertised the fact that she was a former Playmate of the Year. Her use was a permissible, good faith attempt to index the content of her website and permissible under US trade mark laws. Likewise, in *Trans Union LLC v Credit Research Inc*[4], Credit Research's use of the 'Trans Union' name as a metatag constituted fair use since it described the affiliation between both parties and the products available from Trans Union[5].

Playboy were, however, successful in *Playboy Enterprises Inc v AsiaFocus International Inc*[6], where Playboy sued AsiaFocus for trade mark infringement in respect of use by AsiaFocus of Playboy's registered trade marks 'Playboy' and 'Playmate' in its metatags. The court found that AsiaFocus had intentionally misled viewers into believing that the AsiaFocus website was connected with or sponsored by Playboy[7]. If such a connection or sponsorship had existed, but subsequently ceased, continued use of the trade/service mark as a metatag would give rise to a justifiable objection. In *Florists' Transworld Delivery Inc v Originals Florist and Gifts Inc*[8], Florists' Transworld Delivery Inc obtained a preliminary injunction preventing Originals Florist & Gifts Inc from using its trade marks in their metatags (and from displaying these on its website). Since search engines do not perform actual Internet searches each time a request is made, the indexes become out of date over time (much in the same manner as telephone directories) and it was sought to have the website shut down. The court considered that this would be too extreme due to the potential harm to Originals Florist & Gifts Inc and ordered the removal of the metatags.

An assumption that a trade/service mark is being used in a metatag is not by itself sufficient. Evidence that it is contained in a metatag will need to be placed before the courts[9].

1   174 F 3d 1036, 1064 (9th Cir), 1999.
2   The court basically extended the concept of initial interest confusion used in *Dr Seuss* 109 F 3d at 1405 and *Mobil Oil Corpn v Pegasus Petroleum Corpn* 818 F 2d 254, 257–58 (2nd Cir), 1987, to metatag cases. The court stated that 'registration of a domain name for a website does not trump long established principles of trade mark law. When a firm uses a competitor's trade mark in the domain name of its website, users are likely to be confused as to its source or sponsorship. Similarly, using a competitor's trade mark in the metatags of such a website is likely to cause what we have described as initial interest confusion. These forms of confusion are exactly what the trade mark laws are designed to prevent'. (Initial interest confusion occurs where users perform a search for a particular website, only to be diverted by potentially infringing domain names and metatags to competing websites. Once they have realised the website is not the one they were searching for, they decide nevertheless to use that site instead (see *Eli Lilly v Natural Answers*, 233 F 3d at 464–465).) A number of other cases have developed where the claimant has successfully restrained a competitor from using their mark contained in either a domain name or metatag: see *Jews for Jesus v Brodsky* 993 F Supp 282 (DNJ), affd 159 F 3d 1351 (3rd Cir), 1998; *New York State Society of Certified Public Accountants v Eric Louis Associates* 79 F Supp 2d 331 (SDNY, 1999); and *E-Stamp Corpn v Lahoti* CV-99-9287 (CD Cal June 16 2000).
3   78 F Supp 2d 1066 (US Dist, 1999).
4   2001 US Dist LEXIS 3526 (ND III, 2001).
5   A service agreement between the parties enabled Credit Research to use Trans Union's nationwide credit database.
6   No 97–734 1998 WL 724000.
7   See also *Playboy Enterprises Inc v Calvin Designer Label* C-97-3204 (ND, 1997); *Oppedahl & Larson v Advance Concepts* Civ No 97-2-1592 (DC Colo, 1997); *Insituform Technologies Inc v National Envirotech Group LLC* Civ No 97-2064 (ED La, 1997).
8   2000 US Dist LEXIS 16869; 57 USPQ 2D (BNA) 1079.
9   *Movado Group Inc v Matagorda Ventures Inc* 2000 US Dist LEXIS 18196. Matagorda (an on-line watch retailer) advertised Movado's Concord watch for sale on its website, although it didn't actually sell the watch. No evidence that the Concord mark was used as a metatag was provided and this part of the claim was unsuccessful. The judge did, however, find that Matagardo were using the 'bait and switch' scheme by using the Concord watch to lure potential customers to their website.

(b) The position in the UK

5.64   Although *Roadtech Computer Systems Ltd v Mandata (Management and Data Services) Ltd*[1] was trumpeted as the first UK case on metatags, the court was not asked to determine whether the use of a trade mark as a metatag amounted to trade mark infringement or passing off[2]. Nevertheless, provided that the requisite elements of trade mark infringement and/or passing off are present, the indications are that a UK court would find that the use of another's trade mark as a metatag constitutes trade mark infringement and/or passing off. Where registered trade marks are concerned, it is important to remember that where use of the trade mark is to identify goods or services as goods or services belonging to the owner of the trade mark and such use does not take unfair advantage or cause damage to the distinctive character or reputation of the trade mark, such use will not amount to trade mark infringement. *Roadtech* may be indicative of the UK courts' approach to the assessment of damages (should liability be established). Roadtech claimed damages under (i) the user principle, (ii) the cost of corrective advertising, (iii) diversion of trade, and (iv) loss of goodwill[3].

While it is understandable that businesses wish to establish a presence on the Internet, the manipulation of search engines in this manner is most unattractive. Unless the use of the trade mark is legitimate (that is, within the Comparative Advertising Legislation and the TMA 1994), the use of metatags serves to attract traffic to a site which may otherwise be 'traffic-less' or to attract the customers of a competitor.

As trade mark owners become aware of the use by others (and in particular by competitors) of their trade marks as metatags in websites, it is expected that the UK courts will follow the path already paved by the US courts and protect the rights of UK trade mark owners. The use of third party trade marks in metatags should be resisted, unless a business is confident that such use would be legitimate. Clearly, where the trade mark bears no relation to a business's website the use cannot be legitimate. A business must ask whether the higher/additional placing in a 'hit' list is worth the prospect of litigation (particularly when one considers how often one 'clicks' on to the 'next page of hits' returned by the Internet search).

1   [2000] ETMR 970.
2   Notwithstanding, Master Bowman stated that Mandata's actions (Mandata used Roadtech's registered and unregistered trade marks as metatags and within the text of their website, but in the same colour as the background of the home page) were a 'blatant, albeit unsophisticated … unsuccessful invasion of the claimant's intellectual property rights'.
3   The court found that Mandata had taken a ride on the back of Roadtech's very successful website and had clearly intended to obtain a commercial advantage by so doing, and held that under head (i) £15,000 was payable. As regards heads (ii)–(iv): although Roadtech had sought to advertise correctively, it did so too long after Mandata's infringing actions. Had advertisements been inserted promptly at Roadtech's risk, damages might well have been awarded. Insufficient evidence had been demonstrated to conclude that trade had been diverted. Mandata had argued that for Roadtech to succeed, the following assumptions would have to be made in favour of Roadtech: (1) the user had to select particular engines, (2) it had to use Roadrunner, (3) it had to select Mandata (although there is no reference), (4) it had to make the association (although there is no reference).

10.   SPAMDEXING (OR WORD STUFFING)

5.65   Recognising that the repetition of keywords increases a website's ranking by certain search engines, the practice of 'burying' such repetitions within HTML code has developed as a further technique to deceive those search engines. Devious programmers either bury the keywords in the same colour as the website's background (that is, 'fontmatching') or 'stuff' HTML with keywords which bear no resemblance to the content of the website. Regardless of the preferred method, spamdexing or word stuffing (depending on your preferred terminology) is on the whole designed to take advantage of third party trade marks (competitors' marks or otherwise) and provides another example of 'invisible trade mark infringement'[1].

In addition to the actual repetition[2], evidence that the user has not been misdirected to a third party website by such use of a keyword may be relevant. Such was the case in *Trans Union LLC v Credit Research Inc*, where the evidence showed that Credit Research's website did not even rank in the top 50 hits during a search for 'Trans Union' using three popular search engines.

application of laws targeted at off-line advertising. For example, does an advert placed on a website need to comply with the laws of all of the territories of the world, the territories in which the website is based or hosted, or the territories at which the advert is targeted? Can a TV commercial which the Independent Television Commission does not allow to be shown on UK television be broadcast on the Internet? This chapter examines some of the laws applicable to all types of advertising and the regulation of advertising in the UK, before looking at the legal, jurisdictional and commercial considerations which apply to each of the different types of interactive advertising set out in paragraph 6.03 above (except for banner adverts, which are discussed in Chapter 5, E-brand). This chapter does not examine sponsorship, partnering and commercial tie-ins relating to advertising content, or content providers, which are covered in Chapter 2, E-contract. This chapter is not meant to be an exhaustive examination of all legal issues relating to advertising and marketing, but is intended to highlight the additional considerations which arise in respect of using interactive media[1].

1   For a more detailed discussion on the legal issues relating to advertising and marketing under English law, see Crown, *Advertising Law and Regulation* (1998) Butterworths.

2.   SPECIFIC ADVERTISING LEGISLATION

6.05   The regulation of advertising serves two main purposes: to protect consumers from misleading advertising and to restrict unfair competition. In most countries, regulation is through a combination of trade mark, trading standards and unfair competition legislation and codes of practice set up by self-regulatory bodies.

(a) Advertising legislation

6.06   In the UK alone, there are more than 150 different Acts and Statutory Instruments (not to mention applicable European legislation) directly or indirectly affecting advertising and promotions[1]. The main pieces of legislation regulating advertising in the UK are:

■   the Trade Descriptions Act 1968, which sets up various offences of applying a false trade description to goods;

■   the Consumer Protection Act 1987, which contains particular offences relating to unfair pricing;

■   the Control of Misleading Advertisements Regulations 1988 (SI 1988/915) (as amended by the Control of Misleading Advertisements (Amendment) Regulations 2000 (SI 2000/914)), which implements the EU Misleading Advertising Directive 1984 (Directive (EEC) 450/84) and Comparative Advertising Directive 1997 (Directive (EC) 55/97). These Regulations seek to provide minimum standards of protection against misleading adverts, which are likely to deceive consumers by reference to the characteristics of the goods, the price of the goods or the nature of the advertiser. These Regulations and their impact on comparative advertising are discussed further in Chapter 5, E-brand.

1   A detailed list of relevant legislation can be found in the British Codes of Advertising and Sales Promotion, located at www.asa.org.uk.

(b) The Stop Now Orders

6.07   The Stop Now Orders (EC Directive) Regulations 2001, which came into force in the UK as a Statutory Instrument on 1 June 2001[1], give additional powers to consumer protection bodies interested in taking representative action against traders who commit acts contrary to certain consumer protection Directives[2]. The relevant UK legislation which the Stop Now Orders cover includes[3]:

- the regulation of misleading and comparative advertising, except regulation specifically in relation to food and tobacco;

- the regulation of the content, amount and distribution of television advertising and programme sponsorship;

- the Medicines (Advertising) Regulations 1994 (SI 1994/1932); and

- the regulation of the sale and supply to consumers of goods and services.

Other UK legislation is covered, including consumer credit legislation, the Unfair Terms in Consumer Contracts Regulations 1999 (SI 1999/2083) and the Consumer Protection (Distance Selling) Regulations 2000 (SI 2000/2334) (see further, Chapter 2, E-contract).

The UK does not have a history of empowering individuals or special consumer interest groups in relation to enforcing public laws protecting consumers. Historically, if rogue traders breached the consumer protection legislation covered by the Stop Now Orders, consumers would have had to rely in the majority of cases on complaints to trading standards officers who would be responsible for enforcing the relevant law. Even if trading standards officers did investigate and enforce relevant law, the penalty for non-compliance was often a small fine[4], with the result that many carried on afterwards as before[5].

Under the new Stop Now Orders, if a trader commits an act contrary to the UK legislation as set out in the Stop Now Orders, either the Director General of Fair Trading or qualifying consumer interest bodies may bring proceedings under section 35 of the Fair Trading Act 1973. The aim of bringing proceedings is to prevent the infringing act continuing. In April 2002, Dixons Group, Harvey Furnishings and Magnum agreed to amend advertisements relating to 'interest free credit' after the Office of Fair Trading (OFT) consulted and put pressure on the retailers (using the threat of bringing proceedings under the Stop Now Orders) in relation to the offer of 'interest free credit' being misleading[6].

1   SI 2001/1422 (see www.legislation.hmso.gov.uk/si/si2001/20011422.html).
2   The Stop Now Orders, Sch 1.
3   For a non-exhaustive list of UK laws covered, see the Stop Now Orders, reg 2(3).
4   For example, under section 32(2) of the Consumer Protection Act 1987 any person who intentionally does not comply with a requirement imposed on them by an officer of an enforcement authority in relation to consumer safety or misleading price indications is guilty of an offence and liable to a maximum fine on the current scale of £5,000.
5   DTI Press Release 10 April 2001 (see www.nds.coi.gov.uk).
6   For a discussion of the likely remedies and enforcement of the Stop Now Orders by the OFT, see www.oft.gov.uk/business/legal+powers/stop+now+orders+action+informal+assurances.htm.

6.08   Under the Stop Now Orders, in order to qualify as a consumer interest body who is entitled to bring proceedings, objective criteria must be satisfied, such as:

- the organisation is controlled and managed independently;

- the organisation has demonstrated the ability to protect the collective interests of consumers by promoting high standards of integrity and fair dealing; and

- the organisation is willing to co-operate with the Director General of Fair Trading in respect of the sharing of information with other relevant consumer bodies[1].

The Stop Now Orders will add another layer of sanctions and control to existing legislation regulating advertising in the UK (and on top of industry self-regulation which is discussed below), in that they will make it easier for qualifying interested bodies to take immediate action to prevent or stop acts which are contrary to consumer interests. At the time of writing, the Office of Fair Trading had not received any applications from consumer bodies interested in registering as a qualifying body entitled to bring proceedings under the Stop Now Orders. For the time being, therefore, the only bodies who can bring proceedings under the Stop Now Orders are the OFT and the other public bodies specified in the Orders[2].

1   The Stop Now Orders, reg 4(2).
2   Trading Standards authorities, the Information Commissioner, the Civil Aviation Authority, the Gas and Electric Markets Authority, the Director General of Electricity Supply for Northern Ireland, the Director General of Gas for Northern Ireland, the Director General of Telecommunications, the Director General of Water Services, the Rail Regulator, and the Department of Enterprise, Trade and Investment in Northern Ireland.

(c) Applicable law regulating specific industries

6.09   Any legislation or regulations governing a particular sector will still apply to communication via interactive methods. This could include:

- the Financial Services Act 1986 (see Chapter 9, E-finance);

- the Banking Act 1987 (see Chapter 10, E-banking);

- the Personal Pension Scheme (Advertisements) Regulations 1990 (SI 1990/1140);

- the Consumer Credit Act 1974;

- the Consumer Credit (Advertisements) Regulations 1989 (SI 1989/1125);

- the Betting, Gaming and Lotteries Act 1963 (see Chapter 14, E-gambling).

3.   INDUSTRY SELF-REGULATION

6.10   Historically, most regulation of off-line advertising in the UK has taken place within the context of industry self-regulation. Some of the bodies which regulate off-line advertising have extended their remit to on-line and Internet advertising. Set out below is a brief explanation of the different ways in which the advertising industry regulates itself in the UK.

(a) The Advertising Standards Authority Codes

6.11   The Advertising Standards Authority (ASA) was established in 1962 and is the independent body that promotes and enforces standards in principally all non-broadcast adverts (for example, print, press, sales promotions and electronic media). The regulation of advertising falling under the remit of the ASA is split up into three bodies: the ASA, the Advertising Standards Board of Finance (ASBOF) and the Committee of Advertising Practice (CAP). CAP is independent to the ASA and currently comprises all of the trade and professional associations which in turn represent all advertising agencies, advertisers, media owners and advertising service providers. CAP, being representative of the advertising industry, is responsible for updating and devising the British Codes of Advertising and Sales Promotion (the ASA Codes), which regulate all adverts in newspapers, magazines, brochures, posters and other print media in public places. The ASA Codes do not apply to broadcast commercials on TV or radio, but do cover video and cinema commercials together with direct marketing and sales promotions[1].

CAP also provides a Copy Advice Team free of charge to advertisers, which provides help and advice on the content of advertising to try and pre-empt potential problems and breaches of the ASA

Codes[2]. Funding for the ASA and CAP is found by ASBOF through levies to advertisers charged on the value of paid for media (where such media falls under the remit of the ASA). The current levy charged by ASBOF is 0.1% of the cost of media of all display advertising which falls under the remit of the ASA (such as press, print, poster), and 0.2% of the value of certain types of direct marketing.

1 A full list of the types of advert covered by the ASA can be found at www.asa.org.uk.
2 CAP's copy advice can be obtained free of charge by calling 020 7580 4100. Guidance notes are also available on CAP's website at www.cap.org.uk.

(i) General principles of the ASA Codes

6.12 Under the ASA Codes:

- all adverts should be legal, decent, honest and truthful;

- advertisements should be prepared with a sense of responsibility to consumers and to society;

- advertisements should respect the principles of fair competition generally accepted in business;

- no advert should bring advertising into disrepute;

- advertisements must conform to the ASA Codes (primary responsibility falls on advertisers, yet agencies, publishers and other service suppliers must accept an obligation to abide by the Codes);

- unreasonable delay in responding to ASA enquiries may be considered a breach of the Codes; and

- the Codes are applied in the spirit as well as in the letter.

The ASA Codes do not have the force of law; rather, they operate alongside the law through a system of industry self-regulation (but see the discussion on complaints below). The ASA Codes are written in 'everyday' language, rather than 'legal' language. However, the fact that the ASA Codes are applied in spirit as well as the letter means that advertisers cannot argue that they comply with the technical language of the ASA Codes if the effect of the advertising is such that it is not within the spirit of the Codes.

In addition to the general principles set out above, which apply to all advertising, there are specific codes relating to adverts covered by the ASA Codes[1]. For example:

- all claims within adverts must be capable of substantiation, and must not exploit the lack of knowledge or inexperience of consumers[2];

- advertisements should not cause serious or widespread offence[3];

- advertisers are normally urged to obtain written permission before using individuals or referring to them in adverts[4]; and

- care should be taken when using testimonials and endorsements in advertising, and any claim must still be capable of substantiation notwithstanding the testimonial[5].

Advertisers should not unfairly attack or discredit a third party's products and should not make unfair use of the goodwill attached to the trade mark, name, brand or the advertising campaign of any other organisation. This Code is now read in conjunction with the Control of Misleading Advertising (Amendment) Regulations 2000, discussed further in Chapter 5, E-brand[6].

In addition, specific rules apply to the advertising of specific products, such as cigarettes, alcohol, betting and gaming, medicines and slimming products. Advertisements and promotions targeted at or featuring children are heavily regulated.

1 For the full text of the ASA Codes, see www.asa.org.uk.
2 Codes 3 and 6 of the ASA Codes.
3 Code 5 of the ASA Codes. This is one of the Codes on which the ASA receives most complaints; for example the Obsession advert featuring Sophie Dahl in 2000 received 971 complaints, which were upheld (see the Yves Saint Laurent Beaute Limited adjudication dated 10 January 2001 in the adjudication section of ASA website).
4 Code 13 of the ASA Codes.
5 Code 14 of the ASA Codes.
6 Codes 20 and 21 of the ASA Codes.

(ii) Breach of the ASA Codes

6.13 Adverts do not need to be pre-cleared by the ASA before publication. Instead, the ASA relies on a system of complaints in order to ensure compliance with the ASA Codes. If an individual or corporate body feels that an advert breaches the ASA Codes they can make a complaint to the ASA. The ASA will investigate the complaint and, if the complaint has merit on its face, the advertiser will be asked to justify the advert and the claims. If it is not able to do so, or the ASA or the ASA Council does not agree that the advert complies with the ASA Codes, the ASA Council may uphold the complaint and may request that the advertiser withdraws or amends the offending advert. All complaints are published in the ASA Monthly Report[1]. Occasionally, upheld complaints attract the attention of the press. In January 2001, an Yves Saint Laurent print and poster advert for Opium which featured Sophie Dahl, naked, achieved notoriety when the ASA upheld complaints that it was offensive and degrading to women. The advert and the surrounding controversy then became front page news in a number of the tabloid newspapers in the UK[2].

The ASA does not have the power to award damages in respect of adverts which breach the ASA Codes. In addition, the ASA cannot force an advertiser to comply with its requests to withdraw or amend an offending advert itself. Some critics of the ASA and the self-regulatory system say that the ASA has no teeth. However, the vast majority of advertisers do comply with the terms of any upheld complaint because of the pressure within the advertising industry to do so. Media owners (such as billboard owners, newspapers and magazines who will be probably be indirect members of CAP themselves through their affiliation to trade associations) will be informed by the ASA of the decision to uphold a complaint, and will themselves be asked not to publish or distribute the offending advert. The media owners' terms and conditions of business with clients will probably stipulate that they will not carry advertisements that breach the ASA Codes, and publishers will also probably wish to avoid alienating readers by carrying adverts that are considered offensive or misleading. Another incentive to comply with the ASA Codes is derived from various industry bodies, who sometimes give incentives and discounts to members, but which often stipulate that membership is conditional upon compliance with the ASA Codes.

An ASA complaint also attracts a certain amount of publicity, and most organisations regard an upheld complaint from the ASA as attracting adverse publicity. However, for some organisations, the threat of publicity related to an ASA complaint would not appear to be considered adverse, and the suspicion has to be that certain advertisers have deliberately disregarded the ASA Codes and courted controversy to attract widespread publicity. The brand most commonly associated with this approach has traditionally been Benetton[3].

1 Available on the ASA website (www.asa.org.uk).
2 See footnote 3 to paragraph 6.12 above.
3 See references to Benetton on the ASA website (footnote 1 above).

6.14 In extreme circumstances of persistent failure to comply with the ASA's rulings, the ASA may refer a case to the Director General of Fair Trading who may take action under the Control of Misleading Advertisements Regulations 1988 (as amended by the Control of Misleading Advertisements (Amendment) Regulations 2000)[1]. Accordingly, the Director General of Fair Trading can seek an undertaking from anyone responsible for commissioning, preparing or disseminating the offending advert that it will be discontinued. In the event that this is not provided or not honoured, an injunction from the court to prevent its further appearance may be sought by the Director General. A defaulter can be found to be in contempt of court, and is liable to be penalised accordingly.

In addition, a number of advertisers who have persistently breached the ASA Codes are now required by the ASA to have their adverts pre-cleared before they are allowed to book media. For example, French Connection UK, which commonly brands itself as 'FCUK', has had a number of complaints made against it by the public, some of which have been upheld by the ASA because of the implied sexual acronym and possible misreading of FCUK[2]. In early 2001 French Connection UK launched a website located at www.fcukinkybugger.com[3], which it advertised using press and print media and which all referred to 'fcukinkybugger.com'. The ASA received a number of complaints about the adverts which were upheld[4]. In addition, the ASA stated that for the next two years French Connection UK would need to obtain pre-clearance from CAP before it would be allowed to place any more poster or billboard adverts. (Since this date, we understand that French Connection UK has voluntarily agreed that it will obtain pre-clearance advice from CAP on all adverts falling under the remit of the ASA, and not just poster adverts[5].)

1 For example, in February 2002, the ASA referred the Data Protection Act Registration Service, a Manchester-based company offering to register business under the Data Protection Act 1998, to the Office of Fair Trading following non-compliance by the Data Protection Act Registration Service with the terms of upheld complaints by the ASA in September 2001 and November 2001.
2 See ASA adjudications against French Connection Group plc from 12 May 1999, 10 January 2001, 20 June 2001, 4 April 2001, and 4 July 2001, available on the ASA website (www.asa.org.uk).
3 The original website and broadcast commercial which was shown on the fcukinkybugger.com website is no longer available at the website. For further discussion on issues arising in respect of this website, see paragraph 6.32.
4 See ASA adjudication from 4 April 2001, available on the ASA website.
5 See the ASA website.

(iii) Cross-border complaints

6.15 The European Advertising Standards Alliance (EASA) was formed in 1991 and comprises European organisations that operate self-regulating codes of practice governing advertising content and practice[1]. EASA is committed to the principle that effective self-regulation of advertising affords the highest level of consumer protection.

The ASA works with its European partners in EASA to promote self-regulation within the legal framework. In June 1992 EASA set up a system to provide a quick and effective means of investigating complaints across national frontiers. The system applies to complaints about all adverts (broadcast and non-broadcast) which appear in one country but originate in another and aims to ensure that European consumers have equal access to the system and that their complaints are treated fairly and swiftly.

For example, a complaint made to the ASA against a direct mailing which originated from an organisation in Italy but which was sent to consumers in the UK would be first sent by way of a complaint to the ASA in the UK. Given that the ASA would not have jurisdiction to deal with the complaint directly, it would then refer the complaint to its Italian counterpart, who would investigate it under its rules and procedures. If upheld, the sanctions imposed would be those allowed under the Italian self-regulatory system. EASA would co-ordinate the cross-border complaint, support information exchange and report on the outcome of the case. Details of cross-border complaints are published on the EASA website[2].

The Stop Now Orders[3], which implement the EU Consumer Injunction Directive[4], will also facilitate cross-border complaints. The Director General of Fair Trading will be able to require enforcement bodies in other EU countries to assist in relation to any cross-border complaint, where the complaint falls under the remit of the Consumer Injunction Directive and the Stop Now Orders.

The ASA Codes and their application to interactive advertising are discussed in further detail in relation to the different types of advertising via new media below[5].

1   A full list of the Alliance's membership (22 members across Europe and 4 non-European members, which are Canada, New Zealand, South Africa and the USA) can be found at www.easa-alliance.org/about-easa/en/easa_members.html.
2   See www.easa-alliance.org/complaints.
3   Paragraph 6.02 above.
4   Directive (EC) 27/98.
5   Paragraph 6.32 below.

(b)   The Independent Television Commission

6.16   The Independent Television Commission (ITC) Code of Advertising Standards and Practice, together with various other ITC Codes (such as the ITC Code of Programme Sponsorship and the ITC Programme Code)[1], regulates all commercial television broadcast adverts in the UK (the ITC Codes). The ITC has a statutory duty under the Broadcasting Act 1990 (BA 1990)[2] to draw up and enforce the ITC Codes in relation to all television programme services licensed by the ITC under the BA 1990[3]. This currently includes Channel 3 (ITV1 and GMTV), Channel 4, Channel 5 and satellite, cable and digital television services provided by broadcasters established in the UK, who are all ITC licensees. The responsibility for ensuring that TV commercials comply with the ITC Codes falls on the ITC licensees. Unlike adverts falling under the remit of the ASA Codes, TV commercials must be pre-cleared before appearing on UK television channels governed by the ITC. Pre-clearance is carried out by the Broadcasting Advertising Clearance Centre (BACC)[4]. If the BACC believes that a TV commercial complies with the ITC Codes, it will issue a certificate which will then enable the advertiser to place the advert on UK television channels falling under the remit of the ITC. Under the ITC Codes, it is not a prerequisite for all UK television commercials to have a BACC certificate. However, in practice, ITC licensees are unlikely to accept adverts without BACC certificates, given that the primary responsibility for compliance with the ITC Codes rests with ITC licensees.

Having a BACC certificate does not preclude complaints being made against an advert, which will result in the ITC investigating the advert and, if it upholds the complaint, either ordering the advert to be withdrawn or amended.

The ITC has the authority under the BA 1990 to claim jurisdiction over broadcast adverts over the Internet. However, at the moment, the ITC has stated that it is not exercising its right under the BA 1990 to state that all adverts on the Internet are subject to the ITC Codes[5]. Instead, the ITC website provides a link to an organisation called Internet Watch Foundation[6]. The ITC Codes are discussed further in relation to interactive TV at section 8 below.

1   Available at www.itc.org.uk.
2   Section 93 of the BA 1990.
3   The ITC Codes also give effect to a number of EU Directives on television broadcasting, including the Television Without Frontiers Directive (Directive (EEC) 552/89).
4   See www.bacc.org.uk.
5   See www.itc.org.uk/about_the_itc/how_we_regulate/Internet_issues/index.asp.
6   The Internet Watch Foundation website can be found at www.iwf.org.uk. The Internet Watch Foundation has been in operation since 1996 and aims to prevent the Internet being used to transmit illegal materials (in particular, child pornography) and to encourage legal material on the Internet to be classified so that users can tailor their surfing to their own requirements.

(c)   The Radio Authority Codes

6.17   Any organisation based in the UK providing a commercial radio station will need a license from the Radio Authority. Radio adverts are governed by the Radio Authority Advertising and Sponsorship Code[1]. This is beyond the scope of this book, but covers all UK independent radio adverts in accordance with the statutory requirements of the Broadcasting Acts 1990 and 1996. The regulatory system is not dissimilar to that operated in respect of television advertising by the ITC (paragraph 6.16 above).

1   Available at www.radioauthority.org.uk.

(d) OFCOM

6.18   The Office of Communications Act 2002, establishing the Office of Communications (OFCOM) as a regulator to the communications sectors, received Royal Assent on 19 March 2002 and came into force on 1 July 2002. OFCOM will merge the functions of five existing regulatory bodies: the ITC, the Broadcasting Standards Commission, OFTEL, the Radio Authority and the Radio Communications Agency.

The stated aim of OFCOM, which is likely to be operational by the end of 2003, is to ensure that regulation in the field of communication is not heavy handed, wherever possible, and that the communications industry is left to the principles of competition wherever possible.

In the future, advertising using interactive media and traditional off-line media may be affected by OFCOM[1].

1   See www.ofcom.gov.uk.

4.   CONTENT OF A WEBSITE

6.19   This section concerns itself with website content which is used by an organisation to advertise its products and services and to promote its brand. It also covers the issues involved in putting existing off-line advertising campaigns, including press and print adverts (such as newspapers, magazines, billboards) or TV or cinema commercials, onto a website.

(a) Jurisdiction[1]

(i)   The Yahoo! Inc case

6.20   The content of any website raises a number of issues relating to jurisdiction over the Internet. Does the content of the website need to comply with the laws of all of the territories of the world? Does it need to comply with the laws of the 'country of origin'? Or does it need to comply with the laws of all of the territories at which it is targeted? The problem of jurisdiction and advertising over the Internet is compounded by the vast differences in advertising law from territory to territory. For example in France, adverts must be in the French language[2] and failure to put adverts in the French language can be a criminal offence. Alcohol advertising is prohibited in a number of Islamic countries, and is severely restricted in many other territories, including France and Sweden (where advertising alcohol in press adverts was until recently banned)[3]. Advertising aimed at children is prohibited or severely restricted in a number of territories, including Denmark and Sweden. The US has much stricter laws relating to obscenity than the UK, but still these vary greatly from state to state. Based on some of the above examples, a UK alcohol brand producing a website in English could face a number of potential legal problems.

The reason for such a proliferation and difference in approach to the regulation of advertising from country to country comes down to the simple fact that advertising and marketing reflects cultural identity. It goes without saying that cultural identity and social ideas of perceived risk differ widely from country to country. The *Yahoo! Inc* case[4] warned organisations of the real dangers in selling or advertising goods or services over the Internet, due to the potential of the Internet to be governed by the laws of all of the territories of the world. In this case, Yahoo! Inc, based in California, was sued in France under French anti-racist criminal laws because of the sale and advertisement of Nazi memorabilia on its website. Yahoo! Inc argued unsuccessfully that the French courts should not have jurisdiction over the website, because the illegal facts were not committed in France, but in the US. The court rejected Yahoo! Inc's arguments on the basis that the website was available in France, and Yahoo! was found liable. This decision confirmed many legal theorists' warning that organisations wishing to sell goods or services or even merely advertise their business over the Internet potentially run the risk of being found liable under the laws of other territories' laws. (The difficulties of enforcing judgments such as this are discussed with direct reference to this case in Chapter 7, E-dispute, para 7.62).

1   The issue of jurisdiction of the Internet is discussed further in Chapter 7, E-dispute.
2   Loi Toubon (Loi No.: 94-88 du 1 Fevrier 1994).
3   ECJ ruling on the Gourmet case (C-405/98) and the Swedish District Court subsequent confirmation of the ruling on 4 March 2002.
4   *UEJF and LICRA v Yahoo! Inc and Yahoo France* 22 May 2000, available at www.juriscom.net/txt/jurisfr/cti/yauctions20000522.htm.

(ii) The E-Commerce Directive and the Electronic Commerce (EC Directive) Regulations 2002

6.21 It was thought that the E-Commerce Directive[1], when implemented into English law, may go some way towards helping organisations in relation to the question of jurisdiction over website content, by implementing a 'country of origin' principle within the EU. A 'country of origin' principle would mean that organisations providing website content would only need to comply with the laws of the country in which it is based, as opposed to the laws of any other jurisdiction in which it can be accessed. The E-Commerce Directive was due to be implemented into Member States' laws by 16 January 2002. In the UK the majority of the provisions of the Directive are transposed into English law by the coming into force of the Electronic Commerce (EC Directive) Regulations 2002[2] on 21 August 2002 (with the exception of regulation 16, which comes into force on 23 October 2002).

The E-Commerce Regulations are discussed at length in Chapter 2, E-contract. The following is intended to be a brief examination of how the Regulations apply to information on an organisation's website which is used to advertise that organisation's products and services, but for further discussion of the Regulations see the detailed analysis at section 4 of Chapter 2.

The E-Commerce Regulations apply to 'information society services' within the 'co-ordinated field', which covers a wide range of on-line activities that are 'normally provided for remuneration'. This definition includes selling goods and services on-line, including offering on-line information by subscription-based information providers and banner adverts on websites. However, the fact that information society services are defined as services which are '*normally* provided for remuneration' means that it is not immediately clear whether the Regulations are intended to cover free website content and information about an organisation found on its website. Following the DTI's discussion set out in its Guidance on the Regulations[3], it seems that the definition of information society services covers a number of activities that are not normally paid for by the receiver of the service, but where the service provider receives remuneration from a third party (such as selling advertising space on-line). The DTI states in the Guidance that the term 'information society service' will 'also extend to services (in so far as they represent an economic activity) that are not directly remunerated by those who receive them, such as those offering on-line information or commercial communications (eg adverts) or providing tools allowing for search, access and retrieval of data'[4]. Therefore, we suggest that free website content about an organisation which is not directly targeting users, but merely offers a *passive* advertisement about the organisation, will probably not fall under the remit of the Regulations as it might not be classed as an 'information society service'. However, content which is *actively* targeting customers or advertising an organisation's products or services may be classed as an 'information society service' and will therefore be covered by the Regulations. By way of example, a simple information-only website, which offers pricing information about an organisation but which does not actively or directly target the potential customer, may not be covered by the Regulations. On the other hand, a website which contains advertisements about an organisation (for example by putting off-line posters or commercials onto the website) may fall under the remit of the Regulations, as putting targeted advertisements on-line is a service for which the organisation receives indirect remuneration (by way of increasing the value of its brand).

1   Directive (EC) 31/2000.
2   SI 2002/2013.
3   'A Guide for Business to the Electronic Commerce (EC Directive) Regulations 2002' Guidance July 2002, available from the DTI website, at www.dti.gov.uk/cii/ecommerce/europeanpolicy/ecommerce_directives.shtml#guidance.
4   'A Guide for Business to the Electronic Commerce (EC Directive) Regulations 2002', para 2.16.

6.22   If an organisation is providing an information society service within the co-ordinated field by providing on-line content or putting adverts onto its own website, a partial country of origin principle will apply within the EU through the implementation of the E-Commerce Directive into Member States' laws. In principle, this should simplify the question of applicable laws and jurisdiction over content provided on-line, at least within the EU. Under English law and the implementation of the E-Commerce Directive through the E-Commerce Regulations, regulation 4(1) states that information society services provided to a person in another state in the European Economic Area (EEA) by a service provider from an establishment in the UK must comply with any applicable UK law that falls within the co-ordinated field[1]. Regulation 4(2) of the Regulations provides that any applicable UK law that falls within the co-ordinated field may not be applied to an information society service provided by a service provider established *elsewhere* in the EEA, *if* this would restrict the freedom to provide that service into the UK. Accordingly, inbound information society services are subject to a restrictions test: UK law *may* apply to the service provided it does not restrict the freedom to provide the service in the UK.

It should be noted that this does not implement a pure country of origin principle as it does not say that any provider of such services who is based outside of the UK will be entirely exempt from the application of UK laws. There are a number of important exceptions to regulation 4(2) of the Regulations, where enforcement authorities can take proportionate measures against a service provider based outside of the UK on public policy grounds, for the protection of public health, public security grounds or for the protection of consumers[2]. One unanswered question from the E-Commerce Regulations and the E-Commerce Directive is whether some of the restrictive advertising laws in various Member States – such as those relating to the advertising and selling of alcohol over the Internet – could be argued to be laws which protect public health. If they are seen to be protecting public health, organisations from other Member States wishing to advertise or sell alcohol over the Internet will still need to comply with the UK's restrictive laws relating to the selling and advertising of alcohol under the E-Commerce Regulations. Similarly, the terms of equivalent laws implementing the E-Commerce Directive in other Member States may mean that UK organisations wishing to advertise and sell alcohol over the Internet will not be able to avoid liability in other Member States, if they fail to comply with relevant national laws relating to consumer protection and the advertising and sale of alcohol.

The E-Commerce Directive and the UK's implementation of it through the E-Commerce Regulations therefore only partially set up a 'country of origin' principle. The laws of other Member States could still apply to the content of the website or the advertisement of goods or services on-line if public policy or consumer protection grounds demand that the laws of another Member State should apply. In addition, free website content which only provides information about an organisation, without targeting or actively aiming it at customers, may not be covered by the Regulations, which will mean that the question as to jurisdiction over the content of the website will still remain. The E-Commerce Directive is discussed in greater detail in Chapter 2, E-contract.

1 See section 4 of Chapter 2, E-contract.
2 Regulation 4(4) to 4(9) of the E-Commerce Regulations.

(iii) Rome II

6.23 In 2001, there were discussions within the EU relating to a proposed 'Rome II' Green Paper based on the Rome Convention, aimed at non-contractual or non-transactional websites and the jurisdiction for consumers who use non-transactional websites. This would directly cover websites providing information and adverts for their own goods and services. It was originally suggested that the laws of the Member State of the consumer would apply to the website, and that consumers would be able to sue in their own home country rather than the country where the organisation is based. This proposal was met with criticism by the Federation of European Direct Marketing (FEDM) and the Advertising Information Group (AIG) as it seemed to fly in the face of recognising a 'country of origin' principle within the EU and replaced it with the principle of 'country of destination'. The AIG and FEDM argued that this would place a burden on EU organisations to obtain legal advice in all of the Member States of the EU, which would have a negative impact on the amount of advertisers wishing to use websites as an advertising medium within the EU. At the time of writing, the EU had indicated that a revised Green Paper on Rome II would be available imminently, but it is unclear as to whether the new Green Paper would back down on proposals for the country of destination principle. In the meantime, a new EU Regulation based on the Brussels Convention came into force under English law on 1 March 2002[1], which states that consumers (but not businesses) can sue organisations selling goods or services on the Internet in either the Member State in which the consumer lives, or the Member State in which the organisation is based. Whether this will mean that the country of destination principle will be kept in the Rome II Green Paper remains to be seen.

Notwithstanding all of the EU legislative proposals and activity, the question of whether an organisation can be liable for the content of its website falling foul of another territory's laws still obviously exists in respect of countries outside the EU. In addition, even once the EU legislative proposals have been implemented into national laws, businesses will perhaps still not be able to advertise goods or services over the Internet without fear of being liable in other Member States.

1 Council Regulation (EC) 44/2001.

(iv) Practical steps in relation to jurisdictional issues

6.24 Given all of the complexities and uncertainty surrounding jurisdiction of the Internet, and the frightening prospect of being liable under all of the laws of the territories in which the website can be accessed, what can an organisation do to minimise the risks involved with advertising its goods and services on-line? Clearly, obtaining legal advice from all of the territories of the world is not a practical or commercial reality. There are however some practical steps which can be taken to attempt to lower the risk of potential liability.

It is accepted practice for disclaimer wording to be added to a website to state that the website has been put together to comply with the laws of a particular jurisdiction, such as English law. The statement should then go on to state how any dispute arising out of the website will be dealt with (for example, by the English courts, or by alternative dispute resolution (ADR)). By adding such a statement or disclaimer to the website, the hope is that organisations will exclude the application of laws from other territories. In order to be valid under English law, the jurisdiction disclaimer will need to be prominent and brought to the attention of users, in order that the statement regarding jurisdiction and dispute resolution of the website becomes a term of a 'contract' governing use of the website between the website owner and the user. From a risk minimisation perspective, disclaimers and statements such as these should ideally be shown on the entry page to the website, with users having to click on an icon saying 'I agree' before being allowed to enter the website. In practice, creative concerns about the design and layout of the website may outweigh the desire to include such a legal statement on the entry page. Therefore, a number of website owners have taken the view that an icon from the home page of their website to a jurisdictional statement will suffice. Currently, the validity of such disclaimers has never been tested in an English court and there is therefore little indication at present as to how prominent a disclaimer needs to be in order to be validly incorporated into the contract governing use between the website owner and the user. Best practice would suggest that organisations are safer to include a jurisdictional disclaimer on their website as prominently as possible rather than not having a jurisdictional statement at all. Above all, however, this needs to be consistent with the actual content of the website itself and what territories it is targeting in practice. Consumer websites will face particular difficulties. The issue is simply flagged in this chapter, but is discussed in greater detail at paragraph 7.27 of Chapter 7, E-dispute.

The terms and conditions of a website could also attempt to disclaim potential liability which may arise out of the content of the website. For example, the website may be linked to a third party's software which can be downloaded by the user, which carries with it a risk of viruses. The website may also be hyperlinked to a third party's website, over whose content the original website owner does not exercise control, and which could lead to some other kind of liability. For example, a linked website offering negligent home improvement tips could itself raise the possibility of the owner of the linked website being in breach of contract (under an implied term to provide safe information) or under negligence. One practical step which can be taken (subject to the usual caveats relating to limitation of liability which are further discussed in Chapter 3, E-liability) is to attempt to disclaim potential liability arising out of third party software or content by stating that the website owner will not be liable for any loss or damage caused by such third party software or content. However, where the law restricts disclaimers of liability, website owners may not be able to rely on the disclaimer to avoid all possible liability arising out of the use of the website, for example, if such a term was unreasonable or unfair[1]. It is therefore recommended that audits as to the legality of third party content are carried out by the website owner and virus checks be undertaken on any software made available for users to download from the website from time to time in addition to using any legal disclaimers on the website.

1   Section 2(2) of Unfair Contract Terms Act 1977, which states that '... a person cannot so exclude or restrict his liability for negligence except so far as the term or notice satisfies the requirement of reasonableness' (and which applies to contracts with businesses as well as consumers). Under the Unfair Terms in Consumer Contracts Regulations 1994, consumers are not bound by a standard term in a contract with a seller or supplier of goods or services if that terms is 'unfair'.

6.25   An example of a disclaimer which could be added to the website incorporating the above points and some other useful points in relation to the protection of the organisation advertising over the Internet is as follows:

> This website has been put together in accordance with and complies with the laws of England and Wales and is intended to be accessed by UK residents. All visits to this website shall be governed by the laws of England and Wales and shall be subject to the jurisdiction of the courts of England and Wales.
>
> Whilst every effort has been made to ensure the accuracy of information on this website, no guarantee is given and [*name of website owner*] accepts no responsibility or liability as to the accuracy or completeness of the information contained within the website.

Where this website is hypertext linked to any website operated by any third party, [*name of website owner*] accepts no responsibility or liability arising in respect of any content on such website. In addition, [*name of website owner*] accepts no responsibility or liability arising in respect of any use of any software which is available for downloading or copying on this website, or any third party website.

Third party banner ads, pop-up ads and other virtual advertising may be experienced whilst browsing this website. As a result of various pieces of software, such third party ads may not have been approved by [*name of website owner*], and may appear on this website without [*name of website owner's*] knowledge or consent, and [*name of website owner*] accepts no responsibility or liability in respect of the content or display of any such third party advertisements.

No permission to copy, reproduce, modify or download this website (or any part of it) is given other than a single copy for personal use or reference.

All trade marks used on this website belong to [*name of website owner*] or the registered proprietor of such trade marks. All rights relating to such trade marks, copyright and any other intellectual property rights are reserved for [*name of website owner*] or the organisation contributing the relevant materials.

Any information on this website is up-to-date at the time it is posted but is subject to subsequent variation, without notice.

6.26 In addition to including a legal disclaimer such as that set out above, another practical option is to include a warning that if a user is from a particular jurisdiction they should go no further, or to seek to prevent visitors from particular jurisdictions from accessing the website content. This is particularly useful for advertisers of products which may be illegal in other jurisdictions, such as alcohol (and this device is frequently used as part of the terms and conditions of entry for sites with pornographic content). When advertising alcoholic drinks over the Internet it is advisable to ask users to answer questions relating to the country in which they are accessing the website (and to clarify their age). Wherever possible from a technology point of view, filters preventing visitors from problematic jurisdictions from accessing the website in the first place should be used. In practice (and more easily implemented) are safeguards (such as use of IPO addresses and addresses for credit cardholders) to prevent transactions with customers based in particular jurisdictions.

It is recommended that more detailed legal advice is sought in certain key countries where the website is targeted, and also when promoting products which are likely to be heavily regulated (such as cigarettes, alcohol, financial services, on-line gaming and medicines and where any adverts are aimed at children).

However, even if risk minimisation steps are taken, there remains a possibility that an organisation which advertises its goods or services over the Internet still runs the risk of potential litigation or infringement of laws in any jurisdiction in the world!

(b) Intellectual property considerations

6.27 Chapters 4 (E-rights) and 5 (E-brand) contain a detailed examination of this topic, but the following non-exhaustive list of points should be considered when putting content on the Internet.

(i) Infringement of rights

6.28 When putting together an interactive campaign, one question which is frequently overlooked is whether the campaign materials (such as poster adverts, films, drawings, scripts, brand names, logos and trade marks) can be used without infringing the rights of any third parties. This is particularly important when simply moving a campaign from traditional to new media, where it is wrong to assume that content cleared for use on TV or in corporate brochures, for example, additionally allows for use in interactive media.

When putting content onto a website, an organisation should ensure that it has the consent of the copyright owner of all of the materials it proposes to use in respect of its campaign. If the relevant material was written by an employee of the business in the course of his employment, under English law the copyright would normally belong to the employer and organisation in question (subject to any agreement to the contrary)[1]. However, if it was written or prepared by anyone else (including freelancers or external consultants who are not employees), the copyright in the materials will belong to the third party unless the copyright has been assigned by the author of the materials in writing[2].

Therefore, if materials are being used on a website which have not been produced by an employee of the organisation in the course of their employment, organisations will either need a written assignment of copyright from the author of the materials or a licence entitling the organisation to use the materials on the website[3]. Although not essential in order to be legally valid, it is recommended that any licences in respect of copyright are made in writing, in order that disputes over the usage rights for the materials are avoided.

If trade marks are used on a website (whether belonging to a third party or to the organisation which owns the website), care should be taken to ensure that the trade marks are not being infringed unwittingly. In particular, to the extent that a move on-line reflects a shift in geographical target markets, an organisation should treat such an extension of its territories as the creation of new brands in these markets. Trade mark and brand clearances are advisable in order to ensure that use of a trade mark or brand on the website does not constitute trade mark infringement or passing off.

1   Section 11 of the Copyright, Designs and Patents Act 1988 (CDPA 1998).
2   Section 90 of the CDPA 1998.
3   Section 90 of the CDPA 1998.

(ii)   The Newspaper Licensing Authority

6.29   If articles or cuttings from newspapers, journals or magazines are being used, permission should be obtained for the use of the article or cutting, even if it was based on a press release which was drafted by the organisation itself. Some organisations may have licences from the Newspaper Licensing Authority, which entitle them to reproduce and copy a certain number of newspaper articles for use within their business, without having to contact the newspaper or journal in question for permission to copy the article. However, it will not necessarily be the case that licences with the Newspaper Licensing Authority cover uploading articles onto websites in order that articles from newspapers can be copied and distributed. If organisations have a Newspaper Licensing Authority licence covering copying of newspapers and journals, the exact terms of the licence will need to be checked before assuming that copies can be uploaded onto a website[1].

1   For further details see www.nla.co.uk.

(iii)   Image rights and individuals

6.30   If an advertiser uses a picture of a famous individual or uses their name in an advert without obtaining their consent, the advertiser may be liable under English laws relating to passing off provided that:

■   a significant reputation or goodwill is attached to the individual's image or name; and

- the individual is able to show that the actions of the advertiser using the image or name have caused a false message which is understood by a significant section of the relevant market at which the advert is aimed, that the goods or services in question have been endorsed, recommended or approved by the individual[1].

The advertiser may also be in breach of the ASA Codes or ITC Codes for not obtaining permission from the individual to be featured[2]. In addition, actors appearing in still photographs or in films are likely to have restricted the use of their image under the terms of their contract with the advertising agency which produced the relevant advert. Unless use on the Internet has been specifically agreed, such extended use without prior agreement is likely to constitute a breach of contract. This issue is a constant thorn in the side of advertising agencies with their clients, as advertisers are not always sensitive to this issue, particularly given that the advertiser will not have a direct contract with the actor and any claim made will be against the agency.

1 *Irvine v Talksport* [2002] EWHC 367 (Ch), [2002] 2 All ER 414.
2 See Code 13 of the ASA Codes (available at www.asa.org.uk) and Code 15 of the ITC Code of Advertising Standards and Practice (available at www.itc.org.uk).

(iv) Recommendations

6.31 As with conventional campaigns, advertising agencies or advertisers will need to ensure they have obtained usage rights to feature any actors appearing in the advert and in respect of any other use of a third party's property (such as photographs, drawings or music). The usage rights will normally be obtained by way of licences or assignments of rights. Licences will normally limit the territories in which the advert can be shown (which should be unlimited in the case of the Internet), the media (for example, press, poster or TV) on which the advert is to be shown, and the duration of the usage rights (normally by reference to the first publication or first transmission date of the advert). It is common for the Internet to be treated as a 'territory' in its own right (for example 'territory' could be defined as UK, France, Germany and the US, and also the Internet). The Internet is sometimes also defined as 'media'.

Additional payments or royalties will probably be payable to the artist or other third party in the event that the territory, media or duration is extended. It is recommended that additional payments for extension of use are agreed in advance and set out in the licence.

In order to protect an organisation's materials on a website, it is advisable that corporate copyright notices and trade mark symbols are used[1].

1 An example of a copyright notice is © Hammond Suddards Edge 2002. All Rights Reserved. Next to all trade marks, the ™ symbol should be used. (The ® symbol is not recommended without territorial disclaimers, as to claim that a trade mark is registered when it is not could constitute a criminal offence in some territories.)

(c) Advertising laws applicable to the content of websites

(i) The ASA Codes

6.32 In 1995 the ASA confirmed that the ASA Codes apply to 'non-broadcast electronic media', but since 2000 it has stated that the ASA Codes do not apply to ordinary content on an organisation's website. There is therefore a distinction between, on the one hand, claims made by an organisation in content published on-line on its own website and, on the other, paid for adverts and promotions found on-line. Claims made on a company's website will not fall under the remit of the ASA Codes, whereas on-line advertising in paid for space and on-line promotions do fall under the remit of the ASA Codes. While this distinction may not be evident from the ASA Codes themselves, this is nonetheless the ASA's interpretation of 'advertising'[1]. The ASA Codes will therefore apply to banner adverts and virtual advertising, together with adverts in viral e-mails and sales promotions whenever they appear on-line. The ITC Codes do not currently apply to website content and adverts made on-line[2].

When this policy decision was made by the ASA, it led to many website developers and advertisers reverting to the general assumption held in the mid-1990s that the Internet was less regulated than off-line adverts. The interpretation of the decision of the ASA and ITC not to regulate claims made on a website led many advertisers to believe that even if an advert has had to be withdrawn because it breaches the ASA Codes, or has not been cleared for use on commercial television by the BACC, it could be put onto a website without liability. For example, the French Connection UK website located at www.fcukinkybugger.com in early 2001 (discussed in more detail in paragraph 6.14) included a statement that 'The powers that be have decided that our new TV commercial "kinkybugger" contains an unacceptable level of innuendo and is therefore unfit to be screened on national TV ... Thankfully no such restrictions apply on the Internet'. Unofficial sources suggest that the advertisement in question had not been cleared by the BACC for appearance on television.

However, notwithstanding the ASA policy decision not to regulate the content of a website, all other laws relating to the content of the website apply. Where content has been deemed inappropriate by the ASA or ITC for distribution in traditional UK advertising media, it is possible that it will fall foul of laws relating to areas such as obscenity, defamation or comparative advertising. Any traditional media which is used to advertise the existence of the website will also still fall under the remit of the ASA, ITC or Radio Authority Codes, as applicable[3].

As ever, the problematic issue of jurisdiction over the Internet means that the French Connection UK website may well have been in violation of the more stringent laws of several US States.

1 See the article 'Watching the Web' in ASA Monthly Report No 113 (11 October 2000). This distinction has some interesting consequences. For example, if an advertiser also publishes its brochure on the Internet, any claims made in the brochure would not be considered to be adverts for the purposes of the Codes, yet they would in its traditional printed brochure.
2 See discussion on ITC Codes above, at paragraph 6.16.
3 In relation to the fcukinkybugger.com press and poster adverts, the ASA upheld complaints against the adverts and held that the adverts should be withdrawn. This affected FCUK's ability to advertise the existence of its website through traditional media, and therefore indirectly imposed sanctions in relation to the website itself, even though it is not governed by the ASA Codes.

(ii) The Electronic Commerce (EC Directive) Regulations 2002

6.33 Now implemented, the E-Commerce Regulations (discussed above at paragraph 6.21 and in further detail in Chapter 2, E-contract) mean that various pieces of information will need to be given by the information service provider. If organisations fall within the definition of 'information society service' within the 'co-ordinated field', regulation 6(1) of the E-Commerce Regulations states that the following information must be made available in a form and manner that is easily, directly and permanently accessible (for example by way of a hypertext link to a page containing the information):

■ name of the service provider;

■ the geographical address at which the service provider is established;

■ the details of the service provider, including e-mail addresses;

■ trade registration or authorisation details if any (therefore a public limited company registered in England and Wales must state its registration number; and an investment firm must state that it is regulated by IMRO, SFA or PIA or, in due course, the Financial Services Authority);

- if the service provider is part of a regulated profession (eg lawyer or accountant), the professional body it is registered with, its professional title, applicable professional rules and Member States in which services are regularly provided); and

- the service provider's VAT number.

In addition, an organisation providing any 'commercial communication' (which will definitely include website content, as well as e-mails) must clearly identify:

- that it is a commercial communication;

- on whose behalf the commercial communication is made;

- any qualifying conditions if it is a promotional offer; and

- any conditions for participating if it is a promotional competition or game.

Some of these requirements are already found in the ASA Codes (see paragraph 6.32). In addition, the Business Names Act 1985 states that a company, partnership or individual must state in legible characters on all business letters, written orders, invoices and receipts its name and address for service in the UK. The same applies in effect to companies registered under the Companies Act 1985[1].

1   See section 349 of the Companies Act 1985.

5.   ON-LINE SALES PROMOTIONS

6.34   Sales promotions are useful methods of promoting a brand or product. The term 'sales promotion' is used to cover the following types of promotional activity:

- free prize draws (including instant wins);

- competitions;

- coupons, money-off vouchers and some other loyalty vouchers or incentives; and

- other promotions at the point of sale, such as price reductions, discounts, free gifts, on pack promotions, or 'two for one' giveaways (which are beyond the scope of this chapter).

Sales promotions have proved popular over the Internet and other interactive media, such as WAP phones, mainly due to the reduced printing costs and costs of implementing the promotion and the increased audience which the promotion can reach.

(a)   Applicable laws relating to sales promotions within England and Wales

6.35   Sales promotions are primarily regulated under English law by the Lotteries and Amusements Act 1976 (LAA 1976) and by the ASA Codes. For further details on lotteries, see Chapter 14, E-gambling.

Running an illegal lottery, or being associated with running an illegal lottery (such as by printing tickets or distributing advertisements)[1], is a criminal offence under the LAA 1976. Lotteries were defined in the case of *Reader's Digest Association Ltd v Williams*[2] by Lord Widgery as 'the distribution of prizes by chance when the persons taking part in the operation or a substantial number of them, make a payment or consideration in return for obtaining their chance of a prize'. Lord Widgery went on to describe the key factors of all lotteries as being:

- the distribution of prizes;

- which are distributed by chance; and

- where the participants (or a substantial number of participants) have made a contribution or payment to play in the lottery.

Lotteries are illegal under the LAA 1976, unless expressly permitted (see Chapter 14, E-gambling, section 6). In order to avoid running an illegal lottery, promoters need to ensure that the promotion is structured so as to constitute a free prize draw or a competition.

1 Section 2(1) of the LAA 1976.
2 [1976] 3 All ER 737.

(i) Free prize draws

6.36 The LAA 1976 does not provide a definition of what constitutes a lottery or free prize draw. Instead, it has been left to the courts to decide (in cases such as *Readers Digest*, mentioned above). There are three key elements of a legal free prize draw:

- the distribution of prizes;

- which are distributed by chance (as opposed to involving the skill of participants);

- where the participants (or a substantial number of participants) have *not* made a contribution or payment to enter, or at least have been given a chance to enter the prize draw without making a contribution or payment to the promoter.

The contribution or payment point is crucial, as it is the only factor that distinguishes between free prize draws (which are legal) and lotteries (which are illegal unless authorised). It is also the area of English law regulating sales promotions that attracts the most controversy. It is easy to understand why a payment (for example to buy a lottery ticket or instant win scratchcard) to enter a draw has been made illegal (unless specifically authorised) by the courts and Parliament. If this 'mischief' had not been legislated against there would be the possibility for unscrupulous promoters to run lotteries in which participants stand little or no chance of winning and which unduly influences members of the public to put themselves at financial risk in the hope of financial reward. However, prize draws in which the consumer has had to make a contribution are also illegal under English law. This means that promotions where consumers have to buy a product or service in order to enter the draw are unlawful if this is the only entry route, even if the price of the product is the same as if the promotion had not taken place.

For such a prize draw to be lawful under current law, there must be a genuine free entry route for consumers who do not purchase the product or service and a 'substantial' number of participants in the draw must have entered through such a free entry route. This is commonly known as the 'no purchase necessary' route.

6.37 Promoters often find it difficult to understand why prize draws in which the consumer has to buy their product or service are illegal under English law. From the promoters' point of view, one of the main reasons for running a prize draw promotion may be to encourage customers to buy more of their products or services. Many who disagree with the current law would also argue that, from the consumer's point of view, the inducement to buy the product or service is unlikely to unduly influence the consumer to buy the product unless they also have some intention of using the product. However, as the law currently stands, a contribution to enter, such as buying a bar of chocolate on which the 'free' prize draw details are published, is illegal, unless there is a genuine 'no purchase necessary' route.

How should the 'no purchase necessary' route be structured in order to satisfy the current law restricting prize draws? Problems have arisen with off-line prize draws, where participants have either had to buy a product to enter the prize draw or could enter via a no purchase necessary route because not enough participants have entered through the no purchase necessary route. Under the *Readers Digest* case it was established that a prize draw can become an illegal lottery if the vast majority of participants make a payment or contribution to enter. In *Imperial Tobacco Ltd v A-G*[1], scratch cards in a cigarette pack were available in cigarette packs and a small number of scratch cards were available over the counter for customers who did not want to purchase the cigarettes to enter. This was held to be an illegal lottery because the 'no purchase necessary' route did not make the scratch cards available to many participants and therefore most participants had to make a contribution in order to enter the promotion. More recently, in *Russell v Fulling and Page*[2], a scratchcard promotion in which cards were distributed to customers who bought certain goods but which were also available to customers who had not bought the requisite goods was held to be an illegal lottery. The court held that the promotion was not a free prize draw because in the majority of cases the scratchcards were only given to people who had bought the goods, and the fact that only a tiny proportion of participants came through the no purchase necessary route persuaded the court to hold that the prize draw was an illegal lottery.

It is clear that promoters must therefore actively promote the existence of the no purchase necessary route in order to ensure that it is not an illegal lottery. This will mean more than simply indicating a 'no purchase necessary' entry route on the terms and conditions of the promotion. In practice the 'no purchase necessary' route will involve little more than the opportunity for a consumer to participate in the promotion by sending a post card or stamped addressed envelope to a fulfilment house operating the promotion on behalf of the advertiser. It is generally accepted that the cost of a stamp or a phone call is 'de minimis' for the purposes of constituting a contribution for entry (though care needs to be taken with premium rate telephone numbers). Although this point is undecided in case law, the Crown Prosecution Service (CPS) issued a statement in December 1991 to the Institute of Sales Promotion to say that it would not prosecute a promoter or manufacturer in connection with any illegal lottery unless the public interest required it. This statement also said that a scheme might be lawful if there is a genuine, realistic and unlimited alternative free entry route. This leads to the bizarre conclusion that a prize draw such as an 'open to win' promotion on a bar of chocolate is unlawful even if the cost of the product is the same as it normally is, unless the consumer has the option of entering the promotion for the cost of a stamp which they would not have bought otherwise[3]!

In the context of a free prize draw over the Internet, prize draws may or may not be linked to participants purchasing products or services in order to enter the promotion. If the draw is linked to participants purchasing products or services, promoters will need to ensure that consumers who do not buy the products or services are also able to enter into the draw on-line, in order to satisfy the 'no purchase necessary' rule. At the time of writing, no cases have been decided on this point on prize draws conducted over the Internet. However, in view of the position on entries to off-line prize draws for the cost of a stamp and the CPS statement, it is suggested that prosecutions under English law relating to the running of free prize draws on the Internet are unlikely where the only contribution is the cost of the Internet connection under English law. Using dial-up premium rate lines, however, is likely to be an issue.

1 [1981] AC 718, HL.
2 (1999) Times, 23 June.
3 For a more detailed discussion on the implications of free entry routes, see Circus, *Sales Promotion and Direct Marketing Law – A Practical Guide* (4th edn, 2002) Butterworths.

(ii) Competitions

6.38 Competitions are distinguished from lotteries by the element of skill. Competitions are construed as follows:

■ by the distribution of prizes;

■ by participants demonstrating an element of skill which must be present at all stages of the competition; and

■ by whether the participant has made a 'contribution' or not to enter the competition[1].

The element of skill that is needed has been looked at by the courts, such as in the *Imperial Tobacco* case. Section 14 of the LAA 1976 also gives some guidance, stating that:

'It shall be unlawful to conduct in or through any newspaper, or in connection with any trade or business, or the sale of any article to the public:
(a) any competition in which prizes are offered for the forecast of the result either:
  (i) of a future event, or
  (ii) of a past event the result of which is not yet ascertained or is not yet generally known;
(b) *any other competition in which success does not depend to a substantial degree on the exercise of skill'* (emphasis added).

Therefore, in order to be a lawful competition, the success, or the choosing of the winning entrant, must depend on the exercise of skill. The level of skill need not be high but the success of the winning participant must not depend on chance. Problems can arise with two-stage competitions that initially appear as if they require the exercising of skill, but which have been held to be illegal lotteries because the winner is ultimately determined by chance once a pool of correct entries is established. For example, in *Church v News Ltd*[2], a spot-the-ball competition was held in which participants had to pay to enter, and had to guess where the centre of the ball was in an unmarked photograph of a football match where the ball had been deleted. This was held to be unlawful as, although predicting the approximate likely location of the ball required skill in examining the photograph, predicting the location of the centre of the ball was a matter of chance.

It also follows from section 14 of the LAA 1976 that the element of skill necessary must be present at all times throughout the competition. For example, if the participant pays to enter and answers multiple choice questions, and the winner is then picked at random from the winning entries, the hybrid nature of the structure of the promotion will mean that ultimately it is an illegal lottery.

If a promoter is concerned as to whether a competition contains the requisite level of skill, or that the competition depends at various stages on chance and is therefore a 'hybrid' competition, one solution may be to make the competition free to enter. The above analysis of the required degree of skill only matters if the participant has to contribute or pay to enter the competition, as if they do not, the promotion can be made into a legal free prize draw. A second option would be the frequently used 'tie-breaker' device so that all correct entries are assessed on the basis of how they have completed a specified phrase in a limited number of words.

1 *Imperial Tobacco Ltd v A-G* [1981] AC 718, HL.
2 [1933] SASR 70.

(iii) The future of sales promotion law in the UK – the Budd report

6.39 The Gambling Review, chaired by Sir Alan Budd, has advised on gambling legislation (including legislation relating to sales promotion) in the UK[1]. Its conclusions are covered in detail in Chapter 14, E-gambling. At the time of writing, the Government was seeking views in relation to various proposals which have been made to change the law in relation to lotteries and prize competitions generally in the UK. The Consultation Paper[2] recognises the difficulties in relation to determining what a 'substantial degree of skill' is in the context of competitions and asks whether there is a clear distinction between prize competitions and lotteries. It also asks whether further regulation is needed of prize competitions and how free entry route competitions can be better distinguished from those that require payment.

1 The Gambling Review Report, available on the Department for Culture, Media and Sport website at: www.culture.gov.uk/ROLE/gambling_review.html.
2 Available at www.culture.gov.uk.

(iv) Coupons, money-off vouchers and incentive or loyalty points

6.40 As well as traditional coupons and money-off vouchers, the dot.com boom saw the growth of incentives such as Beenz[1] and ipoints[2]. In offering such incentives the operators will contract with other commercial sites, who will typically offer a stipulated number of 'points' in return for the consumer buying goods or services from the commercial website. The consumer may collect the points and exchange them for other goods and services from the points providers' website.

It is easy to overlook the impact and continuing existence of the Trading Stamps Act 1964 (TSA 1964). This requires that 'trading stamps' (which include vouchers, coupons and loyalty points) have a stated cash value entitling the holder to exchange them for their aggregate cash value provided that this amounts to a minimum of 25 pence[3]. Coupons, vouchers or points which are issued in connection with the purchase of a product or a service and which entitle the consumer to a discount from a future purchase or to claim a product for free once a certain number of vouchers or points have been achieved should contain a nominal cash value on the coupon, voucher or point. For example, if a promoter offers consumers £30 off their next holiday, a cash value of 0.001p should be stated on the face of the voucher, together with a term stating that no cash alternative to the £30 holiday offer can be given. Otherwise, under the TSA 1964, there is a strong argument that the voucher itself is worth £30! Although this may seem to be a theoretically low risk, we are aware of one such case where such a claim under the TSA 1964 was made and settled out of court against a leading grocery brand.

1 See www.beenz.com.
2 See www.ipoints.co.uk.
3 Section 3(1) of the TSA 1964.

(v) The ASA Codes

6.41 The ASA Codes regulate the conduct of sales promotions in the UK. Certain information is required to be given to participants in sales promotions. These include:

■ a copy of the terms and conditions applicable to the promotion, which the entrant can retain together with full details of the promoter and its address;

■ the closing date;

■ a list of prizes;

■ any geographical and age restrictions. (On the Internet, it will be important to set out any geographical restrictions clearly and prominently (see paragraph 6.20));

■ any restrictions for entry;

■ the number of entries allowed per person;

■ the availability of winners and how they will be notified (such as by posting the list of winners on a specified date on the website);

■ the criteria for judging entrants;

- the nature of the prizes in detail;

- any or no cash alternatives; and

- any limitations on the number of prizes or on availability in general[1].

The ASA Codes contain full details of the information that is required to be given to entrants to sales promotions. In addition, the Institute of Sales Promotion publishes helpful advice to assist promoters in drafting terms and conditions for sales promotions[2]. From a best practice point of view, it is recommended that promoters follow the advice given by the Institute of Sales Promotion, as well as complying with the relevant law and ASA Codes. In practice it is surprising how truculent winners of prizes are capable of being and it is often the case that the goodwill generated by a sales promotion can evaporate following an inadequate description of or shortage in prizes.

The terms and conditions for a promotion over the Internet should be made available in full on the website, and the participants should be given an opportunity to read the terms and conditions before entering into the promotion.

1 This is particularly important in view of *Wills v Hoover Ltd* (25 July 1996, unreported), CA, a notorious case where Hoover ran a sales promotion which entitled consumers who purchased a product to free flights to the USA. The demand was much higher than anticipated, and Hoover was faced with an extraordinary number of applications.
2 See www.isp.org.uk.

(b) Jurisdiction

(i) *Problems with current on-line sales promotions*

6.42   The aim of sales promotions is to persuade consumers to buy products or services. Territories other than the UK often view the inducement to purchase by offering sales promotions more restrictively. In certain countries, sales promotions are heavily regulated (and in certain circumstances prohibited) because of the belief that consumers need protecting from a pressurised inducement to purchase.

Promoters wishing to implement sales promotions over the Internet have had to face up to conflicting laws across the world restricting sales promotions. To give an example, until relatively recently[1], any 'two for one' promotions or other discounts and rebates were prohibited in Germany, whilst in France and Belgium, on-pack promotions, discounts and 'two for one' promotions are either banned, or heavily regulated. In Belgium, promotions aimed at children are heavily restricted. The Institute of Sales Promotion sets out a table on its website which summarises the types of promotion which are allowed in Europe and those which are not[2].

How can a sales promotion over the Internet take into account all of these laws? It will probably not be a commercial reality to expect the promoter to obtain legal advice from every jurisdiction around the world and the practical effect is that it is impossible to run a single sales promotion in all of the territories around the world.

Up until now, most sales promotions over the Internet will, in practice, have had to be run on a territory-by-territory basis, or by grouping together a few territories in which the sales promotion can be lawfully run (although, in reality, this often reflects cultural and linguistic implications as much as legal restrictions). Therefore, promoters restrict entry to the promotion to residents from a particular territory or territories, and run the promotion in accordance with that territory's laws. They also clearly state that the terms and conditions for the promotion are governed by a particular territory's law. Philip Sheppard, EU Affairs Manager at the Association International des Marques (an association which includes global brands such as Unilever, Procter & Gamble and Coca-Cola as its members) recently publicly commented[3] on how very difficult it is for a company like Coca-Cola to run promotions in more than one country.

1 In June 2001, the German Parliament (Bundestag) abolished certain of their restrictive retail laws.
2 See www.isp.org.uk/europe/europa.
3 *Marketing Week*, 2 October 2001.

(ii) The E-Commerce Directive and the Electronic Commerce (EC Directive) Regulations 2002

6.43 The E-Commerce Directive and the Electronic Commerce (EC Directive) Regulations 2002 are discussed above at paragraph 6.21. The Regulations apply to sales promotions and competitions provided on-line[1].

As previously mentioned, the Regulations do not implement a pure country of origin principle, but a limited one. Providing sales promotions on-line will fall under the definition of 'information society services' which are 'within the co-ordinated field', even though they are not normally paid for by the consumer, given the DTI's Guidance on this (see the discussion at paragraph 6.21 above). This means that, to a limited extent, organisations based within the EU would only have to comply with the laws regulating sales promotions in the jurisdiction of the Member State in which they are based[2].

However, regulation 4(3) and the Schedule to the E-Commerce Regulations provide for exceptions to the application of regulation 4(1) and (2), which include 'contractual obligations concerning consumer contracts'. According to the DTI in its Guidance, this will include requirements under Member States' laws to do certain things before entering into a contract. A sales promotion could be construed as a 'consumer contract' given that it involves the participant and the promoter entering into an contract to supply a prize, a concession or other benefit, if certain conditions are met by the participant. Conditions which have to be met before the 'consumer contract' is entered into could include restrictions such as the no purchase necessary restriction imposed under English law. It is therefore suggested that the exceptions to regulations 4(1) and (2) found in regulation 4(3) will cover the restrictive national laws relating to sales promotions. It therefore follows that the Regulations will not apply to sales promotions over the Internet and promoters will not be able to take advantage of the country of origin principle set out in the E-Commerce Directive and the Regulations.

1 'A Guide for Business to the Electronic Commerce (EC Directive) Regulations 2002', para 3.2(d)(iii).
2 Regulation 4(1) and (2) of the E-Commerce Regulations.

(iii) Proposals for the future

6.44 The European Commission has made a proposal for a Regulation governing sales promotions across Europe[1]. After a survey on the sales promotion market within the EU in 1996, the EC decided that harmonisation of sales promotion law is needed to ensure the working of the internal market in this area. The proposal is only in draft stage at present, and there have been delays in implementing it. At the time of writing, Spain, France and Austria (who all have prohibitive laws relating to discount promotions) wish to delay implementation of the Regulation pending the full review by the EU of a Consumer Protection Green Paper.

The fact that the EC has decided to issue this as a Regulation rather than a Directive means that once implemented it will be directly applicable within all Member States of the EU, without need for each Member State to implement secondary legislation.

The draft Regulation states that Member States may not impose prohibitions on sales promotions generally, unless required to do so by Community Law[2]. The effect this will have is to remove some of the restrictive prohibitions under national laws, such as those set out above. Therefore, in England and Wales the 'no purchase necessary' routes will no longer be necessary, as English law will not be able to prohibit prize draws which depend on consumers buying a product or service.

The draft Regulation states that the payment of a fee to enter a game of chance or free prize draw may still be prohibited under national laws, but a contribution (by for example purchasing a product or service) in order to enter a game of chance may not be prohibited[3]. Therefore English law will still be able to stipulate that lotteries, prize draws and games of chance which involve the participant paying a fee to enter are illegal (unless authorised). However, promoters will no longer need to worry about the no purchase necessary route to free prize draws as such national prohibitions under English law will be removed. Therefore, if they wish to do so, promoters will be able to stipulate that participants have to buy a product in order to participate in a free prize draw.

In other jurisdictions, bans on discounts (including price reductions, 'two for ones', coupons and vouchers) will no longer be allowed.

In addition to relaxing the restrictive laws across Europe on sales promotions, the draft Regulation states that certain information must be provided to participants and consumers on entry into sales promotions[4]. This largely mirrors the type of information which currently must be given under the ASA Codes. However, not all information needs to be given at the time the participant enters into the sales promotion. Some information need not be supplied by the promoter to all participants but must be made available on request (including certain types of information which must be available before the participant enters the promotion, ie the participant must be able to see the information without needing to buy the relevant product or service).

1 Proposal for a European Parliament and Council Regulation concerning sales promotions in the Internal Market of 2 October 2001, COM 546/2001 final; 0227/2001; found on www.europa.eu.int.
2 Article 3 of the draft Regulation.
3 Article 2(I) (definition of promotional game) and article 3 of the draft Regulation.
4 Article 4 of the draft Regulation.

6.45 Children and minors are given additional protection[1]. The draft Regulation stipulates that:

■ personal data cannot be collected on a child without its parent's or guardian's consent;

■ care must be taken when distributing free gifts and premiums to households where children are present to ensure that the gifts do not pose a danger to the child's health; and

■ free gifts or premiums of alcoholic beverages must not be given to individuals under the age of 18.

The EC has said that the Regulation will make it easy for consumers to take action against promoters which have breached the Regulation, particularly in relation to cross-border complaints[2]. The Regulation would take the form of a back-up to the current self-regulatory codes which exist in the UK through the ASA Codes and in other EU Member States. Under the Regulation, promoters will have to:

■ provide evidence of the information (such as values of their prizes) within six weeks of a complaint from a consumer;

■ provide details of an address to which complaints about the promotion may be directed; and

■ stipulate dispute resolution systems in the terms and conditions of the promotion.

The draft Regulation, if implemented, will be of great assistance to promoters wishing to run promotions in which individuals resident within the EU may participate. However, it still leaves open the possibility of liability for sales promotions outside of the EU. In the meantime, until the draft Regulation is implemented, and in respect of other territories outside of the EU, advice to promoters implementing sales promotion over the Internet is to obtain legal advice from the jurisdictions from which they intend to accept entries to the sales promotion. If the sales promotion cannot be legally run in a particular country, entries from participants with a geographical address in this country should be physically screened out and entry not allowed. This should be coupled with a jurisdictional clause together with a choice of law clause stipulated prominently within the promotion (see paragraph 6.20). The terms and conditions and acceptance of entries should clearly reflect this approach. Until the draft Regulation is implemented, promoters will have to persist with such an unsatisfactory piecemeal approach to sales promotions, and it will probably not be possible to run pan-European or worldwide sales promotions across the Internet.

1 Article 5 of the draft Regulation.
2 'Proposal for a Regulation to remove restrictions on sales promotions: frequently asked questions' 2 October 2001; DN: MEMO/01/306.

6. PAID FOR ADVERTISING SPACE ON-LINE

6.46 The term 'paid for advertising space on-line' includes:

■ banner adverts (discussed further in Chapter 5, E-brand);

■ virtual advertising, which is currently being used mainly in the context of sports events, where advertisers have the opportunity of electronically projecting their brand onto other filmed events (for example, projecting an advert onto the perimeter hoardings on a pitch electronically after the filming of the event, for its broadcast). This is particularly useful in the context of international sporting events, where advertising relevant to each individual market or territory can be added, and the right to advertise in connection with a particular event can be carved-up into local territories; and

■ other paid for advertising space on-line, such as pop-up adverts.

Banner adverts and the legalities of the use of keyword buying are discussed in detail in Chapter 5, E-brand.

(a) The ASA Codes and paid for advertising space on-line

6.47 The ASA Codes, which are discussed at paragraph 6.11 above, will apply to adverts in paid for advertising space on-line. Therefore, advertisers who are based in the UK will need to ensure that they comply with the general principles and codes set out in the ASA Codes. If individuals or corporate bodies believe that paid for advertising space on-line does not comply with the ASA Codes, they may make a complaint to the ASA which will be investigated (see paragraph 6.12 above). If the complaint is upheld, the ASA may ask that the advert be withdrawn, or amended.

Banner adverts and pop-up adverts have attracted some adverse publicity over the years, as many consumers complain of them being irritating and slowing down access to website content by appearing on top of page content. Click through rates of users have certainly dropped dramatically since banner adverts were first introduced[1].

Advertisers occasionally try to deal with this perceived criticism by making banner adverts which do not look like banner adverts, in the hope that more users will be persuaded to click through. For example, 888 Casino created an animated banner advert showing a dialogue box stating 'downloading ...' and which featured flashing lights as if a computer process was in operation, a cancel icon and a mouse pointer hovering over the cancel icon. The banner gave the impression that a file was downloading and many users clicked on the fake cancel icon, to try to stop the operation. After clicking on the fake cancel icon, the user was taken to 888 Casino's website. The ASA received a complaint that the advert was misleading in that it implied that a file was downloading and was designed to shock people into pressing cancel thereby directing them to the advertiser's website. The complaint was upheld in January 2002, in spite of arguments that users would be able to recognise that banners led to advertisements through being exposed to a wide range of advertising on the Internet. 888 Casino were asked by the ASA not to use the advert or a similar approach in the future[2]. Similarly, BTopenworld has had an ASA adjudication upheld against it in March 2002, by distributing a banner advert showing a fake 'error 404' message[3].

1 See Chapter 5, E-brand, para 5.70.
2 See ASA adjudication of 9 January 2002, available at www.asa.org.uk.
3 The complaint relating to the 'error 404' message being misleading as it implied that 404 errors can be eliminated by using BTopenworld instead of other ISPs: see ASA adjudication of 20 March 2002, available at www.asa.org.uk.

(b) The ITC Codes and virtual advertising

6.48 The ITC published a Guidance Note in November 2000 on virtual advertising, to be read in conjunction with the ITC Code of Programme Sponsorship. As virtual advertising works by altering the broadcast signal itself, care needs to be taken to ensure that the broadcaster does not lose editorial control over the broadcast programme. The Guidance Note states that it must be clear to viewers that electronic imaging systems used to create virtual advertising are being used, until audiences understand the concept of virtual advertising.

- if advertising was not permitted or not shown at the event itself, additional advertising cannot be placed through the use of virtual advertising;

- virtual advertising for tobacco products is not allowed;

- ITC licensees must not be involved with the sale of virtual advertising to advertisers[1].

In addition, the EU Television Without Frontiers Directive[2] states that surreptitious advertising is not allowed[3] and that advertisements must not be inserted during programmes in such a way that the integrity and value of the programme is prejudiced[4].

1 See the ITC Guidance Note on Electronic Imaging Systems or 'Virtual' Advertising, found in the Codes and Guidance section of the ITC website at www.itc.org.uk.
2 Directive (EEC) 552/89.
3 Directive (EEC) 552/89, article 10.
4 Directive (EEC) 552/89, article 11.

(c) Jurisdiction

6.49 The ASA Codes will apply to all banner adverts and other on-line paid for advertising space placed by advertisers based in the UK. The EASA (discussed at paragraph 6.15 above) will assist in dealing with cross-border complaints in relation to the content of the banner advert, where advertisers are based outside of the UK but are based in a jurisdiction which is part of EASA.

The E-Commerce Directive and the E-Commerce Regulations (discussed in detail in paragraph 6.21 above) apply to banner adverts as the definition of 'information society service' covers services which are normally provided for remuneration, which will include paid for advertising space on-line. This will mean that the partial country of origin principle set out in the E-Commerce Directive and the implementation of it into Member States' laws will apply. Therefore, organisations based in the UK will need to ensure that the banner advert complies with all relevant UK law. UK organisations may be able to escape liability under other Member States' laws, provided for example that there are no public health, consumer safety or security implications in the content and operation of the banner advert (see paragraph 6.20 above for detailed discussion). The information required to be added to commercial communications under the Regulations set out in paragraph 6.33 will need to be provided on the banner advert in an accessible and printable format.

(d) The legalities of on-line ad-blocking

6.50 Conventional on-line advertising could be in jeopardy because of software which blocks users from seeing banner ads. A US company called Gator.com currently offers free software downloads to individuals, enabling Gator.com to show advertisements to them whenever they surf the Internet. Gator.com in turn obtains advertising revenue from advertisers, who pay for targeted pop-up ads called the 'Companion Pop-up Banner', which appear whenever a user goes to a competitor's site, or a site which runs a competitor's pop-up ad. The Companion Pop-up Banner would then overlay and obscure the competitor's banner ad or site.

If the use of software such as Gator.com increases, the threat to the on-line advertising industry, potential on-line advertising revenue and to website owners wishing to control content on their sites is obvious. Therefore, the Interactive Advertising Bureau (IAB) in the US has challenged the legality of the Gator.com Companion Pop-up Banner in a San Francisco Federal court[1], alleging that the ad-blocking and ad-overlaying business of Gator.com infringes the intellectual property rights of advertisers, and breaches unfair competition rules. In June 2002, a group of web publishers also filed suit in a Federal court against Gator.com, arguing that the user is often not aware where the Gator.com originated pop-up advert came from; the use of such software infringes copyright in the websites on which the Gator.com pop-up advert is overlaid[2].

Following current English case law on trade mark infringement over the Internet, there is a strong argument that the pop-ups generated by the Gator.com software infringe the trade marks of the competitor whose ad is blocked. The software may use the competitor's trade mark in relation to identical or similar goods or services for which the competitor's trade mark is registered, which would constitute trade mark infringement[3]. In addition, ad-blocking such as the Companion Pop-up Banner could make the advertiser of the pop-up banner liable in England for passing off to the website owner or the advertiser whose ad is blocked. If the user is expecting to be taken to a particular commercial website when he types in a URL, but instead receives a pop-up banner from a competitor, he may assume that there is an association between the two organisations. If the original website owner can show that this has caused damage to its goodwill, they may be able to successfully sue under the laws relating to passing off[4].

Gator.com is not the only company offering ad-blocking software, and it is possible that it will be some time before a decision is made on whether Gator.com's practices are unlawful in the US. Until the legalities of ad-blocking and ad-overlaying are settled, it is recommended that organisations should notify users in their terms and conditions that overlaid ads and content on their websites may appear without the consent of the website owner, and may not be under their control[5]. In addition, any contracts between website owners with advertisers who wish to advertise on the website should state that overlaying or ad-blocking software imposed on their site by a third party does not constitute a breach by the website owner. It has also been reported that some advertisers and content owners are screening users accessing their site, so that users who have plugged in ad-blocking software are denied access to the website in the first place.

1 See www.gigalaw.com/articles/2001-all/wood-2001-10-all.html.
2 See www.washingtonpost.com/wp-dyn/articles/A52132-2002Jun26.html.
3 Section 10(2) of the Trade Marks Act 1994.
4 See Chapters 4 (E-rights) and 5 (E-brand) for further explanation of trade mark and passing off laws.
5 See the example disclaimer wording at paragraph 6.25 above.

7. VIRAL E-MAILS AND SMS PROMOTIONS

(a) Viral e-mails

6.51 The term 'viral e-mail' means e-mails sent out by an advertiser (usually containing creative, funny, exciting or newsworthy content), which it is hoped the recipient will want to pass on to friends and family. The e-mail is sent on by the original recipient to another group of individuals, who will hopefully also distribute the e-mail amongst their own group of contacts. The idea is that the e-mail spreads, like a virus, quickly and with minimal cost to the advertiser, across a wide range of users and possibly worldwide. For example, the advertiser might devise a game, or a short film containing the advertiser's brand, which is then sent by e-mail to recipients in the hope that they will find it interesting enough to send on to their own contacts.

(i) Problems with spam

6.52 Viral e-mails can either be solicited (such as when users subscribe to a mailing list and confirm that they may be contacted by the organisation with newsletters or news of future promotions by e-mail) or unsolicited. Mass mailings of unsolicited commercial communications or bulk e-mails are often known as 'spam'[1].

There is increasing consumer concern over the use of spam as a legitimate marketing tool. The problems with spam are that:

- it is irritating to recipients as they have to spend on-line time downloading and reading the spam. As most consumers bear the costs of access they are in effect funding the receipt of something they may not have wanted in the first place;

- it poses a threat to consumer confidence in e-commerce. The Internet's capacity to reach literally millions of customers quickly and at a low cost through spam has been seized upon, in particular by fraudulent operators, for a significant proportion of spam contains fictitious information about the sender, misleading subject lines and extravagant earnings or performance claims about goods and services, or chain letters and pyramid selling;

- it burdens ISPs and frustrates their customers who have to suffer poorer performance levels due to increased volume of traffic; and

- it creates support overheads for ISPs who must deal with spam complaints from (as well as concerning) their customers.

1 The term 'spam' as a word for repetitive and invasive e-mail marketing is thought to have been derived from a Monty Python sketch in which the characters sang 'spam' over and over again at one another!

(ii) Specific laws regulating the dissemination of viral e-mails

6.53 The EU has implemented and proposed a number of Directives and E-Commerce Regulations over the past seven years which impact upon the legality of unsolicited e-mails. Nevertheless, at the moment, Member States still have widely differing national laws and interpretations of EU law aimed at the harmonisation of anti-spamming laws[1].

Five Member States[2] currently ban unsolicited commercial e-mails unless individuals have expressly given their permission and 'opted in' to receive mail of that nature. In most other Member States, unsolicited commercial e-mails are legal, provided that the individual recipient has not 'opted out' of receiving such communications. This has led to the odd situation whereby an advertiser may not be able to send viral e-mails to recipients within its own country (unless individuals have opted in to receiving viral e-mails), but may be able to legally do so in other countries within the EU. The EU has therefore proposed a new Communications Data Protection Directive, which is examined below in paragraph 6.55.

1 For a detailed analysis of the emergence of unsolicited commercial communications as a marketing tool, and the history of the regulatory approach of the EU to this area, see the EC paper on 'Unsolicited Commercial Communications and Data Protection' by Serge Gauthronet and Etienne Droard, published in January 2001 (available at www.europa.eu.int/comm/internal_market/en/dataprot/studies/spamstudyen.pdf).
2 Austria, Denmark, Finland, Italy and Germany.

(iii) Data protection laws in England and Wales

6.54 The Data Protection Act 1998 (DPA 1998) (which implemented the EU Data Protection Directive 1995[1]) applies to viral e-mails and other unsolicited e-mails. Data protection is discussed in detail in Chapter 3, E-liability. Personal data collected on individuals must be collected and processed fairly and lawfully. Under this 'fair processing principle', when personal data is collected from an individual, the collector must tell the individual what the data is going to be used for, and how it will be processed. If the collecting organisation plans to use the data to send unsolicited e-mails, or plans to pass on the information to other organisations to enable them to send unsolicited e-mails, it will need to obtain consent from the individual for the use of their personal information in such a way.

Under English law and the DPA 1998, marketers may generally choose whether to obtain consent by way of the individual opting in or opting out. This could be achieved by way of a 'tick box', when the individual provides personal information about himself to the organisation. For example, the tick box could state 'if you do not wish to be contacted in the future by [name of organisation] or other selected third parties, please uncheck this box', which would constitutes an opt out. Alternatively, the tick box could state 'if you wish [name of organisation] or other selected third parties to contact you with details of future news, offers, and promotions, please tick this box', which would constitute the individual opting in. A structure whereby a positive act is required of the consumer to choose to opt out is most typically used.

If 'sensitive personal information' (which includes information revealing racial or ethnic origin, political opinions, religious beliefs, sexual orientation and so on) is used in extrapolating data for viral e-mails, explicit consent will be needed from the individual. The user must expressly opt in to the use of his data, and it will not be sufficient under the DPA 1998 for the user to have merely opted out.

Under the Directive on Personal Data and Telecom Privacy[2], the use of 'automated calling systems without human intervention of fax for the purpose of direct marketing' was only allowed if the recipient had given their prior consent. When implemented into English law by the Telecommunications (Data Protection and Privacy) (Direct Marketing) Regulations 1998[3] (which were amended and revoked by the Telecommunications (Data Protection and Privacy) Regulations 1999[4]), however, this did not cover unsolicited e-mails, but instead concentrated on telephone calls and faxes.

In respect of viral e-mails, the intention of the advertiser is to send an e-mail out to a database of individuals who then in turn forward the e-mail on to their own contacts. In these circumstances, can the advertiser be liable if a recipient was not sent the e-mail directly by the advertiser, but by one of their friends or family? Under the DPA 1998 it is likely that the advertiser could face liability in respect of the mere fact that the e-mail has been received by the recipient from another party. The proposed Communications Data Protection Directive does not address this issue either. It may be advisable as best practice for advertisers in such circumstances to state in the initial viral e-mail that recipients should feel free to forward the e-mail on to friends and family, provided that they are happy that such individuals would not object to receiving the viral e-mail.

1 Directive (EC) 46/95.
2 Directive (EC) 66/97.
3 SI 1998/3170.
4 SI 1999/2093.

(iv) The Communications Data Protection Directive

6.55 The position on whether the necessary consent to unsolicited e-mails can be obtained by way of individuals opting in or opting out to receipt of unsolicited e-mails is likely to change under the proposed Communications Data Protection Directive[1]. Under the proposed Directive, which is intended to amend the Directive on Personal Data and Telecom Privacy (discussed above), unsolicited commercial e-mails will only be allowed if individuals are 'subscribers' who have expressly 'opted in' to receiving them[2]. At the time of writing, it looked likely that the proposed Communications Data Protection Directive would be rubber-stamped by the end of July 2002, and that Member States would then have 18 months during which to implement the Directive into national laws.

1   EU proposal for a Directive concerning the Processing of Personal Data and the Protection of Privacy in the Electronic Communications sector, at http://europa.eu.int/information_society/topics/telecoms/regulatory/new_rf/documents/com2000-385en.pdf.
2   Article 13 of the proposed Communications Data Protection Directive.

(v) The Electronic Commerce (EC Directive) Regulations 2002

6.56   Since the second edition of this book, the E-Commerce Directive has been implemented through the Electronic Commerce (EC) Directive Regulations 2002 (for further discussion, see paragraph 6.21 above). Regulation 8 of the Regulations states that a service provider must ensure that any unsolicited commercial communication sent by him by e-mail, where permitted, is clearly and unambiguously identifiable as such as soon as it is received. The DTI has stated in its Guidance on the Regulations[1] that the purpose of this regulation is so that users of ISPs can delete such communications (or use filtering software to block or delete them) without the need to read them.

The Regulations do not currently state how organisations will meet the requirement for spam to be 'clearly and unambiguously identifiable'. Presumably, organisations will need to label e-mails as unsolicited communications.

The E-Commerce Directive (see paragraph 6.21 above for further discussion) includes a provision stating that Member States must ensure that distance communications may only be used where there is no clear objection from the consumer. It also states that service providers undertaking unsolicited commercial communications by e-mail must consult and respect the provisions of any opt out registers in which natural persons not wishing to receive such commercial communications can register themselves[2]. However, the DTI has said that it does not propose to implement article 7 of the Directive, which has not been transposed into the Regulations. Nevertheless, the DPA 1998 (see above) will still apply, and the proposed Communications Data Protection Directive (see above) once implemented will undoubtedly cover this area in more depth, meaning that unsolicited e-mails will not be allowed unless individual recipients have 'opted in' to receiving them.

1   'A Guide for Business to the Electronic Commerce (EC Directive) Regulations 2002' Guidance July 2002, available from the DTI website, at www.dti.gov.uk.
2   Article 7 of the E-Commerce Directive.

(vi) Voluntary schemes regulating direct marketing

6.57   In addition to laws and regulations governing viral e-mails implemented at both EU and national levels, there are a number of important existing voluntary codes and schemes which viral e-mail marketers should consider complying with. The Direct Marketing Association (DMA)[1] is the core trade organisation for all companies involved in direct marketing in the UK and is a member of the International Federation of Direct Marketing Associations and the Federation of European Marketing Associations. Most advertising agencies who specialise in direct marketing and who implement direct marketing schemes (including viral e-mail campaigns) on behalf of their advertiser clients in the UK will be members of the DMA.

The DMA Code of Practice for Electronic Commerce was issued in July 2000. This establishes standards of ethical conduct and best practice for e-commerce to which members of the DMA must adhere as a condition of their membership. (Members must also comply with the DMA's main Code of Practice, which covers all direct marketing communication, both off-line and on-line[2].)

The DMA E-Commerce Code applies to members' on-line marketing activity in the UK, directed to consumers or business. On-line marketing is defined in paragraph 1.2 of the Code as 'any commercial communications, including advertisements and offers for goods and services, which take place on line through e-mail, Internet website, interactive digital television, wireless application protocol, CD-ROM or interactive kiosks'.

Paragraph 5.2.11 of the DMA E-Commerce Code provides that:

- unsolicited e-mail must be clearly identifiable as such;

- members must not send random, untargeted, commercial e-mail (spam);

- members must use appropriate e-mail preference services and must not send e-mail communications to individuals who have registered an objection to receiving such communications[3];

- unsolicited e-mail must include a mechanism for the consumer to register an objection to receiving further unsolicited communication; and

- unsolicited e-mail sent as a result of a member-get-member scheme must make clear to the recipient that their personal information has been obtained through such a scheme.

1   See www.dma.org.uk.
2   The specifics of the DMA's Code of Practice are outside the scope of this book, but the main provisions of the DMA Code of Practice mirror those of the ASA Codes, which are referred to earlier in this chapter.
3   Examples of the organisations which individuals can register with are set out on the DMA website.

6.58   All DMA members must also comply with the following General Obligations:

- members' Internet websites must provide a 'hotlink' to the DMA website to allow users to access information on the DMA's Code of Practice and on TrustUK approval;

- members should prominently display the DMA's symbol and must display the TrustUK e-hallmark in all on-line consumer marketing communications;

- members' on-line communications must be clear and unambiguous;

- members must ensure that all contracts to which they are a party are clear, fair and balanced;

- members must comply with the ASA Codes in respect of all on-line advertisements, ensuring in particular that all advertisements are legal, decent, honest and truthful and they are clearly identifiable as an advertisement;

- members must comply with the rulings of the ASA; and

- members must comply with any conclusion reached by the Direct Marketing Authority (which is responsible for monitoring the DMA's Codes), including a decision to take disciplinary action resulting from a breach of either the DMA E-Commerce Code or the main DMA Code of Practice.

The standards of ethical conduct and best practice required by the DMA E-Commerce Code are both comprehensive and self-explanatory, reflecting the requirements of EU and UK legislation. They cover:

- pre-contractual information (ie on-line sellers' details, description and delivery of goods);

- performance/fulfilment of orders (ie the 30-day requirement and acknowledgement of orders);

- privacy policy (ie compliance with the DPA 1998 and the use of unsolicited e-mails);

- security of payment and system security;

- on-line marketing to children (the DMA's specific Code of Practice for Commercial Communications to Children On-Line must be complied with); and

- complaints handling system (including referral to the Direct Marketing Authority).

6.59 Where an individual or company receives direct mail which he believes contravenes the DMA Code of Practice, he may make a complaint to the Direct Marketing Authority. Wherever possible members will be invited to settle the matter directly with the person or company making the complaint. However, wherever there is an apparent breach of the DMA Code of Practice, complaints will be referred to the Direct Marketing Authority for investigation. Where a member is in breach, the Authority can seek an undertaking from the member that the breach will not be repeated, issue a formal written admonition of the member which is made public or, in the most serious cases, suspend or terminate membership of the DMA.

Only members of the DMA are bound by the DMA Code of Practice, although many non-members do comply with it. However, although technically non-members of the DMA do not need to comply with the DMA Code of Practice, they should bear in mind that direct mail and circulars are defined in the ASA Code on Advertising and Sales Promotion as advertising and consequently they are bound by that Code, which as previously discussed contains many similar provisions.

The DMA may not prevent direct marketing activities that breach the provisions of the DMA Code of Practice, but adverse publicity is an effective weapon against contravention of the Code. Moreover, like the ASA, the DMA can refer particularly serious cases to organisations such as OFTEL and the Office of Fair Trading for investigation.

In addition to the DMA, LINX (the London Internet Exchange Ltd) runs the main Telehouse exchange in London's Docklands and was set up in 1994 to provide efficient interconnectivity for the UK Internet. Operating exclusively in the UK, it is a not-for-profit partnership between ISPs, which provides a physical interconnection for service providers to exchange Internet traffic. It currently has over 100 members, representing the interests of over 80 ISPs from nine countries. LINX recognises that it is, to a large extent, ineffective for ISPs to try to block spam once it has been sent, and has issued the 'LINX Best Current Practice for Combating Unsolicited Bulk E-mail'[1]. This reflects LINX's acknowledgement that an ISP's most practical contribution to spam is to minimise or eliminate its sending by its customers or from its systems. To be effective in combating spam, the ISP must:

- ensure that its e-mail systems will not relay e-mail for unauthorised third parties;

- ensure that all e-mail generated within its network can be traced to its source and that the immediate source of e-mail which arrives from other networks can be determined;

- ensure that all e-mail generated within its network can be attributed to a particular customer or system (ie by operating a specialist 'abuse' mailbox such as 'abuse@isp.co.uk');

- operate appropriate arrangements for the handling of reports of abuse by its customers;

- (where abuse is proved) take effective action to prevent the customer from sending further spam; the legal basis on which services are provided to customers must allow such action to be taken;

- disseminate information on the action taken in regard to customers who have sent spam (not only does this improve the ISP's standing in the community, it sends a warning to potential abusers that they run the risk of being detected and having sanctions imposed); and

- educate its customers on the nature of spam and ensure that they have been made aware that sending spam will be treated as unacceptable behaviour.

The Best Practice document also contains suggested specimen clauses for use by LINX's ISP members. E-merchants should check the terms and conditions of their ISPs to see if they have been incorporated.

1 See http://www.linx.net/noncore/bcp/ube-bcp.html. This has been submitted to RIPE's Anti-Spam Working Group as a draft European Standard. See also the 'LINX Illegal Material Best Current Practices' and the 'LINX Traceability Best Current Practice'.

(vii) *Other possible legal regulation of unsolicited e-mails*

6.60 As well as data protection considerations, additional compliance under the E-Commerce Regulations and compliance with any voluntary schemes in place, advertisers engaging in sending unsolicited commercial e-mails could be liable:

■ under the Torts (Interference with Goods) Act 1977;

■ under the Computer Misuse Act 1990;

■ under the Trade Marks Act 1994;

■ for the common law tort of passing off; or

■ for breach of contract with the ISP.

On the final point above, ISPs based in the UK have shown that they are willing to sue users of their services for breach of their terms and conditions in both the US and the UK. In the US, BiblioTech Ltd (a UK ISP) sued Sam Khuri/Benchmark Print Supplies (a US subscriber and sender of 'scam spam'). Although this US action settled, the terms of settlement included a term that Benchmark pay liquidated damages of $1,000 plus legal expenses to any affected party (including Internet users or ISPs) should Benchmark send or assist others to send spam[1]. In the UK, another settled action between Virgin Net Ltd and Adrian Paris suggested that breach of contract, trespass to goods and unlawful interference with goods are the most likely causes of action for spamming under English law.

1   Unreported. See 'A victory against spamming' by Paul Friedman and Sarah-Jane Barker in *E-Commerce Law & Policy*, April 2000, pp 12–13.

(viii) *Content of viral e-mails*

6.61 Given that viral e-mails are intended to be highly creative, interesting and often funny, the content of viral e-mails is likely to be regulated by other laws. The same considerations will apply as to putting together an off-line advertising campaign or campaign to go onto a website (some of which are discussed above at paragraph 6.27).

Additional jurisdictional problems may arise out of the fact that the viral e-mail could easily be disseminated worldwide. As discussed at paragraph 6.20 above, different jurisdictions have widely different laws regulating the content of advertising campaigns. Therefore, unless a viral e-mail marketer creates (an inevitably bland) campaign which complies with the laws of all the territories of the world, there is a risk that the marketer could be liable for the content being distributed. However, it will not be possible to prevent viral e-mails from being sent to addresses outside of particular jurisdictions, and so the practical risk minimisation steps which it is recommended advertisers implement when putting advertising campaigns onto websites may not be possible[1]. In theory, advertisers based in England could put a jurisdictional disclaimer onto each viral e-mail stating that the viral e-mail is governed by English law, and is not intended to be distributed outside of England and Wales. There have been no UK cases to suggest whether such a disclaimer would work and the matter would be likely to be dependent on local laws in the relevant jurisdiction in which any complaint arose. Perhaps more importantly, viral e-mail marketers will probably be reluctant to include such a legal statement on their e-mails, given that they want the content to be so attractive that it is forwarded by the recipients to as many people as possible.

At the moment, there is no clear way around the issue of the content of viral e-mails being potentially subject to the laws of all territories to which the e-mail is forwarded. Advertisers should be aware of the risks of legal liability in a number of territories, tailor their creative content of viral e-mails accordingly, and consider how much risk they are prepared to accept in undertaking a viral e-mail marketing campaign.

The ASA has confirmed since 2000 that the ASA Codes apply to viral e-mails. Therefore, advertisers sending out viral e-mails should ensure that they comply with the ASA Codes, as discussed above at paragraph 6.11.

1 See paragraph 6.20 above.

(ix) The US position

6.62 In the US, various anti-spamming legislative measures are being introduced to stop spam at both a Federal and State level. California, Connecticut, Delaware, Idaho, Illinois, Iowa, Louisiana, Nevada, North Carolina, Oklahoma, Rhode Island, Tennessee, Virginia, Washington and West Virginia are some of the States that have already passed such legislation. In California, in addition to criminal liability for hacking and using the domain name of another (up to a year's imprisonment), e-mail service providers can recover their actual monetary loss or liquidated damages of $50 per e-mail (maximum $25,000 a day). In Washington, recipients can collect $500 in damages for each piece of spam.

These concerns have led large service providers (notably AOL) to bring successful court cases against spammers in the US. If you spam in the US, you will run the risk of being sued by your ISP, who could use any or all of:

■   the Computer Fraud and Abuse Act (for knowingly and intentionally causing the transmission of information to, and accessing, protected computer facilities without authorisation, and as a result of such conduct, causing damage, or recklessly causing damage);

■   the Lanham Act (for false designation of origin);

■   various State Computer Crimes Acts; and

■   an action in conversion or trespass to chattels under common law.

(x) A summary of the recommended steps to take when undertaking viral e-mail campaigns

6.63 When undertaking a viral e-mail campaign, it is recommended that you:

■   Ensure that the database of individual recipients has at least had the chance to opt out of receipt of the viral e-mails and has not done so.

■   Consider only sending viral e-mails to those individuals who have opted in to receipt.

■   Be aware of the risks of sending the e-mail to individuals outside of England and Wales, as more prescriptive anti-spamming laws may apply. The only way of effectively reducing this risk is to ensure that all individuals have opted in to the receipt of unsolicited e-mails.

■   Following the implementation of the E-Commerce Regulations, label the e-mail as being an unsolicited e-mail and comply with other requirements of the Regulations in relation to commercial communications (including information about the advertiser and its address: see Chapter 2, E-contract).

■   Consult opt out registers organised by organisations such as the DMA and, where necessary, comply with the terms of any voluntary codes of practice such as the DMA Codes.

■   Ensure that the content of the viral e-mail is legal and not infringing the rights of any third party, and that it complies with the ASA Codes.

- Take particular care when advertising sensitive products such as alcohol, tobacco, medicines and financial services as the legality of advertising such products will be heavily regulated in different jurisdictions where the e-mail may be disseminated to.

- Weigh up the risks of the content contained in the e-mail being illegal in other territories against the desire to engage in the viral e-mail campaign. Jurisdictional statements such as those mentioned in paragraph 6.21 above may assist in minimising the risks.

(b) SMS marketing

6.64 The use of m-commerce as an advertising tool has increased significantly since the last edition of this book. The use of SMS (short message services, commonly known as text messaging) is one of the most widely used m-commerce tools currently in use in the UK.

Under the Telecommunications (Data Protection and Privacy) Regulations 1999 the use of 'automated calling systems' for direct marketing purposes is not permitted, unless the recipient has expressly consented to being contacted for direct marketing purposes by the organisation in question[1]. 'Automated calling systems' are defined as systems which, when activated, operate to make calls without human intervention. There is an argument to say that some SMS marketing does not involve the use of an automated calling system, although most regulators and commentators now agree that the majority of SMS marketing will originate from an automated calling system. If that is the case, the sending of text messages to individuals for advertising or marketing purposes will be illegal under the 1999 Regulations, unless the recipient has expressly opted in to receiving direct marketing text messages.

In addition, regulation 25 of the Telecommunications (Data Protection and Privacy) Regulations states that unsolicited calls for direct marketing purposes (which includes text messages) shall not be permitted if the subscriber has previously stated that he does not wish to be contacted for direct marketing purposes. Individuals can currently register their wish not to receive calls for direct marketing purposes with the Telephone Preference Service[2]. Advertisers wishing to send direct marketing text messages are required to consult the Telephone Preference Service regularly to ensure that individuals have not registered with the Telephone Preference Service. If advertisers wish to send premium rate direct marketing text messages, they will also need to be aware of the Independent Committee for the Supervision of Standards of Telephone Information Service (ICSTIS) codes of practice. Advertisers sending premium rate text messages who are in breach of the ICSTIS codes of practice can be fined[3].

In addition, the DPA 1998 will apply (which is discussed in detail in Chapter 3, E-liability). In the context of SMS marketing, organisations will need to collect and process data in relation to individuals fairly and lawfully. This will mean that organisations should tell individuals what they intend to do with the data they collect on behalf of an individual. This can be made clear to the individual at the time they sign up, or when they opt in to receiving text messages from the organisation.

1 Regulation 22 of the Telecommunications (Data Protection and Privacy) Regulations 1999.
2 See www.telephonepreferenceservice.co.uk.
3 See www.icstis.co.uk.

6.65 At EU level, the proposed Communications Data Protection Directive[1] states that in respect of 'unsolicited communications', the use of automated calling systems without human intervention, fax machines or e-mail for the purposes of direct marketing shall be prohibited, unless individuals have given their prior consent (and therefore opted in to receipt of such communications)[2]. In addition, unsolicited communications which are sent for direct marketing purposes by means other than automated calling systems, faxes or e-mails shall not be allowed unless the individual has opted in, or has not opted out of receipt of such communications. The decision as to whether opt in or opt out will suffice in these cases will be left to Member States. The aim of this is to ensure that if new methods of direct marketing are developed to use new technologies, the aims of the Directive will not be bypassed.

Article 9 of the proposed Communications Data Protection Directive deals with the use of 'location data'. Location data is defined as 'any data processed in an electronic communications network, indicating the geographic position of the terminal equipment of a user of a publicly available electronic communications service'. Mobile phone networks can now position a mobile user's terminal equipment relatively precisely and it is becoming increasingly possible to use this data for the purposes of targeted direct marketing. Under articles 6 and 9 of the proposed Directive, location data may only be used with the consent of the subscriber. In addition, subscribers must be given means of barring location data-based marketing from time to time.

The ASA Codes will apply to direct marketing text messages sent from the UK. In November 2001, the ASA upheld its first complaint about a text message campaign sent by Eidos Interactive Limited. The message stated 'Please report to your local army recruitment centre immediately for your second tour of duty. Commandos 2 on PC, It's More Real Than Real Life – out today from Eidos'. Unfortunately, one of the recipients of the text message was an ex-member of the British Army who believed that the text message asking him to report to his local army recruitment centre was genuine. Once he realised the misunderstanding he complained to the ASA that the message could cause fear and distress. The ASA upheld the complaint and asked Eidos not to repeat it[3].

1   See the discussion above in relation to viral e-mails.
2   Article 13 of the proposed Communications Data Protection Directive.
3   See adjudication section of the ASA website, www.asa.org.uk.

8.   INTERACTIVE TELEVISION ADVERTISING

6.66   Interactive television gives various opportunities to users to interact with their television to adopt content to reflect their preference or change their viewing options by interacting with the content provider, to participate in polls, quizzes, betting, retail activity, and so on. Interactive television also brings increased opportunities for marketing and advertising, such as interactive participation in promotions, ordering products, samples and brochures, and further information about a product being advertised on the interactive television platform. This in turn can help advertisers find out more about and target their potential customers (subject to the DPA 1998, and other data protection regulations and legislation, as discussed in Chapter 3, E-liability).

The ITC[1] regulates programme content for UK television licensees, and also the advertising which appears on licensees' television platforms. The ITC produced a Guidance Note[2], to be read in conjunction with its other Codes (such as the ITC Programme Code, ITC Code of Advertising Standards and Practice, and ITC Code of Programme Sponsorship[3]). The guidance note sets out how the ITC will regulate the content of interactive television services, including interactive television advertising.

The ITC has taken the view that the area of interactive television advertising requires a light regulatory touch, particularly because a great deal of funding for technological developments in interactive television will come from commercial advertising revenues[4]. In regulating interactive television advertising the ITC makes a distinction between 'dedicated interactive services' and 'enhanced programme services':

1   See paragraph 6.16 above.
2   ITC Guidance to Broadcasters on the regulation of interactive television services, February 2001; available from the ITC website at www.itc.org.uk.
3   All available from the ITC website at www.itc.org.uk.
4   The ITC also recognises the growth in 'Internet via TV' services, where users can gain access to the full range of Internet content, as opposed to the limited content provided by walled gardens. The ITC does not propose to regulate the content of the full Internet content accessed via a television.

(a) 'Dedicated interactive services'

6.67 These are services normally accessed via an electronic programme guide (EPG) rather than directly via a programme. They include walled gardens (ie access to the Internet, but limited to content which the content provider has decided to allow the user to access), portals and electronic shopping malls. The ITC has currently decided not to regulate dedicated interactive services. However, viewers must not be misled into thinking that the content they view is part of an ITC regulated programme, and broadcasters will still be subject to ITC Codes if they provide content over which they have editorial control (such as a programme) for inclusion on a dedicated interactive service. Therefore, in relation to walled gardens, electronic shopping malls and portals accessible via interactive television platforms, organisations will not be restricted by the ITC in relation to the advertising they wish to place (but will be subject to any other relevant advertising and marketing laws within the UK, as above).

(b) 'Enhanced programme services'

6.68 These are interactive services added on to existing television programmes. In relation to potential advertising opportunities, this includes:

- advertising within programmes, where users may access advertising or other promotional messages about an organisation from a programme (for example, an icon appearing during a television programme showing a football match, which leads the user to the opportunity to buy the same brand of football boots as are worn by one of the players); and

- enhancements to advertising, where users can obtain more information about a product or service, or possibly even buy the product or service by clicking on an icon from the advert featured on an interactive television platform.

In relation to enhanced programme services, the ITC's paramount concerns remain the separation of advertising from editorial content and the protection of children. The ITC's main role is to protect the public from unsuitable programming on commercial television, which means protecting programming from commercial intrusions.

The ITC's new guidelines on interactive enhanced programme services as they relate to advertising can be summarised as follows:

- ITC licensees will be required to retain full editorial content for any interactive icons and for all normal television commercials, together with control over any advertising contained on the first screen accessed if the viewer chooses to interact within the programme or the advertising itself. Licensees will not be responsible for advertising content after the first screen, which will fall down to general advertising laws and industry specific applicable laws. Pre-clearance by the BACC and by licensees of all of this advertising content (as is the case with current broadcast television commercials) will not be possible due to the increased volume of advertising. Presumably the ITC will rely on its complaints system to ensure compliance in this respect[1].

- Advertisers may not blur the lines between advertising content and the content of a programme, or editorial content which the user has chosen by interacting with the programme[2]. The guidelines state that no interactive icon from a programme can be commercially branded and linked to advertiser's content. Using the example above, this will mean that in a televised football match, the football boots advertiser will not be allowed to have a branded icon of the football boots within the programme content leading to advertising content about the football boots. In any case, the placing of products within programme content is still heavily regulated. The ITC has not relaxed its rules relating to undue prominence[3], which state that any reference to a commercial product or service within a programme must be editorially justified, and should not be featured as close-up shots, or be referred to by product name. Above all, the product placement should not create the impression of commercial interference with editorial control of the programme.

■ Within programmes, where a viewer chooses to interact, advertising content and direct offers for sale to the viewer must be two clicks away[4]. Therefore, in a televised football match, where a user chooses to interact, the first click must take them to a screen which has at least some editorial content. This first screen could be commercially branded, provided that there is at least some other editorial content. Games, such as voting on the likely outcome of an event (such as 'Who will score the next goal?'), are likely to be considered to be editorial content in this context, provided that they are not construed in such a way as to be entirely for commercial reasons. A second click may then take the viewer to pure advertising content which will not be regulated by the ITC, as it will not be required to be under the licensee's control.

1   ITC Rules for Interactive enhanced programme services, Code 1, found at Annex A of ITC Guidance to Broadcasters on the regulation of interactive television services.
2   ITC Rules for Interactive enhanced programme services, Code 3.
3   Found in Code 10.6 of the ITC Programme Code.
4   ITC Rules for Interactive enhanced programme services, Code 6.

6.69   Advertising content which is not specifically selected by the viewer must not dominate over programme content[1]. The ITC has hinted that commercial messages which are not chosen by the viewer must not fill more than one third of the screen.

Special rules relate to news and current affairs, consumer programmes and children's programmes. For example, a programme which is broadcasting the results of consumer trials on washing machines would be prohibited from containing an interactive link to an advert for the washing machines under trial. Children's programmes may not lead to direct offers for sale through the interactive platform.

The ITC guidelines are fairly loosely drafted due to time pressures and the need to cover fast-changing technological developments, coupled with commercial pressures for light regulation. When considering a strategy for advertising on interactive television, it may be useful to start off by querying whether the intended strategy creates any impression of commercial interference with the editorial content. If the answer to this is positive, the ITC will apply the guidelines in the spirit as well as the letter, and will look to the overall effect of the advertising. If however, the answer is negative, but there is nevertheless a concern that the advertising strategy may not comply with the guidelines, it may be worthwhile to contact the ITC (ideally before a significant amount of money has been spent on development of the advertising) for their opinion on whether the advertising will be permissible under the guidelines.

One important potential of interactive television (and new technologies such as TiVo recorders) is to allow users to screen out advertising breaks. Advertisers and advertising agencies are therefore looking to new methods of getting their messages across to viewers. Programme sponsorship is proving to be increasingly popular with advertisers and programme-makers on interactive television platforms. Programme sponsorship is regulated by the ITC Code of Programme Sponsorship[2]. The Code aims to ensure that programmes are not distorted for commercial purposes, and that editorial responsibility of the programme-maker or broadcaster is not affected. There must be a distinction between advertising and sponsor credits, and between advertising and the programme. Problems will arise if an organisation wishes to carry out the following sponsorship activities on interactive television (or indeed any television), which are banned:

■ sponsorship of news, current affairs and consumer affairs programmes[3];

■ sponsoring or funding programmes, where the sponsor has entered into agreements relating to merchandising goods or products related to the programme[4];

- referring to the sponsor, or to the products of the sponsor, during the programme[5];

- including material from advertising campaigns for the sponsor within the bumper credits around the programme[6] or the programme containing similar content to an advertising campaign or other marketing activity, which is likely to be banned[7]. Where characters are created specifically for advertising or marketing purposes (such as Flat Eric for Levis or Honey Monster for Sugar Puffs), it is likely that the ITC would view the use of the character in a programme (whether funded by Levis or Sugar Puffs or not) as not being permissible.

1 ITC Rules for Interactive enhanced programme services, Code 8.
2 August 2000, found at www.itc.org.uk.
3 ITC Code of Programme Sponsorship, Code 8.1,8.2,8.3.
4 ITC Code of Programme Sponsorship, Code 8.6.
5 ITC Code of Programme Sponsorship, Code 9 and Code 15.
6 ITC Code of Programme Sponsorship, Code 11.2.
7 ITC Code of Programme Sponsorship, Code 17.2.

9. ACCREDITATION SCHEMES

6.70 Various voluntary accreditation schemes are emerging in respect of advertising on the Internet, with the aim of increasing customer confidence in the Internet. Some, such as TRUSTe[1], focus on accrediting websites that adhere to established privacy principles. In the UK, Admark sees itself as playing a wider role.

1 See www.truste.org.

(a) Admark

6.71 Admark[1] was launched to the trade in autumn 2000 and to consumers in early 2001. CAP founded it. Aimed at consumers, on-line advertisers, publishers and agencies, the CAP seeks to mirror the achievements of the ASA Codes and reassure consumers that its members' on-line adverts are legal, decent, honest and truthful (ie in conformity with the ASA Codes). All members' adverts in 'paid for' space (for example banner adverts), sales promotions (appearing anywhere on-line) and adverts/sales promotions in commercial e-mails are covered by the scheme.

In return for undertaking to abide by the ASA Codes and any decisions of the ASA (and payment of the scheme's fees), members may use the Admark icon on banner adverts, on-line promotions, websites and commercial e-mails. It is hoped by CAP that this will send a positive signal to consumers, who can 'click through' to the Admark website to verify the advertiser's membership.

1 See www.admark.org.uk.

10. CONCLUSION

6.72 The globalisation of the advertising industry over the last ten years has been partly stimulated by the increasingly global focus of brands. With this, problems have arisen for advertisers because of vastly differing laws and regulations throughout the world. The growth of the use of the Internet is both a cause of the globalisation of advertising and a symptom. The Internet allows advertisers the potential to communicate to global audiences, but at the same time the growth of the Internet has been partly accelerated by the need for global communications.

The advertising boom of 1998–1999 was fuelled by the rise of the dot.coms, frenziedly competing for subscribers and driving up the cost of advertising slots. However, in context, advertising is crucial to interactivity. In a world where the financing of new technologies has hit a brick wall, interactive platforms look elsewhere for funding. When it comes down to fundamentals there are limited ways for them to generate revenue. One way is by the sale to subscribers of access to content. The other is by selling advertising content. In a world where attractive content such as sports rights are currently regarded as being overvalued, advertising as a generator of revenue assumes a still more critical role.

7

E-dispute

I. INTRODUCTION

7.01 The objective for each party to a dispute must be twofold: to resolve that dispute, in a way that secures for itself, or denies the other, compensation or other redress for any harm inflicted or wrong committed; and to achieve that result at no cost or minimal cost to itself.

An on-line business is likely to be faced with disputes not only with parties with which it has contractual ties, but also with a large number of 'strangers'. Many of these disputes will have a foreign element. A large body of law has been developed, both at national and international level, to deal with such disputes, but e-commerce brings new problems to be solved and the on-line business needs to be able to navigate its way through these laws to meet the above objective.

E-commerce can be viewed simply as traditional business carried on using a new form of communication that is faster, cheaper and more convenient than telexes, faxes and telephone calls. In the same way that the law has coped with these technologies and with communications other than by letter or face-to-face meetings, the law can be expected to cope perfectly well with communications in cyberspace. On the other hand, however, e-commerce is a very different medium and does not identify itself with the language of 'send' and 'receive' or a world described by continents, nations and states; it transcends those familiar boundaries and is intangible.

7.02 The aim of this chapter is to enable the on-line business to make an informed decision as to:

- where it can agree a dispute resolution mechanism and how it should do so;

- in the absence of agreement, how it can try to get the most favourable or at least a neutral forum and influence the governing law for the hearing of the dispute;

- how it should prepare evidence to be used in the hearing; and

- how it can enforce the result of the dispute resolution process.

This chapter is organised to reflect the following basic principles:

- subject to certain mandatory provisions, parties are free to decide how they wish to resolve disputes;

- parties can do so either before the dispute arises, for example in a dispute resolution clause contained in their commercial contract, or after the dispute arises, for example in a subsequent agreement to arbitrate the dispute;

■   parties can agree on:

  –   the law governing the contract, including how conflicts of laws are to be resolved;

  –   the tribunal hearing the dispute;

  –   whether the tribunal will have exclusive jurisdiction to deal with the dispute and, where the tribunal is not a traditional court:

    •   where the tribunal will sit and hear the dispute;

    •   the procedural rules which the tribunal will apply;

■   where the parties fail to agree on any of the above, the tribunal may decide what is the proper law governing the dispute, the rules it will use and even the extent of its own jurisdiction;

■   basically, the parties may decide to have the dispute determined:

  –   by themselves, for example through negotiation, with or without the aid of a neutral mediator;

  –   by an expert;

  –   by an arbitrator;

  –   by a court; or

  –   by a combination of the above;

■   the courts will usually become involved if the parties have failed to agree how they wish to resolve their disputes, for example if the contract is silent or if the action is not based on contract. Even if the parties have agreed on an alternative dispute resolution mechanism, however, the courts may still become involved if:

  –   the parties wish to apply for interim relief which the tribunal does not have the power to award; or

  –   the parties are challenging the appointment, jurisdiction, procedures or decision of the tribunal;

■   the court will then decide:

  –   whether it has and wants to accept jurisdiction;

  –   which is the proper law governing the dispute; and

  –   how it will manage the resolution of the dispute;

■   the final step is enforcement of an order, award or agreement, to ensure that its provisions are complied with. This may have to be carried out in a country other than the one in which the order or award was made, for example where the defendant has assets.

Before we look at the court's approach, we will consider the different methods of resolving disputes away from the courts.

2.   LITIGATION OR ADR?

7.03   There is nothing to prevent a party from bringing a dispute before a court, whether or not it has agreed otherwise. Once the matter is before the court, it will consider whether it has jurisdiction over the dispute and, at least in the case of the English court, the court will invariably accept jurisdiction where the parties are, and the actions or events giving rise to the dispute have taken place, in this country[1]. Where the parties have agreed that another court or an arbitrator should hear the dispute, however, the court might refuse to hear it.

Where the parties have agreed an alternative dispute resolution (ADR) procedure, such as expert determination or mediation, the court will continue to have jurisdiction, but will have the discretion to stay the matter to allow the parties to carry out the agreed procedure.

The word 'alternative' in this context is in general used to distinguish between litigation in the courts and any other method of resolving a dispute, ranging from simple negotiation to arbitration. This spectrum of dispute resolution techniques also embraces mediation and conciliation, with many refinements and combinations being added to the list of different techniques as these are developed through use. Different disputes demand different techniques, depending on the degree of control and flexibility required by the parties. So, for example, the parties are likely to retain maximum control in a straightforward negotiation but minimum control in the courts, where both the adjudicator and eventual outcome are imposed.

1 Note here that by 'country' we mean England and Wales, which form a separate judicial and legal jurisdiction from Scotland and from Northern Ireland, even though politically these form the UK.

(a) ADR clauses

7.04 The historical English law view is that many dispute resolution provisions (apart from arbitration clauses) are merely 'agreements to agree' and are unenforceable because they lack certainty[1]. This cautious approach is declining, at least in relation to dispute resolution clauses that are nearly an immediately effective agreement to arbitrate, as in the case of an expert determination clause[2]. In a recent case, a good faith negotiation and mediation clause was held void for uncertainty as it was not 'determinative of the dispute'[3]. In that case, the court also considered that the mediation clause in question was not a condition precedent to the issue of litigation proceedings. The case was decided, however, before the introduction of the new Civil Procedure Rules (CPR)[4] in the courts of England and Wales in April 1999, which require the parties to help the courts to further the overriding objective to deal with cases justly. At the outset, lawyers need to approach a case by seeking, for example, to save expense, and deal with the case in a manner which is fair, expeditious and proportionate to the amount of money involved, the financial position of the parties and the importance of the case. It is difficult to comply with these obligations without attempting negotiation and considering compromise. Even if parties embark upon litigation without exhausting settlement options, the court will encourage the parties to use an ADR procedure 'if the court considers that appropriate'. The 'allocation questionnaire' which is completed after a defence is served asks whether the parties wish there to be a one-month stay to attempt to settle the case.

In determining who should pay the costs of the proceedings, the court will also consider the conduct of all the parties before, as well as during, the proceedings and the efforts made, if any, both before or during proceedings in order to try to resolve the dispute.

1 *Walford v Miles* [1992] 1 All ER 453, HL.
2 See *Channel Tunnel Group Ltd v Balfour Beatty Construction Ltd* [1993] 1 All ER 664, HL; *Cott UK Ltd v F E Barber Ltd* [1997] 3 All ER 540.
3 *Halifax Financial Services Ltd v Intuitive Systems Ltd* [1999] 1 All ER (Comm) 303. See also *Paul Smith Ltd v H & S International Holding Inc* [1991] 2 Lloyd's Rep 127.
4 SI 1998/3132.

7.05 The objectives of the CPR and pre-action protocols can be reflected in ADR-based dispute resolution clauses, enabling parties to demonstrate that they have:

■ exchanged full information about the prospective claims in any litigation;

- made best efforts to settle; and

- taken steps to ensure that the litigation is managed efficiently and at the least cost.

Not only is it more likely that ADR clauses will be upheld under the CPR regime, but also, where the parties have not included an ADR clause in their agreement, their solicitors will be more willing to agree to use ADR as a settlement tool before commencing proceedings, knowing that their clients may face a stay or directions from the court to use ADR. Overall, the use of ADR is increasing. Organisations like the Centre for Effective Dispute Resolution (CEDR) and ADR Group are seeing a substantial rise in the number of matters referred to them for administration, with reports by CEDR of an increase of 141% in the year after the introduction of the CPR.

A distinction may thus be drawn between determinative procedures and non-determinative procedures. Examples of the former include where the parties agree that certain issues will be finally and conclusively resolved by a third party, arbitration clauses, binding expert valuations and third party certifications. Non-determinative procedures, for example where it is hoped that the procedure will assist the parties themselves in resolving their dispute, include negotiation, mediation, expert appraisal and non-binding opinions from a mediator. In the case of non-determinative procedures, while the contract might provide the appropriate machinery, there is no legal obligation to resolve the dispute in that way, particularly in the case of 'good faith' negotiation, and it may be practically and legally impossible to monitor and enforce the process. Despite the obstacles to enforcement, non-determinative procedures are generally quicker and cheaper, when successful, than arbitration and litigation.

To be effective, ADR clauses should be drafted as '*Scott v Avery* clauses', that is participation in the process should be a condition precedent to court or arbitration proceedings. Any ADR clause must also be very clear as to both the procedure that is to be applied and the time limits for the procedural steps. This will ensure that the clause has at least a chance of being upheld, as a matter of contract, if challenged.

(b) The ADR process

7.06 To emphasise what is involved in the *process* of ADR, a draftsman might consider incorporating the following:

- identification of the process[1] and clear machinery for the identification and appointment of the 'neutral', together with provision for his fees. The ideal scheme, rarely seen in practice, is to name in the agreement several neutrals to be appointed in order of preference with an appointing body as the default[2].

- a timetable, specifying in detail each step to be taken by the parties[3].

- a promise by each party to use its best endeavours to complete the process, coupled with a promise not to withdraw until completion of the process.

- some confirmation of the benefits which the parties hope to achieve can help to establish the value of the ADR agreement. As an extension of this concept, the parties might agree a liquidated damages provision, reflecting a genuine pre-estimate of the costs involved if one party refuses to undertake and complete the process. The increased costs of litigation would be a starting-point for such a calculation.

- provisions for the exchange of information, identifying the nature of the information and the time for exchange. (This has the indirect effect of making the parties more committed to the ADR process, because it involves them in doing something which is probably not consistent with forensic litigation.)

- a promise not to commence litigation or arbitration until the ADR process is completed, coupled with an undertaking not to commence proceedings until, say, six months after a dispute has arisen or has been notified by one party to the other. Thus the ability to commence proceedings is subject to clear pre-conditions and the parties are given an incentive to exhaust the ADR process in order to resolve a dispute in the short term. It should be easier to persuade a court to enforce this sort of negative covenant than an undertaking to negotiate, which cannot be defined or policed with certainty.

- consistency between the dispute resolution provisions in connected contracts[4].

1   In *David Wilson Homes Ltd v Survey Services Ltd (in liquidation)* [2001] EWCA Civ 34, [2001] 1 All ER (Comm) 449, the dispute resolution clause did not refer to arbitration, but to referral of disputes for determination to a Queen's Counsel of the English Bar for determination. The Court of Appeal considered that it was irrelevant that the clause did not specifically mention arbitration. The court considered that it was implicit that disputes were being referred to a body other than a court, whose decision would be binding upon the parties and that, accordingly, it was an arbitration agreement.

2   Care should be taken to ensure that the authority selected undertakes the appointment function. By way of example, in a recent Scottish case, *Bruce v Kordula* 2001 SLT 983, an arbitration clause requiring the appointment of the arbitrator by the 'Dean of the Faculty of Arbiters' was void for certainty as there was no such institution.

3   The timetable and procedure of an ADR organisation can be incorporated by reference to a dispute resolution clause: see *Lobb Partnership Ltd v Aintree Racecourse Co Ltd* [2000] CLC 431.

4   In *MH Alshaya Co WLL v Retek Information Systems Inc* [2000] WL 33116470, there was an arbitration clause in one agreement and no arbitration clause in a related agreement. The Queen's Bench Division considered that the contracts needed to be interpreted consistently and that, since it was not possible to add in an arbitration clause where it did not exist, the arbitration clause in the related agreement was struck out.

(c)   Types of alternative dispute resolution procedures

(i)   *Mediation*

7.07   Mediation is a structured negotiation in which a neutral third party (the mediator) is appointed by both parties. The mediator acts as a conduit to facilitate communication between the parties and assist them in reaching a binding settlement. It is a consensual process which is entirely dependent on the willingness of the parties to enter into, and then to continue, negotiations.

Mediation is by far the most popular form of ADR. The introduction of a neutral third party is one feature which distinguishes mediation from simple negotiation. The parties are themselves responsible for reaching agreement, since no decision is imposed upon them by the mediator; there is no judge or arbitrator to decide issues for the parties. Once a settlement agreement has been reached, according to the laws governing the parties or the mediation, the mediator will invite the parties to make their agreement binding as a matter of contract.

The key elements of mediation are:

- the appointment of a neutral or mediator.

- agreement on who will attend the mediation – in many instances there are a number of individuals and/or entities with a direct or indirect involvement in a dispute and it is important to balance the importance of binding those involved into a settlement against the risk that too many competing interests in a mediation may prevent any issues being resolved at all.

- because the negotiations are intended to achieve a settlement of their dispute, both parties will want the freedom to negotiate without having to worry that information disclosed or what they have said in the course of the mediation will later be used in court proceedings. It is therefore usual to agree that the mediation process is confidential and that all steps taken in connection with the process are entirely 'without prejudice' to ensure that information is protected by privilege.

- an agreement as to the fees of the mediator and the costs of the mediation process.

(ii) Conciliation

7.08 Similar to mediation, conciliation involves a neutral third party who helps the parties to negotiate a settlement of their differences. The conciliator will, however, play a more active role by informing the parties of his opinion on the issues in dispute during the joint meeting, in the hope that they will be guided by that decision to reach an overall settlement. In practice, however, there may be little difference in approach between a mediator and a conciliator. The conciliator's decision is not binding on the parties and they are both free to ignore it.

(iii) Mini-trial

7.09 A mini-trial, sometimes known as the executive tribunal, involves representatives of the disputants making short presentations to a panel of at least one senior member of each party and, usually, a neutral adviser, who assists the panel members in reaching agreement. The chief executives of the parties who form the partisan element of the 'tribunal' may well be assisted by several 'neutral advisers' with legal or technical expertise. The mini-trial seeks to replicate the court process in a short period of time, normally one day. Despite its name, however, the outcome of the 'trial' is not binding on any party unless and until a settlement agreement is executed. This technique is well suited to highly technical or complex disputes where there is an advantage to the formal presentation of technical issues, for example where detailed actuarial evidence may be determinative of issues in dispute.

The mini-trial session will usually commence with opening statements by lawyers of, say, no more than two hours' duration from each side. These will be followed by short presentations from each party's factual and expert witnesses. Thereafter, the executives will retire with the neutral advisers to consider the issues raised in the presentations and work towards achieving a settlement.

(iv) Adjudication

7.10 Adjudication involves the *determination* of an issue by a person or persons appointed by the parties for that purpose. The determination may be binding or non-binding, according to whatever is agreed by the parties prior to, or during, the adjudication session.

This can take the form of:

- an early neutral evaluation, which involves the evaluation by an independent third party, usually a lawyer, of the evidence presented by each party in support of its case; or

- an expert determination, which involves the appointment of an expert to assess the technical issues raised in the dispute and determine how the dispute should be resolved.

The appointment of an adjudicator is appropriate where each party considers that a decision of a third party is necessary in order to resolve their dispute. This will often be a person recognised to be an expert in the subject matter of the dispute. In some cases, parties have chosen to appoint a retired judge to act as a private, judicial arbiter.

There is statutory provision for adjudication in the case of construction disputes in the Housing Grants, Construction and Regeneration Act 1996.

(v) Med-Arb

7.11 Med-Arb (Mediation-Arbitration) is a combined process starting with a mediation where, if no settlement is reached by the end of the time set aside for mediation, the parties then consent to the process becoming an arbitration. The neutral formally appointed to act as mediator then assumes the role of arbitrator and delivers his formal decision, which is binding on the parties.

Med-Arb has been designed to answer a criticism which is sometimes levelled against mediation, that it is non-binding and therefore potentially a waste of time and money because either party can walk out after hours of preparation and negotiation, leaving the dispute no closer to being resolved. Med-Arb is itself open to criticism, however, in that the mediator may obtain confidential information during the first part of the process or express views which are partial, either of which would then disqualify him from acting as an arbitrator in the later stages on the ground that there would be a breach of the natural rules of justice. In addition, parties are less likely to be open with the mediator in private sessions about their strengths and weaknesses if they know that the mediator will opine on the merits later. For these reasons, Med-Arb is largely untested in the UK although elsewhere, for example in Hong Kong and Australia, specific legislation has been enacted to permit its use. The undoubted advantage of the process is that it links negotiation, mediation and arbitration in a way that encourages the parties to behave reasonably under the threat that, if they fail to settle, the arbitrator will simply impose his decision. A novel variation has emerged called Arb-Med, where the process starts as an arbitration, the award is produced but not published to the parties, the neutral/arbitrator commences a mediation and the award is only published if one party withdraws or the neutral feels that the mediation stage has been exhausted. This technique answers most procedural and substantive criticisms of Med-Arb.

(vi) Arbitration

7.12   Arbitration involves the adjudication of a claim by an arbitrator, who considers the legal merits of both parties' cases and makes a binding award based on his assessment of the merits. An arbitrator reaches his decision subject to the formal statutory and other rules governing the conduct of arbitrations. The existence of these very detailed rules has meant that arbitration has tended to be a slow and costly process, but has the advantage that an arbitration award can be enforced internationally even more easily than a court judgment. The Arbitration Act 1996 (AA 1996), which came into force in January 1997, has modernised this process in the UK and encouraged both domestic and international disputants to consider arbitration as a viable alternative to mediation and the other techniques outlined here.

Although arbitration can work for smaller cases as well, on-line sellers should consider carefully whether they wish to make this 'mandatory' in a consumer contract. An arbitration agreement will be 'unfair' for the purposes of the UK Unfair Terms in Consumer Contracts Regulations 1999[1], in so far as it relates to a claim for a pecuniary remedy which does not exceed £5,000. In a US case involving the sale of software to consumers, a clause in the vendor's standard terms and conditions requiring disputes to be referred to International Chamber of Commerce (ICC) arbitration was held to be unconscionable because it necessitated payment by each consumer of a $4,000 administration fee[2].

1   SI 1999/2083.
2   *USA v Visa USA Inc* 750 App Div 1 (NYSC, 1998).

(d)   Principles for designing a dispute resolution procedure

7.13   The design of dispute clauses in contracts is crucial and involves more than a choice of law and jurisdiction clause. Any scheme should appear to be 'seamless'; by this we mean that, from the moment an issue is identified as disputed, progression through each stage until resolution should be relatively smooth, leaving as little room as possible for one of the parties to frustrate progress for whatever tactical or commercial advantage.

There are several consequences of this approach: drafting will tend to be more comprehensive than has been the norm in the past and the procedural steps should be detailed. Preferably, the neutrals to be involved in the process should be identified, simply because that avoids delay. It should be relatively easy for the parties to agree on people that they respect to act as neutrals before a dispute arises, whereas later on, depending on the perceived strengths and weaknesses of their positions, one party or the other will tend to obstruct the appointment of the most suitable neutral. If the parties cannot agree on a team of neutrals when they are entering into a contract, then alarm bells should be ringing.

Obviously, any procedure has to be tailored to the particular relationship. A complex multi-stage procedure designed for a large, business-to-business (B2B) e-commerce joint venture, or ongoing commercial trading relationship, will not be appropriate for a one-off, low value business-to-consumer (B2C) sales transaction.

Factors which will have to be taken into account include:

- **The complexity of the issues involved** A dispute on a narrow technical issue may be more amenable to expert determination.

- **The amount in dispute** For small claims, arbitration may not be appropriate because of its relatively higher costs compared to the small claims procedures available in court or through consumer organisations. On the other hand, bringing or defending a claim in a foreign court, over a relatively small sum, may not be cheap or practicable either.

- **Whether there is an ongoing commercial relationship** A less contentious procedure can take the tension out of litigation and enable the parties to continue to work together. ADR also allows parties to keep their affairs confidential.

Depending on the nature of the business relationship, the parties and the draftsman can choose between consensual and non-consensual resolution procedures, or a combination of both.

7.14 Not only can the draftsman and parties choose one method for resolving any disputes that may arise, but it is also possible to:

- choose a number of dispute resolution options to be used for the specific types of dispute that may arise under the contract in question;

- adopt a seamless approach to dispute resolution that enables parties to start with consensual resolution options and then move on to non-consensual resolution procedures, if the first attempts to resolve the dispute fail;

- entrench the exchange of information and documents as a contractual obligation throughout the life of a contract and as part of the dispute escalation procedure;

- provide mechanisms which split issues and methods of resolution, according to the need for efficiency;

- in some cases, provide for a mediator's report to the parties; and

- use mediation to settle disclosure issues and other major interim battles (linking into the concept of 'proportionality' under the CPR).

For example, Nominet's new dispute resolution procedure for domain name disputes (covered in greater detail in Chapter 5, E-brand) provides for:

- a response within 15 days after a complaint is filed;

- a possible reply within five days of the response;

- a period for mediation which expires within ten days of the reply;

- a decision by a Nominet panellist within ten days of the panellist's appointment; and

- the possibility of appeal following the decision.

(e) Drafting a dispute resolution clause

(i) Simple ADR agreements

7.15 An ADR agreement can be very simple. For example, a mediation might only require the following:

> 'Party A and Party B will endeavour to settle the dispute arising out of [insert short description of dispute] by mediation within [x] days and hereby appoint [y] to act as mediator, whose fees shall be shared jointly.'

This clause can be inserted into the initial commercial document between the parties or can be a subsequent and separate ADR agreement. Such a simple formula leaves the regulation of the process of mediation to ad hoc agreement, as the mediation proceeds. While a competent mediator will probably establish the ground rules for the mediation programme, deal with confidentiality and agree his own contract terms prior to the first meeting with the parties, most ADR agreements seek to describe and regulate the process in more detail. This is generally helpful, as the parties then know what to expect and may find it more difficult to withdraw capriciously. There is, however, a danger in seeking to negotiate the details in circumstances where the parties are suspicious of each other. If there is a risk of breakdown in the negotiation of an ADR agreement, advisers should seek the simplest agreement possible and be prepared to be flexible once the non-binding and without prejudice nature of the process is established.

There are, of course, a few essential terms that must be considered:

- defining the meaning of 'dispute';

- confidentiality – that the entire process is 'without prejudice';

- commitment to resolution – the dispute to be resolved is properly identified and the parties record their commitment to seek a resolution;

- who, when and where? – housekeeping items are agreed; and

- type of ADR – since ADR is flexible, processes can be tailored to fit the requirements of the dispute and the parties, for example through the use of seamless dispute resolution procedure.

(ii) Incorporation of organisational ADR rules

7.16 ADR organisations publish procedural rules which can be incorporated into commercial agreements or the ADR agreement itself. Such organisations suggest clauses for incorporation into commercial contracts which entrench the use of that organisation and its rules in disputes which may arise, or which parties with an existing dispute may want to use as a precedent. These standard drafts (and the associated procedural rules) have a value in that they can be suggested by one party, avoiding any perception that they have been drafted in a partisan fashion. Like all precedents, however, such standard drafting should not be used slavishly and care needs to be taken to ensure that the particular requirements of the parties, and the nature of the dispute, have been taken into account.

Examples of these clauses include:

- International Chamber of Commerce's Model Clauses for ICC Rules of Arbitration and ICC Rules of ADR[1];

- International Centre for Settlement of Investment Disputes' Model Clauses[2];

- World Intellectual Property Organisation (WIPO)'s Arbitration Rules, Mediation Rules and Expedited Arbitration Rules[3];

- United National Commission on International Trade Law (UNCITRAL) Arbitration Rules and Conciliation Rules[4];

- London Court of International Arbitration's Model Clause for Arbitration Rules[5];

- American Arbitration Association's Model Clauses for International Arbitration, Commercial Arbitration, Commercial Mediation, Patent Arbitration, Securities Arbitration, Construction Industry Arbitration Rules and Procedures for Cases under UNCITRAL Arbitration Rules[6].

1 See www.iccwbo.org.
2 See www.worldbank.org/icsid/basicdoc/basicdoc.htm.
3 See www.wipo.org.
4 See www.uncitral.org.
5 See www.lcia-arbitration.com.
6 See www.adr.org.

(iii) More detailed ADR agreements

7.17 A more detailed approach to disputes could be included in the commercial contract entered into between the parties, or left until the first dispute arises, although this will come with its inherent difficulties of entrenched positions and time wasted on negotiating the setting up of the dispute resolution process, rather than resolving the dispute. Whichever option is chosen, the parties can agree, for instance:

- a detailed programme of steps to be taken by all parties;

- a statement to the effect that it is the responsibility of all parties to disclose, with candour, all the facts, theories and opinions on which they intend to rely with regard to the matter in dispute;

- a provision that, where no agreement is reached in the ADR process, either party may request the neutral to provide a non-binding opinion;

- to state the law governing the ADR agreement; and

- to specify the circumstances when the parties can resort to the courts.

(iv) Specimen clauses for consensual dispute resolution

7.18 Here are some examples of the different types of clauses that might be used:

- **Dispute defined** 'A dispute or difference will be deemed to arise when one party notifies the other in writing of its grievance, dispute or claim of whatever nature arising out of, in connection with, or in relation to the negotiation, execution, interpretation, performance or breach of this agreement, including but not limited to any claim based on contract, tort, equity, or domestic or international statute ("the Dispute").'

- **Negotiation** 'The parties must first use their respective best endeavours to consult and negotiate with each other, in good faith and, recognising their mutual interests, attempt to reach a settlement of the Dispute satisfactory to both parties. To such end, the parties must, within [7] days of a Dispute arising, convene a meeting between relevant members of management to attempt to resolve the Dispute. If they do not reach a settlement within a period of [7] working days then, upon written notice from one party to the other, the Dispute shall be managed in accordance with [*outline your favoured binding dispute resolution procedure*].'

- **Single adjudicator** 'Within [7] days of the Dispute arising, the parties must appoint an adjudicator. The adjudicator will be nominated by [for example, the Academy of Experts] at the joint request of the parties. Once appointed, the adjudicator's appointment can only be terminated by agreement of the parties. The adjudication will be conducted in accordance with the procedure described at clauses [ ] to [ ] below [*insert procedure that parties wish to follow*].'

- **Dispute resolution board** 'The Dispute Resolution Board ("DRB") must be appointed within [7] days of the conclusion of [negotiation referred to above] and must consist of [3] persons with experience in [the subject matter of the agreement] and knowledge of how a DRB functions [one of whom must also hold a professional qualification as a solicitor or barrister in England and Wales]. The DRB will conduct their proceedings in accordance with the procedure described at clauses [ ] to [ ] below [*insert provision as to how the parties wish the DRB to function*].'

- **Mediation** 'If, within [14] days of receiving [the DRB's non-binding recommendations or the adjudicator's non-binding adjudication] the Dispute remains unresolved, the parties agree to use their respective best endeavours in good faith to settle the Dispute by mediation before having recourse to [arbitration, litigation or some other binding dispute resolution procedure]. The mediation will be conducted as described at clauses [ ] to [ ] below [*insert provisions as to how the parties would like the mediation to be conducted*].'

- **Seamless dispute resolution procedure** 'If the Dispute has not been settled within [28] days or such other period as agreed in writing between the parties after the appointment of the mediator, the dispute must be submitted to arbitration administered by [for example, Chartered Institute of Arbitrators] under the [*insert appropriate arbitration rules or draft your own*] annexed to this contract, which terms are hereby deemed incorporated.'

(f) Arbitration

7.19 The advantage of a '*Scott v Avery* approach' (that is, participation in the process should be a condition precedent to court or arbitral proceedings) in bolstering the enforceability of ADR dispute schemes is illustrated in the *Halifax*[1] case. In any event, parties now have more flexibility in deciding how their arbitration will be conducted and this can obviously have some cost saving benefits. Under the AA 1996, there is a number of non-mandatory provisions that the parties can choose to follow or disregard. If, however, they do not touch upon the subject matter of these provisions in their arbitration agreement, they will be automatically subject to the terms of the AA 1996. It is therefore worthwhile considering these areas. They are as follows:

- **One arbitrator or three?** If parties fail to make provision, section 15(3) of the AA 1996 provides that there shall be one arbitrator. If there are to be three arbitrators, parties should consider whether one is to be a chairman and what his functions should be. If the parties agree to have a chairman but fail to specify his function, then section 20 of the AA 1996 shall apply.

- **Procedure for appointing an arbitrator** If the parties do not agree on the procedure for appointment of arbitrators, then section 16 of the AA 1996 will apply. In the event that there is a failure of appointment, then the courts, under sections 17 and 18 of the AA 1996, can intervene. It is therefore practical to refer appointments in default to professional bodies such as the Academy of Experts or the Chartered Institute of Arbitrators.

- **Replacing arbitrators** Section 27 of the AA 1996 allows the parties to decide on how to fill a vacancy. For example, they can agree that a professional body appoints a replacement arbitrator.

- **Powers of an arbitrator** The selection of the powers that the arbitrators have should be considered in conjunction with the procedure to be adopted by the parties for the conduct of the arbitration. It is entirely up to the parties what procedure they adopt and what powers the arbitrators may have. Powers to consider are:

  - ruling on their own substantive jurisdiction (this includes ruling on the validity of the arbitration agreement, whether the arbitrators are properly appointed, whether there is a dispute, etc). This power can be given to the arbitrator or left to the courts, under section 44 of the AA 1996;

  - ordering the preservation of evidence (for example, photographing evidence, sampling, storage, sale, etc);

  - consolidation of the proceedings with other arbitral proceedings;

  - sanctioning parties for their failure to do something for the proper and expeditious conduct of the arbitration;

  - procedure of arbitration. The issue is whether the parties wish to allow the arbitrators to dictate the procedure to be adopted or whether the parties wish to decide upon it themselves. If the parties do not agree the procedure in advance, once the arbitration gets underway, the initiative will lie with the arbitrator. The AA 1996 gives the arbitrators wide powers, in the absence of the parties agreeing to the contrary, to decide what procedures are to apply. If the parties are to agree the procedure, consideration should be given to the following:

    - *Pleadings* Are formal pleadings to be used and, if so, what form, and what timetable for supply and amendment?

    - *Experts* Consider the need for experts. If there are to be experts, who should appoint – arbitrator or parties? And how many experts?

    - *Evidence* Do strict rules of evidence apply and to what extent should evidence be given under oath? Or should the arbitration be a paper only procedure?

    - *Security for costs* Does the arbitrator have power to order security for costs?

    - *Costs* Do the parties wish to limit recoverable costs to a specific amount?

    - *Representation* Do the parties wish to allow legal or other representation?

    - *Awards* Under sections 50, 52, 53, 54 and 55 of the AA 1996, the parties are free to agree the time for making an award, the form of the award and its notification. Parties can agree that the arbitrator need not give reasons. This, however, effectively excludes an appeal to the courts on a point of law (see section 69(i) of the AA 1996). Alternatively, a clause can be inserted where the parties agree that there will be no appeal to the court. Consideration should also be given to provisional relief as, unless the parties confer such power on the arbitrators, the tribunal has no such power (see section 39 of the AA 1996).

    - *Costs* Sections 60–65 cover the costs of arbitration and the parties are free to agree how they are to be borne. If there is no agreement between the parties, the arbitrators will award the costs on the principle that costs should follow the event except in circumstances where that is not appropriate. Under section 60, an agreement that one party is to pay the whole or part of the costs of the arbitration in any event is only valid if made after the dispute in question has arisen.

- *Intervention of the courts* The parties can agree the extent of the courts' intervention in the arbitration proceedings. See sections 44 and 45 of the AA 1996. What intervention there is will depend upon what powers are given to the arbitrators.

1 *Halifax Financial Services Ltd v Intuitive Systems Ltd* [1999] 1 All ER (Comm) 303.

(g) Human rights

7.20 The European Convention on Human Rights has been incorporated into English law by the Human Rights Act 1988. Article 6 prohibits restrictions on access to courts and also imposes a requirement of procedural fairness. The article 6 requirement that a party should have a reasonable opportunity to present its case has been found to have no application to adjudication on the basis that an adjudicator's decision is not a final determination[1]. Accordingly, in the context of other non-binding dispute resolution processes, like mediation, article 6 is unlikely to provide a basis for requiring procedural fairness. In addition, where parties have contractually agreed to a dispute resolution method other than the courts, it is likely to be considered that they have contracted out of the article 6 prohibition on restriction of access to courts, which was the approach taken in a recent case relating to an arbitration clause[2].

1 *Elanay Contracts Ltd v The Vestry* [2001] BLR 33, per HHJ Harvey QC.
2 *Mousaka Inc v Golden Seagull Maritime Inc* [2002] 1 All ER 726, CC.

3. JURISDICTION

7.21 As we have already seen, courts asked to determine disputes will only accept those that they are competent to adjudicate. In the context of e-disputes, as with more conventional disputes, the decision to bring court proceedings will necessarily focus on three issues:

- which courts or tribunals have *jurisdiction* to deal with the dispute?

- what is the *proper law* governing the dispute, both in terms of the issues to be resolved and the procedural law to be applied (for example the rules of evidence to be exercised)?[1]

- how and where will any judgment be *enforced*?

These questions are also likely to be answered inconsistently, in that different courts around the world will approach them in their own way and devise their own answers. On-line sellers must be aware of this likelihood and endeavour to keep abreast of the law in this area as it develops. By familiarising themselves with the concepts of jurisdiction, applicable law and enforcement, they will ensure that they do not waste time litigating in the wrong forum and that, wherever possible, they retain some control over where they are sued.

Many of the rules on jurisdiction and choice of law affecting England have existed for over 200 years. Although these rules were substantially revised and updated by the Brussels, Lugano and Rome Conventions, to which the UK is a signatory, the principles governing jurisdiction stem from the late 1960s, while those concerning choice of law clauses in contracts were drawn up in 1980[2]. The Conventions have been undergoing amendments, which impact on e-commerce. In particular, the Brussels Regulation[3] has replaced the Brussels and Lugano Conventions, in respect of those bound by the Regulation (currently all EU and EFTA States except Denmark), and came into force on 1 March 2002. For ease of reference in this chapter, the States bound by the Regulation will be referred to as Member States.

In essence, jurisdiction has been assigned by reference to geographical borders. E-commerce, however, does not acknowledge geographical borders and is flourishing precisely because it is unfettered and supranational. Jurisdictional principles that recognise states, unions and trade areas, but not networks, domains and servers, thus leave the courts ill-equipped to deal with the issues of legal competence and governing law that will arise in almost every e-dispute. On-line sellers therefore face considerable uncertainty as to how a dispute, arising in the course of conducting business electronically, is likely to be resolved.

1 This is an extension of the discussion in Chapter 3, E-liability, where the context was the drafting of contracts so as to include choice of law clauses, in view of the consequences (summarised there and also in this section) of failing to do so.
2 The Brussels Convention (1968) was brought into force in the UK by the Civil Jurisdiction and Judgments Act 1982, which came into force on 1 January 1987; the Rome Convention on the Law Applicable to Contractual Obligations (1980) was brought into force by the Contracts (Applicable Law) Act 1990, which came into force on 1 April 1991. The Lugano Convention (1988) is a parallel Convention between the EC Member States and the members of EFTA. With the entry into the EU of Austria, Finland and Sweden, the Lugano Convention applies as between the EU and the three remaining members of EFTA, namely Iceland, Norway and Switzerland. The Lugano Convention was implemented into English law by the Civil Jurisdiction and Judgments Act 1991.
3 Council Regulation (EC) 44/2001.

7.22 The arbitration model suggested below can go some way to removing this uncertainty. The opportunity to negotiate and agree a suitable dispute resolution mechanism will not, however, always arise and the involvement of the courts of one or more jurisdictions may be inescapable. Traders therefore need to be aware of the complex rules relating to jurisdiction, governing law and enforcement. They also need to recognise the impact these rules are likely to have on many, if not all, of their e-commercial relationships. Indeed, it will be prudent, and often vital, for business people to fashion and revise their trading strategies and policies so as to reflect the way in which these principles are applied by the courts.

Most courts around the world are still very unfamiliar with the practice, if not the concept, of conducting business on-line. With development in the law in this area over the next two to five years, new rules that emerge will be a very important part of the culture and customs of e-commerce. An indication of the future comes from Singapore, which is probably foremost in its desire to become an e-commerce hub. The judiciary in Singapore launched an on-line mediation facility in September 2000, which enables commercial and e-business concerns to resolve disputes without going to court or indeed entering a physical presence in a court or hearing room. The scheme, known as e@dr, operates as follows:

- a claimant visits the scheme's website[1];

- the claimant gives particulars and those of the respondent in a form and proposes a solution to the dispute. The form is submitted electronically;

- the claimant receives an acknowledgement and a case number;

- a moderator sends an e-mail to the respondent to the claim;

- on receiving the e-mail, the respondent can either reject the whole process of e@dr, or accept it by completing a form and submitting it back by e-mail;

- on receiving the respondent's e-mail, the moderator decides which forum will be used to resolve the dispute, for example the Small Claims Tribunal. The case is referred to a mediator in the chosen forum;

- the parties are informed and then the mediator contacts all parties by e-mail;

- the mediation process begins.

The following issues require the attention of common and civil law courts around the world and need to be considered carefully by any trader who has established, or is intending to establish, himself as an on-line seller:

■ the express terms of contracts with customers with respect to jurisdiction and the governing law of the contract;

■ the express terms of contracts with his own suppliers as to jurisdiction and governing law;

■ the country or countries in which proceedings might be commenced against a third party for breach of contract, infringement of the trader's rights or other damage to his business or reputation;

■ the country or countries in which proceedings might be commenced against the on-line seller by his customers or suppliers or by third parties, alleging infringement of their rights or other damage to their business or reputation; and

■ the impact of national and cross-border regulators and supervisory bodies established or empowered to regulate and control the on-line seller's activities.

1 See www.e-adr.org.sg.

(a) General principles

7.23 The question of whether a court in England or Wales has jurisdiction over a case is governed by the common law and the Brussels Regulation, which replaced the Brussels and Lugano Conventions[1].

This regime governing jurisdiction allocates jurisdiction in civil and commercial matters and provides for the reciprocal recognition and enforcement of judgments within the territories of the EC and EFTA. The regime determines which Member State's court (if any) has jurisdiction to hear a dispute and whether an order by the court of one Member State must be recognised and enforced by the court of another Member State. The regime will always be the starting point for any assessment of where a party must sue or be sued. Only where it is clear that the regime has no application is it appropriate to consider jurisdiction according to common law rules. It is also important to consider the regime from the point of view of enforcement of any judgment obtained from a court. Courts of Member States can refuse to recognise judgments of other Member States, in certain limited circumstances. Clearly, traders will not want to go to the effort and expense of bringing and proving a claim, only to find that it is unenforceable because the claim was determined by a court that assumed, but did not actually have, jurisdiction.

1 Any major differences between the Brussels Regulation and the Conventions will be identified in this chapter.

(b) Scope of the Brussels Regulation

7.24 The Brussels Regulation applies:

■ **Where an international element is involved (except in the case of consumer disputes, as to which see further below)** A dispute involving an English claimant and defendant concerning a contract to be performed in England will not have an international element. Where both parties are English but the contract is to be performed via or in another country, there is likely to be an international element. In relation to a disputed electronic transaction, it may be difficult to identify where, other than in cyberspace, the material obligation contained in the contract is or was to be performed. In this situation, the mechanics of payment for the particular goods, services or information may provide clues as to whether there is a non-English element that brings the Conventions into play.

- **In civil and commercial matters only** Revenue, customs and administrative disputes are specifically excluded, as are family, bankruptcy, insolvency, social security and arbitration proceedings.

- **Where the proposed defendant is domiciled in a Member State** The basic rule under article 2 of the Brussels Regulation is that persons domiciled in a Member State shall, whatever their nationality, be sued in the courts of that Member State. Accordingly, if the defendant is domiciled in Denmark (currently not bound by the Regulation), or if jurisdiction is conferred on Denmark (for example, via a jurisdiction clause), the Brussels Convention rules of jurisdiction remain applicable.

(c) Importance of the defendant's domicile

7.25   The domicile rule mirrors the English common law principle that the English court has jurisdiction over defendants physically present in England at the time that the claim is brought. The common law rule is, however, secondary to the Brussels Regulation, such that the English court cannot claim jurisdiction where the Regulation dictates that another court has jurisdiction.

Essentially, however, subject to the various exceptions under the Regulation and at common law, the English courts will have jurisdiction to hear a claim against an overseas company with a place of business in England or Wales.

Before looking at any of the other provisions in the Regulation, traders might reflect on the practical effect of the domicile rule where dealing with a potential defendant domiciled within a Member State. Although the Regulation often allows a claimant a choice as to where his claim may be brought, the onus is on him to show that he may bring his claim in the courts of a Member State other than the one where the defendant resides.

A seller may get around this difficulty by ensuring that sales are made subject to a contractual term that the courts of England or another country have jurisdiction over disputes arising. Alternatively, he might decide to provide for arbitration along the lines of the English model. An English court will usually uphold a contractual term providing for a dispute to be referred to itself or to a foreign court. Article 23 of the Regulation requires all Member States to give force to clauses giving jurisdiction to the courts of another Member State, save where limited exceptions apply.

In the case of:

- **Individuals** Whether a person is domiciled in a particular Member State is determinable by reference to that state's national laws (article 59 of the Regulation). Domicile in the UK[1] is defined as residency or 'substantial connection' under section 41(2) of the Civil Jurisdiction and Judgments Act 1982. In general, three months or more residency will usually be regarded as sufficient to meet the domicile test. If a person, according to this test, is not resident in the UK, one must then consider whether he is domiciled in, say, Portugal, by reference to Portuguese law.

- **Corporations** Article 60 of the Regulation defines domicile as the 'statutory seat', 'central administration' or 'principle place of business' of a company or other legal person or association. For the purposes of the United Kingdom and Ireland, 'statutory seat' means the registered office or, where there is no such office, the place of incorporation, or, where there is no such a place, the place under the law of which the formation took place.

---

1   The three jurisdictions that make up the UK have similar approaches towards determining what domicile means and how it is determined. Of course, disputes may still arise as to in which of these three jurisdictions a litigant is himself actually domiciled.

7.26 Where an individual or company has more than one domicile, it is likely that the courts of more than one Member State will have jurisdiction. This means that the claimant can choose where to sue and that, provided he selects a state with which the individual or corporation has some substantive connection, the court of that state will accept jurisdiction. This makes it important for on-line sellers to obtain confirmation from their customers and suppliers of the address from which they are buying, supplying or otherwise operating and, ideally, confirmation of the period for which they have been operating from that address.

The courts within the EU have tended to take the view that the relevant date of domicile, for the purpose of the domicile test, is the date on which proceedings are issued[1]. This makes it easier for potential defendants both to evade service and contest jurisdiction, by moving around frequently.

1 *Grupo Torras SA v Sheikh Fahad Mohammed Al-Sabah* [1995] 1 Lloyd's Rep 374, per Mance J; *Petrotrade Inc v Smith* [1998] 2 All ER 346, per Thomas J.

(d) Exceptions to the domicile rule

7.27 The main exceptions to the basic principle that the defendant must be sued where he is domiciled arise in the following situations.

(i) *Claims in contract*

7.28 Consumer contracts are considered separately below (paragraph 7.35). Where the claimant can show that, although the defendant is domiciled in a Member State, a court in another Member State has jurisdiction because the matter concerns a contract, a claim may be brought in the 'place of performance of the obligation in question' (article 5(1) of the Brussels Regulation).

To this extent, the Regulation maintains the Brussels Convention rule regarding contractual obligations. The problem with the latter was that 'obligation' was determined by reference to the contractual right on which the claim was based. This meant that, on the same facts, the court that had jurisdiction could differ, according to who was bringing the claim. For instance, in the case of a sale of books on-line, where the buyer refused to pay, the obligation on which a claim by the seller would be based was most likely to be the buyer's obligation to pay. Conversely, where the buyer brought a claim, this would be founded most likely on the seller's obligation to deliver the books to the agreed destination. The place of performance of each of these obligations could have been different. Also, the English court confirmed that not only an express term, but also an implied term, can form the basis of an 'obligation' for the purposes of article 5 of the Brussels Convention[1].

To remedy the shortcomings of applying the rules of private international law of the state whose courts are seized, paragraph (b) of article 5(1) of the Regulation now gives an autonomous definition of the place for performance of the obligation in question in two specific situations – the sale of goods and the provision of services. This determination of the place of performance applies regardless of the obligation in question, even where this obligation is the payment of the financial consideration for the contract. It also applies where the claim relates to several obligations. The rule may, however, be displaced by an explicit agreement by the parties on the place of performance. Where the effect of the autonomous definition is to designate a court in a non-Member State, rule (a) will apply rather than rule (b) in article 5(1) of the Regulation. Jurisdiction will lie with the court designated by the rules of private international law of the state seized as the court for the place of performance of the obligation.

1 *Raiffeisen Zentralbank Österreich AG v National Bank of Greece SA* [1999] 1 Lloyd's Rep 408.

7.29 The Brussels Regulation defines 'place of performance' as:

■ in the case of sale of goods, the place in a Member State where, under the contract, the goods were delivered or should have been delivered (article 5(1)(b));

■ in the case of provision of services, the place in a Member State where, under the contract, the services were provided or should have been provided (article 5 (1)(b)); and

■ in other cases, it is determined by the court before whom the dispute is brought, by reference to the law applicable to the contractual obligation in question (whether that be the governing law chosen by the parties to the contract or, in the absence of a choice of law, the applicable law according to the conflict of law rules of the particular court): article 5(1)(a). Applicable law is dealt with at section 4 below (and has also been considered from the perspective of liability in contract in Chapter 3, E-liability).

In the case of contracts where services are supplied or software downloaded in cyberspace, it may still be difficult to identify the place of performance of the obligation in question. An Internet trader should put an agreement in place with his customers as to the law applicable to their contracts.

(ii) Claims in tort (including the US position)

7.30 Where the claimant can show that, although the defendant is domiciled in a Member State, the court of another Member State has jurisdiction because the dispute concerns a tort (including negligence, defamation and the infringement of intellectual property rights), the claim may be brought in the courts of the place where the harmful event has occurred or may occur (article 5(3) of the Brussels Regulation). By covering cases where the harmful event may occur, article 5(3) offers litigants a ground for jurisdiction for preventative measures.

Identifying the place of harm is often difficult in relation to e-commerce, since the harm may affect the claimant in several places and in different ways, or may consist of harm that is incapable of being assigned a 'place' in terms of geography.

The draft Hague Convention on Private International Law (discussed below at paragraph 7.45) provides, by way of comparison, at article 10 that the plaintiff may bring an action in tort in the courts of the state in which the act or omission that caused injury occurred, or in which the injury arose, unless the defendant establishes that the person claiming to be responsible could not reasonably have foreseen that the act or omission could result in an injury of the same nature in that state. This article aims to limit the jurisdictional risk, although the problems in applying this to the Internet have been identified by the Hague Conference, in particular that the proof required to show lack of foreseeability would be difficult to adduce (for example, a person who uploads defamatory information on to a site can reasonably foresee that it may be read anywhere in the world).

An alternative limitation on jurisdiction could be to limit claims to those jurisdictions at which the act was directed or targeted. An English court took this approach when determining a passing off dispute about use of the name 'Internet World'[1]. The plaintiffs were a US company and its English subsidiary, while the defendant was a German company which had used the name at trade shows in Germany and on its website advertisements. The court had to decide whether it had jurisdiction to determine the dispute in the face of an argument by the defendant that the 'harm' occurred in Germany, such that Germany was the appropriate forum. The plaintiffs, however, contended that the harm that had occurred, as a result of the defendant's use of the name, had been directed at, and took effect in, England, where the plaintiffs had substantial goodwill in the name. The court accepted jurisdiction, agreeing that it was at least arguable that the plaintiffs owned the goodwill in the name in England and that, if the defendant's use of the name caused damage, that damage would occur in England rather than Germany.

In an Italian case, the Court of Cessation in Rome held that it had jurisdiction over foreign-based websites containing defamatory material because end-users could view it from within Italy's territories[2]. However, the Court of First Instance in Italy declared that it had no jurisdiction, as the judge considered that to find jurisdiction, the author of the offence had to have its address in the state, or the computer to which the material had been sent had to be located there[3].

1 *Mecklermedia Corpn v DC Congress GmbH* [1998] Ch 40, [1997] FSR 627.
2 *Re Moshe D* Corte di Cassazione, Rome, 27 December 2000.
3 *Internet e Pedopornografie – Art 600 ter C.P. una questione di competenza per territario* Tribunale di Torre Annunziata, 24 November 2000.

7.31 The extent to which harm is caused by posting information or replicating another's trade mark on a website, and the issue of where that harm is suffered, has also exercised the US judiciary on numerous occasions over the past few years. Most US States[1] have enacted a 'long-arm statute' by which they might acquire jurisdiction over a non-resident defendant. Under these statutes, the test is generally whether the defendant has 'systematic and continuous' contact with the particular forum or whether the plaintiff's cause of action relates to the defendant's contacts with the forum.

For a US court to assume jurisdiction, the application of this test in practice means that the defendant must be shown to have committed some act in the forum constituting a 'purposeful availment' of the privilege of conducting activities in the forum. In *Weber & Jolly Hotels*[2], the Italian defendant corporation had advertised its hotel facilities on its website, which was viewed by a resident of New Jersey who then visited the hotel and was injured during her stay. Her local (US) court declined jurisdiction, finding that mere advertisement of hotel services did not constitute continuous and substantial contact with the forum. Had the hotel actually allowed the plaintiff to book a hotel room or purchase other services over the Internet, however, it is likely that the court would have accepted jurisdiction. However, a different approach has been taken by another US court. An Illinois court considered a dispute involving an accident suffered by someone who bought a boat, not from the manufacturer but from a third party[3]. The defendant manufacturer had a website that offered e-mail facilities for inquiries about its products and advertised trade shows at which its boats would be sold. It did not, however, use its website to sell its boats or any other products or services. The court ruled that it did have jurisdiction to determine the dispute because the defendant's website was accessible within the jurisdiction and it knew that the third party who sold the offending boat to the plaintiff marketed the defendant's products at the advertised trade shows.

In a Massachusetts court, the defendant's regular solicitation of business in the forum state and its attempt to do business with the plaintiff found its jurisdiction in Massachusetts in a case involving trade mark infringement, cyber pirating and unfair competition[4]. An Illinois court found personal jurisdiction over an Irish retailer using the Crate & Barrel name on the basis that the defendant's activities, including soliciting Illinois residents to buy its goods, constituted doing business in the forum[5]. A Federal court has also ruled that personal jurisdiction existed over a Minnesota corporation that sold its products via its website to Texas residents, despite the small percentage of business that transactions brought to the corporation[6].

Nevertheless, the US cases show that US courts require something more than merely posting information on a website to found jurisdiction. A Federal court found that a defendant was not subject to jurisdiction based on its website, which allowed residents of a foreign state to place orders and communicate with the company by e-mail. The court looked at the extent of actual contacts (which, in this case, was only one item sold and five e-mail messages exchanged), as well as the degree to which the defendant's activities were directed toward the foreign state (in this case, the website was equally accessible from all states)[7]. In another case, the defendant's website allowed viewers to send e-mail, but did not allow them to enter into contracts with the defendant on-line, and required them to print order forms and mail/fax them back to the defendant. This was considered insufficiently interactive to confer jurisdiction over the defendant[8]. In a further Illinois case, involving a trade mark action against a British company operating a website, the court held that personal jurisdiction in Illinois could not be based solely on a website that promoted the sale of goods. In that case also, the website required customers to print out an order form from the site and mail/fax it back to the defendant's office. Although the sales were made to Illinois residents, the court held that the site's interactivity did not rise to the level of transacting business required for the exercise of the personal jurisdiction[9]. In a Pennsylvania case, a website was found not to be sufficient to establish general jurisdiction over a defendant where it was merely a promotional or informational resource and did not allow purchases to be executed on-line. The court rejected arguments by the plaintiff that the site was interactive based on e-mail addresses, hyperlinks and a 'click-wrap' agreement. The court rejected these arguments on the basis that these were standard features of the website, not related to any e-commerce transactions[10]. In a Texas case, the defendant in a patent suit was not subject to jurisdiction in Texas as the only contact site by the plaintiff was a passive website, and there was no evidence that the defendant made any sales in Texas through its website[11].

While these cases are consistent with the view that US courts tend to require 'something more' than a mere posting of information on a website to found jurisdiction, they demonstrate that a US court will not require very much more before it assumes jurisdiction.

Website owners therefore need to be aware that if they conduct any activity from or via their site, they run the risk that they will be exposed to litigation in a foreign court in respect of tort because the latter will decide that it has jurisdiction over them. This means that traders really need to be aware of who their customers are and where they are based, and to consider the implications of potentially having to submit to the jurisdiction of the courts where those customers are located.

1 As with the three jurisdictions that comprise the UK, it is to be borne in mind that each State in the US is a separate jurisdiction for these purposes.
2 Civ 96-2582 977 F Supp 327 (DNJ, 1997).
3 *Jami R Vitullo v Velocity Powerboats Inc* No 97 C8745 1998 US Dist LEXIS 7120 (ND Ill, 1998).
4 *Northern Light Technology Inc v Northern Lights Club* 97F Supp 2d 96 (D Mass, 2000).
5 *Euromarket Designs Inc v Crate & Barrel Ltd* No 99 C6926 (ED Ill, 2000).
6 *American Eyewear Inc v Peeper's Sunglasses and Accessories* 106 F Supp 2d 895 (ND Tex, 2000).
7 *S Morantz Inc v Hang & Shine Ultrasonics Ltd* 79 F Supp 2d 537 (ED Pa, 1999).
8 *Mink v AAAA Dev LLC* 190 F 3d 333 (5th Cir, 1999).
9 *Ty Inc v Clark* No 99 C5532 (ND Ill, 2000).
10 *Westcode v RBE Electronics* 2000 US Dist LEXIS 815 (ED Pa, 2000).
11 *Nutrition Physiology Corpn v Enviros Ltd* 87 F Supp 2d 648 (ND Tex, 2000).

7.32 The real problem with liability in tort, as opposed to contract, is that traders cannot control where a party who alleges that a tort has been committed against it commences proceedings. Particular care must therefore be taken not to publish defamatory statements or to give or use information that infringes intellectual property rights (see Chapters 3, E-liability and 4, E-rights, respectively), since these activities tend to have the widest reach and can, potentially, expose website operators to litigation right across the globe.

If the law is applied so as to permit actions to be brought wherever a website is accessed, it could lead to trade mark or copyright infringement actions being brought anywhere in the world, including in jurisdictions where the intellectual property right has never been asserted or registered and so does not, in any other recognisable sense, exist. This would be an unfortunate outcome as it would lead to conflicts where rights to a mark or copyright had been divided and to the position where no one could use the mark or work without the agreement of all of the owners of the right.

Jurisdiction might be limited by treating publication as occurring only at the location of the server carrying a website, on the basis that a website has to be accessed to be viewed. This is technically the better solution and analogous to accessing a hard copy at the moment of physical delivery.

Both of these approaches are problematic, however. If there is deemed publication worldwide, rights enforceable in one country might be enforceable worldwide. By contrast, restricting the bringing of legal actions to the courts of the place where the server carrying the website is located could encourage unscrupulous website owners to set up their site in some far-flung jurisdiction, in order to evade proceedings against them.

The publication issue has been considered by the Court of Appeal in England. The case involved publication of pornography in violation of the Obscene Publications Act 1964, although the websites in question were located in the United States. The defendant had argued that, in so far as jurisdiction was concerned, although there was publication of a website in the US, there was no publication in England. The Court of Appeal considered that publication could take place when the data was uploaded on to a website abroad and then, again, when it was downloaded elsewhere[1].

The publication issue has also been considered in an Australian case. In *Joseph Gutnick v Dow Jones & Co Inc*[2], the defendants were the publishers of Barrons Magazine, a US publication that appeared both in print and in the form of an on-line subscription service. The plaintiff brought an action in respect of an alleged defamation contained in an article published on the defendants' Internet subscription website, which was available to subscribers in Australia. The plaintiff argued that since people in Victoria could access the article, thereby defaming him where he is best known, the case should be heard in that state. The defendants applied to the Victorian court, seeking a declaration that the appropriate forum for the plaintiff to bring an action was in the US. They argued that the article was written by an American for an American audience and, accordingly, should be heard in the US. The first question that the court sought to address was the jurisdiction in which the alleged defamation was published. The court considered various options, including the place of uploading, the place where damage was suffered, the country in which substantially the circumstances giving rise to the claim occurred, and the place of downloading. Hedigan J held that the place of publication of a defamation is the place of perception of the defamation, the key element being that the material is available to a party other than the plaintiff in a manner which is clearly understandable. The court concluded, therefore, that the publication for the purposes of defamation occurred at the point of downloading and Victorian courts had jurisdiction to try the case. The defendants' application to stay the plaintiff's action on forum non conveniens grounds failed. The defendants are appealing the decision.

Another solution in defamation cases is to allow the claimant to sue anywhere, but to limit his relief to that which is appropriate to the jurisdiction in which he is suing, rather than his worldwide loss[3]. The flaw in this approach is that, while it ensures damages awards are limited, if an injunction is sought it cannot be effective if its application is limited to a single jurisdiction.

1   *R v Waddon* (6 April 2000, unreported), CA (on appeal from a decision of HHJ Hardy on 30 June 1999).
2   Case Number 7763 of 2000, [2001] VSC 305, Hedigan J.
3   Case C–68/93 *Shevill v Presse Alliance SA* [1995] ECR I-415, ECJ. This approach was not followed in *Marinari v Lloyds Bank plc: C-364/93* [1996] QB 217, where the ECJ held that article 5(3) of the Brussels Convention could not be construed so widely as to cover every place where the consequences of an event which had already caused damage elsewhere could be felt.

(iii) *Operation of a branch or agency*

7.33   Where the defendant is domiciled in a Member State, but the dispute arises out of the operations of a branch, agency or other establishment of the defendant in another Member State, the claim may be brought in that other Member State (article 5(5) of the Brussels Regulation).

This exception throws up the possibility of a company based in one Member State, but with a subsidiary in another and the server through which its server is operated in yet another state, being exposed to the jurisdiction of the courts in all three states.

(iv) Multiple defendants

7.34   Where a dispute involves more than one defendant, each of the defendants domiciled in any Member State may be sued in the country of domicile of any one of the others, provided that the claims are so closely connected that it is expedient to hear and determine them together to avoid the risk of irreconcilable judgments resulting from separate proceedings (article 6(1) of the Brussels Regulation). The proviso has been added by the Regulation to reflect case law of the ECJ under the Brussels Convention.

(v) Consumer disputes

7.35   If article 15 of the Brussels Regulation applies, article 16 provides that:

■   A consumer may bring proceedings either in the Member State where the other party is domiciled or in the courts of the place where the consumer is domiciled (not the Member State where he is domiciled): article 16(1). This departure from the rule applies only to international jurisdiction and not to jurisdiction within a Member State and is warranted by the concern to enable the consumer to sue the other party as close as possible to his home.

■   Proceedings may be brought against a consumer by the other party to a dispute only in the courts of the Member State in which the consumer is domiciled (article 16(2)).

Article 15 sets out the circumstances in which article 16 will apply, as follows:

■   a contract for the sale of goods on instalment credit terms or a contract for a loan repayable by instalments, or for any other form of credit, made to finance the sale of goods, provided in either case that the consumer has concluded the contract for a purpose outside his trade or profession (article 15(1)(a) and (b));

■   contracts which have been concluded with a person who pursues commercial or professional activities in the Member State of the consumer's domicile or, by any means, directs such activities to the Member State or to several states including that Member State, and the contract falls within the scope of such activities, provided that the consumer has concluded the contract for a purpose outside his trade or profession (article 15(1)(c));

■   contract entered into by a consumer with a party who is not domiciled in the Member State but has a branch, agency or other establishment in one of the Member States (article 15(2)).

Article 15 seeks to protect consumers as the weaker parties to a contract. The contracts traditionally covered by this article (sale of goods on instalment credit terms and contracts for loans repayable by instalments and other similar credit arrangements to finance the sale of goods) automatically entitle the consumer to sue in the courts of his domicile. In this respect, there is no change to the content of article 13 of the Brussels Convention.

The criteria given in article 13(3) of the Brussels Convention have, however, been reframed to take account of developments in marketing techniques. The condition in the old article 13 that the consumer must have taken the necessary steps in his state has been removed. This means that article 15(1)(c) of the Regulation applies to contracts concluded in a state other than the consumer's domicile. This removes a deficiency in old article 13, namely that the consumer could not rely on his protective jurisdiction when he had been induced, at the other party's instigation, to leave his home state to conclude the contract.

The concept of activities pursued in or directed towards a Member State has not been defined in the Regulation, and it will be up to the courts to define the ambit of those terms. The intention, according to the Commission's Explanatory Memorandum, is to make clear that article 15(1)(c) applies to consumer contracts concluded via an interactive website accessible in the state of the consumer's domicile. The fact that a consumer simply had knowledge of the service or possibility of buying goods by passive website access in his country or domicile may not trigger the protective jurisdiction.

7.36 The distinction between 'interactive' sites, which facilitate the making of a contract, and 'passive' sites, which simply provide information, is an easy one to make, but may not provide the consumer with the protection intended. For example, a website may be targeted at consumers in a particular country, but may require the contract to be made by fax or post. In that case, the necessary link is made by directing activities towards the consumer's state. The test of 'direction' is therefore a better one and aims to distinguish between suppliers who actively seek out and direct their activities to foreign consumers and those who are sought out by foreign consumers, although that particular distinction may raise practical difficulties. Some sites can easily be identified as 'directed' at a foreign state, for example by the nature of services provided. Other sites are clearly purely local. Between those extremes, however, the distinction may be unclear. The factors which might be relevant are the address of the site (for example, the '.co.uk' extension might suggest that the UK is the target of the site), its language and the currency used on the site, although the Council of Members and the European Commission has suggested in negotiations relating to the Brussels Regulation that the language and currency of a site are not relevant factors and whether the site actually solicits conclusion of foreign contracts will be the determining factor. Whether courts take this view is to be seen.

Guidance on the meaning of 'directing' activities may come from various sources:

■ US cases provide an insight. In *Zippo Manufacturing Co v Zippo.Com Inc*[1], a plaintiff in Pennsylvania sued a defendant in California for trademark infringement in the US District Court for the Western District of Pennsylvania. The defendant argued that there was a lack of jurisdiction. The court identified three types of web activity: substantial business through the Internet (type 1 activity); interactive sites (type 2 activity); and purely passive advertisement sites (type 3 activity). The court considered that jurisdiction is warranted for type 1 activity, unwarranted for type 3 activity and uncertain for type 2 activity. The court concluded that the defendant's connections to Pennsylvania were type 1 as it had entered into several contracts with Internet access service providers to furnish its services to their customers in Pennsylvania. However, as illustrated by the range of US cases referred to above in the context of tort, US courts have been prepared to find jurisdiction over a defendant even in cases where it seems clear that there has been no active targeting or directing on the defendant's part.

■ The regulatory sphere may also provide a guide. Promotions of financial products over the Internet from other countries may be caught by the UK regulatory regime (for example, section 397 of the Financial Services and Markets Act 2000) if the invitations or inducements were 'directed' at persons in the UK. Financial Services Authority Guidance[2] outlines the factors that the regulator will take into account when determining whether there has been 'direction':

– whether the website is located in the UK;

– the extent to which the underlying goods or services are available to UK investors who respond to any advertisement on the website;

– the extent to which any advertisement on the website is directed to people in the UK (including the nature of warnings and disclaimers, the nature and the content of the website in general and whether the website has been advertised in a UK publication);

– the extent to which positive steps have been taken to ensure that UK persons do not obtain goods or services as a result of an advertisement issued over the web; and

– the extent to which positive steps have been taken to limit access to the website.

- The draft Hague Convention (discussed further below at paragraph 7.45) also provides further guidance. It states that a consumer may bring a claim in the courts of the state in which he is resident if the claim relates to a contract which arises out of activities which the other party 'directed' to that State (draft article 7.2). Activity is not 'directed' to a state if the non-consumer demonstrates that it took reasonable steps to avoid concluding contracts with consumers resident in that state (draft article 7.3).

1   952 F Supp 1119 (WD Pa, 1996).
2   FSA, 'Treatment of material on overseas Internet world-wide websites accessible in the UK but not intended for investors in the UK', Guidance 2/98.

7.37   If the broad approach of the courts in some of the US States is taken, which would be consistent with the aim of providing the consumer with protection, companies may face the possibility of litigation in the 15 Member States. The European Commission has noted that the wording of article 15 of the Brussels Regulation has given rise to anxieties amongst the e-commerce industry, relating primarily to the fact that companies engaging in e-commerce will have to contend with potential litigation in every Member State, or will have to specify that their products or services are not intended for consumers domiciled in certain Member States. The latter will undermine the EU Single Market and the growth of e-commerce.

In this context, article 7 may provide some comfort, in that the consumer provisions in the Regulation may be departed from by an agreement:

- which is entered into after the dispute has arisen;

- which allows the consumer to bring proceedings in courts other than those indicated in the consumer provisions in the Regulation; or

- which is entered into by the consumer and other party to the contract, both of whom are at the time of conclusion of the contract domiciled or habitually resident in the same Member State, and which confers jurisdiction on the courts of that Member State, provided that such an agreement is not contrary to the law of that Member State.

The Commission will report on the application of article 15 within five years, at which time the concerns of the e-commerce community can be properly evaluated.

(vi) Exclusive jurisdiction for some matters

7.38   Whether or not the defendant is domiciled in a Member State, the courts of a particular Member State have exclusive jurisdiction over some disputes because the subject matter of the dispute is closely connected with that Member State (for example, a dispute concerning real property situated in that Member State: Brussels Regulation, art 22).

Where an intellectual property right is registered, article 22(4) also provides that the courts of the place of registration have exclusive jurisdiction over the validity of that registration (article 22(4)). The English courts have held, in patent cases, that invalidity is so bound up with infringement that an English court cannot hear an action for infringement of a foreign patent[1]. The effect of this ruling is that an application for a declaration of non-infringement of a non-UK right also cannot be heard in England, but must be heard where the patent is registered[2]. The Dutch courts, when faced with the same problem, arrived at a different solution. They said that jurisdiction could be asserted where the defendant is the hub of the infringement for all Member States. If, however, the defendant was not at the centre of the hub, the Dutch courts would assert jurisdiction only over a Dutch defendant.

Where an intellectual property right is not registered, such as copyright, the ordinary rules as to jurisdiction apply. Thus, the claimant may sue in the place of domicile of the defendant or where the harmful act occurred. An English claimant can therefore opt to sue an English domiciled defendant for infringement of Dutch copyright in England, or in The Netherlands by reason of article 5(3)[3]. Because of the multiple defendants rule, under article 6(1), the claimant may sue in England or in The Netherlands even where there are Dutch defendants as well as an English defendant.

1   *Coin Controls Ltd v Suzo International (UK) Ltd* [1997] 3 All ER 45; *Boston Scientific v Cordis Corpn* (1997) IPD 20 (10), CA.
2   *Plastus Kreativ AB v Minnesota Mining and Manufacturing Co* [1995] RPC 438.
3   *Pearce v Ove Arup Partnership Ltd* [1999] 1 All ER 769, CA.

(vii) Jurisdiction agreement

7.39   Where the disputants have agreed that the courts of a particular Member State will have jurisdiction under article 23 of the Brussels Regulation, the courts of any other Member State will invariably honour that agreement, provided that the agreement is in writing and signed by all parties. The Regulation now defines 'writing' to include any communication by electronic means which provides a record of the agreement (article 23(2)).

The rules are slightly different depending on whether one or more of the parties is domiciled in a Member State. Where this is so, article 23 confers exclusive jurisdiction on the court of the Member State nominated. Where none of the parties is domiciled in a Member State, the nominated court has the option to decline jurisdiction based on national law principles. Where jurisdiction is declined, the courts of any other Member State may then assume jurisdiction, based on their own respective national laws.

An English court has confirmed that where a contract incorporates a clause giving the court of a Member State non-exclusive jurisdiction, that court retains a discretion to decline jurisdiction on the basis that it is more appropriate for another court to determine the dispute[1].

Where the parties agree that the courts of a non-Member State shall have jurisdiction, article 23 does not apply. In this situation, national jurisdiction rules will be applied to determine whether the court before whom the dispute has been brought has jurisdiction. Where a dispute is brought before an English court and the parties have agreed, say, that the courts of the US State of Washington will have jurisdiction but the defendant is based in England, the latter's domicile in a Member State may mean that the English court accepts jurisdiction and refuses to stay the proceedings so that a claim can be brought in Washington.

1   *Mercury Communications Ltd v Communication Telesystems International* [1999] 2 All ER (Comm) 33.

(viii)   Submission to the jurisdiction

7.40   Where the defendant submits to the jurisdiction of a particular court, that court will accept jurisdiction unless, under article 22 of the Brussels Regulation, another court has exclusive jurisdiction (article 24).

(ix) Agreements to arbitrate

7.41   An agreement to arbitrate under English law is enforceable as under contract law. Where an arbitration clause is appropriately worded, it will therefore be upheld by a court and the dispute will be referred to arbitration. This respect for arbitration agreements is enshrined in section 9 of the AA 1996, which requires the court to stay proceedings before it, unless the arbitration clause is void or does not cover the subject matter or scope of the dispute. This requirement applies whether the seat of the arbitration is England or anywhere else and also where the seat has not been chosen by the parties. The national courts of the Member States and of the other countries that have implemented the New York Convention will also, invariably, uphold arbitration agreements and refuse to accept jurisdiction.

The Brussels Regulation does not apply to arbitrations. As a result, one might expect that none of the rules in the Regulation as to jurisdiction, choice of law and enforcement can have any application to arbitrations. In fact, however, the English courts have power to make interim orders, such as injunctions, under section 44 of the AA 1996, notwithstanding the existence of a valid arbitration clause. The powers apply, however, only where the arbitral body itself would not have power or is, for some reason, unable to take equivalent action. In addition, courts of Member States may order interim relief under article 31 of the Regulation, in support of an arbitration[1]. This means that, even where an arbitration clause validly and effectively excludes the jurisdiction of the court to determine the substantive dispute, either party may still apply to the appropriate court for an injunction or other interim measure.

It is not clear whether the right to seek interim relief under the Regulation can itself be excluded, by careful wording to this effect, in the arbitration clause. The right under section 44 can be excluded, provided the exclusion is worded carefully. This point has been considered by the English courts, which ruled that words giving exclusive jurisdiction to the arbitrator were not sufficiently specific and unambiguous to preclude applications for ancillary relief under section 44 (in this case, a Mareva (asset freezing) injunction)[2]. Had the parties included wording to the effect that 'neither party shall bring any action or other legal proceedings in relation to this dispute', however, the court indicated that these words would have been sufficient to exclude applications for interim relief. It is doubtful that the right to apply for relief under article 31 of the Regulation can, with appropriate wording, be excluded in the same way.

The other potential difficulty with arbitration is that, notwithstanding that an arbitration clause is drafted in terms that effectively exclude the court's jurisdiction, a court may decide to strike down the clause on public policy or some other ground, for example for unconscionability. Clearly, the risk of a clause being struck down on such grounds is likely to arise only in the context of dealings with consumers, rather than with other on-line sellers. It does, however, highlight the need to consider carefully whether and, if so, where the parties to a contract containing an arbitration clause are likely to launch any challenge to its validity and the attitude of the courts in that place.

1 Case C-391/95 *Van Uden Maritime BV v Kommanditgesellschaft in Firma Deco-Line* [1999] QB 1225, in relation to the equivalent article in the Brussels Convention.
2 *Re Q's Estate* [1999] 1 Lloyd's Rep 931.

(x) Protective measures

7.42 As we have already seen in the context of arbitration clauses, article 31 of the Brussels Regulation supplements the rules on the jurisdiction of a particular court to hear and determine the substantive issues. Article 31 allows disputants to apply to a court other than the court that has jurisdiction over the matter, for interim relief. Interim relief includes preservation and detention orders, freezing injunctions and searching orders and any other form of temporary relief necessary to maintain the status quo so as to safeguard rights in relation to the substantive proceedings, whether those proceedings are already on foot or imminent. The Regulation does not specify the type of interim measures available and this is a matter for the practice and procedure of the court to which the application is made. As a result, article 31 can give rise to forum shopping as parties select a jurisdiction, according to which court is likely to order the relief most likely to protect their position. These measures are available even where the defendant is not domiciled in a Member State.

Thus, for example, a supplier based in the UK seeking to recover payment from a business based in the US, but with a UK branch and assets in France, might choose to sue the defendant in the UK. The supplier may, however, also apply to the court in France for an injunction preventing any transfer of the defendant's assets out of the jurisdiction, or to stop payment of rapidly depleting funds being made to a third party.

Article 31 is wide enough to allow applications to be made for relief against a third party and not simply against the defendant to proceedings. For instance, an on-line banking instruction to a bank from its customer to make payment out of his account to a supplier might be followed by a failure by the supplier to supply the goods for which payment has been made. While the customer is likely to bring proceedings against the supplier for breach of contract, he might also apply under article 31 for an interim order against the supplier's bank, so as to freeze the payment in the payee's account pending determination of the claim for breach.

(e) Jurisdiction at common law

7.43 Outside of the Brussels Regulation, physical presence of the defendant in England and Wales is sufficient to give jurisdiction over the dispute to the English courts. The courts will not, however, automatically hear the dispute and may stay the proceedings where there is a more appropriate forum in another country (forum non conveniens), where the parties have agreed that another court will have jurisdiction or where the dispute relates to land overseas.

It is for the defendant to raise the question of appropriateness of the forum. He must then convince the court that another court is more appropriate to hear the dispute in order for an English court to decline jurisdiction. The court will take into account such factors as the governing law of the contract (if any), or the place where a tort has been committed, in deciding whether the action should be decided elsewhere. If the defendant persuades the court that there is a more appropriate forum elsewhere, the claimant can still keep the case in the English court if he can show that justice would be best served if the claim were determined by the English and not a foreign court. This somewhat nebulous test allows the court to take a pragmatic approach and consider whether, for instance, the case is likely to be handled more efficiently or more speedily in England or elsewhere. For instance, where the governing law of the contract is not English law, an English court may be keen to decline jurisdiction because another court is a more appropriate forum.

The English court has declined jurisdiction in defamation cases where there has been minor damage within the jurisdiction but the real damage has been suffered outside the jurisdiction. The court has also taken into account the anticipated difficulties in proving the foreign law that would be applicable to the dispute, if heard in England[1].

Where the defendant is abroad but the claimant wishes to sue the defendant in an English court, the claimant must first obtain leave from the court to serve the claim outside the jurisdiction. The court will apply the same forum conveniens test in deciding whether to give leave, as well as requiring the claimant to satisfy it that:

- it has a good arguable case on the merits; and

- the claim concerns or involves the following:

    - an injunction ordering the defendant to do or not to do anything within the jurisdiction;

    - a claim to enforce, rescind, dissolve, annul or otherwise affect a contract, to recover damages or to obtain other relief in respect of a breach of contract:

        • made within the jurisdiction;

        • made by an agent in the jurisdiction;

        • governed by English law; or

        • containing a clause giving jurisdiction to the English court; or

    - a tort where the damage was sustained in, or resulted from, an act committed within the jurisdiction.

1 See *University of Glasgow v Economist Ltd* (1990) Times, 13 July; *Chadha v Dow Jones* (1999) Times, 18 May, CA; *Berezovsky v Michaels* [2000] 2 All ER 986, HL.

7.44 It is important to note that the test for jurisdiction in relation to contractual claims differs from the test under the Brussels Regulation, in that it is *where the contract is made* that is crucial, rather than where it is to be performed.

In the case of torts committed by a trader based in a non-Member State, the test is, once again, different. A claimant will be able to sue in England where it can show that damage was sustained in England or resulted from an act committed there. However, identifying where the damaging act or its consequences took place is not going to be easy where the effects of, say, a negligent misstatement or defamatory message are manifold. Where, for instance, shares are bought on-line in reliance upon information about the company that is posted on a broker's website and which proves misleading, the place where the damaging act took place is probably cyberspace. The subscriber for the shares, meanwhile, may have logged on while travelling from his usual place of business to a client (maybe whilst on an aeroplane) and so there may be no natural starting point for an assessment of where the damage occurred.

Situations like this demonstrate, yet again, the importance of including, as an express term of any on-line trading agreement, a contractual jurisdiction clause that has regard both to the convenience to each party of having their disputes heard by a particular forum(s) and the ease with which any judgment may be enforced. Even where information is being supplied, it is perfectly possible to make access to that information subject to a contractual arrangement that provides for jurisdiction and choice of law, in the event of a dispute as to its accuracy. Saying this, there will, of course, be situations where it is not open to the parties to regulate their relationship by means of a contract and if the only grounds for a claim lie in tort, they will not have been able to choose which court shall have jurisdiction. This does not, however, preclude them from reaching agreement on jurisdiction once a dispute has arisen. An agreement at this late stage may well be a prudent alternative to expensive litigation over jurisdiction issues.

(f) International Convention on Jurisdiction

7.45 An International Convention on Jurisdiction and Foreign Judgments in Civil and Commercial Matters (also referred to as the Hague Convention), which is currently in draft, aims to create an international agreement on which courts should have jurisdiction in civil and commercial matters. Discussions on this issue commenced in 1993. The current draft allows companies to agree by contract which courts will have jurisdiction, but consumers will have the right to take action in their own courts. The US has opposed the Convention on the basis that it will limit the development of e-commerce as the Convention has the effect of opening up e-business to potential liabilities all over the world. A major issue still to be resolved in drafting this Convention is whether it should include special rules in relation to the jurisdiction of courts in disputes arising from communications taking place over the Internet. The paragraphs above on consumer contracts (paragraphs 7.35–7.36) and claims in tort (paragraph 7.30) provide an overview of some of the relevant provisions in the draft.

(g) Alternative dispute resolution

7.46 Despite considerable debate of this issue, the Brussels Regulation does not expressly require parties to make use of ADR mechanisms. The rationale is that the European Commission is promoting ADR, both generally and in the context of e-commerce, in various ways, which will be discussed further in section 7 below.

(h) The E-Commerce Directive

7.47 It has been suggested that the Brussels Regulation conflicts with the E-Commerce Directive[1]. Article 3 of the E-Commerce Directive requires e-businesses to comply with the rules of the Member States in which they are established (the principle of 'country of origin'). This appears to conflict with the Brussels Regulation, which allows consumers to bring proceedings against e-traders in their home state ('the country of destination' principle). However, the Directive only provides a framework for Member States to regulate their ISPs, whereas the Regulation provides rules for private international law. It is for this reason that the Directive expressly provides that it does not deal with the jurisdiction of courts. The *Yahoo! Inc* case provides an illustration. The Tribunal de Grande Instance de Paris considered the case[2]. Yahoo! Inc, which is based in California, was sued in France, alongside Yahoo France, by the International League against Racism and Anti-Semitism (LICRA) and the Union of French Jewish Students (UEJF). The Yahoo.com auction site proposed for sale Nazi objects, and it also hosted on its 'Geocities' service various anti-Semitic pages. Under French law, it is a criminal offence to exhibit signs or uniforms adopted by the Nazis, and spreading racist ideas, which may include selling objects with racist overtones, is illegal. The French judge ordered Yahoo! Inc to make it impossible for consumers based in France to access the auctions or any other sites which are promoting Nazi ideas. Yahoo! Inc claimed that the case was not within the jurisdiction of the French court because the illegal facts were not committed in France but in the United States, and in the US the Constitution protects freedom of speech. The court rejected this argument on the ground that users can access Yahoo.com from France. Yahoo! Inc claimed that it was technically impossible to monitor access. Initially the court rejected this argument, on the basis that Yahoo! Inc could identify the geographical origin of the recipient of its services through their Internet protocol address. This issue was reconsidered by the French court when Yahoo! Inc claimed that it could not comply with the court's order. The French Tribunal considered that it would make a final decision on this particular point after hearing a report from a panel of experts. Ultimately, on the basis of the experts' report, the Tribunal ordered Yahoo! Inc to perform the previous order[3]. The *Yahoo! Inc* case shows that, even if content on sites may be legal in the country in which the site is established ('country of origin' principle), there is a risk that the content could infringe the laws in other countries. The issue of enforcement of the French court's order is considered further below.

1   Directive (EC) 31/2000.
2   *UEJF and LICRA v Yahoo! Inc and Yahoo France* 22 May 2000, available at www.juriscom.net/txt/jurisfr/cti/yauctions20000522.htm.
3   The further considerations by the French Tribunal were on 11 August 2000 and on 20 November 2000 (available on the same site referred to in footnote 2 above).

(i) The future

7.48 Although there has been considerable debate as to how the Brussels Regulation will transform the rules on jurisdiction, it may have little impact if, as the *Yahoo! Inc* case shows, EU courts are prepared to seize jurisdiction in the case of disputes relating to foreign on-line traders without the assistance of the Brussels Regulation.

4. APPLICABLE LAW

7.49 We will restrict the scope of this section to basic observations governing the applicable law in relation to contract and tort. Further issues may affect the choice of law in litigation where, for example, the concern is with title to land or to moveable goods, or to choses in action such as shares in a corporation, which are beyond the scope of this book.

(a) Contract[1]

7.50 The applicable or 'proper' law of a contract governs the validity, interpretation, performance, termination and consequences of breach of that contract. Under English conflict of law rules, parties to a contract are free to choose the law that will govern their rights and obligations under the contract. A choice of English law as the applicable law of the contract is separate from a choice as to jurisdiction and does not automatically mean that an English court will have jurisdiction to hear the dispute.

As with jurisdiction, there are two sets of laws that apply to choice of law. The first is the English common law and the second is the Rome Convention, the terms of which were finalised in 1980 and subsequently ratified by Belgium, Denmark, France, Germany, Italy and Luxembourg. The provisions of the Rome Convention were implemented into English law by the Contracts (Applicable Law) Act 1990, with effect from (and applicable to contracts entered into on or after) 1 April 1991. The common law rules still apply where the Convention has no application.

The Rome Convention applies, with some exceptions, to contractual obligations in any situation involving a choice between the laws of different countries[2]. This embraces more or less any foreign element, including one or more parties being domiciled abroad, the contract having been made abroad or the performance of one or more obligations abroad. The Convention applies irrespective of whether the parties have chosen a governing law for their contract or omitted to do so.

Where a governing law clause appears in the contract, the Convention makes clear that the contract will be governed by the law chosen by the parties. In practice suppliers favour the application of their own national laws for all contracts conducted on their website. A supplier should incorporate on his website an explicit clause of the applicable laws. If the other contracting party accepts this clause, it will govern the contractual obligations of the parties based on the principle of party autonomy. The clause can be on a mandatory page and also in the general terms.

This choice is, however, subject to the overriding effect of any 'mandatory' rules of the country whose law has been chosen or with which the contract is closely connected. The expression 'mandatory rules' is not defined in the Rome Convention, but is treated in the UK as referring to any laws which are expressed to be overriding, notwithstanding the choice of foreign law. This includes many laws introduced to protect consumers, for example provisions relating to exclusion clauses set out in the Unfair Contract Terms Act 1977. In accordance with the Rome Convention, specific rules are applicable to certain consumer contracts, in particular contracts for the supply of goods or services to a consumer. Although parties to these consumer contracts can choose the applicable law, this choice cannot deprive the consumer of protection afforded him by mandatory rules of the law of the country in which he has habitual residence. Mandatory rules, therefore, cannot be limited or excluded by contract.

1 For a parallel discussion and illustrations from case law, see Chapter 2, E-contract.
2 The Convention does not apply to contractual obligations arising under negotiable instruments (such as cheques and bills of exchange), or to arbitration agreements, questions governed by the law of companies or their winding up, the capacity of agents, EC-based insurance contracts, the constitution of trusts or evidence and procedure.

7.51 In the absence of an express choice by the parties of the applicable law, the contract is governed by the law of the country with which it is most 'closely connected'. 'Closest connection' is established by reference to the country where the party who is to effect the performance that is 'characteristic' of the contract has, at the time of making the contract, its habitual residence or, in the case of a company, its central administration. Where the contract is entered into in the course of a trade or profession, the relevant country will be that where the performer's principal place of business is situated. If, under the contract, performance is to be effected through another place of business, such as a branch office, the country where that branch is situated is the determining location. A B2B on-line contract is most closely connected with the country of the establishment of the provider of the product or service. Under the E-Commerce Directive, the place at which an e-business is established is determined in accordance with the case law of the Court of Justice. It recognises that a place of establishment of a company providing services via an Internet website is not necessarily the place at which the technology supporting its website is located or where its website is accessible. Usually, the place of establishment is the place where the business is legally registered. In the case of multiple establishments, the competent Member State will be the one in which the supplier has the centre of its activities.

If 'characteristic performance' cannot be identified, this method of establishing the 'closest connection' is to be disregarded and closest connection is identified by reference to other factors. In a simple contract for the supply of goods or services, the 'characteristic performance' will be the supply of those goods or services, such that the law of the country where the seller's business is located will be the applicable law. In a complex agreement where both parties assume a number of obligations, it will be impossible to identify the characteristic performance and so this test will not apply. In that situation, it is for the court that has jurisdiction over the dispute (or, where jurisdiction has yet to be determined, the court before whom the dispute is brought) to assess with which country the contract is most closely connected.

In the case of consumers, in the absence of a choice of law under a contract, the governing law is that of the country in which the consumer normally lives. Accordingly, in the absence of a choice of law under contract, suppliers are potentially subject to the national laws of 15 different EU Member States when they transact with consumers.

Because of the uncertainty caused by these rules, it makes considerable sense for on-line sellers to specify which law will govern their contracts. As we have indicated above, however, freedom of contract does not permit parties to exclude the effect of 'mandatory rules' favouring the consumer or to exclude rules which are otherwise considered desirable[1].

As well as determining the rights and obligations of the parties under the contract, the applicable law governs issues of validity, including whether a contract has actually been formed, whether it is unenforceable for failure of consideration, whether it is void on the grounds of illegality or mistake and whether it is voidable for duress, misrepresentation or undue influence.

1   For instance, the Hague-Visby Rules on the carriage of goods by sea.

7.52   The E-Commerce Directive also establishes rules relating to the validity of electronic contracts. The Directive requires Member States to ensure that their legal system allows contracts to be concluded by electronic means, except in the case of (article 9):

■   contracts that create or transfer rights in real estate (except rental);

■   contracts governed by family or succession law;

■   contracts requiring the involvement of courts or public authorities; or

■   contracts requiring surety and collateral securities supplied by persons acting for non-professional reasons.

Article 10 of the Directive requires Member States to ensure that, except when otherwise agreed by parties who are not consumers, at least the following information is given by the service provider prior to an order being placed by the recipient of the service:

■   the technical steps to follow to conclude the contract;

■   whether or not the concluded contract will be accessible;

■   the technical means for identifying and correcting input errors prior to the placing of the order;

■   the languages offered for the conclusion of the contract;

- any relevant codes of conduct to which the service provider subscribes; and

- contract terms and general conditions, which must be available in a way that allows the recipient to store and reproduce them.

In the case of disputes submitted to arbitration but where there is no choice of law clause, the presumption is that the applicable law is the law of the seat of the arbitration. This means that if the seat of the arbitration is England, English law is likely to be applied by the arbitrators, although this is subject to anything in the rules of the particular arbitral body giving power to the arbitrator(s) to assess which law should apply. In the case of such a provision, the arbitrator(s) will, in practice, apply the law that has the closest connection to the dispute.

(b) Tort

7.53 In May 1996, the English common law rules on the proper law of torts were replaced by the Private International Law (Miscellaneous Provisions) Act 1995. This Act substituted for the existing rules a new rule that the law of the place of the wrong is the applicable law, save where the law of another place is more appropriate. Prior to May 1996, English law recognised the 'double actionability' rule, by which an act done in a foreign country was actionable as a tort in England only if it was actionable as a tort under both English law and the law of the foreign country where it was committed. This rule severely restricted the opportunities for claimants to recover damages in tort in England and, after years of criticism, was revoked in respect of most torts by the new Act.

The new test focuses on the place or places where the events constituting the tort occur. Where there are several events occurring in different countries, the applicable law is the law of the country in which the most significant element or elements of those events occurred. However, the general rule is displaced if it appears that there are significant factors connecting the tort with another country. In the case of a negligent misstatement, the place where the significant element of the tort occurred is likely to be the place where the statement was acted upon, rather than where it was made.

This important change in the law is likely to lead to an increasing number of disputes being heard by the English courts where the law that is being applied is a foreign law. This practice is one with which the courts are familiar, but which they are nevertheless happy to avoid, where they have a discretion, by declining jurisdiction on the grounds of forum non conveniens.

The double actionability rule will, however, continue to apply to defamation actions.

A proposal for a new Rome Convention addressing non-contractual obligations is under preparation in the Commission (called Rome II). It is being proposed that in a dispute involving non-contractual obligations, the applicable law would be the country where the 'harm' occurred. E-businesses fear that the consequences of Rome II will be that they will be subjected to local laws in tort claims even if they did not intend to direct activities to foreign States – much the same as the concerns expressed by e-businesses in relation to the Brussels Regulation.

5. CLAIMS IN THE ENGLISH COURTS

(a) Proportionality under the Civil Procedure Rules

7.54 Since 26 April 1999, the court's approach to disputes with an international element has been modified by the Civil Procedure Rules, which introduced new practices and procedures for litigation in England and Wales. The new rules encourage speedier resolution of disputes and promote far greater control and management of disputes by judges. The conduct and actions of parties pre-litigation is also now subject to the court's scrutiny and to enhanced powers to impose costs sanctions. In consequence, parties must seriously consider whether it is appropriate to launch proceedings or to negotiate, in a way that was never previously contemplated.

A keystone of the CPR is the overriding requirement of proportionality, which involves the court in a continuous reassessment, throughout the conduct of a dispute, of whether the costs and timescales involved are proportionate to the complexity of the dispute and to the amount being claimed[1]. This principle may well affect the court's thinking when it comes to consider whether it should accept or decline jurisdiction. The requirement will not affect the mandatory application of jurisdiction provisions, but is likely to influence the exercise of the court's discretion to decline jurisdiction on the grounds of forum non conveniens, or to allow service of a claim out of the jurisdiction. The English court in this context has already refused to allow a malicious falsehood claim involving a server situated in the US and a footnote to a Securities and Exchange Commission filing to be heard in England. The claimant could neither prove that anyone had read the footnote, nor that, if they had read it, the damages suffered would be anything more than minimal. The court decided that the cost of allowing the claimant to proceed in the English courts would have been disproportionate to the resultant damages and so declined jurisdiction[2].

1 On the issue of proportionality, consider *Biguzzi v Rank Leisure plc* [1999] 1 WLR 1926, CA; *Wright v Manchester City Council* [2000] CLY 424; and *Grundy v Naqvi* [2001] EWCA Civ 139, [2001] All ER (D) 08 (Feb).
2 *Seer Technologies Ltd v Abbas* [2000] 07 LS Gaz R 40, Jacob J. Permission to appeal the decision was set aside on the grounds of delay: Court of Appeal, 2000 WL1480116.

(b) Proceedings in the English courts

7.55 Under the CPR, claims are allocated to one of three tracks according to their value and the complexity of the issues in dispute. The Small Claims Track is for claims under £5,000, while the Fast Track is for claims up to £15,000. Claims above this amount and non-monetary claims (for instance, for an injunction) are assigned Multi-track status. The Small Claims and Fast Tracks are essentially scaled down versions of the Multi-track, reflecting the objective that the costs of conducting and determining claims should not become disproportionate to the amount in dispute. In the case of each track, a claim is brought by the issue and service of a claim form.

The court by which the claim form has been issued decides to which track the dispute should be allocated. Once it has done this, it will fix a timetable for trial and arrange a case management conference. The purpose of this conference is to establish how the case should be prepared for trial; the court will discuss with the parties the extent to which documentary evidence is likely to be relevant and, if so, how and when documents should be disclosed, as well as whether any of the issues in dispute can be narrowed. It will also involve discussion as to the nature, extent and exchange of any witness and expert evidence on which the parties wish to rely.

In England, costs usually 'follow the event', which means that the winning party can require the other to pay a proportion of its legal costs. In the case of Small Claims and Fast Track cases, these costs are fixed at a low level. With Multi-track cases, however, the amount of costs recovered by a successful party can be sizeable. Because orders for costs are almost entirely within the discretion of the court, however, parties must be aware of the risk that they will not recover costs if the court believes that they have failed to conduct their case economically and expeditiously. A party might win at trial but fail to recover more than, say, half its costs, because it has exaggerated its claim or has made unnecessary applications, perhaps for injunctions that were never likely to be ordered.

The courts will also compare the financial resources of the parties and may penalise a corporate entity on costs where it has had greater resources at its disposal to bring or defend litigation than its opponent.

Prior to the case management conference, the parties will have served their particulars of claim and defence, together with any key documents in support of their respective cases. There are fixed time limits for service of particulars, which can be extended by agreement or by permission of the court. If the defendant wishes to contest jurisdiction, he must acknowledge the claim and apply to the court within 28 days of service of the claimant's claim form[1]. Service of an acknowledgement will not constitute 'submission to the jurisdiction' of the court, but service of a defence or any other step probably will.

1 CPR Part 11, r 4.

7.56 Where jurisdiction is not contested but the defendant fails to serve an acknowledgement or to serve a defence within the specified time period, the claimant can enter a default judgment. In the case of a foreign defendant served with the claim form abroad, the claimant must satisfy the court that service has been properly effected and that the English court has jurisdiction before it will give judgment[1].

While court actions can take several months, if not years, to progress to trial, this can be short-circuited by making an application for early, or 'summary', judgment. This option is available to both the claimant and the defendant and is designed to dispose of weak claims and defences without the parties having to incur the expense of having the matter determined at trial. The court also has the power to order a summary judgment hearing, at which one of the parties will be required to show that it has a reasonable prospect of success, where it takes the view that the claim or defence is weak. Summary judgment can be obtained within a period of two months or so although, if the defendant has contested jurisdiction, the process is likely to take longer as the court will hear the defendant's application first.

There are also detailed rules governing the making and effect of offers to settle disputes, whether made before or during litigation. Parties are given incentives to make early and reasonable offers to dispose of claims in the form of costs awards or penalties. These incentives are greatest in the case of claimants, who are encouraged to indicate the level at, or terms on which, they would be prepared to settle, in the knowledge that if the offer is refused and then beaten at trial they will be awarded extra interest and the entirety of their legal costs[2]. This new regime represents a huge tactical weapon for the parties and forces litigants to recognise and assess the risks of continuing litigation in the face of an opportunity to settle.

A further weapon available to defendants domiciled in the UK, against a foreign claimant, is the application for security for costs. The purpose of this application is to give a defendant some protection against the risk that, if the claimant fails to prove his claim, he will simply disappear and prevent the defendant, as the 'winning' party, from ever getting any of his costs back. Security is usually given by payment of moneys into an account at court or provision of a bank bond or guarantee from a third party. The main grounds for security for costs orders are that the claimant is resident outside the EU or is impecunious. This rule is one which foreign, non-EU claimants need to bear in mind when bringing claims in England. Defendants facing claims by foreign claimants should also take this rule into account, since an application for security might well repel a claim because the claimant does not wish to provide security.

The E-Commerce Directive provides, in article 18, that Member States should ensure that court actions available under national law concerning information society services' activities allow for the rapid adoption of measures, including interim measures, designed to terminate alleged infringement and to prevent any further impairment of the interests involved. The CPR deals with interim remedies in Part 25 and makes provision for interim injunctions, declarations, freezing injunctions and search orders.

1 CPR Part 12, Practice Direction, para 4.1.
2 *All-in-one Design and Build Ltd v Motcomb Estates Ltd* (2000) 144 Sol Jo LB 219, where the validity of CPR Part 36, r 21 was tested. The court considered that the CPR seeks to ensure compliance with the rules by the imposition of sanctions, which are valid.

6. ENFORCEMENT

(a) Methods of enforcement in the UK

7.57 Judgments of the English courts and, to a large extent, recognised arbitration awards, may be enforced in the UK using any of five methods, namely:

■ seizure and sale of the judgment debtor's goods;

■ expropriation of sums in the judgment debtor's bank account (a 'Third Party Debt Order', previously known as a 'garnishee order');

■ charging orders over land owned by the judgment debtor;

■ attachment of earnings in the hands of the judgment debtor's employer; or

■ insolvency proceedings (by the winding-up of a company or bankruptcy of an individual).

For obvious reasons, enforcement by any of the first four of these methods is likely to be difficult unless the enforcing party has comprehensive and up-to-date information about the location and value of the debtor's assets. The risk associated with insolvency proceedings, conversely, is that the enforcing party will only recover a small portion of the sum due to it, because the remainder of the debtor's assets have to be distributed amongst a large pool of creditors with prior or equal rights of claim.

(b) Where should the judgment be enforced?

7.58 Some judgments lead to the losing party simply complying with its terms and paying over the damages awarded, or doing whatever else has been ordered. In some instances, however, the successful party must take steps to enforce its judgment to secure compliance with its terms. Where parties are in different countries or the defendant has spread its assets around a number of jurisdictions, the prospects of recovery without enforcement are likely to be very small. Internet trade is likely to involve parties who are both far apart and have very little knowledge of the whereabouts and value of their opponents' assets, thus making enforcement necessary in the majority of disputes.

It is to be hoped that the exercise of establishing which court has jurisdiction and what governing law should apply will reveal sufficient information about the whereabouts of the defendant and his assets to allow a claimant, armed with his judgment, to select an appropriate court for enforcement. This will not, however, always be the case. For instance, a consumer who has downloaded software from the Internet that proves to be corrupt or out of date may sue in his home court in England, but find that the Spanish software house fails to appear. The consumer may obtain judgment quite quickly in the absence of a defence but, as a result of the defendant's failure to appear, he is likely to have very little information to allow him to make an informed decision about where to enforce. The costs of enforcement might, in this situation, be an expense which the consumer does not think worth incurring because he has no certainty of any recovery. As a result, the judgment becomes virtually worthless.

The consumer can expect to obtain some ultimate redress where the activities of the trader are subject to the supervision of a regulator, who may well impose sanctions on any member found by a court to have committed a civil wrong. This will protect the consumer where he is buying securities, obtaining on-line investment advice or conducting Internet banking transactions. Many trading activities, however, are not yet subject to any supervision or control by a centralised body and so the unscrupulous may evade enforcement and escape penalty altogether[1].

1 It would not be appropriate, however, to raise the hopes and expectations of investors or depositors in relation to judgments sought to be enforced against investment firms, banks, etc, in overseas jurisdictions. Within the EU, there are compensation schemes in place in relation to failed investment firms and banking institutions, but the jurisdiction of such schemes is related to the failure of these institutions as such, and not to the success in court of litigants claiming against them. Generally, while a regulator may be interested to know that a firm which it regulates is failing to honour judgment debts in different relevant jurisdictions, it does not have a direct right to require these debts to be satisfied (even if it has sufficient regulatory powers to sanction that firm for rule breaches, the effect of which may be to persuade it to pay up).

(c) Enforcement and recognition of judgments of Member States

7.59 The Brussels Regulation , which on 1 March 2002 replaced the Brussels and Lugano Conventions in respect of those Member States regulated (all EU and EFTA states other than Denmark at this stage), provides that any judgment or order made in a Member State will (subject to certain exceptions) be recognised in other Member States, without the need for special procedures to be followed (article 33). The grounds for non-recognition include public policy grounds, judgments obtained in default of appearance and a judgment which is irreconcilable with another judgment given in a dispute between the same parties (article 34). For example, where a trader successfully sues his customer for payment in the US and the customer then obtains a declaration from a German court that the contract is void, he will not be able to enforce the German judgment under the Regulation if the US judgment is enforceable under the New York Convention. No review on the substance is possible (article 36). The Regulation has narrowed the grounds for non-recognition that were available under the Brussels Convention in the following manner:

■ the addition of 'manifestly' underscores the exceptional nature of the public policy ground for non-recognition.

■ the ground most commonly relied on by debtors to oppose enforcement, when judgments against them are obtained in default of appearance, has been modified to avoid abuses of procedure. It is sufficient for the defaulting defendant in the state of origin to have been served with a notice in such a way as to enable him to arrange for his defence. Accordingly, a mere formal irregularity in the service procedure will not debar recognition if it has not prevented the debtor from arranging his defence. In addition, if the debtor was in a position to appeal in the state of origin on the grounds of a procedural irregularity and has not done so, he is not entitled to invoke that irregularity as a ground for non-recognition.

■ the ground of failure to abide by a rule of private international law in the state in which a recognition is sought relating to personal status and capacity of natural persons has been deleted.

The provisions relating to enforcement of judgments in the Member States are set out at articles 38–56 of the Regulation. Application is made to the court or competent authority in Annex II of the Regulation. The procedure is governed by the law of the Member State in which the enforcement is sought. The procedure in the Regulation has been streamlined. A judgment will now be declared enforceable immediately on completion of the formalities set out in article 53. There is no review of grounds for non-enforcement at that first stage. The court is limited to making formal checks of the documents presented in support of the application. The party against whom an enforcement is sought cannot make submissions at this first stage. In terms of the formalities, article 53 specifies the need for a copy of the court judgment and a certificate which is required to be in a standard form, provided in Annex V to the Regulation (article 54). Although appeal is available (article 45 and Annex IV to the Regulation), the grounds have been narrowed (the grounds are set out in articles 34 and 35).

For example, where a court wrongly assumes jurisdiction in breach of an exclusive jurisdiction provision in article 22 of the Brussels Regulation, challenge is possible. Actions against consumers in the trader's rather than the consumer's home court, in breach of article 16 of the Regulation, would be challenged. Challenge does not extend to judgments by a court which the parties have agreed should have jurisdiction under articles 17 and 23 of the Regulation. However, a judgment which has been given by a court of a Member State in defiance of an arbitration clause is unlikely to be enforceable. This defence to enforcement can only be relied upon by the party against whom a judgment has been obtained where that party had refused to participate in those proceedings. If the party had submitted to the jurisdiction of the court, it cannot later rely on the dispute resolution clause to avoid enforcement.

(d) Judgments outside the EU and EFTA

7.60 A number of statutes and treaties govern the enforceability of judgments and orders made by courts in non-Member States and those made in Member States but outside the terms of the Brussels Regulation . The Administration of Justice Act 1920 provides for the enforcement in England of judgments given by superior courts of Commonwealth countries, while the Foreign Judgments (Reciprocal Enforcement) Act 1933 provides for the recognition and enforcement of judgments given by courts in countries with whom the UK has entered into reciprocal treaties and those party to a number of international Conventions. Both statutes require registration of the foreign judgment in England before it can be enforced here, although registration is only discretionary under the Administration of Justice Act 1920. Similar grounds for refusing to recognise or enforce a foreign judgment as appear in the Regulation are set out in both statutes.

Where neither the Acts nor the Regulation apply, a judgment of a foreign court may be enforced at common law, provided that it satisfies three conditions:

- the original court must have been a court of 'competent jurisdiction', that is a court in a country with which the defendant had some connection or to whose jurisdiction the defendant submitted;

- the judgment must be final and conclusive; an interlocutory or interim order will not satisfy this test, although a final judgment with a right of appeal will; and

- the judgment must be for a fixed sum of money – foreign injunctions and orders for specific performance are not enforceable in England.

Even where the above conditions are satisfied, however, defences may be raised to prevent enforcement. Where a foreign judgment breaches English principles of natural justice or conflicts with an earlier judgment of the English court, the court in the UK may refuse to enforce the judgment. Breaches of natural justice include where the defendant was not given notice of the proceedings or was denied an opportunity to present his case. If the proceedings raised an issue of fraud and the party seeking to resist enforcement can produce new evidence of fraud, the English court may review the grounds on which the judgment was based and, if fraud is then proved, refuse to recognise the foreign judgment. Equally, where there is an allegation of fraud in relation to the conduct of the foreign proceedings, the English court may refuse to enforce the judgment. Another ground for refusing enforcement arises when the parties agreed that a court, other than the one that gave judgment, was to determine the dispute.

The draft Hague Convention on Jurisdiction and the Recognition and Enforcement of Judgments in Civil and Commercial Matters aims to create an international agreement on the recognition and enforcement of judgments.

(e) Enforcement of foreign arbitration awards

7.61 International arbitration awards are relatively easy to enforce under the New York Convention 1958, to which well over 100 countries are signatories. These include all the EU Member States and all the EFTA countries, with the exception of Iceland. An award is a New York Convention award, and thus entitled to recognition in accordance with the Convention's terms, if it was made in the territory of a state which is party to the Convention. The Convention was first implemented into English law by the Arbitration Act 1975, the equivalent provisions of which were replaced by the AA 1996. The Convention is designed to ensure that national courts respect arbitration agreements and decline jurisdiction for themselves, and to provide a simple mechanism for the enforcement of awards.

As with foreign court judgments, there are, however, grounds for refusing to enforce a foreign arbitration award. These include invalidity of the arbitration agreement, excess of jurisdiction, failure to comply with the applicable procedural rules, failure to treat the parties equally and public policy grounds. Where any of these grounds is proven, the court nevertheless retains a discretion to allow enforcement.

In the case of arbitration awards made in states which have not implemented the New York Convention, enforcement will be subject to common law principles. The defences to enforcement are broadly similar to those under the Convention, save that the burden of proof is on the enforcing party to establish, in the first place, that the award is valid, final and binding. Enforcement of awards made in Scotland and Northern Ireland is also possible under the Civil Jurisdictions and Judgments Act 1982. Various other statutes offer limited enforcement regimes and a number of Conventions also provide for reciprocal enforcement as between signatories[1].

1   Enforcement of certain awards may be made under the Administration of Justice Act 1920, the Foreign Judgments (Reciprocal Enforcement) Act 1933, the Arbitration Act 1950 and the Arbitration (International Investment Disputes) Act 1966, amongst others.

(f)   Lessons from the *Yahoo! Inc* case

7.62   On 7 June 2001 District Judge Jeremy Fogel, sitting in the US District Court for the Northern District of California, granted summary judgment in favour of Yahoo! Inc[1], thereby defeating attempts by the French Anti-Racism and Anti-Semitism League to enforce the ruling of the French court concerning Nazi memorabilia and materials sold on the Yahoo website (see paragraph 7.47 above). The issue considered by the court was whether it is consistent with the US Constitution for another country to regulate the speech of a US resident on the basis that such speech can be accessed by Internet users in that foreign country. The US court considered that it could not enforce a foreign order that violates the protections afforded to US citizens by their Constitution. The court considered that its decision would have been different had the party in breach of French law been physically present in France, and the US court did not consider that it had been in this case. The case, therefore, shows that, although the French court did not follow the 'country of origin' principle (that is, it required Yahoo! Inc to comply with the foreign law, not just its own US law), the 'country of origin' approach prevailed on enforcement[2].

1   *Yahoo! Inc v LICRA*, Case No C00-21275-JF-RS, filed 13 April 2001.
2   Refer also to http://www.techlawjournal.com/alert/2001/08/14.asp.

7.   REFORMS IN EUROPE

(a)   Article 17 of the E-Commerce Directive

7.63   In December 1999 the European Commission launched its 'eEurope Initiative' at the Helsinki Summit. Since then, the mood of the politicians and civil servants has changed markedly. Because of work which had started in 1998 and matured into a draft Organisation for Economic Co-operational Development (OECD) recommendation for 'Guidelines for consumer protection in the context of electronic commerce' in September 1999, one of the key issues identified within the Initiative is the need to promote rapid and effective redress mechanisms to resolve potential disputes encountered by businesses and consumers buying goods and services across borders over the Internet.

The common position adopted by the European Council on 28 February 2000[1] related to an article on out-of-court dispute settlement in the proposed (as it then was) E-Commerce Directive.

At the extraordinary Lisbon European Council in March 2000, the rapid deployment of ADR schemes to help create confidence in e-commerce was identified as a priority. It is rare for arbitration and ADR to be on the political map of Europe.

Upon the request of the European Commission DG Information Society, terms of reference for an exploratory study of out-of-court settlement systems for e-commerce were prepared in January 2000 and the report of the EU Joint Research Centre was released on 20 April 2000. This rapid work revealed the new catch-phrase: 'ODR', or 'On-line Dispute Resolution'. The results of this work will have a bearing on the regulatory process in Europe[2].

Article 17 of the E-Commerce Directive now provides that Member States should ensure that, in the event of disagreement between an information society service provider and recipient of the service, their legislation does not hamper the use of out-of-court schemes available under national law for dispute settlement, including by appropriate electronic means. It also provides that Member States should encourage bodies responsible for out-of-court settlement, in particular of consumer disputes, to operate in a way which provides adequate procedural guarantees for the parties. Finally, article 17 provides that Member States should encourage bodies responsible for out-of-court dispute settlement to inform the Commission of significant decisions they take regarding information society services.

The Recitals to article 17 in the proposal for the Directive provide an explanation of the Commission's aims, as follows:

> 'Recital 17
> Whereas each Member State should be required, where necessary, to amend any legislation which is liable to hamper the use of schemes for the out-of-court settlement of disputes through electronic channels; whereas the result of this amendment must be to make the functioning of such schemes genuinely and effectively possible in law and in practice, even across borders; whereas the bodies responsible for such out-of-court settlement of consumer disputes must comply with certain essential principles, as set out in Commission Recommendation 98/257/EC of 30 March 1998 on the principles applicable to the bodies responsible for such settlement of consumer disputes.
>
> *Recital 17a*
> Whereas in the context of this Directive, notwithstanding the rule on the control at the source of Information Society services, it would appear legitimate under certain circumstances for Member States to take measures to restrict the free movement of Information Society services; whereas, however, such measures must be taken in accordance with Community law and must be necessary to achieve one of the following public interest objectives pursued: public policy, in particular [...] consumer protection; whereas such measures must be strictly proportionate to their objective and must not go beyond what is necessary to achieve it.'[3]

The Commission has not, however, inserted a provision similar to Recital 17 in the Brussels Regulation. Although the Commission considers it desirable for parties to resolve disputes on an amicable basis rather than going to the courts, it considers that in practice consumers will prefer non-judicial solutions where these are available and, in this regard, the Commission considers that there are a large number of projects underway to promote the establishment of such schemes. The Commission does not consider that, in the current state of progress, it is possible to make the options available to consumers under the Brussels Regulation in terms of jurisdiction subject to an obligation to go to ADR first. The Commission considers that this submission could raise constitutional difficulties in certain Member States. Also, the Commission is concerned that the out-of-court schemes are not yet either in operation or fully operational. Finally, the Commission is also concerned that the procedural relationship between ADR and the courts (for example, in relation to limitation periods) are complex and need further study.

1   14263.1.99 REV 1.
2   Wilikens et al, *Out-of-Court Dispute Settlement Systems for E-Commerce* (Joint Research Centre, EU Commission, 20 April 2000).
3   OJ L115 17.04.98 p 31.

(b) The issues examined in the Joint Research Centre study

7.64   There are two facets to the Joint Research Centre (JRC) study (see paragraph 7.63 and footnote 2 to that paragraph), which looked first at settlement systems for resolving disputes related to e-commerce transactions, and second, at the use of on-line means to support the operation of such dispute settlement systems. Whilst the focus of this work is on consumers and small and medium-sized enterprises purchasing relatively low value goods and services, the issues examined are much the same for larger B2B transactions and it is likely that the developments in this arena will be mimicked in other spheres.

Whilst recognising that arbitration is predominantly used in the international B2B sector and the value of the New York Convention in enforcement of arbitral awards, the following were described by the JRC as the critical issues in cross-border e-commerce:

■   are arbitration agreements valid which were concluded on-line, for example by the clicking of a screen button indicating consent?

■   the seat of the arbitration in cyberspace: where is the seat of the arbitration if the arbitrators 'meet' and make their decision from different places on-line?

■   multi-party arbitration in cyberspace.

■   the law applicable to the dispute and cross-border e-commerce: in circumstances where the Brussels and Rome Conventions do not apply; where there is no effective choice of law can the arbitrator choose a transnational law (a lex mercatoria of e-commerce)?

■   the procedural law to be applied in cyberspace (electronic filing of documents, electronic evidence, audio and videoconferencing).

■   the making of an electronic award on-line: does an electronic award comply with the requirements of international arbitration law? What recourse is there against an electronic award and would it be enforced and recognised?

Institutional rules and the application of sympathetic statute law (for example, the AA 1996) can help to solve partly some of these issues but, as a generalisation, the (perhaps unfair) perception that institutional arbitration is slow and costly will have to be changed. The JRC also considered mediation/conciliation and consumer complaints boards/Ombudsmen as alternatives to arbitration.

In addition, the JRC examined available ODR projects.

(i)   Arbitration

7.65

■   Virtual Magistrate[1];

■   Eresolution[2];

- I-Courthouse[3];

- Cybercourt[4];

- Ford Motor Co has, in conjunction with the Chartered Institute of Arbitrators in London, launched an on-line arbitration service for Ford customers in Europe who buy a Ford car on-line[5].

1 See http://vmag.org.
2 See www.disputes.org.
3 See www.i-courthouse.com.
4 See http://cybercourt.de. The three projects above are North American, whereas this is the first European-based arbitration ODR scheme. It is rooted in a private German law firm and uses e-mail combined with chatbox technology.
5 www.arbitrators.org – with a link from Ford on-line shopping site at www.fordjourney.com.

(ii) Mediation

7.66

- IRIS Mediation (France)[1];

- InternetNeutral (US)[2];

- On-line Mediators (US)[3];

- On-line Ombuds Office (US)[4];

- Transecure[5].

1 See www.iris.sgdg.org/mediation. This is a private initiative, with volunteers (and therefore no cost for the consumer).
2 See www.internetneutral.com.
3 See www.onlinemediators.com.
4 See www.ombuds.org. A free service, sponsored by e-Bay.
5 See www.transecure.org.

(iii) Trust seals in combination with mediation

7.67

- BBBOnline (US/Canada)[1];

- Which?Webtrader (UK)[2];

- Trusted Shops (Germany)[3].

1 See www.bbbonline.org: reliability seals and privacy seals, consumer complaints handling, industry sponsored.
2 See www.which.com/webtrader; the seal of Which? consumer association. Provides reimbursement of the first £50 of loss in case of credit card fraud; a European network for cross-border complaints in the making. See also Chapter 4, E-rights.
3 See www.trustedshops.org; a seal of Trusted Shops Guarantee. Provides a reimbursement guarantee for on-line shoppers from an insurance company, as well as consumer complaints handling.

(iv) Automated settlement/negotiation of claims

7.68

- SettleOnline[1];

- ClickNsettle.com (US)[2];

- CyberSettle (US)[3].

1 See www.settleonline.com.
2 See www.clickNsettle.com. Provides on-line negotiation of settlement amount.
3 See www.cybersettle.com. Offers on-line computer assisted method for settling insurance claims.

(c) Further initiatives

7.69 In 1998 the Commission adopted a 'Communication on the out-of-court settlement of consumer disputes' that included Recommendation (EC) 257/98 on the principles applicable to out-of-court settlement (by arbitration) of consumer disputes[1]. This established a number of minimum guarantees that out-of-court bodies should offer their users. The Commission Recommendation (EC) 310/2001 (which applies to mediation) establishes similar principles[2]. There are seven principles:

■ **Independence** The independence of the decision-making body or person should be ensured in order to guarantee the impartiality of its actions.

■ **Transparency** Appropriate measures should be taken to ensure the transparency of the procedure.

■ **Adversarial principle** The procedure to be followed allows all the parties concerned to present their point of view before the responsible body and to hear the arguments and facts put forward by the other party, and any experts' statements.

■ **Principle of effectiveness** The effectiveness of the procedure is ensured through measures guaranteeing that the consumer has access to the procedure without being obliged to use a legal representative, that the procedure is free of charges or has only moderate costs, that only short periods elapse between the referral of a matter and the decision, that the responsible body is given an active role, thus enabling it to take into consideration any factors conducive to a settlement of the dispute.

■ **Principle of legality** The decision taken by the body may not result in the consumer being deprived of the protection afforded by the mandatory provisions of the law of the state in whose territory the body is established.

■ **Principle of liberty** The decision taken by the body concerned may be binding on the parties only if they were informed of its binding nature in advance and specifically accepted this. The consumer's recourse to the out-of-court procedure may not be the result of a commitment prior to the materialisation of the dispute where such commitment has the effect of depriving the consumer of the right to bring an action before the courts for the settlement of the dispute.

■ **Principle of representation** The procedure should not deprive the parties of the right to be represented or assisted by a third party at all stages of the procedure.

1   OJ L115 17.04.98.
2   OJ L109/56 19.04.2001.

7.70 Due to the increase in cross-border consumption, the Communication foresaw the need to create a cross-border network of out-of-court bodies to overcome the obstacles facing a consumer in accessing the out-of-court bodies of other Member States. Council Resolution (EC) 7876/2000 of 11 May 2000 proposed the 'EEJ-Net' (the European Extra-Judicial Network)[1]. A single contact point, a 'Clearing House', is being established in each Member State and these will work together as the EEJ-Net. It is thus a communication and support mechanism. The challenge for arbitration will be to provide methods which comply with the seven principles and become entrenched within the EEJ-Net. A database is being developed which lists the out-of-court bodies which satisfy the criteria[2].

The Webtrader project, co-funded by the European Commission, started at the beginning of 2000 and is a good example of a likely model for the growth of ODR. It is managed by a consortium of independent consumer organisations in seven European countries and provides an on-line certification and arbitration programme. It is based on a code of conduct that suppliers subscribe to in order to receive use of the Webtrader logo. It is conceivable that similar codes of conduct will arise in specific sectors of the B2B market.

Another initiative is the on-line ADR system being developed by European Chambers of Commerce and Industry. There are 82 Chambers of Commerce and Industry, with more than three million business members, participating. The rationale is that Chambers of Commerce and Industry are well placed to act as trusted third parties and neutral facilitators. Businesses will be offered a Trust Mark to display on their websites, provided that they agree to adhere to a code of conduct backed up by an on-line ADR mechanism, which will involve two steps. First, there will be automated complaint treatment, an automated process which involves only the parties, who will aim to reach agreement by communicating directly on-line; and, second, on-line mediation will take place if the dispute has not been resolved by automated complaint treatment.

In light of the collaboration between the London Chamber of Commerce and the London Court of International Arbitration (LCIA), the trend may be toward a two-tier system, whereby the Euro-Chambers of Commerce provide mediation and Ombudsmen services and an institution such as the LCIA provides arbitration services for the higher value and more complex disputes.

The European Commission is also funding the Grotius ADR Programme, a European programme which involves research and surveys on the use of ADR across the continent; education of mediators, lawyers, judges and business people about mediation; and recommendations to the European Commission on the further development of ADR.

1   http://europa.eu.int/comm/consumers/policy/developments/acce_just/acc_just07_cr_en.pdf.
2   The European Commission's website provides information about the national clearing houses and participating ADR bodies: http://europa.eu.int/comm/consumers/policy/developments/acce_just/index_en.html.

8.   A SOLUTION IN THE CONFUSION?

7.71   Although this cannot be used for smaller business-to-consumer transactions, we would propose a model solution to the problems presented by jurisdiction and conflicts of law that answers most of the key questions in a predictable fashion. This model offers a practical way forward for B2B e-commerce, until such time as further laws and conventions are agreed between states and established sufficiently to meet the demands of e-commerce[1]. The features of this model are:

- at the point of contracting, the parties agree and identify the law governing their transaction;

- the parties agree that all disputes between them will be resolved by arbitration, and they select an institution to administer the arbitration, according to internationally accepted rules – for example, the LCIA in London, the ICC in Paris or the American Arbitration Association (AAA);

- the place where the arbitration will be conducted should also be agreed (this is called the 'seat' and imports the law governing the arbitration process – London is the suggested seat for this model);

- as a precursor to the commencement of the arbitration, the parties can agree to set aside a period during which they will attempt to negotiate a resolution, either informally between themselves or with the assistance of a third party neutral, using a process such as mediation.

Because the parties agree to appoint their own tribunal and select the substantive law of their contract by agreement, the questions of jurisdiction and proper law are answered: those agreements will be respected and applied in most cases and states.

The real advantage of this model is apparent in relation to enforcement, because of the widespread and increasing adoption of the New York Convention on the Recognition and Enforcement of Foreign Arbitral Awards 1958. This renders an arbitration award enforceable in signatory countries (numbering over 133), provided it complies with the Convention. The model therefore comprises an effective enforcement mechanism which has global coverage.

To ensure that an arbitration clause is all-embracing in terms of the subject matter, and that applications for injunctions or interim payments prior to determination of the substantive dispute by the arbitrator are proscribed, you will need to include appropriate wording to this effect. Even the most comprehensive wording may, however, be circumvented where your opponent can demonstrate that the dispute falls within the Brussels Regulation and that they are thus entitled to make applications under article 31.

1 For a recent application of a similar model in the B2C market, see the 'fordjourney' scheme (www.ford.co.uk) and the related arbitration scheme (at www.arbitration.org). WIPO is also finalising (with the Mediation Centre and the Application Service Provider Industry Consortium) a set of guidelines and best practice for settlement of Internet disputes: see http://arbiter.wipo.int/asp/report/index.htm/.

(a) E-international arbitration

7.72 The suggested model raises the question of on-line arbitration, since parties to an e-commerce transaction may expect to be attracted to effective and respected on-line methods of dispute resolution.

Can an exchange of e-mail messages containing an arbitration agreement satisfy the formal requirements of the New York Convention? The short answer is yes because, although there are technical differences, there is in substance no difference to an exchange of telexes which has been accepted as sufficient for some considerable time. While encryption provides secure communication, some simple steps provide the necessary degree of certainty:

- verify the context and content of the e-mail so that it is attributed to the sender. The forgery of letters and faxes is just as possible as a forged e-mail, yet an e-mail message comes with a considerable amount of routing information which provides a means for cross-checking;

- print out copies of all e-mails; and

- use the return receipt facility found on most e-mail programs.

Suppose, therefore, that a message from a seller is transmitted to a buyer. The message should conspicuously set out the terms of the agreement which is offered, including the arbitration clause. An example would be:

> 'Any dispute arising out of or in connection with this contract, including any question regarding its existence, validity or termination, shall be referred to and finally resolved by arbitration under the Rules of the LCIA[1], which Rules are deemed to be incorporated by reference into this clause.

> The number of arbitrators shall be [*one* or *three*] [*consider whether to name potential arbitrators*].

> The place of the arbitration shall be [*London, UK*].

> The language to be used in the arbitral proceedings shall be [*English*].

> The governing law of this contract shall be the substantive law of [*England and Wales*].'

The buyer would then be asked to signify acceptance by perhaps inserting data specific to the transaction and then clicking an 'accept' button embedded within the message, whereupon the modified version of the message is transmitted back to the seller. In this way there has been an exchange of information which appears to be identical to an exchange of faxes. In these circumstances, an arbitration agreement has been validly formed, in accordance with article II(2) of the New York Convention.

1 By nominating the rules of the LCIA, issues such as the administration of the arbitration, the appointment of arbitrators and the costs of the arbitration process are automatically resolved by those rules; if such rules are not specified, the agreement should specifically deal with these points.

(b) Conduct of arbitration on-line

7.73 Most international arbitrations are conducted with the parties meeting with the arbitrators for a hearing when evidence is presented and oral submissions are made. Directions for the conduct of the arbitration may be given by telephone or videoconference. However, it is entirely feasible for the parties to embed within their arbitration agreement, or agree thereafter, that the proceedings are to be conducted entirely on-line so that communications with the arbitrators and between the arbitrators themselves are entirely electronic[1]. However, such an arbitration should be set up carefully so that the rules adopted by the parties are amended to delete references to documents 'in writing' and substitute appropriate words, since e-mail is not physical writing.

The Swiss Supreme Court has decided that arbitrators need not meet in person and are free to conduct deliberations by electronic means, including e-mail, provided precautions are taken[2]:

> 'the only mandatory requirement ... is that all the arbitrators must participate in a real way in each discussion and decision.'

The law does not mandatorily impose any particular procedure concerning the deliberations of the arbitrators and their decision-making process; it authorises both decisions made in the presence of all the arbitrators – generally orally – and decisions made 'amongst absent people' – generally in writing.

Thus, the arbitration contract can contain a clause that it be conducted electronically. In the absence of such a clause, but given the law's silence, the procedure to be followed must be determined by agreement between the parties or, in the absence of agreement, by the arbitral tribunal.

Thus, provided the parties agree or the tribunal decides, the arbitrators can make an award after discussing the case by telephone and videoconference, with drafts of the award being then circulated by e-mail.

Where institutional rules are adopted, a clear and explicit agreement between the parties, expressed to modify contrary provisions in the rules, would avoid later difficulties in enforcement under article V(1)(d) of the New York Convention.

As regards the form of the award, most jurisdictions currently require it to be on paper and signed in ink and by hand, so the award will have to be sent by registered post to the parties prior to enforcement. In due course, however, electronically signed awards are likely to be accepted as new laws are introduced.

Provided some basic steps are taken, and the necessary agreements are put in place, an arbitration agreement can therefore be concluded by electronic means, and the arbitration itself conducted in cyberspace. Not only does this make arbitration highly attractive as a means of efficient adjudicative resolution of e-disputes, but also parties can choose arbitrators from around the world according to who is best qualified to resolve the dispute. Since they do not need to congregate in one place (save electronically), substantial cost savings can be achieved, as can greater quality within the tribunal. This should endear arbitration to the business community, which needs certainty and consistency at the lowest cost.

It may well be the case that an international tribunal will be set up, along the lines of the International Court of Justice, to meet the demands of e-disputes. This will require political reconciliation between the main trading blocks and will, therefore, probably take some time.

At the moment, an agreement to arbitrate, alongside an agreed choice of law and procedures, as described above, represents the best available mechanism to avoid the uncertainties created by cross-border disputes in this rapidly developing market.

1 M Scott Donahey reports that it has already been used successfully as part of the Virtual Magistrate Project, a US joint venture involving the American Arbitration Association: (1998) 15(4) JIA 127 at 161.
2 See *Sociétés v Société K 1ère Cour Civile* 23 October 1985 (ATF III Ia p 336).

(c) E-mediation

7.74 On-line mediation allows the parties to tackle their dispute without the delays, cost and further disagreement likely to be associated with setting up a face-to-face meeting. This is the opportunity which the e@dr scheme in Singapore is seeking to realise.

Mediation in cyberspace has already occurred[1]. The Online Ombuds Office in Massachusetts also reports experience of on-line mediation since it was set up in 1996[2]. Several other on-line mediation services have also been established recently in the US and Canada, including the CyberTribunal in Montreal, whose services are offered free of charge[3].

A mediation using electronic means of communication will have a different character to one where the parties are able to meet in one place. As we become more relaxed about electronic communication, a new culture of on-line mediation may develop.

Mediation using e-mail is also intrinsically a much slower process than the usual forum where all parties are physically present. The parties and the mediator can take much longer to consider and phrase their responses than happens in face-to-face discussions. The non-verbal communications (eye, hand, face and body movements, and speed and tone of voice) are absent, so that the written word is the only form of communication, unless videoconferencing is added. By sending or receiving private messages, the mediator can act as a filter to communications and hence steer the process in the right direction. The process can, however, lack momentum and will proceed only at the rate of the slowest party.

1 Jeffrey Kravis, adjunct professor at Pepperdine University Law School and a private mediator, recounts a case he handled a few years ago: *CPR Alternatives*, Vol 14, No 10 November 1996.
2 See http://128.119.199.27/center/ombuds/narrative1.html.
3 See (1998) 15(4) JIA 127 at 164.

7.75 To ensure the process does maintain some sort of momentum, the mediator can use skills such as 'issue framing' to show the parties that their messages have been understood and define the matters that need to be considered, while sidelining certain issues that might cloud the options for settlement.

This technique has obvious advantages where parties live far apart and in different time zones, so that it is impractical to meet. The downside is that there may be limited opportunity to dissipate the emotions which may fuel the dispute. For mediators, Jeffrey Kravis[1] lists his ten tips for on-line ADR (which are useful for the parties as well):

'1. Develop non-verbal ways through your keyboard of creating credibility without being arrogant. A short biography demonstrating your computer literacy, knowledge and mediation skills is useful.
2. Create a confidentiality agreement that describes the on-line process. Include rules about responding to e-mail; the importance of disclosing information only to the mediator; managing delays in responding on-line; and notifying the mediator of travel plans to maintain uninterrupted communications over the Internet.
3. Set the agenda for on-line discussions early on, by instructing the parties to send you an e-mail with their suggested list of issues in dispute.
4. Develop a set of on-line "ground rules" which include artificial time limits.
5. When responding to e-mail messages, filter angry or emotional replies so that the other party receives a response that does not create further hostility.
6. Post no more than two or three short questions per e-mail that are like trial balloons in a mediation. Keep them short and make sure that you are not viewed as favouring one side or the other.
7. No matter how contentious the parties might become on-line, keep the conversation moving forward by reminding the parties of the goal of the mediation.

8. Be prepared to provide an evaluation of the case after the parties have exhausted their efforts at reaching an acceptable solution.

9. If you are providing an evaluation of the case, make sure that you have strong factual and legal support that cannot be overcome by the parties.

10. Know the correct e-mail address of the parties and make sure you know which ones are used regularly and which ones are rarely used.'

Business people need to know that their disputes will be resolved quickly and cost-effectively and that there is a predictable system in place for dealing with e-disputes. Dispute resolution in the courts offers the opportunity to go forum shopping but is fraught with uncertainty and inconsistency. Although the position is likely to change, judges tend to be unfamiliar, if not uncomfortable, with the principles and customs of e-commerce.

Arbitrators and mediators, conversely, can be selected for their experience and expertise in this forum. Combine this advantage with on-line dispute resolution procedures and e-commerce disputes are likely to be resolved satisfactorily. The outcome is also likely to be recognised and enforced wherever the parties live in cyberspace.

1   (1998) 15(4) JIA 127.

9.   EVIDENCE

7.76 Every dispute is decided on its facts and how and which 'facts' are brought to the attention of the tribunal is determined by the laws and rules of evidence governing that tribunal. These are very specific and this section will focus on an English law perspective.

(a) The ongoing revolution

7.77 E-commerce and the use of interactive media generates electronic evidence. Individuals and companies trading electronically expect the legal system to protect their commercial interests in respect of this trade as much as those undertaking trade in more traditional ways, where the 'paper trail' of available evidence may be greater.

The frequent absence of paper-based original documentation relating to e-commerce (for example, the absence of paper-based signed contracts) and the relative ease with which electronic data can be altered, lead to two potentially conflicting requirements for the legal process in dealing with electronic evidence:

■   that there ought to be recognition of 'electronic evidence' including digital signatures for identity and contracting purposes; and

■   that the lawyers and judges become more sophisticated in assessing the proper 'weight' to be given to such evidence once accepted as admissible evidence, given the particular technological basis of its generation or recording.

In addition to the technological changes in business practice and trade, there is another independent basis driving the courts to respond positively to electronic evidence, namely the cost of paper-based evidence.

In the UK, prior to the coming into force of the CPR, parties to even moderate-sized commercial disputes had endured onerous discovery obligations which tended to generate enormous quantities of discovery and trial files and copying costs, most of which were subject to the 'winner takes all' principle of costs recovery.

Under the CPR, not only has discovery now become a less onerous 'disclosure' requirement, but the parties' cost expenditure must be 'proportionate' to the issues and sums in dispute (see paragraph 7.54). Making better use of electronic evidence (for example exchanging respective database files for analysis, rather than printing out a hard copy of the contents) may well assist parties to a dispute to analyse and assess each other's evidence for less cost than would otherwise be the case.

The era where 'good' litigators were defined by how much money they could make their opponents waste in the conduct of litigation will surely draw to an end in favour of 'smart litigators' who use electronic evidence to assist them in assessing the merits of their case or defence at a much earlier stage than their paper fetishing forbears ever did.

(b) What is a document?

7.78 The admissibility of evidence (considered below at paragraphs 7.85–7.89) in civil cases is not as contentious as it once was, in that the disclosure (previously discovery) procedures developed last century mean that parties to this kind of litigation will have been given sight of each other's documents relevant to the dispute, and there is likely to have been mutual consent as to their admissibility. The 'forewarning' of each side's evidence gives the parties time to have prepared any necessary attacks on the 'weight' that should be afforded to any particular document.

The question therefore is whether certain types of electronic data and their storage media are 'documents' for the purpose of discovery and, hence, potentially admissible evidence.

The courts in the UK have long since recognised that the meaning of 'documents' for evidential purposes should not be restricted to paper, print or writings. For historical purposes, some of the case law relating to particular technologies is set out below, but the key point to note is that a 'document' can extend to anything upon which evidence or information is recorded in a manner intelligible to the senses or capable of being made intelligible by the use of equipment. CPR Part 31, r 4 provides that a document:

> 'means anything in which information of any description is recorded'

and a 'copy' in relation to a document:

> 'means anything onto which information recorded in the document has been copied, by whatever means and whether directly or indirectly.'

These are self-evidently very broad definitions and are consistent with the continued general trend against issues of admissibility and special procedures for electronic evidence, in favour of allowing all relevant evidence to be considered in the context of an evaluation of what weight should be attached to it.

In Scotland, the Criminal Procedure (Scotland) Act 1995 provides that a 'document' includes:

> 'in addition to a document in writing—
> (a) any map, plan, graph or drawing;
> (b) any photograph;
> (c) any disc, tape, soundtrack or other device in which sounds or other data (not being visual images) are recorded so as to be capable, with or without the aid of some other equipment, of being reproduced therefrom; and
> (d) any film, negative, tape, disc or other device in which one or more visual images are recorded so as to be capable (as aforesaid) of being reproduced therefrom.'

7.79 The position set out below illustrates the acceptance of a wide range of non-paper based evidence as documents for disclosure/discovery purposes.

(i) Computer databases

7.80 In *Derby & Co Ltd v Weldon (No 9)*[1], Vinelott J held that the database of a computer's on-line system or data which is recorded in back-up files was a document within the meaning of RSC Ord 24:

'It must, I think, apply a fortiori to the tape or disc on which material fed into a simple word processor is stored. In most businesses, that takes the place of the carbon copy of outgoing letters which used to be retained in files.

In the case of *Alliance and Leicester Building Society v Ghahremani*[2], a word processing file was found to be a document for the purpose of an order preserving documents in connection with proceedings.

Similarly, there can be no distinction in principle between the tape used to record a telephone conversation in *Grant v Southwestern and County Properties Ltd*[3], which was an ordinary analogue tape on which the shape of sound waves is, as it were, mimicked by the pattern of chemical deposit on the tape, and a compact disc or digital tape on which sound and speech, as well as music, is mapped by co-ordinates and recorded in the form of groups of binary numbers.

And no clear dividing line can be drawn between digital tape recording messages and the database of a computer on which information which has been fed into the computer is analysed and recorded in a variety of media in binary language.'

In the case of *Elvee Ltd (t/a Track Direct) v Taylor*[4], CDs containing copies of computer files including digital images were found to be documents containing potentially evidential data. For this reason a search and seizure order of the CDs was justified in order to preserve the physical evidence contained on the CDs.

1 [1991] 2 All ER 901, [1991] 1 WLR 652.
2 [1992] RVR 198.
3 [1974] 2 All ER 465.
4 [2001] EWCA Civ 1943, [2001] All ER (D) 79 (Dec).

(ii) E-mail

7.81 E-mails are no different from any other form of document and can be used for, or against, a party in a dispute as evidence. There is therefore no protection against the use of e-mails in the discovery process.

The nature of the medium of e-mail can produce problems in relation to the disclosure process. From CPR Part 31, r 4 it is clear that e-mails come within the definition of a document, which may be subject to an obligation to disclose.

From CPR Part 31, r 8 there exists an obligation to disclose documents which are, *or have been* in the control of the party subject to the disclosure order. E-mails which have been deleted would fall within this description rendering them discoverable. Deleted e-mails may be difficult to locate, as this would require the search of electronic databases and computer archives.

CPR Part 31, r 10 requires the party disclosing the documents to include a disclosure statement setting out the extent of the search which was undertaken to locate discoverable documents. If the discoverable documents included electronic documents, the search undertaken would have to include a search of electronic databases and computer archives and the disclosure statement should reflect this. Proceedings for contempt of court may be brought against anyone making a false disclosure statement (CPR Part 31, r 23).

Employees sometimes treat the use of e-mail differently to other office or company communications (more of a form of 'chat') and this can result in 'unguarded' comments being made. Such comments could be detrimental to a party's case and employees should be aware of the future potential discovery of these communications and their consequent use as evidence.

An example of this was in the recent case of *Takenaka (UK) Ltd v Frankl*[1], where a series of e-mails were found to be defamatory. The e-mails were traced to a particular computer to which the defendant had access as an employee and this was sufficient in order to prove authorship and incur liability.

While the courts will accept e-mail computer evidence as simply another form of documentary evidence, given the particular ease with which such communication can be forged, the UK courts will have to address the problem of authentication as it applies to e-mail communication, especially until the use of digital signatures and encrypted e-mail communication becomes more widespread.

1   [2001] EWCA Civ 348, [2001] EBLR 40.

7.82   Electronic mail can be used on both intranets (self-contained networks of computers, normally within one organisation) and the Internet (the global connection of networks).

When an e-mail message is received, it contains 'header information'. This information normally includes the name of the sender, the name of the recipient, and the date and time the message was sent. In addition, however, most e-mail programmes allow the recipient to view additional header information, including the electronic path that the e-mail travelled to reach the recipient. (Sometimes the user has to enter a command for the programme to display the expanded header information.)

The computers through which an e-mail message travels are identified in the header information by each such computer's 'Internet protocol' unique IP.

The fundamental problem evidentially with e-mail rests in determining their true point of origin. Unlike a fax communication, they cannot show on their face a written signature. The authenticity of e-mail gives cause for concern since it is relatively easy to create either an anonymous e-mail or a message with false header information. Forging e-mails requires little specialised skill because the Internet's e-mail system (which was designed over 30 years ago for academic discourse) has no automatic or inherent provisions for declaring a message to be authentic.

The normal way that messages are authenticated is via header information. This information is notoriously inadequate because of the security flaws present in the mail protocol used on the Internet. By analogy, using an IP address from header information as the means of authentication of an e-mail message could roughly be equated with assuming a letter was authentic simply because of the type-written return address on its envelope.

The view that e-mail should, for the purposes of evidence, be treated largely like a traditional letter simply because both are capable of being forged, is somewhat flawed. E-mail raises a number of particular features which distinguish it from a traditional letter and raise different considerations as to evidential value.

For example, you cannot place a handwritten signature and an e-mail's header information (the nearest e-mail equivalent to a signature) on an equal authentication footing. In contrast to forging handwriting, forging the header information on an e-mail requires no technical or artistic skill. While a handwriting sample could be shown to a jury or judge considering a disputed signature, header information is not a corporeal object that can be displayed and compared by the court. It is data that can simply be altered to undermine its intended purpose.

The most likely technical solution to the problems of authentication of e-mail communication is digital encryption. Applying a digital signature to an e-mail communication could alleviate most of the authentication concerns identified above.

The Electronic Communications Act 2000 gives effect to the Electronic Signatures Directive[1] and, by virtue of section 7, acknowledges electronic signatures as admissible evidence. Section 7(1) of the 2000 Act reads:

'(1)   In any legal proceedings—

(a)   an electronic signature incorporated into or logistically associated with a particular electronic communication or particular electronic data, and

(b)   the certification by any person of such a signature,

shall be admissible in evidence in relation to any question as to the authenticity of the communication or data or as to the integrity of the communication or data.'

Pressing the 'delete' button on a computer system is no guarantee that an offending or potentially prejudicial e-mail has actually been deleted from the system. In most instances it can easily be recovered as the message continues to exist in a number of forms, especially where the system is subject to regular systematic back-up routines.

From an evidential perspective, it is important to appreciate that, even after a recipient deletes an e-mail message from their 'mailbox', the message is stored by the recipient's Internet provider on a back-up tape. Depending on the archival system of the Internet provider company, e-mail communications from as far back as ten years could, in principle, be retrieved.

1   Directive (EC) 93/99.

(iii) Fax

7.83   In *Ralux NV/SA v Spencer Mason*[1] the question regarding sending a document by fax was not directly in issue, but the Court of Appeal appeared attracted to the argument that, if a document in fact came into the hands of a party to be served, that was good service as far as ordinary service was concerned.

In *Hastie & Jenkerson v McMahon*[2] the Court of Appeal held that the use of a facsimile transmission of a document (other than one to be served personally or one originating process) constituted good service, providing it could be proved that the document, in a complete and legible state, had in fact been received by the person on whom service was to be effected.

In the case of *Re a Debtor (Nos 2021 and 2022 of 1995), ex p IRC v Debtors*[3] it was held that a faxed copy of a duly signed proxy form sent by a creditor, was valid for the purposes of rule 8.2 (3) of the Insolvency Rules[4]. The receiving fax was, in effect, instructed by the transmitting creditor to reproduce his signature on the proxy form.

1   (1989) Times, 18 May, per O'Connor LJ, Mustill LJ.
2   [1991] 1 All ER 255, [1990] 1 WLR 1575.
3   [1996] 2 All ER 345.
4   SI 1986/1925.

(iv) Other forms of evidence

7.84

Audio and video tape recordings

Tape recordings of evidence or information are documents[1].

Microfilms

Microfilms used to keep records are 'books' for the purpose of the Bankers' Books Evidence Act 1879[2] and are therefore 'documents' for the purposes of civil proceedings.

Photocopies

Photocopies of documents are generally discoverable since they are equally capable of assisting the parties in the preparation of their case[3]. In the case of *Bank of Baroda v Patel*[4] photocopies of a lost original guarantee were admissible as secondary evidence of the lost original.

Photographs

The fact that photographs may be documentary evidence is well established. In *Lyell v Kennedy (No 3)*[5] the Court of Appeal held that photographs of tombstones and houses were documents for the purposes of discovery and hence admissible. It follows from the fact that photographs were accepted as documents that any moving film should also be considered a document.

In *R v Fellows*[6] it was held that data kept on a computer disk which came from a photograph and could be converted into a screen image came within the definition of 'photograph' for the purpose of the Protection of Children Act 1978. This Act has since been amended to incorporate this broader definition of a photograph.

Radar

Radar recordings of echoes of ships in collision have been held as admissible evidence[7].

Telex

The issue of the authenticity of electronic documents produced by electronic means and the identity of communicants was considered in the case of *Standard Bank London Ltd and Bank of Tokyo Ltd*[8]. The case involved letters of credit and a related 'tested telex' system rather than the use of e-mail computer communication, but the decision has some general implications when considering authentication. The letters of credit in question were authenticated by 'tested telexes', which incorporated a form of digital signature. The digital signatures turned out to be forgeries.

It was argued that there were sufficient suspicious circumstances in the transactions to have put the recipient of the telex 'on enquiry' in relation to the authenticity of the documents. Although the dubious circumstances might have been picked up by an expert in fraud, it was decided that the use of the 'tested telex' system was sufficient to alleviate suspicion such that the recipient could be considered as having acted reasonably in not making further enquiries and that the 'tested telex' could be relied upon.

The concept of the 'tested telex' is one in which a code, known only to the sender and the recipient, is included in the telex so that the recipient can be confident about the identity of the sender. Banks arrange for signatures to be authenticated by the use of such a 'tested telex'. This process clearly bears analogy in certain aspects to encrypted digital signatures used in e-commerce.

1 See *Grant v Southwestern and County Properties Ltd* [1975] Ch 185, [1974] 2 All ER 465. Walton J, in rejecting the argument that a tape recording is not a document (because the information is not capable of being visually inspected), stated:
    'the mere interposition of necessity of an instrument for deciphering the information cannot make any difference in principle. A litigant who keeps all his documents in microdot form could not avoid discovery because, in order to read the information, extremely powerful microscopes or other sophisticated instruments would be required. Nor again, if he kept them by means of microfilm which could [not] be read without the aid of a projector.'
    See also *R v Maqsud Ali* [1966] 1 QB 688, [1965] 2 All ER 464, CCA (recordings made by mechanical means without human intervention are to be treated as real evidence).
2 *Barker v Wilson* [1980] 2 All ER 81, [1980] 1 WLR 884.
3 *Dubai Bank Ltd v Galadari (No 7)* [1992] 1 All ER 658, [1992] 1 WLR 106.

4 [1996] 1 Lloyd's Rep 391.
5 (1884) 27 Ch D 1.
6 [1997] 2 All ER 548, CA.
7 See *The Statue of Liberty* [1968] 2 All ER 195.
8 [1995] 2 Lloyd's Rep 169.

(c) Rules of evidence

7.85 English courts of law will only allow evidence to be placed before them if it is admissible in accordance with the rules of evidence.

Two particular rules have been historically important when considering the issues raised by electronic evidence.

The first was the 'best evidence rule', which required that only an original document could be put in evidence. The courts have now recognised that a strict adherence to the best evidence rule is inappropriate in a world where accurate copies of originals may now be made. Lloyd LJ in *R v Governor of Pentonville Prison, ex p Osman*[1] stated:

> 'We accept that it [the best evidence rule] served an important purpose in the days of parchment and quill pens, but since the invention of carbon paper, and still more, the photocopier and telephone facsimile machine, that purpose has largely gone.'

A general exclusion on copies of original documents is therefore no longer deemed appropriate. Nevertheless, it remains the case that an original document should still be produced if it is available.

In the case of *Krediethank Antwerp v Midland Bank plc*[2] it was said that article 20(b) of the UCP 500 (Uniform Customs and Practice for Documentary Credits 1993) was intended to widen the class of documents that banks would accept as originals. A photocopy could be accepted as an original so long as it was marked as such.

In the case of *Springsteen v Flute International Ltd*[3] the Court of the Appeal (leave to the House of Lords from this decision was refused) pronounced the death of the 'best evidence' rule:

> 'In my judgement, the time has now come when it can be said with confidence that the best evidence rule, long on its deathbed has finally expired. In every case where a party seeks to adduce secondary evidence of the contents of a document, it is a matter for the Court to decide, in the light of all the circumstances of the case, what (if any) weight to attach to that evidence.'[4]

The second rule was the rule against hearsay evidence, which applied to oral and documentary evidence in civil proceedings until the CEA 1995 (CEA 1995). This rule proved to be of significantly greater impact, and much more recently, than the best evidence rule. The history of the rule and its continued application in some jurisdictions is discussed below.

1 [1989] 3 All ER 701.
2 [1999] Lloyd's Rep Bank 219, CA.
3 [2001] EWCA Civ 563, [2001] EMLR 654.
4 [2001] EWCA Civ 563, [2001] EMLR 654, Jonathon Parker LJ.

(d) Hearsay

7.86 The so-called 'hearsay rule' precluded the admission or giving of any evidence in proceedings other than that capable of being given directly by a person via oral evidence of matters within his direct knowledge. Thus, evidence from Bob that 'Fred told me Jim stabbed Johnny' is wholly inadmissible as evidence of the assertion that Jim stabbed Johnny, but will be admissible only of the fact that Bob claims Fred told him something.

It will be immediately apparent that the full application of the hearsay rule effectively precludes all sources of mechanical or computer evidence, despite the fact that, by their very nature, mechanical and computer capabilities are of value to the creation of valuable evidence. In addition to the obvious inconvenience of the rule in an age when enormous amounts of good reliable evidence are created continuously by electronic process, to rule such evidence inadmissible has long since been recognised as highly undesirable. Within the UK, the status of the hearsay rule and the treatment of hearsay evidence has been different in England and Wales, Scotland and Northern Ireland.

Despite the fact that electronic evidence produced to the court in the form of computer statements or 'print-outs' was often agreed in terms of what it evidenced by the parties, in the absence of agreement, and prior to the CEA 1995, computer evidence could only be admitted under section 5 of the Civil Evidence Act 1968 (CEA 1968) as hearsay evidence provided the following conditions were satisfied:

■ the computer had been regularly used to store or process information over a period which included the date when the print-out was made;

■ during such period, information of the kind which was contained in the print-out (or of a kind from which such information was derived) had been regularly supplied to the computer;

■ the computer had been operating properly throughout such period (or, if not, such malfunction as had occurred would not have affected the accuracy of the material contained in the print-out); and

■ the information contained in the print-out reproduced or was derived from information supplied to the computer in the ordinary course of its activities.

There were potentially three witnesses who could attest to the fact that these conditions had been satisfied:

■ the person who was managing the business whose activities were recorded by the computer, since he would be expected to have been aware of any errors produced in the supply of information;

■ the person responsible for overseeing the input of information to the computer; and

■ the person responsible for the 'hardware' and programming of the computer.

7.87 RSC Ord 38, r 24 provided that a 'Civil Evidence Act notice' must be served in respect of such computer statements identifying each of the three persons referred to above and confirming that the computer had been working properly during the relevant period. The other party was entitled to give notice under RSC Ord 38, r 26 requiring the attendance of any of these named persons at the hearing for cross-examination.

All of this has now changed with the coming into force of the CEA 1995, which has had the welcome effect of abolishing the rule against admission of hearsay evidence in civil proceedings. This reforming legislation was largely an implementation of recommendations made in a Law Commission Report in 1993[1]. The entirety of sections 1–10 of the CEA 1968 dealing with hearsay exceptions were repealed by section 15(2) of the CEA 1995.

The requirement for evidence from one person that a computer was 'operating properly' clearly became increasingly unrealistic in the context of highly sophisticated and powerful PCs networked within organisations and connected via the telephone system to the global Internet. This requirement still exists in Northern Ireland (see the end of this section, paragraph 7.88), but the law elsewhere has now recognised the social and business fact that such systems could not be used and relied upon in the way that they are if there were not a high degree of trust invested by all of us everyday in the integrity of computer capabilities in terms of their routine operation. Protection is still afforded to those who wish to challenge computer-derived evidence by way of attacking the weight to be afforded to it, but the reversal of the burden for acceptance of computer-generated records and evidence is to be welcomed both in principle and in practice.

In the US context, there has been a recent attempt to admit hearsay evidence under the exception for 'business records'. This was in the case of *United States v Jackson*[2], where the material sought to be admitted existed on the websites of non-parties to the proceedings, and it was argued that it was the 'business records' of the ISPs of these sites. This argument was rejected by the court.

The relevant statutory provisions now governing proof of statements contained in documents are provided by sections 8, 9 and 12 of the CEA 1995, which state:

'**8** (1) Where a statement contained in a document is admissible as evidence in civil proceedings, it may be proved:

(a) by the production of the document, or

(b) whether or not that document is still in existence, by the production of a copy of that document or of the material part of it,

authenticated in such manner as the court may approve ...

(2) It is immaterial for this purpose how many removes there are between a copy and an original ...

9(1) A document which is shown to form part of the records of a business or public authority may be received in evidence in civil proceedings without further proof ...

12 Document means anything in which information of any description is recorded ... "copy", in relation to a document, means anything onto which information recorded in the document has been copied, by whatever means and whether directly or indirectly ...'

1 'The Hearsay Rule in Civil Proceedings' (Law Com No 216, Cm 2321, 1993).
2 208 F 3d 633 (7th Cir), 2000.

7.88 Despite the fact that no statutory guidelines regarding the weight to be attached to hearsay evidence have yet been issued, it is clear that the general doctrine is moving away from the emphasis on admissibility (which originally sought to protect juries from the perceived intrinsic complexities of computer evidence) towards the basic assessment of probative value.

There remains a residual notice requirement under section 2 of the CEA 1995 in respect of hearsay evidence to be adduced in civil proceedings. The difference now is that failure to comply with that notice procedure does not render the hearsay evidence inadmissible, but it may be taken into account by the court when considering both costs and the weight to be given to the evidence. This is consistent with the Law Commission recommendation that litigants wishing to rely on hearsay evidence should give notice of that intention where it was reasonable and practicable to so and was likely to assist the notified party in dealing with any issues over the weight to be given to the evidence as a result of it being hearsay. This principle is also embodied CPR Part 33, r 2 and the corresponding Practice Direction (33), which refers to the notice requirement of section 2 of the CEA 1995.

The CEA 1968, and indeed the recent CEA 1995, do not extend to Scotland, which has evolved its own and much simpler rules of evidence. Scotland is subject to the Civil Evidence (Scotland) Act 1988, which, like in England and Wales, followed a comprehensive review of the law by the (Scottish) Law Commission[1].

Reforms in Scotland need to be reviewed against other major differences of procedure with the remainder of the UK. In the absence of a compulsory system of disclosure or discovery of documents, the situation in Scottish proceedings is significantly different to that in England and Wales. Documents which form part of a party's case must either be recited in full in the pleadings or incorporated by express reference.

Where a case depends on disputed questions of fact which require resolution at trial, either party can make an application to the judge for an order that the other party produce documents or items in its possession which are required for resolving the issues in the case, whether or not they are adverse to the interest of the producing party.

The scope of such an order for the production of documents or items within the possession of one or other party is limited to such documents or items of a class which are relevant to the issues in the case. Within those limits, the terms of such an order may be fairly wide. Specific documents do not need to be particularised and there is no requirement on the applicant to demonstrate the existence of specific documents or items. While there are certain classes of documents which are privileged from production (such as those passing between lawyer and client), such orders could cover most forms of electronic data and media, and the print-outs of information contained within such media.

The Civil Evidence (Scotland) Act 1988 abolished the rule against both simple and multiple hearsay. In one sense the Act went further than its later English equivalent in that it did not retain any requirement of notification of intention to rely on hearsay evidence. This was felt by Parliament at the time to risk reintroducing the hearsay rule by the back door. Instead, provisions were made for the calling of witnesses where a party could reasonably claim to have been 'surprised' by the reliance on a particular piece of hearsay evidence. The failure to call an available witness in such circumstances would not prohibit reliance on the evidence, but would rather go to the assessment of its weight.

Like England and Wales, no statutory guidelines were or have been given to the courts to assist them in assessing the weight of hearsay evidence.

The situation in Northern Ireland is now to be significantly contrasted with that in the rest of the UK in that the Northern Ireland courts still recognise the rule against hearsay. The main legislation governing exemptions to the hearsay rule is contained in the Evidence Act (NI) 1939 and the Civil Evidence Act (NI) 1971. In terms of the exemptions applying for computer evidence, these are similar to those which applied in England and Wales under the CEA 1968.

There can be little doubt that the legislation is dated and in need of urgent replacement. Litigants in this jurisdiction should be alert to the fact that compliance with notice requirements will be a precondition for admission of almost all electronic evidence.

1 'Evidence: Report on Corroboration, Hearsay and Related Matters in Civil Proceedings' (Scottish Law Commission Report No 100, 1986).

(e) Legal professional privilege

7.89 Documents which are subject to legal professional privilege do not have to be disclosed in legal proceedings. Privilege will attach to documents which are:

- correspondence between a client and its layers which is confidential and written for the purpose of giving or obtaining legal advice, whether or not litigation is pending or contemplated; or

- correspondence between a client, its lawyers or agent and a third party prepared for the sole or dominant purpose of either giving or obtaining legal advice in connection with litigation, as well as experts' reports and witness statements when litigation is pending.

Problems may arise when the document which is subject to privilege is in the form of an e-mail. The original addressee of a privileged e-mail will be afforded the privilege. However, it is unclear as to whether privilege will remain if the e-mail is forwarded to a third party or is widely circulated.

To avoid the loss of privilege, such e-mails should only be circulated to the necessary persons. They can be submitted to an external lawyer for advice in order to attract privilege, should this be absent.

(f) Forensic computing and electronic evidence

7.90 Ultimately, the detailed consideration of the reliability of computer evidence is now addressed by the science of forensic computing. This new discipline analyses reliability as a combination of:

- the trustworthiness/integrity of the content of particular computer evidence; and

- the trustworthiness/integrity of the process by which that content was produced.

When these two factors are evaluated together, they reveal the overall integrity or reliability of the computer-derived evidence. Elements which should be considered in determining the overall integrity should include:

- the integrity of the original source data;

- the extent and quality of the internal computer functions in respect of that data;

- the degree to which control or audit procedures were in place to mitigate errors;

- the presence of corroborative mechanisms;

- the integrity of the derivation process by which electronic evidence has been obtained;

- the integrity of manipulation/handling processes by experts/investigators prior to its submission of a particular electronic evidence exhibit in court.

The integrity of evidence existing on the Internet was considered in the American case of *St Clair v Johnny's Oyster and Shrimp Inc*[1]. The court in this case held that where the only evidence was from an on-line database, this evidence was too unreliable to be admitted, as there was no guarantee it was accurate and unaltered.

A consideration of these elements should assist in generating work practices and protocols to protect the likely status of computer evidence generated by a party aware of these considerations, and likewise provide a useful basis for attacking an opponent's computer-derived evidence. To the extent that such considerations have already led to formal standards being developed, these are considered in paragraph 7.91 below. A detailed consideration of the technical basis of forensic computing is beyond the scope of this book, however.

1 76 F Supp 2d 773 (SD Tex, 1999).

(g) Good practice in electronic evidence record-keeping

7.91 Electronic evidence is likely to be given most 'weight' in litigation and other proceedings where it can be demonstrated to have been created, compiled or stored in accordance with procedures and protocols that enhance or support its reliability.

Such considerations inevitably lead to considerations of best corporate practice and relevant British Standards. There are two relevant standards, one British Standard and one British Standard Code of Practice providing guidance to business, courts and lawyers in relation to the management of computer evidence and its reliability:

- British Standard 7799-1: 2000 – Code of Practice for Information Security Management;

- British Standard 7799-2: 2002 – Information Security Management – Specification with Guidance for Use;

- British Standard Code of Practice DISC PD0008: 1999 – A Code of Practice for Legal Admissibility and Evidential Weight of Information Stored Electronically; and

- British Standard Code of Practice DISC PD5000-1-5: 2002 – International Code of Practice for Electronic Document and E-business Transactions as Legally Admissible Evidence.

(i) British Standard 7799-1 (2000) and 2 (2002)[1]

7.92 BS7799 is the closest standard applicable in the UK to a general code of best practice for electronic information management. The standard has been adopted in a number of other countries, including Australia, New Zealand and The Netherlands.

1   BS 7799-1: 2000 replaced BS 7799-1: 1999, and BS 7799-2: 2002 replaced BS 7799-2: 1999.

(ii) British Standard Code of Practice DISC PD0008: 1999[1]

7.93 This code was developed largely out of the work of academics who created a consortium of business interests to press for legal equivalence of electronic images vis-à-vis printed and handwritten documents.

The code is constructed around compliance with the 'Five Principles of Good Practice', namely:

- recognition of all types of information;

- understanding of legal requirements and execution of duty of care obligations;

- identification and specification of business processes and procedures;

- identification of enabling technologies to support business processes and procedures; and

- monitoring and audit procedures being in place.

The BSI[2] comment on their code:

> 'PD0008 does not guarantee legal admissibility. It seeks to define the current interpretation of best practice in document management and provide a common framework, which if followed, will help maximise the value and integrity of your information in a court of Law.
>
> Of major importance to the Code is the CEA 1995. The Act introduces a flexible system whereby all documents and copy documents, including computer records, can be admitted as evidence in civil proceedings. The court judge will still have to be persuaded to treat that evidence as reliable, and so organisations would be best advised to put in place procedures to prove the authenticity and reliability of the record.
>
> The Code offers guidelines for the procurement, planning, design, management, and operation of electronic document management systems and aims to remove much of the doubt and confusion. It pays particular attention to setting up authorised procedures and subsequently the ability to demonstrate, in a Court of Law, that these procedures are being followed.'

Compliance with the Code will not guarantee that electronically stored documents will be treated as reliable evidence, but it does, however, provide a framework for a court to work within when considering admissibility and weight and strengthen a party's claim that its electronically stored documents should be treated as reliable evidence to support or defend a claim.

Clearly, if a party to litigation was looking for lines of attack in relation to its opponent's computer evidence, requesting that opponent to specify with full particularity whether and how each and every piece of their computer evidence has been handled to comply with these standards is likely to prove exceptionally onerous.

Failure to respond, or an indication that the evidence has been handled in such a way as to have repeatedly violated the standards set out within these documents, could lead to a request to the court to have that evidence excluded.

1 This replaced British Standard 7768: 1994 – Management of Optical Disk (WORM) System for the recording of documents that may be required as evidence.
2 BSI can be contacted at: British Standards House, 389 Chiswick High Road, London W4 4AL. Tel: +44 (0) 20 8996 9000; www.BSI.org.uk.

(iii) British Standard Code of Practice DISC PD5000-1-5: 2002 – International Code of Practice for Electronic Documents and E-commerce Transactions of Legally Admissible Evidence[1]

7.94 This Code is a set of five international codes of good practice, including:

■ Information stored electronically (PD5000-1: 2002);

■ Electronic communication and e-mail policy (PD5000-2: 2002);

■ Identity, signature and copyright (PD5000-3: 2002);

■ Using certification authorities (PD5000-4: 2002);

■ Using trusted third party archives (PD5000-5: 2002).

1 The Code replaces DISC PD5000: 1999.

(h) Legal time requirements for records

(i) Introduction

7.95 In addition to implementing best practice in the systems and management of electronic data and record-keeping, the issue arises as to how long data and records should be retained.

In this regard, the law makes no distinction between electronic data and other types of record. It may be that the increased ability to store large quantities of electronic data will encourage legislators to extend the periods of time for which individuals and companies are statutorily required to keep records of certain matters because it is stored:

■ cheaply (because less space is required than for paper documentation); and

■ for longer periods of time without physical deterioration.

In many cases, legislation makes no specific reference to the length of time particular records should be retained. It is therefore frequently up to individuals and companies to draw up their own policy for the retention of records and documents relating to their affairs.

(ii) Company records

7.96 Company records need to be retained for various statutory reasons, such as:

■ auditing;

■ taxation purposes; and

■ employment legislation.

All company records relating to the incorporation of a company, the company's constitution, meetings of the company and resolutions passed should be retained for the life of the company.

Minute books containing the minutes and proceedings of any general meetings, together with class meetings, must be kept at the registered office.

Section 222 of the Companies Act 1985 states that accounting records of a company must be preserved for a period of three years from the date when they were made in the case of a private company and six years for a public company. The records must be kept at the registered office of the company or such other place as directors think fit.

In addition, a company must also show that it complies with other statutory requirements such as those contained within the Taxes Management Act 1970, the Limitation Act 1980 (LA 1980), the Value Added Tax Act 1994 and the PAYE Regulations. It may therefore be more desirable to keep all accounting records for at least six years, even in the case of a private company.

The LA 1980 imposes time limits within which claims must be brought. An action founded on a simple contract must be brought within six years from the date from which the course of action accrued and in the case of a personal injuries action within three years. In an action upon a contract under seal (that is, a deed), the action must be brought before the expiration of 12 years from the date on which the cause of action accrued.

Under this Act, no claim in respect of defective products can be brought on or after the expiration of ten years from the time when a product was supplied to another.

(iii) Employee records

7.97   All personnel records should be kept for six years after employment ceases. There is no statutory guideline pertaining to personnel records per se, but the need to retain them is apparent from other statutory requirements as set out below.

It is advisable to keep all job descriptions and job applications for six months in the event of any claim under the Sex Discrimination Act 1975 or Race Relations Act 1976.

An employer must retain the following records for three years:

- all records in relation to maternity pay;

- all records in relation to statutory sick pay; and

- all records of notifiable accidents, dangerous occurrences and reportable diseases.

(iv) Tax records

7.98   There used to be no statutory time limit for retaining records or documents for the purposes of corporation tax. Nevertheless, an inspector could (and still can) issue a notice in writing requiring a person to deliver any documents which he believed contained or possibly contained information relevant to the actual or possible tax liability of any taxpayer.

There are also circumstances where the Inland Revenue can call for documents from third parties (that is, the Inland Revenue can request the production of documents in relation to someone else's tax position).

Under the new self-assessment provisions (which are basically the pay-and-file regulations for companies), where a return is required from a company, that company must keep sufficient records to enable it to make a correct and complete return for the year concerned. These records will include:

- details of the amount and description of all receipts and expenses in the course of trade;

- details of purchases and sales (if the trade involves dealing in goods); and

- supporting documents for the first and second items above (including accounts, books, contracts, receipts, etc).

A company will be required to preserve the records until the fifth anniversary of the 31 January following the end of the year of assessment (that is, broadly speaking six years). If the Inland Revenue enquires into a return, the records will have to be preserved until the enquiries are complete if that is later than the 'fifth anniversary' date.

It is possible for a company to preserve the information contained in the records rather than the records themselves and those documents preserving the information would be admissible as evidence in proceedings before the Commissioners.

A company which fails to keep or preserve records in accordance with these provisions will be liable for penalty.

For VAT purposes, business and accounting records, the VAT account and copies of all invoices, credit and debit notes and other documents which evidence an increase or decrease in consideration, must be kept for six years. It may be possible to agree with Customs & Excise on a shorter period, but this is within their discretion and there would have to be a good reason.

Since the requirement to keep records for direct taxation purposes is (basically) six years anyway, this in itself would normally militate against trying to agree a shorter period with Customs & Excise.

(i) Service by electronic means

7.99 Under the CPR there has been some welcome updating of procedure rules to recognise new technology and business practices. CPR Part 5, r 3 deals with 'Signature of documents by mechanical means' and provides:

> 'Where any of these Rules or any practice direction requires a document to be signed, that requirement shall be satisfied if the signature is printed by computer or other mechanical means.'

This is supplemented by Practice Direction 5, which, in paragraph 1, directs that where a signature is printed electronically, the name of the person whose signature appears must also be printed so that person may be identified.

Service itself is dealt with at CPR Part 6. Part 6, r 2 provides for methods of service, including:

> '6.2 (1)   A document may be served by any of the following methods—
> ...
> (e)   by fax or other means of electronic communication in accordance with the relevant practice direction.'

The practice direction on service sets out the following more detailed requirements for compliance with Part 6, r 2(e):

> '*Service by facsimile*
> **3.1**   Subject to the provision of para 3.2 below, where a document is to be served by facsimile (fax):
> (1)   the party who is to be served or his legal representative must previously have indicated in writing to the party serving—

(a) that he is willing to accept service by fax, and

(b) the fax number to which it should be sent.

(2) if the party on whom the document is to be served is acting by a legal representative, the fax must be sent to the legal representative's business address, and

(3) a fax number

(a) provided in writing expressly for the purpose of accepting service where the party to be served is acting in person, or

(b) set out on the writing paper of the legal representative of the party who is to be served, or

(c) set out on a statement of case or a response to a claim filed with the court,

shall be taken as sufficient written indication for the purposes of para 3.1(1).

3.2 A legal representative's business address must be within the jurisdiction and is the physical location of his office. Where an electronic address or identification is given in conjunction with the business address, the electronic address will be deemed to be at the business address.

3.3 Service by other electronic means may take place only where:

(1) the party serving the document and the party on whom it is to be served are both acting by legal representative,

(2) the document is served at the legal representative's business address, and

(3) the legal representative who is to be served has previously expressly indicated in writing to the party serving his willingness to accept service by this means and has provided

(a) his e-mail address, or

(b) other electronic identification such as an ISDN or other telephonic link number.

3.4 Where a document is served by fax or other electronic means, the party serving the document is not required in addition to send a copy by post or document exchange, but if he does not do so and the document is proved not to have been received then the court may, on any application arising out of that non-receipt, take account of the fact that a hard copy was not sent.'

(j) Summary

7.100

■ Relevant computer data and records (including fax and e-mail communications, whether printed or stored electronically) are admissible evidence in civil proceedings both in England and Wales and Scotland.

■ The fact that such communications and/or the electronic data associated with such communications may constitute or contain hearsay evidence does not make the evidence inadmissible in civil proceedings in England and Wales or Scotland.

■ The general movement in the treatment of civil evidence (and, to a lesser degree, criminal evidence) is away from questions of admissibility and towards assessment of its probative value (or 'weight').

■ The probative value of computer evidence is open to challenge in different ways to that of paper-based documentary evidence. Attacks on the probative value of computer evidence can be best rebutted by showing high levels of compliance with relevant British Standards, in particular BS 7799-1: 2000 and BS 7799-2: 2002, Code of Practice DISC PD0008: 1999, and International Code of Practice DISC PD5000-1-5: 2002.

- The CEA 1995 made no special provision for computer-generated documents, and actually repealed the special requirements of section 5 of the CEA 1968. The CEA 1995 has introduced a flexible system whereby all documents and copy documents, including computer records, can be admitted as evidence in civil proceedings.

- A court will still have to be persuaded to treat such evidence as reliable and there will continue to be issues about the weight to be attached to computer evidence, especially where the possibility of tampering exists.

- The starting point for electronically stored documents is now exactly the same as any other document stored in hard copy form.

8

E-taxation

1. INTRODUCTION – STRUGGLING TAX LAWS?

8.01 As our society continues to move from an economy based on manufacturing to one based on information, the value added in that economy is becoming increasingly intellectual and international. In contrast, tax law is based on principles which evolved decades ago and which relate primarily to tax transactions involving tangible products within a single jurisdiction. That tax issues arise seems inevitable with new technology – a hundred years ago, the sort of question that the courts were required to answer was whether a telegraph operator would be liable to account for tax in relation to international telegraph messages[1].

There is an obvious commercial concern that e-commerce may be constrained by unclear and outdated tax laws, particularly if double taxation increases as tax authorities struggle to exercise their rights to tax a new profit source. Taxing authorities are concerned that existing tax laws will not be able to capture electronic transactions properly, reducing the tax base. They also fear a loss of that tax base to lower tax jurisdictions as businesses move the centre of their operations. The increasing sophistication of communications and range of purely electronic businesses mean that it will not be difficult (in theory) for businesses to move from one jurisdiction to another, in search of more favourable tax rates. The areas most likely to be affected by tax base erosion in the short term are those where products are easily digitised and easily available via electronic media: books, music, travel arrangements, software and information supply, and banking and financial services of various sorts.

There is also the potential for transactions to be hidden. E-commerce encompasses not only the Internet, but also the transactions conducted on private networks. Even on the Internet, the sheer scale of on-line activity could make discovery of transactions very difficult. The increasing use of non-traditional methods of access, such as interactive TV, will open up the home retail market even further. The effectiveness of a tax system depends, ultimately, on the consent of taxpayers to be taxed. The collection of taxes is based on the voluntary disclosure of information by individuals and businesses to the tax authorities. The process is policed by those authorities who are given powers to encourage and enforce compliance. Audit trails and records are required, usually based on normal accounting systems. It might sound unduly alarmist to suggest that businesses carrying on e-commerce will engage in massive tax evasion. However, it is true to say that the new ways of conducting business bring new challenges to tax compliance.

The key point to note at the outset is that there are (as yet) no separate taxes that apply to e-commerce. Taxpayers and taxing authorities are both required to apply general principles of tax law to e-commerce and, at present, governments seem content with this approach. It is beyond the scope of this book to discuss those principles in detail. In this chapter, we will focus on the key issues and 'pinch points' where those general rules are ill-suited to e-commerce. We will first consider some of the general challenges and issues facing the tax system in relation to e-commerce, before looking more specifically at the taxation of profits arising from e-commerce and the application of VAT and customs duty to electronic transactions. The chapter will conclude with some comments on the impact of e-commerce on tax administration.

1   *Erichsen v Last* (1881) 8 QBD 414, 4 TC 422, CA.

2.   CHALLENGES AND ISSUES

8.02   The problems of taxation and tax administration in the world of e-commerce have not, of course, escaped attention and analysis; rather, they have actually been reviewed at great length, at a national and international level. The US *Framework for Global E-commerce* was published in July 1997, advocating no immediate new taxes; and the Organisation for Economic Cooperation and Development (OECD) report 'E-commerce: Opportunities and Challenges to Government' in November 1997 called for governments to work together to begin formulating policy. This direction was developed at the OECD conference in Ottawa, in October 1998, by the adoption of the following framework conditions for taxation of e-commerce:

- there should be no new taxes – existing tax rules should be amended if necessary;

- consumption taxes, such as VAT, should be levied in the country where consumption takes place; and

- the supply of digitised products should be categorised as a supply of services rather than of goods.

The focus is now increasingly on ways to resolve the issues raised by e-commerce, not simply to identify the issues themselves. In many cases, it seems that fears that the existing tax system would be inadequate for the challenge of e-commerce have been exaggerated – at least as regards the immediate future.

In 1998 the US Congress passed the Internet Tax Freedom Act, providing for a moratorium on new Internet taxation for the following three years, allowing time for co-ordinated approach. Although the Act expired on 21 October 2001, Congressional approval has been given to a Bill extending the moratorium for a further two years.

(a)   The UK Government's position

8.03   In the UK, the Inland Revenue and Customs & Excise issued a joint statement[1] shortly before the Ottawa conference setting out the Government's policy towards the tax issues arising from e-commerce. In particular, the statement sets out the view (which is broadly consistent with the outcome of the conference) that the following general principles should apply to the taxation of e-commerce:

- **Neutrality** The taxation of e-commerce should seek to be technology-neutral, so that no particular form of commerce is advantaged or disadvantaged.

- **Certainty and transparency** Tax rules should be clear and simple, so that businesses can anticipate the tax consequences of the transactions they enter into.

- **Effectiveness** Tax rules should not result in either double taxation or unintentional non-taxation – the overriding aim should be that the right amount of tax is paid at the right time and in the right country. Tax rules should be sufficiently flexible to continue to achieve this as technology develops.

■ **Efficiency** Tax rules should be efficient, keeping the compliance costs of business and the administration costs of government to the minimum compatible with effective tax administration; measures to counter evasion or avoidance should be proportionate to the risks which they seek to address.

Subject to these guiding principles, the UK tax authorities consider that major changes to the current tax system are not necessary to deal with the issues raised by e-commerce. However, the position is being kept under review and it is recognised that some adjustments may be needed to ensure that the tax base is preserved.

1 News Release 25/98.

(b) Challenges posed by e-commerce

8.04 Traditional methods of taxation rely on being able to verify location. This may be the location of the seller, the buyer or the goods sold. Most countries only seek to tax the people in that country or goods and services in or transferred to that country. However, where people, goods and services move across international borders, there may be competing claims to tax by the various countries involved. For example, if a UK company carries on trade through a branch office in, say, the US, both the UK and the US will claim the right to tax profits generated by that branch. The UK claims the right by virtue of the company having been set up in the UK, the US by virtue of the trading activity taking place in the US. A system of bilateral treaties between trading countries seeks to balance these competing tax claims without unduly restricting commerce. At present, however, the treaties and most tax laws assume a physical exchange is involved in an international transaction. The Internet provides an environment in which automated functions can undertake significant business with little or no physical presence or activity. These functions can be easily and quickly moved from one jurisdiction to another.

(i) No geographical identification

8.05 The correspondence between Internet addresses and geographical locations is very weak. Country suffixes (.uk or .au, for example) are more a matter of choice than obligation – it is not difficult to register an Internet address in another country, and addresses using higher level domains such as .com and .org, originally intended to indicate a US location, are now in widespread use outside the US. Even where there is a link between an Internet address and a country, there need be no correlation between an Internet address and the physical location of a connected person – all you need is a mobile telephone and you could connect from anywhere on the planet.

(ii) Nature of the Internet

8.06 The nature of the Internet only adds to the problem. The 'radical decentralisation'[1] that is taking place means that there is little technical difference between electronic transmission within a country and between countries. To the consumer of an intangible, ordered and supplied electronically, there is no practical difference between a supply from one country compared with another; indeed, the consumer may not be aware of the country of supply. Many website operators arrange for their primary websites to be 'mirrored', meaning that a copy of the website is operated from one or more other servers around the world. This speeds up the service provided to consumers, but adds to location confusion. Using mirrors reduces the amount of electronic traffic to a web server, but it is not always easy to tell whether you are looking at the original server or a mirror. If websites become significant indicators of location of a business, mirrors could cause problems. Global trading also causes location problems: companies can more easily move to favourable tax regimes, or keep moving from one to another, never settling permanently in one place.

The increase in international trade also brings potential, unintentional, compliance problems, especially from smaller businesses which may not have the resource or experience required to deal with international tax compliance. The sheer volume of information, commercial and non-commercial, traded on the Internet means that it is impossible realistically to track commercial activity on any reasonable scale. Even where transactions could be seen to be occurring, the wide availability of military-grade encryption would make monitoring impossible.

Finally, the dynamic nature of e-commerce development presents its own problems. For example, the increasing use of 'intelligent' agent software on a web server, gathering information and presenting conclusions without the intervention of a human, adds to the confusion over where a business is conducted.

1   US Treasury, 'Selected Tax Policy Implications of Global Economic Commerce', November 1996.

(c) Issues

8.07   For taxation to be effective, there are certain fundamental requirements which need to be met. All of these are challenged by e-commerce to some degree.

■   **Jurisdiction** Identification of the location where an electronic business conducts its trade, to establish where the liability to tax is incurred.

■   **Identification** What the liability is.

■   **Enforcement** Information is required about the taxpayer and the transaction and subsequent collection of tax.

Each of these issues is discussed in more depth below, with particular emphasis on the difficulties raised by the nature of e-commerce.

An awareness of the potential tax issues is necessary when establishing an e-commerce business, whether as a new business or as a development of an existing business. It is necessary both because a business should be structured as tax efficiently as possible and because no definitive stance has yet been taken by taxing authorities with regard to these issues.

3.   TAXATION OF E-COMMERCE PROFITS

(a) Where does the tax charge arise?

8.08   In order to be able to impose tax on profits, a taxing authority must have jurisdiction over the taxpayer. Historically, jurisdiction has required some physical presence in the country where that tax authority has power to tax. Physical presence is increasingly less important to e-commerce – it is not always possible to know where a trader has a physical presence, or in which country a transaction has taken place.

The issue is also complicated by the various ways in which electronic media can be used for commerce: besides conducting sales electronically, the graphical potential of the World Wide Web means that businesses can use websites as shopfronts. Businesses which use the Internet to advertise, or to solicit sales then completed by more traditional methods (such as telephone or fax), need not also actually transact business electronically. However, is having advertising space on a website sufficient to give the business a taxable presence in the jurisdiction in which the server hosting that website is located? Some US States have considered laws which would ensure that it would be sufficient.

(b) Determining jurisdiction

8.09 A taxpayer is generally taxed by the country in which he lives, but is assessed on his worldwide income (*residence* basis). Tax authorities generally also tax income arising or profits earned in their jurisdiction by foreign taxpayers (*source* basis).

- **The country of residence** This is the country where a taxpayer has the closest personal links and is usually established by some physical criteria. For companies, the OECD Model Treaty deems this to be the country of *effective management and control*, whereas the US view is that all companies *incorporated* in the US are resident there, regardless of where they are managed. The management test in the OECD Model Treaty is increasingly open to manipulation with the rise of global communications and ease of travel. This is recognised in a discussion paper from the OECD's technical advisory group on monitoring the application of existing treaty norms for the taxation of business profits[1]. The group has suggested a number of alternatives to the place of effective management test, including establishing a hierarchy of tests, one of which could be the place where the economic nexus of the company is strongest.

- **The country of source** This is the country with which an item of income has the closest links. The link may be that the asset which generates the income is physically or legally located in the country (for example, intellectual property rights which are licensed to produce royalties). Alternatively, the link may be that the foreign taxpayer is carrying on a trading activity in the country through a branch or agency or some other physical presence. It is in this area that e-commerce has the potential significantly to erode the source basis of taxation, as it allows the link between an income producing asset or activity and a specific location to become blurred.

Where a double tax treaty is in place, the treaty will generally ensure that the country of residence gives credit for the tax paid in the country of source. It will also limit the right to impose tax in the country of source: only trading profits linked to a 'permanent establishment' in that country may be taxed and the right to tax income derived from ownership of assets (often collected at source by deduction or withholding) may be reduced or eliminated. Most modern tax treaties are based on the Model Treaty devised by the OECD, which sets out basic rules for establishing which country has the authority to tax a transaction. Treaties based on the OECD model restrict the taxing powers of source countries and define who has jurisdiction to tax. They also generally deal with the identification of income. Treaties are usually preferred by developed countries, as they tend to be net exporters and consequently prefer to restrict the taxing powers of the countries which are their customers. Less developed countries tend to be net consumers and would prefer to maintain taxation based on the source of income, but they rarely have enough political influence for treaties to favour them. In the absence of an appropriate bilateral treaty, domestic legislation will govern the taxation of a non-resident conducting business in the country. The status of the same type of business can therefore vary depending on the country of origin.

1 OECD, 'The Impact of the Communications Revolution on the Application of "Place of Effective Management" as a Tie Breaker Rule', February 2001.

(i) *Taxation of a UK business trading electronically*

8.10 A UK business starting to carry out business electronically must accept that it will be liable to UK tax on the profits it generates. These will be calculated in the same way as applies to traditional trading methods. However, a key issue is whether the electronic trading will expose the business to any tax liability outside the UK. This is not an issue if trading occurs entirely within the UK, where the website is hosted in the UK and transactions only take place with UK customers. But this relatively simple situation is unlikely to arise in practice: both non-UK websites or servers and/or non-UK customers are likely to be involved. The question is, therefore, whether trading in this way gives the UK business a taxable presence in either the country where the website or server is located or where the customers are located. In most cases the location of the customer does not determine the liability to tax on profits[1]. More uncertainty exists in relation to websites. Can a website amount to a taxable presence in the country where the host server is situated?

1 Contrast the VAT rules considered below, where the location of the customer can affect the liability of a transaction to VAT.

(c) Permanent establishment

8.11 Permanent establishment (PE) is a concept used in the OECD Model Treaty to determine whether a business is within the jurisdiction of a tax authority. Broadly speaking, under a treaty, the business income of a non-resident can be taxed only if it can be attributed to a PE in the tax authority's country. The principle is used by some countries in their domestic legislation as well as applying where there is a treaty in place with the country of residence of the parent business.

A PE is defined[1] as a fixed place of business[2] through which the business of an enterprise is carried on. It specifically includes:

- a place of management;
- a branch;
- an office;
- a factory;
- a workshop.

Various functions are excluded from creating a PE, including:

- advertising or information provision;
- storage, display, delivery;
- purchasing;
- servicing a new patent or know-how contract.

An *independent* agent acting for a business will not generally give rise to a PE, although a dependent agent will be considered to give the business a PE in the country.

The guidelines to the OECD Model Treaty for determining whether something amounts to a PE include:

- the existence of a fixed place of business (offices, plant and machinery, with some degree of permanence);
- business conducted in that country, either directly through personnel or through automated equipment.

It will be appreciated that the concept of a PE is not fully compatible with electronic business. This is not surprising as the principle was drafted in 1963 and examples in the Model Treaty rely on physical presence. Despite the OECD Model Treaty, individual countries are still free to interpret the concept of PE in different ways. This can have surprising results. For example, a 1996 case in Germany[3] declared a pipeline owned by a Netherlands company and crossing German territory to be sufficient to create a PE under German domestic law. This was despite the passive nature of the presence in Germany: the pipeline was supplied with pressure outside Germany and the company had no employees in Germany (maintenance was carried out by third party contractors).

1   Article 5 of the OECD Model Treaty.
2   Place of business includes any 'premises, facilities or installations'. It can include gaming and vending machines maintained and operated by a non-resident for profit. Lack of personnel in the country is not a barrier to a place of business being a PE.
3   BFH decision of 30 October, 1996 II R 12/92, BStBl II 1997 p 12; www.xs4all.nl/~marvl/pipeline.html.

(i)   Permanent establishment and e-commerce

8.12   Leaving aside territorial differences, the major questions about PE in the context of e-commerce are:

■   whether a website or a web server can be considered to be a PE;

■   whether an Internet service provider (ISP) can create a PE for businesses utilising their services to engage in e-commerce;

■   having established that an enterprise has a PE in a particular jurisdiction, to what extent can profits of the enterprise be attributed to its PE.

(ii)   Can a website/server be a permanent establishment?

8.13   On 22 December 2000, the OECD Committee on Fiscal Affairs updated the commentary on the OECD Model Treaty to clarify the application of the PE concept in the context of e-commerce[1]. The clarification was incorporated in the October 2001 draft update of the OECD Model Treaty.

The changes to the commentary emphasise that, in order for an enterprise to have a PE, it must have something that constitutes tangible property in the relevant jurisdiction. A website, as a combination of software and electronic data, cannot amount to a 'place of business' because it has no physical presence.

This general principle was not, however, accepted by the fiscal authorities of Spain and Portugal, who do not agree that physical presence is a requirement for a PE to exist. Therefore, both countries consider that, in some circumstances, an enterprise carrying on business in a particular jurisdiction through a website could be treated as having a PE in that jurisdiction.

The updated commentary goes on to say that a web server, as a piece of equipment with a physical location, could constitute a PE of the enterprise that operates it. This is the case even though no personnel of the enterprise is required at the relevant location for the operation of the equipment. The important issue is whether the enterprise carrying on business through a website has the server at its own disposal. If it owns (or leases) and operates the server on which the website is stored and used, the place where the server is located could constitute a PE of the enterprise if the other elements of the definition of PE outlined above are present. On the other hand, if the website is hosted on the server of an ISP, such an arrangement will not result in the server and its location being at the disposal of the enterprise (even if the enterprise is able to determine that its website should be hosted on a particular server at a particular location). In such a case, the enterprise will not be considered to have acquired a PE by virtue of the hosting arrangement.

A server at a given location will only constitute a PE if it meets the requirement of being fixed. The updated commentary says that what is relevant is not the possibility of the server being moved, but whether it is in fact moved: the server would need to be located at a certain place for a sufficient period of time so as to become fixed within the definition of PE. The commentary does not give any indication of what would be a 'sufficient period of time' in this context. However, the OECD Committee on Fiscal Affairs has commented that it is unlikely that much tax revenue will be raised on the basis that a server at a given location constitutes a PE, due to the ease with which the equipment may be relocated.

The UK Inland Revenue has taken the view that in no circumstances do servers, of themselves or together with websites, constitute Pes[2].

1 OECD, 'Clarification on the Application of the Permanent Establishment Definition in E-Commerce: Changes to the Commentary on the Model Tax Convention on Article 5', December 2000.
2 Inland Revenue Press Release, 'E-commerce: Tax Status of Websites and Servers', 11 April 2000.

8.14 The updated OECD commentary contains helpful guidance on what would be regarded as preparatory or auxiliary activities (which would not amount to a PE) in the context of e-commerce. The examples given of such activity are as follows:

- providing a communications link – much like a telephone line – between suppliers and customers;

- advertising of goods or services;

- relaying information through a mirror server for security and efficiency purposes;

- gathering market data for the enterprise;

- supplying information.

The updated commentary emphasises that where the above functions in themselves form an essential and significant part of the business activity of the enterprise as a whole, or where other core functions of the enterprise are carried on through the equipment, these would go beyond preparatory activities and there would be a PE if the relevant equipment amounted to a fixed place of business of the enterprise. What would constitute a core function for a particular enterprise would clearly depend on the nature of its business. For example, an essential part of an ISP's business is to operate its server for the purposes of hosting websites or other applications for other enterprises. Therefore, these activities would not be considered as preparatory or auxiliary, as far as an ISP is concerned.

(iii) Can an ISP be a permanent establishment?

8.15 A major issue has been whether an ISP can be deemed to constitute a PE of an enterprise that carries on e-commerce through a website operated through a server owned and operated by the ISP. The updated OECD commentary says that this would be the case only in very unusual circumstances. An ISP would normally fall within the 'independent agent' exception and so not be a PE. It will not have authority to conclude contracts in the name of the enterprise whose website is hosted on its server and will not regularly conclude such contracts. Alternatively, the ISP will constitute an independent agent acting in the ordinary course of its business, as evidenced by the fact that it hosts the websites of many different enterprises. The updated commentary also provides clarification that a PE cannot exist by virtue of a website being an agent of the enterprise because a website is not a 'person' as defined for the purposes of the OECD Model Treaty.

(iv) Attribution of profits to a permanent establishment

8.16 The OECD has also turned its attention to the issue of the attribution of profits to a PE which carries on e-commerce activities[1]. The current treaty rules are contained in article 7 of the

OECD Model Treaty. Broadly, these provide for the attribution to the PE of those profits it might be expected to make were it an entirely distinct and separate enterprise dealing on arm's length terms with the enterprise of which it forms a part. Under the arm's length principle, the amount of profit to be allocated to the PE depends on the nature of the functions it performs, taking into account the assets used and the risks assumed[2].

The OECD paper highlights the difficulty of applying these general rules to a PE which carries on e-commerce activities. It considers the basic business model of an enterprise carrying on retail e-commerce activities through a website on a server situated in a jurisdiction where the server is such as to amount to a PE. One difficulty that arises in relation to such a business is to determine the extent to which the PE should be treated as 'owning' or creating the intangible assets it uses to carry on the business. These would normally include the software used to carry on the business, part of the value of the enterprise's brand and the value of the website design and content.

The OECD paper emphasises that the profits associated with intangible property do not necessarily accrue to the part of the enterprise making use of it, but rather to the part of the enterprise that developed or otherwise contributed the intangible. In the context of a PE with no or limited personnel, the PE is likely to perform only routine functions and would be reliant on other parts of the enterprise to provide the intangible assets necessary for it to perform most, if not all, of those functions. The OECD paper therefore concludes that, in these circumstances, the PE should not be attributed with a substantial share of the profits associated with the distribution activities of the enterprise conducted through the server.

This is contrasted with the situation in which the PE itself is assumed to have developed the website. In this case, the PE will have assumed sufficient development risks to be considered the economic owner of the intangible property developed to operate the website and, therefore, will be entitled to the profits associated with the exploitation of such property.

Problems arise where the activities of the PE fall somewhere between the two extreme cases outlined above. Clearly, it will be difficult to value some intangible assets and not always easy to decide what rights in such assets should be regarded as transferred from the enterprise to its PE. Assessments have to be made about the entrepreneurial risks associated with an activity, about the economic ownership and exploitation of assets and about adequate compensation for services provided. In making these assessments, there are no objective guidelines and it would be difficult for any two analysts to reach the same conclusions. In addition, the OECD's paper is limited to an analysis of an 'e-tailing' situation. The OECD has not yet considered the issues raised by other, possibly more complex, business models when considering the question of profit attribution.

1   OECD, 'Attribution of Profit to a Permanent Establishment involved in E-commerce Transactions'. Draft discussion paper, February 2001.
2   OECD, 'Attribution of Profit to a Permanent Establishment involved in E-commerce Transactions'. Draft discussion paper, February 2001.

(d) Liability of a non-UK business to UK tax on e-commerce profits

8.17   For a non-UK business dealing electronically through a UK website or with UK customers, the issue is whether it will be liable to UK tax on its profits. The UK follows the usual practice in developed countries of taxing non-residents on their UK source income. This may arise from trading in the UK through a branch or agency. In practice, the concept of a branch or agency is synonymous with that of a PE, particularly if the company is resident in a country with which the UK has a tax treaty.

Trading *in* the UK is distinguished from trading *with* the UK, which does not give rise to a UK tax liability. There is no statutory definition of what constitutes 'trading in' or 'trading with' and the case law relating to the subject is not particularly relevant to e-commerce. In principle, a trade is carried on in the UK if the contracts for sale of goods or services are entered into in the UK, unless the substance of the business profits are derived from activities carried on outside the UK. The ability to provide services on-line via e-commerce can change the place in which such activities are carried on. For example, as videoconferencing over the Internet increases in capacity, services which have traditionally required face-to-face presence may no longer need to be carried out in the UK. The recent test runs of a system which allows a doctor in one country to conduct an operation in another, remotely, are probably the most extreme instance of this at present.

English law is not sufficiently clear on where electronic contracts are formed for there to be certainty over where contracts for sale are executed in e-commerce. However, as the parties to the contract can specify which jurisdiction applies to the contract, this is not likely to be an issue for tax purposes where there is a formal contract.

As has already been discussed in Chapter 2, E-contract, in the case of a 'webstore', where goods are advertised and customers can place orders, the store site will generally be designed to form an 'invitation to treat', so that the customer makes the offer. The place of the contract is then the jurisdiction in which the customer receives the vendor's acceptance of the offer. Webstore vendors should ensure that the terms and conditions of sale on the webstore define the applicable jurisdiction, to avoid possibly becoming liable for tax in a number of jurisdictions as a result of contract formation.

Although it seems possible that a company that is resident in a non-treaty country could become liable to UK tax without a branch, agency or PE located in the UK, in practice it would be extremely difficult to enforce a tax liability when there is no physical presence in the UK. For businesses conducting trade on-line from outside the UK, trading with a UK customer alone should not, therefore, give rise to a tax liability.

(i) UK branch/agency

8.18 Due to the problems of collecting tax from non-residents, the Inland Revenue is more concerned with businesses which may have a branch or agency in the UK – a physical presence which enables practical tax collection. A branch or agent located in the UK is liable to tax on the UK profits of the non-resident business, although there are specific exemptions for third party, independent agents. In general, an agent will be exempt if there is no *regular* agency being carried on. If the non-resident business is in a country that has a tax treaty with the UK, there will be no liability for an independent agent even where there is a regular agency carried on.

In the context of e-commerce, the most likely party to be an agent is the ISP who provides access to the Internet and web space for the business to be conducted. However, the concept of agency requires more than mere passive provision of enabling services. If the ISP provides back-office support for the website, making commercial decisions as to conclusion of contracts, then it may be classed as an agent of the non-resident business. If there is a tax treaty that applies, even in the above circumstances, the ISP will not be required to account for tax incurred by the non-resident business provided it is independent of the business. Where there is no treaty, the ISP should ensure that it obtains an indemnity from the non-resident business in respect of any tax liability assessed on the ISP.

(e) What is taxed – identifying income

8.19 Traditionally, tax rules distinguish between different types of income and profits, often applying different rules to quantify the amount of income that is subject to tax. This is particularly true in the UK, where the schedular system applies[1]. For example, profits arising from trading activity are differentiated from income generated from the ownership and exploitation of property, such as royalty income from intellectual property or interest earned on money. These distinctions are increasingly less important but pose particular issues in relation to e-commerce. The blurring of the distinction between goods, services and intangibles on the Internet makes assessment of the nature of a tax liability complicated.

There are three basic types of income:

■ that from sale of goods;

■ that from the use of assets (which may be tangible, such as land, or intangible, such as software); and

■ that from the provision of services.

Tax law presently requires a distinction to be made as the tax treatment of transactions in most jurisdictions depends on what is being taxed. For example, as we have seen, profits from the sale of goods are generally not taxable in the country of sale unless the seller has a 'permanent establishment' there. However, profits from the exploitation of property tend to be taxable in the country where the income has its source, whether or not the seller has any presence in that country. The local tax may be collected by deduction or withholding from payments by the buyer to the seller. The rate of withholding tax will vary from country to country and may be reduced or eliminated by the provisions of a tax treaty[2].

1 The schedular system has been part of income tax throughout its 200-year history and was originally designed to protect taxpayer confidentiality. A different official collected tax under each schedule so that no single civil servant could know the total income of a taxpayer. This tax collection concept did not last long, but the division of the schedular system remains.

2 Entitlement to the reduced rate of withholding tax may require the prior authorisation of the local tax authority. This is the case in the UK.

(i) Royalties

8.20 Particular problems arise with royalties, as different jurisdictions have different approaches to what does or does not constitute a royalty. For example, the sale of software may be treated as the receipt of a royalty in the buyer's country, subject to a withholding tax, and as a sale of goods in the seller's country, subject to full taxation. It will then be a question for the local tax laws in the seller's country whether the seller can claim any relief for the withholding tax it has suffered.

The OECD has revised the commentary to the OECD Model Treaty on the characterisation of payments for the use of software. This depends on the nature and extent of the rights acquired by the purchaser. Complete or partial rights, such as the ability to alter the source code of software or to distribute it, would continue to generate royalty income. Limited rights, generally those required to operate the program, would be classified as profits (the US describes this as the sale of a 'copyright article'). The right to copy software for internal use only would also give rise to profits, not royalties. These definitions would apply regardless of the way in which the rights are transferred so that no distinction is made between physical transfer on disk or CD (a 'shrink-wrap' licence) or electronic transfer (a 'click-wrap' licence).

The amendments to the commentary in respect of computer software are important for e-commerce because of the ability to use the Internet to transmit digital goods – information which has been traditionally sold in a physical format but which can now be sold in digital format, transmitted directly to the buyer. Music is a good example of this type of increasingly intangible 'good'. Until recently, buying recorded music meant buying a CD or similar physical music storage. This was categorised as a sale of goods, not subject to withholding tax even if purchased by mail order from overseas. Now, it is possible to buy music over the Internet, downloaded to the buyer's computer. This is the transfer of copyright material which, in some countries, would be regarded as giving rise to royalties. The buyer should, in theory, withhold tax from the payment if required to do so by local tax legislation. In practice, enforcement would be a burdensome issue, particularly where the buyer is an individual.

8.21 The OECD advisory group considering the characterisation of income arising from e-commerce has concluded that the vast majority of e-commerce transactions should be regarded as giving rise to business profits, not royalties[1]. The group found that, in the case of transactions that permit the customer to download digitised products (such as software, images, music or text) for the customer's own use or enjoyment, the payment made should not be characterised as a royalty. The act of copying the digital signal onto the customer's hard disk might constitute the use of copyright under the relevant domestic law, but this was merely incidental to the transaction and should not affect its characterisation for tax purposes.

This was contrasted by the OECD advisory group with a transaction involving the grant of the right to use a copyright in a digital product. This would be the case, for example, for a book publisher who would pay to acquire the right to reproduce a copyrighted picture that could be electronically downloaded for the purpose of inclusion on the cover of a book produced by the publisher. In this transaction, the payment would be made for the acquisition of rights to use the copyright in the digital product, and should therefore be characterised as a royalty.

The recommendations of the report, and in particular its suggestion for changes to the commentary, are in the process of being examined by the OECD Committee on Fiscal Affairs with a view to making the appropriate changes to the OECD Model Treaty.

Assuming that the changes are made, for international transactions between countries with tax treaties, the distinction between goods and intangibles that is created by the delivery mechanism should not be an issue for tax purposes and neither the seller nor the buyer will be penalised for opting to transfer digital rather than physical goods. Where the buyer is not in a treaty country, the seller needs to be aware of the possibility that a withholding tax could be imposed. It may be necessary to exclude sales to non-treaty countries if there is a practical likelihood of tax being withheld, or to increase the price payable in such countries to cover the tax which should be withheld.

1   OECD, 'Treaty Characterisation Issues Arising from E-Commerce', February 2001.

4.   QUANTIFYING TAXABLE INCOME

8.22 Normal tax rules will apply to quantify the amount of income arising from e-commerce that is subject to tax. As has been seen, the rules will depend on the characterisation of that income for tax purposes – treatment of income as a royalty (seen as passive investment income) may result in a different outcome from that which would apply if it were treated as trading income. This issue is one that has been faced in the past by banks and other financial institutions. They deal in money in the same way as a manufacturer deals in widgets. Income derived from money (that is, interest) was traditionally taxed as investment income with limited ability to offset expenses associated with earning that income. That treatment still applies to most taxpayers. However, for a bank, the commercial reality is recognised by the Inland Revenue: banks will treat financial transactions as a trading activity so that interest earned on loans and deposits is treated as part of their trading income.

It is not within the scope of this book to examine the detailed computational rules that apply to calculate taxable income. However, given the cross-border nature of much of e-commerce, two specific issues are worth highlighting – transfer pricing and the ability of the Inland Revenue to attribute profits of non-UK subsidiaries to a UK company. Both are areas where tax authorities around the world are concerned at the potential loss of tax revenue and use anti-avoidance provisions to police international groups.

(a) Transfer pricing

8.23 Transfer pricing is the mechanism by which a multinational business allocates benefit and reward, setting the prices at which goods, services and assets are transferred between international parts of the business and consequently affecting their taxable profits.

So far, e-commerce has not created fundamental questions for transfer pricing in the way that it has for the concept of PE. It has, however, created a business process which can more readily give rise to issues of transfer pricing. The Internet, and private extranets, allow global businesses to operate 24 hours a day; the financial sector is already conducting business this way. Electronic communication enables the increasing integration of businesses. Each part of a business can become more specialised, making it difficult to allocate the benefit and cost of administrative functions or to assess the effect and value of intangibles such as product technologies and marketing databases. All these things make it more difficult to evaluate the contribution of a single part of the business to the whole.

The OECD has put in place a set of guidelines[1], which attempt to codify international legislation. These now form the basis of many countries' transfer pricing policies[2]. The OECD model is based around the arm's length principle: profits should be allocated for tax purposes between affiliated businesses on the same basis as they would arise on transactions between independent parties. Taxpayers must justify the methodology they use by use of independent comparable data and auditing procedures. This can involve a considerable administrative burden.

For business, a key issue raised by e-commerce is that of obtaining external comparable data against which to check an arm's length allocation of profit. As internal transactions and resource-sharing become more complex, it creates unique transactions. Even businesses in the same industry sub-sector may conduct their global operations in completely different ways.

The issues raised by e-commerce for transfer pricing are not related to fundamental principles of transfer pricing but, instead, to compliance and enforcement. The risk is that, as global business grows, the lack of recognition for the new business models being created by e-commerce and a lack of consensus amongst individual countries as to the methods to be used for transfer pricing will become more of a frustration for business. Consistent interpretation of the OECD guidelines will help ensure that businesses are not required to negotiate their transfer pricing methods with each tax authority.

1 OECD, 'Transfer Pricing Guidelines for Multinational Enterprises and Tax Administrations', July 1995.
2 For example, the UK has incorporated the OECD guidelines into its updated transfer pricing rules: see the Income and Corporation Taxes Act 1988, s 770A and Sch 28AA, which apply to accounting periods ending on or after 1 July 1999.

(b) Controlled foreign companies

8.24 One apparently attractive way for a UK business conducting e-commerce to reduce UK taxation would be to make use of a foreign subsidiary, perhaps in a tax haven where profits would not be taxed. As we have seen, simply using overseas websites or servers would not reduce the UK taxation of the parent, but the profits of a subsidiary would not be subject to UK tax until they were remitted to the UK by dividend.

Unfortunately, it is not always possible simply to set up a subsidiary in another country for this purpose. The controlled foreign companies rules allow the Inland Revenue to tax a UK parent company on the profits of its offshore subsidiaries unless those subsidiaries fit into one of the available exemptions[1]. A subsidiary may be exempt either because it carries out an exempt activity or is located in an excluded country. A list of excluded countries is published by the Inland Revenue and includes most non-tax haven jurisdictions[2]. If the company is not set up in an excluded country, it must carry out exempt activities in order to avoid taxation of its profits in the UK or distribute most of its profits by way of dividend[3].

Exempt activities are negatively defined and the following activities do *not* qualify for exemption:

- investment business, including holding intellectual property rights and leasing such intellectual property;

- delivery of goods to/from the UK or to/from connected/associated companies;

- wholesale, distributive or financial business if more than half of gross receipts are from connected/associated persons.

Even where a subsidiary would appear to fit within an exemption, it still needs to have a business establishment (with employees) in the foreign jurisdiction – a website/server alone would not be enough. To qualify as exempt, the subsidiary must effectively be managed in the foreign country, so that decision-making is carried out there and there must be enough of a physical presence for there to be a requirement for that decision-making.

Using foreign subsidiaries to support an e-commerce business requires careful planning, both to ensure that the subsidiary is substantial enough to qualify and that it falls within an exemption. If it is not exempt, the tax advantage is lost.

1   The Income and Corporation Taxes Act 1988, Part XVII, Chapter IV. Similar rules exist in other countries.
2   See Schedules 1 and 2 to the Controlled Foreign Companies (Excluded Countries) Regulations 1998, SI 1998/3081.
3   Since the dividends will be taxed in the hands of the UK parent, the opportunity to roll up profits offshore tax-free is lost and there is no need for the Inland Revenue to invoke the controlled foreign company rules.

5.   VALUE ADDED TAX

(a) VAT in conventional transactions

8.25   VAT exists throughout the European Union and is governed by EC Council Directive 388/86 (otherwise known as the Sixth Directive). The provisions of the Sixth Directive are substantially enacted into the law of the UK by the Value Added Tax Act 1994 (VATA 1994). VAT is transaction-based and is levied at each stage of a supply chain. Because it is intended to be a tax on consumers, businesses in the chain can usually obtain a credit for VAT incurred on purchases.

A charge to UK VAT arises when:

- there is a supply of goods or services;

- the supply takes place in the UK;

- the supply is made by a taxable person;

- the supply is made in the course or furtherance of a business carried out by the taxable person; and

- the supply is a taxable supply and is not exempt from VAT[1].

As with direct taxation, the key issues for e-commerce arise in relation to identifying what is being supplied, where it is supplied and by and to whom it is supplied. To put these issues into context, some general comments on the meaning of the elements of a transaction that make it subject to VAT may be helpful.

1   VAT is also charged on imports of goods and some services into the UK.

(i) What is a supply?

8.26   The legislative definition of a supply[1] merely states that a supply includes all forms of supply, although anything which is not done for a consideration, whether in money or in kind, is not a supply for VAT purposes. Case law tells us that 'supply' must be widely construed and the general rule is therefore that where something is done or given in return for a consideration, a supply takes place. A supply is either of goods or services. A supply of goods generally involves the transfer of ownership of a physical asset. Any other supply is one of services. The characterisation of what is supplied can affect the rate of VAT that applies and the place where the supply is treated as made. This can be particularly important in relation to e-commerce transactions.

1   The VATA 1994, s 2.

(ii)   When does a supply take place in the UK?

8.27   This is one of the most challenging questions arising out of e-commerce transactions and is considered below.

- **Who is a taxable person?** A taxable person is a person who makes or intends to make taxable supplies and is, or is liable to be, registered for VAT. Registration is normally required if taxable turnover exceeds a certain limit in any 12-month period[1].

- **When is a supply made in the course or furtherance of a business?** A supply is made in the course or furtherance of a business when it is made for the purposes of the business, rather than being a purely private transaction.

- **When is a supply a taxable supply?** All goods and services supplied in the UK are taxable supplies unless they are expressly classified as exempt supplies[2].

1   £55,000 for the financial year to 5 April 2003.
2   The categories of exempt supply are derived from the Sixth Directive and are set out in Schedule 9 to the VATA 1994. They include, for example, finance, insurance, education, healthcare and land transactions (although this last is subject to numerous exceptions).

(b)   VAT on e-commerce

8.28   The main VAT problems resulting from e-commerce are similar to those encountered in direct taxes, although the emphasis is often somewhat different because of the transactional nature of VAT. Since VAT is chargeable by reference to turnover rather than profits, the potential scale of any difficulties is exacerbated by the sheer volume of business which is capable of being conducted via the Internet (not to mention its rapid growth). For instance, by the year 2002 it has been estimated that the value of on-line music sales will top $1.6 billion, or 7.5%, of the global market.

To a greater or lesser extent the problems presented by e-commerce for VAT are not new. It is more a case of technology increasing the existing tax difficulties inherent in cross-border transactions and, in particular, place of supply and compliance issues for non-resident suppliers of services. In the 1980s and early 1990s, technology, together with deregulation, allowed overseas suppliers of telecommunications services to supply services into the UK (and other EU Member States) without charging VAT. This gave them a significant competitive advantage as against EU-based suppliers, who had to charge VAT to their customers. This problem was resolved in 1997 when all Member States were permitted to derogate from the strict rules of the Sixth Directive. VAT is now charged on such supplies by a device known as the 'reverse charge', under which the recipient business accounts for VAT on receipt of such a supply from outside the EU.

The fact that the telecommunications problem was addressed by the Member States demonstrates an ability to deal with novel concepts. However, the need for consensus (and, in some cases, unanimity) can slow the decision-making process. The risk is that solutions to problems caused by e-commerce will not be introduced quickly, nor indeed necessarily before the inevitable advance of technology, enables non-EU suppliers to gain a substantial competitive advantage.

The European Commission agrees with the OECD principles and recognises that, because any new VAT rules will have to be introduced uniformly across the EU (and preferably across the world), its long-held plans for a definitive harmonised VAT system for Europe may now be closer to fruition than might have been predicted. However, the dangers posed by e-commerce to the tax base of Europe have destroyed the Commission's underlying rationale for the definitive system: that it should be source- or origin-based rather than based on the place of consumption. Under the Commission's original plans, all supplies of goods and services would be chargeable to VAT in the country in which the supplier is established, regardless of where the supplies are consumed. However, given the intangible nature of the Internet it is easy for suppliers to establish themselves in low tax jurisdictions and to make supplies which would not be subject to VAT in an origin-based system. Businesses inside the EU making similar supplies would suffer as a result as their supplies would be subject to VAT.

8.29 In June 2000, the Commission published business-to-business (B2B) and business-to-consumer (B2C) transactions proposals to update EU VAT law to accommodate e-commerce[1]. The existing rules cope reasonably well with transactions involving physical goods and the proposals focus on the supply of services, including digitised products that can be downloaded from the Internet. The proposals distinguish between business-to-business and business-to-consumer transactions:

- With B2B transactions, the existing reverse charge mechanism would be extended to require EU recipient businesses to charge themselves VAT at the relevant domestic rate – a UK recipient charges UK VAT, a French recipient charges French VAT, and so on. The aim is to remove the incentive for EU businesses to buy services from outside the EU in order to avoid paying VAT. As noted above, this route has already been followed for telecommunications services. Non-EU traders would not need to concern themselves with EU VAT for this category of customer.

- With B2C transactions, the supplier would continue to charge VAT at its domestic rate, even where the consumer is located in a different EU country. For non-EU traders, the Commission proposes that the trader should be required to register for VAT purposes in the EU and charge VAT to non-VAT registered customers. The trader would be allowed to choose which country to register in and, therefore, pick its VAT rate. Registration would depend on the fact of selling products into the EU rather than having any physical presence in the EU. The proposals note, but do not fully address, the problem arising from how EU VAT laws could be enforced against a non-EU business which may have no other taxable presence in either the country in which it is VAT registered or any other Member State. There is also the prospect of tax competition between Member States (an issue that already exists and encourages cross-border trade within the EU) – the standard rates of VAT currently vary from 15% in Luxembourg to 25% in Denmark. It is a long-standing objective of the Commission to harmonise rates across the EU. The introduction of a system that encouraged non-EU businesses to pick the countries with the lowest rate applies pressure on all EU countries to bring their rates into line. It also brings closer the prospect of a single European VAT registration for each business under which VAT suffered in any Member State can be reclaimed through a single VAT return.

The proposals for B2C transactions have met with fierce criticism from, in particular, the US. A US Treasury spokesman has commented that the 'plan has the potential to operate in a non-central manner, both from a legal and administrative perspective'[2]. He went on to make a number of points:

- the plan carried 'possible unintended consequences' in important non-tax areas. 'We would not want to see a proposal ... that would end or affect the current debate over which country's consumer protection rules should apply.'

- 'we would not want a tax directive that would ultimately require e-commerce retailers to be forced to declare to the authorities the addresses and buying habits of their customers, or alternatively and unintentionally encourage governments to track on-line activities.'

- the plan was potentially harmful to businesses which would be required to register for VAT in the EU to the extent that it would promote comparison shopping. Those that did not register for VAT could sell cheaper than those required to register. The result would be to 'punish the good guys in contrast to those who do not participate'.

- there was a lack of specific information on the administration of the proposed system as to how a customer's status would be determined by a non-EU trader. Problems would also occur with enforcement.

1 Proposal COM (2000) 349 was published on 7 June 2000 by the Commission and is available at www.europa.eu.int/comm/taxation_customs/proposals/taxation/com349_2000/com 2000_349en.pdf.
2 Statement by Treasury Deputy Secretary Stuart E Eizenstat on 7 June 2000.

8.30 The UK has proposed, pending a global solution, to remove VAT from supplies of digitised services to private individuals in the EU. As expected, these proposals have not been accepted by the other Member States. The effect has been, unsurprisingly, to deadlock negotiations.

Further proposals were published by the Commission in relation to EU VAT law and e-commerce in July 2001.

The proposals can be summarised as follows:

- for services supplied by a non-EU trader to an EU customer, the place of taxation will be within the EU and accordingly they will be subject to VAT;

- when services are provided by an EU trader to a non-EU customer, the place of taxation will be where the customer is located and they will not be subject to VAT;

- when an EU trader provides services to a taxable person (that is, to another business) in another Member State, the place of supply will be the place where the customer is established; and

- where an EU trader provides services to a private individual in the EU, or to a taxable person in the same Member State, the place of supply will be where the supplier is located[1].

Comments are still expected from interested parties on these revised proposals.

1 Document 500PC0349(02), 'Proposal for a Council Directive amending Directive 77/388/EEC', p 12.

(c) The essential e-commerce VAT questions

8.31 In any transaction, a number of fundamental questions must be asked to determine whether it is subject to VAT. They are:

- Who is the supplier?

- Where is he located?

- How can the customer know?

- Who is the customer?

- Where is he located?

- How can the supplier know?

- Should the customer pay VAT to the supplier?

- Should the supplier charge the customer VAT?

- If so, should he charge VAT at the rate prevailing in his country or at the rate prevailing in the customer's country?

- How should he account for the VAT to the fiscal authorities in the customer's country?

- What will happen to him if he does not account for the VAT to the authorities?

(d) The VAT treatment of goods physically delivered

8.32 At present, the most common kinds of supply involving e-commerce are those of goods which are ordered through an extension of the concept of mail order shopping via an on-line shopping mall through which a contract is concluded between the supplier and the customer for delivery of goods. There is very little difference between this type of transaction and a conventional mail order sale. Most of the essential VAT questions will be capable of being answered and the answers to those which cannot will not affect the ability of Customs & Excise to collect the VAT in the UK. It is not this type of transaction which poses a threat to the tax base.

The VAT treatment of this type of transaction can be summarised as follows:

- if the supplier and the customer are both in the UK, VAT will be charged by the supplier at the UK rate (17.5%) and will be accounted for by it to Customs & Excise;

- if the supplier is in the UK and the customer is a private individual in another EU Member State, VAT will be charged by the supplier at the UK rate (17.5%) and will be accounted for by him to Customs & Excise;

- if the supplier is in the UK and the customer is a VAT registered business in another EU Member State, no VAT will be charged by the supplier (so long as he holds his customer's VAT registration number) but the customer must account for VAT in his own Member State on the acquisition[1];

- if the supplier is in the UK and the customer is outside the EU, the transaction will be zero-rated as an export and no VAT will be chargeable[2];

- if the supplier is outside the UK, but within the EU, and the customer is a private individual in another Member State (including the UK), VAT will be charged at the rate applicable in the supplier's Member State and will be accounted for by him to the fiscal authorities in that state;

- if the supplier is outside the UK, but within the EU, and the customer is a VAT registered business in another Member State (including the UK), VAT will not be charged by the supplier (so long as he holds his customer's VAT registration number), but the customer must account for VAT in his own Member State on the acquisition[3];

- if the supplier is outside the EU and the customer is in an EU Member State, both customs duty and import VAT must be paid by the customer.

There is an anomaly for goods with a value of £18 or less. If a typical CD is supplied from outside the EU, no VAT (or customs duty) need be paid but VAT will be due on a similar supply made inside the EU. Far from attempting to address the anomaly, Customs & Excise is committed to a relaxation of import controls for such goods to facilitate quick release at the ports and airports. In addition, where goods are imported from outside the EU with a value in excess of £18, it is the importer who must bear the cost of any VAT and customs duty, that is the person with title to the goods at the time of importation. Although the contract between the parties may provide for transfer of title at any stage of the transaction, it is unlikely that many suppliers based outside the EU will wish to retain title to goods up to the point of importation because a liability to register for VAT in the country of importation may result.

It can be seen, therefore, that where there is a physical delivery of goods, the supplier knows (or should be able to establish fairly easily) where the customer is and whether or not he should charge

VAT. Deliveries from outside the EU are 'caught' by import procedures as they cross the frontier into Europe (with the exception of low value consignments).

1 Proof of the goods leaving the UK is required to obtain zero rating. If delivery is in the UK, UK VAT is chargeable.
2 Again, proof of export is required.
3 Proof of delivery to the other Member State is required.

(e) On-line delivery

8.33 Where there is no physical delivery and where a supply (for instance a software package) is delivered on-line, matters are not quite so simple. On-line supplies are the cause of the doomsday scenario commentaries and the reason why governments worldwide are worried about losing significant amounts of tax; as much as anything, this is what led the EU Commission to make its proposals in June 2000 to amend EU VAT rules. If one considers such supplies in the context of the essential VAT questions, it becomes easy to see why. It is not necessary for the efficient conduct of the transaction for many of them to be answered. Using the example of the supply of a software package on-line, the answers to the questions may well be as follows:

- **Who is the supplier?** Presumably the supplier will be known by name or reputation to the customer (or he is unlikely to enter into a contract) but it is not necessary for this information to be known (particularly if there is a time limited try-before-you-buy arrangement available).

- **Where is the supplier located?** Not necessarily known.

- **How can the customer know?** He cannot (and by extension neither can the tax authorities).

- **Who is the customer?** Not necessarily known.

- **Where is he located?** Again, this is not necessarily known and certainly not essential for the purposes of the transaction.

- **How can the supplier know?** He cannot – but what if he needs to know whether to charge him VAT or not? And how can the tax authorities know that a supply has taken place if the onus of paying VAT is on the customer?

- **Should the customer pay VAT to the supplier?** Only if he is certain that the supplier is located within the EU (assuming that the customer is similarly located) – but can he be certain?

- **Should the supplier charge the customer VAT?** Yes, *if* the customer is located in the EU *and* the onus of declaring VAT is on the supplier – but how does the supplier know where the customer is located?

- **If so, what rate of VAT should be used?** If the supplier is from inside the EU then the relevant rate is that which is in force in his country, but if the supplier is from outside the EU then the relevant rate is that which is in force in the customer's country. These two rates will not be the same, in all probability, and, in any case, this analysis presumes that the supplier has sufficient information to identify the correct Member State.

- **How should the supplier account for VAT to the tax authorities in the customer's country?** The only method available is by registering for VAT in each country of the EU to which supplies are made (this includes supplies from the UK to other Member States).

- **What will happen if VAT is not accounted for to the fiscal authorities by the supplier?** If the supplier is outside the jurisdiction of the EU, the practical answer is 'nothing'. One can imagine the response of an overseas supplier on being told that he *should* register for VAT in each of the 15 Member States of the EU.

8.34 It is against the background of these difficulties that the solution promoted by the OECD – that VAT should be accounted for in the country of consumption – makes sense. One answer would be to treat the supply of the software package on-line in the same way as the supply of the same package in a shrink-wrapped box: as a supply of goods. The relatively simple rules for taxing supplies of goods would apply and everyone would know where they stood. There would, however, be a major difficulty. Because the supply would not physically cross any frontiers, it would not be 'caught' by import procedures (which rely on the physical presence of goods at the ports and airports) and release could not be made conditional upon the payment of VAT (and, where appropriate, customs duty). No rules exist for cross-border supplies of goods from outside the EU to be declared voluntarily and outside of customs controls by customers to the tax authorities. An extensive rewrite of those rules would be necessary in order to achieve that result. This would not be acceptable in the context of customs duty and customs controls, particularly in respect of the management of preferential duty rates for the lesser developed nations of the world.

It was consideration of these practical problems, and in response to lobbying by the UK and the EU amongst others, that led the OECD to propose that the supply of digitised products, such as the on-line software package, should not be categorised as a supply of goods. It follows that, for VAT purposes, the supply would be of services. Under current rules, this categorisation can produce the odd situation that a book is zero-rated for VAT in the UK when sold in its physical form, yet subject to 17.5% VAT if sold on-line. Nevertheless it is more rational that the rules for taxing services, rather than goods, should be utilised for digitised products because they are more flexible and do not depend to the same extent on the physical location of the product.

(f) The indirect tax treatment of services

8.35 The VAT treatment of the supply of services depends on where the services take place or are deemed to take place. The rules for determining exactly where the supply is treated as taking place are flexible but far from simple.

The general rule is that services are supplied where the supplier has established his business or has a fixed establishment from which the service is supplied[1]. This rule has been the subject of much litigation about whether or not a supplier has a fixed establishment in a particular country and whether it can be said that particular supplies have been made from such an establishment. This will be discussed in greater detail later in this section, but it should be noted here that the concept of fixed establishment is not synonymous with the concept of PE that is used to determine a taxable presence in a country for direct tax purposes.

However, some services are treated as supplied where the customer is established, that is where the services are received[2]. For example:

- transfers and assignments of copyrights, patents, licences, trade marks and similar rights;

- advertising services;

- services of consultants, lawyers, accountants and other similar services, as well as data processing and the supply of information;

- banking, financial and insurance transactions.

Where these services are received by a UK VAT registered business from outside the UK, the business must apply the reverse charge procedure. In effect it charges itself VAT at the appropriate UK rate. This eliminates the competitive advantage enjoyed by non-UK suppliers over their UK counterparts. However, non-VAT registered consumers do not, at present, have to apply the reverse charge procedure. They can buy these services VAT free.

1 The Sixth Directive, art 9(1).
2 The Sixth Directive, art 9(2)(e).

(g) Reverse charge

8.36 The European Commission has now proposed that the reverse charge procedure should form the basis of future attempts to tax the supply of on-line digitised products in the B2B sector. This procedure ensures the collection of VAT from the recipients of digitised products. It also avoids the need for suppliers to register for VAT in one or more EU Member States, and removes the potential for tax evasion should a supplier choose not to do so. It will also not be necessary to harmonise VAT rates across Europe or provide for a single place of registration in order to secure the tax base and prevent unfair competition from overseas service providers (no matter how desirable that might be in the longer term). As has been seen, the reverse charge procedure has already been amended to bring within its scope supplies of telecommunications services. That amendment, itself, was the first action taken by the tax authorities of Europe in the battle for taxation of e-commerce, although it may well be that the authorities did not fully appreciate, at the time, the wider significance of their response.

The Commission has adopted the definition of telecommunications services provided for by the Melbourne Agreement at the World Administrative Telegraph and Telephone Conference in Melbourne in 1988[1]. It is widely accepted that the provision of access to the Internet should be treated as falling within this definition of telecommunications services and should therefore be taxed for VAT purposes where the customer receives the service, by means of the reverse charge procedure. This treatment is currently only applicable to Internet access and related e-mail facilities. The importance of this treatment is not just to show that Internet access services have already been taxed but also to demonstrate the flexibility of the procedure and its adaptability in the face of technological advances.

Some digitised products are already taxed under the reverse charge mechanism if they fall within any of the definitions of services specified in the list. For example, the sale of an on-line book is a supply of information. Unfortunately, it is not always possible to say with any certainty whether a particular product fits squarely within the current list of services. For example, the supply of an on-line software package could be:

■ a supply of information;

■ a supply of a licence (intellectual property rights) – in which case it is caught by the reverse charge;

■ more than either of those (perhaps a vehicle by which a function is performed, such as an accounting package) – in which case the supply is taxable by reference to the location of the supplier, resulting in no VAT being chargeable if the supplier is located outside the EU; or

■ a mixture of all those things – in which case the liability to VAT can best be described as confusing (probably requiring an apportionment between the various component parts).

Whatever the answer to this question, and others like it, it is obvious that much work needs to be done to define the type and description of supplies made electronically before the list of services to which the reverse charge applies can be meaningfully extended. In the meantime, the facility exists for overseas service providers to steal a march on providers based inside the EU by providing products which are not currently subject to the reverse charge procedure.

1   The definition reads: 'Telecommunications services shall be deemed to be services relating to the transmission, emission or reception of signals, writing, images and sounds or information of any nature by wire, radio, optical or other electromagnetic systems, including the transfer or assignment of the right to use capacity for such transmission, emission or reception.'

(i)   Defects in the reverse charge procedure

8.37 The place of supply is at present only changed from the place where the supplier is established to the place where the customer is established for supplies made to *taxable persons* (unless the customer is outside the EU, in which case no differential is applied). This means that supplies of services to private individuals in the EU are not subject to VAT if the supplier is located outside the EU. The implications of this are potentially enormous for both tax authorities and EU suppliers. Musical, literary, artistic and dramatic works, which have been traditionally delivered in physical form by means of compact discs, cassette tapes, videos, magazines and (the oldest form) books, may now be delivered electronically, free from dependence on a physical carrier and potentially free from VAT – the danger for EU suppliers of such products does not need to be spelled out. Such digitised products are now categorised as 'services', as distinct from 'goods' in their physical form, and no VAT will be due on the supply of such products by an overseas supplier to private individuals in the UK or anywhere in the EU.

Two approaches might be taken, but it will be seen that neither is totally satisfactory.

■ **Extend the reverse charge procedure to private individuals** Some countries have experimented with this approach[1] but without any obvious success. This is perhaps not surprising. One supplier could sell, say, a thousand copies of a software package on-line to individual consumers across the UK. The number of individual supplies and the impossibility of monitoring electronic trading activity carry immense resource implications for the tax authorities. It is difficult to see how such a system could be made to work.

■ **Require the supplier to register for VAT purposes in the country (or countries) where its customers belong** This is the route now preferred by the EU Commission for B2C transactions. The supplier would be responsible for charging VAT at the appropriate rate and accounting for it to the relevant tax authority. A system along these lines already exists for some mail order trading. For businesses, it is clearly unattractive to have to deal with up to 15 tax authorities (assuming trade was limited to the EU alone). The Commission proposals address this by requiring non-EU businesses to register in only one country and charge that country's VAT to all EU customers, regardless of which Member State they live in, so requiring the business to deal with no more than one tax authority. However, this can only be described as an inducement to register for the most compliant of businesses because the difficulty in tracing transactions would still exist. The Commission places weight on peer pressure and the adverse commercial effect on a business that has accumulated a tax debt in the EU. But there would still be problems for those businesses which did register for VAT in the EU: how would a supplier dealing with customers over the Internet know where his customers are located? Further, how could he verify whether the information given by a customer is correct? How then would he know whether to charge VAT to the customer, even if he intended to pay over to the relevant EU tax authority any VAT properly charged?

Until the publication of its proposals in June 2000, it appeared that the Commission and the Member States were reasonably relaxed about the issue of supplies to private consumers and did not foresee any substantial threat to their tax revenues as a result[2]. There were a number of reasons for this:

■ the current level of supplies (whether physical or electronic) from outside the EU to private individuals remains small when compared to supplies to VAT registered businesses;

■ the resource implications of controlling collection of VAT and customs duty for small value consignments outweighs the potential revenue gains which might be realised;

■ it is 'difficult' (but not 'impossible') to tax an individual receiving on-line supplies.

The Commission's proposals anticipate the growth in the volume of trade to private individuals before it becomes a significant threat to the tax base. Pressure also comes from EU businesses who, unless they are able to shift the centre of their operations to outside the EU, are not operating on a level playing field. The example of telecommunications services shows that if the threat is perceived as large enough, action will be taken.

1 Switzerland and Canada.
2 See News Release 25/98.

(ii) Fixed establishment

8.38 It will be recalled that the basic rule for taxing those services which are not subject to the reverse charge is that the place of supply, and thus the place of taxation, will be:

- where the supplier has established his business;
- where the supplier has a fixed establishment from which the service is supplied; or
- in the absence of either, where the supplier has his permanent address or is usually resident[1].

For a company, the place of supply will normally, therefore, be the country in which it is incorporated. However, if it has a fixed establishment in a different country that is more closely connected with the supply, then the supply is treated as taking place in that other country. A branch office carrying out its own trading activities would normally be a fixed establishment. A number of general principles can be derived from the case law.

A fixed establishment must have a 'sufficient minimum strength in the form of a permanent presence of the human and technical resources necessary for supplying specific services'[2]. Accordingly, the mere presence of gaming machines on a ferry did not amount to a fixed establishment. On this basis, a business using a website or server should not have a fixed establishment in the country in which the website or server is located.

European law looks to the substance of the arrangement rather than the legal form. On this basis, a subsidiary company may constitute a fixed establishment of its parent (implying that the VAT registration should be in the name of the parent) if it does not operate independently from the parent company[3]. In contrast, a company supplying goods selected from dealers in a different Member State did not have a fixed establishment in that Member State[4]. This suggests that a website that merely operates as a shopfront should not constitute a fixed establishment.

The service must be supplied from the fixed establishment and not from the main place of business. The place where an entity markets the services and, even, collects payment will not necessarily amount to a fixed establishment[5]. This again is helpful in relation to e-commerce.

Under the Commission's proposals, the fixed establishment rules would be modified for B2C supplies. Non-EU businesses would be required to register for VAT in a Member State, regardless of whether they had a fixed place of business there. The criterion for registration would be the making of supplies to non-VAT registered customers in that (and other) EU Member States.

1 The Sixth Directive, art 9(1).
2 *Bergholz v Finanzamt Hamburg–Mitte–Alstadt: 168/84* [1985] ECR 2251, ECJ.
3 *Customs and Excise Comrs v DFDS A/S: C-260/95* [1997] STC 384, ECJ.
4 *ARO Lease BV v Inspecteur der Belastingdienst Grote Ondernemingen, Amsterdam: C-190/95* [1997] STC 1272, ECJ.
5 *Customs and Excise Comrs v Chinese Channel (Hong Kong) Ltd* [1998] STC 347. See also the *ARO Lease BV* case.

6. CUSTOMS DUTY

8.39 Customs duty is regulated by Council Regulation (EC) 2913/92, which has direct effect in all Member States of the EU, including the UK. Customs duty is due on the importation of goods into the territory of the EU. Generally, payment of duty must be made before the imported goods will be released into free circulation within the EU, although major importers will often operate a deferment account with Customs & Excise whereby duty is paid after the goods have been released. Customs duty must be paid by the importer, who may be the vendor or the buyer depending on who has title to the goods at the moment of importation. This will be a contractual matter between the parties.

VAT is also due on imported goods and is applied as if it is customs duty[1]. As with customs duty, therefore, VAT must, generally, be paid before the goods are released (although this VAT may be claimed as input tax through the importer's VAT return).

Interestingly, and not without some significance in e-commerce (as noted above in paragraph 8.32), relief from customs duty is permitted for consignments of goods (other than goods subject to excise duties such as alcohol, cigarettes and perfumes) where the value of the consignment does not exceed £18.

At present the vast majority of e-commerce still involves the physical delivery of goods to consumers and to businesses. Typically, the Internet is only used as the means of communication/advertisement, order and payment. In order to simplify and speed up the process of importing goods, Customs & Excise have shifted the emphasis from a paper system to an electronic one. The Customs Freight Simplified Procedures (CFSP) allow customs declarations to be made by e-mail, enabling goods to pass through customs control more speedily.

The CFSP assists in the administrative process of charging duty (and VAT) on goods entering the UK. It may provide the model for an EU-wide system. However, it does not address the fundamental point that customs duty can, at present, only be charged on the physical delivery of goods across borders.

1　The VATA 1994, s 1(4).

7.　ENFORCEMENT

8.40　Digital technology increasingly makes the transmission of information easier; but, by doing so, makes tax administration more complicated – for tax authorities and taxpayers. Ease of tax administration may be one of the ultimate driving factors in any decision made about the taxation of e-commerce. It is pointless to put in place a system that is too difficult to comply with.

The OECD, through its Committee on Fiscal Affairs, has commissioned a number of papers in the area of tax administration and e-commerce. The resulting papers[1] were published between December 2000 and February 2001, and public comment was invited by 30 April 2001. At the time of writing the OECD had not published or commented on the responses received.

Issues surrounding the administration of tax recently formed the subject matter of a global conference hosted in Montreal, Canada by the Canada Customs and Revenue Agency entitled 'Tax Administrations in an Electronic World'[2]. This conference was attended by representatives of the tax administrations of over 100 countries, including the UK. It recognised the importance of developing a system of taxation which would provide 'a fiscal climate within which e-commerce can flourish' whilst at the same time being fair and predictable[3].

1　For the full text of the reports, see: www1.oecd.org/daf/fa/e_com/ec_6_WP9_REPORT_Eng.pdf; www1.oecd.org/daf/fa/e_com/ec_8_TECH_TAG_Eng.pdf; www1.oecd.org/daf/fa/e_com/ec_9_FSM_REPORT_Eng.pdf; www1.oecd.org/daf/fa/e_com/ec_10_PDA_TAG_Eng.pdf.
2　For further information, see: www.ae-tax.ca.
3　See www.ae-tax.ca/pressreleases.eng/communique_3.htm.

(a)　Identifying the parties to a transaction

8.41　Fundamental to any successful system of taxation is the identification of the parties to a transaction. When a party declares its identity, for example, whilst placing an order over the Internet, it is crucial that this identity can be authenticated in order to establish the place of consumption.

The difficulty when using an address provided as part of the purchasing process over the Internet is that it may not be reliable: it would be quite easy for a customer to provide an address outside the jurisdiction of the vendor when he is in fact a resident of the same jurisdiction. Moreover, some Internet sites which are involved in the sale of digital products do not necessarily require the details of the physical location of their customers as their product can be e-mailed and subsequently downloaded.

OECD research has shown that using the credit card details of a purchaser is not a feasible method of identifying a customer as the information kept by credit card providers is not stored in a manner which can link the number on a credit card to the billing address of a cardholder. It is also likely that problems would be encountered with domestic laws governing the use of such information for such purposes. More importantly, whilst credit cards are currently the dominant method of payment over the Internet, regard must also be had to the development of other methods of payment, such as digital cash, which could potentially become a more favoured method of payment in the longer term.

The use of Internet protocol (IP) addresses has also been explored by the OECD. In principle, the use of IP addresses should be feasible as they can be used to link the ordering of a product to an individual computer which could then be cross-checked with other information provided at the point of ordering as a means of verification. Whilst in principle the use of IP addresses should work, their viability as a method of pointing to an accurate location is questionable for reasons such as the availability of 'anonymiser' software, which is designed to disguise the IP address of individual computers. Moreover, OECD research has shown that some ISPs do not take into account the location of a user when allocating an IP address. The difficulties involved when individuals place orders through computers located at Internet cafes and when employees place orders over the Internet whilst at work are obvious.

Other ideas that have been looked at by the OECD are digital certificates and digital signatures. These provide an independent method of verifying the identity and location of the holder and are usually provided by organisations which guarantee the authenticity of the information. They are acknowledged by the OECD as being very useful but are not in widespread use.

(b) Audit trails

8.42 Most 'off-line' commerce leaves a paper trail: invoices, credit card slips, cheques, bank transfers. All these provide information for tax authorities to follow, to check back that the figures reported by a business are supported by the records. The structure of the Internet makes audit trails more difficult to establish and, in consequence, more difficult to follow. It is difficult to monitor electronic transmissions, certainly more difficult than monitoring trade in tangible goods. Electronic cash has the potential to leave no trail. Unlike physical cash, there is no physical limit to the amount of electronic cash that can be transferred – it does not weigh down your pockets. Similarly, the use of banks in countries with less than forthcoming reporting requirements can eliminate any paper trail. Tax haven jurisdictions are also an area of concern, not only because of the potential for avoidance but also because of the bank secrecy available in most havens.

Tax authorities rely on average businesses, average records, to get an idea of whether a business tax return 'feels' right – significant discrepancies from the norm in declared turnover, for example, may prompt an enquiry. The new businesses, and new business models, enabled by e-commerce will not fit the established averages. Even where the reported figures of a business do match expectations, where these can be established, it may still be impossible to tell *where* those sales were made. If a source basis of taxation is chosen, there may still be insufficient audit trails even for the most prudent of businesses to be confident of compliance with the requirements of tax authorities.

If the tax authorities cannot obtain the information they need from businesses, they may turn their attention to individuals. To date, most tax authorities have been more concerned with the details of businesses because it is in the revenue of businesses that their greatest opportunity for tax arises. If sales cannot be adequately monitored at the level of the seller, they may look to the purchaser. This is more likely to be a problem for sales taxes, such as VAT, but if a source basis of taxation is developed for direct taxes, such as corporation tax, then it will become a wider issue.

As part of its research the OECD considered possible solutions to the questionable integrity of electronic documents. Its preferred solution is for electronic documents to be 'time stamped' when they are created. This time stamping would prevent the document from being altered after its creation without such changes being logged within the time stamp. Alongside the use of time stamping, the OECD has recommended the use of data encryption as a means of securing information.

(c) Collection

8.43 The OECD has considered five main methods of collecting tax:

■ self-assessment;

■ registration of non-resident suppliers;

■ taxation at source;

■ collection by an intermediary; and

■ the use of technology-based solutions.

Under a system of self-assessment, taxpayers would be required to calculate the tax liability themselves and remit it to the appropriate tax authority as they do at present. For B2B transactions the OECD's view is that such a system is feasible as it is currently operated successfully in most OECD Member Countries for cross-border trading activities. Such a system of collection, however, does not exist in all OECD Member Countries with regard to consumption taxes and appropriate legislation may need to be adopted.

A system of self-assessment for use with B2C transactions is currently operated by only a small number of OECD Member Countries and has not proved effective. Accordingly, self-assessment is viewed by the OECD as not being a viable option for B2C transactions.

The envisaged system of registration would require non-resident businesses to register in a jurisdiction and for it to be responsible for the remission of tax. It is felt by the OECD that problems would be encountered when enforcing such a tax regime on non-residents. Increased costs of compliance may also serve to dissuade non-resident suppliers from entering particular foreign markets. If such a system were adopted, it is likely that de minimis thresholds such as those adopted for distance selling purposes for VAT would be used. The OECD views the registration method as imposing too high a cost on business, which may hamper the development of electronic business.

A system by which tax would be deducted at source has immediate advantages over methods such as the registration method outlined above simply because the associated compliance costs are likely to be lower. The OECD envisages that deduction at source would require the collection of consumption tax on exports to non-residents, which would then be remitted to the tax authority in the country of consumption. Inherent disadvantages in such a system centre around the amount of national co-operation that would be required between OECD Member States. The difficulties that are likely to be encountered during negotiation of the appropriate treaties make this option impractical in the short to medium term.

One other possible solution explored by the OECD involves the collection of tax by a third party, such as a financial institution. The OECD doubts, however, whether such a collection method would be sufficiently profitable to encourage financial institutions to become involved.

OECD research has concluded that for B2B transactions a system of self-assessment is to be favoured. It found that for B2C transactions there is no ideal solution in the short term, although the most viable method is that requiring the registration of non-resident suppliers. As it is unlikely that the chosen method will be the same for both B2B and B2C transactions, it is important that a distinction can easily be drawn between businesses and consumers.

A technology-based solution would involve the development of bespoke software to calculate automatically, collect and remit tax to the appropriate tax authority. In order to facilitate the verification process the OECD considers that a series of bilateral treaties would be needed. As no appropriate software currently exists, this is a longer-term solution but carries with it the advantage that tax authorities and businesses can be involved from the outset.

In the US, various proposals have been put forward to cope with the collection of tax arising in respect of e-commerce as far as inter-state relationships are concerned.

One concept gaining ground is that states should get together and apply a voluntary code to deal with collection of tax on remote sales. Its rationale is that businesses which are not required to charge, collect and pay tax under current law should elect to do so in return for incentives. The most compelling of these incentives is the promise of a low cost solution by the provision of free software that does the accounting for them through an elected representative (that is, the software house) possibly without a tax authority audit.

Opponents advocate that coercion is the only safe and fair alternative and that states are constitutionally prohibited from collusive action.

(d) Attitude of the UK tax authorities

8.44 The Inland Revenue and Customs & Excise are both keen advocates of the use of new technology. In their joint statement issued in 1998[1], they stated:

'The [revenue] Departments are increasingly taking advantage of modern methods of communication, processing of information and payments. They will consider extending the use of Internet technology in particular, so as to continue to improve the quality of service to their taxpayers, simplify and streamline procedures where possible, reduce costs to business and Government and encourage voluntary compliance. In particular, the Departments:

- will continue to develop their websites. They will aim to provide clear, easily accessible guidance on tax obligations and how to meet them.
- will consider, as cryptography systems and digital signature technology develop, wider use of e-mail as a means of secure communication with their customers. This could speed up communications and reduce costs to taxpayers and Government alike.
- have developed systems for the electronic filing of returns and will seek to encourage their greater use. And they are currently developing electronic "intelligent" forms in close co-operation with the private sector.
- are already using facilities for direct bank to bank payment and repayment of tax. Developments in other electronic payment systems will be monitored and their use considered once security problems have been overcome.

As technology develops, the Departments will explore, together with the private sector, how it might be used by businesses to collect and process information relevant to their tax liabilities. By facilitating more accurate return information, less time will be spent by both business and the tax administrations in correcting errors and tracking down missing information, and compliance costs will be driven down.'

The UK has welcomed the publication of the OECD papers on tax administration referred to in paragraph 8.40 above. The Paymaster General, on 12 February 2001, reiterated that the UK views e-commerce as a global issue and that it is important for countries to work together.

1 News Release 25/98.

8. CONCLUSION

(a) The way forward

8.45 The main outcome from the deliberations and pronouncements of the various international forums, particularly the OECD, is that taxation of e-commerce remains in a state of flux. A number of principles have been established by consultation between governments and businesses, the most important perhaps being that of neutrality. Nonetheless, little has been decided and much is still being monitored.

(b) Neutrality

8.46 One of the principles underlying both the US taxation proposals[1] and the OECD recommendations is that of neutrality, to ensure that the tax treatment of a transaction remains constant regardless of the medium in which it is undertaken. This is especially important for e-commerce because of the ease with which transactions can be amended to fit the most advantageous taxation result, for example by changing the method or location of distribution.

At present, the sale of a book is the sale of a good, but the sale of the text of the book in electronic format may be the sale of services or the provision of copyright material. If the tax system is to be neutral, these differences must not affect the taxation of the transaction. This has implications for both direct and indirect taxes, despite the fact that what is provided – the information in the book or text – remains the same regardless of the nature of the transaction. It may be that a fundamental reconsideration of the nature of certain transactions is required to achieve this neutrality, to look through a physical product and consider what is in fact being supplied.

For direct taxation, neutrality must also take into account the location of the income. There are three ways of considering neutrality with respect to location:

- **Capital export neutrality** This ensures that a taxpayer pays the same tax regardless of the location of the transaction. This could be achieved by taxing income on a residence basis alone, or where 100% credit is given for source basis taxation.

- **Capital import neutrality** This ensures all occurrences of a transaction in a particular jurisdiction would incur the same tax, regardless of the location of the taxpayer.

- **National neutrality** This ensures the total benefit to a nation remains constant, regardless of the location of the transaction. Generally, allowing a *deduction* for foreign tax, not a credit, would achieve this.

However, no one form of locational neutrality can exist without violating another. Internationally, a mixture of systems is used – the UK and the US use the residence/credit system of capital export neutrality. Neutrality must also be equitable so that taxpayers in similar positions should pay the same tax on a transaction (horizontal equity), and the tax borne by taxpayers should reflect their income (vertical equity). Equity is a national rather than an international issue, and its scope is wider than e-commerce.

1   See www.iitf.nist.gov/eleccomm/ecomm.htm.

(c) No new taxes

8.47 Part of the problem in coming to a definitive international tax regime for e-commerce is the difficulty in establishing the agenda between nations as businesses. The governments of many developed countries are concerned to ensure that there are no new taxes imposed on e-commerce. The suggestion that a bit tax be introduced, to tax the transmission of information, has been rejected by most authorities as too difficult to enforce.

The OECD conference in Ottawa recommended that authorities should use existing tax principles and fit those to e-commerce. Legislation is to be altered only where it will not discriminate between electronic and traditional commerce.

This ideal is already being eroded, as many less developed countries are concerned that they are being pressured into accepting a taxation regime for e-commerce that favours the developed countries. Those countries that do not participate in the OECD are not constrained by its recommendations, and there is little to stop them setting up favourable tax regimes specifically to attract e-commerce businesses. While the UK's controlled foreign companies legislation (and similar initiatives in other countries) may restrict the benefits of such a regime for companies that remain located in the UK and other OECD countries, truly electronic businesses – delivering digital goods, for example – could relocate easily.

(d) The future

8.48 The OECD's 'wait and see' approach means that the next few years are unlikely to bring a radical change in the taxation of e-commerce. Instead, governments will continue to monitor how e-commerce is affecting their tax base. Existing tax principles can cope with e-commerce, albeit not entirely to the satisfaction of all tax authorities.

Change, though, is almost certain if tax authorities see their tax base eroded. If there is a significant increase in e-commerce, as predicted, the changes may accelerate. At present, however, it is indirect taxation that has received primary attention, with the OECD settling on a place of consumption basis for indirect tax. This may result in new taxes for countries such as the US, where there is no national equivalent to VAT, but should not affect the UK dramatically.

The enforcement of indirect taxes will require further international discussion and co-operation to find a reasonably workable environment in which businesses can comply with reporting requirements. Being source-based, implementation of indirect taxation of e-commerce could also provide a negotiating ground against which to develop direct taxation on a residence basis.

9

E-finance

I. INTRODUCTION

9.01 Preceding chapters in this book have concentrated on what might be called procedural issues in e-commerce; for example, what it is to contract on-line, to protect intellectual property rights and to settle disputes in cyberspace. This chapter, and the four that follow it, will consider substantive aspects of e-commerce in the corporate, financial and property sectors:

- in the case of the present chapter, we are concerned with the operation of the financial services industry on-line;

- Chapter 10, E-banking will look at banking on-line, as well as electronic payment and settlement systems;

- Chapter 11, E-insurance will consider the impact of the on-line environment on insurance law and the interesting questions posed for e-commerce businesses, and their brokers and underwriters, vis-à-vis how new species of e-risk are catered for;

- Chapter 12, E-corporate will consider how the world of e-commerce is changing the law and practice of corporate governance and corporate communication with shareholders; and

- Chapter 13, E-property reviews the impact of e-commerce on property transactions.

(a) The brave new world of electronic financial services

9.02 The financial services industry was among the first to appreciate the true commercial potential of the Internet. There are a variety of explanations for this enthusiasm, some of which will become apparent in the course of this chapter. It is also germane to consider whether this enthusiasm has proven in any relevant respects to have been misplaced or premature.

One common feature within the worldwide market place for financial services is the potential for an investment firm or bank to supply its entire range of products and advisory services wholly electronically. For the sale of physical goods, or services such as travel and leisure, the Internet can only ever be a means towards an end. But the potential exists today to transform the manner in which banking, share dealing, life assurance and pensions, mortgages, mutual funds, personal loans and general insurance are provided to the consumer (and it does not in principle matter whether that consumer is a private individual or a multinational corporation).

The Internet has initially been used to make it simpler to provide financial services of the sort traditionally provided through conventional channels. Instead of phoning your broker to place an order to buy or sell shares, websites now exist where you can place an order electronically, leaving it to be processed in a fully automated fashion by a broker who is, in effect, an electronic processing agency. These types of service have existed in the United States for over a decade now (although the take-off of the commercial side of the Internet in the past four or five years has seen them develop substantially in size). During the past few years, on-line dealing services have become readily available in the UK and we are beginning to see further developments in the manner in which the Internet is used to provide financial services. One growth area at the moment is the use of the Internet to bring venture capital investors and companies seeking funding together. Another trend has been the rise of on-line initial public offering (IPO) services. In time, you will not merely be able to place orders for share trades on-line, but also to use websites to plan very much more complex personal financial transactions, relying increasingly on research solicited from Internet websites.

Ultimately, it is likely that the vast majority of financial services will be provided to consumers on-line, with little if any supply-side human intervention. In time, you may even find that your dealings with your 'broker' (or directly with the market) will be conducted wholly electronically: your PC will host a piece of software programmed to profile you to the market place and to look for investment opportunities marketed to your PC by pieces of software found on the Internet at websites of brokers, banks, etc. Neither you nor any individuals working for the broker(s) or bank(s) involved need even be aware, at first, that transactions are being completed through this medium.

(b) Sources of financial services law

9.03 The UK's financial services industry was until 30 November 2001 regulated in accordance with the Financial Services Act 1986 (FSA 1986). When the Labour Party assumed power after the 1997 General Election, it became known that the FSA 1986 was to be replaced in due course by the Financial Services and Markets Act 2000 (FSMA 2000). The FSMA 2000 has replaced the regulatory framework which existed under the FSA 1986, the Insurance Companies Act 1982 and the Banking Act 1987. The provisions relating to the financial services industry came into force on midnight on 30 November 2001 (known as N2), as did much of the secondary legislation made under the FSMA 2000. The FSMA 2000 provides for a single regulator, the Financial Services Authority (FSA), and a new 'financial promotions' regime to replace the 'investment advertisements' and 'cold calling' provisions of the FSA 1986. The FSMA 2000 aims to cure a number of defects of the old regime: for example, the separation of the regimes governing cold calling and investment advertisements; the failure of the regulatory system to deal with and adapt to technological changes; and the confusion over the territorial scope of the FSA 1986.

2. WHAT DO WE MEAN BY 'FINANCIAL SERVICES'?

9.04 The concept of 'financial services' means different things to different people and the context in which one asks the question may lead to a variation in the sort of answers one gets.

The paramount distinction between 'private customers' and 'non-private customers' underpinned the FSA 1986's regulation of financial services. This distinction has been followed but fine-tuned by the FSMA 2000. Under the FSMA 2000, before conducting designated investment business, ie most types of regulated activities carried on by way of business with or for a client, a firm must take reasonable steps to establish whether a client is a 'private customer', an 'intermediate customer' or a 'market counterparty'[1]. The Statement of Principles for Business in the FSA Handbook[2] impose express requirements on firms in relation to their treatment of clients and customers. The nature of these requirements depends, in part, on the characteristics of the client or customer. Accordingly what is considered to be 'due regard' (in Principles 6 and 7), 'fairly' (in Principles 6 and 8), 'clear, fair and not misleading' (in Principle 7), 'reasonable care' (in Principle 9) or 'adequate' (in Principle 10) depends on the client's or customer's characteristics[3].

A customer firm which carries on investment business or is an overseas financial services institution is a 'market counterparty' unless classed as an intermediate customer. An 'intermediate customer' (essentially the same as 'non-private' customer under the FSA 1986) is a firm/financial services institution with whom a firm undertakes inter-professional business where that firm/financial services institution acts for an underlying customer and the firm and that firm/financial services institution agree to this classification in order that the interests of the underlying customer be protected. In the case of non inter-professional business, a firm/financial services institution is an 'intermediate customer' where, inter alia, it has not indicated that it acts on its own behalf. Listed companies, unregulated collective investment schemes and other companies satisfying various criteria are also classified as 'intermediate customers'. Essentially, a 'private customer' is a private individual. However, a firm may classify any client (other than a firm or services institution) as a private customer. Depending on his experience and understanding, a firm may, having taken reasonable care to determine these factors, classify a client as an 'intermediate customer' with his consent. The Internet will not dismantle these distinctions; what it does is bring into focus different aspects of the firm-customer relationship, namely the degree to which a consumer of financial services requires (as a matter of law or of pure practicality) advice on what he proposes to undertake. The lower or less significant the advisory input, the simpler (in theory) it becomes to convert the provision of the service from a 'face-to-face' or 'paper' one, to one based on the Internet.

1   FSA Handbook, Conduct of Business Sourcebook at COB 4.1.4.
2   The FSA Handbook can be found at www.fsa.gov.uk/handbook.
3   FSA Handbook, Principles for Business at PRIN 1.2.1.

(a) Nil-advisory or low-advisory products and services

(i) Retail banking

9.05 Although retail banking involves the provision of increasingly complex products and services, its core business of receiving, holding and allowing access to money can be provided with minimal advice. Cash withdrawal has been automated for some years, and the emergence of Internet banking continues to have increasing import. This is considered more fully in Chapter 10, E-banking.

(ii) Share dealing services

9.06 The 'popular capitalism' of the 1980s made shareholders out of several million private individuals in the UK who had never dealt on the financial markets themselves. After the major utilities and state-owned industries were sold into private ownership, further mass ownership of shares was boosted by the demutualisation of mutual building societies and mutual insurance companies.

This trend has led to significant developments in the means by which individuals can deal in shares (including dealing through high street banks and building societies). Transferring this sort of service to the Internet is not complicated and several websites offering on-line share dealing services have been active in the UK for a number of years.

In the US, on-line dealing services experienced a period of great success, fuelled by the longest and most significant bull market in history. Progress in the UK has been more modest, and of course got underway much more recently as well[1]. Nonetheless, those wanting to deal on-line are actually now quite spoiled for choice in the UK, with many service providers available. The main difference between the UK and the US environment is, however, cost. Dealing and settlement costs in the UK are still generally higher per trade than in the US, and the persistent refusal of the Chancellor of the Exchequer to abolish or at least mitigate stamp duty on share purchases is certainly not helping the on-line industry to prosper[2].

On-line brokers, even those offering execution-only services, usually offer a variety of services, ranging from research on companies and markets to portfolio management tools and share watching/alert services. A number of financial portals have emerged offering services such as financial and market news and information, share price quotes, product and service comparison tools, 'knowledge banks', charting facilities and investor bulletin boards and 'chat rooms'. The Internet has also made it possible for private investors to trade directly using specialised software and to access markets which were previously beyond their reach. These days, you can buy Dutch stocks as easily as German stocks, using the same account, and monitor the value of your portfolio.

Although the difficult stock market conditions resulting from the bursting of the 'dot.com bubble' have had a detrimental effect on on-line stockbrokers, with fewer customer accounts being opened and the consolidation of firms, the availability of on-line stockbroking services remains one of the most significant developments of the Internet for consumers.

1 By way of comparison, 30% of UK customers were expected to use on-line brokerage services by 2003 compared with 50% of US customers (according to a study conducted by the Boston Consultancy Group (www.bcg.com)).
2 Commission charges in the UK can be between one to three times higher than in the US and the US does not have an equivalent of UK stamp duty (which is currently charged at the rate of 0.5% of the transfer value of a share transaction).

(iii) General retail insurance

9.07   Many forms of retail insurance require relatively little advice from the provider. Take, for example, extended warranties on household appliances: if you buy a new TV or fridge these days, the warranty policy is normally available at point of sale as an optional extra. The sort of risks covered by general insurance are usually relatively uncomplicated, even where the customer's status is relevant. Often the possibility of risk assessment is not presented to the customer for consideration. With motor insurance, for example, relatively simple criteria apply: your car will fall into a set insurance band, and your age, profession and current record of claims will be relevant factors. But even though there is a measure of competition in the market for motor policies (in particular), there are few differentiating factors which apply when choosing the company to insure your car. For example, nobody offers advice as to the underwriters who offer best performance or have fewest claims made against them. Further, motor insurance is – of course – compulsory if you own a car. Annual risk insurance policies may generally be renewed with a minimum of human contact, even if the initial proposal might have required the services of a broker. An added service from some insurance brokers involves comparing premiums payable to a range of underwriters and offering the best value policy come renewal of the insurance policy (which may mean a new underwriter or continuing with the old one). Nonetheless, this service is usually completely automated as far as the insured is concerned. Renewal will come through automatically at the best available rate, with no consultation. Telephone insurance services are now commonplace in the UK. Direct Line Insurance is perhaps the best known and one of the longest established, but it is far from the only service of this kind. Most of the major insurers now offer a direct telephone service, sometimes operated in parallel with their more conventional forms of product distribution, and are exploring and developing platforms to offer insurance services which consumers can access solely by means of the Internet, as exemplified by Churchill Online[1].

1 See www.churchill.co.uk.

(b) Medium-advisory products and services

(i) Mortgages

9.08 Offering a mortgage often requires some degree of advisory input from or on behalf of the prospective lender. How this is addressed in the context of offering on-line mortgage services is discussed more fully in Chapter 10, E-banking.

(ii) Packaged products

9.09 This term refers to products linked to life or term assurance policies, unit trusts, Personal Equity Plans (PEPs), Individual Savings Accounts (ISAs) and certain similar arrangements. PEPs date back to 1986, and were originally vehicles for tax-free investment in UK equities admitted to the Official List of the UK Listing Authority (previously the Official List of the London Stock Exchange). Over the years, the PEP concept was progressively broadened to allow investment in all manner of UK equities, bonds, unit trusts and in the equities of a single company (as opposed to a basket of different issuers). The PEP (along with another vehicle, the Tax-Exempt Special Savings Account or TESSA) was abolished as from 5 April 1999 and has now been replaced by the ISA. An ISA may be used for simple cash deposits, the purchase of stocks and shares, the purchase of life assurance, etc, and is subject to an annual contribution ceiling lower than that of the PEP. Proceeds accumulated within an ISA are tax free and consequently savers are entitled to exemption from income tax and capital gains tax on their investments. In addition, a 10% tax credit will be paid for the first five years of the scheme, that is until 5 April 2004, on dividends from UK equities and unit trust distributions. Such products are almost always sold subject to a duty of 'best advice'. Even though 'best' is a relative term, when you set up one of these arrangements the fact that you are advised at all is significant: *the system expects no less*. The system expects far more by way of advice and disclosure from an investment salesman than it does from a salesman of, say, washing machines or package holidays. It is debatable whether this expectation is fair or realistic. In spite of the discussion of the common law principle of caveat emptor in the Joint Committee of the Houses of Parliament, which scrutinised the first draft of the Financial Services and Markets Bill (March–April 1999), the duty of best advice and the extent to which it has made some inroads into caveat emptor look set to stay with us[1].

The degree to which it is possible to reduce the necessary amount of contact between the financial services product provider and the ultimate purchaser of the product (a process which has become known as 'disintermediation') will vary. One of the more interesting recent developments in this area has been the emergence of a number of on-line 'supermarkets' offering access to UK authorised unit trusts and open-ended investment companies (and in some cases, to ISAs as well). This trend suggests that there is a capacity to disintermediate this market which not all that long ago would not have been considered possible. The premise underlying these on-line services is that subscription for units in the funds is offered on a self-advised basis only. This has not met with instant regulatory approval, although logic dictates that if a customer is given all the information that the law requires a customer to be given concerning the funds available for purchase, then the customer should be entitled to be left to make his mind up. Before the FSMA 2000 there had been a mismatch between the views of two of the UK's financial services regulators. The Securities and Futures Authority required the firms it regulated to avoid advising on, or assessing the suitability of, a transaction for an 'execution-only customer'. Once such a customer gave instructions to trade, the broker was entitled to process it without more. In contrast, the Personal Investment Authority's view was that personal financial advisors had to treat a 'direct offer advertisement' (one that describes a specific investment, such as a unit trust) as constituting investment advice (albeit generic, rather than specific to an investor's circumstances) and therefore as incapable of founding the basis for an execution-only transaction. These two regulatory bodies have now transferred their regulatory functions to the FSA. In general, the FSA Conduct of Business rules are expressed to apply to financial promotions communicated by any means, including e-mails and websites[2]. Accordingly, in principle, the requirements which apply to financial promotions of packaged products by non-electronic means apply equally to such financial promotions by electronic means. More specifically, those who wish to operate funds supermarkets on the Internet must do so on the basis that all documentation relevant to any fund investment (scheme particulars, key features documents, etc) should be found on or through the website (hyperlinks to the website operated by the fund manager will suffice for these purposes provided they are not hidden in the body of the text)[3]. Hard copies should be available on request.

1 See now the FSMA 2000, s 5.
2 FSA Handbook, Conduct of Business Sourcebook at COB 3.2.2G.
3 FSA Handbook, Conduct of Business Sourcebook at COB 3.14.5G.

9.10 It would also be prudent for representations of 'what's new' or 'what's hot' to be avoided, so that you are not misled (by the actual words used or by your misunderstanding of them) into thinking that these amount to some sort of investment steer.

Packaged products are in general much more complicated to analyse than general risk-related insurance policies (and it will be appreciated from the commentary above regarding funds supermarket websites that they are being treated by the UK regulators as rather more complex than stocks and shares acquired via on-line brokers as well). The amount of factual and mathematical disclosure which is required has been the subject of considerable debate within the UK financial services industry. Rival schools of thought have debated for a number of years whether the consumer requires full and candid disclosure of the finest detail of a product's cost and surrender value(s) and so forth, or instead requires clear and concise details, with a minimum of technical data on matters such as performance and projections. Whichever prevails, it seems likely that for some time to come many investors will need the comfort of talking to a human being before making an investment decision. Nevertheless, this is probably the area where software agents can – in time – make the greatest inroads into the work presently done by salesmen and intermediaries.

(c) High-advisory products and services

(i) Portfolio management

9.11 If you have an agreement with an investment manager for portfolio management services, you are very likely to require contact that is regular or intensive (sometimes both) with your investment manager. Firms which provide such services have traditionally prided themselves on the degree to which they maintain close relationships with their clients. This is driven to some extent by the manager's regulatory reporting requirements. Many investment management agreements give almost complete discretion to the manager in respect of day-to-day matters (subject only to compliance with an overall investment objective and a duty to keep that objective under review). Yet, even so, many investment managers are pleased to provide their clients with means to keep up to date on investment opportunities and portfolio values over the Internet.

(ii) Corporate finance business

9.12 'Corporate finance business'[1] covers a variety of activities which involve the provision of investment advice or the arranging of deals in investments. Generally, the circumstances under which a corporate finance adviser acts for a client (such as a public company which might be looking to mount or defend a takeover bid) are so case-specific that it is difficult to imagine this type of service migrating to an electronic format in the near future.

There is, however, another side to this. Deal arranging in, for example, the shares of a newly floated high-risk company has become a more streamlined business with the development of services such as OFEX (a deal-matching system operated by OFEX plc). Presently, the service operates by means of orders telephoned into a broking team, who in effect make a 'market' for the stocks which are 'listed' by OFEX. New issues require a prospectus which complies with the Public Offers of Securities Regulations 1995[2]. In time, the Internet almost certainly will become the logical place for both the publication of new issue prospectuses and the marketing of new issues.

1 As defined in the glossary of the FSA Handbook.
2 SI 1995/1537.

3.   SOURCES OF E-COMMERCE REGULATION FOR FINANCIAL SERVICES

(a) The present system

9.13 When people first started to say that the Internet was a 'jungle' with little, if any, regulation, the riposte from the legal community was that the Internet was actually subject to rather a lot of regulation. However, most of it predated the advent of e-commerce and it was often mismatched. This was perhaps no more true than in the area of financial services law. With the replacement of the FSA 1986 by the FSMA 2000 and a mass of new subordinate regulation, we now have a body of legislation governing the provision of financial services which has been drawn up in the full knowledge of the importance of the Internet.

(i)   The Financial Services and Markets Act 2000

9.14 As already stated, those provisions of the FSMA 2000 relating to the provision of financial services substantially came into effect at midnight on 30 November 2001 (N2). The FSA 1986 was repealed with effect from then. The FSMA 2000 had a tortuous path to the statute books, with much consultation and comment. A first draft for consultation of the Financial Services and Markets Bill appeared in July 1998, followed in the spring of 1999 by various draft Statutory Instruments to be made under the new law. The first draft of the Bill was roundly criticised for a variety of reasons, most notably that it failed conspicuously to establish a Financial Services Authority whose powers were subject to appropriate checks and balances. The Bill was presented to a Joint Committee of both Houses of Parliament for scrutiny in March–April 1999 (an unprecedented move in the history of UK law reform, in as much as this took place before a first reading of the Bill in either House of Parliament). The Committee issued two reports, in April and May 1999. In addition, consultation was carried out by HM Treasury in March and November 1999 on the content of the draft Financial Promotions Order and in February 1999 on the draft Regulated Activities Order. A revised draft of the Bill was published in June 1999 and was laid before the House of Commons for first reading in July 1999. This was carried over into the 1999–2000 session of Parliament by consent of the Conservative Opposition, underwent further changes and amendments during a complex committee stage in both the House of Commons and the House of Lords, and finally received Royal Assent on 14 June 2000. A further consultation document was issued in October 2000 and the FSMA 2000 finally came into effect with respect to financial services on N2.

The FSA 1986 conferred on the Secretary of State extensive powers to regulate the promotion of investments, whether by advertising or the making of unsolicited calls. The scope of the definition of 'investment'[1] covered all forms of securities and debt instruments, bonds, warrants, units in investment funds, derivatives and life assurance. 'Investment business' was defined[2] to include, among other things, dealing and arranging deals in investments, managing investments, safekeeping and administration of investments, operation of certain types of investment fund and provision of advice to investors on the merits of investing.

1   FSA 1986, Sch 1, paras 1–11.
2   FSA 1986, Sch 1, paras 12–16A.

9.15   In the Consultation Paper published by the Treasury in March 1999, in connection with the Financial Services and Markets Bill and the draft Financial Promotions Order, the Treasury stated that the new regime 'aimed to avoid, as far as possible, discriminating between different communications media, and also to ensure that the legislation is sufficiently flexible to adapt to further technological changes'. The old regime under the FSA 1986 was based on the idea that it was possible to distinguish between different communications media. Consequently, it tried to draw a distinction between 'investment advertisements' and 'unsolicited calling'. A breach of the provisions relating to the former carried criminal sanctions, while a breach of the provisions relating to the latter carried civil sanctions. Because of the difficulty of reconciling the use of electronic media with these two concepts, the FSMA 2000 introduced the more media neutral concept of a 'financial promotion'. By virtue of section 21(1) of the FSMA 2000, 'a person must not, in the course of business, communicate an invitation or inducement to engage in investment activity', unless that person is an authorised person or the communication has been approved by an authorised person.

However, the FSMA 2000 is different from its predecessor in a number of respects. Even more than the FSA 1986, it creates a legislative 'framework' setting down broad parameters within which the FSA operates. The FSMA 2000 also provides for numerous Statutory Instruments to implement its terms. These Statutory Instruments run alongside various rules, guidance and codes issued by the FSA. The relative ease with which new secondary legislation can be introduced and existing secondary legislation can be amended means that the new regime can keep abreast of technological advancements and evolving markets. Further, the FSMA 2000 consolidates and replaces the regulation of investment, insurance and banking business which existed under the FSA 1986, the Insurance Companies Act 1982 and the Banking Act 1987. Thus, the main provisions of the FSMA 2000 deal with the following:

- the constitution and objectives of the FSA;

- the grant to the FSA of regulatory duties and powers to achieve its objectives (including powers to make rules, gather information and investigate and impose financial penalties on authorised persons who breach the regulatory regime or on those persons that abuse markets);

- a number of safeguards and checks and balances to ensure that the FSA is accountable for its actions. The FSA is under a general duty to consult with both a practitioner panel and consumer panel to ensure that it is exercising its legislative and other powers properly. The FSA has set up a complaints scheme which provides independent investigation into complaints against the FSA. A person who is the subject of an enforcement action by the FSA has the right to refer the matter to the Financial Services and Markets Tribunal, an independent body, which will consider the matter afresh and may issue directions to the FSA;

- the introduction of a new 'civil offence' of market abuse which applies equally to those who are regulated under the FSMA 2000 and those who are not;

- the introduction of a unified financial promotions regime covering all kinds of financial promotions;

- the introduction of a single authorisation process under which a person seeking to carry on regulated activities either (i) applies to the FSA for a Part IV 'permission', or (ii) automatically receives authorisation (subject to certain conditions) if exercising passport rights under EC Directives or EC Treaty rights; and

■ the introduction of a new single compensation scheme and a single financial Ombudsman scheme.

(ii) The Financial Services Authority – the single regulator

9.16 The FSA 1986 established a system of self-regulation. Powers vested in the Secretary of State were mostly transferred to the Securities and Investments Board (SIB). (SIB was renamed the 'Financial Services Authority' in October 1997[1].) SIB, in turn, recognised a range of self-regulating organisations (SROs), which were empowered to make and enforce rules for the regulation of different sectors of the financial services industry. These SROs originally numbered five but by 30 November 2001 there were just three: the Securities and Futures Authority (which regulated those who dealt in securities and derivatives, market-makers and corporate finance advisers); the Investment Management Regulatory Organisation (whose members included institutional fund managers and trustees) and the Personal Investment Authority (which regulated companies concerned with the issue and promotion of personal investments, such as life assurance, unit trusts and pension plans).

Each issued its own rulebook, as well as other materials such as guidance notes, consultative proposals and newsletters for members. On 1 December 2001, the above three SROs ceased to have regulatory functions and, as provided by the FSMA 2000, the FSA became the single UK regulator with responsibility for the financial services industry. (Powers to regulate the banking industry had already been transferred to the FSA in June 1998[2] (known as N1).) Each of the SRO's rules and guidance have now been consolidated and rationalised in a new single Handbook. This contains all the rules and guidance issued by the FSA pursuant to the FSMA 2000 and governs the entire financial services industry.

The FSA, in exercising its general functions[3], must – in so far as is reasonably possible – act in a way compatible with the following regulatory objectives[4]:

■ maintaining market confidence in the financial system (being the financial markets, activities connected with the markets and regulated activities);

■ promoting public awareness and understanding of the financial system;

■ protecting consumers; and

■ reducing financial crime.

In addition, the FSA must have regard to the principles of good regulation[5], which include inter alia 'the desirability of facilitating innovation' and 'the international character of financial services and markets and the desirability of maintaining the competitive position of the United Kingdom', both of which principles should bode well for e-commerce.

1 See the Financial Services (Change of Name of Designated Agency) Rules 1997, which came into force on 28 October 1997.
2 By the Bank of England Act 1998.
3 The FSA's general functions, as set out in section 2(4) of the FSMA 2000, are making rules, preparing and issuing codes, giving general guidance and determining the policy and principles by which it performs particular functions.
4 The FSMA 2000, ss 2(2), 3, 4, 5 and 6.
5 The FSMA 2000, s 2(3).

(iii) European Directives

9.17 Superimposed on UK financial services law and regulation are the financial services aspects of the European Union's 'Single Market'. Of primary interest is the EC Investment Services

Directive[1], which provides a framework for the provision across borders within the EEA of 'investment services' (as defined in article 1) by 'investment firms'. The definition of 'investment services' under the Investment Services Directive is not, however, entirely the same as the definition of 'regulated activities' under the FSMA 2000. Likewise, the concept of an 'investment firm' in the Investment Services Directive is not exactly the same as that used for firms which require authorisation under the FSMA 2000. The general approach of the Investment Services Directive is to allow an investment firm which is prudentially regulated in its home state in the EEA to provide investment services in other Member States of the EEA without requiring ab initio authorisation there. However, this is subject to the requirement that the investment firm complies with non-prudential regulations (conduct of business rules) in each 'host state' in which it does business. Moreover, such an investment firm is entitled to unrestricted access to all regulated markets in each host state in which it does business itself, again subject to compliance with local conduct of business rules. The Investment Services Directive does not, in detail, determine the content of conduct of business rules that each Member State is required to make. Rather, it establishes the areas in which conduct of business rules are required to be made (for example conduct of business itself and investment promotion) and stipulates that such regulations ensure that firms act honestly and fairly; with due skill, care and diligence, in the 'best interests' of their clients, etc. As a matter of general EU law, the conduct of business rules must be non-discriminatory and must not be anti-competitive.

The Investment Services Directive and its sister Directive, the Capital Adequacy Directive[2], were officially supposed to have been implemented into the laws of all EEA Member States by 1 July 1995, and to have come into operation there on 1 January 1996, though several EEA Member States took much longer than this to implement these measures. There is a parallel Single Market regime for the investment services (as well as the credit and deposit-taking services) provided by banks and credit institutions in the Directive Relating to the Taking Up and Pursuit of the Business of Credit Institutions[3], which consolidates and repeals previous regulations in this field.

One further aspect of EC legislation that should be mentioned is the UCITS (Undertakings for Collective Investment in Transferable Securities) Directive[4], one of the earliest Single Market measures in the financial services field, which provides a framework for the cross-border offering of certain classes of investment fund. The UCITS Directive applies to funds constituted in corporate form, as unit trusts or on a contractual basis. However, the fund must be dedicated to investment in 'transferable securities' (investments in other instruments such as money market instruments will also be permitted under the proposals which have been made vis-à-vis the UCITS Directive regime: see paragraph 9.51 below), it must be open-ended (or arrange for units/shares to be admitted to listing such that they can be sold on-exchange at prices corresponding with net underlying asset value) and investments must be made on the basis that risk will be spread rather than concentrated. The approach of the Directive is to permit a fund which meets the criteria in the Directive and which has been registered in the EEA Member State where it or its operator is resident, to offer shares/units in the fund to residents in other EEA Member States after notifying regulators in those other EEA Member States of its intention to do so. Provided only that local marketing laws are complied with, there is no jurisdiction in the other EEA Member State's regulator to prohibit the offering[5].

1 Directive (EEC) 22/93, as amended.
2 Directive (EEC) 6/93, as amended.
3 Directive (EC) 12/2000.
4 Directive (EEC) 611/85, as amended.
5 The Directive assumes that it is the operator who will want to promote the fund in host states. Increasingly, however, it is intermediaries offering fund supermarket services of the sort discussed in paragraph 9.09 above who wish to sell retail funds across European borders. The Directive is of little help or relevance to them. See further in paragraph 9.51 below.

4. AREAS OF REGULATION

9.18 If it is your business to offer financial services in the UK (including investment promotional materials via the Internet), you are likely to wish to know whether you should seek authorisation under the FSMA 2000 before doing so (or whether, perhaps, one of the exemptions or exclusions might be relevant). Before considering the present position under the FSMA 2000, it is useful to consider the position as it was under the FSA 1986 and how it failed adequately to deal with the advent of the 'information superhighway'.

(a) The old regime

9.19 The FSA 1986 sought to categorise communications as either 'investment advertisements' or 'unsolicited calls'.

(i) Investment advertisements – scope of section 57 of the Financial Services Act 1986

9.20 Section 57 of the FSA 1986 required an investment advertisement that was issued other than by an authorised person or caused to be issued in the United Kingdom to be approved by a person authorised under the FSA 1986, unless one of the exemptions in section 58 of the FSA 1986 or the orders[1] made under section 58(3) applied. The issue of an unapproved, non-exempt advertisement other than by an authorised person was a criminal offence and also had potential civil law consequences for the issuer[2]. Section 57 had been understood during the 15 years prior to its repeal as follows:

- the words 'issue or cause to be issued' meant that a person would fall within the scope of the section whether he issued his own advertisement or he reissued another person's advertisement[3];

- an 'investment advertisement' was defined as an advertisement,

    'inviting persons to enter or offer to enter into an investment agreement or to exercise any rights conferred by an investment to acquire, dispose of, underwrite or convert an investment or containing information calculated to lead directly or indirectly to persons doing so'[4];

- the general view was that 'calculated' was to be understood, in an objective sense, as meaning 'likely'[5];

- an 'investment agreement'[6] was defined widely enough to include any form of agreement where (among other things) dealing in, managing and advising on investments was under consideration (or even if such matters were not under consideration per se, information was being proffered as to how to go about obtaining such services, or giving reasons as to why the recipient might wish to do so);

- practically any form of public display or announcement was an 'advertisement'[7]; and

- it was irrelevant with whom the recipient subsequently contracted. If you posted an advertisement which you considered to be calculated to lead X to sell you shares, but instead Y did so, this was still prima facie within the scope of section 57.

The regime of exemptions under section 58(3) of the FSA 1986, referred to above, made no specific provision for the Internet. For example, article 11(3) of the 1996 Exemptions Order established a list of persons or types of person to whom one could issue an investment advertisement without the approval of an authorised person. The list included investment firms, governments and local authorities, corporate or unincorporated bodies satisfying certain membership or net worth criteria and trustees of trusts over a certain minimum net worth, etc. However, there was no straightforward way to create mechanisms which ensured that only such entities (and not also private individuals) saw the relevant website. This created a particular difficulty for websites originating outside the UK. The difficulties of ensuring that only the 'right' kind of persons in the UK had access to the website often outweighed the benefit of making the services available to UK persons in the first place. This is considered further in paragraphs 9.21 and 9.22 below.

1   The Financial Services Act 1986 (Investment Advertisements) (Exemptions) Order 1996 (SI 1996/1586), as amended by the Financial Services Act 1986 (Investment Advertisements) (Exemptions) Order 1997 (SI 1997/963); and the Financial Services Act 1986 (Investment Advertisements) (Exemptions) (No 2) Order 1995 (SI 1995/1536).
2   See, respectively, section 57(3) and section 57(5)–(10) of the FSA 1986.
3   This was a real trap for the unwary, in view of the fairly free use that was made of banners and hyperlinks that linked one website to another.
4   Section 57(2) of the FSA 1986.
5   See, for example, SIB Guidance Release 4/94.
6   Defined in section 44(9) of the FSA 1986, and including not merely agreements which fell squarely within the definitions of the various activities constituting investment business but also agreements related to activities specifically excluded from that definition by Schedule 1, paras 17–27 to the FSA 1986.
7   Section 207(2) of the FSA 1986 had to be read this way. However, it was generally accepted that the material or medium must have had the characteristics of an advertisement.

(ii)   The problem with section 207(3) of the Financial Services Act 1986

9.21   The old 'investment advertisement' regime deemed an advertisement to have been issued in the UK if it was received in the UK. This, perhaps, worked well enough in the pre-Internet era. After all, if you were a company in another country which was in the process of offering securities for subscription, it required some effort on your part to procure that physical copies of prospectuses and offering memoranda were made available in the UK and went into general circulation in the UK. Because there was no guaranteed way to prevent an overseas publication, such as a newspaper or an overseas broadcast, carrying an investment advertisement from coming to the attention of a UK investor, section 207(3) provided an exception for overseas newspapers and broadcasts. They were not caught provided that they did not circulate, or were not transmitted for reception, in the UK. Section 207(3) specifically provided as follows:

> 'An advertisement ... issued outside the United Kingdom shall be treated as issued in the United Kingdom if it is ... made available to [persons in the United Kingdom] otherwise than in a newspaper, magazine, journal or periodical publication published and principally circulating outside the United Kingdom or in a sound or television broadcast transmitted principally for reception outside the United Kingdom.'

However, though this exception was useful in the realms of printed and broadcast media originating, principally for consumption, outside the UK, its limitations in relation to the Internet become immediately apparent. The Internet was not regarded as a broadcast medium and it was always debatable whether the exception in section 207(3) applied to Internet editions of a newspaper or magazine.

There was accordingly a risk that the firms behind thousands of websites worldwide would be deemed to be committing an offence under section 57 of the FSA 1986 simply because UK-based PC users could find their websites through perhaps purely random surfing of the Internet.

In an attempt to clarify the position, the Financial Services Authority issued Guidance Release 2/98 in August 1998. Commentary was offered as to the sort of factors which would make it less likely that the FSA would wish to exercise its enforcement powers in relation to an overseas website operator. However, the FSA did not set out any clear-cut formulae following which an overseas website proprietor could safely design and operate its website without cutting across section 57.

(iii) Unsolicited calling

9.22   The FSA 1986 dealt with unsolicited calling in relation to investment advertisements under a different framework from that already considered above. An unsolicited call was defined in section 56(8) of the FSA 1986 as a personal visit or telephone call made on a person without his express invitation.

The regime under section 56 of the FSA 1986 differed from that under section 57 in two respects. First, although the civil law consequences of making an unlawful cold call were identical to those which applied to the issuer of an unlawful advertisement, the making of a cold call did not amount to a criminal offence. Second, whilst it was prima facie lawful for any authorised person to issue an investment advertisement (in compliance with the rules of his regulator, of course), section 56 did not permit authorised persons as such to make unsolicited calls. Regulations produced by SIB set out specific circumstances in which cold calling was permitted, but these did not accord with the exemptions from the 'investment advertisement' regime in section 57 of the FSA 1986.

(b)   The new concept of financial promotion

(i)   Limitations in the old system

9.23   The FSMA 2000 amalgamates the old investment advertising and cold calling regimes into a single regime controlling 'financial promotion'. The logic behind the merger of the two regimes was driven by recent developments in Internet and telecommunications technology. For example:

■   the advent of 'chat rooms' and 'discussion forums' on the Internet has created an environment where e-mail can be used for virtually simultaneous exchanges between the correspondents. Under the old regime, where a correspondent received an investment tip in a chat room, it fell to be treated under the old system as a cold call, even if the presentation of that tip was to all appearances no different from routine e-mail.

■   more confused still was the treatment of unanswered telephone calls. If somebody were to call with an investment deal and the telephone was answered, the old regime would treat the call as an unsolicited call. However, if the call were not answered and voice-mail took a recorded message, this arguably amounted to an 'investment advertisement'. To make a cold call was not an offence, but to engage in 'investment advertising' in principle was. In short, whether a caller committed a serious criminal offence was determined by whether the recipient picked up the telephone – a matter completely out of the caller's control. The problem became more acute with the emergence of messaging and alerting services on mobile phones.

(ii)   Financial promotion – the Financial Services Market Act 2000, s 21

9.24   Section 21 of the FSMA 2000 introduced a single regime, under which – in essence – it is a criminal offence for a person in the course of business to 'communicate' an unauthorised invitation or inducement to engage in investment activity. The civil law consequences of such an unauthorised communication are the same as those which applied under sections 56 and 57 of the FSA 1986, in relation to both cold calls and investment advertisements, which were not authorised or sanctioned by the FSA 1986. Any resulting contract is unenforceable against the other party.

Section 21(5) of the FSMA 2000 also provides for exemptions from the basic prohibition to be made by the Treasury. Three exemption orders have been made to date, being the Financial Services and Markets Act 2000 (Financial Promotion) Order 2001[1] (First Order), the Financial Services and Markets

Act 2000 (Financial Promotion) (Amendment) Order 2001[2] and the Financial Services and Markets Act 2000 (Financial Promotion) (Amendment No 2) Order 2001[3] (together, 'the Orders').

In addition, section 238 of the FSMA 2000 prohibits an authorised person from promoting unregulated collective investment schemes in or from the UK, subject to exemptions which are in most respects substantially similar to the corresponding exemptions to section 21.

1   SI 2001/1335.
2   SI 2001/2633.
3   SI 2001/3800.

(iii) Key elements of the prohibition

9.25

- **'In the course of business'** Section 21 provides that communications have to take place 'in the course of business'. The intention was to eliminate the chance that this otherwise quite sweeping section might catch casual remarks and exchanges that were never intended to be business-like representations. The sentiment is justified. However, the term 'business' is capable of a broad construction. Under section 21(4) of the FSMA 2000, the Treasury has the power to specify circumstances in which a person is to be regarded as acting (or not acting) in the course of business. The Treasury has not exercised this power; nor does it intend to do so for the time being. The term 'business' should therefore be given its ordinary meaning. The view of the FSA is that it requires a commercial interest on the part of the communicator, which does not necessarily have to be a direct interest[1]. In the case of individuals, the FSA has stated that the 'in the course of business' test is not intended to include genuine non-business communications, for example friends talking in a pub and e-mails sent by individuals using an Internet chat room or bulletin board for personal reasons[2]. However, there are still areas of uncertainty. What is likely to be of concern (and it may take a test case to resolve the matter) is the extent to which an employer becomes vicariously liable for the personal use made by employees of the employer's e-mail server and system. This may be of more concern, oddly enough, to businesses that are authorised to provide investment services (since it might be more difficult to argue that, if your company is not so authorised, a message sent by one of your staff using the office e-mail, which refers to investments, has a bearing on that employee's role and duties within your organisation). If we presume that a broker's e-mail is set up so as to include the sort of introductory and disclaimer language that is so commonly found on business e-mails these days, and it states that the firm is appropriately regulated to carry on investment business, what is the effect of this on an ostensibly private purpose e-mail sent by a member of staff which makes some reference to investments or their availability[3]?

- **'Communicate'** The meaning of the word 'communicate' includes 'causing a communication to be made'[4]. The FSA's view is that a person is making a communication where he imparts information to the recipient or is responsible for physically transmitting the information on behalf of another person[5]. Furthermore, the FSA considers apart from the originators of a financial promotion, that publishers and broadcasters of websites carrying banner advertisements and intermediaries redistributing a person's communication probably with their own communication are communicating a financial promotion[6]. The 'mere conduit' exemption in article 18 of the First Order ensures that, subject to certain conditions, the restriction in section 21 does not apply to those who merely transport the financial promotions to others, for example postal and Internet service providers and telecommunications companies[7]. The conditions include requirements that the person acting as a mere conduit does not select, modify or otherwise exercise control over the content of the financial promotion before it is made, the financial promotion is wholly devised by another person, and the person acting as a 'mere conduit' communicates it in the course of a business carried on by him, the principal purpose of which is transmitting or receiving material provided to him by others. A person is not, however, selecting, modifying or exercising control merely as a result of having power to remove material which is illegal, defamatory or in breach of copyright, or at the request of a regulatory body, or where the law requires it. The FSA has further stated that a person who operates a website will not be able to take advantage of the 'mere conduit' exemption by simply providing a chat room or bulletin board as this will not satisfy the principal purpose business test[8]. However, in the FSA's view, as long as the required principal purpose is carried on and represents a discrete business, the principal purpose test can be satisfied.

- **'An invitation or inducement'** Although the heading to section 21 refers to 'financial promotion', the body of this section does not refer to this concept – which was one of the chief criticisms of section 21. The absence of the concept of 'promotion' on the face of section 21 arguably means the restriction captures all communications regardless of how private[9]. The Treasury refused to qualify communications to those with a promotional element but stated in consultation that only communications containing a degree of incitement would amount to inducements and that communications comprising purely factual information would not do so, provided that the facts were presented in such a way that they did not also amount to an invitation or inducement[10]. In the FSA's view, an objective test should be applied in deciding whether a communication is an invitation or inducement whereby the communication 'must both have the purpose or intent of leading a person to engage in investment activity and be promotional in nature' and accordingly a communication with no element of persuasion or incitement will not be an invitation or inducement under section 21[11]. FSA guidance states that an invitation is a communication which 'directly invites a person to take a step which will result in his engaging in investment activity'[12]. According to the FSA, an inducement is a form of communication which does not in itself amount to an invitation but is a step in a chain which leads, ultimately, to a person engaging in investment activity[13]. However, only links in the chain that are a 'significant step' in persuading or inciting or seeking to persuade or incite a person to engage in investment activity will be caught by section 21[14].

- **'To engage in investment activity'** The definition of 'investment activity' is not the same as 'regulated activity' (the performance of which requires authorisation). Section 21(8) defines 'investment activity' as entering into or offering to enter into an agreement, the making or performance of which constitutes a 'controlled activity', or exercising any rights conferred by a 'controlled investment'[15] to acquire, dispose of, underwrite or convert a 'controlled investment'. Controlled activities and investments are defined in the First Order and the resulting investment activity is similar to 'regulated activities', except that none of the exemptions from the concept of a 'regulated activity' apply and there are differences in connection with funeral plans and certain credit agreements.

- **'Having an effect in the United Kingdom'** Section 21 provides that a communication should not make its originator culpable unless it is 'capable of having an effect in the UK'. We noted above that this was the concept which caused difficulties under section 57 of the FSA 1986; yet the Treasury proposed throughout the draft stages of the Financial Services and Markets Bill that this would remain a central feature of the proposed new regime. Not surprisingly, this attracted significant opposition from practically all sides. It amounts, in effect, to an attempt by the UK authorities to regulate conduct by persons in other countries who are, for practically all other purposes, outside the UK's jurisdiction. The Treasury refused to climb down over the 'capable of having effect' concept in the Bill itself, and this provision is now found in the FSMA 2000, s 21(2). The Treasury stated in the October 1999 consultation[16] that, in its view, a wide conception was needed in the primary legislation to allow for future developments, but that the relevant order would provide the correct measure of interpretative precision for the comfort of persons operating outside the UK and their professional advisors. This was met by the argument that it is undemocratic to use secondary legislation as a device to define or amend fundamental concepts in primary legislation. However, article 12 of the First Order provides that section 21 does not apply to communications which are not directed at persons in the UK (see further discussion under paragraph 9.33 below).

1   FSA Handbook, Authorisation Manual at AUTH App 1, para 1.5.2G.
2   FSA Handbook, Authorisation Manual at AUTH App 1, para 1.5.3G.
3   There are other issues as well. For example, what is the significance of a 'casual' remark made during the course of a 'business' lunch?
4   The FSMA 2000, s 21(13).
5   FSA Handbook, Authorisation Manual at AUTH App 1, para 1.6.1G.
6   FSA Handbook, Authorisation Manual at AUTH App 1, para 1.6.2G.
7   The Financial Services and Markets Act 2000 (Financial Promotion) (Amendment) (Electronic Commerce Directive) Order 2002 (SI 2002/2157) amends the 'mere conduit' exemption (see paragraph 9.33 below).
8   FSA Handbook, Authorisation Manual at AUTH App 1, para 1.12.20G.
9   Crosthwait, 'Financial Services and Markets Act, UK; A Critical Assessment of the New Financial Promotion Proposals' [2001] JIFM 1 at 5.
10 HM Treasury, 'Financial Promotion: Third Consultation Document', October 2000, para 2.2.
11 FSA Handbook, Authorisation Manual at AUTH App 1, para 1.4.4G.
12 FSA Handbook, Authorisation Manual at AUTH App 1, para 1.4.5G.
13 FSA Handbook, Authorisation Manual at AUTH App 1, para 1.4.7G.
14 FSA Handbook, Authorisation Manual at AUTH App 1, para 1.4.7G .
15 Controlled Investments as defined by article 4 and part II of Schedule 1 to the Financial Services and Markets Act 2000 (Financial Promotion) Order 2001 (S1 2001/1335) include deposits, rights under a contract of insurance, most forms of shares and stocks, all forms of debt instrument, warrants, units in a collective investment scheme, rights under a stakeholder pension scheme, options, futures, derivatives, funeral plan contracts, agreements for qualifying credit and rights to or interests in investments.
16 HM Treasury, 'Financial Promotion: Second Consultation Document', October 1999, Part II, para 2.14.

(c) E-commerce concerns and relevant exemptions under the Orders

9.26 A large part of the material contained in the Orders does not impact upon e-commerce specifically. We set out below the principal provisions of the FSMA 2000 and exemptions which are relevant to e-commerce.

(i) Host or home state regulation

9.27 Although the trend in relation to e-commerce regulation, derived from the European Commission in Brussels, is for greater emphasis on home state regulation, the view which the Treasury takes is that 'the argument has not yet been made' for a move away from the host state regulation of financial promotion which exists at present. Given that one of the fundamental aims of the EU is to create a Single Market (which has been most recently underwritten by the issue of the notes and coins of the Single European Currency on 1 January 2002), it is unsurprising that a Single Market in financial services in the EU was set for completion by 2005 by EU heads of government at the European Council in Cardiff in 1998. Although the Treasury maintained its position on host state regulation in the October 2000 consultation document[1], it did welcome the E-Commerce Directive[2], which takes a home state or 'country of origin' approach to transactions (although not applying to all financial services). As home state regimes develop, section 21 of the FSMA 2000 permits the Treasury, by Statutory Instrument, to remove restrictions on promotions from outside the United Kingdom. The Treasury intends to move to a home state regime once other countries move to a home state regime. In the interim, the Treasury take the view that UK consumers may be vulnerable to financial promotions not controlled under an adequate regulatory framework. The Treasury, however, intends to amend the First Order (see further discussion under paragraph 9.33 below) to take account of amendments to be introduced by the implementation of the E-Commerce Directive.

1   HM Treasury, 'Financial Promotion: Third Consultation Document', October 2000, paras 2.8–2.12.
2   Directive (EC) 31/2000.

(ii) Hypertext links

9.28   Since section 21 the FSMA 2000 is expressly restricted to invitations or inducements, the Treasury's view is that there is no need to consider a special regime for regulating hypertext links in any detail. That is to say, if a link is an invitation or inducement it will fall within the scope of section 21 (unless exempted for some other reason) and, if not, it will fall outside the scope of the FSMA 2000 altogether[1].

Notwithstanding this, the Treasury's views, as expressed in its October 2000 consultation, are that the link itself (and not just the destination website) must constitute an invitation or inducement in order to be caught by the section 21 regime. Simply clicking on a hypertext link and reaching a website does not amount to causing the communication of an invitation or inducement to engage in investment activity contained in that website. Only if the link by itself invites or induces someone to engage in investment activity would it be caught by the financial promotion restriction[2]. Links which include narratives or references may be financial promotions depending on whether they incite persons to use the links. Accordingly, it will be a question of fact whether the hypertext link will amount to a financial promotion, depending on its nature and the context in which it is placed. The FSA is of the view[3] that:

■   taken in isolation, a hypertext link which is purely the name or logo of the destination is unlikely to be a financial promotion by itself; however, banners or changeable text may be a financial promotion depending on the facts of each case;

■   material on a host website which contains the hypertext link may itself be a financial promotion if it contains text seeking to encourage or incite persons to activate the link, with a view to engaging in investment activity;

■   a directory of website addresses or e-mail addresses is unlikely to be a financial promotion unless the website page contains some other inducement to contact the named addressee with a view to engaging in investment activity; and

■   website operators who host or create links to the websites of unauthorised persons are responsible for the contents of their own website. However, in most cases the website operator will not be causing the communication of any financial promotion contained in those other websites and accordingly need not be concerned with these destination websites complying with section 21. If and only if the website operator (the Operator) has made arrangements with the website operator of the destination website under which the Operator is to procure users of his site to access the hypertext link produced with a view to their engaging in investment activity will the Operator be causing the communication of a financial promotion on the destination website for which the Operator's website if not exempt will need to be approved if a breach of section 21 is not to occur.

Despite the above guidance, it may be that this issue will be resolved by the courts where the merits and demerits of the promotional elements (for example, the prominence, size and location of banners and links on a page, and design and text, and any other action which draws attention to the link) will be discussed. This will be of particular concern to websites managed by on-line brokers who give users the chance to follow banners and hyperlinks to other pages for the purposes of gleaning information about particular stocks and the opportunities to trade them.

1   HM Treasury, 'Financial Promotion: Second Consultation Document', October 1999, paras 2.22–2.26.
2   HM Treasury, 'Financial Promotion: Third Consultation Document', October 2000, para 2.29.
3   FSA Handbook, Authorisation Manual at AUTH App 1, para 1.22.3G.

(d) 'Exemptions concepts'

9.29 Taking a similar approach to the 'investment advertisements' regime under the FSA 1986, the ambit of the restrictions on 'financial promotion' is scaled back by the exemptions contained in the Orders. Before considering the exemptions applicable to e-commerce, it is useful to consider briefly three concepts introduced by the Orders.

(i) 'Real-time and non real-time communications'

9.30 The First Order draws a distinction between 'real-time communications' and 'non real-time communications'. Article 7(1) defines a real-time communication as 'any communication made in the course of a personal visit, telephone conversation or other interactive dialogue'. In the FSA's view, the equivalent of a telephone conversation conducted by e-mail will be a real-time communication where persons are expected to respond immediately. A non real-time communication is any communication which is not a real-time communication, and includes communications made by e-mail, by letter, in a publication, via a website, by radio or television broadcast and by a message placed in an Internet chat room[1]. In the FSA's view, a financial promotion which may exist in enduring form will be a non real-time financial promotion, whereas a real-time financial promotion is a promotion which allows interaction[2].

1 FSA Handbook, Authorisation Manual at AUTH App 1, paras 1.10.5G(1) and 1.10.7G.
2 FSA Handbook, Authorisation Manual at AUTH App 1, paras 1.10.5G and 1.10.7G.

(ii) Solicited and unsolicited real-time communications

9.31 The First Order, in article 8, classifies 'real-time communications' as solicited or unsolicited, that is in the latter case made 'cold'. A real-time communication is solicited where it is made in the course of a personal visit, telephone call or other interactive dialogue, for instance in using a chat room, if that visit, call or dialogue was initiated by the recipient or takes place in response to an express request from the recipient[1]. On the basis that recipients require more protection in unsolicited situations, there are fewer exemptions for unsolicited real-time communications than solicited.

1 Article 8(1) of the Financial Services and Markets Act 2000 (Financial Promotion) Order 2001.

(iii) 'Made to' and 'directed at'

9.32 Article 6 of the First Order draws the above distinction – a financial promotion is 'made to' persons when it is addressed to a particular person or persons, that is by letter or telephone call. A financial promotion is 'directed at' persons where it is addressed to persons generally or to a group of persons as in a website. In relation to the latter, it is the FSA's view it does not matter if the financial promotion reaches persons other than those it is intended for, provided it was not directed at them[1]. However, it will be an indication that a financial promotion in a website is directed at the United Kingdom if the website is registered with a UK search engine[2]. It is important to ascertain whether a financial promotion is 'made to' or 'directed at' persons, as some exemptions, in particular, in relation to real-time communications only apply for a financial promotion 'made to' persons. Exemptions exist for 'financial promotions' which are directed at or not directed at certain persons, for example communications not directed at the UK.

1 FSA Handbook, Authorisation Manual at AUTH App 1, para 1.12.8G.
2 FSA Handbook, Authorisation Manual at AUTH App 1, para 1.12.8G.

(e) Overseas exemptions

9.33 There are exemptions contained in article 12 of the First Order for financial promotions which either:

- are made to a person who receives them outside the UK; or

- are directed at persons outside the UK.

These exemptions will apply whether or not the financial promotion is made from the UK with the exception that, if it is an unsolicited real-time financial promotion, it must be made from a place outside the UK for the purposes of a business carried on entirely outside the UK[1]. The 'directed at persons outside the UK' part of the exemption was designed principally for overseas websites. Six tests are set out to assess whether or not a financial promotion is 'directed at persons in the UK'. If some tests only are satisfied, or none, it will remain an evidential matter as to whether or not the financial promotion is targeting the UK.

If a financial promotion is directed from a place outside the UK, even if received by a person in the UK, it will not be treated as directed at persons in the UK if, broadly speaking, the following two conditions are satisfied:

- the financial promotion is not referred to in, or indirectly accessible from, another communication (that is an advertisement in a UK newspaper or UK website) which is itself made to, or directed at persons in the UK by or on behalf of the same overseas person; and

- there are proper systems and procedures in place to prevent recipients in the UK from engaging in the investment to which the communication relates[2].

As discussed above in paragraph 9.28, it would appear that (based on the Treasury's reasoning on hypertext links), that as long as a 'hypertext link' connecting to a website containing the financial promotion is not itself an 'invitation or inducement', the first of the conditions above can be satisfied. The First Order does not, however, include a definition of 'proper systems and procedures'. The FSA has stated that persons seeking conclusive proof that the exemption applies must consciously establish arrangements to prevent their dealing with recipients in the UK[3]. These arrangements may include password protected access to information and/or software programming to recognise and reject UK addresses. The FSA has stated that the fact a procedure may fail on an isolated occasion does not mean the exemption ceases to apply 'provided the systems were and remain proper'.

1   Article 12(2) of the Financial Services and Markets Act 2000 (Financial Promotion) Order 2001.
2   Articles 12(3)(b) and 12(4)(c) and (d) of the Financial Services and Markets Act 2000 (Financial Promotion) Order 2001.
3   FSA Handbook, Authorisation Manual at AUTH App 1, para 1.12.6G.

9.34 In respect of a financial promotion made from within the United Kingdom, to satisfy the exemption, in addition to satisfying the two safe harbours set out above, the communication must be accompanied by an indication that:

- it is directed only at persons outside the UK; and

- it must not be acted upon by persons in the UK[1].

There are two further indicators which are not conditions as such, but which are to be taken into account in assessing whether a financial promotion is directed only at persons outside the UK, namely whether:

- a website, newspaper or magazine is principally accessed in or intended for a market outside the UK; or

- a radio or television broadcast is transmitted principally for reception outside the UK[2].

In addition, a communication may still be treated as directed only at persons outside the UK where it is also directed at persons in the UK provided those persons are limited to 'investment professionals' or 'high net worth persons'[3].

Article 12 of the First Order provides only a marginal clarification of the term 'capable of having effect' in the primary legislation. A general and overriding criticism is that article 12 still means the proprietor of every overseas website should take account of, and advice on, compliance with the UK financial promotions regime. Why should this be so?

1 Article 12(4)(a) and (b) of the Financial Services and Markets Act 2000 (Financial Promotion) Order 2001.
2 Article 12(4)(e) of the Financial Services and Markets Act 2000 (Financial Promotion) Order 2001.
3 Article 12(5) of the Financial Services and Markets Act 2000 (Financial Promotion) Order 2001.

9.35 Overseas websites can be viewed as falling into one of three distinct groups for analysis of whether they are caught by section 21 of the FSMA 2000:

■ those which expressly target UK investors (in which case it follows that the website proprietor must take care to comply with appropriate regulations and restrictions on promotion);

■ those that contain features which are clearly designed to attract the attention of UK investors (among others) and which do not take any precautions to discourage the interest of UK investors (for example, by incorporating a rubric which states that UK residents cannot deal through the website in question, or password protected access, or certain software programming); and

■ those which have no ex facie relevance to the UK at all.

The law in the UK ought to provide that those in the third category should not have to be concerned over falling foul of the section 21 prohibition. It seems heavy-handed that at present, as with the FSA 1986, the FSMA 2000 can be construed as requiring *every* website worldwide to incorporate systems and procedures preventing UK recipients gaining access, and to make express mention of its irrelevance to the UK and/or the absence of any intention on the part of its proprietor to deal with UK investors.

Even with the second category of website mentioned above, there ought to be a clear procedure for the proprietor to be able to assess whether its presentation and content are of a character which should discourage the UK investor, without his needing to incorporate procedures and language for excluding UK investors. The problem, of course, is that such extra material on a website is calculated to reduce its impact or appeal and detract from its primary purpose, that of selling investments to those lawfully entitled to purchase them in other countries. However, in the FSA's most recent formal view, the requirement to include indications in a website to satisfy the above exemption requirements 'may be satisfied by putting information on separate pages which can be accessed through a link, or one of the pages, which contains the financial promotion'[1].

It should be noted that as originally enacted article 12 of the First Order conflicted with the E-Commerce Directive[2]. However, the Financial Services and Markets Act 2000 (Financial Promotion) (Amendment) (Electronic Commerce Directive) Order 2002, which came into force on 21 August 2002, amended the First Order.

It was discussed above in paragraph 9.27 that the E-Commerce Directive promotes a home state or country of origin approach to the regulation of information society services (ISS)[3]. EAA Member States are prohibited from restricting the freedom to provide ISS from other EEA Member States for reasons falling within the co-ordinated field. The Order includes the following amendments:

■ the exemption contained in article 12 of the First Order be amended to remove its application to an electronic commerce communication made from a place of establishment in the UK to persons in other EEA Member States (that is, an outgoing electronic commerce communication) together with consequential amendments to other exemptions in the First Order;

■ a new general exemption for communications made from EEA Member States other than the UK and which constitute the provision of ISS (that is, an incoming electronic commerce communication). This general exemption is in line with the E-Commerce Directive and will not apply to communications constituting an advertisement by the operator of a collective investment scheme which falls under the ambit of the UCITS Directive[4] of units in that scheme, communications in respect of insurance or an unsolicited commercial communication made by e-mail; and

■ an amendment to article 18 of the First Order dealing with the 'mere conduit' exemption, which removes electronic commerce communications from the general 'mere conduit' exemption but inserts a new article 18A in the First Order whereby an electronic communication which falls within and satisfies the conditions of paragraph 1 of any of articles 12, 13 or 14 of the E-Commerce Directive (dealing with 'mere conduit', 'caching' and 'hosting' respectively) at the time of, or prior to, making the communication is exempt from the provisions of section 21 of the FSMA 2000.

In order to satisfy the mere conduit condition, the ISS provided will consist of 'the transmission in a communication network of information provided by a recipient of the service, or the provision of access to a communication network'[5], and the provider must not initiate the transmission, must not select the receiver of the transmission and must not select or modify the information contained in the transmission. An Internet service provider (ISP) should be able to satisfy these tests, which echo the tests under article 12 of the First Order. Caching consists of the service of the transmission in a communication network of information provided by a recipient of the service and hosting is the service of storing information of a recipient of a service, both of which have various conditions that need to be satisfied to benefit from the 'mere conduit' exemption[6].

1 FSA Handbook, Authorisation Manual at AUTH App 1, para 1.22.3G(5).
2 Directive (EC) 31/2000.
3 See discussion on the E-Commerce Directive in Chapter 2 in particular for the meaning of information society services and co-ordinated field.
4 See the discussion on the UCITS Directive at paragraph 9.51 below.
5 2000/31/EC, art 12.
6 2000/31/EC, arts 13 and 14. In respect of 'caching', the service must be performed for the sole purpose of making more efficient the information's onward transmission to other recipients upon their request, on condition that (1) the provider does not modify the information; (2) the provider complies with conditions on access to the information; (3) the provider complies with rules regarding the updating of the information, specified in a manner widely recognised and used by industry; (4) the provider does not interfere with the lawful use of technology, widely recognised and used by industry, to obtain data on the use of the information; and (5) the provider acts expeditiously to remove or to disable access to the information it has stored upon obtaining actual knowledge of the fact that the information at the initial source of the transmission has been removed from the network, or access to it has been disabled, or that a court or an administrative authority has ordered such removal or disablement. In respect of 'hosting' a service provider will not be liable under section 21 of the FSMA 2000 provided that (a) the provider does not have actual knowledge of illegal activity or information and, as regards claims for damages, is not aware of facts or circumstances from which the illegal activity or information is apparent; or (b) the provider, upon obtaining such knowledge or awareness, acts expeditiously to remove or to disable access to the information.

(f) Carrying on a 'regulated activity'

(i) The general prohibition under the Financial Services and Markets Act 2000

9.36 The FSA 1986 provided that a person who carried on 'investment business' in the UK had to be authorised to do so, unless he could benefit from an exemption or a specific exclusion. This general prohibition has been carried over into the FSMA 2000. Section 19 of the FSMA 2000 provides that a person is prohibited from carrying on a 'regulated activity' in the UK, or purporting to do so, unless he is an authorised or exempt person. Although the terminology employed in the FSMA

2000 is a little different from that in the FSA 1986 ('regulated activity'[1] as opposed to 'investment business', for example), the basic approach in this area is much the same. Thus, it is a criminal offence to carry on a regulated activity whilst unauthorised. Likewise, as was the case under the FSA 1986, such behaviour has civil liability consequences for the person concerned.

Therefore, a failure on the part of an (unauthorised) proprietor of a website offering investment services in the UK to operate within the scope of an exemption may well mean that the proprietor has committed a criminal offence under section 23 of the FSMA 2000 as a result of contravening section 19 the FSMA 2000. While there is a general common law presumption (rebutted or removed altogether in certain statutory contexts) that the UK courts do not have jurisdiction over criminal offences committed outside the jurisdiction, there are examples of cases where offences committed overseas have been capable of being heard in the UK courts where they have had some tangible effect in the UK itself.

Of equal importance in cases of unlawful investment activity is the power of the FSA under section 382 of the FSMA 2000 to seek restitution of investors' property and compensation for losses. Moreover, the FSMA 2000 also provides that a person who has been carrying on unlawful investment activity may not enforce its agreements against UK investors with whom it has been doing business (even though such investors have a right to treat the relevant contract(s) as enforceable against that person, if they so wish).

1   The Financial Services and Markets Act 2000 (Regulated Activities) Order 2001 (SI 2001/544), which came into effect at midnight on 30 November 2001, except for the provisions dealing with mortgages and funeral plans, listed the regulated activities as including: deposit taking (Chapter II); effecting and carrying out contracts of insurance (Chapter III); investment activities, that is dealing in investments as principal or agent (Chapters IV and V); arranging deals in investments (Chapter VI); managing investments (Chapter VII); safeguarding and administering investments (Chapter VIII); sending dematerialised instructions (Chapter IX); establishing a collective investment scheme (Chapter X); and agreeing to carry on any of these activities (other than establishing a collective investment scheme) (Chapter XVI). New regulated activities include establishing and operating a stakeholder pension scheme (Chapter XI); activities in relation to Lloyds (Chapter XIII); activities in relation to funeral plan contracts (Chapter XIV); and providing regulated mortgage contracts (Chapter XV). It does not include offering to carry on any of the activities as provided under the FSA 1986.

(ii) Holding out offence

9.37   One particular offence established under the FSMA 2000, of interest to those offering services via websites, is the so-called 'holding out offence'[1]. It is an offence for a person to hold himself out as being authorised or exempt if he is neither of these. The offence will be committed by a person where he:

> 'behaves, or otherwise holds himself out, in a manner which indicates (or which is reasonably likely to be understood as indicating) that he is (i) an authorised person; or (ii) an exempt person in relation to the [relevant] regulated activity.'

A fine can be imposed for this offence, together, if appropriate, with a sentence of up to six months in prison. Section 24(4) of the FSMA 2000 clarifies, however, that where the offence involves or includes any 'public display of material', the fine may be imposed *per day* for each day of that public display. Implicitly, this is aimed at display media such as the Internet, as well as at conventional printed media[2].

It is unclear what sort of activities or behaviour will be sufficient to constitute this offence. It seems likely that the offence can be committed by a person who either intentionally or recklessly engages in a course of conduct. The words 'reasonably likely to be understood' imply a degree of objective assessment of the behaviour in question. For criminal law purposes a person may be held to have engaged in reckless conduct even where he has not fully intended to do so[3]. If, therefore, you are the proprietor of a website (of any sort), the extent to which the structure of your website, including hyperlinks and banners featured there, might lead the PC user to infer that you might yourself be authorised will be of interest. What is the position where, for example, your website 'X' (general non-financial site) is hyperlinked to, or advertises a banner for, website 'Y' (a regulated investment business)? There is clearly cause for concern that you as proprietor of X might be holding yourself out as arranging deals between persons viewing X and the proprietor of Y, or making representations in the nature of advice to click on the link to Y. What makes the position yet more complicated is that the analysis in this sort of case probably turns on matters of presentation or artwork as much as substantive content.

1   See the FSMA 2000, s 24.
2   Repeated use of audio media does not appear to fall within the scope of this provision but probably constitutes a separate offence on each occasion.
3   See *Metropolitan Police Comr v Caldwell* [1982] AC 341, HL; *R v Lawrence* [1982] AC 510, HL. Establishing that the defendant has been reckless requires that the defendant must take an obvious and serious risk (assessed objectively) and must do so in a way that demonstrates (assessed subjectively to the defendant) that either he has given no thought to there being any risk at all, or that there was some risk which he nevertheless chose to take. This conception, which departed from previous case law precedent in relation to recklessness in criminal law, has caused a lot of difficulties, primarily in relation to the sort of case where the defendant argues that he assessed the situation and concluded that there was not in fact any risk at all.

5.   ISSUES FOR THE INTERNET SERVICE PROVIDER

9.38   So far, we have principally considered the impact of the FSMA 2000 regime on those who (lawfully or otherwise) provide regulated services in the UK. It is important to consider the role and place of the ISP in this context and the extent to which the ISP may become liable under the law as a secondary party.

(a)   The position in criminal law

9.39   The ISP might be involved in the affairs of an investment firm in a number of different ways. At one end of the spectrum, the ISP could operate entirely passively and function as a mere conduit through which information passes to and from a firm (much as telephone companies and postal services have operated for many years, in relation to telephone conversations and document deliveries). It would be oppressive to hold an ISP liable for the consequences of its being used as a conduit in this fashion. Accordingly, the FSMA 2000 has created, as outlined in paragraph 9.25 above, a specific exemption for 'mere conduits', which may be relied upon by ISPs in relation to financial promotions. A mere conduit falls outside the financial promotion regime created by section 21 of the FSMA 2000.

The FSMA 2000 also makes some changes to the incidence of the criminal liability under section 23 of the FSMA 2000 in relation to unauthorised carrying on of a regulated activity for mere conduits.

The Treasury has created a mere conduit exclusion under the Financial Services and Markets Act 2000 (Regulated Activities) Order 2001 (the RAO)[1]. By virtue of article 27 of the RAO, a person who provides arrangements which solely enable a party 'to communicate with other parties' to a transaction is not taken to be carrying on the regulated activity of 'arranging deals' described in article 25(2)[2] (essentially arrangements for dealing in general). Consequently, ISPs and other website providers who provide hypertext links to websites which provide investment products will generally not require precautionary authorisation (assuming their own websites do not contain financial promotions). It is debatable whether the ISP or website provider is excluded from the scope of the regulated activity of making arrangements for another person to deal in a particular investment defined in article 25(1)[3] (essentially arrangements relating to a specific deal). Article 26 of the RAO provides that making arrangements which do not bring about the transaction in question is not a regulated activity. Accordingly, whether providing a link to a website for executing specific transactions with a product provider is a regulated activity and requires the ISP to be authorised will depend on the facts of each case.

1 SI 2001/544.
2 Making arrangements with a view to a person who participates in the arrangements buying, selling, subscribing for or underwriting investments, which are securities, contractually-based investments or an investment of the kind specified by article 86 or article 89 of the Financial Services and Markets Act 2000 (Regulated Activities) Order 2001, including but not limited to, securities and contractually based investments.
3 Making arrangements for another person (whether as principal or agent) to buy, sell, subscribe for or underwrite a particular investment which is a security, a contractually-based investment, or an investment of the kind specified by article 86 or article 89 of the Financial Services and Markets Act 2000 (Regulated Activities) Order 2001.

9.40 At the other end of the spectrum, where the ISP takes a more active role, there are also a number of exemptions. Article 29 of the RAO contains a new exclusion (for those who arrange deals through authorised persons). This may help ISPs and on-line businesses. Article 29 provides that such a person does not require authorisation for the activity of arranging deals in investments (whether generally or in relation to particular investments) described in article 25(1) and (2), where the client in his capacity as an investor has not sought advice from the ISP or the on-line business, and a deal is to be entered into with an authorised person. These conditions are usually likely to be satisfied by an ISP. However, if the ISP receives any commissions or fees from a person other than the client (say the product provider by way of commission based on volume of traffic), for which it does not account to the client, the exclusion does not apply. This may limit the commercial usefulness of the exemption.

If an ISP is involved in the financial services industry and does not wish to be authorised, it will have to be careful to stay within the confines of any relevant exemption if it is to escape prosecution. The ISP should also be aware that there may be circumstances where its own actions (or inaction) can be interpreted as – in some measure – assisting or aiding the conduct of persons involved in unlawful investment business on the Internet[1]. Generally, the UK courts do not claim jurisdiction over criminal acts committed outside the UK[2]. However, where the offence is taken to have been committed in the UK via an agent resident there, both the overseas offender and the UK resident agent can be indicted[3]. Whether or not the ISP is a purely innocent agent in respect of offences under section 23 of the FSMA 2000 committed by an overseas person, or is actually complicit, will depend on the degree of its knowledge and involvement. To be guilty as an accomplice, the ISP must be aware of the circumstances of the crime being committed by the overseas person. Even if it lacks actual knowledge, case law suggests that turning a 'blind eye' to the obvious can constitute a sufficient degree of knowledge or involvement[4]. Subjective recklessness may also be sufficient to attract liability[5].

Further issues arise in relation to the operation of collective investment schemes – section 235(1) of the FSMA 2000 defines the concept of 'collective investment scheme' for the purposes of UK financial services regulation. Article 51 of the RAO has the effect that the establishment, operation or winding up of a collective investment scheme in the UK requires authorisation. For this reason, it is often the case that scheme operation is exported and located offshore (with investment advice to the scheme operator or manager provided from within the UK). Nonetheless, problems may arise. The ISP who facilitates communications between UK-based investors and the overseas operator may be arranging a deal in a specific investment, which is a regulated activity and for which the mere conduit exemption may not apply (see discussion above) to arrangements to deal in a specific investment.

1 Although a more general analysis of the criminal liability of an ISP lies beyond the scope of this chapter, it does not seem unreasonable to conclude that the principles set out here might be of wider application than merely financial services information. Chapter 3, E-liability examines issues arising under the UK's laws regarding obscenity, for example.
2 See *R v Jameson* [1896] 2 QB 425; *Air-India v Wiggins* [1980] 2 All ER 593, HL. There are, of course, a number of statutory exceptions to this principle.
3 *R v Baxter* [1971] 2 All ER 359, CA, approved in *DPP v Stonehouse* [1978] AC 55, HL. In *Baxter*, the defendant was based in Northern Ireland and was convicted of attempting to obtain football pools winnings by deception (mailing letters in false names) from English pools companies, contrary to section 15 of the Theft Act 1968 (which does not apply in Northern Ireland).

4 *Cook v Stockwell* (1915) 84 LJKB 2187 (conviction of a brewer for supplying alcohol to another, knowing that he was reselling it illegally); *Cafferata v Wilson* [1936] 3 All ER 149, DC (conviction of a firearms wholesaler for selling a weapon to another, who kept it in his shop and resold it without a requisite licence to do so, since the defendant knew he had no licence and ought to have appreciated that he might resell the weapon).

5 *Carter v Richardson* [1974] RTR 314 (a driving instructor was guilty of aiding and abetting his pupil to drive with excess alcohol in circumstances where the instructor thought this excess was 'probable'). The significance of this case is that the defendant was at all times in control of what was happening in the vehicle (in the sense that a normal front seat passenger would not have been). The same might be said of the ISP, manifested perhaps by the fact that it is increasingly common to find servers denying PC users access to material on the Internet which is of an obscene or politically unacceptable nature.

9.41 ISPs and related service entities in the Internet community should consider the question of secondary liability arising from their passive association or semi-active involvement with companies not authorised to provide investment services in the UK[1]. In fact, the problem is no less profound for the ISP which associates itself with the activities of a regulated entity.

The following two difficulties may arise:

■ an ISP seeks to provide content for its own subscribers by furnishing a link from its home page to the home page of an on-line dealing firm. A mere hyperlink or banner is not usually a problem[2], unless, for instance, the ISP adds language of its own to the surround for the hyperlink. This problem is made worse if there is an agreement between the ISP and the broker for sharing commission generated by referred clients[3]; or

■ a broker (which is regulated) comes to an arrangement with a technology provider of some sort (an ISP, a telecommunications company or maybe even a web designer) whereby the latter will introduce the broker to its customers and contacts. Although this is commercially the reverse of the point above, as it is the content provider that is looking here for outlets, the problem is the same[4].

1 The jurisprudence for this argument comes from a series of analogous cases, in which the defendant is technically incapable of committing the offence as a principal but can be convicted of aiding and abetting others to commit it. See, for example, *DPP v Morgan* [1976] AC 182, HL (husband and three friends have forced sexual intercourse with wife; the husband could not be charged with rape, but was convicted of aiding and abetting the other men to commit rape).

2 On the basis that the broker has issued the promotion or approved its content for issue in accordance with section 21 of the FSMA 2000. However, the financial promotion needs to disclose that it is issued or approved by the relevant authorised person.

3 The ISP cannot rely upon the usual exclusion for mere introductions in article 33 of the Financial Services and Markets Act 2000 (Regulated Activities) Order 2001 because the broker will not be appointed to provide independent advice or exercise independent discretion. Under the RAO the mere introductions exemption does not apply to the regulated activity of 'arranging a deal relating to a particular investment' – regulated under article 25(1).

4 And it should be added that the broker, though regulated to carry on its own investment business, may be liable for aiding and abetting another entity (which is not so authorised). The jurisprudence for this argument is explained in footnote 1 above.

(b) Civil liability

9.42 The civil liability regime under the FSA 1986 has largely been replicated in the FSMA 2000, though there have been some changes.

(i) *Being 'knowingly concerned'*

9.43 Section 382 of the FSMA 2000 allows the court, on the application of the FSA, to make restitution orders against a person who has contravened a requirement imposed by or under the FSMA 2000. This would include breach of section 19 (unlawfully carrying on a regulated activity). The FSA can also take action against any person who has been 'knowingly concerned' in the contravention. The same powers exist where there has been an unauthorised financial promotion (contrary to section 21 of the FSMA 2000) and where any of the criminal offences in section 397 of the FSMA 2000 (generically categorised as misleading statements and practices) has been committed[1].

A person who has contravened or is 'knowingly concerned' in a contravention may be subject to a restitution order where profits have accrued to him or where others have suffered losses or been otherwise adversely affected by the contravention. The restitution process is slightly different from that which operated under the FSA 1986, in that payments are made to the FSA for it to distribute to persons affected in accordance with the court's directions. (This means, of course, that if the person against whom the order is made defaults, the FSA can take action to recover against the defaulter, rather than the affected individuals, who might find it too expensive a remedy to pursue.) The court also has wide powers under section 382(4) of the FSMA 2000 to require contraveners and those knowingly concerned to provide information on profits they have received or losses they have caused to others. This might cause ISPs to consider what records they might reasonably keep of the material which passes through their servers, at least in so far as money payments are concerned.

'Knowingly concerned' under the FSA 1986 was judicially considered in *SIB v Pantell SA (No 2)*[2]. The first defendant, a Swiss company, carried on unauthorised investment business in the UK, causing loss to UK investors by selling them effectively worthless shares. The third, fourth and fifth defendants were English solicitors who had been involved with the mechanics of the share selling (collecting and banking subscription moneys, etc). However, they took no money for themselves. The Court of Appeal held that they were 'knowingly concerned'. Scott LJ held that there was no requirement that a person 'knowingly concerned' should have been involved as a beneficiary of the unlawful transactions. Steyn LJ suggested that the FSA 1986 equivalent of section 382(1) of the FSMA 2000 required actual knowledge of, or involvement with, the unlawful conduct.

On the basis of *Pantell*, it would, at first, appear that an ISP must be actively involved in the making of agreements breaching section 19 of the FSMA 2000 (or financial promotions that the issuer has no right to issue under section 21 of the FSMA 2000, etc). However, since in *Pantell* the solicitors had *actual knowledge*, there was no need to consider whether some form of constructive knowledge might have sufficed. If the ISP is aware (even constructively) that unauthorised investment services are being offered or advertised through its server, and does nothing to stop this traffic, there must be a risk that the ISP has become 'knowingly concerned' in such activities. By way of background, it should be recalled that the Securities and Futures Authority wrote in 1996 to all ISPs putting them on notice of the possible position under the FSA 1986; the risk of 'knowing' involvement is clearly increased now that ISPs have been alerted.

Nothing in any of these provisions of the FSMA 2000 indicates any change to or development in our understanding from *Pantell* of the meaning of 'knowingly concerned'; the same applies for the concept of restitution in this statutory context. It would therefore be prudent to assume that the incidence of liability will be no less than in *Pantell*.

It is also relevant that section 384 of the FSMA 2000 confers on the FSA more or less identical powers to those in section 382 in respect of contraventions by authorised persons, apparently without the need for court proceedings.

1 Section 397 of the FSMA 2000 refers to a person who:
  (i) makes a statement, promise or forecast which he knows to be misleading, false or deceptive in a material particular;
  (ii) dishonestly conceals any material facts whether in connection with a statement, promise or forecast made by him or otherwise; or
  (iii) recklessly makes (dishonestly or otherwise) a statement, promise or forecast which is misleading, false or deceptive in a material particular.
2 [1992] 1 All ER 134, CA.

(ii) Injunctions

9.44 Section 380 of the FSMA 2000 sets out the powers of the FSA to seek injunctions to restrain regulatory contraventions which the FSA considers are about to occur or are likely to continue or to be repeated. There is also power in section 380(2) for the court to order an enjoined person, or one 'knowingly concerned in the contravention, to take such steps as the court may direct to remedy it', provided that the court is satisfied that it is possible for such steps to be taken. This would allow the court to direct an ISP to take down, or block access to, a website which is being operated in contravention of the FSMA 2000.

(c) Criminal liability for misleading statements and practices – section 397 the Financial Services and Markets Act 2000

(i) The offence

9.45 Section 397(1) and (2) of the FSMA 2000 essentially re-enacts the offence created under section 47(1) of the FSA 1986. The only change of substance is that it relates to statements which are false, etc, 'in a material particular'.

No single provision of the FSA 1986 gave those operating in the financial services industry and their professional advisers more difficulties than section 47(1). The same is likely to be the case with section 397(1) and (2) of the FSMA 2000. The offence created by section 397 is complicated to analyse, and it is therefore worth setting out the provision in full:

'(1) This sub-section applies to a person who:
(a) makes a statement, promise or forecast which he knows to be misleading, false or deceptive in a material particular;
(b) dishonestly conceals any material facts whether in connection with a statement, promise or forecast made by him or otherwise; or
(c) recklessly makes (dishonestly or otherwise) a statement, promise or forecast which is misleading, false or deceptive in a material particular.

(2) A person to whom subsection (1) applies is guilty of an offence if he makes the statement, promise or forecast or conceals the facts for the purpose of inducing, or is reckless as to whether it may induce, another person (whether or not the person to whom the statement, promise or forecast is made)—
(a) to enter or offer to enter into, or to refrain from entering or offering to enter into, a relevant agreement; or
(b) to exercise, or refrain from exercising, any rights conferred by a relevant investment.'

Section 397 of the FSMA 2000 requires the actus reus of the offence to have a connection with the UK and section 397(6) and (7) specifically set out the requisite proximity required. In essence, the statement must either be made in or from the UK; the intended inducee must be in the UK (although, strangely enough, the *actual* victim need not be); or, alternatively, the contemplated agreement must have been entered into in the UK, or the investment rights are or would be exercised in the UK. In relation to the mens rea, the inclusion of recklessness as an alternative to intentional conduct is highly relevant, in view of the objective test of recklessness.

Section 397(9) of the FSMA 2000 defines a 'relevant agreement' as including an agreement the entering into or performance of which by either party constitutes activity of a specified kind or one which falls within a specified class and which relates to a 'relevant investment'. Specified kinds of activity[1] essentially include a controlled activity[2], providing funeral plan contracts or providing qualifying credit (from 1 September 2002) or agreeing to carry on any of these two latter activities. A 'relevant investment'[3] is a controlled investment, a funeral plan contract or an agreement for qualifying credit (from 1 September 2002).

1 See article 3 of the Financial Services and Markets Act 2000 (Misleading Statements and Practices) Order 2001 (SI 2001/3645).
2 As defined in Part 1 of Schedule 1 to the Financial Services and Markets Act 2000 (Financial Promotion) Order 2001 (SI 2001/1335).
3 See article 4 of the Financial Services and Markets Act 2000 (Misleading Statements and Practices) Order 2001 (SI 2001/3645).

(ii) Relevance to the Internet

9.46 Criminal liability for misleading statements and practices applies to *any* person, whether or not authorised under the FSMA 2000. If you were to publish an offer document or advertisement, you might be held to be reckless, in an objective sense, as to the misleading nature of a statement contained in that document. This might be the case, if, for example, you had simply not taken the trouble to subject the statement to formal verification. A statement will be made in the UK for the purposes of section 397(6)(b) of the FSMA 2000 if a PC user in the UK is able to see it on a website maintained by an overseas person. This means that an offence under section 397 could be committed by an overseas person making a statement in a web page established somewhere other than in the UK, intending it to be seen and acted upon by PC users in an overseas jurisdiction (for whom it is not misleading), the overseas person having been reckless as to whether it may induce a UK-based person to enter into a 'relevant agreement'.

A further and yet more alarming possibility arises from the *Thomson Holidays* case[1], which was a prosecution under section 14 of the Trades Descriptions Act 1968. As with the FSMA 2000, this Act provides an offence for the making of false or misleading statements. In *Thomson Holidays*, the defendant published two million copies of a travel brochure containing a misleading statement and was successfully prosecuted in respect of one instance where a customer had been misled. Trading standards officers in another part of the country brought a prosecution in respect of another customer. The defendant's claim of autrefois convict, ie that it had already been prosecuted for the offence, was rejected by the Court of Appeal. Lawton LJ held that each of the two million brochures effectively constituted a separate offence. Might this imply that each time a different PC user sees a misleading statement, satisfying the intent or recklessness test which induces him to do any of the things indicated in section 397(2) of the FSMA 2000, a separate offence is committed under that provision by the statement-maker? The quantitative implications for the website proprietor and, by implication, for the ISP as a secondary party are truly worrying.

Section 397 of the FSMA 2000 is generally unsatisfactory, as it appears to criminalise trivial incidents. If an ISP, objectively speaking, is aware that false or misleading statements are made via the Internet to PC users who subscribe to it for access to the Internet, it may have done enough to be guilty of aiding and abetting the commission of the offence by the statement-maker under section 397(2). By whose yardstick this objective test is established is unclear. These were issues under section 47 of the FSA 1986. It is regretful that they remain issues under section 397 of the FSMA 2000.

1   *R v Thomson Holidays Ltd* [1974] 1 All ER 823, CA.

(d)   Civil liability for behaviour amounting to market abuse

(i)   Introduction

9.47 The FSMA 2000 introduced a new 'civil' offence of market abuse[1]. This has been the subject of much comment and debate for the following reasons:

- the offence of market abuse can be committed by any person and not just a person authorised under the FSMA 2000; and

- the penalties for market abuse are an unlimited fine or public censure[2], though the FSA may also seek injunctions to restrain market abuse[3], remedial injunctions[4], freezing injunctions on assets[5] and orders to surrender any resulting profits, and to make restitution to everyone who has suffered any resulting loss[6]. The possible imposition of unlimited fines seems to render the offence a criminal one rather than a civil one and, accordingly, a person should have available all the procedural protections under the European Convention on Human Rights which have been incorporated into UK law by the Human Rights Act 1998.

1   The FSMA 2000, ss 118–131.
2   The FSMA 2000, s 123.
3   The FSMA 2000, s 381(1). On the application of the FSA, the High Court must be satisfied that there is a reasonable likelihood that a person will engage in, continue or repeat market abuse.
4   The FSMA 2000, s 381(2). On the application of the FSA, the High Court must be satisfied before granting an injunction that market abuse has occurred and action could be taken remedying the market abuse.
5   The FSMA 2000, s 381(4). If the High Court is satisfied that any person may be engaged in or may have been engaged in market abuse.
6   The FSMA 2000, ss 383 and 384. Restitution orders may be made by the court on the application of the FSA but also by the FSA exercising its power to require restitution.

(ii)   The offence

9.48   Market abuse is defined as behaviour which 'occurs in relation to qualifying investments traded on a market to which this section applies'[1]. Qualifying investments are any investments admitted to trading on any of the markets which are established under the rules of a UK recognised investment exchange[2], ie basically securities.

Three different kinds of behaviour may constitute market abuse, namely:

- using information which is not generally available to the relevant market but if available to a 'regular user' of the market would, or would be likely to be, regarded by him as relevant when deciding the terms on which transactions in the relevant investments should be effected[3];

- behaviour likely to give a regular user of the market a false or misleading impression as to supply, demand, price or value of the relevant investments[4]; and

- behaviour which a regular user of the market would, or would be likely to, regard as behaviour which would or would be likely to distort the market in the relevant investments[5].

Behaviour will not constitute market abuse unless it 'is likely to be regarded by a regular user of that market who is aware of the behaviour as a failure on the part of the person or persons concerned to observe the standard of behaviour reasonably expected of a person in his or their position in relation to the market'[6].

'Behaviour' can comprise action or inaction[7]. Persons who 'by refraining from taking any action'[8] require or encourage another person to engage in market abuse may also be prosecuted. This new offence applies to corporates as well as individuals, ie both regulated and unregulated.

Importantly for non-UK persons, including on-line businesses and ISPs, behaviour can constitute market abuse not only if it occurs in the UK but also if it occurs in relation to investments traded on a market which is situated in the UK, or which is accessible electronically in the UK[9].

The FSA, pursuant to section 119 of the FSMA 2000, has published a Code of Market Conduct giving guidance as to what behaviour amounts to market abuse[10].

Most importantly and controversially, market abuse can in many cases be committed without an intention to abuse the market: 'it is not essential for such an intention or purpose to be present in order for behaviour to fall below the objective standards expected'[11]. Section 123(1) creates a second offence under which a person by taking or refraining from taking any action has required or encouraged another person to engage in behaviour which if engaged in by the encourager would amount to market abuse. This offence will be of most concern to an ISP/on-line intermediary.

1   The FSMA 2000, s 118. The Financial Services and Markets Act 2000 (Prescribed Markets and Qualifying Investments) Order 2001 (SI 2001/996) as amended by article 2 of The Financial Services and Markets Act 2000 (Prescribed Markets and Qualifying Investments) (Amendment) Order 2001 (SI 2001/3681) stated that all markets established under the rules applicable to companies published by a UK recognised investment exchange would be covered, which would include the Alternative Investment Market, the Official List of the UK Listing Authority and OFEX.

2 Articles 4 and 5 of the Financial Services and Markets Act 2000 (Prescribed Markets and Qualifying Investments) Order 2001 (SI 2001/996) as amended by article 2 of The Financial Services and Markets Act 2000 (Prescribed Markets and Qualifying Investments) (Amendment) Order 2001 (SI 2001/3681).
3 The FSMA 2000, s 118(2)(a).
4 The FSMA 2000, s118(2)(b).
5 The FSMA 2000, s118(2)(c).
6 The FSMA 2000, s118(1)(c).
7 The FSMA 2000, s118(10).
8 The FSMA 2000, s123.
9 The FSMA 2000, s118(5).
10 See www.fsa.gov.uk/handbook/bl2marpp/mar/toc.pdf.
11 FSA Handbook, Market Conduct Manual at MAR, para 1.2.5.E.

(iii) Relevance to the Internet

9.49 Obviously the Internet can be used as a medium through which the offence of market abuse could be committed. The dissemination of false or misleading information could be effected by posting fake or misleading statements relating to, for example, the takeover of a company on an Internet bulletin board or in a chat room.

The liability of on-line intermediaries or an ISP through which a person carries on an activity which amounts to market abuse is unclear. If the intermediary or ISP knows that its customer is engaged in abusive behaviour and does nothing it may be regarded in certain circumstances as having encouraged a market abuse. There is no 'mere conduit' exclusion for intermediaries/ISPs from the market abuse regime.

The FSA has stated, however, that where an originator of a transaction appears to have engaged in market abuse and in the course of so doing has acted through an intermediary, 'the intermediary's behaviour will not amount to either requiring or encouraging market abuse unless the intermediary knew or ought to have known that the originator was engaging in market abuse'[1]. This introduces a test of negligence. Essentially, whether a person acting as an intermediary by taking or refraining from taking action might be regarded as 'requiring or encouraging' others will depend on circumstances such as 'acceptable market practices, the experience level and skill and standard of knowledge of the person concerned, and the control or influence the person has in relation to the person who engages'[2] in the abusive behaviour. The FSA, however, pursuant to section 123 of the FSMA 2000 may not impose a penalty on a person if there are reasonable grounds for it to be satisfied that either:

■ the person concerned (for example the ISP/on-line business) believed on reasonable grounds that its behaviour did not constitute 'requiring or encouraging' market abuse; or

■ the person concerned took all reasonable precautions and exercised all due diligence to avoid behaving in a way that amounted to 'requiring or encouraging' market abuse.

Only time will tell whether this 'effect-based' code will require an ISP/on-line intermediary to take precautions to ensure that misleading information is not posted on its websites. However, some comfort may be taken from the Chairman of the FSA, Howard Davies', speech entitled 'N2 Plus 3' on 5 March 2002 to the Institute of Chartered Secretaries and Administrators, where Mr Davies stated that the FSA aims to 'prioritise rigorously' and only investigate those cases which are 'material and significant' and any response will be proportionate[3]. The FSA is interested in cases that pose a threat to confidence in the UK's financial markets and not in 'pursuing technical or inadvertent infringements of the rules'.

The future of the market abuse regime will also be shaped by the European Commission's proposed Directive on insider dealing and market manipulation (market abuse) presented by the European Commission on 30 May 2001, a proposal arising out of the consensus that a single financial market is a key factor in promoting competition in the European economy. The Directive aims to safeguard the integrity of European financial markets throughout the Common Market. To ensure convergence in this area, the Directive proposes that each Member State designates a single regulatory and supervisory authority which will have a common minimum set of responsibilities and which authorities will work together and share information in the prevention, detection, investigation and prosecution of market abuse. According to the European Commission, the new proposed framework is not intended to replace national provisions but give some convergence between the different EEA Member States' existing regimes.

1   FSA Handbook, Market Conduct Manual at MAR, para 1.8.8.G.
2   FSA Handbook, Market Conduct Manual at MAR, para 1.8.4.G.
3   See www.fsa.gov.uk/pubs/speeches/sp93.html.

6.   THE EUROPEAN DIMENSION

9.50 Consideration of the impact of a range of existing European law measures in this area of financial services shows that some are outdated as far as e-commerce and Internet usage are concerned.

(a)   The UCITS (Undertakings for Collective Investment in Transferable Securities) Directive – marketing of collective investment schemes

(i)   Present purpose and effect

9.51 The UCITS Directive[1] was adopted in 1985, and was fully in force in ten of the then EU Member States by 1 October 1989. Greece and Portugal had a derogation until April 1992. EEA Member States were obliged to implement the Directive as part of their accession to the EEA Treaty in 1994, meaning that Austria, Sweden and Finland, upon full accession to the EU, had also already given effect to the UCITS Directive as a result of their accession to the EEA Treaty. Norway, Iceland and Liechtenstein, though outside the EU, are still within the compass of the UCITS Directive.

The UCITS Directive provides a basis for the cross-border promotion within EEA Member States of certain classes of collective investment fund. Essentially, once a fund coming within the scope of the Directive has been authorised in the EEA Member State where it or its operator is based, a simple procedure exists whereby the operator can 'notify' regulators of investment funds in any other EEA host state, of an intention to promote the fund there. Broadly, the host state regulator cannot go behind the authorisation of the fund and only has jurisdiction to refuse to allow the fund to be offered to investors in the host state if the manner of that offering, as proposed by the fund's operator, would be in breach of host state marketing rules. As well as compliance with marketing rules, the other paramount responsibility on the operator is to maintain an agency presence in the host state, for the purpose of receiving orders from host state investors to acquire or redeem their shares, and for handling correspondence and complaints regarding the fund, etc.

An undertaking for collective investment in transferable securities may be a corporate vehicle (UCITS) (if so, it must be open-ended), a unit trust or a contractual arrangement. The first two of these forms are now common in the UK. The contractual form is found in other EEA Member States (for example the *fonds commun de placement* in France), but does not exist in the UK. On the whole the unit trust model is found in the UK and Ireland alone, since the trust is a concept alien to civil law jurisdictions. A UCITS must operate on the principle of risk-spreading, as opposed to risk concentration. It must facilitate the redemption of the shares/units issued to investors, more or less upon demand, and at a price corresponding to their net asset value. Assets of the fund must be entrusted to a trustee or depositary for safe-keeping, and there must be a measure of independence between the fund/operator and the depositary/trustee. The UCITS Directive also makes provision for the publication of reports and accounts for UCITSs.

1   Directive (EEC) 611/85, as amended.

9.52   It is germane to note that there are currently proposals for reform[1] of the UCITS Directive. These reforms will permit managers of UCITSs to engage in a wider range of activities.

However, in terms of its investment profile, until the reforms to the UCITS Directive regime come into force, a UCITS must be a scheme dedicated to investment in 'transferable securities', meaning stocks, shares, debentures, bonds, gilts, warrants et alia and (subject to certain further conditions) units in collective investment schemes. Investment in land is not permitted, and interests in derivatives are only permitted to the extent that these are acquired in connection with the 'efficient portfolio management'[2] of the UCITS, or the avoidance of currency or interest rate exposure under article 21[3] of the Directive.

Article 21 of the UCITS Directive has led to difficulty and inconsistent interpretation throughout the EEA. UK regulations take a very restrictive approach to this provision. By comparison, in Ireland, the holding of assets through an intermediary company is considered to fall within these parameters if this allows for greater efficiency with tax planning. In Luxembourg, UCITSs commonly hold hybrid securities, where the commercial benefit of the security is referable to an underlying basket of other assets, while the commercial risk is usually associated with the issuer of a debt instrument of some sort that, in itself, may be completely unrelated to the profile of the fund in question.

1   The proposed reforms provide that a UCITS may carry out transactions in financial derivative instruments, provided that the exposure relating to such instruments is covered according to the rules laid down in a new article 24b. If the UCITS carries out transactions in financial derivative instruments which are not dealt in on a regulated market (over-the-counter derivatives), the counterparties to such transactions must be qualified institutions belonging to the categories approved by the UCITS's competent authorities.
2   The reference to 'efficient portfolio management' in article 21 will disappear, as the reference has been criticised for having no precise meaning (given that the scope of this term has been interpreted widely in EEA Member States).
3   Under the current UCITS Directive, investments are strictly limited to those made for the purposes described in articles 21(1) and (2) of the Directive.

(ii) Implementation of the UCITS Directive in the UK

9.53   The UCITS Directive applies in the UK to classes of authorised unit trust schemes dedicated to securities (including gilts) and warrants[1], and since January 1997 it has also been permissible to constitute as UCITS open-ended investment companies dedicated to the same range of investments[2].

1   Several other classes of authorised unit trust exist, which fall outside the scope of the UCITS Directive.
2   Pursuant to the Financial Services (Open-Ended Investment Companies) (Tax) Regulations 1997 (as amended) and the Open-Ended Investment Companies Regulations 2001 (SI 2001/1228).

(iii) The UCITS Directive and the Internet

9.54   The UCITS Directive was conceived in the pre-Internet era. It deals in concepts which depend on the production of printed documents which can be difficult to apply in the e-commercial world, other than by analogy. It is necessary to ask and answer two questions concerning the increasing use and potential of the Internet in relation to the marketing of investment funds:

■   **What are the consequences of using the Internet at all?** In general terms, the commentary in paragraph 9.23 above in relation to financial promotions via the Internet applies to the use of a website to publish a prospectus for a UCITS. A website at which the prospectus appears, accompanied by an on-line application form, or a clear procedure to be followed to apply for securities, runs a significant risk of constituting a financial promotion. The operator of a UCITS in another EEA Member State would therefore almost certainly be deemed to be offering securities to UK investors if, without more, he used an Internet website in this fashion. It is important to bear in mind that section 21 of the FSMA 2000 applies to communications outside the UK if the communication is capable of having an effect in the UK. So, in principle, a website based in France built with the purpose of promoting a UCITS into Germany might still be deemed to be a promotion to UK persons if visible in the UK. However, article 12 of the First Order provides that section 21 does not apply to communications which are not directed at persons in the UK. Article 12 sets out certain requirements for a communication to meet if it is to take advantage of the exemption (eg clear indications that the communication is not intended for UK-based investors as detailed in paragraph 9.33 above). Whilst it is clearly advantageous for an operator of a UCITS to benefit from the exemption, if these requirements are not complied with, as its website clearly targets UK investors, the operator of a UCITS would be required to make the necessary notification application to the FSA under section 264 of the FSMA 2000, describing in full the methods by which promotion in the UK were proposed to take place. If the FSA permits such a promotion, the operator is required to comply with the financial promotion rules in the Conduct of Business Rules of the FSA Handbook.

■ **Do current regulations permit a UCITS to be promoted *exclusively* via the Internet?** There has been no clear regulatory guidance on this matter from the UK regulators. This leaves us with the task of extrapolating what we can from the way in which the relevant regulations are worded. Broadly, there are three issues:

– The first is whether, when the operator of a UCITS is required to produce 'documents', he may do so using purely electronic records of the information in question. The FSA Handbook[1] sets out the obligations of regulated collective schemes, inter alia, with respect to the production of prospectuses and other documents. It must now be regarded as conclusive that the word 'document' may be understood to mean the electronic version of something capable of reduction to printed form[2].

– Second, if the operator of an overseas UCITS must maintain facilities at an 'address' in the UK, can this be an electronic address (an e-mail address or a website)? The case of *R v Bishop*[3] indicates a judicial willingness to construe 'address' as meaning the place or location at which one would come to expect to find the person concerned. In *Bishop*, service of a document required by statute was not possible on the relevant person at a conventional postal address as he was homeless, though known to frequent a certain area where other homeless persons also congregated. That area, therefore, was his 'address'. It may be a logical leap to apply a 40-year-old case concerning homeless persons to the use of Internet address protocols, but in the absence of a little imagination from the regulators in this respect, these are the very jumps that are having to be made to accommodate the potential of e-commerce into an outdated regime where tangible documents and physical presences are the norm.

– Third and last, there are the facilities themselves. Broadly, these are as follows:

  • various documents (in, or translated into, English) must be available for inspection, and copies must be available from the requisite address. These include the UCITS's constitutional documents and prospectus, and its most recent annual or periodic accounts;

  • price details for issue and redemption of units in the UCITS must be available from the address for those merely making a routine enquiry;

  • the address must also serve as a place to which orders for issue and redemption of units may be addressed by UK investors (even if in principle they can also contact the UCITS operator in its home state directly);

- some UCITSs issue bearer certificates (this is rather more common elsewhere in Europe than in the UK). Bearer certificate holders must be able to apply at the address for dividends to be paid and to request copies of the UCITS's report and accounts, and any notices issued by it (being bearer holders, their details are not registered by the UCITS's administrator, so none of these things will have reached them automatically); and

- investors must be able to write to the address with any complaints they may have about the UCITS, the operator and related matters.

1 FSA Handbook, Collective Investment Scheme Manual at CIS.
2 *Victor Chandler International Ltd v Customs and Excise Comrs* [2000] 1 All ER 160, per Chadwick LJ.
3 [1959] 2 All ER 787 at 791.

9.55 In principle, facilities which merely envisage one-way or two-way written communication can be provided across the Internet. Documents for inspection can be reproduced on a website maintained by the operator, and then either printed off or reviewed on-screen by the PC user. Complaints can be sent (and answered) via e-mail. Price details can form part of the operator's website (there are already a number of fund managers who offer this service). Orders to purchase or redeem units can be given through the website or via e-mail. Processing claims from holders of bearer certificates for receipt of their dividends is more complicated, but could certainly be managed over the Internet (for example by requiring the bearer holder to submit a unique certificate code for electronic verification). Money payments (as distinct from the instructions which give rise to them) may for the time being still have to be sent through existing methods outside the framework of the Internet, rather than through any of the developing 'e-cash' systems. However, in time, this too may change.

(iv) Proposals for reform

9.56 In concluding this section, it is appropriate to emphasise that proposals[1] for a new UCITS Directive have been discussed and finalised by the Council. These proposals are primarily for the purpose of creating a more liberal regime for promotion of different types of investment fund. The revisions include increasing the range of permissible UCITS investments[2], and making more onerous the disclosures[3] which must be contained in the UCITS's prospectus, particularly with respect to additional information requirements. Clarification of procedural matters, such as whether a website may be the exclusive means of marketing a UCITS, are likely to be left up to the EEA Member States to address when developing their own marketing regulations.

In this context, we should refer to a point made in paragraph 9.09 above regarding the emergence of funds supermarkets on the Internet. The UCITS Directive presumes that the entity most likely to wish to offer a UCITS to investors in another EEA Member State is the UCITS operator. It is debatable how true this really ever was. The likely flow of investment from host state investors is generally not likely to outweigh the cost of setting up arrangements for a facilities agent in each relevant EEA Member State, to receive and process orders, etc (other, perhaps, than with respect to funds established in Ireland by UK houses that arrange for their promotion to UK investors, and similar arrangements in Luxembourg, with respect to investors in France or Germany). The Internet offers a less expensive means of cross-border distribution for UCITS operators (if ambiguities over the meaning of address, etc, indicated above, can be overcome). But it is the independent sector which is now very much coming into its own. The UCITS Directive makes no allowances for these types of activity (though, to be fair, the Investment Services Directive, considered below, does make some provision). However, the supermarket operator in the UK seeking to market funds to investors elsewhere in the EU finds that the streamlined approach of making all UK funds available to all investors breaks down. Some of those funds are UCITSs. Of those, some have not been registered in some, or all, EEA Member

States. This is quite apart from the various UK authorised unit trust schemes which are not within the scope of the UCITS Directive at all. Host states have different requirements in relation to this form of cross-border marketing, and, as will be seen at paragraph 9.58, the funds supermarket is bound by the conduct of business and promotional regulations in each EEA Member State where it wishes to do business.

1   The final Commission Proposals are contained in COM 0329/2000. A common position was adopted by the Council on a new UCITS Directive in June 2001.
2   Following clear demands by the European Parliament, investments in over the counter derivatives would be fully covered as eligible investments. The assets contained in the portfolio of the UCITS would no longer be distinguished between being for 'general investment purposes', 'hedging purposes' and 'purposes of efficient portfolio management'.
3   The proposals redesign the current article 24 of the Directive in order to incorporate new, more onerous disclosure requirements for the different types of funds.

(b)   The Investment Services Directive – offering of other investment services

9.57   The other major part of the framework underpinning the European Single Market in financial services is the Investment Services Directive[1]. The Investment Services Directive and its sister provision, the Capital Adequacy Directive[2], were part of the programme of Single Market legislation that was expected to have been completed and implemented by 1 January 1993. Significant difficulties over negotiation of the Investment Services Directive delayed its adoption until the early part of 1993 itself. Although the Investment Services Directive provides that EEA Member States were supposed to have made all necessary legislative changes to give effect to the Investment Services Directive/Capital Adequacy Directive regime by 1 July 1995, many had not, and in fact it has taken a number of EEA Member States until relatively recently to give effect to the Investment Services Directive at all.

1   Directive (EEC) 22/93, as amended.
2   Directive (EEC) 6/93, as amended.

(i)   Present purpose and effect

9.58   It is not proposed in this chapter to review the full structure and operation of the Investment Services Directive[1]. The principle behind the Directive is that if an investment firm is authorised in an EEA Member State to provide one or more of the various 'investment services', it may provide those services in other EEA Member States freely (subject to notifying the local regulators and compliance with relevant local laws on the conduct of investment business and investment promotion). If so the firm need not seek authorisation in any such host states.

The Investment Services Directive provides a framework in which EEA Member States have to draw up their own conduct of business rules and other 'non-prudential' regulations, but it does not prescribe in detail what these should be. Accordingly, article 11 of the Investment Services Directive sets down basic principles that such rules shall follow (for example that an investment firm shall act honestly and fairly, exercise due skill and judgement, have requisite numbers of staff, etc). Article 13 prescribes that an investment firm may use all relevant means to promote its services in a host state, but this will be subject to whatever advertising regulations the host state shall have adopted 'in the interests of the general good'.

Access to the investors in a host state is permitted to an investment firm via the opening of a branch in the host state or through the provision of cross-border services. Somewhat different systems of notification to host state regulators apply depending on whether the firm wishes to operate through a host state branch or across borders without the establishment of a branch. Setting up a branch takes up to five months to process. Notification for provision of cross-border services is, in effect, not subject to any time constraints (see below).

A further component of the Investment Services Directive regime is the automatic right of access that any qualifying investment firm established in a given EEA Member State has to 'regulated markets', as defined in the Investment Services Directive, in each and every other EEA Member State. According to article 15 of the Investment Services Directive, a 'regulated market' is one that is operated by an exchange established and regulated in the EEA Member State in question, on which investments falling within the scope of the Investment Services Directive are regularly traded. By way of example, in the UK the markets in question are the various markets operated by the London Stock Exchange, UK Listing Authority, LIFFE, and Virt-x plc. So, a UK-based investment firm can arrange to transact business on an exchange in another EEA Member State via an electronic link, if it so wishes, rather than through the establishment of a branch office in the host state itself (though if using a link in this fashion, the rules of the relevant exchange will almost certainly require a UK-based investment firm to appoint a local clearing broker and custodian to represent its interests in that market).

1   For a useful overview of the structure and purpose of the Investment Services Directive, published practically as the Investment Services Directive first became relevant to the operation of UK financial services, see Carol L'Hévéder, 'The Investment Services Directive and its Implications for Participants in Europe's Financial Markets' (1996) 1 JIBFL 5.

(ii)   What is the position with a wholly electronic establishment in a host state?

9.59   Is the operation in a host state of a wholly electronic service tantamount in any circumstances to the operation of a branch? As far as the Investment Services Directive itself is concerned, the position is not completely clear. In article 3(3) (and see also the fifth recital), the Investment Services Directive indicates that EEA Member States shall require that the investment services provided through a branch operating in that EEA Member State be under the supervision of at least two appropriately qualified persons (the so-called 'four-eyes rule'). This can be understood in two different ways.

It could mean that if you set up a purely electronic presence in a host state (with no human supervision), this by its very nature is not capable of being characterised as a branch. Presently, the European Commission takes this view. But you could draw the opposite conclusion; namely that operating your 'branch' in a host state via an electronic local system is unlawful because it has no human supervision.

There is no easy way of resolving this dilemma. The position is still largely hypothetical in relation to most investment firms. Although bank Automated Teller Machines (ATMs), used for processing cash deposits and withdrawals, can be controlled across jurisdictions by a single computer system, this sort of development in the world of investment retailing is a little difficult to envisage at this stage. Where this development has arisen is in relation to the installation of 'dumb terminals' in the offices of hosts in different EEA Member States. Certain exchanges routinely do this for the purpose of communicating price data for investments traded on-exchange. However, if you were involved in placing a terminal with a host, surely this would merely be a service to the host (rather than the operation in the host's office of a branch of your own)?

The question is also beginning to assume importance for firms which develop pan-European retail investment dealing operations on the Internet, because the computer centre that processes those deals has to be resident somewhere, and it may make economic sense to place this in a location in a different EEA Member State from that in which the firm's head office is based. Resolving whether such a computer centre constitutes a branch may depend on whether the state where the machinery is based regards this as the establishment of a taxable presence there. However, even this is not a clear-cut solution because this might just disclose that the given EEA Member State has a policy for deeming a non-resident entity to be resident for tax purposes.

It is a little difficult to foresee the way in which this sort of market may develop. Perhaps in the next few years we will begin to see ATMs appearing for the purpose of allowing people in the street to make investments or communicate with their brokers. Another possibility is 'sensitivity points', at or near to which communications with brokers over mobile telephone systems will be facilitated. The potential for the ATM system to be used for investment as well as banking business suggests that the rigours of the Investment Services Directive, in characterising as a 'branch' an office supervised by at least two investment staff, may not be practicable in the e-commerce age.

Further, the European Commission has stated in a draft Communication that if a firm provides services in a host state through electronic equipment based in the host state, which is not itself managed or operated by the firm's staff or agents in the host state, this is a provision of services only, not the establishment of a branch office.

(iii) Cross-border transactions

9.60   Despite the continuous speculation in relation to electronic branches, the Investment Services Directive in principle raises more concerns in relation to the manner in which services are offered cross-border. It is in this area that the Internet is destined to fulfil a very substantial role. It is worth examining article 18 of the Investment Services Directive in detail, and the manner in which the European Commission and the UK regulators interpret this provision.

The starting point is article 18(1), which provides:

> 'Any investment firm wishing to carry on business within the territory of another Member State for the first time under the freedom to provide services shall communicate the following information to the competent authorities of its home Member State:
> - the Member State in which it intends to operate;
> - a programme of operations stating in particular the investment service or services which it intends to provide.'

Following this, the first part of article 18(2) provides that the firm's home state's competent authorities shall, within one month, inform their counterpart in each relevant host state, and the firm consequently becomes free to commence provision of those services at once. The second part of article 18(2) imposes upon the host state authorities an obligation 'where appropriate' to draw to the firm's attention the conduct of business rules to which it will be subject in the host state.

Interpretation of article 18 has been problematic from the outset. If a firm proposed to engage in conventional cross-border activities (including mailshots, telephone calls, or even data transmission 'down the wire' to dedicated hosts), it would be expected to register these proposed activities – and would find it difficult to operate in a host state without doing so – the advent of the Internet makes this a much less precise area to regulate. If a firm in the UK puts its information onto a website, but does not in fact overtly target investors in another state, it may perhaps be taken to be doing no more than advertising locally within the UK. An investor in another EEA Member State who finds the relevant website and attempts to interact with it will not become a person who his local regulator has a direct interest in protecting. The converse is also true. A website operated by an overseas firm does not amount to a promotion – under the Financial Services and Markets Act (Financial Promotions) Order 2001 – if the information on the website is not directed at UK recipients and there are proper procedures in place to prevent UK recipients engaging in the proposed activities.

In summary, if an investment firm – in any EEA Member State – can argue that an investor in another Member State came to it, and not the other way around, then is the notification procedure under article 18f the Investment Services Directive necessary at all?

9.61 In understanding the views of the European Commission on article 18(1) of the Investment Services Directive, regard should be had to the various materials on the identical point generated by the Commission and other EC institutions in relation to the equivalent provisions of what was article 20(1) of the EC Second Banking Co-ordination Directive (2BCD)[1] (now replaced by article 21 of the Directive of the European Parliament and the Council Relating to the Taking Up and Pursuit of the Business of Credit Institutions[2]). This was identical in all material terms to article 18(1) of the Investment Services Directive. (It is a matter of regret that the Commission, in spite of several approaches requesting it, has never issued an equivalent communication in relation to the Investment Services Directive specifically.)

Both 2BCD, art 20 and the Investment Services Directive, art 18 mention providing services in the host state 'for the first time'. The Commission concluded in its draft Communication in relation to the 2BCD that a firm that had already provided the relevant services in the host state, prior to its coming into force, was apparently not affected by the 2BCD, art 20(1) requirements, and could continue to provide those services without having to notify anybody. If we take this to apply to the Investment Services Directive, then if a firm was providing relevant services to another EEA Member State on or before 31 December 1995, the firm is not required to notify anybody under the terms of the Investment Services Directive as a condition of being allowed to continue to do so. Moreover, it is the *fact* of provision which is relevant, not the *method*: if the relevant firm used to send mailshots to investors in another EEA Member State, it can now use the Internet to reach them.

Both of these Articles refer to provision of services 'within the territory' of the host state. The Commission's interpretation of this provision is one of the least satisfactory aspects of the draft Communication and it therefore attracted significant critical comment. The stated view was that, if a firm wanted to solicit investors in a host state, the notification regime would apply to it; but if those investors were to approach the firm unsolicited, then it did not. In the case of services conveyed by telephone, fax, e-mail and similar media (where the service moves, rather than the service provider), an identical analysis applies.

In addition, if a firm merely advertised itself and its services, as distinct from actually offering services to investors, it would not be required to go through the notification procedure. The definition of advertising its services is cited from the Misleading Advertising Directive[3] as 'the making of a representation in any form in connection with a trade, business, craft or profession in order to promote the supply of goods or services, including immovable property, rights and obligations'. (Where precisely one draws the line between what, in Internet terms, amounts to advertising and what goes beyond this is difficult to discern.)

1   Directive (EEC) 646/89 established a regime for banks and credit institutions to provide banking and investment services across borders on a passported basis.
2   Directive (EC) 12/2000.
3   Directive (EEC) 450/84.

9.62 Having considered the possibilities for excluding a firm from the scope of the Investment Services Directive, if a firm concludes that it is within the scope of the notification requirement and is required to notify its home state regulator, the requisite firm is thereby permitted to commence provision of the services in the relevant host state(s), without more. A firm need not wait until the end of the one-month period during which the regulator is obliged to communicate the notification to relevant host state regulators, nor await any sort of response from the latter[2].

In response to criticism of the draft Communication, the Commission clarified its thinking, in a Commission Communication issued in July 1997[1]. Essentially, the Commission took the view that the only way to determine the legal and regulatory system having jurisdiction over an investment service was to look at where the services were performed. In effect, where an investor in, say, France, approaches your firm in the UK, you can treat the French investor as contracting for the performance of investment services in the UK, rather than in France on a cross-border basis. Of course, this may lead in some cases to a tug-of-war between the regulators in the firms', and the investors', home states (and if there are investors from all around the EEA involved, forum-shopping among the laws of 18 different countries is theoretically possible).

The case of *Alpine Investments BV v Minister van Financiën*[2] should be briefly considered. In this ruling of the European Court of Justice, the Dutch regulatory authority was held capable of ruling that a Dutch investment firm should not be permitted to make unsolicited calls on investors both inside *and outside* The Netherlands. The freedom of the firm to provide services across borders through the making of unsolicited calls was not denied, but the regulator was entitled to override this for exceptional policy reasons.

Here is a case, the facts of which predate the coming into force of the Investment Services Directive, under which the ECJ is clearly of the view that a *home* state regulator has powers in relation to the control of a firm's cross-border non-prudential business. The point is that the *Alpine* case and the Investment Services Directive, art 18 are now apparently in conflict and it may take a further visit to the ECJ to resolve this matter[3].

One might care to ask, therefore, whether a case such as *SIB v Vandersteen Associates BV*[4] remains correctly decided in the light of *Alpine*.

In that case, SIB obtained an injunction to restrain a company in Belgium from making unlawful cold calls on UK investors. The case was a hollow victory for SIB since the defendant was insolvent at the time and was not represented in court. However, if in similar circumstances a firm in question were to argue that its home state regulator has no difficulty with the nature of its cold calling, would the English court be bound to accept this as the inevitable effect of *Alpine* and dismiss the Financial Services Authority's petition?

1   OJ C204/9, 10.7.97.
2   C-384/93: *Alpine Investments BV v Minister van Financiën* [1995] ECR I-1141, ECJ. Advocate-General Jacobs delivered his opinion on 26 January 1995 and the decision of the full court was given on 10 May 1995.
3   Article 11 of the Investment Services Directive poses similar problems for the e-commerce environment as those raised by article 18. In particular, the article 11 formula, which provides that each EEA Member State 'in which a service is provided' may impose its conduct of business rules, is singularly inappropriate in an e-commerce environment where a firm which provides services via a website accessed by investors from other EEA Member States may, in theory, be subject to the conduct rules of all the EEA Member States.
4   [1991] BCLC 206.

(iv) *Other EU legislation*

9.63   A variety of other EC legislation, actual and proposed, will apply in relation to financial services. In particular there is the ISDN Directive[1], the Data Protection Directive[2] (now implemented in the UK via the Data Protection Act 1998), the still proposed Financial Services Distance Selling Directive[3], which provides a consumer with a right to withdraw from a financial services contract in certain circumstances, and the E-Commerce Directive[4]. These and other measures are, however, considered elsewhere in this book and no further commentary is required at this point.

1   Directive (EC) 66/97.
2   Directive (EC) 46/95.
3   COM 385/1999. The Directive applies to any contract concerning financial services entered into between a supplier and a consumer by means of electronic communication, in circumstances where the supplier and the consumer are not face-to-face, up to, and including, the time of conclusion of the contract (that is through mail order services, telesales and the use of the Internet).
4   Directive (EC) 31/2000.

7.   SPECIFIC ISSUES

9.64   As a final section to this chapter, it is appropriate to look ahead at some issues that are likely to influence the thinking of law-makers and regulators in the financial services field as e-commercial means of conducting investment business become more common.

(a) Electronic prospectuses and filings

9.65 We have already considered, in paragraph 9.51, whether a UCITS can be offered to UK investors on (or exclusively on) the Internet. But what is the position with regard to prospectuses and similar documentation for more routine forms of share promotion?

(i) The UK Listing Authority and London Stock Exchange

9.66 Flotation of a company on the Official List of the UK Listing Authority or on the Alternative Investment Market of the London Stock Exchange remains for that company one of the most important methods of raising capital. The admission of securities to the Official List is a process governed under the terms of Part VI of the FSMA 2000. Section 74(4) of the FSMA 2000 requires 'the competent authority' to make rules (termed 'listing rules') for the purpose of governing the admission of companies to the Official List. On 1 May 2000, this function and oversight of admissions to the Official List (for many years vested in the London Stock Exchange itself) was transferred to a body called the UK Listing Authority (UKLA), which is a manifestation of the Financial Services Authority. Listing rules were produced in time for this transfer of functions to the UKLA, but apart from the abandonment of the traditional yellow cover for its rules (in favour of purple), there were very few differences between the old Stock Exchange *Yellow Book* and the rules of the UKLA (UKLA Rules). No doubt, there will be further developments with time.

A prospectus must be issued where the securities to be listed are offered to the public for the first time[1]; in other circumstances, the document published is referred to as 'listing particulars'[2]. The latter are described as being 'a document ... in such form and containing such information ...' as the UKLA Rules require. The same wording is used in relation to prospectuses, though the word 'document' is not applied to them.

The provisions of the old Stock Exchange *Yellow Book* lagged somewhat behind the technology available for electronic publication of prospectuses and the like. The UKLA Rules are currently no different. The UKLA requires that a variety of different types of document are provided to it in draft prior to issue[3]. The 'cover' of a set of listing particulars is not deemed to form a part of them, though its presentation and content must not be misleading[4]. Drafts are required to be annotated 'in the margin' to indicate where the documentation in question makes provision for various requirements of the UKLA Rules[5]. Amended drafts, when submitted, are required to be marked up in red to show changes required by the UKLA, and in blue or black to show all other changes from previous versions of the document in question. Interestingly enough, however, Rule 5.11 then states:

> 'Alternatively, a draft submitted by facsimile transmission *or other electronic means*[6] is acceptable provided the UKLA has agreed in advance to the methods proposed to distinguish the two types of change.'

1 The FSMA 2000, s 84.
2 The FSMA 2000, s 79.
3 The UKLA Rules, Rule 5.9.
4 The UKLA Rules, Rule 5.8.
5 The UKLA Rules, Rule 5.11.
6 *Emphasis added.*

9.67 This is the only indication in the UKLA Rules, in relation to the principal format and mechanics of listing particulars, that electronic means may be used, in agreed circumstances, to compile listing particulars. It may be reading too much into these words to suggest that the UKLA is in any sense encouraging electronic filing of draft or completed listing particulars (it is more likely that this allows for on-screen amendment of listing particulars using a colour hierarchy such as that provided by Microsoft Word). Rather, whilst electronic drafts may be permitted, the end product is still required to be printed and published in the time-honoured fashion. There is no general facility to file documents with the UKLA (or issue them to the general public) via websites, on CD-ROMs, etc. However, in the United States, the US Securities and Exchange Commission (SEC) will require all non-US companies and non-US governments from 4 November 2002 to make all SEC filings electronically through the SEC's Electronic Data Gathering, Analysis and Retrieval (EDGAR) System, which operates at present for most public companies in the United States.

It should be added, of course, that migration of a filing from printed to electronic format offers the opportunity for a measure of imagination and web space planning (assuming that the line of least resistance – a .pdf format file containing the prospectus – is not universally used). Although one talks in terms of 'pages' as physical divisions of a pamphlet or book, a web 'page' is something with rather less precise boundaries than its printed equivalent. Further, the reader of an electronic prospectus can avoid reading the whole document, or reading it from beginning to end in the right order, because a chain of links from sections allows the reader to bypass materials that are important. The UKLA has carried forward the former *Yellow Book* restrictions on the use of internal graphics. As already noted, the cover to listing particulars is considered not to form a part of the listing particulars in question, yet UKLA still regulates the use of illustrations and text used on the cover (significantly restricting the opportunities for either). All of this indicates a continued desire on the part of the UK's new listing authority to regulate both form and content. As a result, in practice, it would not greatly assist if the UKLA Rules were to be amended to expressly permit electronic filings without more, as the full and ever-developing range of opportunities to employ hyperlink technology and graphical techniques (and for that matter moving images and sound files) would still remain unavailable.

(ii) Other offerings

9.68 The Public Offers of Securities Regulations 1995[1] establish a regime for the publication of a prospectus in relation to an initial offering to the public in the UK of certain classes of security, in circumstances where admission of the security to the Official List is not being sought and where therefore the UKLA Rules and the Official Listing regime discussed above do not apply. The POS Regulations define what is meant by an 'offer to the public'[2] and 'securities'[3]. It is also important to remember that a POS Regulations prospectus is required where securities are to be admitted to trading on the London Stock Exchange's Alternative Investment Market.

The POS Regulations make extensive provision as to the required content of a prospectus and also impose a requirement that the information in a prospectus be presented in as easily analysable and comprehensible a form as possible[4]. Nothing, however, is said expressly about use of an electronic medium to reproduce and disseminate a POS Regulations prospectus and indeed regulation 4 provides that when securities are offered to the public in the UK for the first time, a prospectus must be made available to the public, free of charge, at an address in the UK. When drafted, this contemplated a paper version of the prospectus, although there would not seem to be a problem in electronic versions being available as well.

1 SI 1995/1537, as amended by SI 1995/3275, SI 1999/734 and SI 1999/1146.
2 See 1995/1537, reg 6. 'The public' may include any defined section of the public. However, see also the numerous exclusions in reg 7.
3 Essentially, investments, subject to some exceptions, are shares, instruments acknowledging indebtedness, warrants entitling the holder to shares or creating indebtedness, which have not been admitted, nor are subject to an application, for official listing: SI 1995/1537, reg 3(1).
4 See SI 1995/1537, reg 8(3).

9.69 It will also be important to consider the increasing use of the Internet as a medium for offering securities in a private fashion, where the POS Regulations are not applicable. The following is a set of ten guiding principles which assist the company looking to raise equity, and the broking house that may be involved in assisting it:

1. What sort of offering is it to be?	Will this be a 'public offer' for the purposes of the POS Regulations? ■ A public offer requires a prospectus compliant with the POS Regulations. ■ If not a 'public offer', the offering document is highly likely to be a financial promotion governed by section 21 of the FSMA 2000. The POS Regulations create several exclusions for those seeking to avoid producing a prospectus. Most common is the exemption for offers made to 50 or fewer persons[1]. This is simple to monitor when issuing a paper document: it can be marked with a serial number and the name of the intended recipient, and state that no other person is authorised to treat it as an offer. Posting a document on a website is not as foolproof, unless only the intended offerees have access. You could e-mail it to the intended offerees. In either case, you and the offerees would have to be vigilant, so that they did not pass the material on to others. The exercise is somewhat less precise than with a printed offer document.
2. How do I avoid turning a prospectus into a promotion?	A POS Regulations prospectus alone is never within the scope of the section 21 regime. But if it is integrated into a website where other material could be construed as forming a part of the offer representations, the totality could very well be treated as a financial promotion. You could avoid this by ensuring that the prospectus is housed in a clearly separate part of a given website, with no 'padding' (or better still, a website all of its own).
3. How do I target the right people?	With a POS Regulations prospectus, you will generally not be concerned to limit access rights of the UK general public (unless we are talking about a private placing, and even then no harm is done if the public can read the prospectus even if they cannot subscribe for shares). With respect to an offer memorandum, which is a financial promotion, the issue of suitability arises. This touches upon a question concerning the use of the Internet for many forms of financial service. In essence, you need to ensure that your investor base is tied into an arrangement under which they have password protected access to the relevant parts of your website. This will restrict access to those for whom you consider the offer to be suitable.

4. How do I keep an offer from percolating overseas?

This is a somewhat imprecise science, particularly where the website is open-access in the UK. Share offers in (or into) other countries – and in some cases, to nationals of those countries and to nationals of those countries while resident in the UK – are typically regulated by overseas security commissions. If the website is open-access then, in principle, a PC user overseas can see the material posted for UK eyes. It is generally accepted that in such circumstances you cannot do better than:

- to include wording prominently on the website, making it clear that the offering is not being made in, or in to, overseas jurisdictions, or to overseas nationals as appropriate;

- to use devices on the website which screen out overseas persons (such as requiring them to confirm a UK address before proceeding to the next page);

- to include in the application appropriate confirmations by the applicant that he, she or it is not an overseas person; and

- to prime those who receive applications to look out for material which is sent from overseas or which looks as though it bears a false or forged UK address.

Alternatively, you can register the share offer in overseas jurisdictions – but the expense of doing so is usually likely to outweigh (massively) any benefit from saved compliance costs of screening out overseas applications.

5. Are there any relevant financial promotions exemptions to consider?

This question is primarily of relevance to issuers, and the answer here is that the same exemptions apply to a Internet offering as to a paper offering. It is a question of how effective these can be made in practice. For example:

- the facility to publish exempt financial promotions to institutional investors, authorised persons, etc[2], allows you to register investment funds, pension fund trustees, etc, as authorised to access your restricted website; and

- the same may also be possible where you wish to use the Internet to communicate with your shareholders in exempted circumstances (for example to tell them about a rights issue or an agreed cash bid)[3]. You could, for example, amass details of their e-mail addresses and distribute material by e-mail[4].

6. What considerations affect the form of the offer document?

The POS Regulations govern the content of a prospectus which is required to comply with them, but not its form. The regime for financial promotions makes no demands as to form but in connection with content, a financial promotion should be fair and not misleading and specified wording is required to take advantage of certain exemptions. This all said, if the offer is conducted partly via the Internet and partly by conventional means, it is wise to ensure that the document which appears on the Internet matches its printed equivalent[5].

The best way to ensure consistency between the two is for the Internet version to be a .pdf format document, which is photographically identical to the printed original. The investor will need a .pdf reader such as *Adobe Acrobat* in order to gain access to the material. But this is nowadays a widely distributed piece of software, often sold with new PCs or available from the Internet.

Broadly similar considerations will apply where the prospectus or offer document is sent as an e-mail attachment or on a CD-ROM.

7. Can I accept applications on-line?

The answer under present regulations is unclear. At present no powers under the Electronic Communications Act 2000 have been used to make dispensary regulations[6] regarding share application forms. However, nothing in the Companies Act 1985 specifically requires share application forms to be a printed document and/or to be submitted under signature or seal of the applicant.

8. What is my liability for hosting a document on my website?

Make sure the creator(s) of the offer document assume responsibility for it. The directors of a company publishing a prospectus must accept personal responsibility for the accuracy of its factual content and its compliance with the contents requirements. If you are supporting the issue (whether by placing or offering the shares, or merely by providing a temporary Internet home for the offer document), you should take warranties and seek indemnities from the issuer which protect you against claims arising from the terms of the offer. It is not immediately apparent that these need to be radically different from the sort of warranties and indemnities that have been in circulation for many years in standard placing and sponsorship agreements.

You do need to address one area with care, however. If the offer document or prospectus becomes embedded in your website, and therefore causes a proportion of the website as a whole (above and beyond the document itself) to be concerned with the offer, then merely taking protection from the issuer in relation to the terms of the offer document may not be sufficient. Investors might consider that the context of the offer in the website amplifies the express language used in the offer document itself. Whether they are correct will depend upon the circumstances of the website.

It is best to avoid getting dragged into potential post-offer litigation by posting clear language wherever relevant that the terms of the offer are no less and no more than those contained in the document itself, regardless of whatever other representations may be perceived by investors in the surrounding web material.

9. What if I actually approve the document for issue?

First, this is all the more reason for seeking as much protection from the document's issuer as you can secure through the warranty and indemnity route outlined above.

More importantly, make sure the material is properly verified. If you are responsible for approving the issue of an offer document, you will need to say so in express terms on the website. The accuracy and reasonableness of its content are thereupon no longer just a matter for the issuer but become your responsibility as well.

10. What is the position with a prospectus published after close of the offer?

This is actually a rather subtle question.

Some issuers do like to give publicity to an expired or closed offer on their websites and re-publish the prospectus used to conduct that offer. In the 19th century House of Lords case of *Peek v Gurney*[7] it was held that the terms of a prospectus are not considered to amount to binding representations to investors buying shares in the after-market. But this makes the reasonable assumption that once the offer has closed or the placing is concluded, the prospectus is spent and is never going to be republished. Also, the decision in *Peek v Gurney* was in any event questioned in a 1996 case *(Possfund Custodian Trustee Ltd v Diamond*[8]), where it was held that an after-market purchaser in the case of shares admitted to the Unlisted Securities Market (now defunct) should not be able to rely on representations in the relevant prospectus.

If a prospectus is republished for historical purposes only, it is accordingly wise to append wording to the relevant web page(s) which states that this republication is not an offer to any persons, etc, and that nobody may place reliance on the prospectus in relation to after-market trading[9].

---

1   SI 1995/1537, reg 7(2)(b).
2   See the Financial Services and Markets Act 2000 (Financial Promotion) Order 2001 (SI 2001/1335), art 19.
3   See the Financial Services and Markets Act 2000 (Financial Promotion) Order 2001 (SI 2001/1335), art 43.
4   But the problem is usually that your company registrar will not have these details uniformly to hand, principally as there is no reason under the Companies Act 1985 to require them.
5   There is another reason in relation to POS Regulations prospectus documents: they are required to be filed with the Registrar of Companies (where the offer relates to a UK company) and, presently, the Registrar does not have a facility to accept an electronic filing.
6   For a discussion of the mechanics of the Electronic Communications Act 2000, see Chapter 2, E-contract.
7   (1873) LR 6 HL 377.
8   [1996] 2 All ER 774.
9   There is always the risk that a 'spent' prospectus which is republished in this fashion after close of the offer might otherwise be interpreted as being a financial promotion, or part of one.

(iii) The future

9.70 The future, without doubt, will involve the evolution of an electronic filing and offering system in parallel with the current printed document system, and in time the latter will probably be phased out. (The same should in time apply to the parallel regime for filing various documents with the Registrar of Companies. Moves towards this are considered further in Chapter 12, E-corporate.)

Doubtless before the UKLA can feel comfortable about this it will need to train existing staff (and recruit further staff) to review websites that are prospectuses. Protocols may have to be agreed that prevent amendments to prospectuses in cyberspace without UKLA approval, but the filing of an amendment and the approval process could both be electronic and this would considerably speed up the process. In time, the streamlining of offer documents may lead to the development of a partially electronic scrutiny system, which would check for basic compliance of an electronic filing with certain standard details.

In relation to offers that do not have to comply with the UKLA Rules, the principal concern will be to fully automate the offer and acceptance process. Here, again, we await deregulation through the making of appropriate rules under the powers in the Electronic Communications Act (or, perhaps, just a measure of bravery by the Financial Services Authority in framing its own rules on electronic offer and acceptance of investment transactions).

(b) Intelligent agents selling financial services

9.71 One of the most significant developments which is largely still awaited – though it is surely only a matter of time – is the arrival of software on the Internet which is intelligent enough to profile an investor, search the Internet for suitable investments based on the profile and make a range of recommendations. For the sake of simplicity, we shall label such software as an 'intelligent agent', an expression coming into use to refer to search engines with a capacity to memorise criteria used by a PC user, to refine and further refine searches, and eliminate material assessed as irrelevant. The analogy with the search for investments is good, if not perfect, so the label will do for now[1].

There are a range of issues which we need to explore in order to be prepared for the advent of the intelligent agent selling financial services. This section is not intended to be exhaustive.

1   An alternative might be the 'electronic IFA' ('IFA' being independent financial adviser), since without doubt the rise of such software will impact on the market for the sort of advice and service which IFAs provide in the UK.

(i)   Standard of advice

9.72 Presently, in a world in which financial services are provided to humans by humans, there is a reasonable understanding of the sort of standards by which the salesman is expected to operate. The regulators prescribe examinations that the salesman is required either to have passed or to have been deemed to have satisfied in other ways (for example by experience). The salesman is amenable to supervision from his superiors and from his company's compliance officer(s). Ultimately, if he transgresses, he will find himself liable to discipline from the regulators as well, ranging from fines and reprimands to expulsion from the industry (in the severest of cases)[1].

A piece of software is not in the same position. How are we to assess the competence of a software agent? Who is going to test software in a self-disinterested fashion to determine that it does what it says it is supposed to? How do we know, for example, that a given software product has not been 'toppled', so as (all other things being equal) to favour the products of one company over those of another? Regulators are interested in software which is used in the industry, of course. But none has yet shown the sort of interest that is likely to require it to re-evaluate the emphasis of regulation in years to come, so as to be able to target not just banks and brokers but also certain software houses, to ensure that agent software that arrives on the Internet is at least prima facie in a fit and proper state to advise the PC user on what to buy.

1   The FSMA 2000, s 56.

(ii) How can we prevent the stifling of innovation?

9.73   Search engines generally select websites on the basis of linguistic matches. Sometimes the search engine can be fooled into thinking a site is particularly relevant on account of the repeated occurrence there of the word that forms the backbone of the PC user's enquiry. What is of concern is that if those who operate websites selling financial products are aware that their sites are going to be analysed in this fashion, there is likely to be a significant measure of standardisation of approach, in order that those websites establish a sense of priority among the intelligent agents looking around the Internet for the right sort of information. The concomitant risk is that innovation in investment techniques and products may give way to the need for product houses to ply their trade with tried and tested products in order not to lose market share.

(iii) Will there remain a role for the independent financial adviser as we know him?

9.74   The issue here is not whether the independent financial adviser can continue to function as he currently does, or used to do (clearly he cannot operate oblivious to the march of technology), but even whether the advice provided is good enough to be called 'best advice'. If you, as an IFA, render 'best advice', in theory you roam the entire market for selections and choose the best to offer your client. In practice, you are allowed to discharge this duty in law by making a reasonable selection to start with and narrowing it down to something smaller and more manageable. You and your client both have a human mind, which does not have infinite capacity to memorise and regurgitate facts and figures. Moreover, you will inevitably have been influenced by marketing teams from investment companies which have reached you in person[1].

But the intelligent agent is not subject to such limitations. It has the capacity to search for relevant information all over the world and maybe distil a list of recommendations from tens of thousands of choices, all perfectly memorised, compared and analysed[2]. In the light of this, can the human IFA stand up to the fully functioning electronic IFA? Will it ever again be possible to call the choices of the former best advice?

The most vexed question of all is how we determine the manner in which the burden of liability should fall in the event of an intelligent agent making a mistake – for, competent or not, this is bound to happen.

The problem with the intelligent agent is less the characterisation of the error made than the fact that in the real world it is likely to be designed and operated by persons of considerably less substance than the companies whose products it recommends. The intelligent agent's proprietors may be legally almost invisible. Even if they can be located, it may be more than we should expect of the small investor to locate the agent's owners and controllers and sue them in some far-away jurisdiction. The approach of the European Commission in respect of the liability of agent entities providing services from websites (and therefore, implicitly, the liability of the sort of intelligent agents we are considering here) is that they must be rendered 'visible' and amenable to justice[3]. But is this a really practicable approach?

A more practical approach is to hold that it is in the interests of the financial services industry, in a world where product companies are represented to investors primarily or exclusively by intelligent agents, for those product companies to be liable – perhaps even strictly – for the consequences of sales of investments issued by them to investors who used intelligent agents that were faulty[4]. One would like to think that it will be in only the most exceptional few cases that bad advice is given. The product company might still be entitled to the defence that the fault lay not with the agent but with the erroneous or incomplete information provided to it. But since intelligent agents of this nature are liable to make the process of selling investments very much less expensive for the companies in question, there is sound commercial logic in making them liable for the financial consequences of the odd mistake[5]. Moreover, it would encourage the product companies concerned not to take for granted the competence of intelligent software and, perhaps, even to take a hand in developing appropriate agent software for themselves.

1 This is not unique to the financial services industry, of course. For example, when a GP prescribes a common form of drug (such as a pain-killer or antibiotic), the patient entrusts to his skill and judgment, as well as his Hippocratic Oath, that the GP has chosen the most appropriate drug. But since the GP cannot have the time to get to know *all* the alternatives from which to choose, his information will be based at least in part on how successful representatives from drug companies have been in reaching him with their own marketing techniques.

2 It follows from this that product companies will need to design even more sophisticated marketing methods, so as to take full advantage of this global roaming capacity of the electronic IFA.

3 See articles 5 and 6 of the E-Commerce Directive.

4 Compare this with the position under Directive (EEC) 374/85, under which producers have been liable as a matter of European law for a number of years to compensate ultimate consumers (with whom they may have no direct contract at all) for certain losses caused by defective products, on a no-fault basis.

5 Although the 'agent' epithet was adopted for convenience in this part of the chapter, the suggestion of binding product companies to the consequences of the defaults of such 'agents' is, indeed, wholly compatible with the conception in the common law of agency, that the principal warrants the authority of his agent and is bound by the consequences of its exercise.

10

E-banking

1. INTRODUCTION

10.01 Since the last edition, there have been significant developments in the field of e-banking. A new regulatory regime affecting Internet banks has come into force (and another affecting issuers of electronic money is expected), Europe has continued to churn out legislation in the field of financial services and as the dot.com boom turned to bust at the dawn of the new millennium, many of the providers of on-line banking services have been forced to review their operations.

In light of these developments, the aim of this chapter is to address some of the issues facing those operating in the e-banking sector today. It begins with a brief introduction to Internet banking before moving on to consider various aspects of the English legal framework within which Internet banks operate. It continues with a look at various on-line payment systems, including the use and development of electronic money, and concludes with an overview of some of the more specialised systems that exist today to facilitate the conclusion of a variety of financial transactions on-line.

2. INTERNET BANKING

10.02 In today's heavily disintermediated environment, the term 'banking' inevitably encompasses a wide range of activities. It is no longer true to say that banks are simply the custodians of our funds as, today, many have transformed themselves into global institutions offering a broad range of products and services to their customers. Whilst it is true to say that some of these products and services remain the province of real-world providers, others are successfully migrating to the e-world. What follows is a summary of only some of the legal and regulatory issues which are relevant to e-banking. Unsurprisingly, given the rate at which e-commerce generally is evolving, the law is, in many instances, at a formative stage only.

(a) What are Internet banks?

10.03 In the current personal banking market, there are two types of Internet bank in operation: the 'stand alone' Internet bank, which operates almost exclusively on-line, and the cyberbranch, effectively the on-line arm of an existing bank or building society.

Stand alone Internet banks operate almost exclusively on the Internet, where accounts are opened and transactions concluded. Examples of stand alone Internet banks include Egg[1], Smile[2] and Cahoot[3] and although the majority offer telephone and postal support to supplement their Internet operations, non-Internet communication is kept to a minimum. The idea behind stand alone Internet banks is that, as they have no need to maintain vast networks of expensive premises and call centres, the cost per transaction is reduced and, as a result, they are able to offer highly competitive products to their customers. At present, all stand alone Internet banks are either owned or controlled by well-established players in the financial services sector[4].

In contrast, cyberbranches are the on-line operations of existing high street banks and building societies. They work on the assumption that consumers want flexibility in the way they access their banking services, and exist to supplement, rather than replace, traditional forms of high street and telephone banking. However, because the institutions that operate cyberbranches still have the overheads that stand alone Internet banks have all but dispensed with, the disadvantage is that their products are often not as competitive[5].

Intelligent Finance[6] falls somewhere in between these two business models for Internet banking. In an attempt to create a market between the stand alone Internet bank and the traditional high street lender, it operates both telephone and Internet banking services.

1 See www.egg.com.
2 See www.smile.co.uk.
3 See www.cahoot.com.
4 Egg is controlled by Prudential Banking plc. Smile and Cahoot are owned by The Co-operative Bank plc and Abbey National plc respectively.
5 In October 2001, the interest rates offered by stand alone Internet banks on current accounts (with a typical credit balance of £500) ranged from 3 to 5.5%, whereas those offered by cyberbranches were generally under 1% (Source: MSN Money).
6 See www.if.com. Intelligent Finance is a division of Halifax plc.

(b) What services do Internet banks offer?

10.04 Internet banking has not attempted to promote new products or services: only the media for selling and operating such products has changed. At present, the private consumer market, and its vanilla product, remains the prime focus for Internet banking providers.

To give an overview of some of the products and services currently available on-line, let us take the stand alone Internet bank Egg as an example.

Listed on the London Stock Exchange, Egg is a division of UK-based financial services provider Prudential Banking plc. At present, Egg offers savings accounts, credit cards, personal loans and residential mortgages[1], together with a variety of insurance[2] and investment products[3], through a variety of media including the Internet, mobile phones and digital TV.

Egg operates by allowing customers to apply for a range of products on-line. Application forms are completed and submitted on-line and, in the majority of cases, an immediate on-line decision can be given. However, as the law stands, it is not possible to complete the entire application process via the Internet and in order to finalise it, customers are sent written documentation to sign and return. Reasons for this include the fact that various documents such as regulated credit agreements (which will generally be entered into when applying for personal credit cards and loans) must (currently) be completed on paper[4]. Furthermore, mortgages over property must be executed as a deed and, as the law stands, it is debatable whether a digital signature will be effective to satisfy signature requirements in relation to deeds[5]. Finally, as with all other financial institutions, Egg is under an obligation to comply with current money laundering regulations which, amongst other things, require it to obtain sufficient evidence of the identity of its customers[6].

However, once the initial application has been accepted, customers are able to access their accounts and carry out a variety of financial transactions on-line. They can pay bills and transfer money, set up standing orders and direct debits and monitor the status of their savings accounts, mortgages and loans, all from the comfort of their own homes.

Customers are also able to access their accounts using WAP-enabled mobile phones and digital TV. Using Egg's digital TV service, Egg TV[7], customers are able to service their credit cards and savings accounts and monitor the balance on their mortgages and loans. In addition, using certain WAP-enabled mobile phones[8], Egg customers can check the balance on their credit cards and savings accounts; and, by linking the service to Reuters, they can keep abreast of current share prices[9]. However, Egg customers are unable to carry out any kind of financial transaction via mobile phone, though, at the time of writing, Egg claimed to be looking at ways of improving this service.

The majority of Internet banks (whether operating on the stand alone or cyberbranch model) offer broadly similar services to private consumers, though some remain more developed than others. Cahoot, for example, allows customers to carry out financial transactions using WAP-enabled mobile phones, whereas Smile offers no mobile banking service at all. On the other hand, Smile offers ISAs, whereas Cahoot does not[10]. Although the range of products that Internet banks offer to private consumers will undoubtedly converge over time, at present certain Internet banks will only suit certain needs.

Whilst stand alone Internet banks exclusively focus on the private consumer market, many of cyberbranches increasingly are looking to tap the potentially lucrative corporate market. However, beyond the basic range of on-line account management packages currently on offer[11], cyberbranches offer very few 'business' products to corporate customers. Where highly tailored and specialised banking products are required, simple on-line application forms are not really appropriate and, as a result, cyberbranches' websites tend to be more of a shop window for their high street banking operations than an interactive corporate banking tool.

1 Mortgage provision is one of the last significant areas of the financial market place which is still substantially unregulated. However, this is due to change as the Financial Services and Markets Act 2000 (Regulated Activities) Order 2001 (SI 2001/544) has specified 'entering into a regulated mortgage contract as lender' and 'administering a regulated mortgage contract' as regulated activities for the purpose of the Financial Services and Markets Act 2000 (FSMA 2000) (a regulated mortgage contract being, for these purposes, a contract under which a lender provides credit to a borrower and the obligation of the borrower to repay is secured by a first legal mortgage on land in the UK, at least 40% of which is or is to be used as or in connection with a dwelling by the borrower or a related person). The new regulatory regime affecting mortgage provision is scheduled to come into effect on a date known as N3 (31 August 2002).

2 Including household, motor, travel, critical illness and life insurance.

3 Including Individual Savings Accounts (ISAs) and share dealing services.

4 For further details, together with a discussion of the proposals for reform in this area, see paragraph 10.17 below.

5 For further details see Chapter 2, E-contract, paragraph 2.10. In relation to mortgages, another reason the entire application process cannot be completed on-line is that offering a mortgage requires some degree of advisory input from or on behalf of the prospective lender. If you wish to borrow money for a property purchase, a UK lender (or its agent) traditionally requires some sort of direct contact with you, if for no other reason than it has to obtain a survey of the property you want to buy. Furthermore, and from a purely legal perspective, unless there is some direct contact between the parties, the lender runs the risk that one or more joint parties to a mortgage may be unaware of the true legal nature of his position, and at some future date when the lender seeks to enforce its security, is able to defeat the lender's action: see *Barclays Bank plc v O'Brien* [1994] 1 AC 180, HL; and now *Royal Bank of Scotland plc v Etridge (No 2)* [2001] UKHL 44, [2001] 2 All ER 449.

6 For further details of the money laundering requirements that Internet banks must comply with, see paragraph 10.14 below.

7 At present, customers are able to access Egg TV on Sky Digital's interactive service, Sky Active.

8 Currently the Nokia 3330, 6210 and 7110. It should be noted that WAP (Wireless Application Protocol) technology has not lived up to users' expectations owing to slowness of connection and problems with service. GPRS (a broadband network) is expected to replace WAP in the near future.

9 Egg offers customers the option of receiving text messages alerting them of share price movements. Customers choose the upper and lower limit on up to 15 specified shares on the London Stock Exchange and when the share price reaches either limit, they are sent a text message. All data is supplied by Reuters, the financial information and news group.

10 Correct at the time of writing.

11 The majority allow corporate customers to check their accounts, view statements, pay bills and invoices, set up standing orders and transfer money.

(c) **What are the benefits and drawbacks of Internet banking?**

10.05   One obvious benefit is convenience: accounts can be managed electronically, direct debits cancelled via mobile phone and bills paid and money transferred at the touch of a button. Anyone with a PC, Digital TV or WAP-enabled mobile phone is given the freedom to bank 24 hours a day; and with the ability to access their accounts at any time, users of Internet banking services can keep on top of their finances more than ever before.

Another benefit is the highly competitive products that stand alone Internet banks are able to offer as a direct result of their not having to service large overheads. In October 2001, Smile, for example, paid over 30 times the amount of interest offered by high street banks on current accounts and charged almost half as much on debt.

But what of the drawbacks? For many, a perceived disadvantage of Internet banking is lack of security. There is a fear amongst consumers that by banking on-line, hackers will gain access to their accounts and steal their money. However, although this may be a valid concern, in reality, Internet banks are very secure. Intelligent Finance, for example, uses state-of-the-art 128-bit encryption and Secure Socket Layer (SSL) technology to ensure that the highest levels of security are maintained. Indeed, all of the major players in the market use similar technology as in today's highly competitive market place, the maintenance of a robust security system is seen as essential. Moreover, in the mobile and TV banking sectors, the services offered to customers are similarly secure. Egg, for example, provides its customers with individual identifications and passwords, and uses 128-bit encryption for all communications made via these media.

Of course, other problems face those banking on-line. Computers can develop faults, websites can crash and the Internet can experience delay due to sheer volumes of traffic. However, these problems are common to other Internet service providers. Perhaps the popularity of Internet banking will grow alongside the increase in broadband Internet connection, which should go some way towards addressing these problems.

3.   THE INTERNET BANK/CUSTOMER RELATIONSHIP

10.06   To find out about an Internet bank's relationship with its customer we have to look at an Appeal Court decision from more than 80 years ago.

In *Joachimson v Swiss Bank Corpn*[1], the Court of Appeal held that the relationship between a customer and his bank was essentially a matter of contract.

When a customer opens an account with a bank (or rather with a branch of a bank), Atkin LJ noted that a 'single and indivisible contract' arises to govern their general relations. This contract is basic to all transactions and is to be distinguished from contracts for specific banking services that only arise by subsequent agreement[2]. The contract is formed in the usual way (by offer on the part of the customer to open an account and subsequent acceptance of that offer by the bank) and creates the basic rights and obligations that form the basis of the banker-customer relationship.

In the *Joachimson* case, it was observed that the basic relationship 'depends either entirely or mainly upon an implied contract'[3] and in that case, Atkin LJ went on to list the implied terms of that contract as follows:

> 'the bank undertakes to receive money and to collect bills for its customer's account ...
> *and* ... borrows the proceeds and undertakes to repay them[4] ... *The bank promises* ... to repay at the branch of the bank where the account is kept, and during banking hours;
>
> *the bank promises* ... to repay any part of the amount due against the written order of the customer[5];

> the bank will not cease to do business with the customer except upon reasonable notice; and

> the customer ... undertakes to exercise reasonable care in executing his written orders so as not to mislead the bank or to facilitate forgery[6].'

When the courts clarified the nature of the banker-customer relationship in the early part of the last century, the use of written terms and conditions was uncommon in the banking industry[7] and the provision of Internet banking services undreamed of. However, technology has raced ahead of the law and, as commentators have observed, these implied terms are no longer written in stone[8]. Today, they must reflect developments in telephone and Internet banking and, in particular, the fact that Internet banks do not have physical branches. However, subject to modifications where necessary to reflect changes in technology and banking practice, these implied terms continue to bind users and providers of Internet banking services. Therefore, Internet banks remain obliged to receive money and collect bills for their customers' accounts, are required to repay deposits on demand and must not cease to do business with their customers, except upon reasonable notice. Failure to abide by these terms will expose Internet banks to suit from their customers.

1   [1921] 3 KB 110.
2   As commentators have observed (see *Paget's Law of Banking* (11th edn, 1996), p 110), '[t]he essential distinction is between obligations which come into existence upon the creation of the banker-customer relationship (*pursuant to the terms of the "single and indivisible contract"*) and obligations which are subsequently assumed by specific agreement; or, from the standpoint of the customer, between services which a bank is obliged to provide if asked, and services which many bankers habitually do, but are not bound to, provide' (*emphasis added*). The obligation to honour cheques drawn by a customer falls within the category of services that banks are bound to provide. However, the provision of services such as direct debits, banker's drafts and letters of credit probably fall within the category of services that banks habitually do, but are not bound to, provide: *Libyan Arab Foreign Bank v Bankers Trust Co* [1989] QB 728 at 749.
3   *Joachimson v Swiss Bank Corpn* [1921] 3 KB 110, per Bankes LJ.
4   In the *Joachimson* case, it was confirmed that the ordinary banker-customer relationship is that of debtor and creditor and not trustee and beneficiary. When a customer deposits money with a bank, the bank owns the money (and is therefore free to deal with it as it sees fit) and merely owes a debt to the customer which it undertakes to repay on demand. If the bank had fiduciary duties in respect of the deposited funds, it may have to account to the customer for any profits made from their use; see also *Foley v Hill* (1848) 2 HL Cas 28.
5   Atkin LJ did not determine whether a demand had to made in writing.
6   *Emphasis added* throughout.
7   The observation of Bankes LJ in *Joachimson v Swiss Bank Corpn* [1921] 3 KB 110, that the relationship depends 'entirely or mainly upon an implied contract' no longer holds true today given the widespread use of written terms and conditions throughout the banking industry.
8   See Penn & Shea, *The Law Relating to Domestic Banking* (2nd edn, 2000), p 105.

10.07 In addition to the implied obligations outlined above, it is important to appreciate that banks owe (or in certain circumstances may owe) a whole range of additional tortious, fiduciary and other contractual duties to their customers[1]. A detailed discussion of this complex range of duties is beyond the scope of this book and a dedicated banking law textbook should be consulted for further details. However, in the context of an analysis of Internet banking, one of these duties is particularly worthy of note.

English law imposes a rather onerous duty of confidentiality on banks in relation to the personal information they hold on each individual customer[2]. This is a legal duty arising out of contract[3] and if injury to a customer can be attributed to its breach, a substantial claim in damages can ensue. In addition to this legal duty, most banks and financial institutions also subscribe to codes of conduct which set out principles of good banking practice. The Banking Code[4], for example, specifically addresses issues such as disclosure of customer information and the marketing of banking services. Although purely voluntary, the Code is nevertheless adhered to by the majority of banks and building societies operating in the UK and, as a result, it further entrenches the legal duty of confidentiality that banks owe[5].

In the context of Internet banking, the problem with the duty of confidentiality is that until a 'fail safe' Internet security system is devised, Internet banks cannot guarantee that their customers' personal information will be kept secure from hackers[6]. As a result, given that many banks are prepared to indemnify their customers against losses from accounts which arise as a result of a breach of their Internet security systems (provided that the customer concerned has followed the recommended guidelines on security[7]), the greater risk for a customer who banks via the Internet is a loss of privacy rather than any threat to his wealth[8]. This raises serious questions as to whether Internet banking is fundamentally incompatible with the duty of confidentiality imposed upon banks.

Furthermore, if Internet banks are to avoid falling foul of this duty on a day-to-day basis, then given that the Internet allows information to be disseminated around the world at the touch of a button, they must ensure that adequate systems are in place to ensure that this dissemination is strictly controlled. Except in closely defined situations[9], banks must ensure that they do not disclose details of their customers (or their accounts) to third parties (including members of the bank's own corporate group), which obviously has implications for banks when deciding how to market their products or whether to pass information on to credit reference agencies and the like. Paragraphs 8 and 13 of the Code, which reinforce the legal duty of confidentiality, deal with advertising and marketing and the disclosure of information, and set out strict requirements that banks must adopt when dealing with any personal information that they hold. The Code reiterates the fact that banks must ensure that they do not disclose this information to third parties (other than in cases permitted by law[10]) and sets out additional requirements to ensure that all advertising and marketing material is clear, fair, reasonable and not misleading.

Banks should therefore review their standard terms and conditions in light of these duties and the safest course of action for them to adopt is to ensure that they have their customers' express consent before they pass personal information on to third parties for any purpose[11].

Although all institutions are bound by relevant data protection and consumer legislation[12], only banks are bound by the strict banker's duty of confidentiality. As a result, there is a risk that Internet banks will lose out to other institutions which are active in e-commerce (such as payment service providers [13]) which are not bound by the same rules[14].

1   Examples include the banker's statutory and common law duties of care (see, for example, section 13 of the Supply of Goods and Services Act 1982), their duty to avoid making negligent misstatements (see *Hedley Byrne & Co Ltd v Heller & Partners Ltd* [1964] AC 465, HL) and their fiduciary duties in respect of trust funds. A dedicated banking law text should be consulted for a discussion of this complex range of duties.

2   This is a special duty imposed on banks which exists alongside the equitable duty of confidentiality that applies to all.

3   See *Tournier v National Provincial and Union Bank of England* [1924] 1 KB 461, CA. The banker's duty of confidence is based on an implied term of the 'single and indivisible contract' that arises between the customer and the bank.

4   The Banking Code (and a list of banks and other institutions that support and do not support it) is available at www.bankingcode.org.uk. The Code is reviewed from time to time and the current version was adopted in January 2001.

5   It is, however, important to appreciate that the Code deals only with the relationship between banks and their personal customers and has no relevance to the manner in which banks are expected to treat their corporate clients.

6   Although we have already noted that most Internet banks employ state-of-the-art security systems, we cannot say (and probably never will be able to say) that these systems are 100% secure.

7   For general guidance, see paragraph 14 of the Code.

8   Often, a threat to one's privacy is a very real concern. In *Tournier v National Provincial and Union Bank of England* [1924] 1 KB 461, CA, the bank disclosed to their customer's employer that he was a gambler and was indebted to the bank. As a result of this disclosure, the employer refused to renew the customer's contract of employment.

9   Being where a disclosure is made under compulsion of law, where there is a duty to the public to disclose, where the interests of the bank require disclosure or where disclosure is made with the express or implied consent of the customer: *Tournier v National Provincial and Union Bank of England* [1924] 1 KB 461, CA, and the subsequent cases in this line of authority.

10 See footnote 9 above.

11 Detailed consent provisions concerning the distribution of information for advertising and marketing, credit reference agency and other purposes should be included in the bank's standard terms and conditions. It should be noted that, under section 13.3 of the Code, banks must give their customers 28 days' notice of any intention to pass information on to a credit reference agency.

12 See Chapter 3, E-liability and Chapter 2, E-contract respectively. See also the commentary on the Consumer Credit Act 1974 (CCA 1974) and the Data Protection Act 1998 in paragraph 10.17 below.

13 The Payment service provider (or PSP), which does what it says it does, may be non-bank or even non-financial in character. PSPs such as Worldpay (www.worldpay.com) offer a variety of single or multi-currency payment processing solutions based on encryption technology.

14 See the arguments to this effect in, for example, 'Internet Banking: the Digital Voyage of Banking and Money in Cyberspace' (1999) 8(3) *Information and Communications Technology Law*.

4. INTERNET BANKS AND REGULATION

10.08 In any modern financial system, the effective regulation of the financial markets is key. Investors want markets that are stable, solvent and free from crime, and in order to achieve this, banks and other financial institutions are forced to comply with certain minimum standards.

To give an overview of some of these minimum standards and the ways in which they impact on the banking industry, this section is divided into two parts. The first deals with the provisions that exist to ensure that, through proper supervision, banks maintain appropriate systems and controls to actively manage their risks and the second; those provisions that exist to ensure that banks co-operate in the fight against crime.

Of course, the regulatory regime applying to those operating in the financial services sector is far wider than this. The market abuse[1] and financial promotion[2] provisions, for example, are just as applicable to banks as they are to other financial institutions and, as such, this section should be read in conjunction with Chapter 9, E-finance, which examines current legislation and regulations affecting those operating in the financial services sector in more detail.

1 Part VIII of the FSMA 2000 introduced a new civil regime relating to market abuse. This supplements the existing criminal regimes for insider dealing (Part V of the Criminal Justice Act 1993) and market manipulation (section 397 of the FSMA 2000). For further details see Chapter 9, E-finance.

2 The financial promotion regime prohibits a person from communicating (in the course of business) an invitation or inducement to engage in investment activity unless that person is an authorised person or the content of the communication has first been approved by an authorised person (section 21 of the FSMA 2000). The territorial scope of the financial promotion regime is far reaching and applies to all communications that are capable of having an effect in the UK. In the context of Internet banking, it is important to bear this prohibition in mind as a communication posted on a website in France, for example, is caught (subject to certain exceptions) if UK residents can access it. For further details see Chapter 9, E-finance.

(a) Regulation, risk and supervision

10.09 Banks are exposed to a wide variety of credit, market, liquidity and operational risks. When these risks are not actively managed, the danger is that banks may be unable to meet their liabilities to depositors and if this is allowed to happen, loss and lack of confidence in the financial system as a whole can ensue.

In an effort to address these problems, the FSMA 2000 requires banks intending to carry on business in the UK to first seek permission from the Financial Services Authority (FSA) and, thereafter, to submit themselves to a stringent regime of continuing supervision and regulatory control.

It should be noted that, from a regulatory perspective, there is no special regime in existence for the regulation of on-line as opposed to off-line, traditional banks. The regulatory environment is just the same and although the FSA recognises that it may need to deploy some of its supervisory techniques with differing degrees of intensity, its stated aim is to be e-neutral[1].

The FSMA 2000 provides that a person is prohibited from carrying on a *regulated activity in the UK*, or purporting to do so, unless he is authorised or exempt[2]. Contravention of this prohibition (often referred to as the general prohibition) is a criminal offence[3] and any agreements entered into as a result are generally unenforceable[4].

The *'regulated activities'* are specified in secondary legislation and have already been discussed at length in Chapter 9, E-finance. However, in the context of an analysis of banking regulation, the *regulated activity* of 'accepting deposits' is particularly worthy of note. Article 5 of the Financial Services and Markets Act 2000 (Regulated Activities) Order 2001 provides that a person will be regarded as 'accepting deposits' (and hence carrying on a *regulated activity* for the purposes of the Act) if '... money received by way of deposit is lent to others' or 'any other activity of the person accepting the deposit is financed wholly, or to a material extent, out of the capital of or interest on money received by way of deposit'. Accepting deposits is one of the core business areas of most banks and, as such, it is one of the main activities for which they require authorisation[5].

1 See the speech of Carol Sergeant (29 March 2000), the then Director of Banks and Building Societies at the Financial Services Authority. The full text of this speech is available at www.fsa.gov.uk.

2 See section 19 of the FSMA 2000. Commercial banking concerns are not exempt from this prohibition, although municipal banks, local authorities, charities and industrial and provident societies that limit their activities to 'accepting deposits' are.

3 The maximum penalty being two years' imprisonment and an unlimited fine. It is a defence if the accused can show that he took all reasonable precautions and exercised all due diligence to avoid committing the offence. See section 23 of the FSMA 2000.

4 See section 26 of the FSMA 2000. It should be noted that if the *regulated activity* in question is 'accepting deposits' (one of the primary activities of most banks), then any agreements entered into in the course of carrying on this activity are specifically excluded and will not be rendered unenforceable by this provision. That said, if the depositor is not entitled under the terms of the agreement to recover without delay any money deposited by him, then in these circumstances, he may apply to the court for an order directing the deposit-taker to return that money to him. Of course, if banks enter into agreements in the course of carrying on any other regulated activity then these agreements will be unenforceable and the other party to the agreement will be entitled to recover any money or property paid out or transferred by him and, moreover, may be entitled to claim compensation for any loss sustained. See generally sections 26–29 of the FSMA 2000.

5 We have already noted that most banks offer a wide range of financial services and, in doing so, inevitably engage in other regulated activities. As a result, banks that engage in multiple regulated activities will require additional authorisations from the FSA to do so. However, it should be noted that under the single authorisation procedure established under the FSMA 2000, a single application can now be made for permission to carry on any number of regulated activities.

(i) The problem of jurisdiction

10.10 Before considering the ways in which Internet banks obtain authorisation under the FSMA 2000, it is important to determine which Internet banks require authorisation in the first place.

If an Internet bank is established in the UK and offers its services to UK residents, then it must apply to the FSA for permission to carry on *regulated activities*. However, what about the Internet bank that is established outside of the UK? Given that UK residents can still access its website, does this mean that its operations fall within the scope of the general prohibition so as to require it to obtain authorisation if it is to avoid criminal charge? By similar reasoning, what about the Internet bank that is established in the UK? Could it too find itself subject to interference from foreign regulators? Potentially, the answer to both these questions is yes as, by its very nature, cyberspace knows no jurisdictional boundaries.

For the majority of Internet banks, the prospect of multiple regulators attempting to assert jurisdiction over their operations is likely to cause considerable alarm.

When considering the position in the UK, it is important to appreciate that the general prohibition only applies to those persons carrying on regulated activities *in the UK*. Accordingly, if a person is to require permission from the FSA, then it must be possible to establish a link between his activities and the UK. In general, this link will arise where the activity in question is carried on or managed from an establishment in the UK[1]. However, as the FSA has made clear, it may still be possible to establish this link notwithstanding the fact that the person concerned does not maintain a place of business in the UK[2]. In this context, the FSA cites persons offering services over the Internet and makes it clear that if on-line service providers operate their websites in such a way that they can be said to be carrying on regulated activities *by way of business* in the UK[3], then the necessary link will be established.

The circumstances in which a person will be regarded as carrying on a regulated activity *by way of business* are again specified in secondary legislation[4] and differ depending on the regulated activity in question. If we take the *regulated activity* of 'accepting deposits' as an example, then we find that this activity will not be regarded as being carried on *by way of business* if the person concerned '... does not hold himself out as accepting deposits on a day-to-day basis' and 'any deposits ... he *does accept* are accepted only on particular occasions...'[5].

1   See section 418 of the FSMA 2000.
2   See the FSA Handbook, Authorisation Manual at AUTH 2.4.
3   This is because section 22 of the FSMA 2000 provides that an activity is only a *regulated activity* for the purposes of the Act if it is carried on *by way of business* in the UK.
4   The Financial Services and Markets Act 2000 (Carrying on Regulated Activities by Way of Business) Order 2001 (SI 2001/1177).
5   *Emphasis added.*

10.11   As it is perfectly possible for a bank to hold itself out as accepting deposits via its website, then Internet banks that are established outside of the UK are faced with a choice. If they decide to hold themselves out as accepting deposits from UK residents, then they will have to apply for authorisation if they are to avoid criminal charge. If, however, they decide that they do not want to submit themselves to the jurisdiction of the FSA, then they will have to ensure that their websites clearly state that their services are not available to UK residents and, moreover, actually refuse to accept deposits from anyone resident in the UK[1].

For Internet banks that are established in the UK, similar jurisdictional issues arise. As their websites can be accessed in foreign countries, they must consider whether their operations fall within the jurisdiction of foreign regulators. Let us take the position in the United States as an example.

Under US law, it is generally the case that a non-resident defendant will be subject to the jurisdiction of the forum state if the *minimum contact* test is satisfied. In *Zippo Manufacturing Co v Zippo Dot Com Inc*[2], the court reviewed the authorities and concluded that the likelihood of jurisdiction being exercised over a website was directly proportionate to the nature and quality of the commercial activities that the entity conducted over the Internet. It was of the view that passive websites, which merely display information to those in the forum state, do not satisfy the minimum contact test[3]. However, where the website allows electronic contracts to be formed with residents of the forum state, it concluded that this minimum contact will generally be established[4]. In between these two extremes, where the website allows some level of interactivity but falls short of allowing the user in the forum state to enter into electronic contracts, the court held that '... the level of interactivity and commercial nature of the exchange of information that occurs on the website'[5] will determine the issue[6]. Clearly, therefore, the potential exists for UK Internet banks to satisfy this minimum contact test (and presumably similar tests across the world) and, accordingly, the prospect of interference from foreign regulators is very real.

If UK Internet banks are to avoid such interference, then the safest course of action for them to adopt is to ensure that their services are only available to UK residents. Prominent notices should therefore be used to highlight this fact and their operations be vetted, to ensure that effective procedures are in place to reject applications from non-UK residents.

As regards regulated activities other than accepting deposits, the FSA Handbook, Authorisation Manual at AUTH 2.3.3 states that whether or not an activity is carried on by way of business is a question of judgment. Factors to be taken into account include the degree of continuity, the existence of a commercial element, the scale of the activity, the proportion which the activity bears to other activities carried on by the same person but which are not regulated, and the nature of the particular regulated activity. If factors such as these are satisfied, Internet banks based outside the UK who carry on regulated activities in the UK other than accepting deposits will also require attention.

If an Internet bank based outside the UK carries on in the UK an activity which is not a regulated activity, then that Internet bank need not apply for FSA authorisation. Under the E-Commerce

Directive[7], an Internet bank based in an EEA state needs to comply with its provisions, but the Directive does not provide the same degree of protection to customers as that given by the FSA's requirements. This is important, as providers of information society services may gain exemption from the need to seek authorisation under the FSMA 2000[8]. The E-Commerce Directive applies to providers of information society services (defined as any service normally provided for remuneration, at a distance, by electronic means and at the individual request of a recipient of services). A service provider is defined as any natural or legal person providing an information society service. These definitions include business-to-business and business-to-consumer services and include on-line financial services. The Directive provides basic regulatory protection for recipients of information services, such as providing that general information relating to the provider and any contractual terms and conditions be provided to the recipient, that unsolicited commercial communications be clearly identifiable as such and that certain information be provided before any orders are placed by a recipient.

1   A prominent notice such as 'This website is only intended for use by residents of (Country X)' should therefore be used. It is also prudent to build into a website a feature that is capable of recognising and rejecting applications from residents of countries in which the bank does not want to face regulation.
2   952 F Supp 1119 (WD Pa, 1996). This case involved an Internet domain name dispute in which the court had to decide the extent to which Pennsylvania's Long Arm Statute (42 PaCSA 5322) applied to the Internet operations of Zippo Dot Com, Inc, a company with its principal place of business in California, and with no offices, employees or agents in Pennsylvania.
3   See further, *Bensusan Restaurant Corpn v King* 937 F Supp 295 (SDNY, 1996).
4   See further, *Compuserve Inc v Patterson* 89 F 3d 1257 (6th Cir), 1996.
5   See further, *Maritz Inc v CyberGold Inc* 940 F Supp 96 (EDMo, 1996).
6   In the *Zippo* case, the court concluded that the *minimum contact* test had been satisfied because Zippo Dot Com, Inc had sold passwords to some 3,000 subscribers in Pennsylvania.
7   Directive (EC) 31/2000 on certain legal aspects of Information Society Services, in particular electronic commerce in the Internal Market.
8   The implementation of the E-Commerce Directive in the field of on-line financial and other services will be facilitated in the UK by the introduction of new Statutory Instruments. The Financial Services and Markets Act 2000 (Regulated Activities) (Amendment) (Electronic Commerce Directive) Order 2002 will exclude from the definition of 'regulated activity' the activities of providers of information society services (ISSs) (eg on-line financial service providers) established in other Member States. The Financial Services and Markets Act 2000 (Financial Promotion) (Amendment) (Electronic Commerce Directive) Order 2002 (SI 2002/2157) exempts communications of providers of ISSs established in other EEA states made to persons in the UK from the financial promotion regime established under the FSMA 2000. The flipside of this is that providers of ISSs established in the UK must comply with national legal requirements (eg compliance with the FSMA 2000 financial promotions regime), but not be entitled to exemptions for communications made or directed to persons outside the UK.

(ii) Authorisation

10.12 Assuming that the Internet bank in question falls within the jurisdiction of the FSA, it must apply to the FSA for permission to carry on its activities and achieve the status of 'authorised person'. There are two main types of authorised person under the FSMA 2000:

■   First, there are those who are authorised because they qualify for authorisation. Under the Banking Consolidation Directive[1], banks that are authorised in one EU Member State are entitled to a 'passport' to provide their services in other Member States. As a result, subject to compliance with certain notification and other basic requirements[2], Internet banks that are authorised in their home Member State qualify for authorisation under the FSMA 2000 as of right.

■   Second, there are those who are authorised because they have a Part IV Permission. This is the appropriate method of obtaining authorisation for any other bank wishing to carry on regulated activities in the UK and, as such, Internet banks that are unable to take advantage of the above 'passporting provisions' (as they are generally known) must apply for authorisation in accordance with the procedures laid down in Part IV of the FSMA 2000[3].

In addition to ensuring that the bank itself is duly authorised, banks must obtain individual approval for any employees that are to perform *controlled functions* on their behalf and apply for them to be accorded the status of *approved person*[4].

In contrast to the simple authorisation procedure laid down for those taking advantage of the 'passporting provisions', the procedures involved in obtaining a Part IV Permission are detailed and involved. In addition to satisfying the 'threshold conditions' set out in Schedule 6 to the FSMA 2000[5], banks will be expected to demonstrate that they are ready, willing and able to comply, and to continue to comply, with the regulatory requirements accompanying the regulated activity (or activities) that they intend to carry on. This will involve submission of the prescribed application form together with a variety of other detailed documentation, including business plans, analysed financial budgets and projections, details of compliance procedures to be adopted, details of the individuals to be involved in running the business and such other information as the FSA reasonably considers necessary in the circumstances. The FSA will expect banks to discuss their plans with them before submitting an application for a Part IV Permission.

The FSA will then consider the application and determine whether or not to grant a Part IV Permission. The process is complex and time consuming and should not be undertaken lightly.

It should be noted that when the FSMA 2000 came into force, banks that held authorisations under previous regulatory regimes (notably the Banking Act 1987) were deemed to have permission to carry on equivalent regulated activities under the new Act. As such, there was no need for them to re-apply for authorisation: by virtue of the 'grandfathering' process (as it is known), this was deemed to be automatically granted[6].

1 Directive (EC) 12/2000 as amended by Directive (EC) 28/2000. The reader should note that it is also possible to qualify for authorisation if the institution concerned is as a *Treaty Firm* or an *UCITS Qualifer*. For further details see Schedules 4 and 5 to the FSMA 2000.
2 For further details see the FSMA 2000, s 31(1) and Part II Schedule 3. A list of banks taking advantage of the 'passporting provisions' is available at www.fsa.gov.uk.
3 For a detailed analysis of the of the procedures involved in applying for a Part IV Permission see Chapter 9, E-finance.
4 Broadly, *controlled functions* are those functions that are seen as key to the proper performance of the regulated activities undertaken by the firm. For further details see Chapter 9, E-finance and the FSA Handbook, Authorisation Manual at AUTH 6.
5 Which include requirements as to legal status, location of offices, the effect of close links on supervisability, adequacy of resources and suitability. For further details see Chapter 9, E-finance, Schedule 6 to the FSMA 2000 and the FSA Handbook, Authorisation Manual at AUTH 3.
6 See further the Financial Services and Markets Act 2000 (Transitional Provisions) (Authorised Persons etc) Order 2001 (SI 2001/2636). It should be noted that the transitional provisions give the FSA the right to require a specific class of firm (but not individual firms alone) to re-apply for authorisations granted under the grandfathering process.

(iii) Prudential supervision

10.13 Obtaining authorisation is only the first stage in the regulatory process as, once authorised, banks must comply, and continue to comply, with the detailed prudential standards laid down by the FSA. These are set out in the 'Interim Prudential Sourcebook: Banks' and take the form of rules and evidential provisions that the FSA has made under Part X of the FSMA 2000[1]. The rules are designed to ensure that banks maintain capital resources commensurate with their risks and that they have adequate systems and controls in place to enable them to actively manage those risks. As the FSA has made clear, the rules require banks to maintain adequate capital against their risks (capital enables banks to absorb losses without endangering customer deposits), to maintain adequate liquidity, and to ensure that they identify and control their large credit exposures – which might otherwise be a source of loss to the bank on a scale that might threaten its solvency[2]. The specific requirements are detailed, rigorous and ongoing and by attempting to ensure that banks actively manage their credit, market, liquidity and operational risks, their aim is to prevent sequels to some of the spectacular banking collapses that we have seen in recent years[3].

1 It should be noted that only the rules and guidance on liquidity and fraud apply to banks that have taken advantage of the 'passporting provisions'. The 'Interim Prudential Sourcebook: Banks' is available at www.fsa.gov.uk.
2 For further details see the FSA Handbook at IPRU.
3 The collapse of Johnson Matthey Bankers Limited, the Bank of Credit and Commerce International and Barings testify to the need to ensure that adequate safeguards are in place.

(b) The fight against crime

10.14 In addition to the regulatory controls that exist to ensure the stability of institutions operating within the financial markets, further requirements are imposed on banks and other financial institutions in an effort to rid those markets of crime.

Criminals frequently use the financial system to launder the proceeds of crime. However, as the Preamble to the 1991 Money Laundering Directive[1] makes clear:

> 'When credit and financial institutions are used to launder proceeds from criminal activities … the soundness and stability of the institution concerned and confidence in the financial system as a whole could be seriously jeopardised, thereby losing the trust of the public.'

Money laundering is the conversion of the proceeds of crime into 'clean' untraceable cash or other assets and is a huge, international problem[2]. Money launderers attempt to conceal or disguise the proceeds of crime by channelling them through the financial system and, by so doing, their aim is to make those proceeds appear as though they have come from a legitimate source. Often, these funds are then re-used to finance terrorism, drug trafficking or other organised crime. The rationale behind current money laundering legislation is to detect and deter money laundering activities, therefore indirectly attacking the criminals themselves by starving them of their funds.

The primary money laundering offences are contained in the Criminal Justice Act 1988[3]. This makes it an offence to:

- assist another to retain the benefit of criminal conduct;

- acquire, possess or use the proceeds of criminal conduct;

- conceal or transfer the proceeds of criminal conduct; or

- tip-off another of a current or impending investigation into money laundering, or to disclose to any other person any knowledge or suspicion that a 'disclosure'[4] has been made to a constable or 'appropriate person'[5] and, by doing so, disclose any information, or other matter, which is likely to prejudice any current or future money laundering investigation.

The above offences relate to the proceeds of general criminal conduct. Similar money laundering offences exist in relation to the proceeds of drug trafficking and terrorist activity. However, where the proceeds of drug trafficking or terrorist activity are involved, there are important extensions, as the current legislation creates additional offences of failing to report knowledge or suspicion of money laundering offences in this context[6].

1 Directive (EEC) 308/91 on prevention of the use of the financial system for the purpose of money laundering. On 13 November 2001, the European Parliament approved the text of a draft Directive to amend the Money Laundering Directive and this was enacted on 4 December 2001. The amended Directive extends the coverage of the Money Laundering Directive to a series of non-financial activities and professions and obliges Member States to combat laundering of the proceeds of all serious crime. Prior to this amendment, the Money Laundering Directive only applied to the proceeds of drug-related offences and, moreover, its provisions were confined to those operating within the financial sector.
2 A former managing director of the International Monetary Fund recently estimated worldwide money laundering at 2 to 5 per cent of the world's gross domestic product – some US $800 billion at the low end of the range and perhaps as high as US $2 trillion.
3 Inserted by the Criminal Justice Act 1993.
4 A 'disclosure' being, for these purposes, a disclosure of information or other matter on which a knowledge or suspicion of money laundering is based.

5   An 'appropriate person' being, for these purposes, a person who is designated by an employer as the point of contact for employees in relation to money laundering.

6   See section 52 of the Drug Trafficking Act 1994 and section 19 of the Terrorism Act 2000 respectively. This legislation requires banks to disclose any information, or other matter, on which knowledge or suspicion of money laundering is based to a police constable as soon as is reasonably practicable after it comes to their attention. Should the bank's employees become aware or suspicious of money laundering activities in this context, they must either disclose the information, or other matter on which their knowledge or suspicion is based, to a police constable or to the person designated as the 'appropriate person' for the purposes of the bank's internal reporting procedures. It is a defence to a charge under these sections to have a reasonable excuse for not disclosing the information or other matter in question.

10.15 In addition to the primary offences outlined above, the Money Laundering Regulations 1993 (SI 1993/1933) attempt to take the fight against crime further. In an effort to ensure that the primary offences are actively policed, the Regulations attempt to insert 'choke points' into the financial system in order to deter and detect money laundering schemes. Effectively, the Regulations require banks and other financial institutions to police the financial system through the establishment of appropriate detection and reporting procedures, so as to highlight money laundering offences. The Regulations are stringent and banks must ensure compliance, as non-compliance can result in criminal penalties for them and, in certain circumstances, their individual employees[1].

The Regulations require all institutions engaging in 'relevant financial business'[2] to ensure that they adopt and maintain the following compliance procedures:

■   appropriate measures to ensure that clients are required to produce satisfactory evidence of their identity (this is often referred to as the 'know your client' requirement)[3];

■   appropriate procedures to ensure that all records of identities and transactions are maintained[4];

■   appropriate internal and external reporting procedures to highlight suspected money laundering transactions[5];

■   such other procedures of internal control and communication as may be appropriate for the purposes of forestalling and preventing money laundering; and

■   appropriate training programmes for employees to highlight relevant money laundering legislation and to enable them to recognise and handle suspect transactions.

Finally, in order to comply with its statutory obligation to contribute to the reduction of financial crime[6], the FSA has recently published the Money Laundering Rules[7]. The Rules apply to the majority of firms carrying on *regulated activities* in the UK[8] and impose additional obligations on those firms so as to further reduce the scope for the commission of money laundering offences. Unlike the Regulations, the Rules are regulatory (and not criminal) in nature and, as such, should not be taken as guidance on how to discharge obligations under the Regulations[9]. In effect, the Rules introduce a new and separate regime.

In essence, however, the Rules and Regulations cover much the same ground. Subject to certain limited exceptions[10], firms are required to obtain sufficient evidence of the identity of any client, maintain proper records, and ensure that adequate training and awareness and internal and external reporting procedures are in place. In addition, firms are required to appoint a Money Laundering Reporting Officer (MLRO), who must be individually approved by the FSA[11]. It is the responsibility of the MLRO to act as the focal point within the firm for all money laundering issues and to liaise with the criminal authorities where necessary[12]. The MLRO, and the 'appropriate person' appointed under the Regulations, can be one and the same person.

The obligations imposed on banks and other institutions in relation to money laundering are onerous and, given the criminal and regulatory penalties that can flow from a breach, they must be complied with diligently and in full. This is particularly true today. Now that the issue of money laundering is high on the political agenda in the wake of the recent terrorist attacks in the United States, it is unlikely that the criminal and regulatory authorities will look favourably on any firm that falls short in the discharge of its duties[13].

For Internet banks, the need to ensure that they have adequate compliance procedures in place is even more acute. Given the potential anonymity that the Internet can offer, Internet banks must take the utmost care to ensure that they are able to discharge their obligations and, in particular, ensure that they take diligent steps to ensure that they really do 'know (their) clients'.

1 Regulations 5(2) and 6.

2 The term 'relevant financial business' is widely defined. As far as banks are concerned, this covers any of the activities listed in points 1 to 12, or 14, of Annex 1 to the Banking Consolidation Directive. This brings all banks within the scope of the Regulations.

3 In accordance with the provisions of regulations 7 and 9. A recent report by the FSA ('The Money Laundering Theme: Tackling our New Responsibilities', July 2001) highlights the fact that, currently, many institutions do not do enough to comply with this requirement. The report makes it clear that the requirement to 'know your client' should involve firms actively seeking out evidence of identity and should not be considered a matter of mere form filling.

4 In accordance with the provisions of regulation 12. Generally, these records must be maintained for a period of at least five years.

5 In order to comply with these requirements, an 'appropriate person' must be appointed to receive internal reports and to liaise with external law enforcement agencies (see regulation 14). The 'appropriate person' is required to receive, weigh up and consider any suspicious transaction report made to him and decide whether to make a disclosure to the authorities.

6 See section 2(2)(d) of the FSMA 2000.

7 See the FSA Handbook at ML.

8 Other than the limited number of firms specified in the FSA Handbook at ML 1.1.2R. These firms are excluded because they are subject to adequate regulatory control by other supervisory authorities.

9 The Joint Money Laundering Steering Group (JMLSG) issues Guidance Notes on the application of the Regulations. A court may have regard to these Guidance Notes under regulation 5(3) when deciding whether the Regulations have been complied with. The JMLSG has recently issued Guidance Notes on the application of the Rules and their interaction with the Regulations. These detail how compliance with the Rules and Regulations should be achieved.

10 For example, the duty to obtain evidence of identity under ML3.1.3R need not be complied with where the client is a credit institution or financial institution covered by the Money Laundering Directive.

11 The function of acting in the capacity of the MLRO has been specified as a *controlled function* for the purposes of the FSMA 2000.

12 Generally, the MLRO should liaise with the National Criminal Intelligence Service (NCIS) in relation to suspect transactions. For further information visit www.ncis.co.uk.

13 Since 11 September 2001, governments and law enforcement agencies around the world have begun to take a tough stance on money laundering, particularly where terrorist funds are involved. In the UK, numerous bank accounts containing terrorist funds have been frozen and their proceeds confiscated. The Anti-Terrorism, Crime and Security Act 2001, which received Royal Assent in December 2001, now gives authorised officers wide ranging powers to seize, detain and apply for the forfeiture of 'terrorist cash'. In addition, the Act gives the Treasury the power to make freezing orders prohibiting persons from making funds available to or for the benefit of a person or persons if, inter alia, the Treasury reasonably believes that action constituting a threat to the life or property of one or more UK residents or nationals has been or is likely to be taken by that person or persons.

5. THE WIDER LEGAL ENVIRONMENT

10.16 In addition to the domestic and cross-border regulatory issues outlined above, it is important to consider some of the wider legal issues effecting consumers and providers of Internet banking services in the UK. Transactional level issues, such as choice of law and jurisdiction, are particularly important when entering into contracts (with Internet banks or other institutions) over the Internet. These issues have been dealt with generically elsewhere in this book[1], but at this stage it is worth reiterating that consumers attempting to deposit money, or indeed enter into any other type of agreement, with Internet banks[2] should bear these issues in mind, as from the point of view of convenience and cost, it is always preferable for any dispute to be resolved in the consumer's national courts and under his national laws.

However, as the recent decision in *Standard Bank London Ltd v Dimitrios Apostolakis*[3] serves to show, in the context of *consumer* financial services at least, the issue of jurisdiction should be more of a concern for banks than private consumers. This decision highlights the fact that if banks solicit consumers[4] in foreign countries (either directly or through an intermediary), then in cases where the Brussels Convention applies[5], banks must accept that any dispute is likely to be dealt with in a foreign court. Although this is well understood, it nevertheless should be made clear that even in cases where the Brussels Convention does not apply, banks must ensure that their standard jurisdiction clauses are specifically drawn to the consumer's attention and, moreover, that adequate translations of those clauses are provided if they are to stand up to challenge under UK consumer protection legislation[6]. If they fail to do so, then any clause attempting to confer jurisdiction on the English courts is unlikely to be upheld.

1 See in particular Chapter 7, E-dispute.
2 Assuming of course that the Internet bank in question makes its services available to foreign consumers for the regulatory reasons outlined above.
3 [2001] Lloyd's Rep Bank 240.
4 Contractual clauses conferring jurisdiction on the English courts will generally prevail where the customer contracts in the course of business. However, as the *Apostolakis* decision shows, even in cases where the customer is a high net worth individual taking on large exposures, he will still be regarded as dealing as a private consumer as long as he acts outside the course of business.
5 Article 13 (the relevant article for current purposes) applies where a foreign consumer resident in a Contracting State (being the EU Member States, Switzerland, Norway and Iceland) has been solicited in his home state and concludes the contract in that state. Where this criteria is satisfied, clauses attempting to confer jurisdiction on the bank's national courts will not be upheld. However, it is not entirely clear how article 13 applies to e-transactions as it does not obviously cover situations where a consumer is domiciled in one state but concludes the contract by Internet connection to a business in another. That said, a new Council Regulation (EC) 2001/44 on jurisdiction and the recognition and enforcement of judgments in civil and commercial matters was introduced on 1 March 2002. This clarifies the situation by broadening the existing definition of consumer contract in article 13 to include all contracts where a company pursues commercial or professional activities in the Member State of the consumer's domicile or, by any means, *directs activities* to that state (and/or others). This ensures that contracts that are concluded on-line are brought within the scope of the Council Regulation as, by offering their services to foreign consumers via their websites, banks will be regarded as directing their activities to the state of the consumer's domicile.
6 The Unfair Terms in Consumer Contracts Regulations 1999 (SI 1999/2083) provide that an 'unfair' term in a consumer contract is not binding on the consumer. In the *Apostolakis* decision, the court found that Standard Bank's jurisdiction clause was 'unfair' within the meaning of the Regulations, as it had failed to draw the clause to the foreign consumer's attention and, moreover, it had failed to provide an adequate translation of that clause.

10.17 In addition to the transactional level issues that users and providers of Internet banking services must consider, a variety of general consumer protection measures – some deriving from UK statute, others from EU legislation – are also relevant and need to be mentioned here:

■ The CCA 1974 is not of relevance to the opening and operation of simple bank accounts (on-line or via a physical bank branch), but does affect certain other services which banks provide. Perhaps the two most obvious are (i) personal (unsecured) loans and (ii) credit card facilities[1]. The CCA 1974 does not regulate credit where the amount of credit involved exceeds the current operational maximum set for the purposes of the CCA 1974 (currently £25,000)[2]. However, for a bank to escape regulation under the CCA 1974 on this account, it would have to ensure that *all* its relevant transactions were for credit exceeding this threshold – which is very unlikely in the circumstances. The main problem in the e-banking world with the CCA 1974 is that it derives from an era when electronic service provision was unheard of. In order to protect consumers of the past from unscrupulous consumer credit practices and extortionate credit bargains, a highly prescriptive system was provided for under the CCA 1974, involving the execution of contracts and the service of cancellation notices on paper. The result, for the time being, is that those who wish to offer regulated credit on-line are forced to stop short – well short – of actually extending the credit over the Internet.

That said, the Department of Trade and Industry has now recognised this problem and since the last edition of this book, it has conducted an external consultation to determine the extent to which it should relax the 'in writing' requirement so as to allow authorised institutions to offer regulated credit over the Internet[3]. The initial consultation closed on 3 October 2001, but at the time of writing the DTI had yet to publish a response. We must, therefore, wait to see whether this consultation results in modification of the CCA 1974 and, if so, the extent to which any modifications facilitate the development of a true e-credit market in this country[4].

■   It is also important to mention the Unfair Contract Terms Act 1977 (UCTA 1977) and the Unfair Terms in Consumer Contracts Regulations 1999, as both of these measures have implications for banks, and the standard terms and conditions that they employ. Whereas the UCTA 1977 specifically targets the reasonableness of the exclusion clauses that banks use, the Regulations go further and generally address the fairness of the contractual terms that they employ. The importance of ensuring compliance with the Regulations was highlighted recently in *Standard Bank London Ltd v Dimitrios Apostolakis*[5]. Although strictly not relevant to the outcome of the case, Standard Bank's jurisdiction clause was found to be 'unfair' within the meaning of the Regulations (and therefore non-binding on the foreign consumer) as before the contract was concluded, the clause had not been drawn to the foreign consumer's attention and, moreover, no translation of it had been provided. This decision therefore serves as a warning to banks and means that their standard terms and conditions should be reviewed regularly in light of both the UCTA 1977 and the Regulations[6].

■   As well as ensuring that consumers are adequately protected from oppressive consumer credit practices and unfair contractual terms, further levels of protection are available for consumers when concluding contracts at a distance[7]. In this regard, two consumer protection measures need to be mentioned: the EC Distance Selling Directive[8] and the Directive on the distance marketing of consumer financial services[9].

Although the former does not apply to the provision of financial services, Internet banks nevertheless need to be aware of its sweep, as they are likely to be affected in a secondary capacity. Cancellation rights in relation to investment agreements have led in the past to simple but effective scams involving the passing of cheques representing bogus accounts or sources of laundered money[10]. Even where cancellation has nothing to do with dishonesty on the part of the supposed purchaser, there are issues for banks to consider, in relation to credit analysis and credit risk. Assuming that electronic money does not become considerably more popular and widespread than it is, then consumers will continue to depend for their on-line shopping on the use of their credit cards. Since many more categories of contract will become cancellable, however, the number of transactions which are booked to credit cards and then unravelled will increase, and this in turn could well impose strains upon the credit system of a magnitude which it has not previously had to bear.

When the Directive on the distance marketing of consumer financial services comes into force, however, it will have a much greater impact[11]. The Directive is designed to regulate distance selling of consumer financial services and ensure that consumers are adequately protected in situations where the parties to the transaction never meet.

The Directive itself regulates 'distance contracts'[12] for 'financial services'[13] between 'suppliers'[14] and 'consumers'[15]. Since it was first proposed in 1998, it has been the subject of fierce debate. In order to ensure that consumers are fully aware of the terms of the contracts they propose to enter into, the Directive provides that, in general, suppliers must provide consumers with certain specified information[16] prior to contract formation[17]. This seems reasonable and, in the majority of cases, banks should already be supplying much of this information as a matter of course. However, the more controversial provisions surround the consumer's proposed right of withdrawal from the distance contract. In certain circumstances, the Directive will give consumers a right of withdrawal from a distance contract without penalty and without having to indicate grounds. This is designed to provide consumers with a 'cooling-off' period to reflect on their decision. Depending on the nature of the financial service offered, this withdrawal period will be exercisable within 14–30 days from the later of either:

–   the date on which the distance contract is concluded; or

–   if the distance contract is concluded at the consumer's request before all of the specified information has been supplied, the date on which the last piece of specified information is supplied.

It is the Member State in which the supplier is established that will determine the applicable withdrawal period. Therefore, suppliers need not comply with the potentially different withdrawal periods in the Member States in which their customers reside.

Although there are key exceptions to this right of withdrawal in relation to certain specialised financial services (whose prices depend on market fluctuations outside the supplier's control)[18], the effect will be to produce uncertainty for suppliers during this cooling-off period. Therefore, unless the consumer otherwise consents, suppliers should not begin to provide their services until the cooling-off period has expired[19].

■ In the context of consumer protection in the e-banking sector, the Financial Services Compensation Scheme is also worthy of note[20]. All Internet banks authorised under the FSMA 2000 (other than those taking advantage of the 'passporting provisions' contained in the Banking Consolidation Directive are required to join and contribute to the Scheme. The Scheme replaces the old Deposit Protection Scheme and is designed to protect ordinary retail customers (private individuals and small businesses) in the event of an institution covered by the Scheme being unable to meet its liabilities. Larger companies[21] are therefore excluded from protection, as they are considered better able to evaluate the security of their investments and sustain a loss in the event of a failure.

The Scheme is designed to ensure that money deposited with an institution covered by the Scheme is protected up to certain set limits[22]. In the event that the institution is then unable to repay this deposit, an eligible claimant is entitled to claim under the Scheme. Once this claim has been considered by the Scheme's manager, the claimant may be entitled to compensation (up to the set limit) from a central fund, in order to off-set any loss that he has sustained[23].

■ Further protection for consumers of Internet banking services comes under the Financial Ombudsman Scheme (the FOS). The FOS is established under the FSMA 2000 and membership is compulsory for all firms authorised under that Act. The FOS covers all *regulated activities* and its rules require authorised firms to establish and operate internal complaints handling procedures as the first avenue of redress for customers who are dissatisfied with their services. If, however, after eight weeks the matter has not been satisfactorily resolved, then assuming that the necessary criteria for eligibility are satisfied[24], the complainant will be entitled to apply to the Ombudsman for redress.

The FOS is available to private individuals and small businesses[25] and if a complaint is upheld, the Ombudsman can grant an award up the current maximum of £100,000[26]. Alternatively, or in addition to making a monetary award, the Ombudsman may direct the firm to take such steps in relation to the complainant as he considers just and appropriate in the circumstances. As with many other consumer protection measures, large companies are prohibited from using the FOS, on the basis that it is designed to provide an alternative dispute resolution mechanism for those otherwise unable to afford the courts[27].

■ A final measure of vital importance to Internet banks is the need to ensure compliance with relevant data protection legislation. Like other consumer protection measures, this legislation is not confined to Internet banks and, as a result, a full account of its provisions are given in Chapter 3, E-liability. However, given the amount of 'personal data' that Internet banks gather in the course of their businesses, data protection is also of importance here. In summary, the Data Protection Act 1998 requires a 'data controller' (in this case the Internet bank) to comply with the eight data protection principles laid down in the 1998 Act, so as to ensure that any 'personal data' it holds is not misused. Internet banks must therefore ensure that adequate systems and controls are in place for dealing with this 'personal data'. In particular, procedures for sending e-mails and other forms of communication by electronic means must be reviewed, as the Data Protection Act 1998 makes it an offence to export 'personal data' outside the European Economic Area (other than to countries that provide similar data protection).

1 Though not, incidentally, debit cards such as Switch.
2 Set with effect from 1 May 1998, by the Consumer Credit (Increase of Monetary Limits) (Amendment) Order 1998 (SI 1998/996). At the time of writing, the Department of Trade and Industry was in consultation to determine whether this limit should be increased. See 'Tackling Loan Sharks – and more: Consultation Document on Modernising the Consumer Credit Act 1974' at www.dti.gov.uk.
3 See 'Tackling Loan Sharks – and more: Consultation Document on Modernising the Consumer Credit Act 1974'.
4 The DTI indicated that it would continue to consult on various substantive issues, including removing the requirement for all credit agreements to be concluded in writing, until June 2002 and that it would issue a second Consultation Paper on this particular issue in the autumn of 2002.
5 [2001] Lloyd's Rep Bank 240.
6 For further details, see Chapter 2, E-contract.
7 Such as by mail, telephone, fax or electronic means such as the Internet.
8 Directive (EC) 7/97. The Directive has been implemented in the UK through the making of the Consumer Protection (Distance Selling) Regulations 2000 (SI 2000/2334), which came into force on 31 October 2000. See the more detailed commentary on the sweep of the Directive in Chapter 2, E-contract.
9 Proposal for a European Parliament and Council Directive concerning the distance marketing of consumer financial services and amending Directives 97/7/EC and 98/27/EC.
10 In 1998, a number of arrests were made of persons who were scamming personal equity plan (PEP) providers. The scam was a straightforward process that involved passing a worthless cheque to subscribe for the PEP and then cancelling at the point at which the plan manager had presented the worthless cheque for banking but had yet to discover that it was of no value. Hence the cancellation was honoured through reimbursement of the fraudulent subscriber with a good value cheque drawn on the plan manger's own funds. Extending the same conceptual cancellation rights to a range of routine consumer contracts under the scope of the Directive increases the risk of this sort of fraud permeating other areas of commerce.
11 The Directive was first proposed in 1998 and was to be implemented by Member States by 30 June 2002. On 27 September 2001, the Commission announced that the Internal Market, Tourism and Consumer Affairs Council had reached political agreement on the draft Directive.
12 A 'distance contract' is any contract concerning financial services concluded under an organised distance selling scheme without the supplier and consumer meeting. This includes contracts concluded purely by means of telephone, WAP, e-mail or the Internet.
13 The term 'financial services' is widely defined. It includes any banking, insurance, investment or payment service.
14 The term 'supplier' is defined to include the actual supplier of the financial service as well as any intermediary that may be involved in the supply of the service or in the conclusion of the distance contract.
15 A 'consumer' being, for these purposes, any natural person acting for purposes which are outside his trade, business or profession.
16 Such as the identity and address of the supplier, the main characteristics of the financial service, the global figure that the consumer will be expected to pay and the existence of the consumer's right of withdrawal. A list of information that must be supplied is set out in article 3 of the Directive.
17 The contract can be concluded before all of the specified information has been provided if the consumer expressly consents. However, in these circumstances, the withdrawal period will not begin to run until all of the specified information has been provided.
18 Including foreign exchange services and the reception, transmission and/or execution of orders related to, and services in respect of or related to, products including financial futures and options, money market instruments and exchange and interest rate instruments. A list of exceptions is contained in article 4 of the Directive.
19 For a detailed account of the EC Distance Selling Directive and the Directive, see Chapter 2, E-contract.
20 For further details of the Scheme, see the FSA Handbook at COMP.
21 Being companies which do not qualify as small companies under section 247 of the Companies Act 1985.
22 100% of the first £2,000 and 90% of the next £33,000 deposited. As a result, the maximum compensation payable under the Scheme is £31,700. This is an improvement on the old Deposit Protection Scheme, which only covered 90% of the first £20,000 deposited. Consequently, the maximum compensation payable under the Deposit Protection Scheme was £18,000.
23 The scheme is funded by levies on industry on a 'pay-as-you-go' basis.
24 The rules that apply in determining eligibility are complex and the reader should refer to the rules for specific details. Broadly, however, in determining whether a complaint is eligible for referral under the FOS, the complainant himself must be eligible to use the FOS and the complaint itself must be one that falls within the scope of the FOS: see the FSA Handbook at DISP2.2.
25 Being a business which has a group annual turnover of less than £1m.
26 The Ombudsman may, if he considers that fair compensation requires the payment of a larger amount, make a non-binding recommendation to the firm that it pay the balance.
27 For further details of the mechanics of the FOS, see Chapter 9, E-finance and the FSA Handbook at DISP.

6. INTERNET BANKING – A SUCCESS OR A FAILURE?

10.18 To conclude our brief overview of Internet banking, it is perhaps appropriate to consider whether it has, so far, proved to be a success.

Although quite clearly a remarkable concept, it seems that, to date, Internet banking has not been as successful as originally hoped for. As the *Financial Times* reported in October 2001[1], most attempts to implement stand alone Internet banks have, so far, failed. The Bank of Ireland folded its F Sharp offshore Internet bank in October 2001 after losing several million pounds and First-e, the Dublin-based Internet bank, lost at least US $200m before closing its virtual doors in the summer of 2001[2]. Even those stand alone Internet banks that have so far survived have not fared much better. By October 2001, Cahoot had reportedly lost £120m and Egg's losses stood at around £415m.

So what has gone wrong? The overriding problem seems to be that consumers (in the UK at least) have not warmed to the idea of relying on the Internet for their every banking need. Stand alone Internet banks operate almost exclusively on-line and, to a large extent, customers are devoid of any human contact with the bank. However, as Roly Alden, managing director of Bank of Ireland Offshore points out, '... people want a personal and relationship management service too'[3].

If this is the case, have the cyberbranches fared any better? The answer seems to be that they have, but only up to a point. Although consumers continue to show a preference for flexibility in the ways in which they are allowed to access their banking services[4], the providers of cyberbranches retain the overheads that stand alone Internet banks have all but dispensed with and, at the moment, any additional business that is being generated on-line is not being matched by the additional layer of cost that their on-line operations bring[5].

So where does that leave us? The Internet itself is clearly here to stay; so, as independent consultant Philip Middleton, points out, '... to be credible as a broad-based financial services player you have to have Internet distribution because certain segments of the market want it'[6]. Therefore, when one considers that more and more people are becoming IT literate, it seems that the cyberbranch model of Internet banking is here to stay, as the rise in IT literacy is likely to mean that the demand for on-line access will only increase. Accordingly, although the operators of cyberbranches may lose money in the short term, in the longer term a credible Internet operation will undoubtedly pay dividends. But, for the stand alone model, the picture may not be as clear-cut. Current trends seem to show that the majority of consumers prefer the flexibility of the cyberbranch and although this is not universally the case, it remains to be seen whether stand alone Internet banks will survive to see the critical mass of customers necessary to bring their operations into profit.

1 'How the banks poured money down the Internet drain', 24 October 2001.
2 Other casualties include the stand alone Internet banks that Alliance & Leicester and SEB tried (and ultimately failed) to develop. Alliance & Leicester spent £15m developing an Internet bank that was never launched and SEB closed its British on-line banking and broking business after tests showed that it was unpopular.
3 As quoted in the *Financial Times*, 'How the banks poured money down the Internet drain', 24 October 2001.
4 Whether this be by walking into a branch, picking up the telephone or accessing their accounts on-line.
5 In 2000, Barclays and Lloyds TSB spent £325m and £150m on their respective Internet operations.
6 As quoted in the *Financial Times*, 'How the banks poured money down the Internet drain', 24 October 2001.

7. E-PAYMENTS AND ELECTRONIC SETTLEMENT SYSTEMS

10.19 When the Internet started to gain a significant position in the commercial market place in the mid-1990s, the conventional wisdom was that new secure payment systems would need to be developed, as concerns over security meant that consumers would be reluctant to use their credit cards on the Internet. But, by the turn of the new millennium, despite experimentation with various forms of electronic or digital money systems, a vast majority of consumers were still using conventional methods of payments such as cheques and credit cards when they shopped on-line.

At this stage, and in spite of some conspicuous failures in the experimentation and testing of e-money systems over the last few years, we have to assume that the arrival of electronic money has merely been delayed, rather than cancelled altogether. However, significant problems exist for providers of Internet payment services – whether these operate using electronic money, credit cards, or non-cash 'tokens' of value. Anyone wishing to offer such services will need a system that deals successfully with the legal risks involved.

For example, the service must comply with the legal requirements for signed documents in a range of different circumstances, ensure that customers are adequately identified to minimise the risk of money laundering and fraud, and take into account the Internet's global scope. Money and banks are traditionally national conceptions, but successful Internet payment systems have to be truly international and able to work within any country's legal framework if they are to achieve widespread and lasting success.

In order to provide the fullest picture of the available (or soon to be available) payment options for on-line trading, we will consider the following payment methods or systems:

- paper-based systems;

- electronic fund transfers;

- credit cards, debit cards and direct payments; and

- electronic money.

We will examine how each method or system works, as well as the advantages and disadvantages of each system. We will conclude this section by considering some of the legal and regulatory issues that lie in store for users and providers of e-money systems.

8. PAPER-BASED SYSTEMS

10.20   This touches the core of what we understand as 'money'. Our understanding of money traditionally encompasses a system of locally acceptable, government-backed notes and coins. Our familiarity with this system is so strong that we consider past currencies based upon cattle, cloth and spices, among other things, as being laughably eccentric[1]. However, from certain points of view, current paper-based systems will appear equally antiquated. Currency dealers daily transmit billions of pounds, dollars, yen and euros around the world at the touch of a button and yet it can take days for a simple cheque to clear[2]. Furthermore, central banks spend an inordinate amount of time and money designing, producing and transporting paper money that can be forged, stolen or destroyed with comparative ease (and which wears out and must be replaced regularly). In the context of the Internet, where speed and convenience are crucial, the inadequacies of this system of payment become even more evident.

In summary, though electronic systems are not free from the potential for fraud of one sort or another[3], the scope for fraud in paper-based systems, and their inherent slowness and dependence on physical manifestations (be they banknotes, cheques or tokens of some other sort), makes them rather unsuited to the age of on-line transactions.

1   Amusing fictional instances abound. One is reminded of Gladstone Screwer (played by Sid James) trying to pay off a London taxi cab driver in cigarettes (which are all he recognises as legal tender from his tribal island existence) in *Carry on Again, Doctor*. Or the captain of the Golgafrincham B Ark, in Douglas Adams' *Hitch-Hiker's Guide to the Galaxy*, who having crash-landed on prehistoric Earth, creates money by declaring the leaf to be legal tender, and then resolves to deal with the resulting cash oversupply by burning down all the forests.
2   The effect of the Cheques Act 1992 in the UK should also be borne in mind. Though useful as an anti-fraud device, the requirement that cheques in the UK should be treated as accountable to payee only has provided another limitation on the usefulness of cheques within the settlement system.
3   A recent incident involving the Internet bank Egg, where various individuals managed to open a number of accounts by providing false information, has once again highlighted the potential for fraud using the Internet.

9. ELECTRONIC FUND TRANSFERS

10.21 There are two categories of electronic fund transfer system in operation today: the consumer activated and the non-consumer activated system.

The main consumer activated systems are Automated Teller Machines (ATMs) and Electronic Funds Transfer – Point Of Sale (EFT-POS) systems[1]. Developed to give consumers direct access to their accounts, consumer activated systems have revolutionised the way in which funds are accessed and business-to-consumer payments are made.

In contrast, non-consumer activated systems are designed to be used by banks and certain other financial institutions for the inter-bank transfer of funds. The two non-consumer activated systems operating in the UK are BACS and CHAPS. Designed to process bulk and high value fund transfers respectively, these systems are for the exclusive use of banks and certain other institutions and, as such, consumers are denied direct access[2].

The body charged with overseeing the operation of these two systems is APACS[3]. Established in 1985, APACS is a non-statutory association of major banks and building societies, which acts as an umbrella association for three autonomous clearing companies:

- BACS Limited, which is responsible for the operation of the BACS system;

- CHAPS Clearing Company Limited, which is responsible for the operation of the CHAPS system; and

- The Cheque and Credit Clearing Company Limited, which deals with bulk 'paper' clearings[4].

Each clearing company is responsible for the operational efficiency and financial integrity of the clearings that they run.

Finally, and although not technically a clearing system since it has no settlement rules for its members, it is important to mention SWIFT in this context. SWIFT operates an international financial messaging system, which enables payment instructions and other messages to be sent between its members, and facilitates the smooth operation of many payment systems.

By way of overview, the operation of the BACS, CHAPS and SWIFT systems are considered below.

1 EFT-POS systems, such as those operated by Switch and Visa Delta, are used to process debit card transactions. For further details see paragraph 10.25 below.
2 In some cases, the bank's corporate or institutional customers may be given direct access to these systems.
3 The acronym APACS stands for Association of Payment Clearing Services. For further information visits www.apacs.org.uk.
4 Cheques, credit card vouchers and other such instruments. Although cheques are still physically exchanged between collecting and paying banks, the cheque clearing process is now becoming more automated. On the first day of the clearing cycle, the collecting bank sends an electronic message setting out the fundamental features of the cheque (the serial number, the sort code, the account number and the amount) to the appropriate paying bank through a secure data exchange network (see the new section 74B Bills of the Exchange Act 1882, which allows the presentation of cheques by means of electronic or similar message setting out the 'essential features' of the cheque). The cheque clearing cycle takes three days, though banks usually allow four days for clearing before customers can draw on the funds. For further information, visit www.apacs.org.uk.

(a) BACS[1]

10.22 BACS provides bulk electronic clearing for sterling credit and debit transfers, typically dealing with high volume, but low value, transfers of funds[2]. The BACS payment cycle takes three working days and involves member banks and building societies submitting input data to BACS via a telecommunications link known as BACSTEL[3]. BACS then processes this data and produces a series of credit and debit instructions (output data) for BACS members. On the second day of the payment cycle, the output data is dispatched to BACS members who then process this data and adjust their customers' accounts accordingly by the start of business on the third day. Once this cycle is complete, BACS advises the Bank of England of the global settlements that need to be made between BACS members to conclude the clearing process. All global credit and debit positions are then settled across their respective accounts at the Bank of England[4].

1 The acronym BACS stands for Bankers' Automated Clearing System. For further information visit www.apacs.org.uk.
2 Such as standing orders (instructions from a customer to make regular specified payments to a creditor), direct credits (direct payments into a customer's account such as a salary) and direct debits (a pre-authorised debit on the customer's account by the payee).
3 The input data takes the form of a series of credit and debit instructions.
4 The rules governing the operation of the BACS system are set out in the BACS Users' Manuals and various agreements made between the BACS members themselves. For further information, visit www.bacs.co.uk.

(b) CHAPS[1]

10.23 CHAPS is the UK's same day high value real-time gross settlement (RTGS) system. Unlike BACS, CHAPS does not operate a central clearing system. Instead, each CHAPS member is provided with a standard piece of software, known as the Gateway, through which member banks (and other institutions using member banks as their agents) exchange payment messages with other members of the CHAPS network.

Having received an appropriate payment instruction from its customer, the CHAPS member making the payment sends a credit transfer message[2] to the CHAPS member that is to receive it through the Gateway. However, before this message is released to the receiving CHAPS member's Gateway, it is first routed via the Bank of England for settlement across their respective accounts. The Bank of England is therefore able to check that sufficient funds are in place to complete the transaction and, if so, settles the transaction by debiting the paying bank's account and crediting the receiving bank's account in the same amount[3]. The Bank of England then returns a confirmation to the paying bank and, on receipt of this confirmation, the main payment message is released to the receiving bank's Gateway. On receipt of the main payment message, the receiving bank is therefore safe in the knowledge that the relevant funds have been credited to its settlement account[4]. CHAPS Clearing Company Limited used to operate two separate systems known as CHAPS Sterling and CHAPS Euro. However, since August 2001, these systems have been replaced with a single system known as NewCHAPS, which operates as the enhanced RTGS system for the UK. NewCHAPS is capable of supporting both sterling and euro payments via a common SWIFT platform.

The CHAPS system also provides the UK with access to TARGET[5]. TARGET is a pan-European clearing system, operated by the European Central Bank, which links the national RTGS systems of the EU Member States.

TARGET is designed to facilitate high-value cross-border euro payments. In 2000, it processed a daily average of 188,000 payments to the value of €1,033 billion, meaning that it turned over an amount equivalent to the entire euro area's gross domestic product in less than six days[6]. TARGET operates by linking the national RTGS systems of the EU Member States, using the SWIFT messaging system and a series of bilateral correspondent accounts held by national central banks. To initiate a cross-border TARGET payment, a paying bank in the UK first sends a payment instruction to the Bank of England through the CHAPS system. The Bank of England then checks that the payment instruction is in order[7] and, if so, it debits the account of the paying bank. Once this process is complete, the Bank of England generates its own payment instruction and sends that instruction to the national central bank in the receiving bank's home Member State. On receipt of this payment instruction, the national central bank in the receiving bank's home Member State checks that the receiving bank is a participant in its national RTGS system and, if so, credits the RTGS account of the receiving bank. A payment instruction is then sent, through the national RTGS system, to the receiving bank to complete the payment process. At the end of each business day, the European Central Bank checks that all messages sent between national central banks have been received and that the total value of cross-border payments sent and received by each national central bank match.

Like other RTGS systems, the real-time nature of TARGET means that settlement risk is eliminated and certainty in the financial markets is achieved.

1 The acronym CHAPS stands for Clearing House Automated Payments System. For further information visit www.apacs.org.uk.
2 Comprising the name of the payee, the amount of the payment, the sort code of the payee's bank and the payee's account number. Similar information must be given about the payer's account.
3 If insufficient funds are in place, the Bank of England is able to provide intra-day liquidity by purchasing high-quality assets from CHAPS members with insufficient funds in their accounts under sale and repurchase agreements. CHAPS members are required to repurchase these assets at a later date to reimburse the Bank of England.
4 In 2000, the average daily value of payments handled by CHAPS Sterling was £189 billion.
5 TARGET stands for Trans-European Automated Real-time Gross settlement Express Transfer system. For further information visit www.ecb.int.
6 See the TARGET Annual Report, 15 May 2001, which is available at www.ecb.int.
7 The Bank of England checks that the payment instruction conforms to the required standards, that it contains the required information and that the amount of the payment does not exceed the funds available to the paying bank.

(c) SWIFT[1]

10.24 SWIFT operates a financial message transfer system which allows payment messages and other financial information to be transmitted between members. Unlike BACS and CHAPS, SWIFT does not have specific settlement rules for its members. Instead, using a common language to disseminate financial information, its role lies in acting as the messaging system for a number of payment and other clearing systems. SWIFT members gain access to the SWIFT system through regional SWIFT access points, which are interlinked to create the SWIFT network. According to SWIFT, its messaging service enables banks to reduce cost, improve automation and manage risk. The SWIFT messaging system facilitates the operation of TARGET and a number of other major payment clearing systems.

1 SWIFT (Society of Worldwide Interbank Financial Telecommunications) is a co-operative society established under Belgian law, which is owned and controlled by its member banks and financial institutions. The average daily value of payment messages on SWIFT is estimated to be over US $6 trillion. For further information visit www.swift.com.

10. CREDIT CARDS, DEBIT CARDS AND DIRECT PAYMENTS

10.25 Whilst the majority of inter-bank and high value business-to-business fund transfers are carried out using the CHAPS and TARGET systems referred to above, the majority of on-line business-to-consumer transactions are currently paid for by way of one form or another of direct payment transfer. These include:

■ **direct credits** – a direct credit is an electronic payment which allows the business customers of banks to make payments to businesses or to other individuals. Direct credits are commonly used for the payment of monthly salaries to a company's employees, who receive their 'payslip' for the month as confirmation of the credit transfer. Direct credits are processed by the BACS system[1];

■ **direct debits** – a direct debit is an instruction from a customer to a bank to make regular payments at the request of, and to the account of, a specified third party. Direct debits are commonly used for the payment of utility bills, council tax payments and other periodical dues. Again, direct debits are processed by the BACS system[2];

■ **debit card payments** – the cardholder pays for goods or services by presenting to the merchant his account details, which are coded into the magnetic strip on the card, and the merchant is able to arrange to collect electronic payment directly from the cardholder's account. As with credit cards, debit cards can now be used on-line.

Most debit card transactions are processed by one of the major EFT-POS systems operating in the UK. As the Jack Committee observed[3], 'EFT-POS is a payment system designed to allow retail payments to be made by transferring funds electronically from customers' to suppliers' accounts without any need for cash or cheques. With a typical EFT-POS system, a customer passes his card through a reader terminal installed at the supplier's point of sale, and information encoded in the card, and that relating to the transaction, is sent to a central processing point where the validity of the card is authenticated. The customer then authorises the transaction, either by signing a receipt slip produced by the terminal or by inserting his PIN at the special keyboard. Full details of the transaction are then sent back up the line to the central processor, and from there the supplier's account is credited and the customer's account debited automatically.'

Switch and Visa Delta are two of the main EFT-POS systems operating in the UK; and

■ **credit card payments** – the cardholder pays for goods or services by authorising the merchant to collect payment from the credit card company issuing the card. The credit card company then collects this money from the cardholder at a later date.

Of the direct payment methods referred to above, credit cards are by far the most widely used for business-to-consumer payments. Accordingly, it is appropriate to consider their operation in a little more detail.

1 According to APACS, direct credits numbered nearly 1.1 billion payments in 2000. Almost 60% of direct credits arose from the payment of wages, salaries and company and private pensions.
2 Under the rules of the Direct Debit Scheme, should any money be taken in error, the customer's bank or building society must, on request, make an immediate refund to the customer. According to APACS, nearly 2 billion payments were made by direct debit in 2000.
3 'Banking Services: Law and Practice Report by the Review Committee', Cm 622.

(a) Credit cards

10.26 The main advantages of credit cards to the e-merchant are that they are a familiar method of payment for most consumers, are internationally recognised[1] and, as no special plug-ins or equipment are required to be installed by the consumer, they make it easy for customers to shop on-line. For the consumer, there are no extra agreements to be entered into[2], there are no currency conversion problems[3], and the consumer will generally be in a better position than if he paid in cash because of his rights under the CCA 1974[4]. Increasingly, one finds card issuers offering add-on privileges to cardholders, which range from lower than market-rate fees or low interest rates on late payment to unrelated benefits such as air miles awards, free travel insurance or shopping privileges with connected merchants or schemes. Currently, credit card transactions take place over the Internet in much the same fashion as they do in telephone transactions, with the consumer communicating his card number to the e-merchant on-line[5]. This leaves a clear audit trail, which provides the customer, vendor and card company with as much evidence as any of them should require to determine the course of the transaction in case of complaint of any sort.

However, card numbers supplied can be intercepted and misused. This is seen as the biggest disadvantage of using credit cards (and indeed debit cards) on-line from the consumer's point of view[6]. Concerns over security have led to many websites using Secure Sockets Layer (SSL) technology, which is built into most new browsers and automatically encrypts account information during transmission. Some websites will also offer the customer the option of providing credit card details separately over the telephone but this is hardly amenable to the concept of quick and easy Internet trading (particularly where the customer only has one line to use alternately for his telephone and his Internet connection). The Secure Electronic Transfer (SET) protocol in the context of electronic fund transfers is also increasingly being employed in relation to credit card payments over the Internet[7].

There are also significant disadvantages for the e-merchant in using credit cards: the need to sign up first for a merchant account with a card issuer to allow it to accept credit cards, the relatively high transaction costs[8], and the risk of 'chargebacks'.

1 The vast majority of card issuers provide cards linked to the MasterCard or VISA networks. American Express, which does not license its card to independent issuers, is also widely accepted around the world.
2 Over and above the master agreement from the card issuer, which he must accept as a condition of using the card in the first place.
3 Although in the case of a transaction in a foreign currency, the cardholder is likely to get a relatively poor rate of exchange, largely reflecting the fact that the card company is not itself a holder of the relevant foreign currency and must purchase this in the market in order to settle the transaction.
4 For example, section 75 of the CCA 1974, which applies to transactions where any single item is worth between £100 and £30,000 and there is a pre-existing agreement between the card issuer and the supplier. This gives the cardholder the right to pursue either the supplier or the card issuer for misrepresentation or breach of contract, as the CCA 1974 makes the supplier and the card issuer jointly and severally liable in such circumstances.
5 As opposed to the face-to-face sale, where the presentation of the actual card is necessary.
6 A survey conducted in the summer of 2000 by technology consultancy The Gartner Group found that on-line retailers experience 12 times more fraud than their high street rivals.
7 For further commentary on the SSL and SET systems and certain others coming into use in relation to data encryption, see section 10 of Chapter 3, E-liability.
8 The cost of credit card transactions can be high as 3% of each sale for the merchant. If an e-merchant does not have a facility to accept cards, there is the option of outsourcing secure transactions to companies such as WorldPay (www.worldpay.com) or Secure Trading (www.securetrading.com), which charge up to 4.5% commission on transactions.

(b) Chargebacks

10.27 In the UK a consumer cannot generally be made liable for the misuse of his credit card by a third party[1], although the terms of the credit card agreement can make the cardholder liable, once the card has been accepted, for the first £50 whilst the card is not in the cardholder's possession and any loss accrued by a third party who has possession of the card with the cardholder's permission, until the card issuer receives notification of the loss of the card[2].

However, it is still open to the cardholder, within a certain time limit, to dispute a transaction that may be the result of theft, fraud or error. Where that is accepted by the card issuer, a 'chargeback' will occur, so that the e-merchant may find itself not only repaying the sums disputed but also a processing fee, which in some circumstances may be more than the amount in dispute. This is made worse in relation to on-line transactions where the e-merchant will be unable to verify the cardholder's identity in the same way as it can off-line, and therefore the e-merchant faces a significantly higher risk of chargeback occurring.

In addition, the risk of chargebacks is higher with goods and services which can be delivered electronically[3], as they can be denied more easily. With physical goods the e-merchant will be able to prove that the goods have been delivered to the cardholder's address and, assuming that the cardholder and the customer are one and the same person, the customer cannot argue that the transaction never took place and will have to argue instead that the goods were somehow defective or not what was ordered.

1 The CCA 1974, s 83.
2 The CCA 1974, s 84. It should be noted that section 84(1) and (2) do not apply to the use of a credit card in connection with a 'distance contract' (other than an 'excepted contract'), within the meaning of the Consumer Protection (Distance Selling) Regulations 2000 (SI 2000/2334). See the CCA 1974, s 84(3A) and (3B).
3 It is perhaps not altogether surprising that adult content websites report particularly high levels of chargeback.

(c) Legal relationship between the cardholder, card issuer and e-merchant

10.28 The use of a credit card gives rise to three contracts which operate simultaneously. These contracts were identified by Millett J in the leading case of *Re Charge Card Services Ltd*[1]:

'First there is the contract of supply between the supplier and the cardholder (either in his own right or as agent for the account holder); secondly, there is the contract between the supplier and the card issuing company, which undertakes to honour the card by paying the supplier on presentation of the sales voucher; and, thirdly, there is the contract between the card-issuing company and the account holder by which the account holder undertakes to reimburse the card-issuing company for payments made or liabilities incurred by the card-issuing company to the supplier as a result of his cardholder's use of the card. There are thus three separate contracts and three separate parties, each being party to two of the three contracts but neither of them being party nor privy to the third.'[2]

The effect of this finding of the existence of three separate contracts means that a cardholder who tenders payment by means of a credit card has completed his contract with the supplier. Thereafter the supplier must look to the card issuer for payment. This means that although the credit card payment cannot strictly be countermanded by the cardholder once made, if the card issuer fails to pay the e-merchant (for example, if it becomes insolvent), the e-merchant cannot then look back to the cardholder for payment.

1 [1987] Ch 150; on appeal [1989] Ch 497, CA.
2 In connection with this final observation, it should be pointed out that the Contracts (Rights of Third Parties) Act 1999 might now construe such an arrangement as affording rights to the third of the three parties on any given side of this triangular relationship to derive rights from the contract to which it is not expressly a party.

11. ELECTRONIC MONEY – SMART CARDS AND PURE SOFTWARE-BASED SYSTEMS

10.29 What do we mean by the term 'electronic money'? Although it has been observed that a precise definition is difficult to provide[1], the European Parliament has recently given it the following meaning:

'monetary value as represented by a claim on the issuer which is:
(i) stored on an electronic device;
(ii) issued on receipt of funds of an amount not less in value than the monetary value issued; and
(iii) accepted as means of payment by undertakings other than the issuer'[2].

Electronic money is the digital representation of money or, more accurately, the digital representation of currency[3]. In essence, it is an encoded string of digital information representing a given value in a designated currency, which is designed to be accepted as a means of payment. Purporting to operate as the on-line equivalent of cash, electronic money's intrinsic value (and therefore acceptability as a means of payment) lies in the fact that each string of digital information represents a claim on the issuer for the monetary value that it purports to represent.

Electronic money may be carried on a number of electronic devices[4] and downloaded from a variety of sources, including specially adapted ATMs, modified home telephones and the Internet. It may be used in the physical world by inserting a card into a terminal or by using contactless wireless technology and, in the virtual world, over the Internet from a PC or mobile phone.

Capable of instantaneous transfer and immediate re-use, electronic money's similarity to 'real' cash is quite striking. Indeed, in many respects, the similarities are so compelling that many electronic money issuers specifically market their products as a direct electronic equivalent of cash[5].

However, although electronic money purports to operate as the functional equivalent of cash, it is important to appreciate that it is not, as a matter of English law at least, its legal equivalent. Unlike the physical notes and coins that we carry in our pockets, electronic money is not legal tender, as it is not currency issued with the authority of the state[6]. Therefore, although electronic money is in many respects very similar to cash, it does not have the same legal status[7]. This has two important implications. The first is that where money is due under a contract, unless the parties to the contract otherwise agree, the creditor is not bound to accept payment in any way except by way of legal tender[8]. Therefore, although a merchant would not be entitled to object to payment in legal tender, he would be entitled to refuse payment in electronic money[9]. The second, and perhaps more fundamental, relates to the extent to which a transferee can assert good and indefeasible title to electronic money. This issue is discussed further at paragraph 10.39 below.

A number of payment systems have been developed in recent years that have marketed themselves as 'electronic money'. Broadly, these systems can be placed into two categories.

The first relies on smart card technology, which allows monetary value to be stored on a card carried by the cardholder. Smart card-based payment systems were the first form of electronic money to be developed. In essence, smart cards (or 'stored value cards' as they are often known) operate as an electronic warehouse for existing cash deposits. However, in order to overcome some of the specialised hardware requirements associated with smart card technology, various on-line payment systems have been developed in recent years which are purely software-based. Using nothing more than computer software, these systems facilitate the digital generation of electronic value tokens, for use exclusively on-line.

1   Group of Ten, 'Report of the Working Party on Electronic Money', April 1997.
2   Directive (EC) 46/2000 on the taking up, pursuit of and prudential supervision of the business of electronic money institutions (the Electronic Money Directive). It should be noted that when the UK Government implements this Directive into domestic law, it does not propose to adopt this definition in full. For further details see paragraph 10.42.
3   As Geoffrey Turk points out, although used interchangeably and often synonymously, the words *'money'* and *'currency'* do in fact mean different things. 'Money' is simply a means of communicating value, while 'currency' is the physical manifestation of money – currency gives money visible form. See Turk, *Money and Currency in the 21st Century* (1997).
4   Including a smart card, computer memory or mobile phone.
5   It can be used to buy goods and services, be used independently of a bank account and may be exchanged person to person. Mondex International, for example, markets its electronic cash product in this way. For further details see paragraph 10.31 below.
6   As FA Mann observes, 'only those chattels are money to which such character has been attributed by law'. See Mann, *The Legal Aspect of Money* (1992) Clarendon Press. In England, legal tender consists of coins made and issued by the Crown and bank notes made and issued by the Bank of England. See further, section 2 of the Coinage Act 1971 (as amended) and section 1 of the Currency and Bank Notes Act 1954.
7   However, it should be borne in mind that in the context of payments over the Internet, the question of what amounts to legal tender may well fall to be determined by a law other than English law. As Brindle and Cox point out, 'where a contract specifies payment in a given currency, the question of what constitutes that currency falls to be determined in accordance with the law of the country whose currency it is. Application of this principal would suggest that, for example, the question of whether U.S. Dollars in electronic form constitute U.S. currency and, in particular, whether they constitute legal tender would be referred to U.S. law.' See Brindle and Cox, *Law of Bank Payments* (1999) Sweet & Maxwell.
8   *Thomas v Evans* (1808) 10 East 101.
9   The same is of course true of other alternative payment methods. In the past, Marks & Spencer refused to accept payment by credit card.

(a) Smart cards

10.30 Smart cards are plastic cards that contain embedded computer microchips rather than (or in addition to) the conventional magnetic strips. These microchips allow data, including account balances, personal information, PIN numbers, shopping information and loyalty rewards, to be stored on the card. In the context of payment systems, smart cards allow the consumer to turn 'real' money in a bank account into digitally encrypted value stored on the card (and vice versa).

(i) Mondex[1]

10.31 One of the earliest card-based payment systems developed in the UK was the Mondex card, which was designed principally to provide an electronic means of servicing off-line low value transaction payments (or micropayments). However, since its inception, the technology has developed considerably and, today, cardholders are able to use 'Mondex electronic cash'[2] to make payments both on- and-off-line.

Mondex cards contain an embedded microchip[3] which, in turn, contains an electronic 'purse', in which Mondex value is stored electronically. The purse is subdivided into five separate pockets, allowing up to five different currencies to be held at any one time. In addition to the purse, Mondex cards are capable of supporting a wide range of applications, including interactive loyalty[4] and employee identification schemes[5].

Using the Mondex system, the card is first programmed to reflect an amount of 'real' money which is prepaid by the cardholder to the Mondex issuer. The cardholder can load his Mondex card with value by accessing his bank account via a cash machine, modified home telephone or the Internet[6]. The cardholder's bank account is then debited with that sum. Once loaded, the cardholder is able to present the card by way of payment at any outlet which accepts the payment system or, if he has access to a specially modified PC, he is able to transfer Mondex value over the Internet. Payment is effected by debiting the customer's Mondex card and crediting the merchant's Mondex card. As the system does not operate any kind of central clearing system, Mondex value is transferred directly from the customer to the merchant. Once transferred, the merchant then has the option of either redeeming the value with the Mondex issuer for 'real' money or bank credit, or transferring that value on to another participant in the scheme at a later date.

As Brindle and Cox point out, Mondex transactions are therefore analogous to cash payments. Once the cardholder has withdrawn the value from his bank account and credited it (as electronic money) to the card, the value on the card circulates without each transaction being separately recorded – just like cash[7].

The card system is thought to be very secure (a characteristic of smart cards in general). This is because interference with the chips usually destroys them entirely, leaving the cards useless[8]. In any event, as the cards are not intended to store large amounts of cash, any potential risk of fraud is of minimal significance compared to the convenience.

Through the widespread integration of Mondex technology with a variety of products such as mobile phones and digital televisions[9], it is anticipated that, ultimately, Mondex will allow cardholders to download value and make payments across any remote channel.

At the time of writing, however, Mondex is unavailable in the UK – although a number of pilot schemes have been run[10]. Currently, active territories include Japan and Taiwan. Although the system appears to be achieving some success in the Far East, it remains to be seen whether Mondex will become an established method of payment in the UK[11].

1 See www.mondex.com.
2 Mondex International (a wholly owned subsidiary of MasterCard International) licences its principal product, Mondex electronic cash, to more than 80 territories worldwide. In the UK, the territory franchisees are HSBC Bank plc, NatWest and NAG Europe. Together, the UK territory franchisees are responsible for the commercial development and implementation of Mondex electronic cash throughout the UK.
3 This is known as the multi-application operating system – MULTOS. MULTOS is the operating platform on which Mondex International's principal products, Mondex electronic cash and Interactive Loyalty, are based. MULTOS is the first open, high security, multi-application operating system for smart cards and allows the card to perform a range of different functions. Until multi-application smart cards were developed, cardholders had to carry a number of different cards for each smart card application that they wanted to use. For further information visit www.multos.com.
4 Interactive Loyalty is a secure customer relationship management system which enables suppliers to monitor the behavioural and shopping patterns of their customers. It is designed to allow suppliers to target their marketing and promotional campaigns more effectively. For further information visit www.interactiveloyalty.com.
5 Since January 2000, Hitachi employees in Japan have used Mondex cards as both a payment and a staff ID card.

6 Using a specially modified PC.

7 Brindle and Cox, *Law of Bank Payments* (1999) Sweet & Maxwell, p 194.

8 Mondex and the MULTOS operating system have both been awarded ITSEC Level E6 (Information Technology Security Evaluation Criteria), the highest ITSEC security rating available.

9 The new generation of digital satellite receivers known as Digiboxes already contain a Mondex compatible card reader.

10 In July 1995, the first trial of Mondex cards was carried out in Swindon, Wiltshire, which ran for three years. Since then, a number of other trials have taken place around the UK, including on a number of university campuses.

11 At the time of writing, it was understood that no formal plans were in place to make the UK an active territory.

(ii) Visa Cash[1]

10.32 Like Mondex, Visa Cash was designed as a form of off-line electronic money, aimed primarily at low value transactions. However, as with Mondex, Visa Cash can now be used on-line.

Visa Cash cards (which may be disposable or reusable) are loaded with electronic value units via specialised terminals and ATMs and value is then transferred to the merchant either over the Internet or at the point of sale. Payment transaction data is then collected and transferred to a central system for the purposes of clearing between the (customer's) issuing bank and the (merchant's) acquiring bank. The involvement of more than one bank gives rise to the need for a settlement and clearing system[2].

1 See www.visaeu.com/smartcards/main.html.

2 This is in contrast to Mondex, which does not require a settlement and clearing system (as once electronic value leaves the banking system, it can be used at the point of sale and for transactions between cardholders without creating a separately identifiable accounting record for each purpose). This means that individual transaction costs are lower in the case of Mondex cards and hence make the Mondex card more suitable for micropayments.

(iii) The future of smart cards

10.33 Smart cards are increasingly being used for a variety of purposes. This ranges from making telephone calls through BT phonecards and storing personal and account information on credit cards[1] to acting as a travel ticket[2]. In fact it is conceivable that in future we will all carry smart cards which act as our electronic identities and which combine all of these functions and more. However, as various commentators have pointed out[3], because much of the infrastructure has yet to be put in place, smart cards have yet to revolutionise the way in which payments are made. Currently, smart card payment systems are constrained by the fact that there are no universally accepted smart card 'readers', which are essential to facilitate the transmission of data stored on the cards[4]. Therefore, although it is predicted that US$8.6 billion will be spent on-line in Europe in 2003, it is expected that only 7% of this will be attributable to smart card payments[5].

Nevertheless, smart card technology is increasingly being integrated with a variety of products, such as TV set-top boxes and mobile phones. In the future, it is anticipated that PlayStation-type machines and even kitchen appliances will incorporate this technology. If this integration continues, it may well be the case that smart cards will account for a much bigger share of the electronic payment market. However, as set-top boxes and kitchen appliances are not naturally thought of as on-line shopping platforms, whether consumers can be persuaded to use them for this purpose remains to be seen.

1 A number of banks such as Egg, Smile and NatWest now issue credit and debit cards which contain microchips.

2 Transport for London's PRESTIGE project (see www.transportforlondon.gov.uk/abt_prest_intro.shtml) will see the introduction of 'smart travel cards' in 2002.

3 See, for example, PricewaterhouseCoopers, 'Banking Technology Solutions 2001 (No 6) – A slow start for smart cards'.

4 For example, banks in the UK have to date not issued their customers with smart card readers as American Express did to users of its blue credit card in the US in 1999.

5 According to research carried out by Datamonitor and cited in 'Banking Technology Solutions 2001 (No 6)'. For further information, visit www.datamonitor.com.

(b) Software-based systems

10.34   Software-based systems are to be distinguished from those that rely on smart card technology. Whereas smart cards operate as an electronic warehouse for existing cash deposits, electronic money systems that are purely software-based allow the digital generation of electronic value tokens for use exclusively on-line. The programs considered below have, so far, had a limited degree of success.

(i)   DigiCash

10.35   One of the early systems to be developed was DigiCash, which has since gone out of business[1].

The old DigiCash system required each participant (whether buyer or seller) to have a special bank account with an 'e-cash' issuing bank (often nicknamed the 'mint') and suitable software for handling 'e-cash' transactions. Payment was made by the buyer from a 'purse' of digital 'coins' produced by the buyer's PC using the DigiCash software.

1   eCash Technologies Inc, a software company providing payment solutions, has now acquired the DigiCash business.

(ii)   eCoin.net[1]

10.36   Another software-based system is eCoin.net, which operates as a token-based micropayment system. The system is designed to allow consumers to purchase digital products on-line and, in effect, simulates 'real' currency in the virtual world, by allotting each individual digital token (or 'eCoin') a fixed value in a given currency.

In order to use the system, consumers must first sign-up for a user account on the eCoin Server[2]. This account is necessary to allow consumers to purchase, download or upload eCoins and can be linked to a pre-existing credit or debit facility.

Once the consumer has created his user account, he must then download and install 'electronic wallet' software (known as the 'eCoin Wallet Manager') onto his PC. This allows the consumer to communicate with the eCoin Server and to authorise the transfer of eCoins to a merchant.

Once the eCoin Wallet Manager is installed, the consumer is able to log onto his Server account, purchase eCoins using 'real' money and download those eCoins into his eCoin Wallet Manager, ready for payment. When an eCoin is downloaded into the eCoin Wallet Manager, an identical copy is maintained on the eCoin Server, and when that eCoin is transferred, the copy is marked 'invalid' to prevent double spending.

In order to effect a transaction, the merchant's computer first contacts the eCoin Server and is sent an 'invoice tag'. The merchant's eCoin-enabled website then inserts this invoice tag into the merchant's web page and sends it on to the customer's browser. The eCoin Wallet Manger installed on the customer's PC is then able to interpret this invoice tag. When the customer clicks on the invoice tag displayed, the eCoin Wallet Manager sends invoice data and the requisite number of eCoins to the eCoin Server. The eCoin Server then decodes the 'invoice data', verifies the eCoins and transfers the eCoins from the customer's eCoin Server account to the merchant's, thereby effecting payment. In order to give the customer access to the digital product that he has purchased, the eCoin Server returns a redirect command to the customer's browser together with the URL at the merchant's website where the digital product is located. The customer's browser is then able to load that URL and the customer is given access to his digital purchase.

Under normal circumstances, this seemingly involved and intricate series of events takes a matter of seconds.

1   See www.ecoin.net.
2   Merchants wishing to participate in the scheme must sign-up for a merchant account on the eCoin Server and set up an eCoin enabling facility on their websites. This can be done using the EasyWeb and EasyForm construction wizards available on the eCoin.net website.

(c) Are there any problems in store for users of electronic money?

10.37   The provisional answer to this question has to be yes, even though some of these problems are common to many alternative payment methods.

■   What if the computer crashes or the Internet connection goes down? An on-line system of payment will always be affected by inherent risks of a system failure. However, this is also true of the credit card verification systems that are installed by most big stores. And if the failure is with the customer's computer, as opposed to the system operated by the electronic money provider, then he will no more be able to pay on-line with a credit card. There are now very few forms of payment that do not use computers in some form or other.

■   Fault tolerance and software reliability are problems that could emerge over time[1].

■   Consumers can be expected to lose patience if they discover that the system involves possible long connection times when communicating over the Internet[2].

■   Can payments be stopped[3] (and if so, under what circumstances)? This may not be a major problem whilst the amounts of money involved are very small. However, if future use of the electronic money concept were to be expanded to cover more substantial transactions, then this is an issue which will certainly need to be addressed.

1   This is in a sense connected with the question of how providers of electronic money should be regulated, which is considered at paragraph 10.40 below. The simple point is that an unregulated electronic money provider is not accountable to a national or supra-national regulator for the quality of its systems (merely to the customers who use those systems, if they are in a position to hold it to account for system failures).
2   As connection costs continue to fall, the issue of the sheer cost of staying on-line to complete a transaction will cease to be of significance. However, there remains the simple truth that if the customer believes that everything on the Internet can be purchased almost instantaneously, significant delay in closing a purchase with electronic money is likely to deter many from making use of it.
3   Or, better, reversed. Since an entire payment usually takes seconds to complete (assuming no system failures), it matters to know whether the consumer who subsequently receives wrong or defective goods or who has been mislead can hold the system accountable to him for a reverse transaction that sees the return to him of an equivalent amount of electronic money.

(d) Beenz

10.38   Although Beenz.com ceased its operations in August 2001, Carlson Marketing Group, one of the largest marketing services agencies in the United States, has recently announced a multi-million dollar plan to acquire the beenz.com business[1]. Accordingly, as it seems likely that we will see a re-emergence of the beenz.com technology in one form or another, it is perhaps appropriate to consider how it used to operate.

Beenz.com is the creator of Beenz, a rewards-based loyalty program for the Internet. As it stood, Beenz might have been described as a hybrid of a true money system and a token system (akin, perhaps, to Air Miles[2] and similar services). Indeed, it may have been that in legal terms, it was no more than the e-commerce age's equivalent of that 1960s hardy perennial, the Green Shield Stamp. But Beenz set out to be more than a token or reward system, and merits a mention in a chapter dealing with e-payment methods.

By opening an account with Beenz, customers were able to spend and earn beenz currency at any one of a number of participating websites. By downloading certain software (a 'beenz counter' as it was known), consumers could keep track of their account with Beenz, and determine how many Beenz they had earned. Beenz could not be bought, but were awarded for carrying out certain tasks such as registering with, or buying products from, participating websites. Much like the loyalty reward cards used by a number of UK retailers, BeenzBack Shopping (as it was known) entitled customers to Beenz by way of reward for their loyalty (which could then be redeemed at a later date).

The Beenz.com technology serves as a useful illustration of how novel and innovative on-line payment systems are being devised all the time, and although it is true that it has suffered set backs at an early stage, the fact that it is likely to be re-launched serves as a testament to its potential. If it is in fact re-launched, how successful it will become will depend upon how many e-merchant websites can be persuaded to joint the scheme (a point no less true of any of the other schemes described in paragraphs 10.30 to 10.36). More importantly, however, there is the question of whether a re-launched version of Beenz could ever become truly convertible, and therefore compete as a quasi-currency in its own right. With the value attached to a supermarket reward scheme, this is not such an issue, since the value in the scheme is only intended to be redeemed at that supermarket[3]. Beenz, however, aimed to be more than this, by creating something that allowed for the redemption and earning of value at numerous different outlets. The potential therefore exists for something like Beenz to become an international currency of account, because any jurisdiction could adjust its systems to reflect the latent value in Beenz. If re-launched, whether Beenz does in fact become more than a token exchange scheme for small-scale purchases remains to be seen.

1   The acquisition of beenz.com includes hardware and software assets, the beenz brand and all of the company's intellectual property assets including its patents.
2   See www.airmiles.co.uk. The legalities of operating such a scheme in the UK are set out in Chapter 6, E-marketing.
3   One could make certain other observations regarding air miles and supermarket reward card schemes, such as the fact that they represent very little value in real terms: if you relied on accruing one air mile per £20 spent on a NatWest credit card, for example, then Air Miles UK would eventually fly you for free from London to Paris on the basis of £9,000 expenditure, and to New York on the basis of £130,000 expenditure.

(e) Electronic money – legal issues

10.39   As with all technological advances, it is inevitable that it will take time for law-makers and regulators to devise systems that are capable of addressing some of the novel legal issues that arise. Take the following examples:

■   What happens if a smart card containing electronic money is stolen?[1] If real money is stolen and then passed on by way of payment, merchants will generally acquire good title to that money notwithstanding the fact that the thief had no title to it in the first place. This is because 'real' money is a 'negotiable instrument' and, under the Bills of Exchange Act 1882 (BEA 1882), a person acquiring such an instrument for value and in good faith takes good title to that instrument irrespective of any defect in title of the person from whom it was acquired[2].

   Similar protection is not afforded to merchants who accept electronic money by way of payment. In order to take effect as a 'negotiable instrument', the BEA 1882 requires the instrument to be in writing[3] and, as a result, electronic money fails to meet the necessary criteria for negotiability. Therefore, until the law is changed or electronic money acquires negotiable status through mercantile usage, the danger for the merchant who accepts electronic money by way of payment is that a defect in title somewhere down the chain could result in the true owner asserting title to it. Although merchants would be able to bring a claim against the thief in these circumstances, in the majority of cases, any claim is likely to prove futile[4].

■   Electronic money is not legal tender and as a result, electronic money systems depend on a series of contractual relationships for their legal effect. Therefore, although article 3(1) of the Electronic Money Directive[5] will require an issuer to redeem electronic money at par, what will happen in the following situation?

Suppose that a parent gifts a smart card containing electronic money to a hard-up child at university. The parent will have a contractual relationship with the electronic money issuer under which the issuer will be obliged to redeem the electronic money at par. However, the same cannot be said of the student, as he will not be a party to that contract. What happens when the student then attempts to purchase goods with the electronic money? Given that electronic money is not legal tender, the merchant would be well within its rights to refuse to accept it by way of payment[6]. The question that then arises is whether in these circumstances, the student has recourse to the issuer to obtain redemption of the electronic money at par. As there is no direct contractual relationship between the student and issuer, the issuer may (for whatever reason) argue that he is not obliged to redeem the electronic money in these circumstances.

Whilst this may seem problematic, the solution may lie in the following analysis. If a person holds himself out as an electronic money issuer, then it is arguable that, by doing so, he makes a unilateral offer to the world to redeem any electronic money that is presented to him for redemption[7]. If this is the case, then when the student presents the electronic money for redemption, he will accept this offer (by performance) and furnish good consideration (by giving the issuer the electronic money); as a result, the issuer will become contractually obliged to redeem it. Although the point is likely to remain academic whilst the amounts of electronic money in circulation are small, should the sums become greater, a definitive answer may be given by the courts.

- Electronic money also raises issues for those concerned with money laundering, tax evasion and fraud. Although these are all criminal offences and under English law 'fraud unravels everything'[8], the problem with electronic money is that it opens up new avenues for criminals to exploit. The ease with which the 'mint' can be persuaded to issue 'coins' to consumers (under the DigiCash system), for example, begs the question of whether the system can be safe from money laundering problems. Offences may be difficult to detect if buyers use false identities in trading with sellers and the 'mint' is unable to identify which buyers have spent which 'coins'. The opportunity to convert illicit cash into apparently 'clean' electronic money through this mechanism is bound to attract itself to the would-be money launderer. Further problems arise when one considers that payments made using electronic money do not leave the same clear audit trails as those left by cheques or credit cards. The problem here is that these audit trails are often used as the basis for tracing the whereabouts of illicit funds and further assist taxation authorities in collecting taxes that are due.

- Finally, what happens if electronic money is counterfeited? As with counterfeit 'real' money (if we can call it that), any attempt to use it to make payment will not be effective. However, forgeries may be difficult to detect and, as a result, it is quite plausible that counterfeit electronic money could pass through a chain of entirely innocent ownership before the forgery is actually discovered. As commentators have observed[9], although in theory any loss sustained could be forced back down the chain of ownership in these circumstances, in practice, the loss is likely to fall on the person holding the counterfeit electronic money at the time the forgery is discovered (since the original counterfeiter will often be difficult, if not impossible, to locate). Quite how (if at all) the law will attempt to compensate the innocent holder of forged electronic money in these circumstances remains to be seen. Furthermore, any difficulties in differentiating between authentic and forged electronic money is likely to have serious implications for electronic money issuers themselves. If electronic money issuers are unable to make this distinction and end up redeeming substantial amounts of counterfeit electronic money at par, then this is likely to threaten their ongoing ability to redeem genuine electronic money at par and to pose serious threats to their future solvency.

Whilst certain steps are being taken towards addressing some of the problems highlighted above, there remain situations in which the law needs to be modified. The European Committee on Crime

Problems has recently adopted the text prepared by the Committee of Experts on Crime in Cyber-Space (PY-CY), which will be the first international treaty to address criminal law and procedural aspects of cyber crime. This treaty recognises that the technical revolution has expanded the scope for economic crimes, such as forgery and fraud, and sets out to criminalise the manipulation of assets represented or administered in computer systems with the intention of affecting an illegal transfer of property. In addition, as the Treasury has made it clear that all electronic money issuers will be subject to the Money Laundering Regulations 1993[10], these measures should go some way towards addressing some of the concerns that exist in relation to crime. However, other legal problems remain. It is unclear how the law will respond where issuers of electronic money realise that perfectly forged electronic money is in circulation and, moreover, if merchants are to be safe in the knowledge that they will receive good title to electronic money, then legislative reform is necessary[11]. It is often said that technology races ahead of the law. Developments in electronic money are no exception.

1　The Banking Code now recognises the concept of electronic money and affords consumers a level of protection in these circumstances. It provides that unless the issuer can show that the customer has acted fraudulently or without reasonable care, if the customer's 'electronic purse' is credited with unauthorised withdrawals from his account before he informs the issuer that it has been lost, stolen or misused, then the most that he will lose is £50. If, however, he has informed the issuer of this fact before the unauthorised withdrawal is made, then he will be reimbursed in full. Of course, all of this presupposes that the issuer subscribes to the Code in the first place. The Code defines an 'electronic purse' as 'any card, or function of a card, which contains real value in the form of electronic money which someone has paid for before hand'. It is interesting to note that this definition refers to 'any card, or function of a card'. It would therefore appear that this definition does not cover forms of electronic money that are purely software-based. For details of the institutions that subscribe to the Code visit www.bankingcode.org.uk.

2　This should be contrasted with the situation where a person acquires non-negotiable chattels or securities from a thief. Subject to certain well-established exceptions, the general position under English law is that where goods are stolen and subsequently sold, the goods remain the property of the original owner and can be recovered from the transferee. As Scrutton LJ explained in *Banque Belge pour L'Etranger v Hambrouck* [1921] 1 KB 321 at 329, CA:

> '... at common law, a man who had no title himself could give not title to another. Nemo potest dare quod non habet. To this there was an exception in the case of negotiable chattels or securities, the first of which to be recognised were money and bank notes: *Miller v Race* (1758) 1 Burr 452; and if these were received in good faith and for valuable consideration, the transferee got property though the transferor had none.'

3　'Writing' includes typing, printing, lithography, photography and other modes of representing or reproducing words in a visible form. See section 2 of the BEA 1882 and section 5 of the Interpretation Act 1978 respectively.

4　Thieves tend not to be worth suing: they usually disappear or have no assets.

5　Directive (EC) 46/2000 on the taking up, pursuit and prudential supervision of the business of electronic money institutions. See paragraph 10.42 below.

6　See paragraph 10.29 above.

7　As a general rule, an advertisement does not amount to a contractual offer for the purposes of English law: *Partridge v Crittenden* [1968] 2 All ER 421. However, advertisements can be couched in such terms as to be interpreted as offers, if it is clear that no further bargaining between the parties is possible or intended. In *Carlill v Carbolic Smoke Ball Co* [1893] 1 QB 256, CA, the defendants issued an advertisement promising to pay £100 to any person who caught influenza after using one of their carbolic smoke balls in accordance with certain direction. It was held that this amounted to a unilateral offer on the part of the defendant so that when the claimant caught influenza after using the smoke ball, she accepted the offer (and furnished good consideration) and was entitled to receive the reward. In these cases, there is no need to communicate acceptance of the offer, as the offer is accepted by performance of the act or condition in question. By analogy, where an electronic money issuer is in the business of issuing and redeeming electronic money, it is arguable that by holding himself out as an electronic money issuer, he makes a unilateral offer to the world to redeem any electronic money that is presented to him for redemption, as he is obliged to redeem that electronic money at par (and therefore no further bargaining is possible or intended).

8　Per Lord Denning MR in *Midland Bank Trust Co Ltd v Green* [1981] AC 513.

9　Graham JH Smith, *Internet Law and Regulation* (2001) Sweet & Maxwell.

10　For further details, see paragraph 10.42 above.

11　It is possible that over time electronic money will acquire the attribute of negotiability by the custom of merchants, but since the custom of merchants is something which can only be proved by demonstrating an adherence to the custom by the vast majority of merchants, this cannot be achieved overnight.

(f)　Electronic money – regulatory control

10.40　As the law stands, entities that limit their activities to issuing electronic money are unregulated in the UK[1]. However, having said that, two important points need to be made.

First, the activity of issuing electronic money must be carefully defined and, in particular, it must be distinguished from the *regulated activity* of 'accepting deposits'. If an electronic money issuer accepts funds from the public and immediately exchanges those funds for electronic money, it will not be regarded as 'accepting deposits' for the purposes of the FSMA 2000[2]. However, if the received funds are not immediately exchanged for electronic money and result in a credit balance being left on the issuer's account, then issuer will be regarded as 'accepting deposits' and, as a result, will be forced to comply with the extensive compliance requirements surrounding that activity.

Second, the law is about to change. The European Union has recently adopted two Directives[3] requiring Member States to prohibit non-authorised persons from issuing electronic money and, moreover, to implement measures to ensure the financial integrity and stability of electronic money issuers. Member States were required to bring into force laws, regulations and administrative provisions necessary to comply with these Directives by 27 April 2002.

In October 2001, the Treasury set out its proposed approach to the implementation of the Electronic Money Directive in its Consultation Document 'Implementation of the Electronic Money Directive'[4] and in December 2001, the FSA published the draft text of rules and guidance[5] which it proposed to apply to electronic money issuers, and to those firms to whom it would issue certificates waiving compliance with the proposed regulatory regime. What follows in paragraph 10.42 below is a summary of the new regime.

1 Electronic money may be issued by banks or by non-bank institutions. Banks are currently entitled to issue electronic money under the terms of the Directive (EC) 28/2000, subject to them receiving relevant permissions from the FSA. See paragraph 10.41 below.
2 This is probably the case now but the issue will be put beyond doubt when the proposed Financial Services and Markets Act 2000 (Regulated Activities) (Amendment) Order comes into force. The Order will insert a new article 9A into the Financial Services and Markets Act 2000 (Regulated Activities) Order 2001 to make it clear that a sum is not a deposit for the purposes of article 5 of that Order if it is immediately exchanged for electronic money.
3 The first is Directive (EC) 46/2000 on the taking up, pursuit of and prudential supervision of the business of electronic money institutions (the Electronic Money Directive). The second is Directive (EC) 28/2000, which amends Directive (EC) 12/2000 (the Banking Consolidation Directive) in such a way as to include electronic money institutions in the definition of 'credit institution'.
4 See HM Treasury, 'Implementation of the Electronic Money Directive – A Consultation Document', October 2001 at www.hm-treasury.gov.uk.
5 See 'CP 117: The Regulation of Electronic Money Issuers', December 2001 at www.fsa.gov.uk.

(g) Bank and non-bank issuers of electronic money

10.41 Before considering the nature of the new regulatory regime, it is important to appreciate the distinction that is drawn between bank and non-bank issuers of electronic money. Although both may issue electronic money, the new regime will treat bank and non-bank issuers differently.

Commercial banks undertake a wide range of business activities and, by virtue of Point 5 of Annex 1 to the Banking Consolidation Directive, are already allowed to issue and administer means of payment, including electronic money, subject to compliance with the comprehensive prudential supervisory regime applying to them in accordance with that Directive. Therefore, for most banks that issue it, electronic money will merely be an element that will be taken into account by financial supervisors when analysing the bank's overall risk profile and the appropriate supervisory response. For most banks, electronic money issuance is not expected, at least initially, to form a major portion of their business activities.

Under the terms of the Electronic Money Directive, non-bank issuers will, on the other hand, be severely restricted in the activities they may undertake. These will be confined to the issuance of electronic money and the provision of closely-related financial and non-financial services. This means that any non-bank entity that is considering issuing its own electronic money will have to ring fence those issuance activities in a separate subsidiary. As a counter to these limitations on their business activities, non-bank issuers of electronic money will be subject to an altogether more targeted and, accordingly, less cumbersome regulatory regime than that applying to bank issuers[1].

As the Preamble to the Electronic Money Directive makes clear, '... the introduction of a separate prudential supervisory regime for *non-bank issuers of electronic money*, which, although calibrated on the prudential supervisory regime applying to *bank issuers* ... is justified and desirable because the issuance of electronic money does not constitute in itself, in view of its specific character as an electronic surrogate for coins and banknotes, a deposit-taking activity ..., if the received funds are immediately exchanged for electronic money'[2].

Unless otherwise indicated, the provisions outlined below apply to non-bank issuers only.

1 Notably as regards reduced initial capital requirements and the non-applicability of various solvency and large exposure provisions.
2 *Emphasis added.*

(h) The new regulatory regime

10.42 Both the Treasury and the FSA are responsible for implementing the regime established under the Electronic Money Directive into domestic law. Whereas the Treasury is responsible for implementing the necessary framework legislation, the FSA is responsible for imposing the specific rules that will apply. The new regime was scheduled to come into effect on 27 April 2002, although entities already operating on that date will have until 27 October 2002 to seek the requisite authorisations and prepare for the full impact of regulation[1].

In order to give effect to the requirements of the Electronic Money Directive, the Treasury has specified the activity of issuing of electronic money[2] as a *regulated activity* under the FSMA 2000. In order to achieve this, it amended the Financial Services and Markets Act 2000 (Regulated Activities) Order 2001 so as to include this activity within the list of regulated activities[3]. As the Treasury's Consultation Document made clear, the effect of doing so is twofold. First, it ensures that persons not authorised to do so under the FSMA 2000 (other than those with a waiver) will be prohibited from carrying on the business of issuing electronic money. Second, it enables the FSA to impose the remaining requirements of the Directive by making rules under sections 138 and 157 of the FSMA 2000.

Once the new regime is effective, it will be unlawful for entities (other than those with a waiver) to issue electronic money in the UK unless authorised to do so. Entities wishing to engage in the activity of issuing electronic money will therefore have to apply to the FSA for authorisation in just the same way as those wishing to carry on other regulated activities, or obtain appropriate waivers[4].

UK-established electronic money issuers (or those established outside the EU and carrying on their activities by way of business in the UK) will have to go through the Part IV Authorisation procedure and obtain a Part IV Permission[5]. Those established in other EU Member States (and carrying on their activities by way of business in the UK) will have to go through the inward passporting procedures established under the Banking Consolidation Directive[6] and comply with the requirements set out in Part II, Schedule 3 to the FSMA 2000[7].

Although the Electronic Money Directive requires Member States to prohibit non-authorised persons from carrying on the business of issuing electronic money, it nevertheless permits the grant, in certain circumstances, of waivers from some or all of its provisions. The waiver regime is designed to take small or locally-based electronic money issuers, such as those operating on a university campus, outside the scope of regulation. The Financial Services and Markets Act 2000 (Regulated Activities) (Amendment) Order gives effect to this waiver regime by giving the FSA the power to issue certificates to small electronic money issuers declaring that the issue of electronic money by them is not a regulated activity[8]. Thus, small electronic money issuers will be entitled to apply to the FSA for a certificate of waiver and, if granted[9], will be relieved of the burdens and cost of regulatory control[10].

1 This grace period was designed to allow electronic money issuers already in operation on 27 April 2002 time to bring their business operations and systems into compliance with the new regulatory regime.

2 In its draft implementing legislation, the Treasury defined 'electronic money' as 'monetary value, as represented by a claim on the issuer, which is: (i) stored on an electronic device; and (ii) accepted as a means of payment by persons other than the issuer.' This definition is a partial copy-out of the definition contained in the Electronic Money Directive. However, it omits the second limb of the definition contained in that Directive (which states that electronic money must be 'issued on receipt of funds of an amount not less in value than the monetary value issued'). The Treasury decided to omit this limb of the definition because it felt that it could give rise to a regulatory loophole, whereby an institution which issued electronic money at a discount could escape regulation altogether.

3 A draft version of the Financial Services and Markets Act 2000 (Regulated Activities) (Amendment) Order is annexed to the Treasury's Consultation Document. This Consultation Document is available at www.hm-treasury.gov.uk.

4 For further details of the single authorisation procedure established under the FSMA 2000, see Chapter 9, E-finance.

5 Non-bank issuers of electronic money will require a Part IV Permission limited to the activity of issuing electronic money. This is because the Electronic Money Directive restricts the activities of non-bank electronic money issuers to providing closely-related administrative services and other functions connected with electronic money issuance. Non-bank issuers of electronic money are expressly prohibited from granting any form of credit. Bank issuers of electronic money must apply for an additional Part IV Permission.

6 Just like banks, non-bank issuers of electronic money (which are already authorised in their home Member State) are entitled to a 'passport' to provide their services throughout the EU. This is because Directive (EC) 28/2000 amends the Banking Consolidation Directive in such a way as to include 'electronic money institutions' within the definition of the term 'credit institution'.

7 In the case of electronic money issuers established outside the UK, it is important to determine whether they can be said to be carrying on regulated activities (by way of business) in the UK. Only those persons carrying on regulated activities (by way of business) in the UK need apply for authorisation. For further details see Section 2.4 of the FSA Handbook, Authorisation Manual at AUTH and paragraph 10.10 above, which discusses (in the context of an analysis of banking regulation) the circumstances in which a person established outside the UK will be regarded as carrying on a regulated activity in the UK.

8 Electronic money issuers benefiting from this waiver regime will, however, have to submit periodic returns to the FSA to demonstrate that they continue to meet the criteria for waiver and to report on their outstanding electronic money liabilities. Should they grow in size so that they no longer qualify for a waiver, they will have to apply to the FSA for a full Part IV Permission.

9 A certificate of waiver may be granted if the amount that can be stored on the electronic money issuer's electronic storage device is limited to a maximum of €150 and at least one of the following criteria are met: (i) the total financial liabilities relating to electronic money activities do not normally exceed €5m and never exceed €6m; (ii) the electronic money issued by the issuer is only accepted as a means of payment by subsidiary, parent or sister companies of the issuer; or (iii) the electronic money issued by the issuer is accepted as a means of payment by not more than 100 persons *and* those persons are *either* located within a limited geographical area *or* they have a close financial or business relationship with the issuer.

10 It should be noted that electronic money issuers benefiting from a waiver will be subject to the requirements of the Money Laundering Regulations 1993 and the Money Laundering Rules. This is because their activities involve 'issuing and administering means of payment' within the meaning of Annex 1 to the Banking Consolidation Directive. For further details on the impact of the Money Laundering Regulations 1993 and the Money Laundering Rules, see paragraphs 10.14 and 10.15 above.

10.43 As alluded to above, the Treasury's implementing legislation is in the nature of a framework and, as such, it has been left to the FSA to impose many of the substantive requirements of the Electronic Money Directive using its rule making powers under sections 138 and 157 of the FSMA 2000. Broadly, the Directive requires electronic money issuers to have initial capital of at least €1m (or its sterling equivalent), own funds equal to or over 2% of the higher of the current amount or the average of the preceding six months' total financial liabilities, and have sound and prudent management, administrative and accounting procedures in place. Moreover, provision is made to ensure that funds held in exchange for the issue of electronic money are only invested in high quality liquid assets, that issuers redeem electronic money at par (for coins and banknotes or by transfer to a bank account) and that they limit their activities to electronic money issuance or closely-related services and under no circumstances grant any form of credit.

These requirements are designed to ensure the financial soundness and stability of electronic money issuers and ensure that bearers of electronic money are adequately protected. In its Consultation

Document, the FSA published the draft text of rules and guidance that will be applied to give effect to these requirements.

The Treasury's decision to use the regulatory framework already established under the FSMA 2000 means that, potentially, a whole range of additional provisions are brought into effect, which go much further than those required by the Electronic Money Directive. At the time of writing, the Treasury and the FSA were consulting on whether, as a matter of policy, these additional provisions should apply to electronic money issuers.

In particular, the Directive does not require electronic money issuers to be brought within the scope of the Financial Services Compensation Scheme, the Financial Ombudsman Scheme or the financial promotion regime. However, unless expressly disapplied, by virtue of the fact that the issuance of electronic money will be specified as a *regulated activity* these provisions would otherwise apply.

The Financial Services Compensation Scheme is designed to protect consumers in the event that a person regulated under the FSMA 2000 is unable to meet his liabilities[1]. The Treasury's preferred view is that the Scheme should not apply to electronic money issuers, as it feels that the risks posed to consumers are relatively low, whilst the cost of funding the Scheme (which would be levied on electronic money issuers themselves) could prove a barrier to entry into a market still very much in its infancy.

Similarly, the Treasury does not intend to make the marketing of electronic money subject to the financial promotion regime. Instead, a preference to rely on the general law of misrepresentation to protect consumers is shown. Again, its rationale boils down to cost[2].

Finally, the FSA has proposed that electronic money issuers should be included within the Financial Ombudsman Scheme from the time that they are authorised. As the FSA makes clear, this could be an important factor in encouraging public confidence in, and acceptance of, electronic money. However, the FSA are currently consulting on the cost effectiveness of this proposal.

1 See Chapter 9, E-finance.
2 As the Treasury makes clear, making the activity of issuing electronic money subject to the financial promotion regime would mean that electronic money could only be promoted by authorised persons or where an authorised person had approved the content of the promotion. Therefore, a retailer that accepted and distributed electronic money would not be able to promote it without first getting the promotion approved by an authorised issuer. This could significantly raise the cost of promoting electronic money.

(i) Electronic money – conclusions

10.44 What does the future hold for electronic money? According to Mondex International's Mike Young[1], in the future 'credit cards will still dominate ... and debit cards will be up and coming'. However, in his opinion, '... electronic cash will become popular in certain market segments where it has unique advantages for consumers or merchants who need its capabilities – such as certainty of payment, its applicability to all ages, two-way payment, and its suitability for lower values and micropayments. This would make it ideally suited to things like games playing, gambling, buying digital content or MP3-Format music, or in on-line auctions'.

Whether or not he will be proved right, only time will tell.

1 See 'The Future of E-Payments' at www.mondex.com.

12. FINANCIAL PRODUCTS

(a) Introduction

10.45 As we mentioned in first section of this chapter, many of the cyberbranches have long had their sights on the potentially lucrative corporate market and, as such, many have begun to offer their corporate clients a basic range of banking and related services on-line. However, in the corporate sphere, the funding requirements of larger players often extend well beyond the operation of simple bank accounts and the procurement of loans.

In addition to borrowing money from banks and other financial institutions, many corporates raise additional funds by issuing shares, bonds or commercial paper to investors. Further, many wish to buy goods from suppliers in foreign countries but need to obtain credit before making payments in foreign currencies. But what happens if the exchange rates move against them? How can they be sure that the supplier has shipped the goods before they pay for them? Equally, how can the supplier be sure that he is going to get paid before he ships them?

Sophisticated markets and paper-based systems have been developed over the years for coping with a range of complex financial transactions, but to what extent are these transactions now handled on-line? In order to give a flavour of some of the products currently available on-line, a few examples are considered below.

(b) E-debt securities

10.46 One area in which the Internet has gained a significant presence is the fixed-income market.

Tapping the debt markets is a more sophisticated process than raising money by way of traditional bank loan. Rather than borrowing money from a single bank or consortium[1] of banks, the bond markets allow the larger corporate borrower to access a broader and cheaper investor base. In return for investors lending money to the borrower, the borrower issues a document (or a series of documents) evidencing its debt obligations to them (a 'debt security') and agrees to repay the capital, together with interest[2], at a specified date in the future[3].

Herein lies the major attraction of the Internet: the ability to access a broader investor base and the relative ease with which a search for new bond investors can be made.

One of the less complex forms of debt security is commercial paper. Issued by large companies to finance short-term working capital requirements, commercial paper has a maturity range of a few months. Given these short maturity periods, investors tend to hold on until maturity, thereby creating far less liquid markets than those found in longer-term debt securities.

According to Jerome Lienhard, Senior Vice-President for Corporate Finance at Freddie Mac, '... commercial paper ... lends itself to direct issuance much more readily than bonds because it doesn't trade as much. It's more of a pure distribution game.'[4] Therefore, platforms have emerged which seek to exploit the Internet's capabilities as a global distribution network for commercial paper.

One system that has attempted to utilise these capabilities is cpmarket.com[5]. This US-based Internet platform provides a real-time link between institutional investors in and issuers of commercial paper. It operates as a conduit, allowing multiple issuers to distribute commercial paper through the platform, and facilitates the conduct of real-time transactions. Unlike other systems[6], the Internet-based software application can be accessed through any Internet browser without the need for specialised hardware applications. In order to gain access to the system, institutional investors must complete an on-line application form, accept an access agreement and obtain authorisation from each desired issuer. At present, institutional 'accredited investors' within the meaning of the US Securities Act 1933 can make use of the system; but, in certain circumstances, it may be made available to persons in the UK[7].

Other on-line platforms include single dealer sites, such as PrimeTrade[8] and JPMorganeXpress[9]. However, as Kelly Martin, global head of fixed-income at Merrill Lynch, has observed, 'single dealer sites are just the first step in a marathon race ... ultimately what clients want in many products is liquidity'[10]. Therefore, only multi-dealer sites, linking several dealers at once, can engender a move to a more liquid market.

1 Known as a syndicated loan. Syndicated loans allow the risk associated with a large loan to be spread between a number of banks.
2 The rate of interest depends on a variety of factors including the length of maturity of the instrument, the prevailing economic conditions and the perceived ability of the issuer to repay the capital. The rate of interest may be fixed or variable and in some cases the instrument will pay no interest at all (in which case it will be issued at a discount to its face value). The interest payable is generally referred to as the 'coupon'.
3 There are no hard and fast rules as to the characteristics of such instruments. Debt securities may be issued at a discount, convertible into shares, listed on a recognised exchange or only made available to a specific class of investor.
4 As quoted in *Euromoney*, July 2000, p 137.
5 See www.cpmarket.com.
6 Such as the system operated by Bloomberg, which requires specialised hardware applications.
7 In the UK, the services are only available to those with professional experience of the wholesale markets in commercial paper.
8 PrimeTrade is an Internet/intranet-based, real-time, global trading system, which is available to registered Credit Suisse First Boston clients. For further information, visit www.csfb.com/primetrade.
9 JPMorganeXpress is JP Morgan's premier electronic trading platform across multiple asset classes and across multiple time zones. For further information, visit www.jpex.com.
10 As quoted in *Euromoney*, July 2000.

10.47 BondVision epitomises this move. Since going 'live' in late August 2001, this European fixed-income trading platform has traded in some 500 euro-denominated fixed-income securities. By September 2001 daily trading had reached levels of €500m, with an average ticket of over €15m.

The new platform is the product of two Internet-based dealer-to-customer trading platforms and heralds the first major consolidation in European fixed-income electronic trading, through the merger of BondVision and BondClick. According to Gianluca Garbi, Chief Executive Officer of MTS SpA, 'This deal is evidence that the fixed-income market is moving towards consolidation at a faster pace than the equity market. The expertise and experience contributed by BondClick and its shareholders will not only ensure consolidation and liquidity in fixed-income on-line trading, but also deliver higher market efficiency and lower transactions costs.'

BondVision now boasts 25 leading market-makers participating on its platform; the most recent additions include Credit Suisse First Boston, Goldman Sachs International and Schroder Salamon Smith Barney.

A further success story in the on-line market is that of TradeWeb LLC[1]. Launched in 1998 with an investment by major bond dealers, the network now offers Internet-based electronic trade execution to institutional customers for US Treasuries. Moreover, the product line has since expanded to include additional highly liquid debt products, including US Agency debt, Euro-Denominated government debt and Agency mortgage-backed securities.

In July 2001, the network announced that its cumulative trading volume had surpassed the $5 trillion mark. The average daily trading volume stands over $20 billion and has reached more than $32 billion on more frenetic days. The unique multi-dealer trading model links 15 of the world's leading dealers of fixed-income securities to nearly 800 investment firms in North America and Europe.

However, along with the burgeoning success stories, there are also failures. In late October 2001, BondBook, LLC, the registered Alternative Trading System (ATS), closed its lines. After eight months of operation, the on-line trading platform for high grade and high yield corporate bonds announced its closure.

The main cause of failure is attributed to falling profits and a weak US stock market. According to BondBook's press release, '… the platform's ambitious model required a degree of behavioural change among market participants that BondBook's sponsors concluded was unlikely to be achieved in an acceptable timeframe given current market conditions.'

It remains to be seen whether BondBook's equity partnership, which is made up of Credit Suisse First Boston, Deutsche Bank AG, Goldman Sachs Group Inc, Lehman Brothers Holdings Inc, Merrill Lynch & Co Inc, Morgan Stanley Dean Witter & Co, Salomon Smith Barney and UBS Warburg re-initiates the enterprise under more favourable conditions.

In a market where many on-line trading platforms are seen to overlap, banks have begun to look at cutting costs. In 2001, the list of casualties included Visible Markets, eBond USA and TruMarkets. As the on-line market matures, platforms will either consolidate or fall by the wayside. Moreover, those wishing to eschew highly liquid US Treasuries may be put to the sword by the less profitable corporate market.

After an edgy start, the market is likely to mature very quickly. Therefore any successful entry or re-entry will depend on gaining a critical mass in a very short time.

1   See www.tradeweb.com.

(c) E-trade finance

10.48   In commercial transactions where the buyer and seller are in different countries, the normal risks associated with the transaction are increased. Often, buyers will be unwilling to make payment until they are sure that the goods are safely in transit and, equally, sellers will be unwilling to ship them until they are sure that they are going to get paid. Moreover, in cross-border transactions, the parties are less likely to know a great deal about the other's credit standing and if one party defaults, the other will be faced with a whole host of legal and procedural problems in trying to enforce the contract against him. In order to try and address these concerns, many turn to the international banking system for help, particularly the documentary credit system.

Broadly, a documentary credit is an undertaking from a bank (preferably in the seller's home country[1]) which provides that, subject to certain conditions being met by the seller, the bank (and not the buyer) will make payment to the seller in satisfaction of the moneys due under the terms of the underlying contract[2]. Usually, the conditions are that the seller must present to the bank certain documents representing the goods after they have been shipped and are in transit[3], within the time frame specified in the credit. Often, this is satisfactory for all concerned. Assuming that the seller can meet the terms of the credit, then he no longer has to worry about the inability of the buyer to pay[4]. From the buyer's perspective, this is equally satisfactory, as he is safe in the knowledge that payment will not be made unless and until the seller can prove to the bank that the goods are safely en-route.

Most documentary credits are governed by the ICC Uniform Customs and Practice for Documentary Credits (the UCP)[5]. The UCP seeks to establish an international code governing the operation of documentary credits and, as such, is designed to promote certainty and consistency in international trade. However, it is important to appreciate that the UCP does not, and is not intended to have, any force in law[6]. Therefore, if it is to apply, it must be incorporated, expressly or by implication, into the text of the credit[7].

1   If the parties agree that the seller is to receive an undertaking from a bank in his home country and the bank opening the credit (the issuing bank) has no branch in the seller's home country, it must instruct a bank in that country to act on its behalf (the correspondent bank). Where the correspondent bank agrees to act, it will be asked to confirm the undertaking that the issuing bank has given to make payment. The issuing bank will then give the correspondent bank details of the documents that the seller must present to obtain payment. Once payment is made, the correspondent

bank will look to the issuing bank for reimbursement together with, of course, its fee. As we will see later, sellers do not always receive undertakings from banks in their home country and, in these cases, they are forced to rely on unconfirmed credits which are often less satisfactory.

2 The bank's undertaking creates an obligation which is independent of the underlying sale of goods contract. Having agreed to enter into a documentary credit arrangement, the seller cannot then look to the buyer for payment unless the bank defaults.

3 Generally, these will include a bill of lading (which represents title to goods after they have been shipped and are in transit), an invoice and an insurance policy (to cover the goods during shipment). Other documents, such as certificates of origin and quality, may also be required.

4 Effectively, the seller is able to convert a credit risk on the buyer into a credit risk on the bank.

5 The UCP are drafted by the International Chamber of Commerce (the ICC) and the current edition was issued in 1993. In November 2001, the ICC issued a supplement to the UCP to deal with the growing number of documents that are presented electronically. For further information visit www.iccwbo.org.

6 See *M Golodetz & Co Inc v Czarnikow-Rionda Co Inc* [1980] 1 WLR 495, CA.

7 Article 1 of the UCP.

10.49 The UCP defines a documentary credit as 'any arrangement, however named or described, whereby a bank (the "Issuing Bank") acting at the request and on the instructions of a customer (the "Applicant") or on its own behalf,

■   is to make a payment to or to the order of a third party (the "Beneficiary"), or is to accept and pay bills of exchange ("Draft(s)") drawn by the Beneficiary; or

■   authorises another bank to effect such payment, or to accept and pay such bills of exchange (Draft(s)); or

■   authorises another bank to negotiate, against stipulated document(s), provided that the terms and conditions of the Credit are complied with'[1].

As will be apparent, it is possible to structure a documentary credit arrangement in a number of different ways. Common arrangements, however, include the use of standby credits[2], transferable credits[3] or revolving credits[4]. These may be revocable or irrevocable[5], confirmed or unconfirmed[6] or used in conjunction with a bill of exchange[7] if, for example, the buyer needs additional time to pay. However, the one thing that all documentary credit arrangements have in common is that they operate on a payment against document concept and, accordingly, given the paper intensive nature of documentary credit transactions, it does not take a great leap of the imagination to see the potential benefits that the Internet has to offer.

As Richard Caplehorn, Senior Counsel at Bolero International Limited has pointed out[8], statistics produced by the United Nations reveal that 7% of the total global cost of international trade is attributable to the need to issue paper shipping documentation; amounting to some US $420 billion per year. Therefore, if it were possible to replace this paper documentation with some kind of electronic messaging via the Internet, then the potential benefits to all concerned are obvious – and huge.

1 Article 2 of the UCP.

2 It should be noted that, technically, standby credits differ from true documentary credits. Under a true documentary credit arrangement, the bank's obligation to pay is a primary one. However, under a standby credit arrangement, the bank's obligation to pay only arises on the default of the customer. In effect, standby credits are more akin to guarantees.

3 Transferable credits allow the seller to ask the bank to make payment to a third party. Transferable credits are used to help finance transactions as the seller can, for example, ask the bank to make payment to his supplier.

4 Revolving credits are used when the buyer and seller trade on a regular basis. Under this type of arrangement, the bank agrees to pay the seller any sums due from time to time up to certain set limits.

5 Under a revocable credit arrangement, the bank can revoke its undertaking to the seller at any time up to the presentation of the documents specified in the credit. Under an irrevocable credit, the bank cannot do this. Obviously, for the seller, an irrevocable credit arrangement is preferable.

6 This distinction is only important where an issuing bank uses a correspondent bank in a foreign country. As will be recalled, where this type of arrangement is used, the seller must present the documents specified in the credit to the correspondent bank for payment. If the correspondent bank has confirmed the credit, then the seller will obtain the benefit of a payment undertaking from both the issuing bank and, more importantly, the correspondent bank in his home country. However, if the correspondent bank does not confirm the credit, then the seller will be forced to rely on a payment undertaking from a bank in a foreign country. Obviously, from the seller's point of view, a confirmed credit arrangement is preferable.

- **Crime risks** Unlike professional indemnity insurance, this class of insurance does not have any defined market and is bought relatively infrequently. As a consequence, it has traditionally been viewed as an add-on product to a client's main body of insurances, with the net result being that both proposals and wordings are far from bespoke. The highly variable wording of crime insurance policies can create a degree of uncertainty for the insured that in some ways detracts from its usefulness. As more and more businesses become concerned with Internet trading, the greater is the scope for new and varied forms of fraud. To ensure that crime insurance really is effective to a business, it will be necessary to ensure that a policy is tailored to that business's needs.

- **Employment practices liability** A standard employment practices liability policy, 'EPL' cover[1], is likely to cover losses for claims arising out of race, disability and/or sex discrimination, defamation, unfair dismissal, misrepresentation and breach of privacy and/or confidentiality. The normal policy does not often define clearly how the breach or discrimination must occur and thus can overlap with some proportion of the 'new' coverages. However, the big difference between the old and new is that standard EPL cover does not encompass all allegations which can flow from a company going on-line, for example inappropriate workplace, obscene publications, etc.

1 EPL is a reasonably new form of insurance but is treated as a 'traditional' cover for the purposes of this illustration. It is *not* to be confused with a traditional employer's liability policy covering physical injuries to employees.

(c) Traditional underwriting

11.16 Many proposal forms for the traditional policies do not address the risks arising from e-business. Generally, insurance law requires the insured to bring to the attention of the underwriters all material facts, which the underwriters as reasonable men consider to be relevant and material to their assessment and underwriting of the risk. In the fast changing environment of e-business, it may not always be easy to define what is relevant. This grey area presents a very real risk of dispute between insured and insurer but, nevertheless, the doctrine of utmost good faith in insurance contracts remains.

4. HOW WILL THE INSURANCE MARKET DEAL WITH PROPOSALS FOR E-INSURANCE?

(a) The traditional rule – utmost good faith

11.17 Given that the doctrine of utmost good faith is firmly enshrined in insurance law and practice, insurers were always entitled to rely upon the proposer to disclose every material fact pertaining to his proposal, in order to assess the risk of providing the insurance cover requested. The common law principle was codified by section 18 of the Marine Insurance Act 1906, which provides:

> '(1) ... the assured must disclose to the insurer, before the contract is concluded, every material circumstance which is known to the assured, and the assured is deemed to know every circumstance which, in the ordinary course of business, ought to be known by him. If the assured fails to make such disclosure, the insurer may avoid the contract.
>
> (2) Every circumstance is material which would influence the judgment of a prudent insurer in fixing the premium, or determining whether he will take the risk.'

Although found within a marine statute, the principle is applicable to every insurance policy. This applicability has been tested and firmly approved in recent times. In *CTI v Oceanus Mutual*[1], it was decided that a non-disclosed or misrepresented fact is a material fact if the prudent insurer would have wished to have taken it into account when reaching his decision regarding the risk or the premium. Following the decision in *Pan Atlantic Insurance Co v Pine Top Insurance Co*[2], the insurer in question can avoid a policy on the basis of a non-disclosed or misrepresented fact, but only if it induced him to insure on the terms in which he did. However, the Marine Insurance Act 1906 also provides that an insurer may be presumed to know matters of common notoriety or knowledge. Arguably, therefore, as the Internet becomes all pervading, will insurers be deemed to know what is broadcast on CNN, Reuters or the Internet news services?

1   [1984] 1 Lloyd's Rep 476, CA.
2   [1989] 1 Lloyd's Rep 568, CA.

(b) Will e-risks change the traditional method?

11.18   Can it still be said with confidence that an e-business will know more about its affairs than anyone else? For example, whilst it is commercially advantageous to be trading from one computer to an undefined number of countries using the Internet, how many e-businesses know exactly their responsibilities under the various consumer protection, product marketing or other relevant laws operating in such markets and jurisdictions? If an e-business does not know, how can its insurer?

The difficulty is potentially compounded by the fact that the traditional laws of commercial trading, which are long established, have had to be adapted to the new methods of business communication[1].

In the light of the new environment, an insurer may be expected to undertake a number of pre-policy risk assessments with the proposed insured, either at inception or on renewal, and these might include any or all of the following:

■   a survey by an IT security expert to check the security of the insured's financial arrangements and its arrangements for, amongst other things, data storage;

■   a legal audit of the insured's contractual arrangements, including standard terms of business, if any;

■   a survey by a web designer to check hypertext linking capabilities as well as methods of barring access to contract-making with persons in jurisdictions for which the insurer is not prepared to grant cover;

■   a compliance audit concerning e-mail policies for the purpose of preventing unauthorised use (which might require, for example, that this is restricted to business use only) and restricting the scope for defamatory communications; and

■   domain name vetting, including trade mark usage and entitlement[2].

This may well become a prerequisite for underwriting risk assessment even after the insurance contract between the parties has been created, if, for example, the methods employed in the insured's e-business were to change to a significant degree. The fluidity of the process for analysis and acceptance of e-business risk means we might find that by the end of a policy year an insurer may have determined to refuse to indemnify its insured from risks which prior to the start of the policy year were unforeseen and, by definition, had not therefore been disclosed.

Nevertheless, despite the problems associated with the principle of utmost good faith and its relationship with material non-disclosure, it is already apparent that the above methods are being adopted by insurers and are likely to become ever more sophisticated as time passes.

1   For example, we cannot yet be completely certain whether a contract made on the Internet is consummated through an act of acceptance or an actual communication of that acceptance to the offeror: both are possible.
2   An example of such a service can be found at www.hammondsuddardsedge.com/webvet.

(c)   What are the questions an insurer should ask when addressing a proposed e-risk?

11.19   Examples of areas that insurers will wish to cover in proposal forms are as follows:

■   **Business activities of the insured** Insurers will wish to understand the extent of the insured's e-business activities. For example, does the insured only have e-mail access for sending and receiving e-mails over the Internet, or does the insured have a presence on the Internet for providing information or advertising through a web server? Alternatively, the involvement of the insured on the Internet may be more extensive and the insured may be involved in e-commerce activities, ie the buying and selling of products, services or information over the Internet. Another area of Internet activity is hosting, ie the insured may provide hosting services to third parties. In order to assess the risk, the insurers first need to understand the extent of the e-business activities of the insured. In addition, the electronic world develops at a rapid pace and insurers should also enquire whether the insured is proposing any new business activities during the next 12 months.

■   **Website** Information on the insured's website can give rise to potential claims for infringement of intellectual property rights and/or libel. The insurer will wish to understand the nature of the insured's website, what procedures are in place for authorising the content of the website prior to publication and whether the content and structure of the website has been reviewed by a lawyer. Insurers may wish to raise specific enquiries as to when the insured first established a web presence, the number of visits to the website during the last 12 months and the anticipated number of hits during the next 12 months. Insureds will use their websites for different purposes and insurers will wish to discover whether the website has been set up to provide information only or whether it is a full e-commerce site capable of accepting on-line payments. In relation to authorisation of information on the website, insurers may wish to enquire whether the insured has procedures in place for authorisation of website content prior to publication and whether there is a written protocol in relation to how often and who monitors the insured's website. Further, if infringing material is posted on the website, does the insured have a procedure for removing such material?

■   **Hypertext linking** Some websites have links to other external websites and insurers may wish to confirm that the insured has a procedure in place to obtain consents to use any links or other material on its website. The *Shetland Times* case[1] is an example of the importance of obtaining consents.

■   **Chat rooms or bulletin boards** Insurers will wish to enquire whether the insured has any chat rooms or bulletin boards on its website, and who manages these.

■   **Domain names** If the insured is using brands on its websites, insurers may wish to enquire whether these are protected as registered trade marks in all the territories in which the insured operates.

■   **E-Commerce terms and conditions of trade** If the insured is involved in e-commerce business, insurers may want to confirm that the insured's website is structured in a way that it is an invitation to treat with a view to receiving offers to purchase rather than goods which are being offered for sale. For example, the website should be the equivalent of a shop window display enticing e-buyers to browse the products on display with a view to receiving offers to purchase. This is an important distinction as noted in the case of the £2.99 TVs in 1999[2]. In addition, insurers may wish to confirm that if the insured is involved in e-commerce activities its website is designed so that a potential buyer is forced to hypertext link to the terms and conditions before being allowed to purchase. An insurer's liability for the product liability claim, for example, may well depend upon validity and incorporation of the insured's limitation clauses.

- **Employees and e-mails** Most companies, whether they are involved in e-commerce activities or not, have now introduced computers with Internet access onto the desks of all employees. As a result, the companies may be exposed to claims from employees for, for example, infringement of employee's rights of privacy at work, as well as discrimination, harassment and dismissal claims. In addition, companies may be at the receiving end of claims by third parties as a result of Internet usage by their staff (for example, infringement of intellectual property rights, libel and damage to third party computer systems as a result of transmission of a virus). Insurers may wish to include the following questions in their proposal forms:

  - Does the insured monitor Internet access and e-mails for activities that could be harmful to the company or its employees?

  - Are all employees told never to reveal their passwords to anyone?

  - Have any employees been disciplined owing to malicious computer activity?

  - Does the company have a written protocol concerning e-mail usage by employees and use of the Internet?

  - Do e-mails sent out by employees contain a disclaimer?

- **Computer security** If the insured's computer systems are damaged the insured will suffer costs in restoring computer systems and records, and may suffer financial loss as a result of business interruption. Insurers will wish to consider the extent of the insured's security systems and backups. In relation to security, insurers may wish to enquire whether the insured has a firewall and who is responsible for maintaining and updating the firewall. In addition, insurers may wish to enquire whether the insured has any anti-virus software installed on its computer system and whether the insured has anti-virus scanning software. In relation to backups of computer data, insurers may wish to find out whether insureds have backups and where and how often these are stored. In addition, insurers will wish to be aware of whether the insured has an uninterrupted power supply in place. Insurers may also wish to enquire whether the insured has a disaster recovery plan to deal with situations where they may be unable to access electronic records.

1   *Shetland Times Ltd v Jonathan Wills & Zetnews Ltd* [1997] FSR 604.
2   See paragraph 2.04.

(d) What are the new forms of exclusion to traditional covers?

11.20   Some insurers are attempting to include an exclusion in traditional covers in relation to e-liability. A common exclusion is to proscribe any claim arising from a computer virus or hacker attack.

There are various problems that can arise from these types of exclusion. For example, there is a minimum wording requirement for indemnity insurance for professionals, including solicitors, surveyors and accountants. A policy which restricts cyber/computer virus cover may not comply with the profession's minimum wording. For example, it will be necessary to establish that the insured fell below the standard of the reasonably competent professional before claims can be made under the policy and it would not be sufficient for the loss to be suffered solely as a result of a virus or hacker attack. With or without a cyber exclusion, this will restrict the scope of indemnity under the policy in any event. It is difficult to imagine many situations where successful claims would arise against professionals for losses suffered as a result of computer viruses or hacker attacks where there has also not been negligence on the part of the professionals. In addition, there may be concurrent causes of claims against professionals and whilst one cause may be as a result of a virus or hacker attack, another cause of the same loss may result in the claim being covered under the policy. Each claim will depend upon its facts and a blanket cyber exclusion may well fail.

At present, there are no decided cases on this issue, but it is anticipated that it will not be long before claims are made against firms who transmit viruses, alleging, for example, that they were negligent in not ensuring that they had sufficient anti-virus software or a firewall in place. In such cover, arguments will be raised as to whether the cause of the loss was a failure to engage adequate security measures or contractors, or a pure (and excluded) cyber liability. Whatever the position, the imposition of blanket cyber exclusions is unlikely to succeed in excluding all liabilities arising from using the Internet. Exclusions will be construed by the court narrowly whenever the source of the claim is a normal activity of the insured.

(e) What are the new forms of cover?

11.21 Insurers that are trying to exclude e-liability cover from traditional covers are looking at the possibility of developing a specialist e-commerce policy so that the risks associated with such cover can be assessed.

In addition, some new companies have been set up which provide specialist e-commerce policies and related cover, such as professional indemnity cover for IT consultants and charge back cover.

5.   THE E-COMMERCE DIRECTIVE AND THE INTERNATIONALISATION OF E-LAW

(a) The E-Commerce Directive

11.22 The E-Commerce Directive[1] was adopted on 4 May 2000, and EU Member States were given until November 2001 to implement it[2]. It was implemented in the UK in August 2002.

The purpose of the Directive is the regulation of the EU Single Market in relation to e-commerce. It identifies obstacles to the smooth operation of e-commerce derived from practices in the different Member States and the legal uncertainties which exist in relation to trade between entities in these different jurisdictions.

The Directive's philosophy is one of requiring Member States to facilitate commerce by electronic methods in areas where there are presently inhibitions which can effectively be removed (for example, requirements for printed documents or autograph signatures). The other area of significant impact is in relation to choice of law in cases where the parties to an e-commerce transaction are resident in different Member States. Presently, the Single Market operates on the presumption that applicable law for the conduct of a cross-border service provided within the EU will be the law of the consumer's home state[3]. However, e-commerce opportunities will be severely hampered if an e-business has in effect to make certain it complies with the consumer laws of all 15 Member States, rather than being entitled to oblige those consumers to contract with it subject to the protections in its own applicable law. Thus, the thrust of the E-Commerce Directive is to require Member States to adjust their laws so as to favour home state (that is, service provider state) rather than host state (consumer state) laws for the regulation of e-commerce contractual relationships.

1 Directive (EC) 31/2000 on certain legal aspects of Information Society Services, in particular electronic commerce in the Internal Market.
2 Further commentary on the commercial and contractual aspects of the Directive may be found in Chapters 2 (E-contract) and 6 (E-marketing).
3 Thus, for example, where an investment service is provided pursuant to the passport arrangements under the Investment Services Directive (EEC) 22/93, as amended, the law regulating conduct of business by the investment firm will be the law of the consumer's home state.

(b) Impact on insurers

11.23   In relation to the provision of insurance cover, the jurisdictional approach of the E-Commerce Directive has the following effects:

■   where a UK insurer accepts risk in relation to an e-business in the UK, the latter's risk profile may be simplified if those who contract with it from within the EU are obliged to do so under prevailing law in the UK (rather than the consumer protection laws in their own states); and

■   where the UK insurer accepts risk in relation to an e-business operating from another Member State and engaging in e-commerce with UK customers, the opposite will in principle apply: while formerly the insurer would have had the luxury of assessing risk on the basis of applicability of UK consumer laws, it is likely that the relevant law will now be that of the home state of the e-business[1].

Meanwhile, of course, since the Directive obliges Member States generally to liberalise their legal regimes so as to facilitate e-commerce and eliminate physical obstacles to it, the sort of e-risks which could arise and require insurance cover are likely to multiply. This might be because:

■   moving from a physical to an electronic or virtual environment leads to uncertainty of approach, potential for system failure and the like; or

■   discrepancies in approach will continue to exist between the Member States even after purported implementation of the Directive.

The Directive introduces (or, to be more precise, requires the introduction of) a more streamlined approach to e-commerce within the EU; but the capacity of the Member States (while retaining their own legal systems) to give independent and subjective effect to this sort of measure means that a degree of legal uncertainty or anomaly is bound to remain.

Moreover, the Directive has no direct effect outside the EU. If an insurer in the UK accepts risk in relation to an e-business in the US or Australia, then it will still need to consider the laws affecting that e-business's operations as being the relevant home state law as well as, potentially, the laws in each customer's jurisdiction.

1 The same analysis applies where an overseas insurer based in another Member State is concerned.

(c) Assessing e-risks

11.24   In the light of the E-Commerce Directive, but also in absence of any other prescriptive e-laws agreed through international convention[1], the insurer has to be prudent when assessing e-risks. The insurer should examine its own modes of contracting and may need to consider territorial exclusions where the insured is offering services to customers in territories where relevant laws are considered by the insurer to provide for the creation of excessive exposure. Further (and to the extent applicable in the circumstances), it will need to bear in mind what percentage of an insured's proposed on-line contracts is likely to be of a business-to-business nature and what percentage is likely to be business-to-consumer. Other considerations include the proposer's place of establishment, the requirement for registration before a transaction can take place[2] and the process or mode of contracting which the proposer will use in its business dealings with others. In the context of the last of these points, it will be important to bear in mind:

- how the proposer's website is structured;

- what jurisdiction and choice of law clauses are provided in the contract between the proposer and its customer(s);

- whether there are alternative dispute resolution (ADR) clauses in this contract;

- whether the proposer's website has software enabling the encryption of personal details;

- whether anti-virus software is in use; and

- how often the material contained on the website is monitored, for example to check against intellectual property infringements.

1 Although much of what we think of as e-commerce can proceed in accordance with, and be regulated by, existing legal principles at both national and supra-national level, aspects are crying out for a universally applicable set of rules. In the absence of 'e-laws' agreed in accordance with international convention, some would argue that there is an opportunity for English law to become (through what is in effect a process of passive adoption) the default legal regime for numerous aspects of e-commerce, in the same sort of way, and for broadly similar reasons, that it has been for shipping law and insurance law.

2 This will see insurers registering in several jurisdictions where they wish to trade away from their home domicile. What effect it will have on existing cross-border trading is yet to be seen.

6.   RISK AVOIDANCE AND PRUDENT MANAGEMENT

11.25   An insurance policy is not in itself a risk management programme, although it should form an important part of such a programme. There are a number of reasons for implementing a risk management programme as part of the prudent management of an Internet business, which will impact upon both the cost and extent of insurance cover required. As a result, considerable benefits should flow from implementing a risk management programme, namely:

(a) Reduced insurance premiums

11.26   The insurance premium is likely to be reduced if a business can demonstrate that it has an appropriate risk management programme in place. Indeed, once a business reaches a certain size of turnover or operates in a particular field of risk, it may not be possible to obtain insurance cover at all, or at any rate it may be possible to do so only for limited categories of risk that the business encounters, unless an appropriate risk management scheme can be demonstrated.

As mentioned previously, insurers may require their own independent consultants to carry out a risk audit before agreeing to provide insurance cover for the business. Usually, the cost of the risk audit will be deducted from the premium paid by the business. At the other (smaller) end of the business spectrum, insurers will be content to accept a properly completed proposal form either in writing or, increasingly, on-line.

(b) Reduced numbers of claims

11.27   It may be a comfort to have insurance to deal with a claim, but there is always an operational cost to the business that can be very high for time spent in dealing with that claim. For instance, a business will not usually be able to recover under an insurance policy for the time of the personnel involved in investigating and assisting in the defence of a third party claim, unless the cover specifically deals with those costs. Further, those personnel are unable to generate income for the business whilst they are so involved.

Similar considerations apply to first party claims. In particular, insurance policies do not simply pay fixed sums of money for business interruption but, rather, it is incumbent upon the business to prove the loss that it has suffered. It is time-consuming and expensive to have to prove precisely what loss has been caused to the business by, for example, server down time or a virus infection[1].

1   While business interruption policies may include the cost of commissioning an accountant to calculate loss, the cost of a protracted dispute or the size of the loss is rarely insured within that policy.

(c) Avoiding duplicated insurance

11.28   It is prudent to ascertain that the business is not subject to double insurance. If, for example, insurance cover is already in place under an existing policy for defamation, there is unlikely to be any benefit in including such cover within an insurance policy for 'e-activities' because this leads to a duplication of this cover. Far from providing additional cover, this is a waste of premium and may lead to complex disputes between insurers as to which of them will pay for any claim which may be made and in what proportions. The sensible approach is for the e-business to review the extent of its existing cover before simply proposing for blanket e-liability cover. Purchasing cover for e-liabilities requires a holistic assessment of the whole of the business activities of the insured.

(d) Jurisdiction issues

11.29   Doing business on the Internet can expose a business to claims in potentially every jurisdiction around the globe[1]. It is essential for a business to consider what limitations it needs to impose upon its global exposure and to ensure that its insurance cover matches that exposure. As a starting point, if the business considers that doing business in X presents it with too many legal or regulatory risks of its own, it will want to take steps to make sure that residents of X cannot contract with it through the website, etc. Given that it has taken this step, there will then be little point in having e-liability cover that includes claims arising from dealings in X, and the scope of its e-liability insurance can be negotiated accordingly.

1   Or if not actually in such jurisdictions, then at least subject to the laws of such jurisdictions.

(e) Good employment practice

11.30   A good risk management programme will provide for an IT security policy setting out clear guidelines to the employees of the business as to what is and what is not permitted in the way in which, for example, they utilise e-mails, the Internet and the business's IT systems. This encourages good employment practices and should provide a comprehensive basis upon which employees can operate (as well as laying the ground rules for the discipline or dismissal of employees who abuse or fail to comply with operational procedures).

(f) Establishing the business risks

11.31   Perhaps the most important part of a risk management exercise is to establish precisely what risks the business is prepared to bear and what areas of risk it wants to limit by some means, ie contractual terms or an insurance policy. All business involves risk and a business cannot insure itself against all of its risks in any event. The business also needs to balance the cost of risk avoidance with the likelihood of the risk materialising, for example in terms of lost custom, because of unacceptable contract terms or insurance premium cost. Further, a business needs to consider how much cover it will require in order to give it adequate protection in the event of a claim.

Having established that there are sound reasons for fashioning a risk management programme for an Internet business that complements its insurance cover, it will then be necessary to put such a programme in place. A detailed review of risk management issues for an Internet business is necessarily beyond the scope of this chapter, but the key issues are likely to be or include the following:

- the nature of the business conducted, for example selling products, services or information;

- the nature of the competition, for example a business is likely to be operating in such a way that its competitors might consider it to be infringing their intellectual property rights;

- the number of personnel;

- volumes and methods of payment; and

- jurisdictions in which the business trades.

11.32 It is suggested that the starting point will be the nature of the business and its target market. Anecdotal evidence from insurers which have carried out surveys of Internet businesses suggests that many on-line businesses, particularly when they first start up, do not have rudimentary security such as firewalls and virus checkers in place. These precautions need not be expensive to introduce and should be obtained. Thereafter, an internal security policy for employees of the business should be developed, for example the proper use of passwords and IT equipment[1], and the parameters within which personnel are permitted to use the Internet and, in particular, e-mails.

As regards risk management measures related to insurance issues, discussions with insurers or insurance brokers or visits to their websites will reveal which features insurers require that will reduce the premium and therefore the risk to the business. For example, insurers which are prepared to insure e-businesses will welcome:

- the ability to demonstrate that the website has been vetted to ensure that it does not infringe copyright or trade marks;

- that appropriate terms of business have been incorporated into the website;

- that there is a regular vetting of the website to ensure that any defamatory or obscene material posted on to the website is removed as quickly as possible and is not forwarded through the website to others; and

- the ability to demonstrate that the IT systems used by the business have secure firewalls and encryption processes in line with current industry standards.

1   Which includes ensuring that it is switched off or immobilised when inactive, to prevent breaches of security after hours.

7.   E-CLAIMS

(a) Subrogation

11.33 Subrogation, under newly evolving insurance policies covering e-commerce claims, has, to date, been rarely pursued. Examples of areas where insurers may wish to try to make a subrogated recovery include intellectual property claims and claims in respect of professional negligence of computer security companies. There are, however, potential hurdles to e-subrogation as follows:

- **Contractual terms and conditions** Computer and licensing agreements may include limitation on warranties, limitations on damages (providing for maximum recovery limited to the cost of the product or services rather than consequential damages including lost profits), restrictions or elimination of subrogation rights and other provisions which may make the subrogation effort economically unrealistic. However, whether or not these provisions are enforceable will depend on a case-by-case analysis of the reasonableness of the provisions.

- **Relationship between insurance coverage and subsequent subrogation** Many jurisdictions are still split on the interpretation of 'physical damage' in computers. Some jurisdictions are examining loss of use and loss of functionality of computers as determinative of physical damage. In relation to policy coverage, underwriters will wish to argue that, for example, a power outage did not adversely affect the computer equipment's ability to perform its intended function and its inherent ability to accept the process data. However, underwriters will wish to reverse their position if bringing a subrogated recovery action as a result of the power loss.

- **Quantifying the loss** Losses in e-commerce cases are often very difficult to assess. Claims often result which include lost personnel time in finding the virus or negligent programming in a product, lost production, cost of replacement software and other relatively intangible damages. In addition, protecting evidence on a computer system is not a simple task and the use of experts on site before moving any electronic medium is usually necessary for the protection of the evidence.

- **Economic loss** The doctrine of economic loss states that where a product malfunctions and damages only itself there is no recovery under the law of tort for damages. It is possible to bring claims for negligent misrepresentation as an exception to the doctrine of economic loss. For example, where a computer consultant advises on but does not sell a computer product, or where the consultant both advises on and sells computer products, the critical question will be whether the information is an important part of the product. If so, it may be possible to bring a claim for negligent misrepresentation.

- **Assets of the 'wrongdoer'** If the wrongdoer has no or insufficient assets, the subrogation effort will be an effort without benefit. However, in some cases there may be insurance cover, for example an employee who uses his new employer's computer to destroy the old employer's computer data may trigger the insurance coverage of the new employer.

8. THE INTERNET AND THE LONDON INSURANCE MARKET – LMP 2002

11.34 London is the insurance capital of the world. The London market's survival is dependent upon the ability to accept risks where the local market is uncertain or is exhausted in terms of its capacity. The City of London's square mile has traditionally offered brokers a choice of competing insurers in a single location. It has therefore acquired a unique skill base centred around Lloyd's. Whatever cannot be covered locally can usually find capacity, at a price, in the London insurance market. It is the point at which much of the wholesale reinsurance market deals with the inward retail demand of insurers covering business e-risk from around the world.

But the London market's procedures have become antiquated: production of paperwork is notoriously slow; notifying and reporting to a subscription market of sometimes dozens of insurers subscribing to a substantial risk is slow and expensive for a broker to serve. In response, Lloyd's and the London companies market have responded with the London Market Protocol (currently LMP 2002). This provides for the electronic placing of cover and development of claims reporting procedures and payments controlled by a single lead insurer, with instructions given electronically on behalf of all insurers following the risk.

The first LMP contract slip has now been placed and registered electronically and, having been slow to respond, insurers are now quickly moving to using the Internet to report and communicate. As information technology becomes an increasingly familiar part of the practice of the industry, its underwriters will become more willing to assess the premiums required to spread the costs of business e-risk through insurance.

9. THE WORLD TRADE CENTER AND E-TERRORISM

11.35 The political and terrorist tensions of the world have collided with the commercial assessment of risk in the most dramatic way. Catastrophic losses from 11 September 2001, estimated in excess of US $48 billion, are being shared by insurers around the world. This is restricting available cover, especially in areas of e-risk. It is also driving premiums upwards. This in turn is encouraging new but very cautious capital to enter the market to support new underwriting, especially in Bermuda.

The businesses occupying the World Trade Center were businesses wholly reliant on utilising ever-changing information about the state of the world's financial markets. Cyber traffic and the free flow of digitalised information was the lifeblood of that market. The world's biggest e-commerce claim has therefore begun to unravel. Insurers will be asked to pay the lion's share of the business interruption losses flowing from that catastrophe. Where gaps in cover emerge, new pressures and demands for additional cover will be made.

The incidents on 11 September 2001 have prompted reinsurers to impose terrorist exclusions to available cover. These in turn have restricted the cover available to e-businesses. At the same time, hacktivism (the abuse of the Internet for political rather than solely criminal means) has become an increasing issue and resulted in claims. The 2000 US Presidential election saw the supporters of both sides deface each other's sites. The prospect of on-line elections being manipulated by hacktivists may be arriving soon, while even the Pentagon has had its security breached by hacktivists out to prove a point. Both Palestinians and Israelis have set up bogus websites and stolen credit card details for political ends. Insurers, at least for the moment, are going to exclude from policies any liability to indemnify losses resulting from what will be regarded as random attacks from an unknown source or risk.

10. CONCLUSION

11.36 As this chapter demonstrates, using the Internet exposes businesses to new areas of risk that are not covered by traditional insurance policies, though inevitably there are grey areas where traditional policies may respond.

The insured must appreciate that the doctrine of utmost good faith in insurance proposals and contracts continues to be the fundamental principle upon which insurers are entitled to rely. Therefore they must remain vigilant in informing insurers of material facts. Further, this obligation may well exist during the life of the policy if, for instance, an e-business significantly changes or adds to its area of operation.

E-risk is a new area of business for insurers; thus it is understandable that they are entering it with a degree of caution. At the time of writing, the tendency is either to provide very wide coverage with relatively low limits of cover or to provide much higher limits of cover after extensive third party analysis of the risk and with detailed policy wordings trying to anticipate precisely which eventuality will or will not be covered. Further, UK insurers tend to sell policies to insureds within the same jurisdiction (albeit providing cover for their insureds for claims arising in other jurisdictions) so that any legal dispute with an insured can be dealt with under UK law and, in particular, the principle of 'utmost good faith'.

Insurance for e-liabilities is no substitute for risk management of an e-business, but must properly be part of that process.

The Internet creates a vast new market both for insurers (particularly since insurance is an ideal product that can be marketed on the Internet) and for insurance brokers, whose independent advice on the issues highlighted in this chapter will be sought.

The resolution of the losses and adjustment of the business interruption claims flowing from the World Trade Center catastrophe are shaping the global market's ability to adapt to the insurance demands of e-business. At the same time, the investigation of the incident's commercial losses is identifying where more protection is required. But as the CEO of AIG (American International Group Inc) himself has indicated, although the market can sustain one World Trade Center catastrophe, whether it can sustain a succession of terrorist outrages without imposing blanket restrictions in cover is questionable. As we have sought to demonstrate in this chapter, the Internet is just one more theatre in which political protest and insurgency is made and fought. E-risk is now endemic and impossible for business and insurance to ignore.

Traditional policies will adapt and cover will be rewritten. Specialist broking knowledge and risk assessment will be required. The continued exclusion of cyber liability is likely to recede over time. However, the market's ability to generate profit will dictate how quickly progressive insurers will underwrite e-risk and at what level. While there are a number of signs that substantial insurers are seeking to develop new products, until the financial losses resulting from the World Trade Center incidents are resolved, it is too early to predict how and when the traditional forms of cover will be forced to adapt.

E-corporate

1. INTRODUCTION

12.01 As will be apparent from the earlier chapters in this book, opportunities for companies to use the Internet and other e-commerce applications for their commercial operations have grown enormously in the past few years. Given the sophistication with which many companies can now communicate electronically with their customers (and, of course, internally through the use of intranets linking up their employees), companies, both public and private, are increasingly keen to be able to use similar electronic means to simplify the process of corporate governance and shareholder communications.

This chapter will explore the three main areas where electronic methods of communication are beginning to make an impression on corporate governance and investor relations, and will examine the scope of the existing law in permitting this use, the impact of relevant legislation and areas where further reform may still be necessary:

- **Communications with shareholders** The corporate website and the use of other new media, delivery of certain statutory documents (for example, the annual report and accounts, summary financial statements, notices of general meetings and proxy appointments), annual general meetings and electronic voting systems.

- **Communications between directors/senior executives** The holding of board and other meetings and the corporate intranet.

- **Communications with Companies House** The filing and viewing of documents and the incorporation and re-registration of companies.

Most companies are looking to move as much of their corporate communications material as possible on to the Internet (or other forms of electronic communication), motivated by the twin aims of improving channels of communication and reducing corporate communication costs. However:

- improving communications is still dependent on shareholders having the correct platform(s) for making use of electronic materials. A public company with a large shareholder base will generally have institutional shareholders with highly developed technology for receiving and storing materials sent electronically. The same cannot automatically be assumed of a company's private individual shareholders;

- the cost/benefit advantage in communicating electronically with shareholders is still unclear. There may well not be significant financial savings for a company until the majority of private shareholders elect to use electronic means of communication, because whatever new electronic systems are approved by law reform, the law will still require a company to appeal to the lowest common denominator, and that means printing hard copies of annual reports, etc, for those shareholders who are not on-line.

2. THE LEGISLATIVE FRAMEWORK FOR CORPORATE GOVERNANCE ISSUES

12.02 A general summary of the current legislative framework and reform proposals is set out below.

(a) Sources of law for corporate governance issues

12.03 The primary sources of law governing the manner in which a company established in England or Wales communicates with its shareholders, files statutory returns, etc, are the Companies Acts 1985–89[1] (the Companies Acts). The Companies Acts establish fundamental law for companies in general. They supplement the common law, which is still applicable in relation to aspects of corporate governance[2]. Other relevant sources, as appropriate, include the following.

- A company's articles of association. Every company has default articles of association derived from regulation[3], but (within the limits established by the Companies Acts) may introduce variations to the default set. The articles govern the relationship of the company with its directors, officers and shareholders, and their respective rights against and relationships with each other. One must look first to the articles to check, for example, the procedure for holding board meetings, and whether there are special rights and privileges associated with different classes of share issued by the company.

- If the company's shares are admitted to the London Stock Exchange Official List, then aspects of the UK Listing Authority Rules[4] will be relevant, as these Rules regulate the company's and its directors' duties to the London Stock Exchange.

1 It is understood that the Government is proposing to consolidate the Companies Acts and introduce further statutory reforms of company law. However, it is unlikely that any such legislation will take effect before 2003.
2 For example, directors' fiduciary duties: see *Regal (Hastings) Ltd v Gulliver* [1942] 1 All ER 378, HL.
3 The Companies (Tables A to F) Regulations 1985 (SI 1985/805). Table A contains the default articles applicable to a company (public or private) which is limited by shares.
4 For further details as to the provenance of the UKLA Rules, see Chapter 9, E-finance.

(b) Interpreting current law for an electronic environment

12.04 As with so many areas of law, the Companies Acts were conceived before the Internet and other electronic media came to prominence. As a consequence, there has been some debate as to whether existing company law dealing with corporate governance issues, in particular various provisions of the Companies Acts, could be interpreted in such a manner as to acknowledge and encompass the use of new technologies[1]. Take, for example, the requirement that the notice convening a company's annual general meeting should be '*in writing*'[2]. Since the Companies Act 1985 (CA 1985) does not itself define what is meant by this expression, one has to rely upon the Interpretation Act 1978[3], which provides that in Acts of Parliament, references to writing 'include typing, printing, lithography, photography and other modes of representing or reproducing words in a visible form'. At first sight this would seem to include text on a computer screen. However, the prudent view[4] is that the word *'permanent'* should be implied in addition to *'visible'* and that a document on screen is not *'in writing'* until it is printed out.

It may be informative to debate such points (and in some cases, current legislation may admit a more flexible interpretation than the CA 1985 in relation to the meaning of *'in writing'*). However, this entire area of the law has been transformed through the introduction of an order (perhaps the first of a series in the corporate field) under the Electronic Communications Act 2000 (ECA 2000)[5].

1   See, eg Tunkel, 'Investor Relations, New Media and the Law' (2000) 7 JIBFL 250.
2   The CA 1985, s 369.
3   The Interpretation Act 1978, Sch 1.
4   This view is reinforced by the wording of the CA 1985, s 723, which allows the use of computers for the storing of company records 'so long as the recording is capable of being reproduced in a legible form'. See also, for example, the Financial Services (Regulated Schemes) Regulations 1991, reg 6.02.2 with respect to the keeping of a register for an authorised unit trust scheme, where the register must be maintained 'in a manner capable of being reproduced in a legible form'.
5   The parameters of the ECA 2000 and the power to make orders that facilitate electronic signature and delivery of documents currently required to be in writing and autographically signed have been discussed more fully in Chapter 3, E-liability.

(c) Basic framework of the Companies Act 1985 (Electronic Communications) Order 2000

12.05   On 22 December 2000, following a lengthy consultation exercise undertaken by the Department of Trade and Industry (DTI), the Companies Act 1985 (Electronic Communications) Order 2000 came into force[1].

The Order makes provision for certain types of communication between a company and its shareholders to take electronic form and enables companies to be incorporated at Companies House, and to deliver certain documents to Companies House, by electronic means. In the Order 'electronic communication' has the meaning given to it in the ECA 2000[2]. The definition is intended to cover all known forms of electronic communication and any future ones which new technology may produce. More specifically, it covers communication by telephone, facsimile, e-mail and on CD-ROM.

It is important to note that the Order has a permissive rather than a compulsive approach. In no way are companies, shareholders or Companies House *required* to use electronic communication: the Order simply *enables* them to do so (in circumstances where both sender and recipient agree to this).

The Order is drafted in such a way as to provide safeguards for those shareholders who may prefer hard copies of documents or have no equipment by which to receive information electronically[3]. The approach is that shareholders are required to 'opt in' to electronic communications rather than be taken to agree by default[4]. Equally, it would seem that shareholders will not be able to demand electronic transmission of documents as a right if the company in which they hold shares does not wish to provide them electronically with that information.

The Order amends Table A in line with its other amendments to ensure that, for companies that adopt Table A in the future, full account is taken of the amendments concerning electronic communications[5]. But the Order goes further than this in relation to corporate articles: the Order has the effect that any provisions in a company's *existing* articles that would prevent the company concerned from taking advantage of the amendments in the Order are overridden[6].

1   SI 2000/3373.
2   The ECA 2000 is discussed in greater detail in Chapter 2, E-contract.
3   See, for example, article 12 of the Companies Act 1985 (Electronic Communications) Order 2000, pursuant to which the accounts and annual reports must be sent '... to such address ... notified to the company by that person for that purpose', meaning that if the shareholder has notified a postal address only, then it is that address which must be used.

4   Therefore, the regime of the Order will not permit a company to write to all its shareholders and state that, to the extent that it does not hear from them by a given date to the contrary, their consent to electronic service in future is presumed to have been given. This may be regarded as unfortunate, since it considerably weakens the impact of the Order in circumstances where shareholders are reluctant communicators; it forces the rate of progress to proceed at the pace of the slowest shareholders.

5   Article 32(1) and Schedule 1 to the Order.

6   This provision will be of most use to public companies with large shareholder populations, where seeking an amendment to the articles to give effect to the regime of the Order would in itself be time-consuming and expensive. However, the Institute of Chartered Secretaries and Administrators has recommended that companies should, in fact, consider revising their articles to provide specifically for electronic communication.

(d) The ICSA Best Practice Guide

12.06   The Companies Act 1985 (Electronic Communications) Order 2000 is sparse on prescriptive detail[1], presumably in the interest of providing companies with the flexibility to organise their own approach to electronic communication. The Institute of Chartered Secretaries and Administrators (ICSA) has published a Best Practice Guide on Electronic Communications[2], which many companies will most likely wish to follow. It contains guidance, for example, on the process of offering shareholders the facility to use electronic means of communication and recommends that they have the ability to change their choice at any time.

ICSA's advice on this issue[3] may be summarised as follows:

- companies should (after taking proper advice) take steps to amend their articles of association specifically to provide for the use of electronic communications;

- if a company decides to offer the facility to use electronic means of communication, it should send a letter, by post, to each shareholder, detailing which documents will be available via which means and explaining the procedure that will be adopted in each case;

- the option to continue to receive any and all communications in hard copy by post should be clearly explained. Shareholders should be told how they may register their choices and that, in the absence of any response, they will continue to receive information by post;

- companies will need to make clear to shareholders that they will all continue to be treated alike, whether they take up the option of receiving electronic documents, expressly ask to be notified by post or express no view either way;

- companies will need to explain to those electing to receive information electronically that the obligation is to send the information, and that the company will not be responsible for the material actually reaching the recipients (ie for any failure in transmission which is outside the company's control). Where e-mail is sent to an incorrect address, the system will usually generate a fairly quick, if not immediate, notification that the message cannot be delivered. If this happens, the company would be expected to revert to sending paper copies by post to the shareholders affected;

- in any event, a company should notify shareholders that it reserves the right to revert to postal delivery where there is some reason (for example, a failure of its server) that prevents it from providing an electronic service;

- a company should make available on its website a facility enabling shareholders to change their choice at any time. This will obviously make it easier for any new user of the Internet to elect to use that medium in future;

- a company should give shareholders the opportunity to update their details at least every three years although it is recommended that an automatic reminder is included in each communication sent out; and

■ a prominent reminder encouraging shareholders to keep the company informed of any change in contact details (whether it be a postal address, e-mail address or anything else) should be placed on the corporate website.

1 For example, there is no indication given as to how agreement should be reached between a company and its shareholders to communicate electronically (other than that it seems as though it will not be possible for consent to electronic communication to be presumed from the other party's silence). Nor is any guidance given to companies in relation to the manner of publishing reports and accounts on a website.
2 For a summary of the main recommendations in the Guide, see the review in *The Company Secretary*, November 2000, pp 2–3 or visit the ICSA website at www.icsa.org.uk (note also the Electronic Communications Update Guidance Note, ref 011103, also available on the ICSA website).
3 Appendix 3 of the Guide.

(e) The need for further reform

12.07 There are many areas where methods of electronic communication could prove useful to companies that the Companies Act 1985 (Electronic Communications) Order 2000 does not touch on. These include 'virtual' annual general meetings (AGMs) and electronic shareholder voting[1]. Opinion on these topics appears to be divided and it is clear that there will be much discussion on these, and related issues, in the future as the drive to modernise company law continues[2].

1 A consultative paper issued by the Steering Group in October 1999 entitled *Modern Company Law for a Competitive Economy: Company General Meetings and Shareholder Communications* (URN 99/1144) can be found at www.dti.gov.uk/cld/review.htm.
2 By way of example, the Steering Group has addressed (in the October 1999 consultation document) the question of whether a company should be permitted to hold a 'virtual' general meeting, substituting interactive communication through an electronic bulletin board for face-to-face contact. This issue is further considered at paragraph 12.16 below.

3. COMMUNICATIONS BETWEEN A COMPANY AND ITS SHAREHOLDERS

(a) Using the corporate website and other new media

12.08 The corporate website is an increasingly important tool by which a company can communicate with the outside world. Companies worldwide use their websites to promote their services and products and some companies also use their websites for ancillary or development purposes (for example, recruitment). The use of the website as a focal point for communication with shareholders, however, is still a relatively new matter[1].

For those individual shareholders able to receive electronic communications, the corporate website can be an invaluable source of information. Aside from being a means of receiving the usual communications required by statute, access might also be gained to information previously available only to institutions and analysts (for example analysts' presentations)[2].

Companies may also want to use CD-ROMs to reach shareholders and often these can be designed to integrate with the corporate website, to launch applications on the website, etc. Most home computers have the hardware and software needed to read and work from CD-ROMs. Not as many have state-of-the-art software and modems for the most efficient use of the Internet (though even a basic Internet e-mail system and a 14,400 bps modem will suffice for the purposes of sending and receiving text e-mails).

Other potentially useful applications of new media include e-mail and mailing list technology for sending increased amounts of information to shareholders, 'chat rooms' to host ongoing dialogue with shareholders, corporate promotion via bulletin boards or public discussion areas on websites, and, increasingly, webcasting sessions.

Whilst it is entirely a matter of choice which documents a company displays on its website, the display of certain documents must comply with legal formalities and these are examined in more detail below.

1   In the United Kingdom, that is. Investor relations websites in the United States are now frequently found, even though the standard for content, disclosure, presentation, etc, varies considerably. The US is close to reaching the point at which it will be considered sufficient for a company to publicise significant corporate matters on its website for it to have discharged its duty of fair disclosure, although in relation to SEC Regulation FD (FD stands for 'full disclosure') issued in October 2000, the SEC has held back from making a conclusive statement to this effect.

2   Care is required here to ensure that the sort of material presented in this way does not constitute a financial promotion pursuant to section 21 of the Financial Services and Markets Act 2000. Material which falls into this category and which is circulated to institutional investors and investment firms benefits from exemptions under the regime operating pursuant to section 21 of the Financial Services and Markets Act 2000, but it is very unlikely that any of these exemptions would apply to material which is made available to private individuals. For a fuller discussion of the relevant issues, see Chapter 9, E-finance.

(b) Annual report and accounts – the position under the Companies Act 1985

12.09   The position under the CA 1985 with respect to the format and content of a company's annual report and accounts, and the manner and timing of their sending to its shareholders, is extremely prescriptive, and not all that friendly towards electronic media. Although the Companies Act 1985 (Electronic Communications) Order 2000 has moved these criteria very significantly onwards, it is useful to summarise the previous position as a starting point.

■   **Format and content requirements** There are extensive provisions in the CA 1985 dealing with the format and content of annual reports and accounts, both in relation to the accounts themselves[1] and to the notes that accompany them[2]. Such provisions are indicative of a formal structure to the production of the company accounts, which is easy to accomplish using printed pages. Using new media instead may require a little more lateral thinking. If the intention is to produce an annual report which is structurally the same in electronic format as in printed format, then the simplest solution that makes use of contemporary technology would be to produce the document as a .pdf format file. This file can be sent to shareholders on a CD-ROM or as an e-mail attachment, or can be made available from the corporate website[3].

■   **Signature and approval requirements** The CA 1985 refers to the annual accounts being approved by the company's board of directors and signed on behalf of the board[4]. It also requires the copy of the company's balance sheet, which is delivered to the Registrar of Companies, to be signed on behalf of the board by a director of the company[5]. Failure to comply with these provisions is an offence[6].

The inevitable conclusion is that under the CA 1985, the 'master' set of an annual report and accounts must be a printed document. But this does not, of itself, preclude companies from using this master to create a CD-ROM-based or web-text version for distribution[7].

■   **The reports of the directors and the auditor** The report section of a company's annual report and accounts is also governed by the provisions in the CA 1985, although it has become customary in recent years for the annual report and accounts of public companies to contain rather more information and narrative than is strictly necessary for compliance with the legislation.

The accounts document should contain a directors' report which has been approved and signed by the board[8]. A copy of such report should be delivered to the Registrar of Companies[9].

The company's auditors are required to report on the accounts of the company which are to be laid before the company in general meeting in a separate auditors' report which has to be signed by them and also laid before the company in general meeting[10]. This again points to the fact that a printed version of the accounts is still required.

- **Laying before the general meeting** The CA 1985 provides that the directors of the company shall lay before the company in general meeting copies of the company's annual accounts, the directors' report and the auditors' report[11]. It also provides for delivery of copies of the accounts to the Registrar of Companies and provides civil penalties for failure to do so[12].

  'Laying before' is not defined in the CA 1985. Doubtless, the term follows through from the original Victorian corporate legislation and certainly it conjures up the image of physically laying a printed document on a table at the meeting. But is this essential? Is there perhaps latitude to interpret this constructively, so that, for example, the report and accounts could be projected a page at a time on to a very large screen, clearly visible to all attending the meeting? One would argue that the manner of presentation at a general meeting matters less than that those attending are fully party to that presentation, however manifested[13].

- **Requirements of the Listing Rules** It is also worth making brief mention of certain provisions affecting companies whose securities are admitted to the London Stock Exchange Official List. These companies are obliged in relation to reporting to comply with the provisions of the Listing Rules[14] as follows:

  - Listing Rule 12.40 provides for relevant information to be published in a preliminary announcement adopting the format of the information used in the accounts and Listing Rule 12.41 provides that the company must issue annual accounts.

  - Listing Rule 12.43 makes reference to information to be 'included' in the annual report and accounts including, under Listing Rule 12.43A, significant information relating to corporate governance and directors' remuneration.

1 The CA 1985, s 262 defines the annual accounts of the company as the individual accounts required by section 226 and any group accounts required by section 227. Section 226 states that 'individual accounts' are comprised of a balance sheet and profit and loss account. According to section 226(3), individual accounts shall comply with the provisions of Schedule 4 as to the form and content of the balance sheet and profit and loss account. Additional information must be included by way of notes to the accounts. Pursuant to section 227, similar obligations apply as to group accounts, the relevant form and content provisions being contained in Schedule 4A.

2 The CA 1985, s 231 provides obligations in relation to further disclosure in respect of accounts (related undertakings) and states that 'the information in Schedule 5 shall be given in notes to the company's annual accounts'. Section 232 provides that disclosures in relation to directors' emoluments are to be included and similarly uses the word 'shall' with respect to notes to the company's annual accounts. Section 261 (which is in effect a sweeper provision) provides that the relevant notes to the accounts must be contained either in the accounts or in a document annexed to the accounts.

3 This presupposes first that a shareholder has a computer with access to the Internet and/or a CD-ROM reader and, second, that he has software (such as Adobe Acrobat Reader) for decoding and reading .pdf materials. However, the advantage of .pdf is that the text of the report (and illustrations) are reproduced faithfully and (unlike web text) cannot be tampered with by the recipient or the transmission process.

4 The CA 1985, s 233.

5 The CA 1985, s 233(4).

6 The CA 1985, s 233(5).

7 Indeed, whereas at present a company's annual report and accounts as distributed to shareholders may conform to the copy signed by the board of directors, using the .pdf format to create a file on a CD-ROM with the accounts means that for the first time shareholders will receive a document which actually bears facsimiles of the signatures themselves.

8 The CA 1985, ss 234 and 234A.

9 The CA 1985, s 234A(3).

10 The CA 1985, s 235(1).

11 The CA 1985, s 241.

12 The CA 1985, ss 242 and 242A.

13 In this connection, it is instructive to consider the case of *Barker v Wilson* [1980] 2 All ER 81, which is a robust judicial authority for how a Victorian expression, which in its narrow contextual meaning is outdated, should be interpreted today. The case considers the meaning of the expression 'bankers' books', for the purposes of construing relevant provisions of the Bankers' Books (Evidence) Act 1879. That Act provides that certified copies of entries in the books of record maintained by banks would suffice for court purposes (subject to certain other conditions), since it was a significant imposition on Victorian era banks to have to produce the books themselves in court. But modern banks do not have handwritten records, preferring to commit their records to, for example, microfilm (which in this case was held to fall within the concept of 'bankers' books' for the purposes of the Bankers' Books (Evidence) Act 1879).

14 Although the Listing Rules of the new UK Listing Authority (the Financial Services Authority by another name) are now in force, there is no substantive change in this respect (among many others) from the framework of the old Stock

Exchange *Yellow Book*. However, following implementation of the Companies Act 1985 (Electronic Communications) Order 2000, the Listing Rules were changed to allow companies to send their shareholders any document (which they are required to send under the Listing Rules) in an electronic format or to display that document on a website, provided that certain conditions are met (Listing Rule 1.27). The changes made to the Listing Rules supplement rather than replace existing legal and Listing Rules requirements for the production of printed documents. Paul Geradine, Director of Listing at the UKLA was quoted: 'Companies cannot satisfy their Listing Rules obligations by only publishing accounts or other price sensitive financial information on the Internet. Any information which is, or may be, price sensitive must be published as an announcement on the Regulatory News Service before or at the same time as it is published on a company's website' (PLC, April 2001 Volume XII Number 3, p 10). See further under Chapter 9, E-finance.

12.10 So, then, a formal and old-fashioned regime would appear to apply under the CA 1985 framework which presents a company with little latitude for innovation. Actually, this regime is probably not quite as restrictive as it might appear. Before we go on to consider the changes made to the regime as per the Companies Act 1985 (Electronic Communications) Order 2000, we can draw certain conclusions regarding the capacity for the annual report and accounts to move away from the old printed document to an electronic version on a CD-ROM:

- **Document** Without doubt a CD-ROM with text on it is treated as being a document for contemporary legal purposes[1]. The composite nature of the report and accounts which companies publish these days calls for a printed 'document' of some complexity; the CD-ROM in fact lends itself much more readily to this sort of publication than the printed booklet(s) approach to which companies have been wedded for so long.

- **Copies** For the time being, we must accept that the original version of the accounts will take the form of a printed document, but other than in respect of the version which needs to be sent to the Registrar of Companies (who cannot process anything other than a printed document[2]), all further copies for circulation seem to be capable of reduction to electronic form on a CD-ROM. The prudent approach is for the accounts to be reduced to a .pdf file on the CD-ROM, which is, in effect, a complete visual reproduction of the printed original (rather than just a text document).

---

1 This matter was settled in relation to computer disks as long ago as 1987: see *Huddleston v Control Risks Information Services Ltd* [1987] 2 All ER 1035. See, however, more recent dicta in *Victor Chandler International Ltd v Customs and Excise Comrs* [2000] 2 All ER 315, [2000] 1 WLR 1296.
2 It is worth noting that the Companies Act 1985 (Electronic Communications) Order 2000 does not indicate that the Registrar of Companies is in the process of moving from this position, at least as regards the filing of annual reports and accounts.

12.11 In summary, under the CA 1985 regime, companies that wish to move from the conventional printed document approach as far as is reasonably possible under the then current legislation, are left with two options:

- to send out the current year's report in printed format, as in previous years, and state in it (or in a covering letter) that in future the accounts would be issued in CD-ROM format, unless the recipient specifically wrote to the company requesting a printed document (in which case he would most likely receive the .pdf format file printed off from the CD-ROM or the source used to create it); or

- to send a letter well in advance of the beginning of the 21-day notice period for the AGM which indicates that, as from the current year, the company would be moving to CD-ROM as the primary means of publishing the annual report and accounts. In the absence of specific requests for a printed version, a CD-ROM could therefore follow 21 days or so prior to the AGM.

The one thing that could be problematic is combining formats. Under the CA 1985, the report and accounts cannot safely be considered to be a single 'document' if part is contained on a CD-ROM and part in the form of a printed appendix or abstract. As can be seen, the CA 1985 in its current unamended form actually allows for rather greater freedom for a company to issue its accounts to shareholders electronically than might at first have appeared to be the case. In fact, it is clear that there is not even any form of 'opt-in' requirement for this: the company could require its shareholders to ask to receive old-fashioned paper copies and presume from silence that they were happy with CD-ROMs. However, there is not a great deal of point dwelling at length on this position since, upon the making of the Companies Act 1985 (Electronic Communications) Order 2000, this analysis has ceased for most purposes to be relevant. It is to the effect of the Order that we turn next.

(c) Annual report and accounts – provisions in the Companies Act 1985 (Electronic Communications) Order 2000

12.12 What sort of changes to the above regime are contained in the Order? Indeed, does the Order significantly advance matters? The Order achieves the following:

■ companies are now able to agree with a given member[1] of the company for the annual accounts, directors' report and auditors' report to be sent electronically to that member, either directly (by e-mail or on CD-ROM) or by notifying him (in an agreed manner, which could be by post but would more likely be by e-mail[2]) that the documents have been published on a website or sites identified to him;

■ if companies are making their annual report and accounts available electronically prior to a meeting at which they will be discussed[3], these should be available on the company's website for a full 21 days before the relevant meeting, in line with existing requirements[4]. In view of this approach, companies might wish to ensure that their company's annual report and accounts appear on more than one website, which avoids embarrassment if technical failure or non-availability due to excessive demand causes a website to cease to operate normally;

■ where a member (or debenture holder) exercises his right to ask for an additional copy of the annual report and accounts, a company may send these electronically if the member so agrees[5].

1 Defined in the CA 1985, s 22(2) as being a person who is entered on the register of members as such. For practical purposes, the term is synonymous with 'shareholder'.
2 ICSA recommend that, where an e-mail notice is sent advising that information is being posted on the corporate website, a hyperlink to the appropriate website page should be provided in that e-mail.
3 The CA 1985, s 241.
4 The CA 1985, s 238(1).
5 Article 13, amending the CA 1985, s 239.

12.13 The Companies Act 1985 (Electronic Communications) Order 2000 does not provide for any relaxation in the content requirements of the annual report and accounts discussed above. Moreover, the Companies Acts lay down certain requirements in connection with the publication of accounts, and these still apply[1]. The ICSA Best Practice Guide seeks to set down good practice standards for the publishing of annual reports and accounts on websites. It advises that companies involve their auditors in the process at an early stage to ensure they have no objections to how their reports are represented[2].

It is perhaps a matter of regret that the Order has not been used as a means for even further reform. The following are areas which have not been covered:

■ **'Laying before'** Unfortunately, the Order is of no real assistance in defining this term for the purposes of electronic communication or allowing a company to dispense with such a requirement altogether[3]. The CA 1985 needs a more intelligent definition of the laying before process. If the directors of a company wish to conduct an audio-visual display that conveys the relevant details at the AGM to those present, it is a pity that the CA 1985 could not be amended to make it crystal clear that this is permissible.

■ **Documentary structure for annual report and accounts** It would also have assisted if there had been some guidance in the terms of the Order as to the structure of the annual report and accounts, and what amounts to the appending or inclusion of materials in the annual report and accounts in electronic terms. Using a CD-ROM to package the components of the annual report and accounts effects a binding together of this material in a fashion which is (paradoxically) physically more effective than can be accomplished with printed materials. The same is not entirely true of materials on a website, since relevant components will probably have URLs and, if anything, they are even more loosely connected than are a series of papers served on the shareholder in a single envelope under the same covering letter.

- **De facto requirement for a printed original** It was perhaps only to be expected that if the Order creates an opt-in regime (where shareholders can ask to receive electronic materials but cannot be required to do so), the base document for the annual report and accounts still has to be printed on paper. This conclusion is clear from the silence of the Order in relation to the capacity of directors, auditors, etc, to sign electronically the documents for which they are responsible.

- **Opt-in structure – limitations** The Order is required by the terms of the ECA 2000 to operate on the basis that a shareholder has to agree to a company sending out electronic materials to him; or, conversely, the company has to want to do so, whatever its shareholders may be asking for. This was considered by the DTI to be the fairest solution to the problem that large companies face, where they have a variety of shareholders, including those with no access to, or appetite for, a computer terminal to read their corporate documents. The problem with this approach is that a perfectly reasonable *via media* seems to have been overlooked. There does not seem to be anything inequitable in a company writing to its shareholders and asking them to respond positively if they want to continue to receive documents in printed form. If shareholders do not respond within a reasonable period (and 21 days may not be sufficient for these purposes), then shouldn't a company be allowed to assume they will be happy to receive materials on CD-ROM, for example? The paradox is that there does not seem to be anything in the CA 1985 to prohibit this course of action[4], though this is no longer possible now that the Order has come into operation. This comes down to a question of cost-benefit analysis. The purpose behind electronic media being made available to companies is to reduce their corporate governance and shareholder communications costs. As the Law Society Company Law Committee noted in its response to the DTI Consultation[5], a company which currently prints 10,000 annual reports and achieves a reduction in its print run to about 1,000 with the benefit of opt-ins under the Order will not really have saved much money, because the bulk of the printing and production costs of that annual report are locked up in the first 1,000 or so printed.

1 See, for example, the formalities under the CA 1985, s 240 in relation to the publication of statutory accounts.
2 In relation to the presentation of accounts on-line, it is worth mentioning that the accounting industry is experimenting with a version of HTML known as Extensible Business Reporting Language (or XBRL) which would allow corporate financial data to be placed on a website in a manner which enables it to be viewed through standard Internet browsers in an integral fashion, without being affected either by the process of hypertext transfer or the configuration of the PC on which it is being viewed. The companies supporting the development of XBRL are hopeful that it will eventually become a standard for electronic financial reporting.
3 The Order only deals with 'laying before' in one very minor respect, namely to give a shareholder in a private company the power to serve an electronic notice under section 253 of the CA 1985 to require the company to lay the accounts before the AGM where that company has previously elected to dispense of laying accounts before the AGM under the CA 1985, s 252. (See article 13 of the Order.)
4 Although there might of course be a restriction in a company's articles on the manner of service of documents and formal notices.
5 See 'Law Society Company Law Committee Memorandum 397', April 2000, response to Q1.

(d) Other provisions in the Companies Act 1985 (Electronic Communications) Order 2000

12.14 Other provisions in the Order include:

- **Summary financial statements** The Order[1] amends the provisions in the CA 1985 relating to summary financial statements, so that these may be sent by facsimile or e-mail or published on a website rather than sent by post. Logically, this amendment follows from the changes proposed in relation to the annual report and accounts.

- **Notice of general meetings** It is possible, under the Order[2], for a company to serve a notice of a general meeting (annual or extraordinary) either (i) by e-mail or other electronic means directly to those shareholders who opt for electronic communication; or (ii) by publishing the notice in full on a website or sites (with notification sent to those shareholders that such a notice has been published and of the address of the website or sites).

  As a safeguard, to avoid the risk that a company's shareholders might overlook a notice published on a website, and hence miss the resulting meeting, the Order requires the notification which is sent to shareholders to state:

  – the place, date and time of the meeting;

  – whether it is an AGM or EGM; and

  – that it concerns a statutory notice given under the CA 1985.

  The notice itself must then remain available on the website or sites until the end of the meeting.

  The ICSA Best Practice Guide goes further, stating that the notification sent to shareholders of the publication of a notice on a company's website should draw attention to any special business that may be on the agenda at the relevant meeting.

  The Order amends regulation 115 of Table A, which provides that proof of correct posting is conclusive evidence that formal notice has been given by a company, and that notice is deemed to have been given 48 hours after posting. To deal with electronic communication, the amended regulation 115 provides for the notice to be deemed to have been given 48 hours after electronic despatch[3].

- **Proxy appointments** Under the Order, shareholders will be able to appoint proxies and give voting instructions to proxies electronically, and also to lodge appointments of proxies electronically, where this is agreed and an address for so doing has been provided[4]. This might be an e-mail address, a facsimile number or a telephone number[5]. Table A previously provided that[6] an instrument appointing a proxy had to be 'in writing'. However, the Order has amended this provision. Some company articles already enable voting instructions to be given electronically to a proxy, although pursuant to the Order the right to do this does not now depend upon any specific provision being added to the articles of the company.

  The Order does not contain a requirement for shareholders to provide authentication when appointing and lodging appointments of proxies electronically. It may be wise for a company to require this: for example, it could issue its shareholders with PIN numbers or other personal identifiers, such as electronic signature certificates, and require that they are used in these circumstances. The ICSA Best Practice Guide recommends allocating a discrete identifier to each shareholder. This will then need to be used in order to access an on-line proxy form or be quoted on a proxy form lodged in any other way[7].

  It should be emphasised that the Order does not provide for electronic voting[8]. A shareholder or his proxy will still need to be physically present at a meeting in order to register a vote.

- **Requirement that the annual report and accounts be laid before a company in general meeting** Where a private company has elected to dispense with the laying of the annual report and accounts before a general meeting[9], a member is nevertheless permitted to require that such a meeting is held by giving due notice[10]. Under the Order[11], it will be possible for the member to give this notice electronically, where the company agrees and has specified an address for this purpose.

1 Article 14 and Schedule 2, amending the CA 1985, s 251 and the Companies (Summary Financial Statement) Regulations 1995 (SI 1995/2092) respectively.
2 Article 18, amending the CA 1985, s 369.
3 See Schedule 1, paragraph 8 to the Order. The DTI's earlier draft of the Order did not provide a yardstick for proving that electronic service had been effected properly. The Order now provides that proof that notice contained in an electronic communication was sent in accordance with ICSA guidance shall be conclusive evidence that notice was given.
4 Article 19 and paragraphs 2–6 of Schedule 1 to the Order, amending the CA 1985, ss 372 and 373 and regulations 60–63 of Table A respectively.
5 See article 16, which states that an address 'in relation to electronic communications, includes any number or address used for the purposes of such communications'. This would appear to apply conclusively in favour of e-mail addresses, fax numbers and the like.
6 Regulation 60 of Table A.
7 There ought to be no problem in principle with that identifier being chosen by the shareholder himself when registering with the company to receive electronic materials. The principle is the same as where a new user on any website is allowed to select his password for future use.
8 See paragraph 12.22 for further information on electronic voting.
9 The CA 1985, s 252.
10 The CA 1985, s 253.
11 Article 15 of the Order, amending the CA 1985, s 253. In a similar vein, a shareholder in a private company that has dispensed with its AGM under the CA 1985, s 366A has power to request electronically that the AGM be held: see article 17.

(e) Other communications to and from members

12.15 It is important to remain aware that, in spite of the Companies Act 1985 (Electronic Communications) Order 2000 becoming law, there are still instances of communication between companies and members, regulated by the Companies Acts, that have not been addressed by the Order and where electronic methods of communication cannot be used with confidence. The main examples are listed below (in the first two situations the risk is primarily with members):

■ where a member requisitions an EGM[1];

■ where a member or members requisition a resolution[2];

■ where a private company passes a written resolution[3] (there is no provision under the Order for signatures to be implemented electronically);

■ where a company sends a copy of the memorandum and articles to a member at his request[4];

■ where a company sends notice of a meeting which includes a resolution to disapply pre-emption rights under the CA 1985, s 95(2) (that is, where the disapplication is in relation to a specific allotments); and

■ where a company sends a copy of the register of members to a member at his request[5].

1 The CA 1985, s 368.
2 The CA 1985, ss 376 and 377.
3 The CA 1985, s 381A.
4 The CA 1985, s 95(5) requires a written statement to accompany these notices. Therefore, an electronic notification to consider a resolution would not be appropriate. However, the majority of resolutions to disapply pre-emption rights are general disapplications under the CA 1985, s 95(1) where no written statement is required and the view of ICSA and the DTI is that electronic communications can be used.
5 The CA 1985, s 356(3).

(f) The annual general meeting

12.16 The Company Law Review Steering Group consultation document[1] focused on company general meetings and shareholder communications as part of its ongoing review of modern company law.

The Steering Group acknowledged[2] that current law and practice on AGMs is a matter of widespread concern and sought to examine whether improvements in law and practice could better enable AGMs to serve their intended purpose (as an effective mechanism for control of a company by its members) without imposing undue burdens on company boards or others concerned. It was material to consider whether companies could achieve that purpose as well, or better, by means other than the AGM. Most of the Steering Group's observations are beyond the scope of this chapter, but it is useful to look at the Steering Group's comments on several areas relevant to the use of new technology[3].

1 October 1999, see paragraph 12.07.
2 Paragraph 14 of the consultation document.
3 A full breakdown of all the responses to the consultation document is available as a .pdf file on the DTI's website at: www.dti.gov.uk/cld/reviews/condocs.htm.

(i) What may constitute a 'meeting'

12.17 The Steering Group's provisional view[1] is that, provided there is two-way real-time communication between all locations at which persons nominally 'present' at the meeting are in fact based, there is no reason why an AGM should not be held for the benefit of people physically present in a number of locations.

Views were invited as to whether such two-way communication should be audio-visual or simply audio and replies on this point were divided. For example, the Law Society[2] agreed that, in principle, both should suffice. It noted, however, that the conduct of a meeting relying on sound alone calls for careful chairmanship, particularly in relation to the management of debate and ensuring that everyone present at the meeting is aware of the identity of the speaker at the meeting at any given moment. It suggested that this could be an area where ICSA could usefully develop best practice guidance. The Institute of Chartered Accountants in England and Wales (ICAEW) considered that only face-to-face communication would suffice[3].

1 Paragraph 29 of the consultation document.
2 See 'Law Society Company Law Committee Memorandum No 387', January 2000, para 6 (available at www.lawsociety.org.uk).
3 Paragraph 7 of a memorandum submitted in January 2000 to the DTI by the ICAEW in response to their consultation document.

(ii) Shareholder approval for multi-location AGMs

12.18 If AGMs are permitted, by future company law reform, to be held by some form of remote communication, further questions then arise:

■ should the decision to hold a multi-location AGM require shareholder approval?

■ if so, should this be by ordinary or special resolution?

■ should a distinction be drawn between public and private companies?

Views were invited on the above issues and replies were again divided. For example, the Law Society[1] felt that some form of shareholder approval should be required for public company AGMs to be held by remote communication. There was a slight favouring towards this being by ordinary resolution. Some committee members at the Law Society favour any member of a private company having the right to require a face-to-face general meeting[2]. The ICAEW believe that the decision to hold an AGM without at least one physical meeting point should require shareholder approval comparable with that required to dispense with an AGM, which seems to imply that, so long as there is at least one physical meeting point, no shareholder consent should be required[3]. The ICAEW supported a change to the law for both public and private companies[4].

1 Paragraphs 9 and 10 of the Law Society Memorandum.
2 Paragraph 11 of the Law Society Memorandum.
3 Paragraph 8 of the ICAEW Memorandum.
4 Paragraph 9 of the ICAEW Memorandum.

(iii) 'Virtual' meetings

12.19 The Steering Group noted that it would be possible to go one stage further from the multi-location meeting, thus creating an interactive 'virtual' meeting held in no location; the directors' presentations would be posted on an electronic company bulletin board accessible to shareholders and the shareholders' interventions and the directors' responses would also be posted on the bulletin board. Such a 'meeting' would probably have to remain open for several days. Such a procedure potentially offers even wider shareholder access, but at the cost of the discipline on the directors of face-to-face real-time contact with shareholders.

Questions were posed as to whether 'virtual' general meetings should be permitted and, if so, whether they should require a certain level of shareholder consent and if a distinction should be drawn between public and private companies.

Replies on this issue indicated a general unwillingness for AGMs to be held 'virtually' although most were in favour of companies experimenting at a more informal level. The Law Society is opposed to the idea of public companies being able to hold 'virtual' general meetings. It believes[1] that the importance of conducting meetings through real-time links lies in dealing with the genuinely difficult meeting where the element of personal interaction between individuals is a vital feature. It is also concerned that it could be very difficult to manage debate effectively at a 'virtual' meeting and that this could be hijacked by dissenting elements. It did recognise, however, that these issues were of less concern to private companies[2]. The ICAEW believes[3] that it should be possible for companies to experiment with other communication methods such as 'virtual' meetings, the use of Internet bulletin boards and posting analysts' meetings on the Internet, but that a 'virtual' meeting should not be allowed to constitute a general meeting. Again, the ICAEW made no distinction between public and private companies.

1 Paragraph 12 of the Law Society Memorandum.
2 Paragraph 14 of the Law Society Memorandum.
3 Paragraphs 7 and 10 of the ICAEW Memorandum.

(iv) Deferred voting

12.20 The Steering Group raised the possibility of deferring voting until after an AGM has been held as a possible way of both rationalising the voting procedure and adding substance to the meeting itself.

The idea is that shareholders could perhaps be given an interval of, say, two weeks after a meeting to reflect before voting. Those unable to attend would not lodge proxies before the meeting but would vote themselves afterwards. If this were to happen, votes might be cast either at the place(s) of meeting at the conclusion of business or by post or, if authorised by a company's constitution and agreed by its shareholders, by telephone or electronically.

In some cases boards would not go into meetings knowing that they already have the votes necessary to achieve their desired outcome. This could give the meeting a more 'democratic' significance, leaving open the possibility that the course of the debate might influence the outcome. In particular, institutions could assess the directors' performance at the meeting, and any media or public reaction, before casting their vote.

Opinions among the replies to the deferred voting proposal were mixed. The Law Society has distinct reservations[1] about the practicality of adopting any such system and remains unconvinced as to the argument that it would add substance to the meeting itself. The ICAEW can see some advantage[2] in holding the voting open until a specified date after the AGM but does not consider that this should be required by statute.

1　Paragraph 33 of the Law Society Memorandum.
2　Paragraph 18 of the ICAEW Memorandum.

(v) Other proposals

12.21　Other proposals put forward by the Steering Group, such as enabling public companies to dispense with AGMs altogether[1], would seem to pave the way for electronic voting to be adopted. Indeed, even without the changes under proposal being adopted, the Steering Group recognises that some companies might want to offer electronic voting as an option in the future. Both the Law Society[2] and the ICAEW[3] seem broadly supportive of such a move and the issue in general is covered in more detail at paragraph 12.22 below.

1　Paragraphs 24–27 of the Law Society Memorandum.
2　Paragraph 52 of the Law Society Memorandum.
3　Paragraph 26 of the ICAEW Memorandum.

(g) Electronic voting

(i) What is meant by the term 'electronic voting'?

12.22　The term 'electronic voting' can be used to cover a wide range of voting methods, for example voting by facsimile or e-mail as well as over the Internet. This section highlights the advantages that could be gained by companies adopting some form of quality, secure, electronic voting system via the Internet.

(ii) The advantages of electronic voting[1]

12.23

- **Speed** The less time votes spend in transit means more time for analysis and discussion, enabling more informed decisions and more time to process instructions.

- **Certainty** Electronic voting will improve transparency, reduce the likelihood of simple errors and offer tracking and reporting facilities.

- **Effective use of resources** Electronic voting will reduce the need for staff to process votes manually and enable a company to use its resources more effectively.

- **Authentication** Electronic voting within a secure system will ensure that only the registered proxy cardholder can action the proxy vote and send the information down the chain of command.

1　For more on this, see 'Great Expectations – electronic voting and company meetings', an independent review by Simon Carr, published by E-Vote.

(iii) The US experience

12.24　The Internet is used routinely in the US for receiving shareholder voting instructions, and telephone voting is also fairly commonplace. Some general points are of interest:

- the Internet is an extremely cheap method of transmission in the US;

- PIN numbers are used to ensure that both Internet and telephone voting are secure;

- a 'meeting record date' is commonly fixed ahead of an AGM (ordinarily 35 to 50 days in advance of the meeting date) to determine:

    - a shareholder's right to receive meeting documents;

    - his right to attend the meeting; and

    - his entitlement to vote.

    This simplifies the voting process, by clearly closing the books, to produce a defined group of entitled shareholders, unaffected by subsequent dealings, whose voting can be accurately monitored;

- proxy voting service organisations are commonplace; and

- proxy voting service companies receive their instructions via voting instruction forms (VIFs), which are produced in a standard format and can be scanned and recorded automatically at high speed.

(iv) The need for modernisation in the UK

12.25   The system of shareholder voting in the UK is in urgent need of modernisation. Voting levels are low[1] and it is thought that, for institutional investors at least, this is in large part due to the antiquated proxy voting system. The major issues were reviewed by the Newbold Inquiry and certain of the associated problems have been addressed by the ECA 2000. These are summarised below:

- **The Newbold Inquiry** An independent inquiry, sponsored by the National Association of Pension Funds (NAPF) and chaired by Yves Newbold, published its findings in July 1999[2] into the effectiveness of the voting practices of pension funds and their managers[3].

    The Newbold Inquiry emphasised the weakness of the existing system for executing institutional proxy votes[4]. The current system involves a long and complicated paper trail, particularly for pension funds. Put simply, the process is as follows:

    - the company sets the agenda for its meeting and prepares the notice and proxy materials;

    - these are printed and issued by registrars and then sent to the registered shareholders (usually the custodian where a pension fund is concerned);

    - the custodian then transmits these to the investment fund manager or to the beneficial owner;

    - the fund manager receiving proxy materials analyses them in order to identify those items it has the discretion to decide upon, those items it has specific instructions from the client pension fund to decide upon, and those items where the advice of the trustees is required;

    - once the custodian receives instructions on how to vote, it completes the proxy cards and delivers them to the registrar, usually by post or courier.

    This process is overly complicated and manually intensive, with too many parties involved. There is no doubt that this leads to inefficiencies and there is potential for error as a result[5].

Nor is there any clear way of providing confirmation that voting intentions have been successfully carried out.

One objective of the Newbold Inquiry (and the one most pertinent to this chapter) was to identify and assess the role that could be played by electronic voting systems under current and anticipated technology. Its finding was that electronic voting could be seen as a partial solution[6] to the problems identified. To the extent that the introduction of electronic voting would substantially overcome the complexity and cure the weaknesses of the present system, it would allow institutions to vote more efficiently and encourage them to increase their voting levels. Electronic voting is not however the whole solution, because, as the report itself states[7], 'if the will to vote is not there, the introduction of electronic systems in and of itself will not rectify that absence of will'.

- **Relevance of the Order made under the Electronic Communications Act 2000** The Companies Act 1985 (Electronic Communications) Order 2000 does not specifically address the issue of electronic voting in its present form, though it allows shareholders to appoint proxies and give voting instructions to proxies electronically, and also to lodge appointments of proxies electronically, where the company agrees and has provided an address for doing so[8]. This has been welcomed by those organisations (listed below) that seek to provide electronic (or at least, semi-electronic) voting services.

There is every likelihood that a future order made under the ECA 2000 will specifically address the issue, but we shall just have to wait and see.

1 Pension funds and institutional funds vote on 50% of total company shareholdings ('Great Expectations', see paragraph 12.22).
2 'Report of the Committee of Inquiry into UK Vote Execution (foreword by Sir Adrian Cadbury)', 5 July 1999.
3 At present pension funds cast only about 40% of their votes and are considered to have a particularly poor record in voting on important corporate governance and corporate strategy issues of relevance to institutional investors.
4 The Newbold Inquiry Report, section 2.
5 The Newbold Inquiry Report, appendix 1, which details evidence of some of these.
6 The Newbold Inquiry Report, section 3.
7 The Newbold Inquiry Report, section 3.2.
8 See paragraph 12.14 above for further details.

(v) *Current voting services*

12.26 The following voting services are currently on offer in the UK and are all generally designed for use by institutional shareholders. They all seek to provide, so far as possible under current law, electronic voting solutions for their clients:

- **Manifest Voting Agency** Manifest[1] is an on-line proxy voting agency which was launched in March 1996. Its electronic voting service, Manifest Vote Plus, uses Oracle database technology to offer customers computerised voting 'templates' which can be customised as required. These templates enable investors to sift and screen resolutions on an issue-by-issue basis and also to record and monitor voting decisions. Since votes cannot yet be lodged in electronic form, Manifest is responsible for delivering computer-generated poll cards under the hand of an authorised signatory on behalf of its clients. Manifest will also attend meetings if required.

- **Investor Communication Services (ICS)** ICS[2] was set up in 1989 and is a division of Automatic Data Processing. Part of its service includes the collection and carrying out of client voting instructions. Its electronic proxy management system, ProxyEdge, uses Microsoft Windows-based software.

1 Manifest's website can be found at www.manifest.co.uk.
2 ICS's website can be found at www.ics.adp.com.

4. COMMUNICATION BETWEEN DIRECTORS/SENIOR EXECUTIVES

(a) Board and other meetings

12.27 Communication between directors is not as heavily regulated as that between shareholders, and many companies already distribute board papers, for example, by e-mail. The main company law issue in this area concerns the use of new technology to assist in the holding of board meetings.

(i) The position under existing law

12.28 Existing law leaves the issue fairly open. Regulation 88 of Table A states that 'subject to the provisions of the articles, the directors may regulate their proceedings as they think fit'. Meetings can therefore be highly informal (and in the case of smaller private companies often are) although there has to be an intention that a board meeting is taking place. There is also a requirement for a quorum to be present. Regulation 89 of Table A states that 'the quorum for the transaction of the business of the directors may be fixed by the directors and unless so fixed at any number shall be two'. For a board meeting to be validly held, it is therefore only necessary that the specified number of directors attend, provided that all directors (other than those absent from the UK) have been given notice of the meeting.

(ii) Telephone conference calls and audio-visual links

12.29 It has become increasingly common to find companies providing in their articles for directors to meet through telephone conference calls and audio-visual links where it is not possible for them to meet in person. Directors present in this way are deemed to form part of the quorum and, as such, are entitled to vote. If this is the case and a meeting is held by telephone with all directors in separate locations, the meeting would be considered validly held in accordance with the articles. However, in view of the unusual nature of the provision, it may be advisable to use it where the matters to be discussed are formal and uncontroversial or in cases of emergency[1].

1 See *Shackleton on the Law and Practice of Meetings* (7th edn, 1997), para 22-02.

(iii) Outside the board room

12.30 New technologies will undoubtedly continue to have an increasing impact on day-to-day company life. E-mail, voice-mail, conference calls and videoconferencing facilities are now all commonplace. Software facilitating real-time, web-based meetings is available from various sources[1]. Discussions can be held and documents can be exchanged on-line. This has implications in terms of cost, speed and convenience, not just for the general management of a company by directors and senior executives, but also for areas such as training, marketing and recruitment, as well as webcasting corporate announcements to the press, financial institutions and investors.

1 For example, see Microsoft Windows' NetMeeting at www.microsoft.com, Real Network's RealSystems at www.realnetworks.com and First Virtual Communications at www.fvc.com.

(b) The corporate intranet

12.31 Many companies today make use of corporate intranets to communicate internally in an efficient and effective manner. These can be open to everyone within a company, or it might be decided to restrict access to all or part to senior management and/or directors.

Relevant documents that might be placed on a corporate intranet include:

- board authority levels;

- terms of reference and membership details for board committees;

- matters reserved to the board;

- share dealing rules and associated explanatory documents or forms;

- contact lists and movement details for directors and/or other senior executives;

- director databases;

- lists of key dates (board meetings, committee meetings, etc);

- corporate/financial calendars;

- transaction timetables;

- banking documents and trust deeds;

- corporate procedure manuals;

- policy documents (ethics, environment, compliance, discipline, etc);

- share option information (dates, grant details, rules); and

- share price information.

(c) Notice of removal of a director

12.32 According to the CA 1985[1], notice to a director of a resolution to remove him as a director still cannot be sent by electronic means.

1 The CA 1985, s 304(1).

5. COMMUNICATIONS WITH COMPANIES HOUSE

(a) Filing of documents

12.33 Companies House launched an electronic filing service for the submission of certain statutory documents[1] in the summer of 1998 for the benefit of companies registered in England and Wales. Companies House have stated that they may eventually become an entirely 'virtual' source of information, with companies updating their information on-line. Companies House would then provide the gateway to access information rather than actually hold the information itself[2].

The service permits the electronic transmission of the specified documents via e-mail over an extranet set up by Companies House. No charge is made for the use of the extranet facility but normal statutory fees apply to documents such as the annual return. Forms sent electronically must comply with an approved structure. Therefore, companies wishing to take advantage of the service must use software, or go through a provider, approved by Companies House[3].

All electronically filed documents are automatically validated for compliance with the Companies Acts before receipt is acknowledged. If any problems are detected, the acknowledgement will indicate this. Validated information is transferred direct to the register (thus eliminating problems such as misfiled or lost documents).

1 It is currently possible to submit electronically the following forms (although it is intended that additional forms will be added to this list): change of registered office address (paper form 287), appointment of a director/secretary (paper form 288a), resignation of a director/secretary (paper form 288b) and change of director/secretary details (paper form 288c).

2 'Companies House E-Business Strategy Further Development of Electronic Services', available on the Companies House website at www.companieshouse.gov.uk.

3 Examples of approved software packages include Blueprint and Secretariat. Approved package providers include Jordans Limited and York Place Company Services Limited. A full up-to-date list of approved suppliers can be found on the Companies House website.

(i) Authentication requirement

12.34 Documents sent electronically cannot be signed on behalf of the company in the traditional way. The Registrar is allowed to prescribe[1] how a document required to be signed or sealed under various provisions of the Companies Acts should instead be authenticated. As a result, the Registrar requires all companies using the electronic filing service to have a company authentication code. Prior to any documents being electronically filed, this must be communicated to Companies House in writing, on company headed paper and signed by a serving officer of the company. Every document filed electronically must bear the relevant company authentication code or it will be rejected.

The requirement in the CA 1985[2] for the notification of a new director or secretary to contain a consent, signed by that person, to act in the relevant capacity, is met by the requirement for three items of personal information, which may include place of birth, date of birth, telephone number, house/flat number or name, national insurance number, passport number, mother's maiden name, eye colour or father's first forename.

1 The CA 1985, s 707.
2 The CA 1985, s 288(2).

(b) Viewing of documents

12.35 Companies House Direct[1] is an on-line information service that has been in operation since January 1999. It is a Windows-based Internet service which allows registered users to view or download images of documents filed at Companies House since March 1995 or to place orders for microfiche or hard copy documents.

1 See www.direct.companieshouse.gov.uk can be accessed by registered users only.

(c) Incorporation of companies in England and Wales

(i) The position under the Companies Act 1985

12.36 The electronic incorporation of companies at Companies House was previously impossible due to a number of provisions of the Companies Acts:

- **Attestation of signatures** There is a requirement for the signature of each subscriber to the memorandum to appear on both the memorandum and articles of association of the company, attested by a witness[1].

- **Statutory declaration** The CA 1985 requires there to be a statutory declaration, sworn by the solicitor engaged in the formation of the company, or a person named as a director or secretary of the company, in front of another solicitor or a notary, as sufficient evidence that particular requirements of the Companies Acts have been met[2].

1   The CA 1985, ss 2 and 7.
2   The CA 1985, s 12(3).

(ii) Provisions in the Companies Act 1985 (Electronic Communications) Order 2000

12.37   The Companies Act 1985 (Electronic Communications) Order 2000 removes the statutory obstacles to the electronic incorporation of companies contained in the CA 1985, so that the Registrar is now able to direct the form and manner for effecting incorporation.

The Order deals with the requirement of witness attestation by providing that where the memorandum and articles are signed electronically in accordance with the directions of the Registrar, the requirement for attestation of those signatures no longer applies[1].

The Order overcomes the problem of the statutory declaration by providing that it can be replaced by an electronic statement, which the Registrar may equally accept as sufficient evidence of the matters it contains[2]. False electronic statements will be as serious as false statutory declarations and will attract equivalent penalties[3].

The formation of private and public companies limited by shares as well as guarantee is possible using this method.

1   Articles 2 and 3 of the Order.
2   Article 4 of the Order.
3   Under the Perjury Act 1911, false statements made in statutory declarations constitute perjury, which is punishable by up to two years' imprisonment or a fine. The Order provides for the same penalties to apply to false electronic statements.

(d) Other provisions in the Companies Act 1985 (Electronic Communications) Order 2000

(i) Re-registration of companies

12.38   The Order makes it possible for a company to re-register as a different type of company electronically, for example a private company as a public company, a limited company becoming unlimited or a joint stock company becoming public. The Order[1] provides that the requisite statutory declaration of compliance with the requirements of the Companies Acts can be replaced with an electronic statement. Again, equivalent penalties will apply to false statements as to false declarations.

1   Articles 6, 7, 8 and 24 of the Order amend the CA 1985, ss 43, 47, 49 and 685 respectively.

(ii) Other documents requiring a statutory declaration

12.39   The Companies Act 1985 (Electronic Communications) Order 2000 makes it possible for the Registrar to accept, in certain circumstances, an electronic statement in place of a statutory declaration as sufficient evidence that particular requirements of the Companies Acts have been met. Such circumstances include the following:

- compliance with the share capital requirements of a public company[1];

- the establishment of a place of business in Great Britain[2]; and

- the submission of a memorandum of satisfaction of a charge[3].

Not all instances where a statutory declaration is required under the Companies Acts to be lodged with the Registrar have been addressed by the Order (but, of course, this position may change). Ones that have not been addressed (so far) include payment out of capital for the redemption or purchase of its own shares by a private company[4].

Article 10 of the Order was intended to allow companies to use electronic statements as an alternative to the statutory declaration required by sections 155 and 156 of the CA 1985, which prohibit financial assistance. However, the amendments introduced by the Order are not complete and require amendment as they do not deal with all the practical problems surrounding replacement of the statutory declaration. According to a DTI spokesman, the amendments 'do not provide a workable solution' and the DTI is trying to find a 'better approach'.[5]

1   Article 9 of the Order amends the CA 1985, s 117.
2   Article 26 of the Order amends the CA 1985, s 691.
3   Articles 22 and 23 amend the CA 1985, ss 403 and 419 respectively.
4   The CA 1985, s 173(3).
5   This is likely to be included in a second order, which the DTI is preparing for consultation.

(iii) Future electronic delivery

12.40   The Companies Act 1985 (Electronic Communications) Order 2000[1] provides that *any* document required to be delivered to the Registrar under the Companies Acts may be delivered in electronic form, provided that delivery is in a form and manner approved by the Registrar. Where a document is required to be signed or sealed, it may instead be authenticated as directed by the Registrar.

The current position under the CA 1985 is that 'any requirement to deliver a document to the registrar ... is satisfied by the communication to the registrar of the requisite information in any non-legible form ... approved by the registrar[2]'. Therefore, even before the Order, there was already a measure of flexibility in this area. However, the Order widens the current definition of 'non-legible' to include, for example, communication by telephone and facsimile as well as by e-mail.

1   Article 22 of the Order inserted a new section 707B into the CA 1985.
2   The CA 1985, s 707(2).

6.   CONCLUSION

12.41   It is clear that most companies are increasing their use of new technology to simplify the process of corporate governance and shareholder relations. This is a trend that will continue and has two main consequences: (a) the very nature of corporate governance and shareholder relations could change; and (b) the law will always be playing 'catch-up'.

(a)   The changing face of corporate governance

12.42   It is one thing to look at how new methods of communication can be applied to existing forms of corporate governance but another to recognise how the very nature of such new methods might change those forms. The increased volume of information that can be stored, processed and transmitted, the speed at which this can be done and even the manner in which it can be done (for example, it is much easier to personalise communications using new technology) will have a multitude of effects:

- e-mail and mailing list technology could increase the amount of information sent to shareholders;

- there is the potential for on-line dialogue with shareholders;

- the availability of chat rooms could increase shareholder activism;

- on-line reporting could lead to an increased range of information being provided (financial and non-financial) as the potential to do so is available at little extra cost;

- on-line reporting has the potential to be more up to date;

- on-line reporting could facilitate comparisons between companies;

- electronic voting could lead to more transparent voting systems as organisations make the move to publish proxy voting decisions[1];

- electronic voting could increase voting levels; and

- intranet technology opens up channels of communications within companies.

1   Domini Social Investments has already done this. See its website: www.domini.com.

(b) Can the law keep pace?

12.43   The indications are that the present Government is committed to facilitating the growth of electronic methods of communication between companies and their shareholders. For example, a second order supplementing the Companies Act 1985 (Electronic Communications) Order 2000 is currently being prepared by the DTI for consultation (see paragraph 12.38). However, whilst new laws are an important step in the modernisation process, it is difficult to see how any regulatory framework can keep pace with the opportunities that new technology brings.

Technology meanwhile continues to develop at a rapid pace. It is difficult to predict what applications will come on the market next and what their effects will be. One thing that is clear is that the lack of official standardisation and harmonisation will hinder their use and effectiveness.

(c) Learning from the US experience

12.44   It is fitting to conclude this chapter with a brief commentary on the position of investor relations and corporate communications in the US. The culture of investor relations there is considerably more advanced than it is in the UK and Europe. Shareholder activism in the US is far more common. This is a cultural matter, in the main, since private investors in the US have been accustomed for more than three generations to take stock in companies directly (the crashes of 1929 and 1987 and the recent downturn in the markets as exacerbated by the events of 11 September 2001 notwithstanding).

But perhaps the single largest difference between the position of shareholders in the US and their UK counterparts is that in the US corporate membership registers are available to all shareholders. In the UK, an investor has the right to see the record of his entry on the company's register but nobody else's. It significantly inhibits communication between individual shareholders in a company if they are not actually aware of each other's existence. When an investor in a UK company believes that the company's management is making mistakes and wishes to alert other shareholders and form some sort of action group, he has a few choices. All of them are either unrealistic or clumsy:

- he can ask the board to circulate his proposals – but although the Companies Acts require the board to circulate material of this nature in certain circumstances, if the material is overtly critical of them, they will not be best disposed towards this shareholder and the process is not likely to run smoothly;

- he can advertise for other investors to come forward – but this involves expense and often considerable effort on his part (with the advent of financial websites[1] allowing individuals the opportunity to post their views regarding particular companies on bulletin boards, this has become more commonplace); or

- he can wait until the AGM and use this as an opportunity physically to hand material to other shareholders – but by then it is often too late to have a profound influence on the business of that meeting and, in any case, such meetings can be very poorly attended.

Advertising for shareholder interest may be easier and less expensive in view of the Internet (though not necessarily less time-consuming). But in practice this method of increasing shareholder awareness is still hampered by the lack of a public shareholder register. There is a strong argument for saying that investor relations websites and better communications generally with investors provide a means to a very useful end, namely the cultivation of a more discerning and interested shareholder class. That class will stand behind good management, while being equally enthusiastic to move (or even remove) poor management with the power of their commitment to the companies in which they invest. That in turn leads to better managed companies and thus to better all-round economic performance. In the US, this trend is well-developed. Enabling companies to communicate certain matters to their shareholders electronically is a starting point in the UK. However, there is a great deal more to be done before we have the sort of shareholder motivation that exists across the Atlantic.

1 See, for example, www.iii.com.

13

E-property

1. INTRODUCTION

13.01 Whilst the property industry has lagged behind other sections of the economy in rising to meet the e-commerce challenge, there is no doubt that technology has made an impact. In this chapter we examine the ways in which the property industry has been affected by e-commerce. We will consider how the industry has responded to the challenges of e-commerce and look at new on-line products which facilitate the process of buying property. We will also examine the legislative changes which are now to be introduced to enable e-commerce to revolutionise the conveyancing process itself.

2. THE IMPACT OF E-COMMERCE ON PROPERTY

(a) The market strikes back

13.02 There are those who predicted that the high street would dwindle away to nothing and office blocks would stand derelict, victims of the increasing move towards virtual shopping, teleworking and on-line business. However, whilst an increasing amount of business conducted on the Internet is having an effect on the way that businesses use space, the changes have not been as dramatic as feared. The dot.com crash and global terrorism have undoubtedly been contributory factors but, in reality, the changes that have taken place have been more subtle and complex than those which were originally contemplated.

(b) Retail

13.03 Initially there was a fear in the retailing industry that the high street would be severely affected by e-commerce. However, it proved more difficult for Internet-only business to demonstrate that they could create successful and profitable business models: Amazon[1] does not have any conventional shops and it has taken some considerable time for it to demonstrate that it has a successful and profitable business model. It appears that conventional retailing has undergone something of a renaissance in response to the challenges of e-commerce. Rather than being a threat to in-store sales and shopping centre operations, e-commerce is now looked upon as providing an opportunity for retailers and shopping centre developers to create an extra delivery channel for their goods. Many high street retailers now run their on-line business side-by-side with traditional shops ('clicks and mortar'). Think of almost any branded store and you will find that as well as maintaining a branch network which allows customers to touch, taste, try on and try out the goods, the retailer will also have a website permitting browsers to find an article, compare it with others and purchase it on-line if desired. The success of retailing depends on satisfying consumer desires. Today, besides value, service and the wide variety of goods and services they have always wanted, consumers expect an 'experience' when they shop. Large shopping centres such as Bluewater[2] are now regarded as destinations in their own right, where shopping is simply part of the overall experience. Until recently shopping centres have been largely single-purpose standalone developments dependent on traditional rental income streams. Shopping centres are now beginning to find ways to create new income streams. In the future retail rents may become a less important part of the total revenue which is derived from the shopping centre. Shopping centres such as Bluewater now have their own websites where, in addition to a directory of shops, there is a directory of restaurants, events and concierge services which are all designed to ensure that every possible consumer requirement is met. Increasingly, shopping centre owners are setting up and incubating their own business-to-business (B2B) service companies to provide the additional services which will support the retail function. The services include telecommunication, marketing and building procurement services for tenants, as well as entertainment services aimed at customers. In-store technology will both enhance the customers' experience and a store's utility. The store will not only be a point of sale but also a point of exchange, returns, service and assistance for customers who have purchased items on the web. This in turn will increase sales on the web because customers will know that they will receive the support and follow-up service they expect after their purchase, just as if they had purchased the item in-store. It is clear that the high street and shopping centres will reinvent themselves on a regular basis and technology will simply speed up the pace of change.

1   See www.amazon.com/www.amazon.co.uk, a leading on-line retailer of books, music, DVD, video, etc.
2   See www.bluewater.co.uk.

(c) Distribution

13.04   A critical issue for all businesses, not just e-businesses, is now 'speed to market'. To get your goods to the market you have to have logistical and distribution facilities. Even though Amazon does not have any conventional shops, it does have huge warehouses to carry its stock[1], and it is essential that it has a reliable delivery service. As more and more retailers go on-line, industrial properties have become increasingly sought after and market rents for warehouses in particular have increased due to demand for well-located facilities[2]. Some conventional retailers, however, are making use of their existing buildings to adapt to e-business. Tesco operates an on-line ordering and home delivery service[3] for which orders are fulfilled by picking direct from the shelves of the local superstore. Stock is replenished by the store's usual supplier deliveries, and the only additional step required is to load the orders up and deliver them to the customer. No additional warehousing or stock control is required. However, this method seems to be very much the exception rather than the rule. Demand for property in key distribution locations which are well connected to road, rail and airline interchanges will undoubtedly increase in order to facilitate the prompt delivery of goods which have been bought on-line.

1   In contrast, Dell has been able to dispense with conventional warehousing by creating a system where computers are built to order and delivered without ever being stored in a warehouse.
2   Source : Catella/IPML Regional Rental Indices, July 2000.
3   See www.tesco.com. Tesco is the UK's leading groceries retailer.

(d) Offices

13.05   Just as the disappearance of the high street was foretold by the soothsayers of the dot.com bubble, the centralised office was also predicted to become a relic of a bygone age. It seems that workers are still prepared to commute to their city centre offices, notwithstanding transport problems, particularly so long as their employers would prefer to be able to have some idea of their whereabouts! Nevertheless, the use of office space is becoming more flexible. Cellular offices are by no means the only space planning solution. Partitioning is being taken down and open plan is now seen as boosting productivity, particularly in creative businesses where information and ideas need to be shared. In industries where staff are more mobile, 'hot desking'[1] is increasingly prevalent. Teleworking[2] is still only a viable option for a minority of workers, whether due to lack of investment in equipment or due to having a less than enlightened employer. Traditional businesses still need offices to house their support functions and most e-businesses need access to office space too. Call centres and helpline facilities need to be established where there is a plentiful supply of qualified labour and can take up an enormous amount of space. Start-ups need a presence, too, preferably within easy striking distance of potential customers and (possibly more importantly to begin with) providers of venture capital and professional advisers. Even a start-up successfully incubated in a spare bedroom at home will need to expand beyond that once it takes off.

1   Hot desking is a desk sharing system where desks are not assigned to designated individuals (such areas are now often referred to as 'touchdown space').
2   'Teleworking' means working away from the office connected to business systems by remote network link.

(e) Serviced offices

13.06   The property market has expanded to include property 'products' which provide the flexibility and simplicity which e-businesses require. These include 'incubator' type business centres (aimed specifically at dot.com start-ups) and serviced offices[1]. Both of these concepts provide readily available office space in convenient locations on flexible terms. All standard business facilities will be provided by the operator, some as part of the rental package (telephones and reception services, desks, chairs, storage cabinets), others at additional cost (videoconferencing, catering, meeting rooms, word processing). Space can be rented on a licence only basis[2] by the day, week or month and can be added to or vacated on minimum notice, rather like occupying a hotel room. Market rents for this type of flexible space are generally inflated above the average payable for vacant office space. The rent takes account of the fact that a high level of fit-out and service is included, and also compensates the operator for the fact that the occupier may leave on short notice, leaving it without income generated from that space until another occupier can be found. On the other hand, the occupier does not incur any capital costs in fitting out new offices. Again for a start-up business, 'speed to market' is the key and serviced offices provide an instant office solution.

1   Such as those provided by operators including Regus (www.regus.com) and MWB Business Exchange (www.mwbex.com). The Institute of Directors launched its own serviced offices operation in June 2000 as a joint project with property company MEPC.
2   A licence differs from a lease in that a licence is personal to the occupier and confers no interest in the land or building occupied. In other respects licence and lease arrangements can be similar, with the parties free to negotiate the extent of their respective obligations in respect of repair, access and use of the premises. A licence may be terminated by the owner at any time. Unlike a business tenant whose rights are protected by statute (the Landlord and Tenant Act 1954), a licensee has no security of tenure.

(f) 'Wired up' buildings

13.07   Now, more than ever, buildings located 'on-fibre' are increasingly attractive to sophisticated occupiers needing huge bandwidth available to service business applications[1]. Buildings located close to new cable communication networks are especially popular, as they cut down the amount of additional cabling required in order to connect to the network, and their location provides a high degree of connectivity for very little effort on the part of the occupier. However, the buildings themselves have to be up to the task too. Simply being in the right location is not sufficient in itself. Among other requirements, large amounts of cabling may need to be fitted into floor voids to bring the network to the desktop and the floors themselves may need to be strengthened to cope with additional loading due to the amount of equipment installed. A constant uninterruptable power supply is required (some new developments incorporate dedicated power generation facilities) and security is paramount. Of course, a business may not need a whole building equipped to this specification. Good space planning can keep the area required to a minimum.

1 'Industrial Floorspace Today – July 2000' (Research publication produced by King Sturge International Property Consultants).

(g) Datacentres

13.08 The alternative is to take advantage of a datacentre. A datacentre ('telehotel', 'carrierhotel', co-location facility or 'telehousing') provides facilities for Internet servers to be maintained in a dedicated space within a building which is used in common with others. The building will have all the attributes necessary to provide a high level of connectivity in a well-maintained and secure environment. The user can choose a variety of services from simply renting the racking on which its servers are kept to a full maintenance programme (including rental of servers if required), all of which are provided in return for payment of a periodic fee[1]. Operators in this sector take advantage of the business need for secure server accommodation to cater for 24/7 website and communication maintenance and occupiers are happy to pay for the facility to be provided.

1 Operators in this market include Telecity (www.telecity.com) and Globix (www.globix.com).

(h) Old buildings – obsolete?

13.09 Older buildings frequently do not have the attributes necessary to enable them to support these requirements. However, it is not necessarily the case that old buildings cannot be satisfactorily adapted to meet the needs of high tech or dot.com occupiers. New wireless broadband communications systems such as those provided by Winstar[1] will enable older building stock to be brought up to date with access to increased bandwidth but without the need for cabling. Winstar uses a small pair of antennae located on the rooftop of a building linked through a 'hub and spoke' network to a local switching centre and then to the global telecommunications network. Systems like this one can provide an acceptable and cost effective solution where the cost of laying cabling to connect with existing networks would be impractical due to the type or age of the building, or prohibitively costly due to location. Another approach is to simply make the best of what you already have. The Telecoms Technology Consortium[2] plans to wire buildings owned by its members to enable upgradable fast telecoms access to be routed to the desktop, providing digital voice, data, video and Internet services. The Consortium members own millions of square feet of commercial space between them, occupied by a wide variety of mainly blue chip companies. As the initiative takes off and tenants begin to reap the benefit, the existing but newly wired building stock held by the group will provide strong competition for new developments, and should keep the market for e-commerce occupiers lively.

1 See www.winstar.com.
2 Members of the Consortium include British Land, Canary Wharf Group, Legal & General Property and Prudential.

(i) Televillages

13.10 Another new concept in the world of property is the televillage[1], a hybrid between teleworking and pure serviced offices. The televillage provides cottages and work studios specifically aimed at teleworkers. At the heart of the village is a purpose built telecentre with Internet links and videoconferencing facilities. The aim is not to provide space where companies can put whole teams, but to offer an environment in which individual teleworkers can take advantage of high levels of connectivity to their own remote business whilst enjoying a level of social interaction with others working for different businesses.

1   The first such facility in the UK was the Acorn Televillage, Crickhowell, Powys.

(j)   What next?

13.11   It is clear that the property industry is responding to the opportunities presented by e-commerce. New formats are emerging as traditional forms of property are reinventing themselves. Shopping is now becoming primarily a leisure experience. Soon going into the office may be a purely social experience and we may have to go to the pub or the coffee shop to get some work done!

3.   BUYING PROPERTY ON-LINE

(a)   The digitally enhanced dream home

13.12   Residential and commercial estate agents alike have realised the potential of web-based listings. Accurate property details including photographs, location maps and virtual 'walk-round' tours can be provided cheaply and be made available to a potentially limitless market. Combined with information about local services and amenities, on-line listings can provide a considerable amount of detail about specific properties and their location in return for minimal effort on the part of the buyer. Of course, both sellers and agents must bear in mind the legislative provisions applying to promotional materials advertising properties for sale. The Property Misdescriptions Act 1991 (PMA 1991) applies to on-line particulars as well as traditional brochures and flyers. The PMA 1991 provides that if a false or misleading statement is made[1] about a property in the course of an estate agency or property development business, the person making it is guilty of an offence punishable by fine and (in the case of repeated offences) disqualification. On the assumption that some buyers will rely entirely on the particulars provided by on-line listings, great care must be taken to ensure the accuracy of all statements made. Poor quality digital imaging for photographs of properties in particular could cause difficulty. An unclear image may in fact be misleading, so the quality of delivery and performance of the website assumes crucial importance. The Royal Institution of Chartered Surveyors has issued guidance notes concerning the PMA 1991. Information should be independently verified where possible and third party material should be clearly identified. A sufficient but reasonable disclaimer should be clearly displayed on the website.

1   The provisions apply only to 'prescribed matters' – the PMA 1991 includes a full list.

(b)   Project pathway

13.13   Most on-line property listings[1] at present do not go beyond providing basic information in an accessible format. Websites maintained by residential agencies[2] may offer links to other useful services (mortgage loan advice, solicitors and conveyancers, removals) but none so far seem to permit the buyer to place an offer on-line. Commercial listings have become slightly more advanced. Project Pathway[3] is a project intended to provide the first pan-European property listings service including additional information, commercial data and research resources. The first phase covers the UK, Germany, Spain, Belgium, Ireland, France and The Netherlands. In time (as legislation allows) the service will be expanded to become an on-line transaction exchange.

1   For example, www.propertylive.co.uk (maintained by the National Association of Estate Agents and TM Property Service Ltd, a national on-line property service), www.houseweb.co.uk (for private sales where no agent is instructed).
2   For example, www.foxtons.co.uk, www.winkworth.co.uk.
3   A joint venture between commercial property specialists DTZ, Jones Lang LaSalle, CB Hillier Parker/CB Richard Ellis and Reed Business Information.

(c) Fprop

13.14   One step further on finds First Property Online[1] (Fprop) in business and successfully achieving on-line transactions to the limit which the law currently allows. Fprop operates on an auction type basis (although no contract is formed upon an offer being accepted). Sellers can post information about their property in a standardised form on the Fprop website. The information is made available to potential buyers in three levels. The first level contains brief details only and the second includes full particulars and photographs. The third level information is only available to potential buyers on payment of a fee[2], and includes detailed legal information, search results and standard form contract documents. The fee is returned to the buyer after bidding has closed, provided the buyer made a bid above the reserve price (which is indicated on the listing for each property). Safeguarding from frivolous marketing or bidding on Fprop is maintained by a system of good faith deposits. Sellers pay £1,000 per property in order to register and the deposit is returned once bidding has closed or, in the event of a successful sale, once Fprop's success fee (0.5% plus VAT of sale price, capped at £10,000) has been paid. The seller's good faith deposit is forfeit if it gives in to the temptations of gazumping and accepts a bid only to later reject it in favour of a higher one. Buyers register required information on the website (including both personal details and confirmation of the solicitor who will act on their behalf) and then pay £1,000 in order to bid. Each £1,000 allows the buyer to bid on up to five properties. Further bids can be made on payment of a further £1,000 deposit for each five bids. Transactions are conducted entirely via the website at this stage. Fprop is a secure site[3], which gives added peace of mind to both buyer and seller. As transactions on Fprop are conducted along auction lines, the properties registered on the website are marketed for a maximum period of six weeks before bidding is opened. Marketing is conducted by using traditional methods (including press and viewings) as well as making the property details available on-line. Buyers are recommended to take legal advice and to obtain the level three information before submitting a bid. Bidding remains open for as long as the level three information remains valid (that is, until the local authority search information becomes unreliable due to the age of the search). The bidding process is transparent. Buyers and sellers alike are kept informed of how bidding is progressing. Each registered user of the website is provided with a 'Propmonitor' (this is an e-mail based service which buyers can use to list and monitor properties in which they are interested, and which sellers can use to assess the level of interest shown). The Propmonitor advises every user when a change in bidding takes place, and sellers can access a full bidding history including the number of level one and two hits on their property details and the number of level three information packages issued. The seller may accept a bid at any time provided that it is the highest made. If a bid in excess of the reserve is received, it must be accepted within three business days unless a higher bid is received in the interim. Bids from buyers are kept open for three business days as a minimum. Once a bid has been accepted, the seller and buyer must exchange contracts within two business days. Fprop has indicated that this timescale may well be shortened once legislation permits on-line exchanges to take place. Standard form contracts are made available on-line, and provide the basis of the subsequent agreement between buyer and seller. The form of contract for each property is provided in the level three information package so that the buyer can have notice of the terms before it submits a bid. Exchange of contracts and subsequent completion of the transaction are conducted using traditional methods between the parties and their solicitors. Technology and legislation permitting, it is Fprop's intention to allow buyers to exchange, complete and register their purchase on-line in future, transforming Fprop into a true transactions exchange.

Fprop has enjoyed a period of growth. It acquired both Commercial Property Database Limited and Propertytrade[4] during the course of 2001, and has also expanded its services. As well as providing high level property information, Fprop now also provides a wider range of standardised property documentation, including certificates of title which a buyer or lender may rely on, obviating the need to undertake independent searches and enquiries. Additional services include bespoke loan, valuation and legal quotes[5] and an underwriting service[6].

1 See www.fprop.com.
2 Currently £75 plus VAT.
3 SSL secured (40-bit).
4 An on-line property database and listings service.
5 A panel of commercial property lenders, their valuers and solicitors are invited to review Fprop listed premises which meet their lending criteria, and to provide an on-line indicative financing quote and fees quote. The quotes are subject to further due diligence and to the buyer's status.
6 Fprop can offer sellers either a guaranteed fixed purchase price in return for an agreed underwriting premium or a guaranteed fixed purchase price in return for a share of the profit if the property sells on the market at a price higher than the minimum. Through these mechanisms, Fprop has begun trading in property on its own account.

(d) Legalmove

13.15 As far as residential properties are concerned, on-line services such as legalmove[1] are at the forefront of the latest developments. Legalmove allows buyers and sellers to track their house move completely on-line. On-line fixed fee quotes are followed up by 24/7 real-time on-line access to case details and documents. Telephone support is also available if needed seven days a week. Each legalmove.com account is protected by the use of secure logon, a unique personal account number and password. An enthusiastic response to the service so far promises success in the future and demonstrates an appetite for on-line conveyancing services. Given the moves now being made towards enabling electronic conveyancing (see Section 5 below) it is not difficult to foresee that services such as legalmove will be best placed to deliver the new model.

1 See www.legalmove.com, the on-line conveyancing service operated by HammondsDirect.

(e) Octane and Sitestuff

13.16 Other B2B business models have been developed within the property industry. One example is Octane, an e-business alliance of managing agents and surveyors[1]. Octane works with another e-business, Sitestuff[2], as its primary web-based procurement partner. Sitestuff helps owners and managers of commercial properties streamline their operations by ordering goods and services on-line.

1 Members include CB Richard Ellis, Jones Lang LaSalle and Trammel Crow.
2 See www.sitesuff.com. Sitestuff is a venture backed enterprise. Octane has made a substantial investment in it.

(f) Servista

13.17 Servista[1] allows individual householders who subscribe to its service to have phone, gas and electricity services provided from one source, settled through one composite on-line bill. Servista claims it can offer savings to consumers because it pools requirements in order to bulk-buy, passing the savings on to its subscribers[2]. The Servista offering is intended to be extended to include Internet, mobile phone and ADSL services in the future, but to date the service remains limited to its three primary components[3]. This is perhaps a reflection of the intense competition in the mobile network market, and of the relatively slow take up by consumers in the UK of advanced broadband services such as ADSL.

1   See www.servista.com.
2   Similar enterprises have seen gas and electricity providers branch out to offer their customers a range of services from one source.
3   npower (www.npower.com) provides a similar offering, but also includes domestic appliance repair and home insurance.

(g) The Realm

13.18   It is also now possible to acquire finance, management and accounting services on-line, together with transactional services such as rent collection. The Realm[1] is an e-commerce hub for commercial real estate management which provides all of these services. It offers workflow solutions, standard process automation tools and research facilities.

1   See www.therealm.com (a venture funded e-business hub hosting an applications site, a gateway to hosted transactional services, content channel delivery and real estate industry information).

(h) Arrideo

13.19   E-commerce applications have also been developed to help to streamline the construction process: a large amount of work is required before the ground is broken to begin construction. AEC Venture[1] is a global B2B exchange for the architecture, engineering and construction industry. The UK alliance partner of AEC Venture is Arrideo[2], a joint venture between a group of leading construction companies[3]. It is a new venture and its website has not yet been completed, but it is intended that it will eventually provide facilities for on-line and project co-ordination.

1   See www.aecventure.com (accessible to members by password only). AEC is a joint venture between AMEC, Bovis, Lend Lease, Hochtief Turner and Skanska.
2   See www.arrideo.com.
3   AMEC, Balfour Beatty, Bovis Lend Lease, Kvaerner and John Laing.

4.   BORROWING ON-LINE

(a) Choosing a mortgage

13.20   Most businesses and individuals finance their acquisition of property by means of borrowing. Several aspects of the process have been made easier, for both borrower and lender alike, by making them less reliant on traditional means. The first and most obvious point at which a borrower can be overwhelmed by a deluge of paper and conflicting advice is in choosing a financial product to fund the necessary borrowing. Although it is beyond the remit of this chapter to reflect on the various options available and the merits or otherwise of the products themselves, suffice it to say the choice is bewildering. However, there is now a proliferation of websites available to help the consumer make a choice[1]. Some are maintained by recognised brokers, others have been set up independently. All provide brief details of a large number of loan products, usually with the facility to calculate monthly repayments. The next stage of the loan transaction has not yet been successfully piloted on-line. Credit reference checks must be carried out to verify the financial standing of the borrower, and the lender must also satisfy itself that the property being acquired will provide adequate security for the loan. The borrower's credentials are checked following receipt of a signed application form and supporting documentation[2]. The property itself will be subjected to a survey. At present there is no comprehensive on-line facility available for credit referencing, although some on-line lenders have the facility to provide borrowers with an indication of how much they will be permitted to borrow (subject to full credit checking being carried out at a later stage)[3].

1 Among others, www.fredfindsmortgages.com, www.e-loan.com, www.netmortgage.com, www.moneyextra.com.
2 Salary slips, P60, employer's reference, etc.
3 At best, these indicators are tools to guide the borrower in assessing how much it can afford to repay. On-line credit checking facilities are being developed (by Egg (www.egg.com) among others) but seem unlikely to be made available to the general public given the need to comply with data protection legislation.

(b) Web-based streamlining for the lender

13.21 Once a mortgage application has been submitted and accepted, the lending transaction can be streamlined still further. Although a borrower may only have one transaction to worry about, lenders can have thousands live at any given time. Systems for on-line work management and volume transaction handling come into their own for this type of work. HammondsDirect[1] is one such system. It is a high volume legal support service for lenders and financial institutions. Incoming documents (the application, supporting documents and correspondence) are scanned and inputted onto the work system, which becomes effectively paper-free and thereafter is accessed by PC and web only. The case history of each transaction is made accessible to the client in real-time via a browser, accessed through the HammondsDirect website via a secure link which is password protected. Telephone calls relating to each individual loan transaction are also logged in real-time and become part of the case history. The client can communicate with its service team via the Internet, as well as by conventional means. The level of sophistication which has now been achieved means that the lender has access to up-to-date details of every live transaction at its fingertips. The work management system integrated into the service permits multiple transactions to be processed with the same efficiency as if they were handled individually. The end result is that the transaction benefits from faster turnaround and response times, leading to a shorter time period before drawdown and completion can be achieved. This in turn helps speed up the borrower's purchase and the benefits filter through into the transaction chain.

1 See www.hammondsdirect.com, provided by the lender services department of Hammond Suddards Edge. Clients include Bradford & Bingley, Halifax, Prudential and Britannia.

(c) Redemption on-line

13.22 Although it is not yet possible to create a mortgage entirely by virtual means, it is now possible to release one by an electronic method. The Electronic Notification of Discharge (END) is now accepted by HM Land Registry as evidence that a charge has been redeemed without any certificate or correspondence being submitted. An END is an electronic message sent direct by a lender to HM Land Registry via a secure link. The message confirms that the loan has been repaid and includes the title number of the property against which the mortgage was secured and details of the borrower and the mortgage. The END is held on the Land Registry's computer system until an application is submitted for the loan to be discharged. The END and the application are then matched and processed and the mortgage is discharged[1]. A lender will only transmit an END if it has received sufficient funds to discharge the loan and cannot unilaterally withdraw the END once transmitted. Strict time limits apply to users of the END system. Lenders have 21 working days within which to transmit an END following redemption of the loan, and the Land Registry undertakes to investigate any END-related queries within five working days of receipt[2]. Adherence to these standards will ensure that the paper-free discharge provides an efficient service to all parties. Not all lenders have signed up to the END system. To date, several[3] have taken the plunge. No doubt as the system proves itself, it will become more popular. In fact, the move towards electronic notifications may well be inexorable.

1 At present applications must be submitted on standard Land Registry forms in hard copy accompanied by title deeds. Advances in Land Registry practice will soon enable forms and deeds to be submitted in electronic format.
2 HM Land Registry Practice Leaflet 30, October 1999.
3 49 lenders, according to the HM Land Registry Annual Report 2001 (http://search.landreg.gov.uk/publications/ar/ar2K01.pdf), including Nationwide Building Society, the Woolwich, Derbyshire Building Society and Cheltenham & Gloucester plc.

(d) Dematerialisation of deeds

13.23 A further benefit of the move towards a paperless system of transfer and registration will be ease of storage of title details. At present, millions of title certificates are held by solicitors, individuals, banks and building societies throughout the country. Part of the Land Registry's new role may well be to provide secure storage for the electronic versions of the title certificates created by the new process. In fact, a new system is already in place which makes this vision a reality, at least in respect of those properties which are secured by way of mortgage in favour of a bank or building society. At present, millions of charge certificates (comprising the title to the relevant property, with a note of the bank's interest appearing on the face of the document) are held by banks and building societies in their vaults. The certificates are never used unless a query arises on the title or until the property is transferred and the mortgage is redeemed. In reality, there is probably no need for a certificate to be issued at all, since the title and the record of the mortgage are maintained in electronic form at the Land Registry (for computerised titles at present, and for all titles in future). The Land Registry introduced a new scheme on 1 November 1999, under which it will no longer issue charge certificates for new residential mortgages. The Nationwide Building Society was the first to join the scheme. The register entries maintained by HM Land Registry are clearly marked with an entry indicating that the title details are retained at the Land Registry. When the registration of the transfer and mortgage is completed, only a copy of the register entries is issued. A certificate can be made up at a later date if requested. The Land Registry expects that all building societies and banks which sign up to use the END system will also 'dematerialise' their charge certificates by joining this system. At the time of writing, 70 lenders have agreed to use the dematerialisation scheme[1]. It is hoped that others will follow.

1 A list of lenders is available at www.landreg.gov.uk/info.

5. CONVEYANCING ON-LINE

(a) Introduction

13.24 When the Law Commission published its report 'Land Registration for the 21st Century – a Conveyancing Revolution' in July 2001, it stated that the purpose of the Land Registration Bill (attached to the report) was to create the necessary legal framework in which registered conveyancing can be conducted electronically. The Bill was to bring about a conveyancing revolution: the move from a paper-based system for conveyancing to one that is entirely electronic. Electronic conveyancing, according to the report, is regarded as 'inevitable'.

(b) Registered land and computerisation

13.25 Title to land, whether freehold or leasehold, can either be registered or unregistered. Land which is unregistered becomes registrable when a 'trigger' for registration occurs. Since 1990 a purchaser of unregistered land anywhere in England and Wales has been obliged to apply to have the title registered at the Land Registry after acquiring it and, from 1 April 1998, this requirement has been extended to unregistered land acquired by gift or by will. The grant of a first legal mortgage of freehold or leasehold land will also trigger first registration. As well as extending triggers for compulsory first registration, the Land Registry has encouraged voluntary first registration by reducing Land Registry fees for voluntary applications. As a result of these changes the Land Registry estimates that some 80% of all titles in England and Wales are now registered and of the registered titles 95% have been computerised.

Once a title is computerised this opens the way to electronic access to the Land Register, title plan and any deed referred to in the title. The Land Registry also has an ongoing computer mapping programme to enable staff to carry out the mapping of each registration on-line. This is expected to be completed in 2005.

Electronic conveyancing can only apply to land for which the title is both registered and computerised. The increase in registrable transactions and the computerisation of the register and electronic access have laid the basis for electronic conveyancing.

(c) What is electronic conveyancing?

13.26 Electronic conveyancing means transferring and creating interests in registered land by electronic means. When the system is fully operational, it will only be possible to create or transfer rights over registered land by registering them on-line. Chains of transactions will be managed electronically. Searches and investigation of title will be conducted electronically. Figure 1 shows how an electronic conveyancing transaction might be conducted under the new system.

Figure 1: Electronic conveyancing model transaction

1. Marketing
- By traditional methods.
- By notice on NLIS bulletin board.
- Agent provides copy of sellers pack.

2. Offer
- Offer made, subject to contract.
- Offer accepted.
- Agent notifies conveyancer for each party by e-mail.
- HM Land Registry put on notice.

3. Negotiation

- Single comprehensive property search conducted through NLIS and Land Registry Direct.
- Survey (only if official survey in sellers pack is insufficient for buyer's purpose).
- Mortgage finance arranged on-line.
- Completion date agreed by reference to Land Registry or chain manager.
- Buyer's conveyancer agrees form of new register entry with HM Land Registry.

4. Exchange

- Contract signed by or on behalf of each party using an authenticated electronic signature.
- Exchange contracts electronically under power of attorney from client.
- Conveyancer notifies HM Land Registry and any 'e-settlement authority' of agreed completion date.
- HM Land Registry freezes register and makes provisional new register entry. Entry held until agreed completion date *or* until 30 days after exchange if no completion date is agreed.
- E-settlement authority holds provisional completion statement/disbursements list in electronic format.

5. Pre-completion

- No action required. HM Land Registry will have frozen register of title on exchange. No additional searches or priority required.

6. Completion

- Transfer executed using authenticated electronic signature.
- Completion agreed between conveyancers on authority of client.
- Completion money including stamp duty, Land Registry fees and other financial obligations settled simultaneously by electronic means via e-settlement authority.
- Simultaneous registration.

7. Post-completion

- No further action required (except possibly upon first registration).

(d) NLIS – National Land Information Service

13.27 The NLIS system is being developed alongside the electronic conveyancing system. Under the traditional conveyancing system a buyer must make enquiry of several different agencies to find out relevant information about a property which might influence its decision to purchase. As part of the move towards a more streamlined web-based system, NLIS[1] is now fully operational. NLIS provides an on-line one-stop service for collating search information. It provides a means of searching websites (other than the Land Registry) which hold information about property. Searches are carried out via the Internet and are routed through one of three channels[2] via the NLIS hub. From the hub the enquiries are routed to local authorities and the Coal Authority. The enquiries are related to the specific property not only by address but also by using the National Land and Property Gazetteer (NLPG), a definitive index of land and property[3]. On-line access to large-scale Ordnance Survey digital mapping is also available. Results are returned in electronic format where possible[4].

1 See www.nlis.org.uk.

2 TM NLIS Search, Transaction Online or NLIS Searchflow.

3 NLPG assigns a unique identification number to each property.

4 Over 100 local authorities currently have the capability to return electronic results.

(e) The Homes Bill

13.28 The Homes Bill, introduced during the course of the last Parliament, dealt with the introduction of the seller's pack. The pack was intended to be an integral part of the process of streamlining the house buying process under the House Bill proposals, reversing the established principle of caveat emptor (buyer beware!) which has underpinned English land law for many centuries. In essence caveat emptor means that a seller has no duty to disclose to a buyer anything beyond the bare details of the title to the property being sold. Even when a seller does disclose information about the property to a buyer a seller usually insists that the buyer should not be entitled to rely on such information as being accurate and should rely on its own searches and enquiries. Under the Bill a prospective buyer was to be given a comprehensive pack of information relating to the property it wanted to buy as soon as its offer was accepted. Although the Bill fell when Parliament was dissolved before the last general election and the prospect of a new Homes Bill was not mentioned in the Queen's Speech for the 2001–2002 Parliamentary session, the Government has made a manifesto commitment to making house buying easier. There is a strong possibility that the Homes Bill will be re-introduced with a view to having it enacted by the end of 2004. If it is introduced then it will, in tandem with the Land Registration Act 2002 (LRA 2002), constitute nothing short of a conveyancing revolution.

6. THE LAND REGISTRATION ACT 2002

13.29 The LRA 2002 was introduced to the House of Lords as a Bill in June 2001 and passed to the Commons in November 2001. The Bill arose out of the consultative document 'Land Registration for the 21st Century', which was followed by Law Commission Report No 271 published in July 2001 ('Land Registration for the 21st Century – A Conveyancing Revolution')[1].

The LRA 2002 aims to provide the necessary legal framework in which all registered conveyancing can be conducted electronically. The fundamental objective is to enable an effective system of electronic dealings with land. For this to become a reality, the register should be a complete and accurate reflection of the state of title to land at any given time. This will make it possible to investigate title to land on-line with the minimum of additional inquiries and inspections being required.

The LRA 2002 sets out provisions enabling formal documents to be executed, exchanged and completed electronically. Electronic conveyancing is dealt with in Part 8 of the LRA 2002[2]. It provides for the establishment of a secure electronic communications network for this purpose. Access to the network will be controlled by HM Land Registry.

The LRA 2002 includes amendments to the Land Registration Act 1925 (LRA 1925) and the Law of Property (Miscellaneous Provisions) Act 1989 (LP(MP)A 1989). New land registration rules and stamp duty legislation will also be required to give full effect to the proposals[3]. Contracts and transfers are dealt with separately in the LRA 2002, although the requirements for each are similar.

1 The LRA 2002 received Royal Assent on 26 February 2002.

2 Clauses 91–94 and Schedule 5.

3 The Land Registry published a Consultation Paper containing the draft Land Registration Rules on 27 August 2002. These Rules are available from the Land Registry and comments are invited until 19 November 2002. The LRA 2002 and the new Rules are expected to come into force on 13 October 2003.

(a) Contracts

13.30 A new section 2A of the LP(MP)A 1989 is inserted by the LRA 2002, specifying the criteria for a valid electronic contract (see 'Formalities' at paragraph 13.33 below). Electronic forms of contract will be permissible for use in relation to both registered and unregistered land.

(b) Transfers

13.31 The LRA 2002 sets out a new section 144A for insertion into the LRA 1925. Very similar criteria to those specified for contracts will apply. Electronic transfers will be available for use only in relation to registered land or to unregistered land where the disposition triggers compulsory first registration[1]. It will not be possible to make an electronic disposition of unregistered land which does not require subsequent registration.

1 Compulsory registration of certain types of transfer has applied in England and Wales since 1 December 1990.

(c) Registration

13.32 Why should the proposals not be extended to include all unregistered land? The fact is that unregistered land forms a small minority of the land holdings in England and Wales, and, following the introduction of compulsory registration, is dwindling all the time. Most unregistered interests comprise leases granted for a term of less than 21 years, which are currently unregisterable and which represent a sizeable gap in the registration system[1]. The only valid reason for not extending compulsory registration to these interests was the huge burden it would impose on the Land Registry. However, that burden will lessen considerably with the introduction of an electronic system and the Land Registry believes that its systems are robust enough to handle the anticipated volume of additional applications. Accordingly, the new proposals envisage that all leases granted for a term of seven years or more will be compulsorily registerable[2]. An additional concern about extending electronic dispositions to include unregistered land is that of security. For registered land the Land Registry will keep all necessary records, and will give a guarantee in respect of any registered title; there will be no central repository for the secure transmission and storage of documents relating to unregistered land. The new proposals envisage that completion of a disposition and its registration at HM Land Registry should take place simultaneously (see Figure 2). This would mean that the register would be updated in real time and would give a truly accurate record of all registered titles.

1 Many commercial occupiers prefer to lease rather than own their business premises, taking advantage of the protection offered to business occupiers by the security of tenure provisions of the Landlord and Tenant Act 1954. Although landlords prefer to grant leases for terms of 25 years and over, occupiers prefer shorter terms. Terms of five, ten and 15 years are now common, and none of them are currently registerable.

2 It was proposed that the minimum term triggering registration should be dropped to three years. A three-year lease is already a trigger in one respect in that all leases granted for a term of three years or more must be executed as a deed. There are no special requirements for leases of less than three years' duration. In theory therefore they could already be created by electronic means.

Figure 2: HM Land Registry – electronic conveyancing timeline

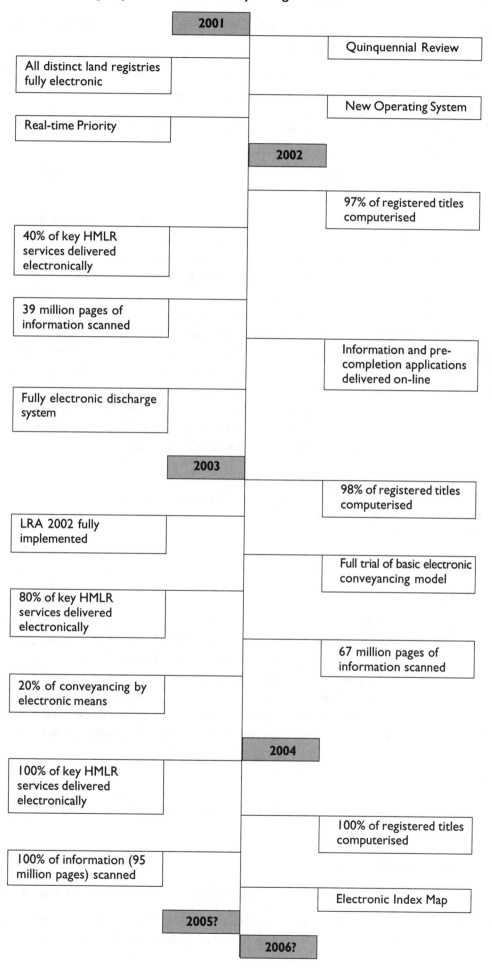

(d) Formalities[1]

13.33 Electronic conveyancing documents will have to meet certain criteria in order to be used for electronic dispositions. The criteria are:

- the document must contain or refer to all of the terms intended to be incorporated into it;

- the document must state when it is intended to take effect;

- the document must be signed using the certified electronic signature of each party required to execute it; and

- the document (if it is a disposition) must be drawn up in a form specified by HM Land Registry[2].

At present, there are statutory and common law requirements relating to deeds and documents. For example, any contract for the sale or other disposition of an interest in land must be in writing and signed by or on behalf of both parties[3]. Any disposition other than the grant of a tenancy for a term of three years or less must be by deed[4]. These will continue to apply to 'paper' documents but a draft order has been made which will deem compliance with them if various criteria are satisfied[5]. The provisions set out in the LRA 2002 do not disapply statutory or common law requirements relating to the execution of documents, but deem compliance with them if the various criteria are satisfied. The deeming provisions will also apply where electronic documents are executed by an agent (for example, a solicitor) acting on behalf of his principal (the client). The agent who executes an electronic document on behalf of his principal will be deemed to have the full authority of that principal to do so as far as any person relying on that document is concerned. This provision will cater for the scenario in which an agent acts for a principal which does not have its own electronic signature, but assumes that every practitioner with access to the network has or will be assigned one.

1   Clause 91. This derives from a proposed new section 144A of the LRA 1925.
2   The Land Registry has not yet published the required formats.
3   The LP(MP)A 1989. The sole exception is at auction, where the contract is created when the hammer falls.
4   The Law of Property Act 1925, ss 52 and 54.
5   It will insert a new section 2A in the LP(MP)A 1989.

(e) Network

13.34   The provisions set out in the LRA 2002[1] enable the Land Registrar to establish an electronic communications network to facilitate electronic conveyancing. Many of the details of this scheme remain to be worked out. It is not made clear whether the most effective form of network has yet been identified or what equipment will be required to access it. The terms on which practitioners will be permitted to access the electronic conveyancing network have yet to be published in detail, but it is clear that HM Land Registry will authorise access to the network and practitioners will be charged for that access. Access will be governed by a network access agreement. That agreement will enable the authorised party to do one or more of the following:

- communicate, post and retrieve information;

- make electronic dispositions and applications which will result in changes to the register;

- issue official search certificates;

- issue office copies of title information;

- 'other' conveyancing-related actions (at the discretion of the Chief Land Registrar).

Variable levels of access will be available. The Registrar will have limited powers to terminate access, those powers being regulated by network access rules. Grounds for termination could include failure to comply with the terms of access, failure to meet imposed conditions or ceasing to be part of a class of people with whom HM Land Registry may contract to grant access[2]. The Registrar will be empowered to impose suspension periods[3].

Network access rules will be made by the Lord Chancellor having regard to various criteria including confidentiality of the information kept on the network, the authorised person's competence to use the network[4] and adequate insurance against potential liabilities being made available.

1   Clause 92, Part 8 of the LRA 2002.
2   For example, licensed conveyancers, mortgage advisers, solicitors.
3   The exercise of the Registrar's powers may be queried by appeal to an adjudicator and to the High Court (on points of law only).
4   Those applying for authorisation to use the network must demonstrate their competence to do so. It is probable that an on-line training and education programme will be introduced, with participation being made a condition of access.

(f)   Registration[1]

13.35   The paper-based and electronic conveyancing systems will operate side by side to begin with, but it is intended that the paper system will eventually be phased out in order to achieve maximum benefit from the efficiencies which a fully electronic system can offer.

1   Clause 93, Part 8 of the LRA 2002.

(g)   Storage[1]

13.36   The LRA 2002 also provides for rules to be made regarding storage of electronic documents, but no details have been finalised. Any rules which are made will have to take account of the progress already made in the use of END[2] and dematerialisation[3].

1   Clause 94, Part 8 of the LRA 2002.
2   Electronic Notification of Discharge, in which a lender whose mortgage over a property is discharged simply notifies HM Land Registry by e-mail rather than by executing a deed. Some of the lenders who now use this scheme include the Woolwich, Nationwide Building Society and Cheltenham & Gloucester plc.
3   Traditionally when a mortgage or other secured loan is registered against a property at HM Land Registry, a charge certificate has been issued to the lender to be held as security for the loan. Dematerialisation relies on the electronic records of title already held at HM Land Registry. No charge certificate is issued in respect of loans advanced by lenders participating in the scheme. Lenders save on the cost of storage, the Land Registry saves on the administrative cost of producing paper copies and the title record is securely held in electronic format until required. The Nationwide Building Society was one of the first lenders to adopt the system.

(h)   Supplementary provisions

13.37   The LRA 2002 will insert a new section 3(ii)(a) into the LRA 1925 to extend the definition of a 'document' to include documents in electronic format which satisfy the various criteria. An additional rule will give the Lord Chancellor the power to make land registration rules under a new section 144(I) of the LRA 1925. The rules will encompass the following:

■   rules regulating the submission of documents in electronic form;

■   rules providing for applications to register notices, cautions or restrictions[1];

■   rules regulating the storage of documents in electronic format;

■   the power for the Lord Chancellor to make electronic conveyancing compulsory for all registered land transactions[2].

1   Common protective measures employed by persons with an interest in land other than the owner.

2   It is not proposed at present that the use of electronic conveyancing should be compulsory – provision has been made for those who do not have access to the necessary technology or who want to do their own conveyancing without engaging the services of a solicitor or licensed conveyancer. A Land Registry advisory unit will be set up to assist in such instances. However, during the consultation which was undertaken prior to the publication of the Land Registration Bill, several responses from practitioners and other professionals indicated a strong preference for the electronic system to be made compulsory within a short period of its introduction so that all users could benefit from the efficiencies it has to offer. If some paper-based transactions were still permissible, the introduction of an electronic system would achieve little more than offering a different method of transacting, but without the benefits of a fully integrated system.

(i)   Timetable

13.38   Figure 2 above shows the projected timetable for the Land Registry to comply with the Government's requirement for all public services to be made available on-line by the end of 2005. As far as electronic conveyancing is concerned, the LRA 2002 should be partially implemented by the second half of 2002 and fully implemented by the second half of 2003. Electronic conveyancing could be partially implemented by the beginning of 2004 and fully implemented by the second quarter of 2005 (although with three of four consultation periods still to come the timetable seems likely to slip by a year or two). Electronic registration should be technically possible by the end of 2003, which is also when it is thought registration of short leases will become compulsory.

7.   REMAINING ISSUES

13.39   As with any new proposal, extensive consultation has been undertaken to canvass the views of those who will be using the new system. The responses to the Lord Chancellor's Department's consultation paper[1] indicate that the respondents see progress towards electronic conveyancing as inevitable, subject to suitable safeguards. Several key themes have emerged as being of particular concern.

1   Lord Chancellors' Department, Electronic Conveyancing – Analysis of the responses to the Consultation Paper on a draft order under section 8 of the Electronic Communications Act 2000 (www.lcd.gov.uk/consult/general/e-convresp.htm).

(a)   Security

13.40   Is current technology sufficiently secure for users to have confidence in it as a mainstay of the new electronic system? Fraud and loss of confidentiality are key concerns. The consultation paper does not propose any mechanism by which a defrauded owner whose property has been transferred without its consent by fraudulent use of its electronic signature or under purported agency can credibly prove that the electronic document giving effect to the transaction was not effected under its authority. Hacking is seen as a potentially damaging problem which current encryption technologies cannot prevent. A determined hacker could access confidential contracts and other transaction documents, and may also be able to perform unauthorised transfers. A degree of global harmonisation may also be required. Different countries permit varying levels of encryption. Without a global consensus as to the level of encryption which is desirable and necessary to prevent abuse of the system, cross-border transactions could be badly affected.

(b)   Electronic signatures

13.41   As far as electronic signatures are concerned, most respondents to the consultation paper had no difficulty in understanding and accepting the concept. However, the consultation paper gave no guidance as to how electronic signatures will be regulated or which systems may be employed. This may be sensible given the fact that technology changes rapidly, but has opened the proposals up to criticism. A common concern is that practitioners and clients cannot be expected to give full support to the proposals when key details remain unclear. More details concerning issues such as the regulation of the certification authority for electronic signatures, liability for those acting as authorised agents and methods for combating fraud will be needed in order for prospective users to be confident on security issues. What seems clear is that users will expect a high integrity system with the close involvement of practitioners and their regulatory bodies.

(c) IT capability

13.42 The proposals seem to suggest that there will be a dedicated linked 'intranet' system enabling registered users to have access at the appropriate level. There is some concern about the level of linkage and degree of interaction which will be possible between what will be a very large number of users, each with their own intranets, deal rooms, extranets and the like. Although many businesses and individuals already have sophisticated IT systems delivered via PC to the desktop, much of the advantage of increased connectivity will be lost if the system is not sufficiently robust or if it will require further investment in costly specialised equipment.

(d) Certified agents?

13.43 A great deal of concern has been expressed by practitioners over the impact of the provisions which deem that an agent (the conveyancer) is acting with the full authority of the principal (his client) without requiring evidence of that authority. Respondents to the consultation paper were particularly concerned about this aspect of the proposals. The analysis of the responses notes that there appears to have been a degree of misinterpretation. The Lord Chancellor's Department's suggestion is that an agent executing an electronic document by or on behalf of his principal with written authority to do so should not be required to produce evidence of that authority in order for a third party to rely on the executed document. However, most respondents to the consultation paper interpreted the provisions to mean that no express authority would be required in order for one party to act as agent for another. This was not intended, and clearly more work will need to be done to ensure that a workable 'best practice' system is put in place to safeguard principals, agents and third parties[1]. One solution might be to replace the 'deeming' provisions with a system in which authority to act on behalf of a principal can be certified. This would deter agents from acting without authority and would give all users of the system greater confidence that they are not an unwitting party to a fraud. The requirement for certification would take some of the immediacy out of the system, but may reap benefits if more doubters could be persuaded to rely on it as a result. It is possible that modifications to the Powers of Attorney Act 1971[2] could be required to give effect to a certification process. If no formal requirements are imposed, it is likely that practitioners will develop a system of 'best practice' which includes some means of certification in order to cover the additional risk that comes with relying on deemed authority.

1 In practice a conveyancer acting on behalf of his client in executing a document would always require written authority to do so, and any practitioner relying on that authority would want to see evidence of it. Many corporate entities have very strict procedures for executing documents, and would be unlikely to be comfortable with delegated authority in any event.

2 The Act requires powers of attorney to be made in writing, signed or sealed by or in the presence of the person giving the power. Without amendment this would require a traditionally executed paper instrument to authorise an electronic transaction.

(e) Effective date

13.44 The new proposals for electronic conveyancing attempt to address the problem of defining the moment at which a contract negotiated and exchanged electronically is created by leaving it to the parties to specify when the electronic document is to take effect. This is one of the main criteria suggested for an electronic document to satisfy the requirements set out in the LRA 2002.

(f) Risk

13.45 From the point of view of practitioners, there seem to be several areas of risk giving cause for concern. The first is that the use of an electronic system and the attendant problems of signature certification, security and unauthorised access give rise to additional risk of speculative fraud carried out by third parties. Second, it also gives no protection against fraud carried out by the parties themselves. Third, unfamiliar practices will leave professionals exposed to potential negligence claims until the limits of their responsibility are defined by case law. In the meantime, practitioners could find that the cost of their professional indemnity insurance rises to reflect these increased risks.

(g) Guarantees

13.46 The proposals make no provision for guarantees. Guarantees are governed by legislation[1], which provides that guarantees cannot be enforced unless made or evidenced in writing. Accordingly, any disposition of land which involves the taking of a guarantee will be thrown back on paper-based procedures unless this omission is rectified.

1 The Statute of Frauds 1677.

(h) Stamp duty

13.47 As a general rule stamp duty is payable at prescribed rates on all dispositions of property made for value. Stamp duty is payable within one month of a disposition being made[1], and applications for registration at HM Land Registry cannot be processed without evidence that the proper rate of duty has been accounted for to the Inland Revenue[2]. The current system involves a visible stamp being impressed onto the original document. Clearly this is not practicable where electronic documents are concerned. The Inland Revenue has set up a policy team to advise on modernising stamp duty, which is advising the Government on the future requirements for stamp duty collection in the electronic age. Current proposals include receipt of stampable instruments via a designated 'gateway', with verification of the digital signatures giving effect to them, backed by some form of money transfer system[3]. An electronic receipt would then be issued recording the fact that duty had been paid. However, it is not possible to say at present how these proposals will interact with those put forward in the LRA 2002.

1 For details of rates, regulations and exceptions see www.inlandrevenue.gov.uk/leaflets/stof.htm. Parts of the proposals for on-line conveyancing suggest that stamp duty should be payable immediately upon completion via an 'e-settlement' authority, which would enable simultaneous registration of the disposition at HM Land Registry, but no details are available.

2 In addition, an unstamped document that should bear duty is generally not admissible in evidence at court in case of dispute.

3 Stamp duty reserve tax (SDRT) provides a precedent for this type of treatment. SDRT applies in relation to transfers of most stocks, shares and certain other securities (which can already be electronically traded).

8. THE FUTURE OF ELECTRONIC CONVEYANCING

13.48 Although many of the respondents to the Lord Chancellor's Department consultation paper and many other commentators have noted with enthusiasm that an electronic conveyancing system will bring greater efficiencies, it has been rather difficult to pinpoint precisely what the immediate benefits will be.

The new systems of electronic conveyancing will not be compulsory in the first instance. Accordingly, the new system offering a streamlined procedure will run side-by-side with the paper intensive and often time consuming traditional methods. Many domestic conveyancing transactions form part of a chain which can become lengthy and in which exchange and completion must be synchronised. It seems unlikely that great efficiencies will be achieved whilst chains have to be managed with two systems in place, and any chain can only move as fast as its slowest participant. The Land Registry has proposed that a chain manager should oversee linked transactions, but details are scant.

Cost savings are another anticipated benefit of the electronic conveyancing model. However, the respondents to the consultation paper reached no general consensus on this point. Many pointed out that even if it is not necessary to make costly investment in new technology to support the system, expenditure will still be required in order to implement the new internal systems and audits required to ensure the integrity of the new model. Having said that, if the electronic model offers clear advantages in terms of time saving and streamlining, many users may be prepared to pay a premium to use it.

An examination of the proposed model has also revealed practical queries which remain to be answered. In particular, many security issues remain unresolved. The Lord Chancellor's Department is launching a new major public consultation during 2002[1], which should hopefully address outstanding concerns.

It is clear that there remains a great deal of work to be done to make on-line conveyancing a realistic and attractive proposition. The ongoing consultative process will help to iron out concerns about fraud, security and other issues. Even with a lot of work still to come, however, it seems that the question is not whether electronic property dispositions will become possible and practicable, but when. The Government, the Land Registry, commercial entities and private practitioners are all working hard to make certain that the system, once introduced, will be as robust and long lived as that which has been in place since land registration was introduced in 1925.

1   With a view to having the system rolled out in 2006. For further details see the Lord Chancellor's statement on the Work Plan for advancing HM Land Registry's Quinquennial Review Recommendations: www.lcd.gov.uk/civil land reg/qrrec.htm.

9. SUMMARY – THE FUTURE OF CLICKS AND MORTAR

13.49 The groundwork has already been laid for an exciting future where e-commerce and real property work in partnership. In future it should be possible to find a property, negotiate, offer, contract, complete and register the acquisition in less time than it currently takes just to find somewhere and instruct a solicitor. And all without forms, without signatures, without documents. People and businesses will always need to occupy space, there can be no doubt about that, but the balance is changing. In 20 years' time the high street may be full of Internet cafes and flexible workspaces rather than shops. Supermarkets may have developed into pleasure domes or distribution centres. Electronic conveyancing will be well-established. The Land Registry and NLIS may have outsourced their server maintenance to a datacentre. Only time will tell. There are technological and legislative hurdles to be overcome, but the key pieces of legislation are already being rolled out. The next task will be to encourage confidence in the new systems and take the opportunity to move firmly onwards into the brave new world of 'propert-e'.

E-gambling

I. INTRODUCTION

14.01 Since the second edition of this book was published, there has been increased interest in, and commercial activity around, on-line betting and gaming. Reputedly, with the exception of the sex industry, this is the most profitable service sector on-line. Due to regulatory constraints, much of the on-line betting and gambling sector had sought refuge in offshore locations (particularly the Caribbean). However, the success of the industry has persuaded the UK Government, amongst others, to relax the regulatory constraints in order to entice more of those businesses into the UK.

This chapter begins with a brief introduction to the gambling industry in the UK before moving on to consider various aspects of the English legal and regulatory framework within which on-line gambling operates. It continues with a reflection on the recommendations made for the future regulation of on-line gambling by the Gambling Review Body and concludes with a consideration of international approaches to on-line gambling.

2. THE GAMBLING INDUSTRY IN THE UNITED KINGDOM

14.02 There are currently 8,500 licensed bookmakers' offices and 116 licensed casinos in England and Wales[1]. A few large operators dominate the traditional off-line gambling and gaming markets in the UK.

The three largest bookmaking operators – William Hill, Ladbrokes and Coral – own 21%, 17% and 9% of the high street bookmaking market respectively and, together, these bookmakers control three-quarters of the UK telephone betting market[2].

The casino industry in the UK has also been marked by a trend towards ownership by three companies, the Rank Group, Stanley Leisure and the Gala Group. Together, they own 75% of all casinos in the UK[3].

The gaming machine industry has experienced 'roller coaster trading'[4] over the last 30 years and whilst some 107,000 new units (worth almost £180m) were manufactured and sold by UK producers in 1999[5] only 50,000 units were sold in 2000.

There are currently 743 bingo clubs that hold bingo gaming licences. The industry has declined year-on-year since 1974, when there was a peak of 1,800 bingo clubs[6]. Two large operators, Mecca Bingo and Gala Leisure, dominate the bingo sector, operating around 40% of all bingo clubs in the UK.

The current operator of the National Lottery is Camelot plc, which runs both lottery draws and instant lottery scratchcards. Since its inception in November 1994, over £36 billion has been spent on all of the National Lottery products and over £10 billion has been donated to good causes[7]. The introduction of the National Lottery has had a significant impact on the other forms of lottery[8]. Of particular note is the fact that local authority lotteries have declined from 148 in 1990 to just four in 1999–2000[9]. Whilst a recent report[10] found that despite an increase[11] in the number of societies lotteries[12], for every £1 used to purchase National Lottery products only 2 pence was spent by the public on societies lotteries. However, ticket sales for societies and local authority lotteries rose from £26.4m in 1990 to £161.1m in 1999, before falling to £103m in 2000[13].

It is difficult to state with any certainty how many on-line gaming and gambling operators exist as, in most jurisdictions, there are no requirements for registration or licensing. Some estimates suggest that there are around 1,500 on-line casinos in the Caribbean alone[14]. Overall, there are already hundreds and possibly thousands of gambling websites around the world, all potentially accessible by British gamblers with Internet access.

1 The Gambling Review Report presented to Parliament by the Secretary of State for Culture, Media and Sport, July 2001. See www.culture.gov.uk/ROLE/gambling_review.html.
2 The Gambling Review Report presented to Parliament by the Secretary of State for Culture, Media and Sport, July 2001.
3 The Gambling Review Report presented to Parliament by the Secretary of State for Culture, Media and Sport, July 2001.
4 The Gambling Review Report presented to Parliament by the Secretary of State for Culture, Media and Sport, July 2001.
5 Maygay Machines Ltd (2000), reported in the Gambling Review Report, July 2001.
6 Bingo Association (2000), reported in the Gambling Review Report July, 2001.
7 National Lottery website: www.national-lottery.co.uk.
8 Small, private, societies and local authority lotteries.
9 The Gaming Board, reported in the Gambling Review Report, July 2001.
10 Department for Culture, Media and Sport – Economics Branch (2000).
11 From 806 in 1990 to 27,334 in 2001: the Gambling Review Report, July 2001.
12 As defined in the Lotteries and Amusements Act 1976 (LAA 1976), s 5.
13 Gellatly and Clarke, *On-line Gambling: The Regulation of Global Sports Betting* (2001) Sport Business Group Ltd.
14 Sutherland J (16 April 2001), reported in the Gambling Review Report, July 2001.

14.03 The available data suggests that, to date, only a small percentage of the UK population have gambled on-line and recent surveys found that less than 0.5% of respondents had gambled over the Internet[1]. Similar percentages have been reported overseas[2]. Identifying the type of person likely to gamble on-line is speculative. Recent submissions made by the betting industry[3] to the Gambling Review Body suggest that the profiles of telephone gamblers and betting shop gamblers are markedly different. It would not be surprising if the profile of a typical on-line gambler also differed from his off-line counterparts. This may have implications when targeting potential customers and will be likely to impact on how protective regulators will be.

The profile of an on-line gambler may be similar to that of a current e-commerce customer, which is in turn based on analysis of Internet users. One report suggests that the typical e-commerce consumer in England and Wales is a 34-year-old male, in social class ABC1, who lives in the south east and has at least one degree[4]. It is also clear that this profile will develop and some industry analysts have commented on the ability of interactive television and on-line gambling sites to reach novice gamblers, such as women[5] and younger people who would not normally enter a betting shop[6].

There is limited data available on the number of people currently registered with on-line gambling sites. Blue Square (the UK-based onshore Internet betting site launched in May 1999) claims that it has 110,000 users registered[7] and that over the Grand National weekend in 2001 it received over 70,000 bets on-line[8]. The interactive television site Open also reported that, by March 2001, it had signed up more than 20,000 active betting customers[9]. These claims are supported by studies that indicate that on-line betting sites rank among the most visited entertainment sites on the Internet[10].

1 Sproston, Erens and Orford (2000), reported in the Gambling Review Report, July 2001.
2 Australian data suggests that in 1998–99 about 0.6% of adults gambled regularly on the Internet. It has also been reported that of the 90 million web users in the US, some 5% have gambled on-line.

3   The Gambling Review Report, July 2001.
4   Retail E-Commerce Task Force (2000).
5   Although women are more likely than men to participate in Bingo, according to a report by Sproston, Erens and Orford reported in the Gambling Review Report July 2001.
6   *Broadband* Media, 9 April 2001.
7   *Broadband Media*, 9 April 2001.
8   *Racing Post* (13 April 2001).
9   *Broadband Media*, 9 April 2001.
10 *Broadband Media*, 9 April 2001.

14.04   Present and future on-line gambling revenues are difficult to estimate because of the lack of verifiable public data[1]. One analyst concluded that the value of the UK Internet betting market was probably approximately in the region of £100m in 1999[2]. This compares to betting office turnover of £6,563m and telephone betting turnover of £729m onshore and £250m offshore in the same year[3]. In relation to betting via interactive television, BSkyB announced that it made £33m from gambling in the second half of 2000, generated by the Surrey Group Internet site and via Open (the TV-based e-commerce platform), which currently carries Blue Square[4]. Open claims that its profit margins exceed 10% per bet.

All of the UK's leading digital TV operators[5] have alliances with individual bookmakers on their interactive platforms although, at the time of writing, the proposed alliance between BSkyB and Ladbrokes appears to have floundered. These alliances reportedly provide partners with lucrative revenue streams, though no interactive betting company has yet published comprehensive details. It is thought that platform operators may take 40%–50% of the profits accumulated by TV bookmakers, usually receiving a tenancy fee plus a commission on all bets.

Whilst analysts talk expectantly about the growth of e-gambling, reports suggest that less than 5% of betting in the UK has gone on-line[6]. Other commentators have suggested that on-line betting now accounts for 2–3% of the UK gambling market[7]. It is possible that very few people are betting on-line but that it is the higher spending gamblers doing so. Indeed, certain operators, such as Betdaq, are deliberately targeting a comparatively small number of high value transaction gamblers on their recently launched peer-to-peer betting site.

The UK gambling market has already attracted the interest of large multinationals, such as Disney and Playboy, and the recent successful application by MGM Mirage for an on-line casino licence based in the Isle of Man is 'an indication that US land-based operations are urgently looking outwards from their core US operations'[8].

As a result, commentators predict that there will be a massive growth in revenues and the investment bank Merrill Lynch has predicted that the global on-line gambling market could be worth as much as $125 billion by 2015[9].

1   Kelly J (2000), reported in the Gambling Review Report, July 2001.
2   Europe Economics (2000), reported in the Gambling Review Report, July 2001.
3   Europe Economics (2000), reported in the Gambling Review Report, July 2001.
4   *Broadband Media*, 9 April 2001.
5   Sky Digital, NTL, Telewest.
6   Sky Digital, NTL, Telewest.
7   Merril Lynch (2001).
8   Gellatly and Clarke, *On-line Gambling: The Regulation of Global Sports Betting* (2001) Sport Business Group Ltd.
9   (2001) Times, 6 April.

3.   LEGAL CLASSIFICATION OF GAMBLING

14.05   The Betting, Gaming and Lotteries Act 1963 (BGLA 1963) establishes no precise definitions for the various forms of gambling and contains only the rather circuitous statement that 'a bet does not include any bet made or stake hazarded in the course of, or incidental to, any gaming'[1].

This characterisation side-steps any definition of the terms 'bet' or 'gaming' and many commentators believe that the lack of precision in the drafting was a deliberate act. In the case of *Seay v Eastwood*[2], Lord Wilberforce described as 'very sound' the principle of magistrates using their local knowledge, experience of the world and common sense to give sensible interpretations to the various forms of gambling. Lord Wilberforce expounded the view that '... It is impossible to frame accurate definitions which can cover every variety [of gambling activity] and attempts to do so may indeed be counter-productive, since each added precision merely provides an incentive to devise a variant which eludes it'.

The characterisation of gambling activities is of paramount importance if an on-line gambling operator is to establish the legislative regime that governs its activities. It can be difficult to distinguish between the myriad of gambling products on offer but, for the purposes of this chapter, the legislative control of gambling within the UK is broadly based upon a division between gaming, lotteries and betting. As such, the starting point must always be an examination of each gambling activity and a close analysis of the contractual arrangements between the various parties involved in the particular gambling activity. In this manner, it should be possible to decide whether each activity should be properly categorised as 'betting', 'gaming' or a 'lottery'[3].

There exists a considerable overlap between the various categories of gaming, betting and lotteries. This overlap is particularly apparent and significant when the gambling activities are offered on-line[4]. These distinctions are old fashioned and artificial.

The conventional methods of differentiating between gambling products are not sufficient when dealing with on-line gambling. As a result, the on-line operator will need to assess the characteristics of each gambling product and the manner in which that product is offered before determining what regulatory controls it is subject to. This is not always a straightforward task. For example, roulette, which is correctly classified as 'gaming' when offered in 'bricks and mortar' casino premises, may amount to 'betting' when offered on-line. This is more than a mere academic exercise. Whilst 'gaming' is regulated by the Gaming Act 1968 (GA 1968) and may not be offered on-line, 'betting' is regulated by the BGLA 1963 and (provided that the operator holds a bookmaker's permit) may be offered on-line.

It is, therefore, necessary for an on-line operator to examine the nature of each of the gambling products it intends to offer on-line so that it may establish by which specific legislation the product will be regulated.

1 The BGLA 1963, s 55(1).
2 [1976] 3 All ER 153, HL.
3 See Lord Buckmaster in *A-G v Luncheon and Sports Club Ltd* [1929] AC 400 at 404, HL.
4 For the purposes of this chapter, the reference to 'on-line' refers to gambling services that utilise a telephone connection. This includes services that are accessed via the Internet, mobile telephony platforms and interactive television.

4. GAMING

14.06 The principal legislation governing gaming is the Gaming Act 1968. Section 52 of this Act defines gaming as 'the playing of a game of chance for winnings in money or money's worth whether any person playing the game is at risk of losing money or money's worth or not'[1].

Whether a particular activity involves 'playing a game' is a question of fact and there is no conclusive test[2]. Case law[3] supports the assertion that there must be *active* participation on behalf of the punters if the particular activity is to constitute gaming. However, to satisfy the requirement for 'active participation' a player need do little more than exercise *some* degree of skill or choice. In addition, the available case law suggests that playing of a game requires communication between the persons involved in playing it[4]. However, judicial interpretation is inconsistent as to the level (or indeed the requirement) of communication that is necessary between the punters[5]. The definition also refers to a 'game of chance'. This has been defined as 'a game of chance and skill combined and a pretended game of chance and skill combined'[6]. However, this definition should be considered in conjunction with section 52(6) of the GA 1968, which provides that 'in determining [...] whether a game [...], is a game of chance and skill combined, the possibility of superlative skill eliminating the element of chance shall be disregarded'. Therefore, irrespective of the degree of skill that is required, the game will be deemed a game of chance provided that the element of chance is not so slight as to render the game one of pure skill. This is a question of fact[7].

It is evident from the definition that even if the persons 'playing the game' do not risk losing any money (or money's worth), they are still 'playing a game of chance' and, as a consequence, 'gaming' within the meaning of the GA 1968. In the case of *Wheeler v Gibbins*[8], police officers who played bingo but could not collect any winnings because they did not hold membership cards were still held to be gaming.

1   This definition is reiterated in *Earl of Ellesmere v Wallace* [1929] 2 Ch 1, CA.
2   *Armstrong v DPP* [1965] AC 1262, HL.
3   See particularly *DPP v Regional Pool Promotions Ltd* [1964] 2 QB 244; *Armstrong v DPP* [1965] AC 1262, HL.
4   *DPP v Regional Pool Promotions Ltd* [1964] 2 QB 244; *Armstrong v DPP* [1965] AC 1262, HL; *Adcock v Wilson* [1967] 2 QB 683, DC; affd [1969] 2 AC 326, HL.
5   At one extreme is the dicta of Lord Parker CJ (in *DPP v Regional Pool Promotions Ltd* [1964] 2 QB 244; *Armstrong v DPP* [1965] AC 1262, HL), which suggest a high level of communication involving physical or geographical propinquity. Later dicta (Lord Morris in *Adcock v Wilson* [1969] 2 AC 326 at 335, HL) suggest that some degree of communication (but not physical proximity) is required between the participants.
6   The GA 1968, s 52. Athletic games and sports are specifically excluded.
7   *R v Tompson* [1943] 1 KB 650, [1943] 2 All ER 130, CCA.
8   [1970] 1 All ER 323, DC.

(a) Casino gaming

14.07   All bankers' games and games of unequal chance are prohibited. The stated exceptions to these rules include American roulette, blackjack, punto banco, French roulette, craps, baccarat, casino stud poker and super pan[1]. These games are permitted provided that they are played only within licensed premises[2], which must be operated as members' clubs and located in certain designated areas of the country, known as 'permitted areas'[3]. Gaming may only be offered on premises where the operator holds a gaming licence[4]. Section 12 of the GA 1968 limits participation in gaming to those members or guests of members 'present on premises at the time when the gaming takes place there'[5] and 'no person may participate in gaming on behalf of another person who is not present on the premises'[6]. Potential casino operators must acquire a certificate of consent from the Gaming Board for Great Britain before any application for a gaming licence can be made to the licensing justices[7]. The application to the Gaming Board must specify 'the premises in respect of which the relevant licence application is proposed to be made'[8] and a certificate of consent will only be issued if the Gaming Board is satisfied that the casino complies with various requirements relating to the character, reputation and financial probity of the potential operator[9]. The certificate of consent may limit consent to a bingo club licence or may give consent to a general gaming licence.

Once the Gaming Board has issued the certificate of consent, the potential operator can, within a specified time limit[10], make an application for the issue of a gaming licence from the Gaming Licensing Committee of the local magistrates' court in a prescribed form[11]. The GA 1968 sets out formal procedures for the hearing of an application and sets out various mandatory and discretionary[12] grounds for refusal to grant a gaming licence[13]. Applications for gaming licences can be refused if it is shown that the applicant is not a fit and proper person[14], that there is insufficient demand for the gaming facilities[15] or that the premises are not suitable[16]. The gaming licence entitles an operator to offer commercial gaming only in those *specific* premises stipulated in that gaming licence and may place restrictions on the gaming licence relating to operating hours[17], gaming areas and games[18]. This effectively prevents an on-line gaming operation being located in the UK.

It can be seen that the GA 1968 is structured in a manner that would prevent an on-line gambling site offering gaming by means of a server located in Great Britain. As a consequence, if such an operator[19] offers gambling products that may be defined as gaming, the requirement that gaming takes place on the premises for which a licence has been granted would preclude the obtaining of a gaming licence for purely Internet gaming. Furthermore, even if the question of premises could be addressed (which is unlikely) an on-line operator would be required to find ways in which it could comply with the numerous restrictions imposed by Part I of the GA 1968. These restrictions include a prohibition on any charge (other than a stake hazarded)[20] or levy[21] being made in respect of gaming. Other restrictions relate to the exclusion of underage players[22], the hours of play[23] or the provision of credit for gaming[24].

1 Provided they comply with the conditions set out in the Gaming Clubs (Bankers' Games) Regulations 1994 (SI 1994/2899), as amended.
2 The GA 1968, s 1 prohibits gaming other than on licensed premises or in registered clubs or miners' welfare institutes.
3 See the Gaming Clubs (Permitted Areas) Regulations 1971 (SI 1971/1538).
4 Part II of the GA 1968.
5 The GA 1968, s 12(1).
6 The GA 1968, s 12(1).
7 The GA 1968, Sch 2, para 3.
8 The Gaming Board Consent Application Form.
9 The GA 1968, Sch 2, para 4.
10 The certificate of consent usually stipulates a period of seven weeks.
11 The GA 1968, Sch 2, para 5(2).
12 The case of *R v Crown Court at Manchester, ex p Cambos Enterprises Ltd* (1973) 117 Sol Jo 222 established that a licensing authority had a discretion to refuse the grant of a gaming licence.
13 The GA 1968, Sch 2, paras 18–23.
14 The GA 1968, Sch 2, para 20(2).
15 The GA 1968, Sch 2, para 18.
16 The GA 1968, Sch 2, para 20.
17 The GA 1968, Sch 2, para 24.
18 The GA 1968, Sch 2, para 25(1).
19 That is, location in Great Britain.
20 The GA 1968, Sch 2, s 14(1).
21 The GA 1968, Sch 2, s 15.
22 The GA 1968, Sch 2, s 17.
23 The GA 1968, Sch 2, s 18.
24 The GA 1968, Sch 2, s 16.

14.08 However, it is important to remember that not all games offered in an on-line casino will necessarily be construed as gaming[1]. It is possible to structure gambling products offered on on-line gaming sites in such a way that they do not constitute 'gaming'. Roulette when played at a casino is a group activity (even though each competitor has his own contract with the bank). However, when played on the Internet, roulette can be offered as a gambling activity in which both the operator and the punter can win or lose. In such circumstances the operator is obligated to settle each winning bet without reference to the other stakes (if any) received from other participants. Each of the players will actively participate in selecting his chosen colours or numbers and could be said to be forecasting the outcome of a particular event (that is, where the electronic ball will finish) and it is therefore more akin to fixed odds betting. Gaming has been defined as 'the playing of a game of chance for winnings in money or money's worth'[2] and in this context it is important to identify whether the activity involves 'playing a game'. This is a question of fact[3]. The courts, in reaching a decision, will consider the whole circumstances of the case and there is no conclusive test of the matter. Lord Parker[4] determined that playing a game of chance involved some participation by the players, either by the exercise of skill, the exercise of a choice or by some physical act. Equally, there are numerous cases that suggest that the playing of a game must involve the physical presence in one location of all the players or some degree of communication between them. That said, there are some modern indications that the participants do not need to be physically proximate to be playing a game. One particular example of this can be found within the GA 1968[5] which establishes that a game of 'linked bingo'[6] may still amount to gaming when played simultaneously in different club premises. However, the requirement for communication is probably still relevant. As a result, it is unlikely that a game is being played if it can be shown that there is no communication between the competitors. This lack of communication is a common theme of gambling activities offered on-line and the on-line roulette product offered on most of the popular casino websites provides no opportunity for the participants to communicate between themselves or with the 'operators'.

Furthermore, case law suggests that the playing of a game normally involves several players in competition with each other, and this is not usually the case with on-line casinos. However, the GA 1968[7] does envisage that a game of chance may be played where there is only one player if it is played against a gaming machine[8].

As a result, if a gambling activity could be offered on the Internet and involved the on-line participation of a number of competitors who were in active competition (and communication) with each other, then the activity may amount to 'gaming'. Equally, and following the reasoning in *Fielding v Turner*[9], an on-line competition that enables participants to interact with the promoter's software in order to win prizes could amount to gaming even if there is only one player.

Whilst it may be more difficult to restructure games such as poker or blackjack on-line so that they are no longer 'gaming' activities, it is possible to structure craps as a fixed odds bet on the next number thrown between the operator and the punter. The difficulty with games like blackjack is that the nature of the game requires active participation and, whilst there are a number of combinations upon which the punter will win, he does not in any real sense 'forecast' a particular winning combination.

1 As defined by the GA 1968, s 52(1).
2 The GA 1968, s 52.
3 *Armstrong v DPP* [1965] AC 1262, HL.
4 *Armstrong v DPP* [1965] AC 1262 at 1272, HL.
5 Section 20(2).
6 See paragraph 14.09.
7 Section 26.
8 See paragraph 14.11.
9 [1903] 1 KB 867, DC.

(b) Bingo

14.09 Bingo is an equal chance game in which each player receives an individual set of numbers that he has not chosen. Numbers are selected at random and announced by a caller, the player then covers those numbers and wins by completing given arrangements (such as a line or a full house or set) of numbers within his individual set earlier than his opponents[1]. The player wins a sum that is pre-determined or is determined by reference to amount contributed by the players.

Commercial bingo may be played only in bingo premises[2] licensed under the GA 1968[3]. There are two main types of bingo:

- prize bingo, to win non-cash prizes, which is frequently found in seaside amusement arcades and is governed by the LAA 1976; and

- cash bingo, to win cash prizes, which is controlled by the GA 1968. Cash bingo is permitted in a restricted number of licensed proprietary clubs[4], registered members' clubs[5] and miners' welfare clubs[6]. There are two notable varieties of cash bingo, known as the National Game (or multiple bingo)[7] and linked bingo[8]. An operator that provides licensed cash bingo may levy charges on players, but only eligible members of a club can play bingo as one of the activities in a private club under section 40 of the GA 1968. The club must be permanent and have at least 25 members. There are no age limits on who may play. Not more than 60 pence per person can charged for participation[9], although there is no limit on stakes, which must be distributed in full as winnings to the successful participants.

1   Department of Culture, Media and Sport website: www.culture.gov.org.
2   As defined by the GA 1968, s 20(1).
3   The GA 1968, s 20(1), Part II.
4   The GA 1968, s 20(1), Part II.
5   The GA 1968, s 40.
6   The GA 1968, s 40.
7   As defined by the Gaming (Bingo) Act 1985, s 1 and regulated by the GA 1968. National bingo is played simultaneously by clubs across the country.
8   As defined by the GA 1968, s 20(2)–(4). Where two or more clubs combine to play a joint game of bingo and aggregate prize moneys.
9   If a club wishes to charge more than 60 pence a day, then it must be registered under Part II of the GA 1968 with the local licensing authority as a bona fide members' club. These clubs do have age restrictions and no person under the age of 18 may be present in the room while bingo is taking place.

14.10   Most bingo should take place only within these specified premises, although there are some exceptions where gaming is also permitted. These include gaming at certain types of entertainment, not for private gain; gaming by way of amusements at bazaars and fetes; and very limited gaming in certain clubs and institutes[1].

Operators that wish to offer licensed bingo[2] require a certificate of consent from the Gaming Board and a licence from the local licensing authority.

The requirement that bingo should be undertaken in certain designated (or exempted) premises would seem fatal to the provision of on-line bingo. However, the decisions in cases relating to the provision of newspaper bingo and bingo by post create some ambiguity. Newspaper bingo (like on-line bingo) is not played 'in premises'. Notwithstanding this, it has been held in relevant authorities, such as *Readers Digest Association Ltd v Williams*[3] and *Imperial Tobacco Ltd v A-G*[4], that newspaper bingo is permitted provided that there is no direct or indirect charge for the opportunity to win a prize. It would not be a quantum leap to infer that on-line bingo is equally permitted in such circumstances. In contrast, and following the decisions in the cases of *Turner v Chief Constable of Liverpool*[5] and *Armstrong v DPP*[6], it is not permissible to offer lawful bingo gaming by post.

However, the Gambling Review Report states categorically that, in its view, the existing legislative arrangements establish that 'it is illegal to set up on-line [bingo] sites in Great Britain'[7].

Some commentators suggest that on-line bingo can be distinguished from newspaper bingo. However, this argument is advanced on the basis of the decision in the case of *R v Interactive Telephone Services Ltd*[8]. This case established that the cost of a telephone call used for connecting to the Internet could amount to a direct or an indirect charge for the opportunity to win a prize. However, the decision relates to premium rate telephone calls and it would be possible to structure on-line bingo using local rate or even free phone call rates. The law governing on-line bingo is therefore unclear, but, on balance, the affirmation of the law stated in the Gambling Review Report adopts the most consistent approach and is more likely to be a correct analysis.

1   Subject to restrictions on levying charges for participation.
2   Or prize bingo, if it is played within commercial bingo clubs, as it will be governed by the GA 1968.
3   [1976] 3 All ER 737.
4   [1981] AC 718, HL.
5   [1965] Crim LR 725.
6   [1965] AC 1262, HL
7   The Gambling Review Report, para 30.5.
8   (1995) unreported.

(c) Gaming machines

14.11   Whilst gaming usually implies that there is more than one competitor and those competitors are competing with each other, the GA 1968 and case law[1] does envisage that gaming may involve only one person competing against a machine. In the case of *Fielding v Turner*[2], a primitive amusement slot machine was held to be gaming on the basis that the owner of the machine 'may be said to back his chance of the money falling into one of the four compartments, in which case it will be retained without return by the owner of the machine'[3]. Equally, the House of Lords in *Seay v Eastwood*[4] dismissed an argument that players using fruit machines in a bookmaker's office were betting with the bookmaker. Instead, they held that the transaction was one in which the player of the machine 'played against or with a machine (the stakes provided by other players)'[5].

Equally, in the case of *Rosenbaum v Burgoyne*[6], it was held that a game was played in connection with a fruit machine each time the handle was pulled, setting the revolving digits in motion.

The GA 1968[7] permits only three types of gaming machine (jackpot, 'amusement with prizes' and all-cash) and these machines may be located only in specific premises.

■   The use of jackpot machines is limited to casinos, bingo halls and clubs[8]. A machine is a jackpot machine if it is constructed or adapted for playing a game of chance by means of the machine and it has a slot or other aperture for the insertion of money or money's worth[9]. The maximum stake is 50 pence and the maximum prize is £1,000 (in casinos), £500 (in bingo halls) or £250 (in clubs).

■   Amusement with prizes machines are most commonly found in arcades or at fairs, but can be located in other premises, such as cafes, with the consent of the relevant local authority[10]. Amusement with prizes machines are governed by Part III of the GA 1968. There is no definition of what constitutes an amusement with prizes machine but, broadly speaking, the kinds of amusements falling within this term consist of light-hearted amusements and can include games of skill, like darts and shooting. The maximum stake is 30 pence and the maximum prize is £5 cash or £8 tokens (or a non-cash prize).

■   All-cash machines can be located in bingo premises, pubs and betting shops[11]. The maximum stake is 30 pence and the maximum prize is £15.

1   See *Fielding v Turner* [1903] 1 KB 867, DC.
2   [1903] 1 KB 867.
3   [1903] 1 KB 867 at 871.
4   [1976] 1 WLR 1117.
5   [1976] 1 WLR 1117 at 1122.
6   [1965] AC 430, HL.
7   Section 35.
8   The GA 1968, s 31.
9   The GA 1968, s 26.
10 The GA 1968, s 34(1).
11 The GA 1968, s 35(5)(e).

14.12   In addition, the GA 1968[1] more widely applies to machines 'constructed or adapted for playing a game of chance by means of a machine'[2]. Case law determined that a game would be deemed a game of chance even if no prize (in money or money's worth) could be won by the player[3] and even if the element of chance could be reduced or eliminated by the exercise of skill on the player's part[4].

Whilst pinball machines, penny pushers and cranes are classified as gaming machines under the GA 1968[5], activities that require skill alone (such as quiz machines or driving games) are not classified as gaming machines and are therefore not subject to any control or regulation under the gaming laws.

Gaming machines such as jackpot machines and amusement with prizes machines are normally regarded as gaming within the GA 1968. In the case of *Seay v Eastwood*[6], the House of Lords held that a fruit machine was being used for gaming and not betting. In this case, the owner of the machine retained a set percentage of all moneys staked and was indifferent to the success or otherwise of an individual punter. This was conclusive proof that no betting was taking place. An on-line fruit machine is also likely to involve gaming rather than betting. A punter using such a machine is unlikely to be 'forecasting' a particular event. Instead he provides his stake to the on-line operator and then activates the machine hoping that he is lucky and a winning combination comes up. Furthermore, if the on-line fruit machine is structured so that it delivers a fixed percentage of stakes to the on-line operator, this is further evidence that the activity is not betting.

Applying these rules to the on-line environment, it is clear that a virtual fruit machine could not involve gaming by means of a machine[7] as there is no slot or other aperture for the insertion of money or money's worth in the form of cash or tokens[8]. It would appear that on-line activities of this nature fall outside the scope of what is permitted by the current legislation and regulatory system.

1　The GA 1968, s 26, Part III.
2　The GA 1968, s 26, Part III.
3　The GA 1968, s 52(5), Part III.
4　See the Irish case of *Gordon v Dunlevy* [1928] IR 595, which concerned the 'Diddler' – a machine where contestants won prizes by stopping a revolving reel.
5　Section 52.
6　[1976] 1 WLR 1117, HL.
7　As defined in Part III of the GA 1968.
8　The GA 1968, s 26.

(d) Overseas gaming operators

14.13　There is no legislation that prevents operators offering on-line gaming to UK residents. There are, however, restrictions on the promotion and advertising of on-line gaming operations to UK residents[1].

1　See Chapter 6, E-marketing.

(e) Taxation of gaming

14.14　Casino gaming is taxed on a sliding scale determined by the level of gross gaming yield[1] and is charged at stepped increases from 2.5 to 40%.

The tax on gaming machines is the amusement machine licence duty. Different rates apply depending on whether it is an amusement with prizes, all-cash or jackpot machine. Companies that are registered for VAT (about 95% of gaming companies) also pay VAT on the gross gaming yield of the machine. History has shown that the fees are prone to increase every year[2].

Currently, duty on bingo is 10% of the stakes of ticket plus VAT of 17.5% plus one-ninth of the amount by which the weekly value of prizes exceeds the duty-exclusive value of the stakes[3].

In the April 2002 Budget, the Chancellor announced that he was considering bringing bingo into line with other forms of betting by changing the tax regime for bingo. Under the proposed regime, tax would be levied on the gross profits of the bingo company, rather than on the bingo players. This proposal is currently under consultation and the Chancellor expects to announce a decision either later in 2002, or in the 2003 Budget.

1　Which is the amount of money paid in, or wagered, minus the money paid out as winnings.
2　Between 1990 and 2000, for example, the cost of an amusement with prizes licence had increased by nearly £300 to £645 per year.
3　The Betting and Gaming Duties Act 1981 (BGDA 1981), s 17(1) and (2).

5. BETTING

14.15 Betting is governed by the BGLA 1963[1]. There is no statutory definition of the term 'betting'. However, it is generally regarded as 'entering into a contract by which each party undertakes to forfeit to the other, money or money's worth if an issue, in doubt at the time of the contract, is determined in accordance with that other party's forecast'[2].

Betting has been variously described in the authorities[3]. Hawkins J in *Carlill v Carbolic Smoke Ball Co*[4] defined a wagering contract as 'one by which two persons professing to hold opposite views touching the issue of a future certain event, mutually agree that, dependant upon the determination of that event, one shall win from the other, and that other party shall pay or hand over to him, a sum of money or other stake; neither of the contracting parties having any other interest in that contract than the sum or stake he will so win or lose, there being no other real consideration for the making of such contract by either of the parties'. If a 'bet' is to be categorised as a 'wager' it must be possible for both parties to win or lose.

The Royal Commission on Lotteries and Betting 1933[5] defined a bet as 'a promise to give money or money's worth upon the determination of an uncertain or un-ascertained event [...] it may involve the exercise of skill or judgement'.

This definition was elaborated upon by Lord Dunedin in the case of *A-G v Luncheon and Sports Club Ltd*[6], who stated '... the essence of a bet is that on determination of an event in one way the first party wins and the second loses'. However, unlike 'wagers' it is not essential that both parties are able to win or lose for the gambling activity to be construed as a bet.

Although the terms 'wager' and 'bet' are used interchangeably, there is a distinction between them. The significance of this distinction is that contracts by way of wager[7] (or gaming) are void and unenforceable whilst certain betting contracts[8], such a spread betting agreements, are not classified as wagering and are therefore binding legal arrangements[9].

The types of bets that are available fit broadly into three categories: fixed odds, pool betting and spread betting.

1   Despite its title, this particular piece of legislation no longer deals with gaming and lotteries.
2   Department of Culture, Media and Sport website: www.culture.gov.org.
3   See, for instance, Lord Dunedin in *A-G v Luncheon and Sports Club Ltd* [1929] AC 400 at 406, HL; Lord Russell LJ in *Ellesmere v Wallace* [1929] 2 Ch 1 at 49.
4   [1892] 2 QB 484.
5   The Royal Commission 1933, Cmd 4341.
6   [1929] AC 400 at 406, HL.
7   Gambling by bookmakers is usually classified as wagering.
8   Which include pool betting.
9   *Tote Investors Ltd v Smoker* [1968] 1 QB 509, CA.

(a) Fixed odds betting

14.16 Only the holder of a bookmaker's permit may conclude fixed odd[1] betting transactions[2]. The betting licensing committees at magistrates' courts issue bookmaker's permits and must be satisfied that applicants are fit and proper persons to hold a permit. If a bookmaker wishes to accept bets on premises[3], section 9 of the BGLA 1963 requires him to have a betting office licence.

A bookmaker can legally offer a bet on anything other than the outcome of the National Lottery.

Applications for a betting office licence are made to the betting licensing committee, who consider whether the premises are suitable and whether there is a demand in the locality for the facilities[4]. Both permits and licences last three years and a fee is payable.

Telephone betting has been undertaken in the UK for many years and, provided that a bookmaker established in Great Britain holds a valid bookmaker's permit, he may also offer fixed odds and credit betting on-line to British punters.

It has already been stated that on-line operators have an opportunity to structure on-line gambling activities in a manner that avoids the prohibitions of gaming by falling under the betting regime (eg structuring roulette as a fixed odds bet). However, some care needs to be exercised. The decision of the Court of Appeal in the *Victor Chandler* case[5] establishes the principle that statutes regulating gambling activities are not static and should be interpreted on the basis that they are 'always speaking'. As such, it is possible that the definition of 'gambling' may be extended by the courts to include activities that have been constructed so as to comply with the definition of 'betting'. Added impetus is given to this interpretation by the Gaming Board, which classifies all activities offered within on-line casinos as a form of gaming[6].

1   'A bet is a bet at fixed odds only if each of the persons making it knows the amount he will win' (the BGDA 1981, s 10).
2   'Betting transaction includes the collection or payment of winnings on a bet and any transaction in which one of the parties is acting as a bookmaker' (the BGLA 1963, s 55(1)).
3   Premises are defined by the BGLA 1963 as including any place or vessel in public or private.
4   Known as the demand test.
5   *Victor Chandler International Ltd v Customs and Excise Commissioners* [2000] 1 WLR 1296, CA.
6   See the Gaming Board website (www.gbgb.org.uk).

(b) Overseas betting operators

14.17   There is no legislation that prevents overseas operators offering on-line betting to British residents[1]. However, overseas bookmakers are subject to additional operating restrictions that are not relevant to UK-based operators, particularly relating to the right to advertise.

1   There are, however, restrictions on advertising and promotion.

(c) Betting exchanges

14.18   A recent development has been the growth of betting exchanges on the Internet. A betting exchange (also known as peer to peer betting) allows individuals to bet against other individuals. Participants can choose to place a bet (known as 'backing') or offer odds to other participants (known as 'laying').

Whilst 'backing' a horse with a bet exchange is no different to betting with a traditional bookmaker, 'laying' allows a participant to 'act as a bookmaker' and offer odds against that horse winning. If the selection loses then the layer collects the backer's stake. If the selection wins, then the layer pays out to the backer.

The winner in each transaction pays a commission based on his net winnings to the betting exchange operator. This commission is usually between 2% and 10% of net winnings.

Some of the most popular betting exchanges include Odds Mad, Bestdaq, Betfair, IbetYourWrong (sic) and Play 121.

An examination of these operations suggests that the individuals who are 'laying' bets are acting as bookmakers in contravention of section 2(1) of the BGLA 1963 which states that no-one may act as a bookmaker on his own account unless he is the holder of a bookmaker's permit.

Betting exchange operators have attempted to address their own legal exposure in two ways. In the first scenario, betting exchange operators have obtained a bookmaker's permit and have acted between the 'backer' and 'layer'. In this sense the 'backer' and 'layer' are not actually betting against each other. Rather, both the 'backer' and the 'layer' are betting against the betting exchange operator[1]. This option may also allow a 'layer' to argue that he does not need a bookmaker's permit as he is, in reality, a punter rather than a bookmaker.

Alternatively, some betting exchange operators have not acted between the 'backer' and 'layer', but rather as the servant or the agent of the layer using the same structure as operators of on-line auctions. In these cases, the operators have obtained a bookmaker's permit to comply with the provisions of section 3(1) of the BGLA 1963. This provision states that a person may only *receive or negotiate* bets as a servant or agent to any other person if he is himself the holder of a bookmaker's permit. In this instance, it would not be difficult for the 'layer' to argue that he is a punter as this would lead to an interpretation that there are two punters and no bookmakers in this transaction! Therefore, technically, as his activities fall within the definition of bookmaking[2], the 'layer' would require a bookmaker's permit. Technically, this raises issues of criminal law and tax liability.

1 It is important to note that the operator protects its commercial position in two ways First it 'accepts' each bet only when it has an appropriate 'backer' and 'layer'. Some exchanges use terminology such as 'matching' bets.
2 Section 55 of the BGLA 1963.

(d) Pool betting

14.19 Pool betting, such as the pool competitions organised by Zetters and Littlewoods, involve the pooling or aggregating the stakes of the entrants, deducting a proportion of the stakes to cover expenses, tax and operator's profits and, when the result is known, sharing the remainder of the prize pool between the winner(s).

'Pool betting' is defined by the BGDA 1981 in the following terms 'a bet is deemed to be made by way of a pool betting unless it is a bet at fixed odds and a bet is a bet at fixed odds, only if each of the persons making it knows, or can know at the time he makes it, the amount he will win'[1].

A less circular description can be found on the Department of Culture, Media and Sport website[2]. The website states that 'Pools Betting involves the pooling of the stakes of the participants, the deduction of a proportion of the stakes to cover expenses, tax and operator's profits, and, when the result is known, the sharing the remainder of the 'prize pool' among the winners'.

To constitute pool betting a competition must have an entry fee; prizes, whether cash, goods or tickets to an event, etc, and a power of selection for the entrants which could determine the winner.

There is no certainty at the time the bet is made as to the amount the punter may win if his predictions prove correct. The rate of return (the odds) which a winning punter receives are dictated by both the total amount staked and by the number of winners.

In the case of *Customs and Excise Comrs v News International Newspapers Ltd*[3], the owner of the *Sunday Times* ran a 'Fantasy Fund Manager' competition. Entrants paid a £5 entry fee to select a portfolio of shares to invest in an imaginary fund. The winning portfolio would be the one that recorded the greatest gains and the winning entrant would receive £100,000. The competitors in this competition were making forecasts of an uncertain future event and the winnings of those who won were not determined by reference to the £5 stake money paid. Instead they were divided among such of the persons, as were winners. As a result, the activity was deemed as 'pool betting' within the meaning of section 10 of the BGDA 1981.

Only registered pool promoters can operate pool competitions and the promoter must be registered with the local authority for the area in which they intend to carry on the majority of their pool betting business[4]. For on-line operators based in the UK, the relevant local authority will be the local authority in which their server or business is based. Once registered the pool operations are subject to strict financial scrutiny by an independent accountant.

There are no statutory limits on the percentage of stakes that may be retained by the pools promoter. However, pools promoters are required to disclose to punters the percentage of stake moneys paid as winnings and, in order to remain commercially competitive, most pools promoters pay out not less than 45–50% of the stakes as winnings.

The registration will continue indefinitely unless it is revoked and the promoter must make payment of an annual registration fee on or before 1 January each year.

Provided that a pool promoter established in the UK is validly registered, he may also transact his business on-line.

1 The BGDA 1981, s 10(1) and (2).
2 www.culture.org.uk.
3 [1998] V & DR 267, CA.
4 This will be the relevant district council, or borough council, or the Common Council of the City of London.

(e) Overseas pool betting operators

14.20 There is no specific legislation that prevents overseas operators offering on-line pool betting to British residents[1].

1 There are, however, restrictions on advertising and promotion.

(f) Spread betting

14.21 Spread betting started out as a method of speculating on financial instruments. Subsequently all spread betting – financial and reporting – is subject to investment regulation and is heavily regulated by the Financial Services Authority (FSA)[1].

Spread betting is deemed an investment for the purposes of the Financial Services Act 1986 (FSA 1986) (as amended by SI 2001/3649) and is defined in the BGDA 1981 as:

> 'A bet that constitutes a contract to which section 63 of the Financial Services Act 1986 applies by virtue of paragraphs 9[2] and 12[3] of Schedule 1 to that Act.'

Because spread betting (whether on financial matters or sporting events) is classed as an investment and is subject to statutory regulation[4], any spread betting debts can be legally enforced in the English courts if one party fails to honour the bet.

The FSA 1986 (as amended by SI 2001/3649) regulates the conduct of all investment business and requires anyone who wishes to carry out such business to be authorised by the FSA or to obtain authorisation through membership of another approved body[5].

There is no requirement for an operator to conduct a spread betting business from any physical location. As a result a spread betting operation correctly established in the UK may also operate on-line on the same terms.

1 www.fsa.gov.uk.
2 Paragraph 9 states that a contract will be an investment contract if the purpose of the contract is to secure a profit or avoid a loss by reference to fluctuation in the value or price of property of any description or in an index or other factor designed for that purpose in the contract.
3 Paragraph 12 only goes on to say that buying, selling, subscribing for or underwriting investments or offering or agreeing to do so, either as principal or as an agent, will constitute dealing in investments.
4 Under the FSA 1986 (as amended by SI 2001/3649).
5 Such as the Securities and Futures Authority (SFA), which regulates market-makers, brokers and securities dealers, but which also applies to betting organisations.

(g) Overseas spread betting operators

14.22 The FSA has stated that it 'is keen not to stifle legitimate commercial development of the Internet to deliver financial services, but is also concerned to ensure that potential investors are not placed in any worse position when dealing with firms over the Internet than they would be if dealing with them using any other medium'[1].

Provided that an overseas spread betting operation has not issued advertisements (including the content of any website) that specifically target UK residents, the FSA is unlikely to take any measures to restrict that operator's activities[2].

There are many factors that the FSA will take into account to ascertain whether or not an advertisement is targeted at UK residents in contravention of section 57 of the FSA 1986. These include:

■ whether the website is located on a server outside the UK;

■ the extent to which the advert relates to UK users specifically, for example many betting sites may only offer their services in foreign currency or they may insist on punters specifying their country of origin;

■ the extent to which the website provider has taken steps to avoid investors using the service in the UK; and

■ the extent of the advertisements in the UK (for example, notifying the existence of the site to a UK search engine).

This is not an exhaustive list. There are many other factors that the FSA will take into account before deciding that the organisation will not need to be regulated because of an overseas persons exclusion.

1   www.fsa.gov.uk.
2   Telephone discussion with the FSA on 20 December 2001.

(h) Taxation of betting

14.23 Only spread betting and off-course betting are subject to duty; on-course betting is not. On 6 October 2001 general betting duty[1] was replaced with a tax on bookmakers' gross profits of 15%. From this date, spread betting firms became subject to a gross profits tax of 3% for financial spread bets and 10% for other spread bets such as those on sports events[2].

Pools have been subject to some of the highest levels of gambling taxation. In 1990, pools were subject to a duty rate of 40%. By 1999–2000, the tax rate had been reduced to 17.5%.

Duty on pools competitions is paid as follows:

■ 17.5% of all stake money paid before any expenses are deducted (this includes any amounts paid to agents or collectors);

■ 17.5% of any payment which allows a punter to make a bet or take part in any transaction liable to pools betting duty; or

■ 17.5% of the promoter's expenses and profits and those of any other person concerned with or benefiting from the betting – but not expenses and profits which are already met out of stake money or have no connection with the betting.

Therefore, a promoter must pay duty on all amounts the punter has paid to make a bet whether this is described as stake money, commission or contributions towards expenses and profits.

There is no requirement to pay duty on a punter's contributions to charity or sports if the donation is for the benefit of:

- a society established and conducted for charitable purposes only *or* a society established and conducted wholly or mainly to support athletic sports or athletic gains but not for private gain; and

- the punter knows at the time of making the payment that a specific amount or percentage will go to such a cause[3]. Therefore, if a punter pays £1.05 to place a bet knowing that 5 pence will go to such a cause, duty is only due on the remaining £1. Any donations made by the promoter of his own accord are not exempt from duty.

A pools competition where *only the profits* would benefit a charity or sports association would be fully liable to duty because the punter would not know at the time of placing the bet the amount he was donating.

Where an entry into a pool competition is made by means of a premium rate telephone call there is no stake. Since there is no stake, there is no liability to pools betting duty.

In the 2002 Budget, the Chancellor announced the abolition of pool betting duty tax on football pools. Instead, pool betting is brought into line with other forms of betting and is now subject to a general betting duty of 15% gross profits tax.

1 Of 6.75% on all stakes.
2 Customs & Excise website: www.hmce.gov.uk. Previously spread betting had been taxed at 6.75% on all betting stakes.
3 HM Customs & Excise Notice 147, para 6.

6.   LOTTERIES

(a) UK lotteries

14.24 The courts have repeatedly stated that there is no static definition of a 'lottery' but the term has been interpreted to include 'a distribution of prizes by lot or chance'[1]. In the case of *Barnes v Strathern*[2], the High Court had to decide whether a particular gambling scheme known as a 'snowball' was a lottery. In his judgment, Lord Justice General commented that 'there is no limit to the ingenuity of the devisers of such schemes and there is, accordingly, no end to the variety of schemes which may constitute a lottery'. As a result, lotteries can (and do) take numerous forms, but three are most widespread:

- the first variety of lottery allows the punter to purchase the right to select his numbers from a selected range. On a pre-determined date, the lottery operator conducts a draw of the numbers and determines the winner(s);

- the second form of lottery is commonly referred to as a 'raffle'. This form requires a player to buy a numbered ticket (the operator may retain a counterfoil). Again, on a pre-determined date the operator then draws one or more counterfoils to determine the winner(s); and

- the third lottery requires a player to purchase a ticket and scratch off or otherwise reveal the concealed numbers or logos to determine instantly whether the ticket is a winning ticket.

Despite the various formats there is no statutory definition of a 'lottery'.

However, Lord Widgery CJ, in *Readers Digest Association v Williams*[3], set out the following three essential features[4] of a lottery:

'First of all, the distribution of prizes; secondly, the fact that this is to be done by means of a chance; and thirdly that there must be some actual contribution made by the participants in return for their obtaining a chance to take part in the lottery.'

Other characteristics of lotteries include the fact that there is a scheme which is designed to attract a number of entrants[5], that the promoter has no interest in the outcome as against the participants and cannot 'lose' in the gambling sense of the word[6], and also that the entrant makes a payment to enter. The case of *DPP v Bradfute & Associates Ltd* established that 'a [lottery] prize need not be a sum of money; [...] an article [...] or anything which can be said to be of value'[7]. As such, the 'opportunity to earn money'[8], 'a gift'[9] and 'a coupon of unknown value'[10] have all been determined to be distributions of prizes.

1   *Taylor v Smetten* (1883) 11 QBD 207, DC; *Re Senator Hanseatische Verwaltungsgesellschaft mbH* [1997] 1 WLR 515, CA.
2   1929 SLT 37.
3   [1976] 1 WLR 1109 at 1113.
4   The courts have repeatedly refused to treat Lord Widgery's comments as a definition of a lottery, using them instead as a description of the essential elements of a lottery that are to be applied with flexibility to the facts in each case.
5   *Barnes v Strathern* 1929 SLT 37.
6   Although a promoter may not make a profit if the stakes received do not exceed the costs of establishing the lottery.
7   [1967] 2 QB 291, per Lord Parker CJ.
8   *Kerslake v Knight* (1925) 41 TLR 555, DC.
9   *Minty v Sylvester* (1915) 25 Cox CC 247.
10 *R v Harris* (1866) 10 Cox CC 352.

14.25   It is clear from Lord Widgery's definition that free prize draws will not fall within the definition of a lottery on the basis that the participants have made no actual contribution in return for their obtaining a chance to win a prize in the draw. There have been numerous cases that illuminate what is meant by a contribution, but the scheme is unlikely to constitute a lottery if there is a clearly promoted means of entering without payment of a contribution and a significant number of entrants actually use that free entry route[1]. Free prize draws are lawful and are subject to no registration requirement, regulatory conditions or controls[2].

Equally, if the winners are not selected on a genuinely random basis, or if pure skill is required, the activity is unlikely to constitute a lottery, but may amount to a prize competition[3]. In the case of *Scott v DPP*, Atkin J stated that 'any kind of skill or dexterity, whether bodily or mental, in which the persons can compete would prevent a scheme from being a lottery if the result depended partly upon such skill or dexterity'[4]. It has also been held that the 'element of skill required might be quite small'[5], but must be 'more than a scintilla of skill'[6]. Whilst it was held that the offer of £1 to anyone who spotted that a single match in a box of matches burned with a green flame did not require any true skill[7] and it is clear that a poetry or art competition would require skill, difficulties arise when the elements of chance and skill are combined. This combination of factors occurred in the case of *R v Interactive Telephone Services Ltd*[8], which required the entrants' skill to answer a series of multiple choice questions on a range of topics. Those entrants that provided correct answers were entered into a series of draws for cash prizes. The stipendary magistrate held that the competition taken as a whole was a lottery as skill had no real effect in determining the winner, but merely reduced the number of entrants to the draw. Prize competition draws are subject to no registration requirement and are dealt with in more detail in Chapter 6, E-marketing.

In the event that the gambling activity is a lottery, the LAA 1976[9] provides that all lotteries which do not constitute gaming are unlawful except for the following:

■   small, or one-off, lotteries[10] that require no registration with any statutory body. Small lotteries are permitted provided that they are incidental features to other entertainment such as dinners, fetes or sporting events[11]. The whole proceeds of the lottery and the entertainment to which it is incidental must be devoted to purposes other than private gain[12];

■   private lotteries[13] that require no registration with any statutory body. As the name suggests, these lotteries are permitted provided that the public is not entitled to participate. They are confined either to society members[14], or to people who work[15] or reside at the same premises[16];

- societies' lotteries[17] that are registered with the relevant local authority if their proceeds do not exceed £20,000[18] (or with the Gaming Board if proceeds in a single lottery exceed £20,000 or if cumulative annual proceeds exceeds £250,000[19]). Societies' lotteries must be run by societies established and conducted for charitable, sporting, cultural or similar voluntary purposes[20];

- local lotteries[21] that require Gaming Board registration[22] and may be promoted by local authorities[23] to raise funds for any purpose for which they have the power to incur expenditure[24]. Each lottery must have a specific object[25] that must be brought to the attention of the entrants to that lottery[26] and must be promoted in accordance with a scheme approved by a local authority[27]; and

- the National Lottery[28] which was established under the National Lottery Act 1993 (NLA 1993) and was launched in November 1994. The current operator of the National Lottery in the UK – Camelot plc – operates two types of lottery. The first lottery is known as the 'National Lottery Draw'[29] in which the player can choose his own numbers which are then matched to a draw. The second kind of lottery is referred to as 'Instants'[30] and is an instant lottery in which a player rubs off a seal to reveal if he has won a prize.

1 *R v Interactive Telephone Services Ltd* (1995) unreported; *Russell v Fulling and Page* (1999) Times, 23 June.
2 Free prize draws are dealt with in more detail in Chapter 6, E-marketing.
3 The LAA 1976, s 14.
4 [1914] 2 KB 868, DC.
5 *Imperial Tobacco Ltd v A-G* [1981] AC 718, HL.
6 Humphreys J in *Moore v Elphick* [1945] 2 All ER 155, DC.
7 *Andren v Stubbings* (1924) Times, 16 October.
8 *R v Interactive Telephone Services Ltd* (1995) unreported.
9 The LAA 1976, s 1.
10 The LAA 1976, s 3.
11 The LAA 1976, s 3(3)(b).
12 The LAA 1976, s 3(3)(a).
13 The LAA 1976, s 4.
14 Defined in section 23 of the LAA 1976 as 'any club, institution, organisation or association of persons by whatever name called'.
15 The LAA 1976, s 4(1)(b).
16 The LAA 1976, s 4(1)(c).
17 The LAA 1976, s 5.
18 In accordance with the provisions of Schedule 1 to the LAA 1976.
19 In accordance with the provisions of Schedule 1A to the LAA 1976.
20 The LAA 1976, s 5(1)(a), (b), (c).
21 The LAA 1976, s 6.
22 The LAA 1976, Sch 2, para 3(1)(b).
23 As defined in the LAA 1976, s 23.
24 The LAA 1976, ss 6 and 7(1).
25 The LAA 1976, s 7(3).
26 The LAA 1976, s 7(2).
27 The LAA 1976, s 6(2)(b).
28 Introduced under the NLA 1993.
29 The original licence was varied by consent to allow a mid-week draw.
30 The NLA 1993, s 6.

14.26 Each of the types of lottery outlined above may be promoted on-line by a UK-based promoter provided that no ticket or chance is sold by means of machine[1]. It could be said that tickets sold on-line by a computer have been sold 'by means of a machine' and this has been recognised by the Gaming Board who have registered on-line societies' lotteries only on the basis that the tickets are sold manually by staff an not by machine.

This is also the case with sales of National Lottery tickets, which are restricted to machines that are attended.

As a result, it would not be possible for an operator to operate an on-line lottery within the UK unless the restrictions on ticket sales via a machine are overcome.

1 The Lotteries Regulations 1993 (SI 1993/3223), reg 5.

(b) Overseas lottery promoters

14.27 As far as lotteries promoted outside the jurisdiction are concerned, section 2 of the LAA 1976 prescribes the sale of tickets and the advertising and promotion of overseas lotteries in the UK. The European Court of Justice upheld the UK's right to ban the promotion of lotteries not permitted by the LAA 1976 in the case of *Customs and Excise Comrs v Schindler*[1].

1 C-275/92: [1994] QB 610, ECJ.

(c) Taxation of lotteries

14.28 The National Lottery is the only type of lottery that is subject to excise duty. It is currently taxed at a rate of 12% of the amount staked[1].

1 National Audit Office (2000) 11–12.

7. PUNTERS

14.29 Although UK-based operators may be restricted by current legislation, there are no rules or regulations to prevent a UK-based punter from accessing or participating in a gaming or betting activity offered on a non-UK website. The Gambling Review Report provides a concise and accurate synopsis of existing legislative arrangements that exist for casino, bingo and machine gaming: '... it is illegal to set up on-line sites in Great Britain. It is not illegal for British residents to gamble on-line. Nor is it illegal for overseas operators to offer on-line gambling to British residents'[1].

1 The Gambling Review Report, para 30.5.

8. ADVERTISING GAMBLING OPERATIONS

14.30 Whilst it is clear that English law does not prohibit British residents from gambling on-line, provisions do exist that severely restrict the ability of on-line operators to promote their gambling operations. As a result, on-line operators need to structure their promotional activities and advertising material accordingly. In addition to the following specific rules, the promotion and advertising of all gambling (on-line or otherwise) is subject to strict regulation by a number of bodies. These regimes are covered in detail in Chapter 6, E-marketing.

(a) Gaming

14.31 The GA 1968[1] provides a general prohibition against advertising gaming activities within Great Britain[2]. In particular, the GA 1968 proscribes the issue of any 'advertisement inviting the public to subscribe any money or money's worth to be used in gaming whether in Great Britain or elsewhere, or to apply for information about facilities for subscribing any money or money 's worth to be so used'[3].

Although this prohibition clearly restricts advertisements in paid for media (including banner advertising), there is an argument as to whether advertising in media which has not been paid for constitutes an 'advertisement' as such. The most likely interpretation is a wide one, so that a direct mailing on an unsolicited basis or a non-paid for banner ad on a betting site promising a related gaming site would be sought by the prohibition. However, a simple hyperlink to an on-line gaming site without a related banner is much less likely to constitute an 'advertisement'. Many of the operators of on-line casinos have produced and distributed CDs that contain the software necessary to participate in gaming activities on-line to punters and potential punters based in the UK. The distribution of such a CD to persons already registered with the casino website is unlikely to offend the provisions of section 42 of the GA 1968, as such a CD is unlikely to be an 'advertisement' and is more analogous to a membership pack being dispatched to a member. Nor is it likely that the issue of such a CD to existing subscribers would be deemed to be an 'invitation to the public'.

However, the definition of 'advertisement' contained in section 42(8) of the GA 1968 is very wide and the distribution of promotional CDs to the general public should be undertaken with caution. Much will depend upon the content and packaging of the CD and any exhortation to 'subscribe money for gaming' or to 'apply for information about facilities for doing so' must be avoided.

Advertising on-line gaming facilities within Great Britain is an offence punishable on summary conviction to a maximum fine of £5,000 and upon conviction on indictment to an unlimited fine and/or a maximum term of two years' imprisonment[4].

It may be difficult for the authorities to enforce the provisions of the GA 1968 in respect of advertisements on the Internet where the provider and server are outside the UK. Any advertisements issued or published within the UK other than on the Internet will, of course, be capable of enforcement.

1   The GA 1968, s 42.
2   Following a deregulation order in August 1999, there are now some exceptions (for example, casinos are now permitted limited advertising in written publications). However, the relaxation of the rules are not relevant here since most apply to premises with a gaming licence.
3   The GA 1968, s 42(1)(c).
4   The GA 1968, s 42(7).

(b) Betting

14.32   The restrictions on the advertising of the services provided by a bookmaker established in the UK are not relevant to on-line operations since they relate to advertising of 'betting offices' rather than the advertisement of betting opportunities per se[1].

However, the BGDA 1981 does contain provisions[2] that were intended to preclude offshore bookmakers from soliciting bets with punters in the UK and thereby avoid the UK's general betting duty of 6.75%, which was levied on all bets placed in the UK. The BGDA 1981 prohibits the issue, circulation or distribution of advertisements inviting or otherwise relating to such bets.

Until very recently, many in the betting industry held the opinion that advertising viewed on television screens in the UK via Teletext or the Internet was not prohibited because the existing law had not anticipated the advent of new technologies. However, the Court of Appeal[3] has established the principle that the legislation regulating gambling activities is not static and should be given an 'always speaking' construction. The *Victor Chandler* case determined that the prohibitions in the BGDA 1981 do include advertisements on Teletext. Whether the 'always speaking' construction could extend the prohibition to advertisements on the Internet is a subject of some debate and it may be possible to make a distinction between the passive availability of an Internet site from the positive acts of transmission necessary to deliver Teletext content.

However, following the introduction[4] of a new system of tax on bookmakers' gross profits[5], the advantage to offshore bookmakers in avoiding the general betting duty is reduced. As a result, section 9 of the BGDA 1981 has lost much of its impetus[6].

An offence under section 9 of the BGDA 1981 carries punishment on summary conviction of a maximum fine of £5,000 and upon a second or subsequent conviction a fine and/or a maximum of three months' imprisonment. Upon conviction on indictment an unlimited fine may be imposed; on a second or subsequent conviction a fine and/or a maximum of one year's imprisonment.

Subject to certain exemptions, the FSA 1986[7] states that no person other than an authorised person shall issue, or cause to be issued, a spread bet advertisement in the UK unless its contents have been approved. It is the view of the FSA that an advert which can be accessed on a computer screen in the UK will have been issued in the UK for the purposes of section 57. In section 207, the FSA 1986 goes on to provide that an advert will be treated as having been issued in the UK if it is either directed at people in the UK or made available to them other than by way of a periodical publication published and circulated in the UK in a sound or television broadcast. The FSA does not consider the Internet to be a sound or television broadcast, however, and there are therefore exceptions that allow Internet companies to avoid falling under section 57. These include whether the website is located on a server outside the UK, the extent to which the advert relates to UK users specifically (for example, many betting sites may only offer their services in foreign currency or they may insist on punters specifying their country of origin), the extent to which the website provider has taken steps to avoid investors using the service in the UK and the extent of the advertisements in the UK (notifying the existence of the site to a UK search engine).

This is not an exhaustive list. There are many other factors that the FSA will take into account before deciding that the organisation will not need to be regulated because of an overseas persons exclusion.

Any contravention of section 57 is a criminal offence punishable on conviction by imprisonment, or a fine, or both.

1   The BGLA 1963, s 10 as amended.
2   See particularly the BGDA 1981, s 9(1).
3   *Victor Chandler International Ltd v Custom and Excise Comrs* [2000] 1 All ER 160; on appeal [2000] 2 All ER 315, CA.
4   In the 2001 Budget.
5   The new system introduced on 6 October 2001 replaces general betting duty of 6.75% on total stakes with a tax (of 15%) on bookmakers' gross profits.
6   It has been argued that the restrictions contained in section 9 could amount to a breach of the Human Rights Act 1998 and/or the regulations governing the free movement of goods and services or freedom of establishment.
7   The FSA 1986, s 57.

(c) Lotteries

14.33   Current lotteries regulations[1] do not restrict the on-line promotion of lotteries and the Gaming Board have registered on-line societies' lotteries on the basis that the tickets are not actually sold, but only promoted, on-line.

The LAA 1976 does, however, prohibit the advertisement or promotion within Great Britain of lotteries based outside the UK[2]. It imposes liability on every person who prints, sells, distributes, offers or advertises tickets for either an illegal lottery, a list of prize winners, or any 'item' which induces people to participate in the lottery. If any offence under the LAA 1976 is due to their neglect, consent or connivance, companies and/or company officers may also be prosecuted.

The European Court of Justice upheld the UK's right to ban the promotion of letters not permitted by the LAA 1976 in the recent case of *Customs and Excise Comrs v Schindler*[3].

1   The Lotteries Regulations 1993, reg 5.
2   The LAA 1976, s 2.
3   C-275/92: [1994] QB 610, ECJ.

(d) Interactive television

14.34   Whilst the Independent Television Commission (ITC) Code of Advertising Standards and Practice prohibits promotion via television for products or services relating to betting tips, betting and gaming, advertising relating to football pools is expressly permitted[1]. As a result, an operator would be able to attract punters to its service (which offers fixed odds and pools betting) by promoting via television only the pools betting aspect of the service.

The ITC has stated that the simple 'labelling and naming' of interactive gambling services on interactive menus does not constitute 'promotion via television' and is therefore permissible[2]. The ITC is currently considering the establishment of a code of conduct related specifically to gambling and this situation may change. It should also be noted that the ITC has recently circulated a consultative questionnaire on interactive television[3] and it is clear from the questions posed that 'access' to interactive gambling services is an issue the ITC is considering[4].

1 ITC Code of Advertising Standards and Practice.
2 ITC website: itc.org.uk; 'The ITC's Approach to Regulating Interactive TV Services'.
3 Interactive Television – An ITC Public Consultation, February 2000.
4 Page 12, question 7 of the consultative questionnaire.

(e) Recent developments

14.35 The Gambling Review Body also recommended that all on-line gambling sites that have been licensed by the proposed Gambling Commission should be permitted to advertise their operations in Great Britain. Whilst overseas operations are currently restrained from advertising in the UK, and will remain so restrained, those operations licensed by the proposed Commission will have 'demonstrated a sufficient connection with the UK to receive the reward of being able to advertise to a market not yet saturated with gambling adverts'[1]. In its response to the Gambling Review Body Report, the Government has accepted this proposal in principle, although further consideration is being given to the extent to which this concept will apply to on-line advertising.

1 Department for Culture, Media and Sport, 'A Safe Bet for Success', 26 March 2002.

9. FUNDING ACCOUNTS AND THE RECOVERY OF GAMBLING DEBTS

14.36 It has been long established by statute that contracts or agreements for gaming or wagering are void and unenforceable[1]. However, as a result of the anomalies within the Gaming Act 1845 (GA 1845), spread betting debts are enforceable and it is also the case that a casino can sue for payment of a cheque[2] (though not on the gaming contract itself). In the case of *Hill v William Hill (Park Lane) Ltd*[3], Lord Green interpreted section 18 of the GA 1845 as making 'gaming and wagering agreements null and void [...] at the outset'. He also held that the GA 1845 'prohibits [...] the bringing of any suit [to] recover any sum of money [...] alleged to be won upon any wager'. Similar decisions were reached in the cases of *Law v Dearnley*[4] and *MacDonald v Green*[5]. In the most recent case on the subject, *Morgan Grenfell & Co Ltd v Welwyn Hatfield District Council*[6], Hobhouse J decided 'if the purpose of the parties was to wager, then the contracts would be void under section 18 of the Gaming Act 1845 and section 1 Gaming Act 1892'. This can have serious implications for any on-line gambling operation and particularly those that intend to offer punters credit facilities.

Of all the methods available for punters to fund their account, credit cards are the most widely used and industry analysts have, for some time, voiced concern that credit cards debts incurred on gambling may not be enforceable.

However, provided that the credit card is being used by the customer only to deposit sums of money with the on-line operator and by the on-line operator only to pay winnings to the customer, it is likely that any debts incurred by customers in England and Wales would be enforceable by credit card companies. It is notable, however, that a number of leading credit card companies do not allow customers to use cards for the purpose of depositing money to be used for gambling.

There exists specific legislation in the FSA 1986 that relates to the enforceability of spread betting contracts. Any spread betting contracts entered into as a result of a contravention of the restrictions relating to the advertisement and promotion of spread betting opportunities[7] may be unenforceable, and any money or property paid by an investor may be recovered together with compensation.

In relation to gaming, *Smith and Monkcom*[8] suggest that the decision on whether a loan or credit advance to another person to enable that person to take part in gaming is or is not recoverable by civil action depends upon a number of factors. First, it is dependent upon whether the gaming concerned is unlawful, in which case the loan is irrecoverable at common law[9]. Second, and assuming that the gaming is lawful, it is dependent upon whether the loans are made to pay off losses already incurred or for future gaming. If the latter, the loan *may* be recoverable[10].

Whatever the legality of credit card payments used to fund on-line betting activities, it is clear that the gambling industry recognises that 'credit cards do not serve the needs of the on-line gambling industry'[11] and as many as 50% of gaming transactions are rejected by credit card companies[12]. Greg S Held, the CEO of layeway.com[13] reports that in the United States 'credit card companies currently charge about $15 for a transaction worth $100'. It has also been reported that new Visa regulations prohibit on-line casinos from paying winnings as credits to punter's accounts[14] whilst American Express prevents their credit cards being used for gaming purposes[15].

1 Section 18 of the GA 1845.
2 But not on a contract.
3 [1949] AC 530, HL.
4 [1950] 1 KB 400, CA.
5 [1951] 1 KB 594, CA.
6 [1995] 1 All ER 1.
7 The restrictions are set out in section 57.
8 *The Law of Betting, Gaming and Lotteries* (2nd edn, 2001) Butterworths.
9 *M'Kinnell v Robinson* (1838) 3 M & W 434.
10 See *Chitty on Contract* (25th edn), Volume 2, 3633–47.
11 *Broadband Media*, 9 April 2001.
12 Interactive Gaming Council website: www.igcouncil.org.
13 A specialist direct electronic fund transfer company.
14 Reported in *Broadband Media*, 9 April 2001.
15 Interactive Gaming Council website: www.igcouncil.org.

14.37 Governments are also contemplating the use of financial controls to disrupt the growth of on-line gambling.

In the US, Representative Jim Leach has proposed the re-introduction of the Internet Funding Prohibition Act[1], which he states prohibits the facilitation of Internet gambling transactions and 'attacks Internet gaming companies where it hurts – in their virtual cash registers'[2].

The Australian Parliament has passed the Interactive Gambling Bill 2001. This law prohibits casinos based in Australia from taking bets from Australian citizens. Amendments to this Bill would entitle the Australian Government to 'block' Australian websites that act in contravention of this law, if the government of the country where the punter is based requests it. Another amendment to the Bill would declare that obligations (such as credit card debts) incurred by Australians on on-line websites would not be enforceable. The Australian Government has until the end of 2002 to formulate the regulations required to implement the bill, but most commentators believe that Prime Minister John Howard will fast track the Bill to ensure that his Liberal Party are seen to be tackling problem gambling in this crucial election year. However there have been suggestions that the provisions of this Bill breach the restraint of trade guidelines issued by the World Trade Organisation.

In Hong Kong, there have been proposals for the Legislative Council to implement a Bill to restrict banks and credit card companies from allowing their customers to pay Internet gambling debts with credit cards.

Commentators suggest that 'prohibitions enforced through financial instrument bans will most likely facilitate the growth of new payment alternatives'[3] and are likely to be unenforceable. Furthermore, there is concern that such controls will adversely affect only legitimate Internet gaming organisations (who will be concerned to ensure compliance) whilst the unregulated operators will continue to thrive.

In March 2002, the UK Government responded to criticisms levelled in the Gambling Review Report[4] and announced its intention to pass legislation that would result in all gambling debts becoming enforceable.

1 R-IA. This legislation was due to be considered by the Financial Services Committee.
2 Interactive Gaming Council website: www.igcouncil.org.
3 Interactive Gaming Council website: www.igcouncil.org.
4 The Gambling Review Report, July 2001.

10. BACK OFFICE SERVICES

14.38 A growing number of betting and casino operators are considering the implications under the current law of establishing administrative or 'back office' functions in the UK whilst their core on-line gambling services remain based overseas. This would mean that the actual operations would continue to be conducted in a jurisdiction which permits such activity (by operating under a local licence and physically locating its services in the same jurisdiction). However, there is sometimes a shortage of suitably qualified back office staff in jurisdictions of convenience.

Whilst the location in the UK of administrative or back office services for an overseas bookmaker offering fixed odds or pools betting would not infringe any UK legislation relating to betting, the position is different for gaming operators. It has already been stated that it is not illegal for overseas operators to offer on-line gaming facilities to UK residents, nor is it illegal for UK residents to game on-line providing the site operates from outside of the UK. However, the provisions of the GA 1968[1] may also prohibit the location in the UK of administrative or back office services for an overseas casino.

The restrictive wording within the GA 1968[2] is drafted so widely that it may catch any UK-based back office administrators whose purpose or function is to administer or promote gaming opportunities available to UK citizens which are not offered on licensed premises. Furthermore, the prohibition against advertising overseas-based gaming in the UK under section 42 of the GA 1968 may also extend to any back office administrators located in the UK. It could be argued that administrators, such as PR or finance personnel, could be said to be encouraging or 'inviting the public to make subscriptions to be used in gaming'. However, many UK operators have taken a bullish view of these issues and at least one major overseas betting and gaming operation has established its 'back office' in the UK. In the context of the forthcoming changes in the law they may have taken a view in respect of the authorities' willingness to pursue this point.

1 The GA 1968, s 8.
2 The GA 1968, s 8.

11. THE GAMBLING REVIEW BODY

14.39 In order to address the fact that the present legislation governing gambling is over 25 years old, the Home Office commissioned the Gambling Review Body to undertake a review of current gambling regulation. Following a change of responsibilities, the Department for Culture, Media and Sport[1] released the report on 17 July 2001.

The Gambling Review Body Report contained many proposals relating to the future regulation of the gambling industry in the UK.

The Report advocated a fundamental liberalisation in the laws relating to on-line gambling. The authors of the Report clearly appreciated the difficulties of enforcing new regulations outside the UK and the recommendations would only have an effect on gambling operations based in the UK. UK citizens would not be prohibited from gambling on offshore sites.

In response to the recommendations of the Gambling Review Report, Tessa Jowell, Secretary of State for Culture, Media and Sport, announced in March 2002, a radical overhaul of the UK's outdated gambling laws[2]. In confirming the Government's intention to implement the key reforms of the Budd Report[3], Ms Jowell acknowledged that the modernisation of the UK's gambling laws was 'long overdue'. She pointed to the fact that both 'society and technology had overtaken the law', prompting government action[4].

The reforms, contained in the document 'A Safe Bet for Success', look set to modernise an industry whose growth has been hampered by legislation that is nearly 40 years old and dogged by the proliferation of overseas-based on-line casinos. However, with these proposals, the Government has reaffirmed its commitment to making the UK *the* place to establish on-line gambling operations.

It is clear that the Government is keen that Britain be seen as a facilitative environment for this highly lucrative industry. Whilst only a small number of the 176 proposals of the Gambling Review Body relate to on-line gambling operations, the Government is eager for opportunities in this area to be exploited as the future revenues could be huge. To achieve this aim, the proposals contain a number of measures designed to allow 'customers, both here and abroad [to] access a full range of gambling sites licensed and located here, safe in the knowledge that the probity and integrity of the gambling operators and the products they offer are assured'[5].

1   Following changes in the departmental responsibilities after the recent election, the report was commissioned by the Home Office but submitted to the Department of Culture, Media and Sport.
2   Department for Culture, Media and Sport, 'A Safe Bet for Success', 26 March 2002 detailed the proposals for new legislation to replace the BGLA 1963.
3   The Gambling Review Report, available on the Department for Culture, Media and Sport website at: www.culture.gov.uk/ROLE/gambling_review.html.
4   Department for Culture, Media and Sport Press Release, 26 March 2002.
5   'A Safe Bet for Success', para 4.48.

14.40   Under the new regime, UK operators will be able, for the first time, to offer on-line gambling and gaming on the Internet or via interactive television. This marks a major shift in policy that previously prohibited UK operations from offering on-line gaming but allowed UK citizens to access overseas on-line gaming facilities. The Department for Culture, Media and Sport was eager to accept the views of the Review Body, saying 'the prohibition of on-line gambling by British customers would be an entirely unrealistic objective, even if it were thought to be desirable'[1].

On-line betting already takes place with a proliferation of websites offering punters enticements to open accounts[2]. The Government was of the view that on-line betting on real-time events should be permitted[3] as it raised no new regulatory issues to those already presented and resolved those in respect of telephone betting.

The ability of British citizens to participate in on-line gaming activities remains an area of great concern to both the Gambling Review Committee and the Government. Whilst on-line betting involves using on-line technology as a means of placing a bet on a real-time event, on-line gaming involves placing a stake on a game which will be generated at random by computer software[4]. This raises a whole host of issues over the validity and transparency of Internet gaming operations.

In addition, there are concerns that allowing gaming on-line will increase the incidence of problem gambling, with punters becoming addicted to gambling on-line where money is not being won or lost in the physical sense and there are not the distractions of an off-line casino to divert attention from the actual gambling. In addition, it was felt that the wide accessibility of the Internet may promote gambling amongst underage people and other vulnerable sections of society.

The Budd Report recommended, and the Government accepted, a number of proposals aimed at minimising the risk of problem gambling and gambling by vulnerable sections of society, such as children. The proposals adopted have received widespread support, not only from those who stand to make commercial gains from the new liberalised regime, but also from those treating problem gamblers who have become concerned with the sheer volume of unregulated gambling websites available[5].

A number of the proposals focused on the need for Internet gaming operators to assist their players in policing themselves. The proposals included measures that enable players to set their own personal maximum stakes and limits and the possibility to ban themselves from the site[6], and the regular display of clocks and timers to remind players of the real time spent on gambling sites[7].

1 Department for Culture, Media and Sport, 'A Safe Bet for Success', 26 March 2002, para 4.46.
2 For example, www.bluesq.com and www.sportingbet.com offer £10 of free bets for all new subscribers, whilst www.bet365.com offer £20.
3 The Gambling Review Report, para 30.27.
4 This distinction was articulated by the Gambling Review Report, para 30.25.
5 'A Safe Bet for Success', para 4.47.
6 The Gambling Review Report, para 30.35.
7 The Gambling Review Report, para 30.36.

14.41 The inevitable failure of these measures in a small number of cases may be combated by the requirement that all websites must provide information about, and direct links to, websites dealing with advice for, and treatment of, problem gamblers[1].

It has been proposed that all punters in on-line casinos should be fully identified before they commence play. It is envisaged that the Gambling Commission will issue guidelines to on-line casinos in order to ensure that their standards of identification are as high as those required in off-line casinos[2]. In addition, there will be provisions requiring all prizes won by minors to be forfeited[3].

Whilst the Government was keen to highlight the safeguards it intends to introduce, it was equally keen that both British and overseas companies would take the opportunity to locate their operations in Britain, encouraged by the liberalised legislation. For this reason, there are a number of proposals for on-line gaming that will encourage and nurture trust in British-based gaming websites.

The Review Body suggested that an on-line gambling operator seeking to be licensed by the Gambling Commission should, as a minimum, be registered as a British company, locate its server in Great Britain and use a UK web address for its gambling site[4].

The Government has indicated that such a requirement would need primary legislation and is considering this issue further. The Government agrees that gambling operators and their systems should be UK-based in order to seek a Gambling Commission licence. However, there is concern over the position of third party servers and, for this reason, the Government has decided to look into this issue further before fully accepting this proposal.

1 The Gambling Review Report, para 30.37.
2 The Gambling Review Report, para 30.32.
3 The Gambling Review Report, para 30.34.
4 The Gambling Review Report, para 30.20.

14.42 The fortunes of the gambling industry in Britain will be closely allied to the success and credibility of the proposed Gambling Commission[1]. This will be a statutory body with overall responsibility for all licensing and regulatory aspects of commercial gambling (be that betting, gaming, lotteries or pools). In addition, the Commission will be granted powers to impose penalties on the operators it licenses.

With respect to on-line gambling, the Commission will licence all operators. Once licensed, websites will be able to display the Commission's 'kitemark' with the aim of reassuring punters that the site they are entering has been fully vetted and licensed by the Commission. It will be an offence to claim falsely to be licensed or make unauthorised use of the kitemark. In addition, the Commission will operate a portal on its website, listing all the on-line gambling providers it has licensed[2].

With respect to on-line gaming, the Commission will be specifically responsible for the inspection and testing of all gaming software which must operate at random[3] and for the setting of parameters for the future development of on-line games[4].

It has already been stated that the Gambling Review Body has recommended that all on-line gambling sites that have been licensed by the Gambling Commission should be permitted to advertise their operations in Great Britain. The Government has accepted this proposal in principle, although further consideration is being given to the extent to which this concept will apply to on-line advertising.

It is clear that the Government recognises gambling as a mainstream leisure activity and as a highly lucrative industry. The proposed measures will rid the industry of outdated restrictions and allow UK companies to compete with offshore-based Internet operations whilst limiting the effects of underage and problem gambling. The Government feels the proposals for the Commission will contain enough flexibility that the pace of technological change will not so easily destabilise the regulation of gambling in this country.

Tessa Jowell conceded that the key changes to the law would require primary legislation. She also acknowledged that bringing on-line gambling within the scope of formal regulation would be such a key change[5]. Whilst the recommendations of the Rothschild Commission, which reviewed gambling in the 1970s, were never acted upon, it is likely that the changes proposed in 'A Safe Bet For Success' may be enacted during 2003.

1 Department for Culture, Media and Sport, 'A Safe Bet for Success', 26 March 2002, para 3.4.
2 The Gambling Review Report, para 30.40.
3 The Gambling Review Report, para 30.29.
4 The Gambling Review Report, para 30.30.
5 'A Safe Bet for Success', para 9.1.

12. DATA AND LEVIES

14.43 Although the UK Government is not directly responsible for horseracing as a sport, it did administer, under the BGLA 1963, a statutory body called the Horserace Betting Levy Board. The function of this organisation is to assess and collect financial contributions from bookmakers to facilitate the improvement of breeds of horses, the advancement or encouragement of veterinary science and education and the improvement of horseracing in general[1].

The Horserace Betting Levy Board is empowered to introduce a levy scheme each year. Although the 41st levy scheme[2] has already been drafted (and includes a new levy on the turnover received by Internet-based bookmakers[3]), there has been much discussion about the apparently imminent abolishment of the Levy Board and the levy scheme itself.

The British Horseracing Board has set out a structure[4] for funding horseracing after the cessation of the levy scheme, which introduces a commercial charging mechanism for the sale to bookmakers of pre-race data[5], pictures, audio and betting shows.

Following nearly two years of legal wrangling between the British Horseracing Board (BHB) and William Hill over the use of pre-race data on the Internet, the BHB announced in April 2002 that it had agreed a groundbreaking five-year deal with the UK's five biggest bookmakers for the provision of pre-race data.

The dispute that had recently been referred by the Court of Appeal to the European Court of Justice[6] and the Office of Fair Trading concerned the computerised database of pre-race information. This database included information on runners, owners, trainers and race times and is collected, verified and distributed by the BHB. This time critical information is constantly revised to ensure accuracy and costs over £4m per year to collate and maintain according to the BHB, who licenses it to the betting industry. The Court found that William Hill had extracted and used the information on their Internet betting service outside the scope of their licence, and were therefore infringing the BHB's database rights in that information. The Court of Appeal referred the matter on to the ECJ, but the contents of the questions to be referred were never agreed. William Hill went on to lodge a complaint with the Office of Fair Trading alleging that the BHB had abused its dominant position as the only supplier of information on UK horseracing by demanding an excessive and discriminatory price for pre-race data licences.

The terms of the agreement provide for the withdrawal of all court proceedings and OFT complaints. Until the announcement of this agreement, many feared the bookmaking industry was on a collision course with horseracing as the ECJ and the OFT prepared to enter the fray. The OFT stated by telephone that complaints made against the BHB had been withdrawn, although a decision on a notification application by the BHB has yet to be made. However, the deal has restored some certainty in respect of pre-race data.

Under the terms of the agreement, those bookmakers whose gross profits from UK horserace betting exceed £150,000 will pay an annual charge of 10% on those gross profits. For those whose gross profits fall below this level, there is a sliding scale of fees that will operate to determine the annual fee payable. A general right of offset in respect of the charges payable to the BHB has been provided to bookmakers in relation to payments made under the horserace betting levy scheme.

The same terms will be offered to on course bookmakers, although they will pay £15 inclusive of VAT for marker sheets in place of the standard data charge for the first year. On course bookmakers who operate from on course betting shops will be treated under the rules applicable to betting shops outlined above.

The agreement was not an easy one to reach. The main stumbling block in the negotiations was the refusal of the smaller independent bookmakers to sign the agreement. The Confederation of Bookmaker Associations raised concerns that, under the new terms, the larger operations will be paying less than the current levy whilst the smaller independent operations could find themselves paying anything between 30% to 100% more. However, with the disappearance of television pictures from bookmakers' offices from 1 May 2002, these companies will find it almost impossible to operate, let alone compete, if they remain adamant in their refusal to sign up to the deal.

1 The BGLA 1963, s 27.
2 For the period 1 April 2002 to 31 March 2003.
3 Levied at 1.2% on Internet turnover less the total of any licensing fee paid to the British Horseracing Board in respect of the levy period up to 1%.
4 British Horseracing Board, The Future Funding Plan for British Racing (2000).
5 Including fixtures lists and pre-race information.
6 *British Horseracing Board v William Hill* [2001] RPC 612, CA.

14.44 Sports data (which is vital to any bookmaker) is emerging as a contentious issue and rights levies on sports data will become increasingly prevalent. That is not to say that the introduction of levies on data has been universally accepted and, as such, the decision in the Swedish case of *Fixtures Marketing Ltd v AB Svenska Spel*[1] is worth noting. This case relates to the reproduction without permission of English and Scottish football fixtures. A crucial factor in the decision in this case was that Fixtures Marketing did not satisfy the courts that Svenska Spel had extracted and re-utilised the football fixtures from Football Fixture's database. As a result, Svenska Spel could not be held to have infringed Fixtures Marketing's database rights. Fixtures Marketing Limited have appealed the judgment on the basis that the Swedish Government had incorrectly incorporated (or interpreted) the terms of the European Database Directive[2].

Whilst the outcome of the *William Hill* and the *Svenska Spel* cases is awaited, it is important that on-line operators who wish to reproduce sports data clarify their position on data rights and obtain the appropriate licences[3].

The horserace betting levy is unique in the UK and there is no statutory levy imposed on other sports betting, although the greyhound racing industry has implemented a voluntary levy of 0.4% of a bookmaker's turnover. The Betting Office Licensees Association estimates that the voluntary levy costs its members approximately £4m per year.

There also exists an entity formed by the FA Premier League and the Football League for the purpose of collecting and licensing various data (such as fixture lists)[4] relating to English football. This organisation, known as Football DataCo, has established a system that requires any person or company that uses or reproduces the fixture lists for the Football League and/or the FA Premier League (including any on-line betting or pools operator) to obtain a licence and pay the appropriate fee. It is known that Football DataCo has begun legal proceedings (in the UK and elsewhere) against a number of offshore gambling operators that have been using unlicensed data. However, at the time of writing, these proceedings have not been concluded.

1   Swedish Court of Appeal, 3 May 2001 – Svea Horvrätt – (Svea Court of Appeal) Case No T350400.
2   Directive (EC) 9/96.
3   For example, it is a requirement of the FA Premier League that website operators obtain a 'website licence' if they wish to reproduce photographs taken within FA Premier League clubs' stadia. Equally, a licence from Football DataCo Limited is required if any website wishes to reproduce fixtures from the English or Scottish leagues.
4   It was established in *Football League Ltd v Littlewoods Pools Ltd* [1959] 2 All ER 546 that the fixture list created by the football authorities is a copyright work capable of protection.

13. TRADE ASSOCIATIONS AND ARBITRATION SERVICES

14.45   Aside from the various licensing bodies, there exist several arbitration service and trade associations that have their own respective part to play in the betting industry. Their main roles are outlined below.

The British Betting Office Association is the leading trade association for independent bookmakers in the UK. The Association operates a variety of functions and represents its members in the assessment of the annual horserace betting levy. At present it does not accept members from on-line operators.

The Betting Office Licensees Association (BOLA) is the main representative body for the UK and fulfils a variety of representative and regulatory functions. BOLA is prepared to accept membership from on-line bookmakers but only if their offices and business functions are located mainly in the UK.

The Bingo Association represents 111 operators with 540 clubs, accounting for 74% of the industry. The Bingo Association will not accept membership from on-line bingo organisations.

The Lotteries Council is the main representative body for lotteries other than the National Lottery. It is a not-for-profit association, which represents, regulates and instructs its member organisations. Membership is open to any person or organisation engaged in activities connected with the promotion of lawful lotteries.

The Pools Promoters Association was established in the 1930s. Its members are Littlewoods Promotions Limited, Vernons Pools Limited and Zetters International Pools Limited. It represents and promotes the interests of its members.

The British Amusements Catering Trades Association represents the manufacturers, operators and owners of gaming and amusement equipment. This Association offers advice and information to help its members comply with laws and regulations. It encourages high standards of business practice through a voluntary code of practice.

The British Casino Association is the trade association of the casino industry in Britain. All licensed casinos are voluntary members of this Association. They do not currently accept membership from on-line organisations but have indicated that they are considering the impact of changing technology and practices.

The Independent Betting Arbitration Service will investigate disputed bets between its members and customers. It will only do this if all other means of amicable resolution have been exhausted. It will conduct arbitration relating to on-line bookmakers but only if they are based in the UK.

Many on-line gambling operators are members of the Interactive Gaming Council, a global and voluntary trade association. Under its Seal of Approval Programme, members[1] are obliged to adhere to the Council's code of conduct, which regulates areas such as truthful advertising, financial probity, privacy, data protection and underage gambling. The Interactive Gaming Council also provides a dispute resolution procedure for on-line gambling disputes[2].

1 Which include casino, betting, bingo and lottery operators.
2 The Interactive Gaming Council website: www.igcouncil.org.

14. ON-LINE GAMBLING IN OTHER JURISDICTIONS

14.46 Because the Internet is a global medium, a website is potentially subject to the laws in each jurisdiction where it website can be accessed. As a result, website developers are increasingly inserting disclaimers and terms and conditions on to websites. These disclaimers and terms and conditions purport to exclude residents of jurisdictions where on-line gambling is illegal from accessing the website. Both the practical and legal effectiveness of these measures are unclear, but they do reflect a growing concern on the part of on-line gambling operators to avoid suffering the same fate as individuals such as Jay Cohen[1].

Set out below is a mere snapshot of the major jurisdiction's attitudes to on-line gambling.

1 Cohen was arrested whilst on holiday in the US and was convicted when the court found that his company, World Sports Exchange, was accepting bets from North America from its offices in Antigua.

(a) The United States

14.47 Gambling in the US is prohibited unless specifically permitted by a particular US State. However, commentators on the patchwork quilt of Federal laws regarding Internet gambling in the US have noted that 'on-line gambling has grown through the gaps in the legislative programme'[1]. It is important to reflect that despite the proliferation of new Bills introduced regularly by US congressmen, there are still no Federal laws that explicitly prohibit the use of the Internet for gambling purposes.

The Federal Wire Act[2] was the 30-year-old legislation used to prosecute Jay Cohen and it has far reaching implications for Internet gambling operators. The Act specifically states that 'bets on sporting events are unlawful if placed over a phone line from a State where phone wagering is illegal'. It is important to note that the legal status of telephone gambling in the US State where the bet is being processed is irrelevant. Equally, the individuals who place bets escape prosecution. This legal loophole allows Americans to place wagers over the Internet and has led to numerous efforts to have Internet gambling banned, most famously by Senator Jon Kyl and Congressman Bob Goodlatte. Kyl introduced a Bill known memorably as S-629. This Bill (and the Goodlatte-sponsored Internet Gambling Prohibition Act) attempted to ban Americans from using their PCs to partake in Internet gambling worldwide. It met with a hostile reception from many other countries. Whilst both bills had little public opposition, effective lobbying on behalf of the casino operators, church groups and Internet service providers (ISPs) ensured that they are currently 'dead' in the House of Representatives[3].

Gambling is banned in many individual States in the US. In *People v World Interactive Gaming Corpn*[4], the court held that permitting New Yorkers, from their home computers, to access and use Antigua-based computers to engage in gambling activities violated New York State's prohibitions on gambling in New York. In addition, it was held that these activities also violated the Wire Act, the Travel Act and the Interstate Transportation of Wagering Paraphernalia Act. The court held this regardless of the fact that gambling was legal in the country in which the wagering was actually taking place: 'The act of entering the bet and transmitting the information from New York via the Internet is adequate to constitute gambling activity within New York State'. In *US v Jay Cohen*[5] the court even went on to prosecute the owner of the company.

The threat of prosecution by the US Government is a deterrent, but this has not stopped Internet gaming sites outside the US continuing to accept bets from US citizens – even in cases where the site owner has been prosecuted. However, there are now signs that prohibition is giving way to regulation. A Bill has been introduced to the Las Vegas Assembly[6] that would allow casinos in Nevada to conduct Internet gaming under licence. The Bill makes recommendations for stringent regulations on security, underage gambling and taxation. It is understood that there are moves to introduce a similar Bill in New Jersey. At the time of writing, sportingbet.com has aimed a series of advertisements at the US authorities lobbying for the liberalising of the on-line gambling regime on the basis that it is happy to pay tax in respect of its US activities.

1 Gellatly and Clarke, *On-line Gambling: The Regulation of Global Sports Betting* (2001) Sport Business Group Ltd, para 5.1.
2 18 USC 1084 (a).
3 Paragraph 14.37 has already considered the issue of the US authorities targeting the providers of the financial infrastructure necessary to facilitate on-line betting and gaming.
4 (NY Sup Ct, 1999).
5 (2nd Cir, 2001).
6 AB466.

(b) Australia

14.48 The Australian Government's position on on-line gambling has moved from 'benevolent oversight to prohibitive injunction'[1]. In Australia, the State Government initially chose to license Internet gambling operators but concern about the level of problem gambling arising from the accessibility of both off-line and on-line gambling led the Federal Government to introduce a moratorium on interactive gambling services, which took effect on 22 December 2000[2]. The Government subsequently undertook a study into the feasibility and consequences of banning interactive gambling and, in April 2001, the Australian Minister for Communications announced the Interactive Gambling Bill. This Bill proposes a prohibition on gambling companies from offering on-line gambling to any Australian resident. Subsequent amendments to the Bill exempted sports betting from prohibition, but the remaining provisions have far-reaching consequences for on-line operations (for example, on-line operators that are found to have knowingly accepted bets from Australian residents face substantial fines of up to $650,000 a day). However, Australian on-line gambling suppliers are permitted to offer their services to people outside Australia[3].

Whilst Australian on-line gambling operators' ability to advertise across State lines has always been limited, the Interactive Gambling Bill prohibits the advertising of any interactive gambling service in traditional print and broadcast media and on billboards and the Internet[4].

1 Gellatly and Clarke, *On-line Gambling: The Regulation of Global Sports Betting* (2001) Sport Business Group Ltd, para 6.1.

2 National Office for the Information Economy website (www.noie.gov.au).

3 Information supplied by NCE, 29 May 2001.

4 Paragraph 14.37 has already considered the issue of the Australian authorities targeting the providers of the financial infrastructure necessary to facilitate on-line betting and gaming.

(c) Europe

14.49 The regulations relating to on-line gambling are far from unified in the various European states, and the decision in the *Schindler* case[1] held that, contrary to the provisions of article 59 of the EEC Treaty[2], a European state can control all forms of gambling within its borders.

Internet gambling laws in Sweden and Scandinavia are some of the most lenient in the world. Test licences for Internet gambling have recently been issued and a new regulatory Act is due imminently. Ladbrokes (in co-operation with a Swedish partner) have recently announced plans to apply for a local gaming licence.

In Norway, prospective gambling organisations need permission before they can set up on-line sites. Companies are not permitted to make a profit from the sites, although no specific laws regulating Internet gambling exist.

Although Denmark is keen to promote on-line gambling within the country, it is not prepared to allow foreign competitors into the market. With the exception of print media, it is illegal to promote non-Danish betting in Denmark. This law was recently enforced when several websites were 'requested' by the Ministry of Taxation to remove banner advertisements for foreign betting operations.

Spanish-based websites do offer on-line betting but they are closely monitored by the Spanish Ministry of the Interior. In Portugal and Greece, on-line gambling has not developed, mainly due to lack of funds, whereas in France, most forms of sports betting are prohibited and there is strict legislation against Internet gambling.

Along with France, Germany has introduced some of the toughest laws relating to the Internet. The German Federal Government has recently decided against an outright prohibition on on-line gambling and has instigated a review of on-line gambling legislation. Some licences have been issued for on-line gambling operations.

1 *Customs and Excise Comrs v Schindler: C-275/92* [1994] QB 610, ECJ.

2 Article 59 prohibits a Member State from placing obstacles on cross-border services.

15. CONCLUSION

14.50 Despite inherent uncertainties in the outdated legal framework in which it has to operate, the UK on-line gambling industry has expanded exponentially over the last five years. Whilst gaming activities in conventional premises remain heavily regulated, UK bookmakers (and overseas gaming operators) routinely offer gambling products to UK citizens via the Internet. The 2002 FIFA World Cup was expected by UK bookmakers to be the biggest betting event in history, and this indeed proved to be the case[1]. The proliferation of on-line bookmakers and specialist betting exchanges allows sophisticated punters a greater degree of choice and value, which in itself generates increased turnover. The recent tax changes, relaxation of advertising rules and the enactment of the provisions contained in 'A Safe Bet for Success' confirm the UK as *the* place to locate legitimate and secure on-line betting facilities. On-line gaming does not look to be far behind.

1 See www.bettingzone.co.uk/football/worldcup.

Index